Legal Linguistics

Marcus Galdia

Legal Linguistics

PETER LANG
Frankfurt am Main · Berlin · Bern · Bruxelles · New York · Oxford · Wien

Bibliographic Information published by the Deutsche Nationalbibliothek
The Deutsche Nationalbibliothek lists this publication in the Deutsche Nationalbibliografie; detailed bibliographic data is available in the internet at <http://www.d-nb.de>.

ISBN 978-3-631-59463-6

www.peterlang.de

Contents in Brief

Detailed Contents

Abbreviations

ADA	Americans with Disabilities Act (US)
All ER	All England Law Reports
BGB	Bürgerliches Gesetzbuch (German Civil Code)
CC	Code Civil (French Civil Code)
CIC	Corpus Iuris Civilis
CISG	United Nations Convention on the International Sale of Goods
ECPA	Electronic Communication Privacy Act (US)
EU	European Union
HTS	Harmonized Tariffs Schedules (US)
OSCE	Organization for Security and Co-operation in Europe
PECL	Principles of European Contract Law (EU)
PTO	Patent and Trade Office (US)
SEC	Securities and Exchange Commission (US)
UCC	Uniform Commercial Code (US)
UCITA	Uniform Computer Information Transactions Act (US)
UNCITRAL	United Nations Commission on International Trade Law
UNIDROIT	International Institute for the Unification of Private Law

Non-English language legal terms are provided an index relating to their origin, e.g. (FR) for French or (CN) for Chinese legal terms. In some contexts American legal terms are marked with (US) and the English ones with (UK). An asterisk (*) marks linguistically incorrect or constructed lexical units.

Preface

Why has this book been written? Questions related to linguistic aspects of law are nowadays dealt with in an interdisciplinary branch of knowledge called by many the Legal Linguistics. The number of material issues as well as theoretical problems discussed in the Legal Linguistics is constantly growing. At this stage of its development it seems to be worthwhile to focus on some fundamental issues in the research that may be helpful for the understanding of the scope of the discipline, its findings and its future tasks. Therefore, on the following pages, we will take a closer look at the theoretical foundations and the material achievements of the Legal Linguistics as two main issues which determine its current and future standing among the interdisciplinary branches of knowledge. By doing so, we will clarify the question of what is the relation between law and language which has been traditionally identified as the focal point for all fundamental legal-linguistic research. With other words, we will make plain what are the linguistic aspects of the law. As a result of this step, prerequisites of the perception of the Legal Linguistics as a particular legal theory will become understandable as well. Meanwhile, a broad definition of the subject seems to be appropriate because of the vast number of problems canvassed in the legal-linguistic research. In the theoretical part of this book the Legal Linguistics will be mainly understood as a subject dealing with two questions, namely how law is created and how it is applied with linguistic means. Both main legal-linguistic features of the law, i.e. its creation and its application with the help of language, are fundamental for an appreciation of this phenomenon as one of the most efficient social institutions. Both creation of the law as well as its application in its different forms such as interpretation, argumentation or translation are complex linguistic operations. Their characterization has always been a challenge for the legal theory and it is equally a challenge for the contemporary Legal Linguistics. Therefore, in this book, we will try to explain how the law is interpreted and translated, and use these exemplary facets of the legal practice in an attempt to better understand the legal argumentation. This theoretical goal is approached through analyses of the legally relevant linguistic materials, mostly court opinions and statutory provisions. The analyses have been carried out in order to demonstrate that the fundamentals of the Legal Linguistics are well anchored in the legal practice.

How is this book structured? The book begins with an introduction into its main theoretical issues based on examples from the legal practice. It demonstrates also in a succinct form what law is actually about when it is seen from the jurists' perspective. This question is not without importance for the shaping of the Legal Linguistics which deals with the linguistic manifestation of law, and all too often presupposes that whoever engages in it masters perfectly the law. Neither is it realistic to assume that those who master law would also master linguistics. Therefore, in the introductory part some thoughts upon law and upon linguistics are presented in a way that should facilitate the understanding of what will follow. Needless to say that those few pages spent on the parent disciplines of the Legal Linguistics cannot make up for thorough studies of both subjects. In fact, interdisciplinary studies have their inherent constraints and those courageous enough to deal with them will always suffer from a lack of sufficiently founded knowledge. The remedy against this shortcoming is the constant awareness of the researcher about own limits rather than a timid reserve and resignation.

After the sketch of preliminaries, material issues of the Legal Linguistics such as the legal terminology and subsequently the linguistic operations that are characteristic for law, especially the legal argumentation, the legal interpretation and the legal translation, will be introduced and discussed. This is the main part of the book which also shows that the theoretical fundamentals which were mentioned in the introductory part are essential for the understanding of all linguistic operations which constitute the legal discourse. Broader aspects of discourse and textuality will also be dealt with in the context of Law and Literature. While keeping in mind the daily needs of professionals dealing with legal-linguistic issues, all over the book practical matters discovered in the research are discussed and, where possible, also suggestions are made for the practical use of the legal-linguistic research. Because the book aims to be of practical importance for jurists, linguistic issues relevant for the emergence of the global law as well as the linguistic legislation are presented in its final part. The book ends, unsurprisingly, with conclusions. In an appendix the reader will find notes and materials which refer to issues and cases mentioned in the main text. This is, in short, the general structure of the book.

What detailed knowledge is provided in the book? Practically important for every professional of law is the mastery of the legal argumentation. Without understanding of this topic no other linguistic operation in law, be it the translation of a legal document or the justification of a court decision can be conscientiously performed. Therefore, the legal argumentation in its relation to all other linguistically relevant aspects of law is the central material topic of the book. The legal discourse which is the overarching structure for the language used in law is by its nature argumentative and law is in fact identical with this specific discourse. Therefore it is practically important to elaborate the requirements for successful legal argumentation. Once the linguistically relevant essence of the legal argumentation is understood, the rest of the Legal Linguistics - with all respect for this fascinating discipline - could be equally well included in footnotes.

Before dealing with the legal argumentation and other linguistic operations in law some time will be spent on scrutinizing the legal terminology. The reason for this specific attention on the legal terminology is that many people still approach the legal language through the legal terminology. We will therefore reflect upon this traditional approach and integrate it into our perspective that is dominated by argumentative features of the legal discourse. In fact, legal arguments are developed around legal concepts which manifest themselves in texts in the form of terms. Therefore, analyses of the legal language should not be reduced to terminological issues. When seen from the argumentative perspective the language used in law appears in its most illustrative context. What is more, in the broader perspective of the legal discourse the legal terminology will become operational in different speech acts. These speech acts will help determine what there is in law that might make it appear as being composed of mere words. Moreover, textual aspects of law are best understood in comparison with literature. We will therefore have a glimpse of the sister discipline Law and Literature to learn from it and benefit where possible. Still more concretely, we will ask why do lawyers speak and write differently than other people do, and reflect upon their purportedly arcane language use. In this context, we will also ask why the language used by lawyers is often ambiguous and we will reflect upon the necessity for remedies. Finally, we will try to sketch out a retrospective upon the original legal language and look back to the times when the basic legal language was constructed as part of our efforts to describe its creation. Some knowledge of Latin is necessary to understand this part of our study. In consequence of all those detailed analyses, the Legal Linguistics will appear as a description of two already mentioned activities exercised by lawyers; i.e. creation and application of law with linguistic means.

What other practical consequences follow from this research? Legal Linguistics has also a role to play in the comparative legal science. It can contribute to the solution of some problems which are discussed there by pointing out that the central legal-linguistic questions must be asked in the comparative law as well. This book is written in a time when global law as a coherent regulative body of generally accepted rules still does not exist. Therefore, a comparative approach to the legal diversity and the legal culture has been adopted here. However, we will not conceal our support for the efforts undertaken by the legal science to overcome the legal diversity and to contribute to the development of the global law. Legal Linguistics can contribute to the development of the language of the global law. This practical task may be perceived as urgent and possibly even more relevant that the main theoretical aspects of Legal Linguistics upon which this book lays the main stress. Both issues are, however, interrelated. They can, therefore, be perceived as two sides of the same coin. Moreover, the Legal Linguistics deals also with regulations concerning language use. Therefore, we included an overview of problems related to this specific area. We deal there with language use in multilingual societies and especially with the development of effective legal mechanisms which support the linguistic cohesion in modern societies. Here, the Legal Linguistics shows again its practical bearing for the legal science.

How can this book be used? This book is written for all professionals interested in linguistic aspects of law. It can become instrumental as a textbook introducing the Legal Linguistics for everyone who is also interested in the theoretical fundamentals of the subject. Courses in Legal Linguistics which are now parts of curricula all over the world address very often the non-legal audience composed mostly of interpreters and translators of legal texts. Also this audience should be able to use this book with some benefit. This book does not contradict the tendency to perceive Legal Linguistics as a course in legal terminology for non-lawyers or a course in foreign legal terminology for lawyers. Yet, it addresses the issue from a broader perspective and aims explicitly to reach lawyers while being also accessible to non-lawyers who wish to acquire specific skills in order to exercise a profession which is related to law. However, this book cannot replace a course in comparative law or in jurisprudence. It has been construed as a complementary part of it. Despite all the inconveniences described, it seems to be well adapted to the needs of teaching law, and it can also serve as an introduction into legal reasoning against the background of comparative law. At least, the author was using the materials on which this book is based in this sense during his teaching of courses on Legal Culture and Comparative Law, U.S. American Business Law and Principles of the E.U. Economic Law, as well as International Business Law and International Law.

From what theoretical perspective has this book been conceived? This book was developed in an interdisciplinary exchange between legal science and linguistics. Contrasting and combining methods of either disciplines or parts of them is an inevitable prerequisite of any work of this sort. Works from philosophical and linguistic pragmatics, analytical philosophy and French *épistémologie* are its main theoretical framework. This theoretical commitment has an additional practical consequence. The focus on one theoretical approach which stresses the linguistic and philosophical pragmatics means also that no exhaustive overview of publications and issues discussed in the legal-linguistic research could be undertaken here. First, recent publications by Heikki E. S. Mattila (2002b and 2006) provide a thorough overview of these issues and include broad if not the broadest available bibliography of the Legal Linguistics. Interested readers should consult them. Second, no encyclopedia of Legal Linguistics was planned by the author, but rather a very specific view upon the subject matter due to unresolved fundamental methodological issues of the subject itself. Readers interested in other conceptions of the Legal Linguistics will find in the chapter *Language and Law* a critical commentary of existing currents in this domain. There, also a state of the art report is outlined for readers who rather prefer a problem-oriented than a methodologically founded approach to legal-linguistic issues.

How and where has this book been written? Legal materials used in this work mostly concern U.S. American and French law due to the author's involvement in teaching at the International University of Monaco between 2005 and 2009, i.e. in the time when the main part of this research was prepared. Nevertheless, the general remarks in the book also aim at reflecting language use in the civil law of European provenance although this has not always been explicitly stated in the text. The reason for this is that the Legal Linguistics is perceived here as uniform in its methodological setting, it does not depend on the specifics of laws in different jurisdictions. Parts of this study were written during professional assignments the author spent in Russia, Macedonia and Montenegro. Access to original publications of some classics there has been difficult. This is the reason why sometimes a German writer is quoted in the Serbian language version of his work. Interested readers in countries were original editions of these books are available should not encounter particular problems with identifying the right paragraphs in the original works. Sources from which only textual examples had been borrowed are not included into the bibliography. Instead, they are mentioned in the current text.

The author's last word (in the preface) The Legal Linguistics in its contemporary shape is a fascinating but also a challenging enterprise. Both, readers and writers who wish to deal with this topic need a lot of enthusiasm and patience to accomplish their relative tasks. Let us therefore reiterate and linguistically reformulate some of the main thoughts of this preface in order to encourage the readers to deal with the chapters which will follow. For the author, law is a type of socially relevant argumentation, a discursive and predominantly institutionalized practice. Language is used in it in a specific way. Language use in institutional settings can be aptly characterized with the help of pragmalinguistic approaches. This broad understanding of law and language makes it possible to perceive the Legal Linguistics (also) as a theory of law. Therefore, the entire book can be perceived as prolegomena to the pragmatic theory of law. This task makes it also necessary to focus extensively on basic paradigmatic and conceptual notions of such a theory, its preliminary questions and prerequisites. The time spent on this reflection is not lost, because the emerging Legal Linguistics needs a solid basis for its future development. Otherwise, it would risk disappearing in details and footnotes and would continue to be perceived as marginal in legal sciences, as well as in linguistics proper. We, instead, aim at preventing this discouraging scenario. Ultimately, the term Legal Linguistics is spelled here with initial capital letters in order to stress that it refers to an emerging and independent – although interdisciplinary - branch of knowledge.

Monaco, March 2009

Acknowledgments

I am particularly grateful for advice and support provided by Prof. Heikki E.S. Mattila (University of Rovaniemi, Finland). His pioneer research into Legal Linguistics was a basis and an incentive for me to engage in this emerging subject. Prof. Mattila kindly read the first and the final drafts of this book and made many comments of principal nature which I tried to incorporate into the final version. I was introduced into Legal Linguistics by Prof. Dr. Edeltraud Bülow and into interpretation of texts by Prof. Dr. Uwe Ebel, both at University of Münster (Germany). To both I remain particularly indebted. Prof. Bülow also friendly read and commented an earlier draft of this book.

Prof. William Lightfoot (International University of Monaco) read and commented the second draft of this book. I had also the pleasure to discuss extensively legal-linguistic problems with Dr. Natalya Voronina (Russian Academy of Sciencies, Moscow) during our common research activities in Russia in the years 2003 and 2004. Likewise, I would like to thank Dr. Doris Wydra (University of Salzburg, Austria) and Mr. Neil J. Brennan (Ottawa, Canada) who supported my work on the linguistic legislation as well as Dr. Jean-Louis Aroui (University Paris VIII, France) for his help with identifying relevant publications on the French *épistémologie.* Prof. Mami Hiraike Okawara (Takasaki University, Japan) and Dr. Wojciech Kwarciński (Poznań, Poland) sent me their unpublished legal-linguistic findings. Dr. Lukáš Hlouch (Supreme Administrative Court of the Czech Republic, Brno) informed me about the development of the legal-linguistic research in his country. Professor Karol Janicki (University of Bergen, Norway) kindly provided me information about publications that were initially not included into the draft of this book. I give special thanks to Mr. Michael Rücker from the Peter Lang Publishing Group for his editorial comments and support during my work on the final version of the manuscript. My students at the International University of Monaco Matthew R. Clevenger, Alexey Manshin, Dimitra Andrianakos, Lorenzo Tolotta, Frédéric Mähl, Darryl L. Jones and Sergii Gromovych helped with proofreading, editing and solving technical problems of the manuscript.

The author

Part 1: Introduction

In the introductory part we will reflect upon some theoretical questions that will be further elucidated in the main part of this book. First of all, we will try to establish what lawyers are actually doing when they create or apply the law. This will help us to understand the law before we specifically approach the Legal Linguistics. Furthermore, we will show in some short narrative examples different aspects of the language used in law. Moreover, in order to make our observations theoretically operational in subsequent chapters we will establish a conceptual framework based mainly upon linguistic and philosophical pragmatics which will be needed later on in our case analyses. We will also show that the conception of language is fundamental to any reflection upon Language and Law. Finally, we will recognize that language in legal contexts conveys ethical values. Therefore, we will include some preliminary observations on the role ethics plays in the law and in its language. The combination of linguistic pragmatics and ethics will enable us to engage in the numerous analyses of court opinions and statutory provisions which will follow in the main chapters of this book.

1.1 Preliminary Questions

1.1.1 Are laws made with words?

Indubitably, the readers of the numerous pages that follow will not be particularly impressed by our initial remark that law and language are closely related. Most legal professionals and also many interested citizens realized this fact long ago without the help of a particular scientific discipline. In fact, many citizens have equally experienced this very loosely formulated statement as a part of their biographies. How shall we react to this experience accumulated by professionals of law and laypersons alike? Shall we become trivial or ironical, or both, when talking about law? Some may wish it so, as they suspect sheer power behind the subtle construct of law. Others would find an ironical or sarcastic reaction more appropriate, because for them law is nothing more than language, mere words. Could both of those observer groups of the legal practice be right; i.e. could it be that law is powerful and while being so it is empty and constitutes a risky analogy to the naked emperor in Andersen's tale? In this study about the linguistic aspects of the law which exposes explicit theoretical ambitions we cannot exclude such fundamental observations. Before approaching the language in law we will have to determine what actually the law is and what the legal science is. How shall we explain the law in terms of language without the risk of appearing naïve? How to avoid falling into the pitfalls of legal reasoning which were thoroughly constructed by generations of lawyers before us? We will try, first of all, to describe what lawyers are actually doing from the perspective of someone interested mainly in the linguistic part of their work. We will identify the aspects of their work which are linked to language and by so doing we will also show which parts of the lawyers' work are less dependant on language. In this way we will make plain that the question of whether there is something more in law than only language is essential for any conception of the Legal Linguistics. This procedure may seem cumbersome, but the Legal Linguistics cannot be developed in a vacuum. To put it more specifically, there is no Legal Linguistics without law. Therefore, understanding law towards the background of the societal experience made with its complex mechanisms is a necessary precondition for its construction. And, there is even one more obstruction to the careless and rather nonchalant start with the Legal Linguistics without law. The Legal Linguistics is profoundly grounded in its parent disciplines; i.e. in the legal sciences and in linguistics which as all modern branches of knowledge speak with different voices. Seen from these different perspectives, law appears sometimes as a wordless fact and sometimes as an endless cascade of words. However, it also appears regularly as a texture of both wordless facts and voiceful arguments. The legal linguist must be able to cope with all those disenchanting situations.

1.1.2 Interdisciplinary aspirations

As mentioned in the preface, the theoretical background in this book is interdisciplinary. The basic theoretical framework has been mentioned already. Yet, it has not been explained. We will therefore outline it on the pages which follow and subsequently apply it as a conceptual framework on legal texts. In the main part of the book these sketched ideas will be described in a more detailed way in combination with case analyses. These case analyses will help us to develop a material theory of law; i.e. a theory that starts with materials which it scrutinizes. This procedure is close to the interest expressed towards the daily experience made with law which was related to in the foregoing paragraph. Moreover, the material analyses will also show that the Legal Linguistics provides not only some insight into the linguistically relevant parts of the legal mechanisms but is also capable of embracing law in a way that it forms a fully-fledged theory of law. Thus, our goal is more ambitious than showing some pertinent relations between law and language. As said, our approach is material; it is based mostly on legal decisions taken by courts while applying statutory provisions and interpreting precedents. We will therefore regularly make reference to court decisions and sometimes even quote them extensively. It is important to show that linguistic aspects play always a decisive role in the application of law. Therefore, reference will be made also to routine cases which otherwise neither substantially nor procedurally represent any points apt to rise particular attention. As noted, this procedure is necessary to prove the ubiquitous character of law and language relations. Our analysis is therefore not limited to spectacular cases, sometimes referred to as hard cases. In the Legal Linguistics all statutes and all court opinions and other documents with legal relevance such as contracts or last wills matter equally. They all show different aspects of the language used in legal contexts. Therefore, the reader of this book should not try to find out why these and not other legal cases or statutory provisions or quotes from administrative documents have been used for this research. With good reasons other materials could have been used as well. Even more so, whatever linguistic sources that relate to law can be used for our purposes. Were the Legal Linguistics selective in its sources, it could not function as a part of our theoretical knowledge about law or language. In consequence, it would not make much sense to study it, either.

1.1.3 Some legal-linguistic narratives

In order to enter into the problems discussed in this book imagine some short narratives taken from the legal practice:

I. A court has to determine the meaning of *chicken*, a word used in a contract on chicken delivery between two parties who disagree. The plaintiff pretends that it includes young birds only while the defendant insists upon all *fowls* being perceived in trade as *chickens* (Cf. Frigaliment Importing Co. v. B.N.S. International Sales Corp. 190 F. Supp. 116 (S.D.N.Y. 1960), quoted also in Notes and Materials nr. 30).

II. An accused in a common law country does not use the honorific form *Your Honor* when addressing the judge.

III. A legal writer introduces a chapter on the Law of the European Union in his text-book for law students with: *The law relating to the European Community is now a wide ranging subject. European Community law* **intrudes upon**, *and affects, an ever increasing volume of domestic law and now represents an important source of law in the United Kingdom* (emphasis added).

IV. A court has to decide whether *protective gear* can be perceived as *accessory* to roller blades under U.S. Customs Regulations (Cf. Rollerblade, Inc. v. U.S. 282 F. 3d 1349; Fed. Cir. 2002, quoted also in Notes and Materials nr. 33).

V. A court considers whether a foreign State can obtain the letter of administration in a case when an intestate decedent according to the provisions of this State inherits as heir. Yet, it may refuse to grant the letter of administration in the same case when the State according to its own provisions obtains the estate as *bona vacantia* (Cf. In re Maldonado - State of Spain v. Treasury Solicitor, All ER 1953, vol.2. p.1579 sqq., quoted also in Notes and Materials nr. 38).

All five above cases refer to law and the legal practice. In all of them language has an important role to play. However, it seems that they represent different aspects of legal practice and reflect various facets of language use in law. Yet, how to grasp this difference? Is this difference a legal problem or a linguistic one? The reader will intuitively realize that answers to such questions cannot be found in a law book. They are different from questions of structural character in law such as: In what statute is the rule of *anticipatory repudiation* in commercial contracts stated in the U.S. law? The right answer is Sec. 2-610 UCC. And the *right to inspection*? In Sec. 2-513 UCC. And the *mailbox rule*? In Sec. 2-206 UCC. These structural questions are not about the application of the law. They simply refer to its inner structure and provide provisional, mechanical information about law which remains irrelevant to the propositional contents of the quoted provisions. Moreover, the content of the few provisions mentioned here does not change through attributing numbers to them or through identifying them with help of the numerical reference. These quotations are doubtlessly also important for lawyers as they pertain to their activity of knowing how to determine sources of law; i.e. where to find the law. However, they definitely will not dominate our investigation because they are accidental to problems of creation and application of law. Indeed, law is more than a mechanical system of references which link legal provisions to numbers. For many, law begins with its inner structure where issues and regulations (facts and rules) are interrelated in a specific order. This specific order is dressed in words. For instance, in the UCC provisions referred to above there is more than pure mechanics. Legal notions such as *anticipatory repudiation* or *mailbox rule* are created and used there. In the legal practice, litigations emerge about the application of such notions. Parties to the litigations will try to convince the judges that their reading of the law is the right one; i.e. the one which the society is ready to enforce with the help of the competent authorities. In the litigation only one of the possible readings of the law will be determined by the judges as the right one, i.e. the one which will be enforced. If necessary, force will be used to provide full credit to a court decision that involves such a technical issue like the scope of the application of a legal notion, be it *anticipatory repudiation* or whatever other not particularly poetically sounding concept. In fact, law is power expressed with linguistic means. In our study we will therefore also have to show this process in the course of our material analyses. All other related problems, e.g. why it is necessary to introduce concepts such as *anticipatory repudiation* or *mailbox rule* into laws are dealt with in the legal science. The legal linguist takes such issues for granted.

Let us now come back to our short introductory cases. They shall illustrate that language use in law differs as the context of use is changing. They show situations of language use; i.e. the contexts in which speakers engage in legal discourses. The legal linguist works differently on those different situations as well. Here, it is decisive to establish the appropriate perspective upon the language, both in the situation of use and in the situation of reflecting upon the use. Otherwise, language will not work properly. It will lead to confusion that expressed in terms of law means injustice. This being said, in case I the judge is dealing with identifying the meaning of the word *chicken* which belongs to the ordinary language. In the legal-linguistic perspective it is necessary to find out how the judge actually determines the meaning of a word that belongs to the ordinary language. As a second step, it is necessary to decide whether the interpretive strategy adopted by the judge corresponds with our knowledge about the language and especially with our knowledge about the way we grasp the meaning of a word. Finally, the legal linguist may decide to make suggestions about the appropriate strategic choice in such situations. This, in short, is the way in which the legal linguist deals with our case I. Similarly, in case IV the judge analyzes a legal term *accessory* and determines its scope of application towards the background of a commercial transaction which involves also the use of words belonging to the ordinary language, in casu *protective gear*. Here again, the legal linguist scrutinizes the way in which the judge understands the ordinary language. Yet, in addition to it, she has to reflect upon professional strategies of language use in law in situations where legal provisions indicate the way in which a legal concept such as *accessory* shall be determined. The legal linguist follows here the instruction provided by the legislator and examines the way the judge reacted to it. Finally, she establishes whether the judge acted in accordance with the rules that determine the way in which legal language shall be understood. Additionally, she may also address critically the legislative regulation, should it not correspond with our professional knowledge of what is language. In case V the judge interprets the doctrine while reflecting upon the intricacies of language use in interpretation. For the legal linguist it is decisive to establish how the judge interprets legal provisions as a professional of law. The legal linguist first studies the techniques used by the legal professional and subsequently evaluates them in order to understand how legal professionals structure the use of language in legal contexts in which they used to act. Needless to say, she may also comment upon these techniques should she feel challenged by them as a professional of language. Finally, in case III a legal writer provides in a scientific text a strategy for the interpretation of legal acts in that he posits that some of them *intrude* upon others. The legal linguist shows in such a case primarily that there is an intention in this contention. She has to prove it because this may not be evident for all language users and she has also to reflect upon the author's strategy to engage in the task of providing this sort of interpretive strategies to readers. And case II? In common law countries judges are usually addressed as *Your Honor* (Mattila 2006: 49). This communicative implication is definitely a pragmatic issue (cf. Levinson 1983: 10) because it is based on a linguistic convention of use. However, its legal implications remain unclear. What would happen if a party in litigation would omit the honorific address? Neither the substantive nor the procedural law in the common law tradition demand from parties to address the judge in this way. The legislation prohibits the parties from offending the judge, but is the omission of the honorific an offence? The legal linguist has to clarify these and other questions which will be addressed in this book later.

In the subsequent chapters we will shed more light on the five short cases which helped to describe the way language works in legal contexts and the way the legal linguist tries to cope with these different situations. We will also establish a perspective for the theoretical reflection upon the distinctions which we have found out among them. The examples illustrated by the short narratives are far from being exhaustive for legally relevant language use. However, they undeniably show the evolving variation of strategies in context-bound language use. In addition, they also demonstrate that the legal linguist's professional reflection upon this use depends on different contexts of use. This is the main result needed in the preliminary part of our Introduction.

1.1.4 Tasks of the legal science

In order to perform her professional tasks the legal linguist needs to know what is the legal science. The utmost reason for this requirement is that the language use that she analyzes is dominated by the professionals of law. Those legal professionals learned their professional language simultanously with their law studies (Mattila 2006: 19). Therefore, the legal linguist must be interested in finding out how the legal science works; i.e. how it provides linguistically relevant professional knowledge. It is evident from the material samples scrutinized above that the knowledge about the numerical reference to the legal provisions or the knowledge of case names alone cannot be perceived as knowledge of law. The specific knowledge about the law which means predominantly knowledge about its contents in a given moment is the task of the legal science.

1.1.4.1 Systematization in law: To infer the content of law from statutes or cases, or both, the jurist has to systematize or classify them according to the subject matter treated in them. Legal provisions or judicial opinions may be classified as belonging to the *private* or to the *public law*. Furthermore, a more precise differentiation can be made and private law provisions be divided into provisions relevant for *contracts*, *torts*, *property*, *family* and *succession*. They can be also devided into *substantive* and *procedural*. The law of the European Union has been classified differently. Notions of *primary* and *secondary law* have been perceived as the most suitable framework for its classification. Enormously many possibilities for classification or systematization of legal provisons or rules exist. As of now, only a few possibilities have been used for this enterprise by the legal science. There is undoubtedly an inherent logic in these attempts to systematize legal provisions or court decisions. Thus far, the results of the traditional classification are mostly coherent and rational, although they may at times divide the social facts which form their background along formalistic lines. This is the case when social facts of a regulation or a case are seen in the light of the *substantive law* and on the other hand in the light of the *procedural law*. In this perspective, the matter which forms a social fact is artificially split which may lead to problems of apprehension and application of the provisions in question. The systematization efforts are nevertheless rather based on tradition than on logic. However, this result is not surprising because the role of systematization or classification is to introduce some preliminary order into the subject matter which is studied. Without this methodological approach jurists would risk getting lost in the law that they try to apprehend. Meanwhile, legal provisions and court decisions are too numerous that they could be known or studied in the chronological order of their promulgation by the legislator or issuance by the courts of law respectively. At this stage, we may maintain that in order to perform the task of systematization some concepts such as *private law*, *contracts* or *substantive law* had to be created with linguistic means in past times by those who first approached the challenging task of systematization.

1.1.4.2 Other legal-linguistically relevant criteria: After the preliminary classification took place it is possible to engage in broader proceedings that are equally relevant for the Legal Linguistics. At this point, the question arises as to what proceedings suit best the study of law on a more advanced level. Historically, it has been proposed to deal with legal concepts and study their function in the provisions and their use in court decisions. However, it became plain very soon that law is not only about concepts, although it undeniably deals with them. Law also deals with evaluations along the established dominant views about right and wrong in society. The values which underlie the decision making process in establishing of the legal provisions by the legislator as well as in the process of their application in courts must also be taken into consideration. Otherwise, only a conceptual skeleton of law would emerge as the result of legal studies. What is needed instead is a multi-dimensional view of intertwined legal provisions, an analysis of rules inferred from them as well as from judicial decisions and values which determine the choices in operating them. Therefore, today, when law is studied, attention is drawn both to the complex legal structure composed of legal rules and to the values which control their application. Here, however, the additional question could be asked as regards the way in which these efforts could be generalized or finalized. We propose a linguistic point of view as the most suitable perspective for studying law. From the linguistic point of view, the legal argumentation is the basis of an advanced structure of law. For us, the legal arguments are the utmost elements of classification or systematization in law. The knowledge about this structure composed of legal arguments within the legal discourse is the knowledge of law. The legal linguist studies the use of these arguments and assists the jurist in his studies of the legal argumentation.

1.1.4.3 Knowledge of the subject matter and knowledge of law: The analysis of the language used in legal texts (written as well as oral) requires substantial knowledge of law. This requirement can be fulfilled through diligent legal studies. More problematic is however the knowledge of the subject matter, i.e. the facts on which a judicial decision is based or those which form the background of a legislative initiative. Access to written sources (mostly files) on which legal decisions are based is almost impossible. Sometimes, direct witnesses of the legislative actions, mostly politicians, mention unknown motives for legislative acts in their diaries. Moreover, facts reported in legal opinions may not correspond with the real course of events and this may be known to the issuers of a court decision and the parties or may remain hidden even for them. All this factual knowledge is however essential in the analysis of argumentative strategies used in court opinions and legislative acts. The lack of such reliable knowledge constitutes an impediment upon the progress in the legal-linguistic research and threatens it by the assumption of naivity when official motivations for legal acts or court decisions are taken at face value (cf. Ross 1966: 57). This methodological problem of the legal-linguistic research is difficult to overcome. Analogously, in literary studies, the narration from the omniscient perspective (Rimon-Kennan 1989: 95) is used in some types of narration. The omniscience is however easily accessible there because it mainly depends upon the author's intention. In dealing with law the omniscient view upon the subject matter is impossible to achieve because factual data are never available in their entirety even if the linguistic strategy of dealing with them in the public sphere, especially in court decisions, may signalize complete factual knowledge. Hence, the only methodological tool which remains at the researchers' disposal is the general rationality test. It includes the coherence test for the motivations provided by the court or the legislative body, and the correspondence test in which this data is evaluated along the experience based on the social practice. This rationality test - as imperfect as it may be - guarantees at least that the perspective taken in the research concentrated upon the language use in law will not be perceived as purely repetitive, and therefore also intentionally or unintentionally affirmative of the analyzed legal text. Furthermore, it prevents the use of a methodology unsusceptible of the risk that motivations provided for in some legal texts may differ from those which were decisive for the decision taken. For the legal linguist, therefore, dealing with language use means to be alerted to all possible contexts and conditions of use, explicit and implicit ones. In sum, understanding of the structural requirements imposed upon the lawyer's work, be they systematization of legal provisions and case law or the determination of facts towards the background of moral evaluations, is an essential precondition of any legal-linguistic approach. The corresponding linguistic stage to it is the knowledge about the creation of language and the underlying signification processes as well as the mechanisms of the linguistic change that affects the language used in law as in all its other varieties.

1.2 Pragmatics for Lawyers

1.2.1 Pragmatic preferences

The legal linguist willing to assist the jurist must base her knowledge on a scientifically founded theory in order to be accepted by the jurist. She has constantly to compete with other professional views about law which can be challenged only with good arguments; i.e. those which convince due to their particular rationality. The legal linguist uses arguments based on the Legal Linguistics. Her problem is that the Legal Linguistics is in the stage of emergence and a lot of work will have to be done until it will be able to compete effectively with other branches of knowledge which also deal with law. How, then, will the legal linguist try to develop her recommendations for the jurist? We may use one of our short cases to understand how theory is developed in the Legal Linguistics. It goes without saying that linguistic habits such as the use of honorifics, e.g. *Your Honor*, while addressing judges are part of the language use before courts. Our question must however be, are they also part of Legal Linguistics? Here, we would like to stress that we favor linguistic use which is relevant to the judicial decision making process. Equally, we are attracted by language use in the legal argumentation as far as it is relevant for the decision as well as for stylistic particularities as long as they matter for the decision taken. These aspects of language use are for us the predominant part of Legal Linguistics. It would be however unjustified to exclude communicative situations or other – even marginal - aspects of language use from Legal Linguistics simply because they seem not to influence directly the decision taken. In the Legal Linguistics, we should try to get hold of all communicative situations in law and of their structures and mechanisms. Otherwise, the Legal Linguistics would impoverish the legal science and be applicable only to some selected aspects of the legal culture. The legal culture embraces a vast area of social phenomena which are sometimes remote from the act of making a decision in a court of law such as the shape or decoration of court rooms or court buildings (Mattila 2006: 13). However, we should not forget that some of them might be more influential than others and we must mark it in our approach to the Legal Linguistics.

In the approach adopted here inferences overtly and intentionally conveyed by speakers in a context (Levinson 1983: 24) are the criterion distinguishing language use which is primarily reflected in the legal-linguistic use and language use which is peripheral to it. This statement can be used in order to formulate a theory for the use of the legal linguist. This distinction is not in contradiction with the tendency in the linguistic pragmatics of the last decades to stress conversational analysis. It leaves enough room for this approach, and does not develop to the detriment of the conversational analysis because the role of the legal discourse remains essential, even if sometimes only parts of it are scrutinized in a different context than the discursive one. This holds true for some issues concerning the legal terminology that doubtlessly have a role to play in the legal discourse but may also be addressed in an isolated surrounding. The later approach is even typical for the legal-linguistic research. It simply means that some approaches and results may be under specific circumstances more relevant than others. What approach should be perceived as dominant in a case is a question of the case itself. Some discourse analysis research, e.g. concerning criminal law shows that this approach may be more prolific than others when fact finding is at stake and witness testimony must be evaluated by the judge. This approach is also helpful in determining the role of the honorific address in our case II. Apparently, the omission of the honorific *Your Honor* especially when done systematically; i.e. constantly practiced by the speaker who personally depends on the decision taken by the judge, may influence the decision making process. However, particular research would be necessary to find out under what circumstances the use or omission of the honorific is essential for the decision making. In turn, deciding whether goods are inherited by the State as *last heir* or whether they are *bona vacantia*, and only subsequently are incorporated into the treasury of the State (our introductory case V), are not dependent on social conventions used by speakers when approaching courts. Here, professional argumentation matters. The professional argumentation is not emotive as is the conversational practice of addressing a judge. Therefore, other aspects of linguistic use may be more relevant for understanding structures that dominate vertically structured discourses. Overall, dealing with the use of language as a starting point for building a theory suitable for the legal linguist leads to its scientific roots. They are for us, as indicated previously, pragmatics and general semiotics. Pragmatic and general semiotic approaches to law offer many examples for fruitful implementation within the legal theory (Jackson 1985: 4). The range of practical application of one and the same theory may cover some aspects of the Scandinavian legal realism, the American legal realism, the speech act theory and the legal semiotics of Algirdas J. Greimas (Jackson 1985: 8-9). Some aspects within these theories, however, may not correspond or may underscore other than legal-linguistically relevant elements. We will therefore remain tolerant to other viewpoints because they may contribute to the Legal Linguistics in a way methodically different from ours while we will be visibly favoring one approach. This specific tolerant approach concerns especially the materials analyzed in the research that has been methodologically differently construed than ours.

The above preliminary remarks on theory building allow for the first summary of requirements that are relevant for the dealing with Legal Linguistics. The Legal Linguistics builds its theory while keeping in mind the needs of the legal science. Methodologically, however, it is not grounded in the legal science but in linguistic and social theories. In this book a choice has been made between these theories and some have been preferred to the detriment of others. This means also that a differently founded Legal Linguistics is possible and this will be shown in the chapter on Foundations of Legal Linguistics where other approaches than the pragmatically oriented one will be discussed. Likewise, our initial short analyses of legal-linguistically relevant materials also brought first theoretically relevant results. They illustrate the first important shift in the modern reflection upon law from the inner-structural perspective to the problems of creation and application of law. In our approach we will show that both can be adequately integrated into a legal-linguistic theory of law based on a pragmatic approach. Yet, first of all we will have to explain why we have chosen this approach and by selecting it we seem to prefer it to others. This preference has a personal background because we simply know this approach better than other ones. In addition, we also assume that it provides innovative insights into problems of the structure and the application of law. Indeed, as many theorists argue, legal and pragmatic reasoning display affinities that cannot be a coincidence.

1.2.2 What is pragmatics about?

We have already mentioned that linguistic pragmatics deals with language use, and that Legal Linguistics in the sense in which we are going to outline it deals with the language use in law. All of it may sound mysterious and the impression might come up that first there is language, then we take and use it and make for instance law of it. On the other hand, neither linguistic pragmatics nor Legal Linguistics is as trivial as this series of issues may suggest. In our preliminary thoughts about law and language many things are commingled. And our task will be to bring order into this amorphous amalgam. To begin with, distinguishing between language and its use is a metaphor (cf. Davidson 2001: 247). In fact, we cannot deal with language without using it. Moreover, distinguishing between law and language in the analysis of their supposed interrelation is another such metaphor. Here, again, the legal language does not exist outside its legal context of use. Seen from the pragmatic perspective, language is a mode of acting in the world, not just a mode of reflection upon it (Enos 1996: 54). Therefore, using language means performing actions (Holtgraves 2002: 177). The minimal linguistic form of such actions is the *speech act*. The speech act may, e.g. convey a promise or a threat, convince the hearer or not. In terms of the speech act theory which deals with the systematization of the speech acts and tries to understand how they function, we undertake different actions when we use language. We may wish to introduce changes to the world around us while using *declarations* or *directives*. We may describe our set of mind with *assertives*; we can also describe our emotions with *expressives*. All these actions are social, because they involve also other people (Holtgraves 2002: 178). The actions which we named as examples for speech acts have a specific grammar and a criterion of correctness of use which is called *felicity* (Levinson 1983: 229). They may be performed in a successful way, but they may also fail. For instance, the speaker who is making a promise may as well convince the hearer as he may fail (Searle 2004: 66). Therefore, we have to know the preconditions for the successful performance of speech acts because we are not interested in performing them in order to fail. In other words, we have to know how to transform our intentions into successful social actions. In order to achieve this competence we need to know a lot about prerequisites of such actions. Some speech acts are rather simple daily routine that we perform without problems. For instance, asking the way from a person on the street. We acquire the knowledge necessary to perform them as we grow up in the community of speakers in which they are used. Other speech acts, such as taking a judicial decision about somebody's criminal responsibility are more complex in their nature. They require additional formal (institutional) training and material (linguistic) competence. The exercise of these actions is analogous to games (Levinson 1983: 227). We play them with others, in society, where it is also determined who can play, who plays according to the rules, as well as who succeeds and who does not. Players may be on equal footing like two judges or two criminals. Their roles as players may also be differently distributed. Imagine a judge and a criminal playing according to the rules of the criminal procedure. Their distance in mastering the rules of successful game may be so big that they can only assume to play the same game as they play on different procedural levels of this game. Also, the grammar they use is often different. These legal games, and we can imagine them as legal discourses composed of legal speech acts, are played in a co-operative mood. Otherwise, they would quickly be terminated. Sometimes, however, the procedures of language use may impose rules upon players and oblige them to play even against their desires. They will then play an adversarial game but the game will continue due to its imposed structure. This is the way our judge plays while using words with the criminal who becomes involved in the game with own words structured according to the rules of his grammar which may also mean that he may remain silent. Our introductory case II concerning a person who addresses the judge as *Your Honor* or omits the honorific address makes plain how the legal speech act functions; i.e. how it can succeed or fail. It goes without saying that some players are more skillful than others. Even in simple discourses of daily routine there is a difference in performance between players. In our example we will rather recommend to the accused to play according to the convention when he defends himself, i.e. when he performs speech acts which are qualified as defense. The defense discourse may be based on a very simple legal speech act, e.g. *It wasn't me, (Your Honor).* It can, however, also include more sophisticated formulations such as *The charges raised against me are statute barred, (Your Honor).* We may additionally assume that the accused will probably be more successful when he includes the honorific *Your Honor* when specifically addressing the judge than when he systematically and ostentatiously omits it. Finally, it may prove that including or excluding the honorific address has been less decisive that we assumed. We have previously mentioned that specific research based on field work would be needed in order to determine this circumstance. Another reason for this indeterminacy of results (felicity of the legal speech act) is that speech acts of defense exercised before the judge by the accused are part of a broader language game that we call legal discourse. Many players engage in them, for instance, during the trial, think of the public prosecutor, the defense lawyer, the panel of judges and the accused personally. Add to it emotional reactions from the public and newspaper reports about the case. All of them contribute to the legal discourse and influence linguistically the final result. In addition, complex games such as legal discourses include linguistic operations that require professional knowledge to be played successfully. This knowledge cannot be acquired in daily socialization processes, unless one is the child of a Supreme Court judge. They take place against the background of complex sets of performance rules defined in institutionalized processes. Therefore, law students first learn the law, then get practical training, and after this they are ready to participate in professional legal discourses. The Legal Linguistics that is based on linguistic pragmatics explains how language mediates the complexity of social interactions where legal discourses take place.

1.2.3 Pragmatic notions

Pragmatics has been frequently perceived as a complicated and controversial concept by the pragmatists themselves as well as in the criticism advanced by its opponents (cf. Note and Materials nr. 1). We will understand it as a tradition of scientific reasoning based foremost on Anglo-American analytical philosophy, especially its ordinary language streaming, and its recent transformations in

American and European scientific reasoning. Central to our work will be the distinction between sentence as a semantic problem and utterance which invokes the actual context (Levinson 1983: 18, 19) that is characteristic for any pragmatic conception. Levinson (1983: 21) puts it as follows: *Pragmatics is the study of the relations between language and context that are basic to an account of language understanding.* Indeed, both aspects of the pragmatic nature of utterance are decisive for legal-linguistic pragmatics because it deals with utterances in legal texts (mostly statutes or precedents) which are conceived as actual in the specific legal perspective; i.e. that law can change. Later on, we will reflect upon this dynamic element in law and we will also ask whether law is an aporetic phenomenon and what does this mean for the prediction of results in judicial decisions. Again, we will see that this is a problem of finding the appropriate way for the interpretation of legal texts. We have also noticed that *language usage* and *context* play a particular role in pragmatics. And indeed, many singular pragmatic approaches to language are based on these concepts. Pragmatics, like all other scientific disciplines, has its own method and its own set of issues upon which it used to concentrate. However, the characteristic feature of pragmatics is that the set of issues the researchers focus upon is still in the making. Some are already fixed, but many others can be discovered and added to it. Until now, the linguistic pragmatics concentrated on *deixis*, *anaphora, conversational implicatures*, *presuppositions*, *speech acts* and *conversational analysis.* The future will show what additional phenomena will be discovered and added to this list. In this book we will mainly use speech acts and discourse analysis. Apparently, also all other named phenomena could be made operative in a pragmatically oriented Legal Linguistics. For example, deixis shows how utterances such as *Come here!* are understood in the contexts in which they were pronounced. In law, it could make plain how time or place specifications contribute to the success or failure of legal speech acts. Anaphora refers to the structure of speech acts in a broader context (Levinson 1983: 86). It seems to have implications for the Legal Linguistics as well because lawyers tend to use constructions in which referring expressions are more frequently or at least differently applied than in the ordinary language (Galdia 2008: 25). Those detailed questions will be discussed later after more pragmatically relevant general examples have been scrutinized. At this place, once again, it is important to maintain that the preponderance of some pragmatic issues in this book does not mean that others are irrelevant.

1.2.4 How pragmatics operates in legal contexts?

As said, in this work we will propose to use pragmatic concepts while analyzing law. Pragmatics in this sense is the philosophical and linguistic theory dealing with the specific aspects of language and its use by the speaker who is also an interpreter. In the Legal Linguistics it is important to determine the role of the speaker because the participation in the legal discourse is based mostly on the professional (institutionally founded) competence, and not only on the pure linguistic competence. This means in practice that it is not sufficient to speak like a judge; one must also have been appointed to exercise the function of a judge by the competent organ. Under these circumstances, only the person involved may pronounce the judgment while using his professional knowledge and his general linguistic competence. That the judge adjudicates does not mean that he simply speaks. It means first of all that in his legal speech acts he interprets the law. The Legal Linguistics does not reduce the judge to a simple speaker of a language. It approaches him as an interpreter of law. What does a simple act of interpretation look like? We will look at it first from the position of a non-professional speaker in order to avoid getting involved in complicated legal matters, in addition to those pragmatic ones which are already intricate enough. Thus, the knowledge about language enables us to distinguish between logically possible meanings of labels such as *smoking* and *non-smoking* which can be defined as denoting premises which are reserved for activities rather than the specific groups, and where even hard smokers can use the premises for non-smokers provided they do not actually smoke there. Moreover, non-smokers can use premises for smokers but they will not be able to prevent the smokers from smoking there. The example may seem a little complicated and not so evident at all, at least linguistically. We have to admit that no one masters a language completely and therefore we sometimes have to test our knowledge by asking others what they mean with what they say. For instance, when we do not understand the expression *Welsh rabbit* we simply ask what is meant by it. We can do the same with the distinction *smokers* and *non-smokers* and easily establish a consensus about its use. Happily, under regular communicative circumstances we will not need to go that far because most such regulatory language is understandable for us without further consideration. Later we will ask why it is so.

At a stage, however, the professional legal competence is necessary to interpret legally relevant language use. The smoker example is particularly significant in our context of law and language because it includes a *legal position*, a *protection of a subjective right* which - before it can be claimed and enforced - must be duly identified. We must understand exactly which actions are allowed and which are forbidden under the sign of *smokers* or *non-smokers* before we formulate a legal claim. But can we do it without knowing the law and rely only on our linguistic competence as English speakers? Strangely enough we cannot, because the linguistic use of captures for premises in which a legal position is protected is inherently linked to law as well as to language in which it has been formulated as a *right*. Therefore, we cannot understand one of the two captures while knowing language only, we understand them properly solely when we grasp the law inherent in the linguistic caption. Again, in life, we usually do not have such problems because the knowledge of the social rules is integrated into our speaker competence.

1.2.5 Environment of pragmatics

Pragmatics is not an isolated science. General semiotics and hermeneutics accompany it in all analyses; the first being omnipresent and thus inevitable wherever signs are used. The other functions foremost as a tool for verifying whether we identify the right issues in the text analysis. We will therefore try to incorporate some of their concepts. In our attempt to synthesize, we will remain loyal to the conceptual realm of semiotics which seems mandatory for any science and at least unavoidable in analyzing texts. As a matter of fact, semiotics which underlies the conceptional work for this research enables us to identify the relevant *legal signs* and shows what operations can be done with them. We will concentrate on the practically most relevant ones, i.e. on argumentation, interpretation and translation. First of all, semiotics draws our attention to the process of creation of signs in law (cf. Jackson 1985). This is essential for the Legal Linguistics because other disciplines dealing with law such as legal theory and legal pragmatics focus mostly on the application of legal rules expressed in language and take the process of emergence of the legal language for granted. The general semiotics and the semiotics of law teach us that legal-linguistic consideration actually begins at the point where legally relevant language use starts to emerge. Also the linguistic pragmatics has been less interested in the process of emergence or constitution of language and concentrated rather on the use of the ready made language. Therefore, the creation of law is construed here as the reference for all other processes and operations with signs in law.

1.2.6. Pragmatic vs. semantic theories of legal language

We have stressed in 1.2.3 the distinction between utterances and propositions, and are now trying to set up a theory which shall be distinct from semantic theories about language, and specifically about legal language. For a long time, legal language has been perceived from the perspective of the traditional semantics alone and researchers used to concentrate upon legal terminology (Mattila 2006: 11). Semiotics and especially pragmatic analysis had to follow suit but were as a matter of fact never fully integrated into what might be called jurisprudence or legal theory. For instance, traditional canons of legal interpretation (i.e. literary, systematic, historical, sociological or teleological interpretation) were recommended in the legal doctrine and it was argued that, if followed, they would ensure the appropriate interpretation of legal provisions (Lasarte 2006: 74-78). Achievements of the linguistically oriented legal theory have not been implemented there. As we will be dealing foremost with the language use in written texts (both in legal provisions and in judicial decisions), or in written quotes of spoken languages, one could question the central role of pragmatics in it. The critics of our approach would stress the semantic rather than pragmatic aspects of law and they would argue that those were central for a theory of law. However, pragmatic concepts expounded above and below show that pragmatics is not only a discipline dealing with what was left by semantics but a theory of communicative aspects of language par excellence. A theory of interpretation makes a part of it; it includes literary interpretation and a question as to whether this type of interpretation is productive in legal interpretation as a part of Legal Linguistics and legal theory or not. Our problem has also a historical background. The development in semiotics opposed the *dyadic* (binary) and the *triadic* sign models (Jackson 1985: 3; Recanati 2008: 138). The evolution of the concept of sign in the semiotic research strengthened our view upon law as a complex sign which cannot cope without its interpreter. The search of meaning in the classical sense, supported by reference to the work of Ferdinand de Saussure based its views on a dyadic concept of *signifiant* and *signifié*. This concept was radically questioned by Jacques Derrida who challenged the space between the sign and the signified. Charles Sanders Peirce went even further and imagined already during de Saussure's lifetime a triadic sign model composed of signs, objects and interpretants (Sheriff 1989). The result of this distinction has been that not only the structural method was challenged but also our static view of a sign composed of two isolated elements had to be abandoned. The interpreter returned on the semiotic scene and made theory more complicated but also more revealing. Why should this distinction matter to the legal linguist? In works such as G. Cornu's *Linguistique juridique* the dyadic sign model is adapted (Cornu 2005: 26). The focus upon *signifiant* et *signifié* in the sense of the term introduced by Ferdinand de Saussure and later, in 1915, published in *Cours de linguistique générale* results in a perspective which stresses semantic implications of the legal language. Cornu (2005: 29) mentions pragmatics as *nom donné à l'étude des relations entre les signes et leurs usagers* and provides an impressive list of speech acts identified in the French legal language (2005: 38). Nevertheless, he finally concentrates in his approach towards Legal Linguistics on semantic aspects of the legal terminology and of the legal discourse. Hence, the dyadic sign model prefigures the subsequent treatment of the legal language. It leads also to the preference of decoding of meaning in texts to the detriment of their interpretation (Jackson 1985: 20). As law is for us an argumentative practice, we will support here approaches to the sign structure that allow an adequate description of the language use in law and that include all three pragmatically relevant components. We will also assume in the following that a semantic theory is truth-conditioned. With this in mind one could ask whether the truth-conditionality is a sufficient criterion to determine the meaning of a legal concept. Were it the case, then taking into account the pragmatic implications in a legal analysis would be an unnecessary burden for lawyers. However, some theories of interpretation, like R. Dworkin's, base the interpretation at least in hard cases on contextual assumptions and cannot infer their 'right contents' through the applying of procedures of formal logics on them. Here, we adhere to these views and therefore cannot support a conception of Legal Linguistics based on concepts and methods of traditional semantics that attempts to decode an alleged unequivocal meaning in legal texts. In the following paragraph we will see that others researchers share our reservations.

1.2.7 Extention of the concept of semantics

The realm of semantics can also be defined broadly and include most if not all issues traditionally allotted to pragmatics (cf. Recanati 2008: 97). This extention of the concept of semantics would invade upon the realm of pragmatics even if defined very narrowly. Indeed, also the opposite operation is possible. At the current stage of discussion about semantics and pragmatics we still have an option and we will exercise it to the benefit of pragmatics. We feel encouraged to do so also by the ongoing discussion in the linguistics about the overlapping areas in both pragmatics and semantics (cf. Pohl 2008). Nevertheless, we shall mention that some researchers still insist upon the necessity to distinguish strictly the semantic and the pragmatic domains (cf. Akmajian 2001: 264). Also in the contemporary legal-theoretical discussion many attempts have been undertaken to redefine the relation between semantics and pragmatics. Canale and Tuzet (2007: 33) identified the drift towards the pragmatization of semantics as a consequence of the strengthening of the pragmalinguistic theory in law. In our view, this drift may also strengthen the overall position of the pragmalinguistic theory as it shows its general utility. When nowadays inferential conceptions of semantics can operate with concepts such as *context sensitivity*, *process sensitivity* or *contextual constraints* (Canale and Tuzet 2007: 40) so it is possible only due to the pioneer work done within the pragmatic research. Traditional semantics does not contribute much to issues which we perceive as central in the Legal Linguistics. Its strength lies in the moment of incorporation of pragmatic concepts in its own theory which is accounted for by Canale and Tuzet (2007: 32) who also admit that for the legal interpretation the pragmatics of the semantic content is useful. Here we may note that pragmatists even in the time when the classics of pragmatics, J.L. Austin or L. Wittgenstein, were at work never had doubts about this result. This can in part explain the reasons for our preferential choice of the pragmatic perspective which in our view can better integrate traditional areas of language description.

1.2.8 Is there more than language in law?

Previously, different perspectives upon law, of which the legal and the linguistic ones are central, have been demonstrated in order to illustrate the specifics of the legal-linguistic point of view. We can now re-enter the discussion of a basic question in this introductory part that is whether laws are made only of words. This question is not a pure intellectual experiment. It concerns the essence of all activities in law and must therefore be approached also as a precondition of the Legal Linguistics. In fact, were law made of words only, which means that it were an amalgam of phrases, it would not make sense to study it as it would not provide any knowledge that could be generalized or systematized. The Legal Linguistics would still be possible but it would be practically useless because law would be based on arbitrary use of language. Some critics of law discouraged legal studies refering to law as a boundle of sophisms. Others were suspicious about law as a subject of academic studies because for them the law provided regularly several and contradictory answers to a legal question. Science, so they claimed, had to deliver a precise answer to a precise question as it were allegedly the case in other branches of knowledge, for instance in natural sciences. These critics underestimated the complexity of language where no mechanism prevents engendering false or contradictory utterances. However, our language allows for the formulation of competing utterances in terms of truth or validity. This is one of the most interesting qualities of language for the legal linguist. Luckily, language has also the capacity to engender coherent worlds. This means that by using language we are able to construct worlds of words which are organized in more complex units such as speech acts. Some of those worlds created with words are quite complex. N. Goodman (1978) pointed out that many of our primary conceptions about the world such as our comprehension of the universe and the stellar bodies are structured around linguistic creations like *Morning Star* and the like. On the other hand, however, we are aware of that there exists also a non-linguistic, non-verbal reality, a world composed with objects without words (Searle 1999: 14). Our interest in the issue is that we wish to position law on the scale between linguistic and non-linguistic worlds. We need to know the place law takes on this scale in order to be able to determine what matters in the Legal Linguistics and what does not. Yet, first of all, the determination of the place law takes on the scale between linguistic and non-linguistic determines the future of this discipline. Here, again, we will start with the analysis of some linguistic examples. In a text sample from the Wall Street Journal: *The Malacca strait links the Indian and the Pacific Oceans and carries half of the world's oil and a third of its commerce* we discover a purely linguistic reality – in an alleged link *Malacca strait* between *two* oceans, all this being a linguistic construct related to nature. The other part of it is metaphorical use. This linguistic construct structures nature in a specific way, many other structures (or none) would be thinkable as well. In its factual background there is solely water. Another example is the one of the *sun set*. We know even with our rudimentary knowledge of school astronomy that in reality the sun neither sets nor rises. Yet, we understand the motivation grounded in unsophisticated daily experience which stands behind the lexicalization of this experience. Cultural phenomena are constructed along the same principles. The famous orientalist Edward Said (1979: 6) stressed that the term *orientalism* were an occidental invention and as such has no role to play in the cultural sciences. It is one more linguistic invention. We create such language because we create culture. Occasionally, someone, like E. Said in the debate about *orientalism*, is able to make clear that this sort of linguistic creation is empty, that is has no material content. Are legal utterances of the same type? Some legal materials may indicate a positive answer. Sometimes the linguistic character of law is explicitly invoked by jurists and one may therefore ask whether this fact is indicative of the nature of the phenomenon law or rather of a specific professional view jurists adopt when they approach legal problems. Let us now illustrate this problem with an example. The Maldonado case, already quoted here among our introductory narratives as case V and known through the decision of the House of Lords as State of Spain v. Treasury Solicitor (All ER 1953 vol.2. p.1579 sqq.) is in this respect a challenge. As far as the claim of the State of Spain to be granted a letter of administration for the estate of its intestate deceased citizen, Ms. Maldonado, is based on Spanish law where the estate is inherited by the State as last heir, the House of Lords might have considered it as in accordance with the laws of England. Were the claim based on the Spanish law understood as providing the right to the estate through an act of appropriation it might have considered it as contrary to the laws of England. One of the Lord Justices while recognizing the linguistic dimension of the case put it this way: *"the distinction between succession by a sovereign State and the appropriation of bona vacantia by a foreign State is said to be* **a mere matter of words**. *This argument is not without persuasive force, but I do not think the question can truly be said to be one of* **distinction without difference**. *The foreign State can only succeed under its own law of succession where the succession is governed by that law. On the other hand, where the case is not one of succession but of appropriation of ownerless property, the right applies to any ownerless property which may be reached by the law of the foreign State concerned, irrespective of the law by which its devolution is governed, provided only that by the relevant law it is in fact ownerless. Then it is said that the foreign State, being omnipotent so far as its own law of succession is concerned, can* **constitute itself successor** *in circumstances in which it could equally well rely on claim based on jus regale. But in accepting the foreign State's law of succession, English law recognizes the foreign State as arbiter of what the succession is to be."* (emphasis supplied)

Does the above quote convince us that there is more behind the legal issue at stake than words? The characterization of a legal problem as a *distinction without difference* or *a mere matter of words* clearly indicates that from the judge's point of view we have here to do with sophisms. On the other side, the judge also argues that a legal argument may also have a *persuasive force* and then it would not be a *distinction without difference,* i.e. a sophism. It would convince him, we may suppose, because it conveys a truth, i.e an utterance which convinces the professional of law. The specific structure of this truth in terms of the legal profession is for the judge of argumentative nature because it has a *persuasive force.* Also Alf Ross (1957) supposed that in law we are able to speak significantly with meaningless words; only the context of use determined for him the meaning of legal notions such as *ownership.* We may therefore retain as a result of our introductory remarks that law appears here for the judge as a linguistic product which transports a very specific truth. This truth is grounded in professional argumentation about the validity of propositions that state the law. The task of the legal linguist is to determine the linguistic constituents of this professionally defined truth. Consequently, when we ask ourselves whether law is in fact language and nothing more than that we ask a fundamental question of the Legal Linguistics. Negative answers would probably come from some branches of social sciences. Some would argue that law makes part of social sciences which analyze societies that fill the law with content. But here, again, it seems that it is first of all the notion of language which stimulates the debate rather than the law itself. Language perceived in pragmatic terms cannot be viewed simply as a system of formally related signs outside the society in which it has been created and in which it functions and evolves. Thus, language even as an abstract notion automatically reflects all social practices because it is grounded in them. In this narrower sense, law is very much about language. More precisely, law refers to and is constituted by acts of legal argumentation. Yet, opinions concerning the notion of *language,* its extension and its limits differ as well.

1.2.9 What conception of language to choose?

Thus, in order to be able to deal with this intricate fundamental question the linguist must reflect upon the linguistic elements in legal provisions. And this task, in turn, requires that the legal linguist as a professional of language has a clear conception of what language is actually about. The reflection upon language is at least as old as the reflection upon law. Therefore, while dealing with these phenomena and especially when dealing with both of them simultaneously a choice is necessary among various conceptions of law and of language. A further choice must be done among interdisciplinary conceptions of Law and Language. In this book, we have constantly exercised choices but we have also justified our preferences. In the introductory part we deal with the theoretical framework of the

Legal Linguistics for which a conceptual network is necessary. While discussing the different approaches we simply describe the way in which we are looking for this framework. Linguistics, however, does not provide for one coherent view of language. Therefore, the legal linguist cannot take the concept of language for granted in the hope that an implicit theory of language would manifest itself in due course of her research. When we pretend – and some may perceive it as truly pretentious – that we are developing here a theory of law which is in its heart linguistic, we will have to state what is language for us. Helpful in this sense are extreme views such as R. Rorty's formula *'there is no such thing as a language'* (Rorty 1992: 373). This means first of all that the concept of language depends upon the linguistic theory adopted for its description. We could use here as a reference for the legal-linguistic research a classical conception of linguistics like the one presented in Jean Aitchison's *Linguistics* (1978: 18) or in J. Lyons' introductory work into theoretical linguistics (1968). Both feature phonetics, phonology, syntax, semantics and interdisciplinary areas in sequence. We could also adopt a circle of linguistic levels starting with a bigger unit like text and ending with phonetics. Yet, by so doing we would have to prove that all these linguistic levels are equally relevant for the emergence of the legal meaning that is central for our view of language use in law. The reader realizes that this cannot be the right answer. Mattila (2002a: 175) attempted a choice in this sense and stressed also its limits. Language clearly is not composed of words that are structured according to syntactic rules. It is much more than that. Formally, one could argue that without a physical act of uttering sounds – which we can localize at the lowest level of the traditional linguistic scheme – no legal meaning would come up. And this is right, but this is a very formal truth. We realize that a sincere answer to problems we are here dealing with cannot be simply reduced to sound emitting. On the other side, an approach which focuses exclusively on syntactic or semantic features of legal language is vulnerable because it is obviously incomplete. Language is a complex mechanism and it does not consist of philosophical traps and paradoxes as it does not consist exclusively of simple physical sound emissions. We therefore need a broader conceptual basis, but it should not be too broad. Too broad is a formal-logical analysis of legal language because it cannot explain the argumentative and interpretive moments in the legal language and especially in norm application (cf. Verschueren/Östman 1995: 60). It also remains incomplete – although on a very high level of abstraction.

For legal linguists, the linguistic pragmatics - and especially the speech act theory and the discourse theory – has the advantage that it covers all levels of language description upside down or vice versa and provides their appropriate evaluation in terms of a pragmatic perspective. The speech act theory grounds its observations in the physical act of voice emitting. The *locutionary act* is the very beginning of the linguistic adventure without which no linguistic act would subsist. But it also insists on the multilayered structure of *illocutionary* and sometimes *perlocutionary* acts which convey propositions and not only sounds and which produce meaning in the sense which interests us here. The basic unit remains the *speech act* and not the more or less indivisible phonem and this is already a good beginning. The speech acts can be analyzed in isolation or as parts of broader units such as *discourses*. In terms of linguistics, a phenomenon that interests us can be perceived as described exhaustively when its role in a discourse has been identified. In Legal Linguistcs, at least, no higher level of speech realization than the *legal discourse* seems to exist. Therefore, we favor the pragmatic instruments for language description. Among them especially the speech act theory proved to be able to provide particularly innovative insights into the way how law functions through language. Yet, before speech acts emerge in the language complex signification processes must take place there.

1.2.10 What is language in terms of pragmatics?

We can explain those complex signification processes on a few examples. An English language speaker will easily be convinced by the enunciation that *strong* collocates with *coffee* in an expression *strong coffee*, but *powerful* does not. On the other hand, in the German language both collocations are effective provided they are transferred correctly. Why is it so? In the daily use of a language speakers make choices from its vocabulary while constructing sentences according to syntactic rules. These choices are the basis for the pragmatic aspect of language next to its syntactic and semantic aspects. However, in language choice is limited. Linguistic rules determine the ambit of our linguistic creativity. Our example has a semantic connotation like the classical question *Is the Buckingham Palace a house?* which is perceived by many as a problem of semantics. While in both examples the semantic and the syntactic aspects are undeniably traceable, the preference of speakers can be explained only from the pragmatic perspective, i.e. from the daily use of language by the speakers. One can test the efficacy of this approach by analyzing the use of the expression *Good Morning!* which is applied only under definite conditions and can be shifted to other conversational situations dominated by irony or threat only with the reference to the conventional use. Hence, the scope of application of this expression can be widened to include ironical greetings that mean exactly the opposite of the affirmative and benevolent aim of a *Good Morning!* To grasp this specific usage we definitely need pragmatics. We realize that speakers understand such ironical expressions without problems. They automatically determine the right context of their use. And this holds true also of a procedure that is necessary for speaking and understanding language: the context cannot be separated from the vocabulary and the syntax. Otherwise, an enunciation would be understandable only to those who understand it anyway; it is to the speakers but not the hearers. As seen, language use involves an interpreter and it does not exist beyond the act of its usage by the speakers. The interpreter tries to identify intentions in speech acts. In our *Good Morning!* - example he will regularly be able to determine whether the speaker uses it as a formal greeting formula or whether he uses it informally, when the morning has began really badly for him or for the hearer. The linguistic and especially the *pragmatic competence* enable the interpreter to figure out what is actually meant with an utterance. This is, in short, the way in which speakers and hearers cope with the language. The approach which will be followed in this book is close to this experience because the act of identifying intentions is crucial for jurists' work with language in their daily practice. The legal linguist can also deal with the language in its abstract form, as it is stated in a dictionary. In such a case, however, many legal-linguistic operations will be overlooked, because they manifest themselves exclusively in the use of the language under changing circumstances. Equally, one could deal with the utterance *Good Morning!* in the sense declared in most dictionaries and English primers. There, we would identify this expression as a *greeting*, but we would not understand that it may also mean an ironical greeting or even a threat. The legal linguist who works with a pragmatic method cannot simply look into dictionaries when she interprets the legally relevant language. She would miss the point would she concentrate on the static and abstract form of language. When we deal with an abstract form of it we deal with linguistic remnants or certain selected aspects of it, but definitively not with *the* language.

Let us look at some additional examples which illustrate how the use determines meaning. Would we agree when a specialist analyzing the enunciations: *War is war*, *Paris is Paris* or *Children are children* would pretend that they express a logical relation of the propositional subject with itself, that they are tautologies? Almost certainly we would argue that our expert does not get the phrases right, although in terms of the formal logics these enunciations are classical examples of tautologies. Yet, they say us much more than their logical form seems to indicate to our specialist, because we are able to identify their metaphorical use. The same concerns enunciations formulated in a negative way, their logical sisters like: *The England of today is not the England of yersterday* which mean more than a simple negation of the subject. Still further, in *A child needs love* or in *A car must be insured* we instantaneously understand that not an individual child or a particular car is meant but rather a general concept embracing all children or all cars. We are able to infer the meaning from the syntactical form of the sentences only because we also understand the use which leads to the emergence of such syntactic structures. In language, levels analyzed by linguists in isolatation, like syntax or semantics, are intertwined. They regularly also imply each other. For example, semantic and syntactic implications are manifest in *The **news is** good.* They are linked to the pragmatics of such an utterance. The pragmatic aspect in the utterance is that speakers form this sort of counter-systemic structures. The principles of their choice making are pragmatic although the linguistic mechanisms implied in the utterances are mainly morphologic and syntactic. A further example may make clearer this interdependence of linguistic levels in the language. How do we construe the difference between *rabbit* and *bunny* or *dog* and *doggie*, the later two words in each pair belonging to infantile use. We are able to differentiate between the lexical variations because we know the context of their use, and therefore properly identify them as in essence equal but belonging to either adult or infantile use. This essence seems to belong to the realm of semantics, the rest is pragmatics. Paradoxically, without the residual pragmatics the essential discovery would remain useless, a pure formality. Therefore, these seemingly trivial examples make plain why we instist upon the eminent role of the pragmatic reasoning in this book. Pragmatics and pragmalinguistics are not limited to speech acts, conversational implicatures etc., although they include all of those aspects. Pragmatics shows how language works in general. Its scope is very broad and we will not be able to use it with all its potentialities in a research limited to preliminary questions of the Legal Linguistics.

1.2.11 The linguistic turn in law

One more fundamental legal-linguistic issue has to be mentioned in the introductory part as an explanation for conceptual choices exercised in this book. In the history of thought this issue is called the *linguistic turn.* The linguistic turn marked the development of philosophy in the last century. Its initial idea had been that fundamental philosophical problems were in essence linguistic problems. Therefore, the hope arose within the analytic philosophy that through the application of linguistic analysis upon philosophical concepts the main philosophical issues could be solved (Rorty 1992: 371). And, as a matter of fact serious progress has been achieved in the philosophical research by means of the linguistic analysis. Fundamentally, notions pertaining to metaphysics were identified as such and excluded from the scientific discourse (Engel 2000: 63). Later on, the conceptions of formal scientific language were developed. In the consequence of these efforts the interest shifted towards the ordinary language and its use. This is also the stage which today might be perceived as most promising within the inheritance of analytical philosophy. Whether analytical philosophy led to the solution of the most pertaining philosophical problems has been an issue of controversial debates. Certainly, it is not up to us to determine the result of these debates. We are foremost interested in the linguistic turn because it did not take place in the legal science although the hypothesis that legal problems are at their bottom problems of language is within the reach of daily professional experience of jurists as well as of people concerned by their decisions. In law, the linguistic turn would accomplish a shift of interest from the isolated systematization of provisions and concepts in the civil law tradition and in the parallel also a shift from analyzing rules and principles in the common law with means perceived as logical towards a linguistic perspective. Law would be seen predominantly as a linguistic phenomenon because it is created and applied in linguistic operations. This shift in perspective is not really revolutionary because it mainly states the factual situation. It does not create any new law, but simply adjusts our perception of law. There is no reason why the fundamental operations in law, i.e. its creation and its application, should be perceived as something else than linguistic operations. But, surprisingly, they are even today approached from all but linguistic points of view. As already demonstrated, systematization efforts in law concerned different linguistic aspects of emergence of legal rules and their application. As mentioned in 1.1.4.1, legal rules had been divided as representing *substantive* law, *procedural* law or *conflict of laws*. Branches of law, such as contracts, torts, administrative, penal or constitutional law had been developed upon the basic distinction traditionally made since the Roman times between *private* and *public* law which itself is a result of systematization efforts of legal rules. In the law of the European Union, the rules have been divided into *primary* and *secondary* law. These different perspectives ground in doctrines and dogmas used in the legal research and in the legal education. It would not be particularly realistic to wish that they disappear from the legal discourse, mostly because they form a substantial part of it. Systematization efforts in law led to a more transparent structure of law. They also improved the rationality of decisions taken in the domain of law. But they also displayed limits of this approach. To be truly operative in law, systematization would have to focus on legal arguments as used in legal discourses and not on legal concepts and their prerequisites. Yet, the systematization of legal arguments did not take place. However, it seems inevitable that issues pertaining to the legal argumentation would be perceived as central for the legal research and the legal education. Still today, legal argumentation is treated mostly as a peripheral phenomenon belonging to legal theory and not to the core activities in the legal research and the legal education. The linguistic turn in law that is supported in this book intervenes precisely at this point.

1.3 Morals for Lawyers

1.3.1 Law without morals?

Some eminent legal thinkers might have opposed this topic fundamentally while saying that law is not necessarily connected to morality (cf. Jackson 1985: 6) and that this negative relation is also true when inversed. Therefore, they would discourage us to deal with this topic in a book dedicated to the Legal Linguistics. Moreover, they would stress that in law we deal with legal institutions and statements which provide us the basis for prediction of future judicial decisions and not about the evolution and the appraisal of values. They would also try to convince us that jurists do not need to deal with ethics because all decisions pertaining to morals in law have been taken already before the stage when jurists begin to work. They would shift the responsibility for the ethical content of the law to parliaments which debate and enact laws within political discourses that embrace all pertinent arguments, not only the legal ones. Therefore, for many specialists the relation between the legal language and the results it produces in law remains unclear. Some claim that bad legislation can emerge from the same legal language as well as good, like a bad house or a good house can be constructed from bricks of the same quality (Pigolkin 1990: 8). In their view, the legal language should be perceived as a *neutral tool* in the hands of the legislator. However, the existence of a neutral language has never been proven with the necessary conviction. Legal language, even the formal if not formalistic language of the Roman private law is value-laden and transports convictions and views about the social practice which are fundamental for the society in which it had emerged. The legal rules are not only a result of value-laden social debates; they are also a part of them (Hare 1952). Discourse about values is an ongoing debate. At times, we are not able to recognize its nature. This happens also when we deal with the Roman law that is remote from the debates of our times and that provides us rather the form, i.e. concepts than their social background. The approach that strictly distinguishes between law and ethics belongs to the legal positivism. Its most negative outcome is that it encourages obedience to immoral law (Minda 1995: 51). This result should be avoided in the Legal Linguistics. Consequently, in the following paragraphs attention will be called to issues concerning ethics, especially ethics as perceived by lawyers who take decisions related to social values. The reflection upon these issues is necessary here because values manifest themselves in the legal language as an inherent part of it. The legal linguist cannot understand the law and, in consequence, also the linguistic aspects of the law without understanding the processes in which values enter into the law and also determine its application.

1.3.2 Some examples of morals in law

We may clarify the ethical residue in the law with the help of two additional introductory cases:

Case VI

Casey Martin, a successful professional golfer who won numerous competitions applied to the golf tournament organizers to permit him the use of a cart. The reason for Martin's request has been his progressing disease that has atrophied his right leg. This degenerative circulatory disorder called Klippel-Trenaunay-Weber syndrom caused Martin pain and fatigue during his walks and created a significant risk of hemorrhaging and fracturing his tibia. The tournament organizers refused to accommodate his request claiming that all competitors had to play on equal conditions. Martin sued the tournament organizers.

The U.S. Supreme Court had to deal with Martin's case. In PGA Tour Inc. v. Martin (532 U.S. 661, 121 S. Ct. 1879, 2001 U.S. LEXIS 4115) it had to decide whether the provisions of the Americans with Disabilities Act (ADA) guaranteed to a handicapped professional golf player the use of a golf cart during the tournaments which obligated the participants to walk during the play. One of the lower courts decided that using a golf cart in a situation where other participants had to walk would *'fundamentally alter the nature of the tournaments'*. The U.S. Supreme Court did not share this view and decided in favor of Martin. However, in the dissenting opinion, the decision is criticized for exercising *benevolent compassion* with the handicapped plaintiff instead of applying law. *'Agility, strength, speed, balance, quickness of mind, steadiness of nerves, intensity of concentration'* says the dissenting opinion *'are not evenly distributed. No wild-eyed dreamer has ever suggested that the managing bodies of the competitive sports that test precisely these qualities should try to take account of the uneven distribution of God-given gifts when writing and enforcing the rules of competition'*. Thus, according to the dissent the plaintiff would have to accept this fact as he had to accept his progressive handicap. The dissenting opinion developes an own rule for the application of the ADA. This rule postulates that in ordinary situations handicapped persons would have to accept their handicap unless the statute provides for explicit guarantees of equal treatment. However, this rule is nothing more than one of possible linguistic interpretations of the ADA. It does not replace the statute; neither does it discover a better law, a better meaning of the provision. Towards the background of social goals on which the ADA is based the majority decision is more convincing. It is better embedded in the ethical rules of the contemporary society which strives to limit the manifestation of physical inequalities and to integrate handicapped persons in all areas of social life.

The introductory case VII will further stress the value-load of law:

Parents of a public middle school student sued the school in order to prevent prayers, benedictions and religious invocations during the graduation ceremony by a clergyman invited by the school. They relied on the establishment clause of the First Amendment of the U.S. Constitution that says: *Congress shall make no law respecting an establishment of religion, or prohibiting the free exercise thereof; or abridging the freedom of speech, or the press; or the right of the people peaceably to assemble, and to petition the Government for a redress of grievances.* The U.S. Supreme Court in its decision Lee v. Weisman (112 S.Ct. 2649 (1992)) found that compelling students to participate in a religious exercise is forbidden by the Consitution. It referred to the generally accepted interpretation providing that the government may not coerce anyone to support or participate in religion or its exercise, or otherwise act in a way which establishes a state religion, or tends to do so. Again, in the dissenting opinion, a contrary view was expressed by pretending mainly that: (1) the establishment of religion clause should not have been interpreted so as to invalidate a long-standing American tradition of non-sectarian prayer at public schools graduation, (2) religious invocations and benedictions during the graduation ceremonies involve no psychological coercion of students to participate in religious exercises, (3) the only coercion that is forbidden by the clause is that backed by the threat of penalty, and (4) the school did not direct or control the prayers during the graduation ceremony so that no involvement of the government with religious activity could have been established.

Doubtlessly, deciding the two above cases without taking an ethical standing, i.e. exercising choices among values at stake is not possible. The application of law does not consist of a schematic or rigid use of preformulated linguistic templets or in decoding of meaning in the concepts challenged before the U.S. Supreme Court. It involves constant decision making processes in a society where a debate about values is ongoing. Pragmatic aspects of the legal language are related to values which dominate the public discourse about the right content of law. The citizenry has its own opinions about what is right and what is wrong in society; what is just and what is unjust. Sometimes it also provides reasons for its choices. Jurists, too, have opinions about which values to support in society and which tendencies to combat. They use these opinions to solve legal cases as those illustrated above.

1.3.3 What is the place of law in our life?

In everyone's biography the presence of law is sensible at least to some extent. We know from our experience that law is neither almighty nor does it fill the room around us totally. In the rapidly changing world some wish rather more law, forgetting that law is not omnipotent, while others wish rather less law and more spontaneous and collective decisions about what is right and what is wrong in society. The later refer to the alleged failure of law to establish sustainable peace in society and among nations. Both share the view that law matters although they weigh its impact differently. We shall therefore ask where law is particularly effective and why it is important to have it there. Law is obviously not as omnipresent as oxygen is in the air around us, nor is it our invisible companion like gravitation or radiation. Neither law nor its fundamental principles can be found in nature nor can nature help us to learn something about law when we have to create or to apply it. Yet still, we often notice and sometimes we are even forced to acknowledge that law exists. Of course, this is only occasionally the case. Law is an elusive companion, it appears in our lives from time to time and its importance varies – it is rather capricious like a cat and not faithful like a dog. But, still, it is domesticated enough to play a constant, although not decisive, role which is taken care of by natural phenomena or moral principles in our daily life. Therefore, law should not be overestimated as to the role that it plays in our lives and compared with oxygen, although it might occasionally function as oxygen for the society or be seen as a tool of a sovereign who exercises power through it. Neither do we constantly need law nor are we its obedient slaves. The legal linguist realizes that law plays a different role in our life than language without which we cannot cope even for a moment. It regulates only parts of our biography and structures only partly our societies. In structuring and regulating individual or social behavior law makes use of sets of values and becomes part of our behavior, i.e. of our *life form* which we used to call daily life. It may still be much less necessary in our life than oxygen or language. Yet, modern societies are aboundantly regulated and become increasingly dominated by the law as the language used in them becomes more and more legal.

1.3.4 Why law matters although it is not omnipotent?

When asked by a policeman on the street to show our ID card without that we would be able to understand the reasons for his demand, or when we are requested to follow him to the next police station we notice the importance of law. If we are employed by someone whom we progressively disgust and he/she feels exactly the same way about us, or when we are demanded to pay tax advances in an amount which makes appear our daily striving futile, we again realize the importance of law. It matters of course on many other occasions as well, but when we sit on a bench in the municipal park or take a sunbath at the seaside, it often does not matter at all. However, if a bellicose person does not appreciate the way we used to sit on a bench or questions our way to make our skin smooth by sunshine and uses force to appear more persuasive, then law matters again, more than ever. Modern law is construed as a mechanism that protects citizens. The interest in studying it is linked to this task. Meanwhile, it also transports elements of control or constraint. What is more, in times of globalization the power of the national state and its law diminishes. The national law does not attract any more by its triumphant mechanisms of enforcement. Its subjects, who became citizens in the course of societal evolution and nowadays perceive themselves increasingly as citizens of the world, abandon realms they dislike. Thus, the legislator who wishes not to become alienated or lonely in the end will have to make laws palpable to the citizens concerned. Pampered and spoiled as they are, the citizens become gradually the real princes of the law. Yet still, even if the legal catering does not always work out, it shows that law matters. The legal linguist knows how to make better laws, i.e. how to use language in a way that the final product of legislative efforts would convince the citizens about the necessity of measures taken. The same holds true for court decisions. Our two initial cases VI and VII have probably proven to most readers that ethical problems can be solved by courts in a satisfying way. Therefore, there is generally no reason to disrespect or ignore the law in critical situations. In fact, as law can be a fine companion, our question will be how to find it and how to cope with it best, uphold its friendship, and construe it properly. As we appreciate friendship but disapprove obstinacy, we are ready to become its critical friends after we have found it. This question demands but also rewards concentration.

1.3.5 Material ethics and formal ethics

Our two introductory examples with ethical load have demonstrated that there is a way to solve such cases. They have shown also that opinions about the right solution of fundamental ethical questions in them may differ even among professionals of law. Indeed, the diversity of opinions about ethical issues dealt with in law is a social fact. Gender, racial or environmental issues, same sex marriage or pornography lead to controversies in societies. We have different opinions about what is right and what is wrong in the society we live in, and we even have views about right and wrong in societies we do not belong to, and which we for instance visit as tourists. Values and opinions about them differ, and change with time. To date, all efforts to establish material provisions related to values which would be acceptable for all members of the society have failed. For many values there is no common denominator which would unify the disparate views about them. Therefore, some were tempted by the idea to establish institutions which ruled authoritatively about what was right and what was wrong in a society. However, this idea is becoming less and less persuasive for most people nowadays.

1.3.5.1 Science shows the way? Science has been perceived by many as the last resort for establishing the right way to go in society. However, scientists have also been in the avant-garde to demonstrate the variety of possible views and opinions about society and its values. Economists, sociologists and psychologists deal with this variety which for them constitutes society and they are not inclined to reduce it along some obscure directives. Jurists or other scholars cannot know it better than other citizens whether pornography or prostitution in a society should be forbidden or legalized. We can assume that they have their own view on these issues as citizens, but this view is not a professional one. Roughly the same could be assumed of other professionals. At best, science can show the material diversity of societal views about values but it cannot establish the right values for a society, neither can it provide instruments for distinguishing right from wrong (Mackie 1977: 35). We increasingly become aware of the circumstance that values in society are a question of debate and that this ongoing debate is unavoidable in every society. Where it does not take place, the society becomes rigid and stagnates. Where it is forbidden, totalitarian, oppressive and inhumane rule puts down roots which are difficult to eradicate once they encroached in society.

1.3.5.2 Establishing rules for social dialogue: As soon as we become aware of that all societal issues are by their very nature subjected to deliberation, science can help. It can work on establishing methods for the efficient deliberation in society about the appropriateness of value-laden choices which are grounded in material ethics (cf. Steinvorth 1990: 48). It can show how is it possible to reach the most advanced solution in a societal debate about a value-related issue such as virtual child pornography, insider trading or tax evasion. The task to set up procedures in which the diverse ethical views could be discussed in society in the most appropriate way coincides with argumentative techniques and procedures. It is therefore crucial to grasp the importance and the place of moral issues in law. They are definitely not excluded from it. Instead, they make part of it; but they do it in a very specific way. Therefore, we can concentrate in this book upon issues relating to language and still remain in the center of the debate about values. Moreover, while talking about the language use in law we would not be able to avoid ethical issues. In sum, the relation between law and ethics can be perceived as a typical academic problem. Like language, ethics cannot be distilled away from law. Equally, language cannot be divided from ethical issues that it vehicles. Thinking these issues together is a challenge for the legal science. Analyzing this challenge is the task of the legal linguist.

1.3.5.3 Professional ethics for lawyers: Jurists would however feel abandoned had they to cope with the diversity of opinions about moral values on their own. Therefore, law provides for its professionals some directives for the appropriate dealing with it. Legal morality is based on issues central for the strengthening of democracy and peace in the world. It is based on principles which with time were filled with substance and which constantly must be refined and modernized. Culture of peace, culture of human rights, cultural diversity and business ethics make part of this moral background of law (cf. Rorty 1993: 115). They make it possible to create general legal rules and to apply them in cases. The closer the jurist, and especially the judge, approaches the most convincing standards of legal morality in his decision the better is the law governing the given society. One could contest this view by the contention that jurists do not need to endorse the law; they solely need to know it. Also this view is problematic as it has a clear positivist background. This approach enables, at best, the systematization of law; the application of law remains impossible without a defined opinion about values which shape the most convincing legal decision. Furthermore, all legal professions, for instance attorneys-at-law regularly set up rules for the exercise of their profession. Other corporate legal professions such as judges have also set up moral standards for their professional acting. This is by far not an exclusive attempt to define morals in terms of professional constraints. Also in the business life a vivid discussion about the business ethics is going on and issues relevant to corporate governance and codes of conduct are perceived as central within modern managerial structures.

1.3.5.4 Volatility of law: One of the most irritating aspects of law, especially for those dealing with this phenomenon professionally, is that it constantly changes. The formulation by Julius von Kirchmann (1938: 37) that three words of the legislator can convert whole juridical libraries into wastepaper became proverbial for generations of lawyers. This is of course a practical problem to which lawyers have to adapt. They do not work on a construction of an edifice which is growing bigger floor by floor. Instead, they are rather engaged in reconstructing the building which should become more convenient for its inhabitants to live in. This volatility of law has consequences for the work with law which includes its setting, its study and its application. Legal science is a method rather than a set of provisions once established. Methodological skills make the jurist and distinguish him from the layperson. Methodological skills embrace a lot of disparate issues like working with definitions and legal terminology, establishing facts from the testimony of others, tracing the appropriate legal provisions at the moment of their application. All these skills are grounded in language use. Therefore, coping with the volatility of law means being able to use the language of law adequately.

1.3.6. How to trace ethics in law?

We were until now dealing with ethical issues in law as if they were unproblematically visible in legal texts. This is definitely not the case and frequently it is necessary to prove that a legal text, e.g. a legal act or a judicial opinion, displays problems which are relevant in terms of ethics. This is the case because ethically relevant issues in law are as a rule not discussed as problems of ethics but as problems of the application of law. In this situation, the sister discipline of the Legal Linguistics, Law and Literature, provides some methodological advice as how to proceed. It analyzes an issue of law as a part of literature, mostly by focusing upon narrative fiction presented by a writer, e.g. Franz Kafka or Fyodor Dostoevsky. There, it can free itself from the boundaries of the rule-oriented legal system and try to focus upon the ethical problems in law in a safe isolation from the immediate boundaries of jurisdiction and its formal-procedural requirements. It can view the problems as such and by so doing it manifests that law does not only deal with the application of legal-technical rules and that it cannot be reduced to such simple activity (Weisberg 1992: 237). Furthermore, it makes plain the ethical dimension of law and prefers to reflect its ends rather than procedures (Weisberg 1992: 242). The Legal Linguistics can contribute to this method in that it concentrates on the issues of creation and use of language in ethically critical situations in law. When dealing with ethics in law we are confronted with hierarchical social structures and power issues which are expressed mostly with linguistic means. Here again, it is necessary to adjust the legal-linguistic method to this specific communicative situation where speakers do not talk to each other in a space determined by perfect equality of weapons, arguments and procedures. Scholars, such as James Boyd White, warned in their writings against this power-oriented language use which may rather seek domination instead of dialogue (Weisberg 1992: 237). R. Weisberg scrutinized three publications by White, *The Legal Imagination* (1973), *Heracles' Bow* (1987) and *Justice as Translation* (1991) in order to show that linguistic communication in law has very specific boundaries. Later on, we will focus upon procedural boundaries relevant to the language use as described by Jürgen Habermas and Robert Alexy. White, in turn, and also Weisberg, were rather interested in the ethical issue of the setting of communicative boundaries in law. They came close to the classical perspective taken by Friedrich Nietzsche who viewed power-dominated communication rather skeptically. He insisted upon distance and distrust towards "*writers and institutions primarily centered around the word*" (Weisberg 1992: 302). The Legal Linguistics must learn the bitter lesson based on these findings. This makes any work on language use in law undoubtedly more challenging. But the effort is rewarded by results which explain the law and not only the language used in it.

1.4 An Introduction Must End

It would be tempting to continue in the introductory part into the Legal Linguistics the list of its epistemological prerequisites which - when woven together - would make a coherent new branch of legal sciences or linguistics. Above, we mentioned ethics as one of its pillars. Previously, the deliberative nature of law, the tasks and methods of the legal sciences as well as the necessity to accomplish the linguistic turn in law have been touched upon. On the other side, general linguistics and also a specific perspective upon the language that is called linguistic pragmatics or pragmalinguistics have been introduced as central for the vision of the Legal Linguistics developed in this book. Certainly, we would also have to discuss additionally at least the anthropological parameters of law which ground in the circumstance that law is made by humans for humans and that it emerges towards the background of their culture. We will nevertheless not enter into this issue. Instead, we will remind the readers that law with all its linguistic and ethical constraints is embedded in a broader practice which is our culture. In this culture, law emerges in signification processes as an amalgam of legal signs. Legal semiotics scrutinizes these processes which are deeply hidden in the structure of our minds and our culture. The Legal Linguistics covers only some of these processes. It concentrates on those parts of the legal culture which are expressed verbally. We must of course be aware of the further implications of the semiotic domain, but we do not necessarily need to explore them here in all detail. We have reached here a perspective that enables us to look at how law is expressed with linguistic means which interests us most. This result enables us to end the introduction, and concentrate now on some more specific aspects of the metaphorical relation between law and language.

Part 2: Language and Law

Under the heading Language and Law we will defend the necessity of a discipline called by us and some others Legal Linguistics. We will look back at the achievements of a highly heterogeneous research into Law and Language and sketch possible developments, especially the pragmatically oriented Legal Linguistics. Legal Linguistics will be characterized in its geographic and epistemological development. Subsequently, the borderline will be drawn between it and subjects which come close to it in order to better expose the legal-linguistic domain and mark the difference between this specific subject and the adjacent branches of knowledge. Once the subject of the Legal Linguistics is characterized, the language use in legal contexts will be scrutinized, mostly referring to established (not always pragmatically oriented) research. Furthermore, we will accentuate specific features of language used in law in the light of pragmatics. Especially, we will closely look at the legal terminology and ask what terminology means in terms of pragmatics.

2. 1. Foundations of Legal Linguistics

2.1.1. Language and Law

The principal theoretical issue in the contemporary discussion about the Legal Linguistics has been the long-standing relation between or rather the interrelation of language and law (Mattila 2006: 6) that we explore here mostly as a metaphor. In the terminology used in the English speaking countries, the caption *Law and Language* has been regularly used in order to characterize research into this particular interrelation. We have reversed the common order of words in the above heading for the needs of this chapter in which the language analysis will dominate our perspective. Notwithstanding this change in the perspective we still hope that the analysis which follows can contribute essentially to the classical topic *Law and Language* in equal degree.

As previously mentioned, the very distinction between law and language or in the reverse order the distinction between language and law seems to be rather of stylistic than of substantial nature. Indeed, there is no law without language and to suppose it seriously would mean to fall into one of the numerous metaphysical traps existing both in the legal theory and in the more practically oriented legal reasoning. It seems that the conception of law existing independently of language had never been earnestly considered (Viehweg 1954: 54). Some exceptions could possibly be found in the studies related to logical formalization of law which began with G. W. Leibnitz's (1646-1716) impressive but failed idea of the law operating *more geometrico*. His fundamental works on this issue *Dissertatio de arte combinatoria* (1666) and *Nova methodus discendae docendaeque jurisprudentiae* (1667) show the limits of any attempt to formalize the law, i.e. to make it work like a calculus. Leibnitz has been aware that law is structured by *topoi*, i.e. by certain common places which are recurrently used in the legal argumentation. However, he hoped to be able to control their use under an arithmetically founded *ars combinatoria.* Nowadays, the discursive nature of law is not questioned any more and a method controlling the use of legal arguments with formalized procedures appeals to some few researchers. Moreover, the research into possible formalization of law rather showed the deep logical structure of law functioning in language than the independence of both. Nevertheless, the failure of the formalization project should not be misunderstood. Although law will never function like a logical calculus, it will never function independently of logics either. Challenging in this respect is nowadays the way in which both aspects could be balanced in the research. The central role of language in the law cannot be replaced by any other communicational mechanism. Hence, the distinction between law and language in the above caption - and not only there - is a question of convention in the developing research into this still unclear interrelation. It is, at best, of administrative importance in the Legal Linguistics and it is typical for metaphorical language use that is acceptable provided one is aware of the metaphorical character of such language. Otherwise, it may give rise to problems that are metaphysical, i.e. caused by the language itself. Dealing with the question of law in the language or language in the law is nothing more than a - probable unavoidable - stage in the development of the Legal Linguistics as a theory of law. To date, in the common law tradition that dominates the English speaking world *Law and Language* defines itself, like *Law and Literature* or *Law and Economics*, as an interdisciplinary field which forms upon the both areas of social practice and scientific research, which are law and language respectively (Schauer 1993: xiv). It deals with the development of the legal (mostly English) language and includes a panoply of perspectives with more or less explicit semiotic background. Especially, issues concerning the indeterminacy of legal language as contrasted with the language of literary works attracted the attention of writers in this area. Here again, it becomes obvious that the determination of what is law and what is language is essential for the debate about the metaphorical interrelation of both if a sterile or blurred debate should be avoided. A particular view of law or of language shapes the argumentative framework and the research results. This relation is undoubtedly an issue for a legal theory which also calls itself linguistic. Otherwise, a somehow unproductive listing of situations in which language is used in legal contexts comes up without that further consequences would follow from it. In fact, to maintain that law is both a product of and dependant on language (Schauer 1993: xi) demands further explanation. With Schauer we can underline that this simple claim already includes a position taking in the legal theory. Further elaboration on the issue leads directly into the solved and unsolved problems of the legal theory. According to Schauer, *the rela-*

tionship between law and language seems in some ways special. To say why that is so, however, or even to maintain that it is so at all, is in itself to take a position on one or another position of legal theory. Schauer (1993: ix) deplores the *intrinsic messiness of the subject itself*, and calls it therefore slippery. Indeed, it took two thousand years to reach the level of theoretical reflection on law and language or language and law that we now have at our disposal. The theoretical debate which begins with the Greek rhetoric (Wolf 1952: 13) and continues in the Roman epoch and the Middle Ages (Curtius 1996: 258), which passes through the tormented waves of the Enlightenment and all theoretical approaches which emerged in modern times (cf. Berman 1983) had produced an amalgam of ideas, perspectives and opinions. Again, it took time to separate the wheat from the chaff and lay foundations for the contemporary legal theory and to prove the necessity of the Legal Linguistics. Therefore, when talking about language and law, we should bear in mind this unusual process of development, its aspects of continuity and discontinuity, turns and breaches in the debate about the conceptual relation we focus upon (Viehweg 1954: 29). Rare are disciplines which can refer to such an edifying past and even rarer are those which can directly benefit from research done into their subject by generations profoundly remote in time. It is worthwhile to ask about the possible reasons for this thematic continuity. First of all, it might be that practical needs of using language in courts, in negotiations with private parties or with authorities forced this continuity of reflection (Mattila 2006: 6). Yet, it could also be that the textual basis of law transferred in form and content from generation to generation imposed a view upon law as a social practice that manifests a stronger link to written texts and through it to language than any other socially relevant practice.

2.1.2 The name-problem

We have frequently mentioned here that the Legal Linguistics is a relatively new discipline. This statement is true and it is false at the same time. It is false because the so-called relation between law and language as the historically first legal-linguistic question had occupied lawyers from time immemorial. It is true because until recently the Legal Linguistics did not exist as an autonomous branch of legal science or linguistics, and its status as an interdisciplinary field of research has not been particularly strong either. Not even the name for this new discipline is assured. Mattila (2002a: 170) and Cornu (2005: 10) refer to the French legal scholar François Gény who used the term *linguistique juridique* already in 1921 in his work *Science et technique en droit privé positif III*. In French-speaking Canada the term *jurilinguistique* is in use (id.), also Polish and Russian denominations *jurysligwistyka* (cf. Pieńkos 1999) and *pravovaya lingvistika (правовая лингвистика)* are in use respectively. In the Czech research, Hlouch (2007/8: 42) uses the term *právni lingvistika* when talking about the development in Germany, in Ukrainian the term *juridichna lingvistika* (*юридична лінгвістика*) is in use (Pradid 2002). In Italian, the term *linguistica giuridica* is occasionally applied (Veronesi 2000). In German, the term *Rechtslinguistik* is used for various theoretical approaches which cover also general philosophical and critical studies about the relation between the language used in law and the dominant ideology. For the German name usage Bülow (1985: 30) pointed to a publication by A. Podlech in 1976 where the concept of (D) *Rechtslinguistik* was developed in contrast to a programatically narrower Law and Language studies. The English speaking world is problematic in the sense of name giving for our undertaking. There, mostly foreign authors apply in their works the term *Legal Linguistics* (Mattila 2002a: 171). The formulation *Law and Language* seems still to dominate the professional language usage in the English-speaking academia.

2.1.3 Legal Linguistics in the World

It is therefore desirable to justify the new general approach to Law and Language and several authors dealing with this issue such as G. Cornu or H. Mattila did it before us. They tried to legitimize the existence of the new discipline differently. They proceeded by focusing on selected topics in the societal and academic discourse which they perceived as decisive for the relation between language and law. We will start with a geographic approach that shall illustrate the spatial distribution in the process in which the Legal Linguistics actually emerged. It is, by necessity, a sketch and cannot cover all geographical regions of the planet due to limited access to publication in Europe from e.g. Latin America (cf. Bulygin 1983) or Africa (cf. Opeibi 2008) where legal-linguistic research develops as well. Finally, German speaking countries with a multitude of approaches could constitute a specific legal-linguistic area of research. There, publications by E. Forsthoff, H. Dölle or H. Neumann-Duesberg relating to current legal-linguistic issues appeared already in the forties of the last century (Bülow 1981). Salas (2001: 209) ties the emergence of Law and Language studies in Germany to the analytical philosophy and refers especially to Eckmann (1969) and Koch (1976). In the German speaking area the vast number of publications concerns various aspects of law and language that are difficult to synthesize. Some of them would merit particular attention in a separate research. Close to the German legal-linguistic tradition is the Italian view upon law and language that is dominated by works of legal theorists such as E. Pattaro, U. Scapelli, M. Jori, L. Gianformaggio and N. Bobbio (Pintore 1995). Finally, in Spain legal argumentation constitutes the essential part of the legal theory developed by M. Atienza (2008); legal-linguistic research that reflects the issue of understandability of the legal language is represented in the works by Prieto de Pedro (1991) and Duarte i Montserrat (1998). The Catalan language *Revista de llengua i dret* publishes since 25 years legal-linguistic contributions.

To date, the geographically oriented description of the legal-linguistic research concentrates mostly on the development in the U.S., in France and in Russia. It focuses on the achievements of some eminent scholars in this field such as Heikki E.S. Mattila in Finland who shaped the subject towards the background of the comparative law or Peter Tiersma in the U.S. who broadened the traditional historically oriented approach there, respectively. Our overview does not cover purely philosophical or legal-theoretical research which is not exclusively legal-linguistic but which has been fundamental for the development of the modern Legal Linguistics like many publications by G. H. von Wright, A. Aarnio or J. Habermas. Instead, it concentrates on achievements which can be explicitly counted as belonging to the Legal Linguistics. Fundamental philosophical and legal-theoretical research is taken into consideration here at places where particular legal-linguistic issues are described. Therefore, e.g. G.H. von Wright is mentioned in parts concerning the role of logics in law and A. Aarnio and J. Habermas in parts concerning the structure of the legal discourse.

2.1.3.1 Tendency towards rationalization of language use in the USA: American authors stressed in the beginning of the research into Law and Language issues such as the emergence of the English legal terminology. They then developed a tendency towards forming a modernized legal language in that they responded to the claims in the plain language movement for a legal language directly accessible for the citizens (cf. Tiersma 1999: 211). This particular interest is anchored in the American tradition initiated by D. Mellinkoff (1963) to deal with the legal language from the most striking perspective for its users. Mellinkoff assumed that this language use is mostly linked to specific legal concepts which draw the attention of the users because they differ from the ordinary language. He tried then to explain the etymology of those concepts with the intention in mind to make the legal terminology understandable; yet he also stressed the necessity of rationalization of the legal English (Mellinkoff 1963: VII). P. Tiersma drew from it the conclusion that the understandability of the legal language can be rather achieved through its modernization than through etymological and historically oriented research, although he also allotted a considerable part of his work to the historical development of the legal English. Another research topic in the U.S. is the analysis of the speech in the courtroom where sometimes methods of the conversational analysis or methods neighboring this specific pragmalinguistic approach are used in relation to narratives, pleadings, cross-examination, why-questions or code switching (Solan 1993; Tiersma 1999: 147-198). P. Tiersma also stressed the importance of the speech act theory in the analysis of the legal language (1999: VII) and applied it in the discussion of some characteristic constructions of the legal language. Other American legal-linguistic specialities are the *forensic linguistics* and a research field called *artificial* *intelligence and law* that includes aspects of formalization in the legal language, esp. the open-texture concepts (Berman and Hafner 1987). Last but not least, the American legal theory includes voluminous contributions to issues that are fundamental for the Legal Linguistics such as argumentation and interpretation in law (cf. Atiyah/Summers 1987).

2.1.3.2 Legal terminology and discourse in France: Legal-linguistic research in France has been traditionally dominated by the issues related to the legal terminology that has been scrutinized from the diachronic and from the synchronic perspective. It started with the idea of distinguishing between the properly legal vocabulary and the non-legal one. J.-L. Sourioux and P. Lerat published in 1975 *Le language du droit* that is until today perceived as one of the fundamental works on the subject. G. Cornu entered into the problems of the Legal Linguistics through the analysis of the legal terminology in his *Linguistique juridique* that is currently available in its third edition. One of the most significant epistemological discoveries revealed in Cornu's *Linguistique juridique* is the step taken by the author from purely lexicological analyses to an overarching idea of the legal discourse (FR *discours juridique*). According to Cornu, the legal discourse unites the terminology into a coherent entity (Cornu 2005: 15). Since Cornu's analysis of the legal discourse based on the legal terminology the Legal Linguistics is no more limited to purely lexicological scrutiny. Another important step for the development of the new scientific domain was the introduction of the linguistic legislation (FR *droit linguistique*) into the realm of the Legal Linguistics. Cornu's broadening of the legal-linguistic domain can be characterized as paradigmatic due to his particularly convincing justification for the introduction of the subject matter which regulates the use of the language with linguistic means (Cornu 2005: 2, 36, 421). As a result, one can maintain that the legal terminology organized within the legal discourse constitutes the focal point for the issues discussed in the French *linguistique juridique*. This paradigm for the legal-linguistic research is well grounded in G. Cornu's lexicographical work *Vocabulaire juridique* available currently in its eighth edition at PUF (2000) and in the sixth edition at Quadrige. Further works that have shaped the silhouette of the modern French *linguistique juridique* had been the classics such as Fr. Gény, *Science et technique en droit privé positif* (1921) and M. Foucault's studies dealing with *épistémologie* of science and with the concept of discourse, especially his *Les mots et les choses* (1966) and *L'archéologie du savoir* (1969) as well as G. Kalinowski's *Introduction à la logique juridique* (1965). Last but not least, Ch. Perelman's epoch-making *Logique juridique, nouvelle rhétorique* (1979) has been incorporated into the general paradigm of the French *linguistique juridique* due to its fundamental importance for the legal argumentation. G. Cornu (2005: 40-51) provides a general bibliography for the *francophone* legal-linguistic research that has developed more or less closely around the main paradigm.

2.1.3.3 Tendency towards formalization of language use in Russia: Russian specialists focused like the majority of researchers on the legal terminology, especially on the unification and the standardization of legal language towards the background of the automatic data processing (Pigolkin 1990: 21). Rationalization of the legal terminology and the standardization of its use are understandable goals of the Legal Linguistics. However, standardization is rather an offshoot than a process in the development of the legal language. The framework for the emerging of the legal terminology is the conceptualization of legal subject matters and their parallel lexicalization. Their products are concepts and terms which the authors of (RU) *Язык закона* (*Iazyk zakona*) also frequently stress in their collective work (Pigolkin 1990: 15). Yet, they do not make this distinction operative for their conception of the legal language. The specific approach in Pigolkin (1990) is therefore useful within the data processing models for the legal terminology. At any rate, legal terminology goes its own ways and it would be challenging to press it into standardized patterns. The tendency to dominate law by means of informatics is perceptible especially in the social practice. Nevertheless, the assumption that some day law will dominate informatics is convincing due to historical experience made with legal mechanisms. Therefore, it would be more important to develop data processing patterns which would fit for the legal terminology, rather than to try to adapt the legal language to the requirements of data processing as it is done in *Iazyk zakona.* Also Vlasenko (1997) developed in his (RU) *Язык права* (*Iazyk prava*) a semiotically oriented approach to legal-linguistic issues which is mostly grounded in research available in Russia (Mattila 2006: 9). The on-line research project *Jurislingvistika,* (RU) *Юрислингвистика,* based at the Altai State University, provides in the Russian language information about the legal-linguistic research in Russia and abroad.

2.1.3.4 Polish legal theory and Polish Legal Linguistics: In Poland, the legal-linguistic research developed on the basis of the legal theory (Petzel 2006: 153). Since the first modern theoretical work on the language of law by B. Wróblewski, *Język prawny i prawniczy* (1948), the research has been dominated by approaches rooted in the philosophy of language and in logics (Kotarbiński 1955). T. Gizbert-Studnicki (1979) published the first research perceived as truly linguistic (Petzel 2006: 153). The linguistic trend was continued by J. Pieńkos (1999) and by K. Brodziak (2004) as well as by W. Kwarciński (2004) who introduced pragmalinguistic concepts into the debate. A position less dependent on the legal theory is represented by B. Z. Kielar (1979) who rather favored terminology-oriented approaches to the legal language. She also published a renowned book on the legal translation (Kielar 1977). The Polish legal-linguistic debate has been dominated by the question whether the language of law that has been identified by legal theoreticians can be construed as language in terms of linguistics (Petzel 2006: 163). Today, pragmalinguistically oriented researchers (cf. Brodziak 2004: 123-124) stress the *pragmatic competence* as a characteristic feature in the functioning of the legal language as language while other scholars rather tend towards a formalized and strict view upon the language as a system of signs or rules that opposes the perception of the language used in law as language (Petzel 2006: 163). The recent monograph on the Polish legal language by A. Malinowski (2006) takes an intermediate standing and combines quantitative research with pragmatic concepts. The Polish contributions to the Legal Linguistics make plain that the determination of the concept of language is an essential precondition of every legal-linguistic research.

2.1.3.5 Diversity of legal Chinese and understandability of legal Japanese: Likewise, a group of Chinese researchers attempted to determine the scope of the Legal Linguistics (Zhou 2003). They dealt with the linguistic legislation and with different private law traditions in China proper and in Hong Kong which had been strongly influenced by common law. They had also to cope with the unusually long history of development of legal terminology from the Tang to the Qing dynasty and within the Occidentalization process in the Chinese law. They also underscored the importance of linguistic legislation in China that in their view results from the power exercised by language. Finally, modern voice analyzing methods as well as quantitative analyses are explored as well (Zhou 2003). Forensic linguistics seems to dominate the practically oriented research, e.g. in Zhang Cuiling's *An Acoustic Study on Disguised Voices*, published 2005 as a PhD-thesis by the Department of Forensic Science of the Nanakai University (Salmi-Tolonen 2008: 380). Also Du Jinbang (2004) published a work dedicated to the construction of forensic linguistics and stressed its systematic structure as well as its theoretical research basis. Explicitly pragmalinguistic research on illocutionary and perlocutionary acts in legal discourses has been undertaken by Weiming Liu (2005). Cao (2008) discussed ambiguity and vagueness issues in the legal Chinese in a cross-linguistic perspective. In Japan, researchers such as T. Okubo, S. Hayashi, E. Iwabuchi and T. Nakano dealt with the Japanese legal register mostly from the perspective of its understandability (Okawara 1998: 73-80). Hayashi pointed already 1959 to the fact that lengthy sentences in legal Japanese texts result from embedded modifiers, conjunction clauses and distant placement of subject and object (Okawara 1989: 74). This initiated the modern discussion about the relation between the length of a sentence and its understandability that is mentioned later in this book (cf. 2.3.2.3).

2.1.3.6 Legal Theory and Language in Scandinavia: Furthermore, it would be important to stress particularly the development in Scandinavia and the Scandinavian legal realism where scholars such as Karl Olivekrona attempted to implement the linguistic turn in law (Olivekrona 1969: 10; cf. also Peczenik 1986: 168-175). The Scandinavian legal-linguistic tradition is far-reaching and particularly important for the development of the legal argumentation (Peczenik 1995). Serpe (2006) demonstrates on the example of human rights that the linguistic analysis in the Scandinavian legal realism was since the forties of the past century embedded in conceptual clarifications. Yet, in difference to any other variety of conceptual analysis the Scandinavian scholars attempted also an ontological determination of concepts used in law and in the legal language in general. In his overview A. Serpe stresses the contributions by T. Eckhoff, P.O. Ekelöf (cf. also Peczenik 1986: 261-263), I. Strahl, A. Hägerström, K. Olivecrona, V.Lundstedt, A. Wedberg, N.K. Sundby, T. Opsahl and F. Castberg. Unsurprisingly, Alf Ross' investigations of concepts in law as hollow words, without independent semantic reference (cf. Ross 1957) take a particular place in the Scandinavian legal-linguistic research. Some aspects of the Scandinavian approaches to legal language are mentioned in Galdia (1995); the research by N. Jareborg (1972) into fraudulous acts committed through the abuse of language is mentioned in Galdia (2008). Mattila (2005: 44) underlines the use of national languages in Scandinavia; Galdia (2003: 124-125) mentions the emergence of the Finnish legal vocabulary based on Swedish lexems; Landquist (2008: 157-171) characterized the influence that D. Ehrenståle Nehrman exercised in the process of formation of legal Swedish. Also the Finnish Legal Linguistics is rooted in the legal theory. The newest Finnish publication *Kielen ja oikeuden kohtaamisia* (2008) shows the diversity of approaches to the legal language there. It focuses on Heikki E.S. Mattila's approach that could be seen as complementing the existing Finnish legal theory in which scholars such as Aulis Aarnio addressed questions of the interpretation of legal texts and legal argumentation (Galdia 2008: 18). Its roots may be found in works by Osvi Lahtinen and Kaarle Makkonen who researched the linguistic and logical basis of the law (Galdia 1995: 33-34). Additionally, Pajula (1960) provided an overview over the history of the legal Finnish; Bonsdorf (1984) sketched the development of the Swedish legal language in Finland. Overall, Finnish scholars have primarily tied their work in with the hermeneutic, pragmatic and general semiotic facets of the legal language and published their findings in occasional volumes (Hirvonen, Tuori (eds.) 1990; Jyränki (ed.) 1999; Salmi-Tolonen (ed.) 2001). Mattila synthesizes most of these views in his conception of the comparative legal linguistics. Therefore, due to the multidirectional and interdisciplinary vision his conception remains open to its further development towards comparative law or towards legal theory as well as towards a merger of both. The particular strength of the legal-linguistic research in Finland is its usefulness for lexicological or forensic-linguistic projects (cf. Mattila 2004; Working Group 2001).

2.1.3.7 Particular research: Mattila (2006) quotes recent studies into particular issues of the legal language. This sort of detailed research into particular aspects of the legal language is and will remain for some time fundamental for the development of the Legal Linguistics. This detailed research concerns for instance the use of the conjunction *hvis* (NO for *if*) in the Norwegian legal language (Mattila 2006: 73), verbal substantives in the legal Swedish (ib.), use of verbs in the legislative language (ib.), use of tenses and modes, especially the conditional (ib.), use of passive mode (ib.), prison slang (Mattila 2006: 6), professional jargon used among jurists (Mattila 2006: 5), legislative drafting (Mattila 2006: 10), forensic linguistics (Mattila 2006: 11), pronunciation of Latin in the common law countries (Mattila 2006: 12), legal symbols in Finland (Mattila 2006: 13) and in Russia (ib.), legal Latin (Mattila 2006: 125-158). A group of Finnish lexicologists prepared an innovative dictionary of legal abbreviations (Mattila 2004) which continues lexicographic efforts undertaken there in the publication of Finnish court terminology (Working Group: 2001). Also in Japan a Standard Bilingual English-Japanese Dictionary of Legal Terms has been completed by a working group of the Cabinet Secretariat in 2006 (Anderson/Okuda 2007: 139). Husa (2007: 52, 53) dealt within his broader research into the Greek legal language with prepositions and prefixes in Greek legal texts. Markhardt (2006) prepared a dictionary of Austrian legal, business and administrative terminology in which the specific Austrian-German lexical units were resembled. Warda-Radys (2006) scrutinized Polish language administrative documents in medieval German-language Dantzig. Znamenáčková (2007) researched nominal, verbal and prepositional word clusters in different text types of the German civil law in the perspective of their stability and variability. In Vilar Sánches (2007) microfunctional linguistic analysis has been applied by different researchers upon German and Spanish language employment contracts. Microfunctions such as conditions or obligations and many others were analyzed there in a comparative perspective. In Heller/Ehlich (2007) terminological, contrastive and communicational aspects of the legal language are discussed. Kredens and al. (2007) insisted upon the international perspective in the legal-linguistic research. Wagner and Cacciaguidi-Fahy (2008) edited a volume on the understandability of the legal language in different legal cultures.

Overall, the increasing number of detailed research centered around the Legal Linguistics is encouraging. Nevertheless, no generalization of the research data is possible at this stage, partly due to the methodological pluralism in the research and partly because the general theory of the Legal Linguistics is still underdeveloped. However, two main fundamental tendencies seem to dominate the research. The first is grounded in the legal theory and the other is rather independent of the legal science, and develops an autonomous view upon the legal language from the perspective of the general linguistic theory. In terms of methodology, we rather favor a synthesis of both because the purely legal-theoretical research stresses mostly the procedural aspects of language use and avoids any involvement in material issues of legal argumentation. The purely linguistic research, in turn, risks drifting into the view of a Legal Linguistics without law that is less productive than the synthetic Legal Linguistics.

2.1.4 Conceptions of Legal Linguistics

In the above description we concentrated on topics discussed in the legal-linguistic research according to their geographic distribution. However, also a conceptual characterization of the research is worthwhile considering. This characterization helps overcome geographic boundaries and it also helps develop a unified Legal Linguistics. This is a task for the future Legal Linguistics as nowadays the interaction between the different tendencies and schools all over the world is not particularly close (Mattila 2006: 9). Therefore, paradoxically, it is easier to characterize tendencies in the development of the Legal Linguistics in terms of geography than in terms of concepts.

2.1.4.1 Legal Linguistics as semiotics of law: The most fundamental approach to legal language is the one based explicitly on the conceptual framework of the general semiotics. As a matter of fact, the general semiotic analysis seems to be the most appropriate tool for the analysis of language simply because language is a sign system (Pigolkin 1990: 4). No other approach can therefore compete with the semiotic one in the attempt to display the legal language in all its complexity. Explicitly semiotic works aim therefore at describing law as a sign system. Sometimes they reveal ambitions to lay foundations for a semiotically sensitive theory of law (Jackson 1985: ix). Sometimes they may attempt at clarifying semiotic presuppositions and perspectives of other theoretical works in which the inherent semiotic foundations have to be uncovered (Jackson 1985: 147-225). Roque Carrión Wam (1982) described the background and the development of the legal-semiotic research until 1980. In his report the origins of legal-semiotic investigations are seen in Félix E. Oppenheim's *Outline of a logical analysis of law* (published in Philosophy of Science 11, 1944) and later in works by George Kalinowski, especially in his already mentioned *Introduction à la logique juridique* (1965). However, only rare are studies which deal with legally relevant material against the background of the semiotic conceptual apparatus. For instance, A. Greimas (1966) undertook an analysis of the French Company Law Statute from 1966, (FR) Loi n. 66-537, but his work remained in every term an exception (cf. Jackson 1985: 33). Nowadays, especially the *International Journal for* *the Semiotics of Law* publishes contributions to this field of interdisciplinary studies.

A semiotically founded pragmalinguistic conception for the Legal Linguistics has been developed in Germany by Edeltraud Bülow, mostly in her teaching on the theoretical fundamentals of the subject in the 80s of the past century. The semiotic basis of law has been seen there in non-verbal signs inventories covering both the spatial and the temporal dimensions of the phenomenon (proxemy and chronomy) as well as in its complementary features such as gestures, mimics or kinetics. According to Bülow, legal signs emerge in this broad spectrum and constitute more specific units such as statute, commentary or contract which can be analyzed as text types. Moreover, many of these text types, mostly specimens of legislation and judicial decisions, come about in institutionalized processes. These text types which reflect narration, exposition, description, argumentation, instruction and so on can be further specified with the help of the speech act theory. There, propositions can be qualified, for instance, as threat or promise. In addition to it, temporal and spatial aspects of the legal language became manifest in the specific use of deixis and anaphora in legal texts. Furthermore, the signs of law are used in discourses dominated by ethical or political issues (Bülow 1986: 105). Therefore, next to the broad context of their spatial and temporal emergence also their particular use in these contexts must be taken into consideration. Only then are the signs of law construed in their entirety as parts of the life form in which humans interact towards the background of their complex culture in which societies are formed as results of historical processes. Bülow's approach (1985: 36) is grounded in general semiotics and anthropology which provide an orientation for the pragmalinguistics that in some other approaches occasionally hangs in a vacuum. In many respects, Bülow's fundamentals of the Legal Linguistics come close to B. Jackson's conception of the legal semiotics. In both conceptions the spatial and temporal spectrum in which legal signs emerge reaches the outer limits of the space in which legal signs are constituted in the societal communication. Bülow adds to it the social-pragmatic perspective in which legal signs are used in a society whereas Jackson concentrates mostly on the process in which the legal signs emerge. Both views are complementary, and when put together they show law in its semiotic complexity. Equally, in the vision proposed here, the Legal Linguistics incorporates also practical goals like contributing to the emergence of the language of the global law.

2.1.4.2 Legal Linguistics as hermeneutics of law: Traditional hermeneutic methods that aimed at determining the objective meaning of texts were broadly used in the legal theory and in the legal sciences (Đorđević 2002: 6). Since G. Gadamer's (D) *Wahrheit und Methode* (1965), (UK) *Truth and Method* (1975), hermeneutic standards have significantly changed. Understanding of texts is based there on a hermeneutic circle which means in essence that the understanding of the whole text depends on the understanding of its parts and vice versa (Juhl 1986: 7). The text is no longer construed in an objective isolation from its reader; its understanding presupposes the fusion of the textual horizon and that of the reader (Juhl 1986: 7). This conclusion is crucial for the interpretation of legal texts in the Legal Linguistics (Gizbert-Studnicki 1987: 478). Finally, authors using contemporary hermeneutic approaches to law such as Jürgen Habermas (1988), stressed the ideological facets of law which they perceive as enclosed in social mechanisms legitimizing judicial decisions. Critical views upon language use in law dominate also in F. Müller (1999), H. Rottleuthner (1981), and H. Rodingen (1977). Other hermeneutic approaches stress the interpretive nature of activities connected to law (Đorđević 2002: 6). Hermeneutic research includes also numerous works about hermeneutics of the judicial decision making process (cf. Forsthoff 1940/54; Rottleuthner 1973; Wróblewski 1988). Judicial decisions are discussed there usually in a broader perspective than ours. Therefore, many of them belong rather to the general legal theory than to Legal Linguistics.

2.1.4.3 Legal Linguistics as introduction into law: For Gérard Cornu (2005) the Legal Linguistics could function as an introduction to legal studies and especially to the legal terminology. In the consequence of this approach law would be perceived as a linguistic phenomenon stated in texts whereby the aspects of the specific legal terminology and the structure of the legal discourse dominate the overall view. Cornu's approach differs from ours in that it is based on semantics, we however, focus on pragmatic aspects of law. Like Cornu, we posit that Legal Linguistics can be instrumental as an introduction to law and additionally we stress that it can even function as its theory. The Legal Linguistics would be thinkable and useful even if the role language plays in law would be much more constrained than it seems to be now. Cornu (2005: 1) notes in a context different from ours the existence of law as a language: *Dans de plus vastes perspectives, on aurait à se demander si le droit même n'est pas, en soi, un language.* Later on, the same author refuses however to consider the existence of a grammar of the legal language: *L'étude grammaticale d'un énoncé de droit est un exercice utile; une grammaire juridique une absurdité* (Cornu 2005: 29). Let us remark at this stage that the destiny of a legal grammar depends very much upon the notion of grammar one is inclined to adopt. For instance, B. Jackson (1985: 111) consecrated a whole chapter to the conception of 'Legal Grammar' in his work on semiotics and legal theory. Notwithstanding some conceptual divergencies, the overall approach to the Legal Linguistics as an introduction into the law is a step worth considering, especially in the legal education.

2.1.4.4 Legal Linguistic as part of comparative law: Heikki E.S. Mattila anchored his conception of the Legal Linguistics in comparative law (Galdia 2003: 271). In his fundamental work *Vertaileva oikeuslingvistiikka* (2002b) as well as in the English (Mattila 2006) and the French editions (in press) of the Finnish original he provided first of all an overview of existing issues within the Legal Linguistics perceived as a product of crossing legal and linguistic systems. His comparative approach is distinct from the monolingual perspective adapted by other researchers, such as G. Cornu or P. Tiersma, who usually focused on the relation between the ordinary language and the legal language perceived as special register. Mattila prepared the ground, both in terms of diachronic and synchronic research, for the mapping of the conceptual landscape in the Legal Linguistics. He identified the method for comparative research into legal terminology and the legal translation. Additionally, he also selected the relevant languages for the legal-linguistic research. Mattila stressed, unlike many other writers dealing with Law and Language, the shaping role Latin has had for the emergence of the legal language and engaged in detailed, also quantitative analyses in this abandoned area (Mattila 2002c). In his approach he revigorated the research into the legal Latin which may have consequences for the processes in which the language of the global law is coming into being. Finally, his research facilitates the broadening of the perspective in the Legal Linguistics, particularly concerning the speech acts in law, towards pragmatic issues which are stressed in this book. Mattila's approach is not only developed along the lines of comparative law, it can be made operative in comparative law as well. Neutrally construed conceptions of comparative law like R. Kraakman's comparative and functional approach towards corporate law stress the necessity to develop an appropriate language in which issues of comparative corporate law could be addressed without confusion and misinterpretation. Kraakman (2004: 4) writes about this goal: "*Of equal importance, we wish to offer a common language and a general analytic framework with which to understand the purposes that can potentially be served by corporate law, and with which to compare and evaluate the efficacy of different legal regimes in serving those purposes*". Innovative concept creation like *corporate constituencies*, *non-shareholder constituencies* or the modified concepts of *legal personality* of *company* or of *agency* (Kraakman 2004: 7) are examples for the efficiency of this approach. Mattila's work is suitable to function as a background source for this sort of detailed legal-linguistic constructions. Also Grossfeld (1990: 103) argued for the area of comparative law that legal language is its essential concomitant which in his view does not make it any easier. Likewise, the emerging global law will also need a new language. Works such as Mattila's are fundamental to its development.

2.1.4.5 Legal Linguistics as forensic linguistics: Forensic linguistics focuses upon the use of language within judicial institutions of different sorts (Mattila

2006: 11). For this part of research not the specific legal register is decisive but the institutional framework in which different varieties of language can be used. Even if legal professionals and laypersons use different varieties of language in different discourses within the legal institutions, they nevertheless used to speak differently there than outside the institutional legal settings. This approach is particularly valuable because it makes plain that language use in law is necessarily bound to institutions and apparently would not survive long without or beyond them. For many, especially in the English speaking countries, forensic linguistics is an applied branch of the linguistic studies which concentrates on the identification of speakers through voice analysis. This part of the forensic linguistics is dominated by technological processes which use phonetic research for investigative or evidential purposes within legal proceedings (Salmi-Tolonen 2008: 375). Common law experience with the forensic linguistics is reflected in Shuy (2006). Last but not least, forensic linguistics is perceived as combining aspects of voice analysis (forensic phonetics) and semantic or pragmatic studies which relate to language use in courts as underlined by Salmi-Tolonen (2008: 393). In this book forensic linguistics is understood in the broader sense described by Salmi-Tolonen.

2.1.4.6 Legal Linguistics as interlingual comparison: The interlingual perspective upon the language use in law comes close to philological research. The researcher concentrates there upon one national language, for instance on Finnish or English. She may elucidate the emergence of the legal language towards the background of the ordinary language or describe the processes which underlie the evolution of conceptual meaning in the legal texts. Works such as Risto Hiltunen's *Chapters on Legal English* (1990) are deliberately situated within philology or linguistics and do not expose any ambitions to contribute to the legal sciences or to the legal theory in particular. In this sort of research documents, mostly historical sources, are used as a basis for the description of the development of the scrutinized language. Thus, they limit their scope to their proper discipline, in the case to the English philology. They make clear how the legal language changes with time and illustrate problems which non-jurists unaware of the legal language encounter when they try to understand legal texts. Also the author of these lines while working on (FIN) *Lakisaksa* (German legal language) used linguistic research on special registers to cope with linguistic terminology. Legal Linguistics emerged in *Lakisaksa* (Galdia 1999) as a matrix of legal systems expressed within one natural language (namely German). This type of Legal Linguistics provides insights that are important for the general linguistics. It is equally interesting for jurists because it influences their daily practice, especially the way how they draft statutes or other legal documents.

As we already mentioned, it is cumbersome if not impossible to characterize the state of the art in the contemporary Legal Linguistics. The reason for this is first of all the vast spectrum of approaches – a characteristic feature which Legal Linguistics shares with other disciplines – and another reason which seems to be particular, unique to it. Observations relevant to Legal Linguistics appear regularly in works of legal doctrine, e.g. on contracts or on property which at least by their main topics are not explicitly related to our domain (Galdia 2008: 20). They risk therefore to be - and in most cases also are - overlooked by legal linguists. In this book we tried to incorporate at least some examples of this sort of legal-linguistically relevant research that belongs to other branches of the legal science.

2.1.5 What is Legal Linguistics and what it is not?

In all above approaches one legal-linguistic feature seems to replicate, namely that language is constitutive for the law (cf. Bülow 1985: 25). Indeed, as we have noticed here regularly and are tempted to repeat at this place – law in its theoretical form is for us predominantly Legal Linguistics. The reason for this is that the Legal Linguistics which focuses on two central issues of the creation of law with linguistic means and its application, i.e. interpretation and argumentation, is its theory. It is *a* theory of law. We will therefore concentrate on the approaches and achievements of the philosophical and linguistics pragmatics which we perceive to be the most advanced theoretical approaches to law and language. We will not try to draw any distinctive lines between the philosophical and the linguistic pragmatics as both are closely related, the linguistic current following the philosophical in time and method. The distinction between both is for us rather a matter of courtesy towards researchers who used to stress this distinction than a theoretical necessity. We address this issue here simply by anticipating possible questions. Despite the mentioned problems with the current state of the art in the Legal Linguistics which we perceive as a practical rather than a theoretical problem we are able to attempt a description of the role philosophical and linguistic pragmatics play in our domain. And, we will do it by asking what Legal Linguistics is and what it is not. This procedure is part of our quest for the Legal Linguistics that was initiated in the introductory part of this book.

2.1.5.1 Legal Linguistics is not philology: Philology concentrates on the reconstruction and the protection of written texts as cultural achievements of mankind. One of its major tasks is to reconstitute the original written text and to determine the time of its appearance and the meaning of words in it at the time of its creation. For instance, a paper by G. Falcone (1991) *Per una datazione del "De verborum quae ad ius pertinent significatione" di Elio Gallo* belongs to this group of works. Philology has therefore a role to play in all attempts to reconstruct historical legal texts and to determine the linguistically appropriate interpretation of historical sources like those of the classical Roman law. Its task is mainly directed towards the preservation of the initial meaning of texts that may be later interpreted differently due to the multitude of approaches towards texts and their interpretation. Furthermore, its methods are crucial for the editing of historical as well as contemporaneous legal texts. The editorial philological methods comprise the preparation of the authentic text for print and the ways of its presentation including a critical commentary. They are used for editing of statutes and case collections, both historical and contemporary. Unlike the Legal Linguistics, philology concentrates on the purely linguistic aspects of legal texts. It does not look at them through the prism of the legal sciences. Therefore, the philological research does not replace Legal Linguistics; it has an auxiliary role to play there. Works such as Hiltunen's (1990) which provide a substantial contribution to the Legal Linguistics but perceive themselves rather as parts of general linguistics or national language-philology must be properly transformed within the conceptual framework of the Legal Linguistics to become truly operative there (cf. 2.1.4.6).

2.1.5.2 Legal Linguistics is not philosophy of law: Legal Linguistics deals with many philosophical issues. One may even have the impression that it deals exclusively with philosophical issues. How should we otherwise understand the signification processes in which legal concepts emerge, the procedures of interpretation and argumentation or the shift of signification when incompatible legal concepts must be translated between two or more networks of legal rules expressed in different national languages? These issues are deeply philosophical in their core and we try to approach them here from the perspective of pragmatics which is not only linguistics; for many it is philosophy. However, the legal philosopher deals with philosophical issues in law differently than we are doing it. Her interest is directed towards the subject matter of the legal provisions which she scrutinizes from the philosophical perspective. For instance, in the constitutional law she would ask the fundamental question what is good governance; in criminal law, what is free will and what is causation; in contracts she would ask how parties of different economic standing can be perceived as equal in law. Additionally, she could ask why the legislator actually prefers to protect the family and treats it differently from many other social groups or why does he protect the environment or deals with issues pertaining to bioethics? Finally, she could ask why the legislator uses rights and not other conceptual forms in which political positions can be termed as an instrument of their expression and protection. Our answer to all these questions would be monotonous and not interesting for the legal philosopher. We would always repeat that all this is a matter of linguistic creation and appropriate legal argumentation. The legal philosopher would certainly be bored by our lack of imagination. What fascinates the legal philosopher is the subject matter of law reflected or evaluated from the philosophical point of view. We, instead, take law in the sense it interests the legal philosopher for granted.

2.1.5.3 Legal Linguistics is not sociology of law (and not legal anthropology): The sociology of law deals with the social reality in which law is created and applied. For it, the question how the doctrine imagines the law to be is of secondary importance. In its approach it is close to Legal Linguistics which also focuses upon the reality in the creation and the application of law. The main distinction in the object of studies is that the Legal Linguistics focuses exclusively on linguistic aspects of law, whereas in the sociology of law issues concerning the use of power in society through law dominate the perspective. Similarly, the legal anthropology supplies narratives used in law which enable us to understand the legal culture. While referring to C. Geertz, M. A. Glendon et al. (1999: 13) speak about stories which not only influence the way "*how legal norms are invented and applied within (that) system, but on how facts are perceived and translated into the language and the concepts of law.*" Again, the Legal Linguistics takes most of these fundamental culture creating processes for granted. It definitely also creates and analyzes the legal culture but it proceeds within a much more limited scope of application. It therefore cannot explain what is law in terms of cultural creation of mankind, but it can explain how we create and use language within our complex legal institutions. And this is already quite a progress. Therefore, the Legal Linguistics is not legal anthropology which is in a sense broader because it includes the use of language in law as part of the human culture. The legal anthropology insists upon the primacy of man and his needs over law (Lampe 1970: 17). It differs from the Legal Linguistics in terms of methodology (cf. Lampe 1970). As far as the legal anthropology deals with social principles and rules governing indigenous societies where legal rules are not reflected in the way adapted in the tradition of the Roman law it differs significantly from the goal of the Legal Linguistics that is to practically contribute to the emergence of a global law. This emerging law will definitely be based on the tradition of creation and application of law grounded in the Roman tradition. However, both the sociology of law and the legal anthropology are in many respects very close to the Legal Linguistics.

2.1.5.4 Legal Linguistics is not law: Legal Linguistics cannot replace the law. Law has next to its linguistic form also another material component which is its subject matter. Law includes rules which provide regulations concerning specific socially relevant issues. A substantial part of the legal training consists of learning what legal provisions concern what subject matters, and in what way subject matters in question are regulated in law. For the legal linguist all these subject matters are an *x*, a *quantité negligeable*. This, however, does not mean that the Legal Linguistics tries to reduce the importance of law or restructure its position among social sciences. As an example, reductive theoretical processes concerning the law are dealt with in the theories of Law and Economics. There, attempts had been undertaken to reduce the role of law as an autonomous social institution. R. Posner and many others were of the opinion that law should have an auxiliary function in the social reality which is determined by economic processes (Posner 1987). According to this view, law would provide the legal instruments which fit best these processes. We might have given rise to the same impression when talking about law and Legal Linguistics. As there is quite a lot of language in law one might be tempted to pretend that also the Legal Linguistics can replace the law or at least replace the legal science. In our view upon law, in which Legal Linguistics definitely plays a preponderant role, such a shift in ontology and methodology remains impossible. For the legal linguist law is a construction made and driven with words. She is not interested in knowing what exactly the legislator regulates in an act relating to the operations of hedge funds in a country. Neither is she interested in the question whether these regulations are justified by the reality that dominates the financial markets. She will exclusively focus on the way in which the legislator uses language while creating such a regulatory legal act. Therefore, the Legal Linguistics cannot replace the law. It cannot replace its teaching and learning either. But it can contribute to that both would be done differently in future.

2.1.5.5 Legal Linguistics is not legal doctrine: We stress the distinction between the Legal Linguistics and the legal doctrine also called *legal dogmatics* in the civil law because of the fundamental difference between both. Legal doctrine proceeds in areas interesting us in a way which presupposes the right solution to a legal problem within the so-called legal system. It establishes a fictitious formal procedure of inferring this solution from relevant legal provisions. We do not believe in this procedure and we extensively exposed reasons for this view in this book. Legal doctrine tends towards the *reification* of legal language. Therefore, not only language but also law and Legal Linguistics constitute an insurmountable obstacle for the legal doctrine as it is practised in the civil law countries. Let us illustrate the problem on a few small examples. A typical doctrinal problem is represented in the distinction between *relative* and *absolute rights*. *Absolute rights* are generally defined as the sum of the applicable legal provisions in a society that take effect against everyone, whereas *subjective rights* concern the legal position of an individual. Usually, in the civil law tradition, rights which emerge under contracts have been perceived as *subjective* because they are binding only on the parties involved. Property rights, instead, have been construed as *absolute* because they are effective against everybody. Needless to say that the quality of a party to a contract and an offender of a property right are only conventional; i.e. they are a matter of perspective. One could say that *subjective* and *absolute* rights provide the same protection for those exposed to the breach of contract or violation of a property right. They do not concern persons who are not involved in the matter. To assume that the property right protects the home owner against all inhabitants of his country is a metaphysical construct. The protection right becomes effective only against those who intend or actively attempt to violate this right. Another doubtful concepual pair is the one of *public law* and *private law* (Guimezanes 1995: 27-28). Law, as we have seen, is effective only within the public sphere. It cannot function on the basis of private arrangements that are otherwise welcome in society (cf. Berman 1993: 4) but they are not law when they cannot be enforced in the public sphere. D. Kennedy (1982) spoke therefore of the *arbitrariness of the public-private distinction*. Finally, we have referred already to the doctrinal tendency to split events relevant to law in a *substantive* and a *procedural* part (cf. 1.1.4.1). Such a method would contradict the legal-linguistic efforts because it imposes metaphysics on the understanding of law. Moreover, the Continental *doctrine of legal sources* usually excludes *precedents*. It is difficult to accept in the Legal Linguistics this artificial and unjustified selection. In the common law the *doctrine of consideration* is equally problematic because it does not respect the daily social (i.e. also linguistic) practice. Cooter/Ulen (2004: 192) characterized the American court decisions that deal with *consideration* as *Humpty-Dumpty jurisprudence*. In sum, the legal-linguistic methodology does not coincide with the methods of the legal doctrine. Therefore, the Legal Linguistics will rather critically follow this sort of doctrinal thinking in law.

2.1.5.6 Legal Linguistics is not logics for lawyers: The linguistic approach to law is complementary or sometimes even identical with the logical one. Logics, however, uses a different language when it characterizes the reality. Therefore, the parallels between linguistic and logical approaches are not always immediately visible. Through the attempts to formalize the legal rules logics goes behind their lexicalization and asks specifically for the form of rules behind the rules in words. It develops forms of legal rules such as $p \rightarrow q$ which suit its epistemological interests best. More specifically, *deontic logics* developed by G. H. von Wright (1951) disclosed the most abstract and formal structure of legal norms. To date, no valid argumentation has been provided to fundamentally question this approach (Atienza 2006: 125). Our approach to law seems to be, however, more practical as it is grounded in the problems of interpreting of concrete legal provisions and in applying concrete rules on concrete cases. In contrast, the strength of the legal logics could be seen in its attempts to generalize our knowledge about the legal language on a very high level of abstraction. Moreover, logic comprises rules for the *descriptive* language as well as rules for *prescriptive* language, like the language of law (Weinberger/Weinberger 1979). In its scrutiny of *prescriptive* language it deals with deontic modalities: *prohibited*, *permitted* and *required* (Frändberg 2001:13). It establishes *validity* as the mode of existence of legal norms. These deontic modalities can incite the legal linguist to look closer to how they manifest themselves in the legal-linguistic praxis. One could for instance ask how Chinese auxiliary verbs *děi* (must) or *gāi* (shall) function in Chinese legal texts. The function of normative language and especially of verbs in it seems to be an area of a possible close cooperation between logics and Legal Linguistics. However, the Legal Linguistics goes beyond deontic operators (cf. Jackson 1985: 47) and comprises the entire linguistically relevant vocabulary of a language or an area which we call the Legal Thesaurus. Another common domain for logics and Legal Linguistics is the legal argumentation. The relation between law and logics has not been free of paradoxes there. Non-valid argumentation in law had been identified by logicians in legal contexts. These specific argumentative structures may appear to logicians as fallacies, (FR) *paralogismes*; they are frequently justified by jurists as a specific way of how jurists speak and write. They were also termed as specific legal rationality. Some researchers therefore maintain that the formal logics cannot be perceived as an exclusive or the most appropriate analytical instrument for the appraisal of the legal argumentation (Verschueren/Östman 1995: 60). The rational argumentation as well as the interest in an argumentative discourse (cf. Aarnio 1987) remain however central for both logics and Legal Linguistics. Regarding other traditional issues in logics, such as the truth, the contrastive approach seems more appropriate. Can we distinguish between truth and interpretation in law? What is the truth in law? We may use Tarski's formulation of a truth condition like: It is true that it was raining in New York at 11.50 today if it was raining there at this time. This statement of truth conditions is not banal at all. Tarski asks himself what is the criterion of a material - not purely formal - truth of an utterance and he provides the simplest and the formally and materially most pervasive test for an utterance about facts. In setting up the test, he provides the most convincing criterion, not an argument, because in the case in which someone would still question the result of the test we simply cannot talk with him in a reasonable way as a rational criterion does not appeal to him. Tarski's most simple criterion is not the end of the search for tests for material truth in utterances; it is only the beginning of it. Providing tests for more sophisticated utterances is more difficult and providing criteria of that sort for propositions about law is impossible. This is the effect of Dworkin's theory of law as an interpretive concept. There, validity of the best argument counts for the truth in law. Indeed, law is about interpretation and argumentation, not about truth criteria. Social facts cannot be verified according to Tarski's test. There is no truth in such utterances, other than the one being subject to legal interpretation. Law is based on linguistic conventions. However, there, where conventions are missing, logics is particularly welcome. Notwithstanding theoretical limits, the specific truth in legal utterances and W. Hohfeld's (1913) fundamental logical relations in law (rights, duties, powers and liabilities) form still a conceptual basis for attempts to formalize the law (cf. Ashley 1990; Bench-Capon/Coenen 1992; Berman/Hafner 1987 and 1993; Branting 1991). Problems connected to the *open-texture concepts*, reasoning with cases to interpret open-texture concepts or conflicting legal rules and concepts as well as adversarial reasoning, i.e. the ability to create persuasive arguments for both sides of an issue seem to be unsolvable in all attempts to formalize the law. Development in this area is described in the periodical *Artificial Intelligence and Law*.

The least problematic in our context is the traditional legal logics. It consists mostly of analyses of legal reasoning and legal argumentation including its specific cases, legal interpretation and legal justification. We have already identified these topics as belonging to the Legal Linguistics and can accommodate them in our pragmatic conception because we basically deal with the same issues. Moreover, traditional logics and the question of a systemic character of law came up in the civil law tradition and were discussed with less interest in the common law countries. Some authors were seeking the reason for this disparity in different approaches to law in both dominant legal traditions (Mattila 2006: 224). The civil law developed as university doctrine based on *substantive law* whereas the common law has been developed by courts which turn their attention to *procedure*. It may therefore be understandable that civil law lawyers were always interested in the systemic character of law which dominates the substantive law and which was determined to provide a solid basis for civil codes. In turn, procedure has been rather neglected in academic teaching and research. In the common law countries procedure has been central, its teaching technique is case analysis and no case exists beyond the procedure. In both legal traditions cognitive interests developed differently, and the consequences are perceptible today in the research. This is also one of the reasons why we insist upon the linguistic turn in legal sciences.

2.1.6 What is Legal Linguistics, then?

We have somewhat categorically cut off the links between the Legal Linguistics and all other kindred disciplines. Nevertheless all these disciplines remain parts of one big family; i.e. the legal science. They approach and characterize the law from different perspectives, but law remains law exactly as all these related disciplines remain kindred parts of the legal science. As members of the same family they have some resemblance. Still, every family member is a distinct creature. This is true also for the Legal Linguistics. It deals with the most essential linguistic phenomena and linguistic operations in law. It approaches and describes law as a linguistic phenomenon based on the conviction that language is constitutive for the law. In this sense, the Legal Linguistics is its theory. As stressed above, problems of law are not always problems of language. However, the problems of the legal theory are essentially linguistic problems; this is why we may call our Legal Linguistics also a theory of law. It is not *the* theory of law, because law can be approached from different perspectives; for us however the linguistic perspective is the decisive one for the description of the theoretical problems in law. All other problems are for us practical problems. But also they may give rise to legal theories.

2.1.6.1 Legal-linguistic conceptual network: Currently, the Legal Linguistics is best positioned on the intersection of semantics and pragmatics, at least as long as the debate about the conceptual borders of both semantics and pragmatics is going on (cf. Pohl 2008). Its background is the theory of syntax that could prove particularly prolific when applied on legal texts and the morphophonology that would also have a role to play in the Legal Linguistics, although a limited one. In addition, the two traditional levels of description of linguistic phenomena, the synchronic and the diachronic one are taken into consideration. To date, the Legal Linguistics operates with conceptual instruments of different value. Several central notions such as *discourse, text type, speech acts, narrative, style, prototype-stereotype, form of life, equivalence in legal translation* dominate texts belonging to the Legal Linguistics. Moreover, substantial part of texts oscillates around *concept* and *term*. In addition, the conceptual apparatus of the general semiotics is often applied in such texts. In a more advanced conception of this new branch of knowledge which would belong to legal sciences or linguistics, or both, this conceptual apparatus would have to be redefined in order to function as a coherent conceptual set of the *Legal* Linguistics. Therefore, the notions of *legal* discourse, *legal* text type, *legal* style and *legal* narrative, *legal* term and *legal* concept must become operational. The current problem of the Legal Linguistics is furthermore that its main concepts are distributed asymmetrically and somewhat capriciously. All concepts identified as central for the Legal Linguistics should operate in a network which provides for their balanced distribution. The pragmatic apparatus proposed here is able to integrate these partly heterogeneous concepts. As long as it is materially related to *legal* texts it is also reliable in the sense that it guarantees the appropriate level of *'legalness'* within the conceptual network. It is suitable to describe some of the linguistic operations in law such as interpretation, argumentation, translation and many others. It is also elastic enough as it does not put any artificial boundaries to the identification and the description of further linguistic operations in law.

2.1.7 Is Legal Linguistics really more than a Legal Linguistics?

Legal Linguistics deals with legally relevant aspects of language use. Occasionally, the attempt to determine whether a specific legal-linguistic operation is relevant in law may become problematic. As a test for such cases the *juridicity* of the text has been used here. Nevertheless, some general semiotic aspects of textual constitution and application go beyond the pure juridicity; i.e. the role a linguistic unit plays for the legal decision taken in a specific case or the choice of a formulation. Therefore, next to the juridicity of language use, also the role that a linguistic or para-linguistic unit (such as a gesture) play in the legal culture must be taken into the consideration as well. Doubtlessly, therefore, the Legal Linguistics makes also part of a General Legal Semiotics which provides for the most exhaustive scientific description of the phenomenon law (cf. Bülow 1986: 93). Furthermore, the results reached in this book until now show that the Legal Linguistics could be equally well perceived as a theory of law. Reasons for this are multiple. First of all, the Legal Linguistics includes the most relevant legal-linguistic operations such as the legal argumentation, the legal interpretation or the legal translation which have been traditionally also dealt with in the legal theory. In the legal theory as in the Legal Linguistics those operations are treated as parts of the legal discourse as an overarching linguistic entity. In addition, in some approaches the Legal Linguistics emerged in the theoretical context of the legal theory or has been supported by the legal theory (Galdia 2008: 16). This is the case also as far as this book is concerned as it is unthinkable without its roots in the legal-theoretical discussion.

2.1.7.1 Family resemblances: The affinity between the legal theory and the Legal Linguistics may also be perceived as challenging. If namely the Legal Linguistics deals with the issues identified as relevant in the legal-linguistic use by the legal theory it could simply be perceived as belonging to the established legal theory. No need would therefore exist for the emergence of a new discipline which doubles the efforts undertaken in the field of the legal theory. However, the partition of tasks among disciplines is not always undertaken with surgical exactness. Academic disciplines, like the tools described by L. Wittgenstein (1984: 243) in his famous metaphor, can resemble each other as family members do. Some features are equal, while others constitute a difference on which personality can be based. The relation between legal theory and Legal Linguistics can be therefore characterized within the argumentative framework of family resemblances. Legal Linguistics seen from the perspective of the legal theory is a linguistic view upon law and the legal theory. This is one more reason why the Legal Linguistics can be – at least as far as the pragmatic perspective adopted in this book is concerned - also perceived as a specific theory of law.

2.1.7.2 Analytical philosophy and Legal Linguistics: Occasionally we have referred here to concepts and conceptions having their origins in the analytical philosophy. Issues such as *meaning*, *truth* and *reference* have been its central notions and also the most relevant areas of scientific analysis. The same holds true for law, although with slightly modified emphasis. Meaning remains central for both. Jurists had established and since R. Dworkin's works they also understand the way in which they interpret legal rules. This will say that they now know how they conceive and create the meaning of legal concepts and rules. In this specific point they may be even more advanced than many philosophers who still inquire into the presuppositions of meaning in texts engendered in their field. Truth, in turn, is a delicate subject for jurists (cf. 2.1.5.6). Legal rules are rather valid or void; propositions about their content rather acceptable or unacceptable, more or less appropriate in a given social context. Truth may concern facts upon which law is applied. It is relevant in briefs provided by the attorneys in the litigation or in witness testimony. Yet, in general, jurists have their institutional and procedural truth that they define in terms of validity which is a construct. This juridical truth is equally constructed as is the world of referents at which the law is pointing. Therefore, jurists have no problems with reference because law refers to a constructed world of concepts and argumentative methods. All this is gratifying as it shows that law is a relatively easy subject, at least when compared with philosophy. But, unlike philosophy, law exists in application and makes sense only in the process of confronting socially relevant action and legal rules. At this point it is much more complicated than is philosophy even in its analytical form. Jurists cannot hide behind general or generalized rules. They have to apply them on concrete cases and they have to document this process which ends with a written and signed legal decision. In the recent years, the linguistic wing of the analytical and post-analytical philosophy came close to cognitive sciences and the philosophy of mind. Towards this background, Recanati (2008: 9) advocates the unity of the linguistic philosophy and the philosophy of mind. The main reason for his claim seems to be the necessity to overcome the split between the reasoning and the language as signalized in the cognitive sciences (Aroui 1993: 127; cf. also Bülow 1985: 29). Indeed, mental phenomena analyzed in the philosophy of mind and notions of the philosophy of language such as *reference, denotation, connotation* or *intentionality* are at least interrelated. Thus, the problems of reference of legal notions, their denotation and connotation may be reappraised in the philosophy of mind and in the cognitive sciences. Within the philosophy of mind three approaches to *interpretation* have been developed (Engel 1994: 93). First, the indeterminacy of meaning thesis defended by W. Quine (Engel 2001: 75); second, the theory of popular meaning that tried to reconstruct the mental background of interpretive processes (Engel 2001: 76), and third, the projectivist conception that warned against overemphasizing rationality in interpretation (Engel 2001: 78). Aspects of the indeterminacy theory are discussed here under 3.7.8. Other findings are equally relevant in the legal-linguistic contexts because spontaneous emergence of meaning in law is limited. Therefore its intentionality is more explicit than the intentionality in the ordinary discourse. Finally, *legal discourses* convey *meaning* that is anchored in the validity of their underlying norms and not in logically verifiable procedures. Discourses about validity of norms are by necessity discourses about rationality. Such discourses cannot be reduced to mental representations; again, the necessity to unify grammar and discourse becomes pertinent (Du Bois 2002: 47). Forensic linguistics may offer a research pattern for this type of innovative legal-linguistic analyses.

2.1.7.3 Legal Linguistics as legal pragmatics: A conception relatively close to ours is the one of the legal pragmatics. Legal pragmatics could be construed as a vision of law, i.e. its theory which stresses its application aspects. Legal Linguistics is in many respects also legal pragmatics and the theoretical exposition of problems in both is roughly the same, only that the Legal Linguistics reflects upon legal issues from the perspective of language use. The broader conceptual frameworks of both do not collide nor are research results known which would show basic difference among both perspectives issued from the same tendency within the social sciences. Thus, the theoretical difference between both is purely distributional in that both occasionally stress different aspects within the same approach. This result cannot take by surprise as both linguistics and pragmatics are unthinkable outside the social context. For the language already the classic of the analytical philosophy, L. Wittgenstein, claimed that a private language could not exist (cf. Ayer 1966: 251-266; Rhees 1966: 267-285). In the social sciences no developed conception of a human being living outside the society and being independent of it has been seriously considered. Moreover, within pragmatic approaches *praxiology* developed by Tadeusz Kotarbiński (1886-1981) has an impact on both, the Legal Linguistics and the legal pragmatics. Kotarbiński's approach to legal language (1955: 16) enables to integrate issues which jurists used to discuss as terminological, especially legal concepts, into a pragmatically founded Legal Linguistics. It has equally further going implications because it mainly concerns effective action (id.: 6). In law, it would be fundamental for the justification of legal decisions or the effective use of arguments in legal contexts.

2.1.7.4 Legal Linguistics for Linguists: The perspective adopted in this book stresses the importance of the linguistic analysis in legal contexts. The most general sense of it is to characterize the linguistic operations in law and to accomplish the linguistic turn in the legal science. It may seem that these results are rather interesting for jurists than for linguists. The sense of the Legal Linguistics for linguists is not only to show that the linguistic analysis, for instance the application of the speech act theory or the discourse theory are possible in law, as no other result could realistically be expected by linguists. However, the analysis of the legal-linguistic operations shows the linguistic means and the linguistic prerequisites of the language use in law. It illustrates in this way what legal language is actually about, at least when seen from the pragmatic perspective.

2.2 Do Lawyers Have Their Own Language?

2.2.1 Paradoxical answers

In their practical argumentation lawyers developed an efficient answer to embarrassing questions. Whenever a controversy about abstract issues threatens to destroy the coherency of their reflections they used to answer: *'yes and no'*. And indeed, this rhetorical trick which at the first glance may appear somewhat infantile may bear in itself a very specific justification. In fact, the Legal Linguistics begins for many with the question whether the legal language really exists. Doubtlessly, lawyers did not develop any genuine language in the sense of natural languages like English or Chinese, and researchers regularly refer to this fact when talking about the legal language (Mattila 2006: 3). In this sense the infantile 'no' from our elusive answer seems to be justified. However, also a 'yes' would be a convincing answer due to the particular way in which lawyers communicate. These 'nos' and 'yes' are in fact too elusive to satisfy our curiosity in the subject. Nevertheless, they constitute a first, although paradoxical, answer. In general, paradoxical answers emerge in our language when our world view is troubled by a logical inconsistency of which we are unaware. In fact, to answer our question by a simultaneous 'yes' and 'no' cannot be sufficient. Reasons for this are not only purely logical. They have their roots in the subject matter. Therefore, we will work on our perspective upon the legal language in order to determine the answer. As a matter of fact, initially, the legal language has been perceived as a question of style (Dölle 1949). Also in Pigolkin (1990: 4, 16) the legal language is characterized as a specific functional style of the literary language. The issues of style have been related to the rhetoric of legal texts and it was stressed that the legislative language is characterized by rhetoric neutrality (Pigolkin 1990: 8). Yet, in this view the concept of style is undetermined. We could define it as a specific way to see the world with linguistic means (Goodman 1978: 3). However, in this perspective the legislative language would appear rather as profoundly rhetorical, abounding in rhetorical figures, emotions and understatements and definitely not as neutral. We prefer, therefore, to integrate the debate relating to style and rhetoric into the legal argumentation where it can be understood in a broader context. Furthermore, other scholars emphasized the specific professional terminology as a characteristic of the legal language. Some scholars, however, questioned the existence of a particular legal language and pointed rather to a specific register than to language (Gizbert-Studnicki 1979: 49-60). By contrast, in some already classical works on this issue like D. Mellinkoff's *The Language of the Law* (1963) the term legal language is used in an equivalent transformation. Therefore, a conclusive answer to the question whether lawyers have their own language depends – as always – on the definition of language adopted in the research. Nevertheless, in general, one can retain from the classical discussion that language used in the legal contexts is somehow specific, although in elderly research this specificity remained rather nebulous. For example, the mentioned questions of style or specific professional register refer to aspects of language use rather than to a language typology. These and many other linguistic aspects of law are the area of the Legal Linguistics. They comprise the whole arsenal of the legal discourse, an organized set of legal-linguistic signs. Nowadays, the legal language can be therefore adequately characterized as language use within a specific type of discourse, i.e. the legal discourse. This is why lawyers have their own language, although they actually do not have any.

2.2.2 How language used in law became special?

As noted, the legal language is mostly perceived as a professional register, i.e. a specific language use based on ordinary language in communicative situations which take place within social (judicial) institutions. Now, this specific use must at a stage be discernible to the language users, speakers and listeners alike. When do language users realize that the appropriate register to use is the legal-linguistic one? We could easily imagine a layperson entering a court of law and speaking the ordinary language. Besides, this happens regularly in the legal practice if not for want of any better linguistic skill as laypersons usually master the legal language only rudimentarily, if at all. Yet, the user of the ordinary language in a court procedure will soon realize that the linguistic situation in which he is expected to act requires a different language use to perform in it in an optimal way; i.e. to produce and understand legal speech acts correctly. Otherwise, his language use which entails producing and understanding of legal speech acts will lead to infelicitous performance; i.e. to legal speech acts which only partly engender the intended consequences and sometimes may produce even the opposite of the intended. Due to this specificity, the Legal Linguistics deals with legal-linguistic operations as the most salient aspects of language use in law.

2.2.3 Text types in law

Speakers and hearers notice the different circumstances in which language is used and they realize that they have to make use of various registers in order to cope with the linguistic situation in which they are acting. Linguistically, this difference can be observed on different text types that emerge as a result of this differentation of language use. In fact, language use in legal texts differs considerably. Until now, these differences have been scrutinized rather intuitively and formal juridical criteria were applied in order to set up a broader matrix of text types in law (Galdia 1998: 551). However, it would be expedient to work out other than juridical criteria for the typology of texts used in law. This typology should be based on linguistic rather than juridical characteristics. It would show whether the intuitively identified text types correspond with a matrix which would be developed by the linguists. At this stage of development, one can assume that some of the text types would coincide with the linguistic criteria while others might overlap and form broader or narrower text types. The typology used today mostly comprises:

- Language of statutes (language of legislation)
- Language of legal decisions including fact description
- Language of the legal doctrine
- Language used by lawyers in professional discussions and pleadings
- Language used by laypersons in legal contexts (testimony, comments on legal decisions)
- Language used by administrative clerks

In turn, the traditional linguistic text typology includes e.g. *narration, description, exposition, argumentation, instruction*. More advanced typologies include *informative, appellative* or *declarative* texts. One can classify one legal text as belonging to several types, for instance: *All rights reserved. No part of this book may be reprinted or reproduced or utilized in any form or by any electronic, mechanical or other means, now known or hereafter invented, including photocopying and recording, or in any information storage or retrieval system, without permission in writing from the publishers* may be perceived as *informative* or *appellative* in the sense that it appeals to the user not to violate its terms. The classification methode is analogous to the indentification of speech acts. Both ways of classification prove the context dependent quality of text types used in law. The text type may convey messages with different pragmatic load that change with time; the samples from different versions of Japan's constitutions illustrate this phenomenon (cf. Notes and Materials nr. 10).

2.2.3.1 Text type dependent transformations of legal language: Basic for any conception of legal text types is the transformational theory of legal language. Its hard core is the contention that all lexical units of an legislative act, i.e. those explicitly belonging to the legal terminology and those taken from the ordinary language become in the transformation which produces a legal act (a law, a decree or others) part of normative language (Pigolkin 1990: 151). The normative character of the act unifies the terminology used in it and transforms it into a normative text without distinguishing the lexical classification of terms. Only lexical units with purely auxiliary character may be excluded from this process. All terms in a legal act should be therefore perceived as having an equal status (Pigolkin, ibid.). This is understandable when scientific terminology (e.g. *multiculturalism, gender, race*) is introduced into the legal language (Galdia 2004: 172). Otherwise, the exclusion of auxiliary lexical units, and the authors of *Iazyk zakona* apparently mean prepositions etc., is not convincing as they may gain specific importance in legal acts and contracts. This has regularly been the case with expressions involving time and calculating deadlines (*until, not before, in three weeks* etc.). It would be therefore more persuasive to perceive the normative language as fully unified through its normative text type, as proposed in Galdia (1989: 330). The normative text type forms also the basis for further linguistic differentiation of text types used in legal contexts.

2.2.3.2 Legal language transgresses law: The Legal Linguistics goes beyond law in that it includes also legal usage which is not acceptable as a proposition of law or as valid legal-linguistic use. For instance, an Incoterm clause such as *FOB Mexico City* is for us part of the legal-linguistic use because it has been applied in a legal-linguistic context. It does not matter that the contractual clause which includes this Incoterm as such does not make sense in law. Similarly, a clause in an English-language contract providing for a guarantee of *good standing* in a case where the application of the German law is agreed upon by the parties does not make sense in terms of law because the German law, unlike the common law, does not know any such guarantee. Legally, the clause does not make sense but as an utterance in a legal context it is a valid object of legal-linguistic interest. In addition, manifestly erroneous court opinions and propositions of law presented there are interesting for us although they may be perceived as useless by the legal profession. Dissenting or concurring opinions are not less interesting for us than the majority opinions. Language in overruled precedents is for the Legal Linguistics equally important as the language in the overruling decision. Practicing lawyers will have to distinguish carefully between them as some of them state the law while others do not. Alleged linguistic mistakes and fallacies also fall within the spectrum of the Legal Linguistics. Uncorrect translations are a source of information for the legal linguist (cf. Notes and Materials nr. 12). For us, such texts represent language used in discourses about law in equal degree. In this sense the Legal Linguistics goes beyond the law.

2.2.4 Legal language as ordinary language

Apparently, the legal language is less perfect and less complete than our ordinary language is. Generally, no particular semantic problems come up in our daily communication. Troubles in understanding in the ordinary language use can be easily solved in a communicative situation. Equally, idiosyncratic linguistic use can be explained or is perceptive in the communicative situation by the participants. Should a semantically ambigous sentence be pronounced in a conversation, e.g. *I like my secretary better than my wife,* a simple question will suffice to disambiguate it (Juhl 1986: 52). Law does not provide us with such comfort. Yet still, would it not be enough to have a look at the use to determine the meaning of a legal concept? In some situations it may even be the case, while in others the interpreter of a legal rule risks to fall into a trap prepared by the users of ordinary language. The repetitive requests for precision in the legal language (cf. Schmidt 1972; Mattila 2006: 65) are the best illustration of this dilemma. The request for precision links the debate to the possible use of ordinary language in law. The idea is not particularly popular among lawyers, partly due to the corporatist view that lawyers are responsible for guarding and passing further their professional terminology (Galdia 2003: 12). Furthermore, the legal language and especially the legal terminology guarantee for many the correct functioning of the judicial apparatus. However, legal terminology and legal language developed and function as an elaborated form of the ordinary language (Gémar 2004: 738). Put into pragmatic terms, the difference between the ordinary language and the special register of law is that the legal language attempts to draw precise semantic boarders among words and the users of the ordinary language are less worried about this task. However, in law the distinction should be made between the postulate of a conceptually clear legal language and the existing legal language. Speakers, even lawyers - with possible exception of some legal scholars - rarely perceive legal language as particularly clear. The constant use of interpretive and argumentative techniques in the application of law proves that the legal language is all but clear; i.e. univocal.

Theoretically, a specialized language such as the legal language presupposes the existence of the ordinary language of which it is the extention. Were it not so, one would not be able to learn it because all knowledge about the specialized language is acquired through the ordinary language (Savigny 1981: 323). Some additional basic assumptions about the relation between the specialized language S and the ordinary language O were stated by Savigny (1981: 348). According to him, any utterance in S can be expressed in O; no utterance in S would make sense would in not at least in some contexts be translatable into O; every utterance in S is meaningful due to rules formulated in O; S develops historically among speakers of O; O must be learned before S is learned; the speaker has to master O in order to master S but not vice versa; some convictions of O are valuable in S; in order to understand S one must share some convictions formulated in O. The main distinction between the specialized language and the ordinary language is that some knowledge is not available in the ordinary language;

instead it is proposed in the specialized language. Yet, this does not mean that this knowledge could not be expressed in the ordinary language. It is not available there simply because some results of science are achieved in specialized communities of experts who speak and write the specialized language. Yet, it could at any moment be translated into the ordinary language. Through this translation the knowledge would not become more or less true or more or less false. The mere circumstance that an utterance containing knowledge is expressed in the specialized language is not a guarantee that the utterance is true. And vice versa, the use of ordinary language in the transfer of knowledge does not make this knowledge less true or less false. The result of the translation from the specialized language into the ordinary language is a quality mark of a branch of science. Wherever this linguistic transfer does not function justified mistrust against scientific theories may come up (Savigny 1981: 322). Therefore, regular and thorough transformation of knowledge available in a branch of science into the ordinary language seems to be in its well understood self-interest. Equally, the concepts used in the transfer of knowledge do not say anything about the existence of objects to which their lexicalization might refer. That the word *unicorn* exists does not mean that the unicorn exists in reality (cf. Recanati 2008: 39). This result does not change even if the sublime tapestry in the Museum of Cluny known as *La Licorne* shows a unicorn in all detail. Even cross-culturally, the statuettes of 'Chinese' unicorns, (CN) *dú jiǎoshòu,* can prove the ubiquity of the image, but not the real existence of this sublime, yet virtual animal. Within natural sciences this issue of possible existence or non-existence of postulated concepts may lead to additional methodological problems of justification (Bülow 1985: 24). In law, the situation is less complicated. The legal language is special in the sense that its concepts generally do not exist in the physical reality; they are pure linguistic creations. In some semantic theories this sort of concepts used in law is perceived as shorthand script. Thus, *adverse possession* or *unjust enrichment* do not exist in reality. Instead, they refer to specific existing social situations in which sets of facts previously characterized as decisive in law are labelled with concepts. This procedure simplifies their use in law. The fate of such concepts is unequal either. Some, mostly vivid concepts which can be easily simplified in the ordinary language like *unjust enrichment* find easily their way into it, others like *adverse possession* or *promissory estoppel* may attract the speakers of the ordinary language only in very specific situations, if at all. This selection may even decide their destiny in law; concepts disappear from law not only through changes in law but also through preferential changes which speakers impose upon the legal language. Therefore, the two concepts, specialized language and ordinary language are not constant. It is occasionally difficult to draw the line between them because they are not only interdependent, they are also in contact. Concepts of scientific language such as *electron* or *unjust enrichment* enter into the ordinary language and it is often only a question of time until a concept from the specialized register of a branch of science is perceived by speakers as belonging to the ordinary language albeit with a simplified meaning. Intralingual polysemy like the use of *instrument* in whatever daily context, for instance music instrument and the use of *instrument* in the international law to describe a legal act, mostly an international convention, are typical situations of the use of same words in two registers. Both registers are also less homogeneous as one would wish in a research partly based upon their mutual distinction. Needless to add that in the contemporary law they have also a multilingual dimension (Mattila 2006: 32). Furthermore, the language of statutes differs from the language of court decisions or administrative correspondence although we used to treat this usage as characteristic for one legal language. Equally, ordinary language used by persons with different levels of formal education usually differs, provided their education has not been a mere formality. The same speakers may use their ordinary language differently in emotionally loaded situations and speak another variety of ordinary language in circumstances which they perceive as emotionally neutral. In addition, there exist specialized languages which are more specialized than others (also within one branch of science) as there exist ordinary languages less ordinary than others (Savigny 1981: 347). In sum, no convincing theoretical reasons exist for not using ordinary language to express law. Legal concepts can be expressed by ordinary language as well in that they are described in it. Furthermore, the legal language is not constituted of concepts alone. For the forming of the modern law, it would be more appropriate to concentrate on description of actions and characterization of legal speech acts, rather than on developing of new legal concepts. Significant progress would be reached in this way and law would become at least more rational and easier accepted. Moreover, in relation to the global law it is important to keep in mind that also national legal languages are sometimes more and sometimes less close to ordinary language (Galdia 2003: 21). A global law expressed in a language which is not adapted to this linguistic usage will not be understood, nor will it be applied properly.

2.2.4.1 Fictions in legal language: Law expressed with linguistic means appears in the semiotic perspective as a fiction. It is a secondary sign system (Jackson 1985: 13) which refers to a primary system of signs, such as society or state. While referring to the primary sign system law provides rules for this system. These rules say how the primary system should be. Therefore, one must assume that law would not exist were the primary sign systems generally reflecting and applying these rules. The ontological difference between *is* and *ought to be* is the precondition for the existence of law. The tension between the two sign systems is focused upon by legal sociologists. The sense of their activity is to research the relation between the secondary and the primary sign systems. The discrepancy between both systems which legal sociologists could succinctly express as *state and society are often not what they should be in terms of law* demonstrate materially the genuine condition of the existence of law. Therefore, again, were rules which we perceive as legal generally known, generally accepted and generally applied in state and society no law would be needed. Almost certainly, under these circumstances, law as a collection of explicit rules would not even come up. Regularly, legal rules are linguistically expressed in forms which may suggest that they simply state facts (cf. Minda 1995: 239). They appear then in the clothes of primary sign systems while being by nature secondary, although not less important. The ontological difference which has been mentioned, helps distinguish legal rules as engendered by a secondary sign system from rules of primary sign systems. This is not a distinction without difference because it makes plain what legal interpretation is about. It does not describe the law as it is. Instead, it tries to set up propositions of law which would fit the requirements of the secondary sign system aiming to provide guidelines for the primary sign systems. Signs in law have therefore a constitutive, not a descriptive function. They engender meaning, instead of only representing it. Generally, the fictitious character of law manifests itself also linguistically. Statutory provisions include numerous formulations, such as (D) *gilt als (is perceived as)* which are instrumentalized to provide equal legal consequences to unequal factual constellations (cf. Lachmeyer 1979). The most basic example of such fictions is the sign *No dogs!*. Placed at the entry of an institution it is regularly interpreted in the sense of the message to animals' owners meaning that animals are - to put it mildly - not welcome there. Other linguistic fictions are eventually more complex. These linguistic fictions were construed by F. Lachmeyer (id.) as a particular boldness of jurists to create equality between evidently unequal things or events. This is definitely the case when, for instance, in the contract law a late acceptance of an offer to enter into a contract is perceived as a new offer (cf. § 150 I BGB or Sec. 40 of the (U.S.) Restatement (Second) of Contracts). Without the understanding of the fictitious character of the legal signs the creation and the application of law cannot succeed.

2.3 Characteristic Features of Language Used in Law

2.3.1 Descriptive models and their sense

The linguistic characterization of the language used in legal contexts can be accomplished within the notional framework provided by general linguistics for the description of natural languages. It may reflect their textual structure and start with *text* or *text types* and go over to their *semantic* and *syntactic constituents* (van Dijk 1980: 41). It may equally well follow a descriptive model that is divided into *linguistic levels* and comprise *phonology* and *phonetics, morphology, syntax* and *semantics* (van Dijk 1980: 19; Akmajian 2001: xi). As an annex to this model, one may mention the communicative levels of language use understood there as *pragmatics* (Akmajian 2001: 3). The legal-linguistic research favors the last model that is based on structural aspects of language to which communicative or functional aspects are added. This model splits the language into discrete units that are easier to handle at the beginning than complex structures where phonological issues are combined with morphological ones or semantical issues combined with syntactical ones. Nevertheless, the description of language is achieved only when these levels are linked, with other words when the structural components of language are combined with its functional properties (Akmajian 2001: 5). As a result, the descriptive model based on the scrutiny of discrete units on different and separated levels is easy to start with but complicates the descriptive task on a more advanced stage. However, the integrative task of linguistic description that focuses on more complex units such as *text* (Mattila 2006: 65) or *discourse* is central to the task of the Legal Linguistics. Therefore, in this paragraph the two-fold descriptive model will be used to make plain what linguists and lawyers found out about the legal language while applying it. At the same time, it will make clear, at least implicitly, why in this book rather the pragmatic approach is stressed and why results achieved within the two-fold descriptive model must be reinterpreted in the Legal Linguistics that is based on the pragmatic model.

2.3.2 Linguistic levels

2.3.2.1 Phonology: The phonology of the legal language provides for a set of issues with a legal background, like e.g. the pronunciation of the Latin legal notions, especially the traditional English pronunciation of Latin and the upcoming Italianized or classical pronunciation in the U.S. (Tiersma 1999: 53-55; Mattila 2006: 151). Pragmatically interesting is, for instance, the voice tone that rules in some courts, the hypercorrectness in the pronunciation or notaries' routine reading of legal documents. Research on phonetical and phonological issues in law is concentrated rather around their practical application within the forensic linguistics.

2.3.2.2 Morphology: Morphological implications in the legal terminology concern primarily the meaning of complex words. For instance, the word *payable* used by a banker who says that a bill is *payable* on October 1 does not mean that this bill *can* be paid on that date but that it *should* be paid (Akmajian 2001: 49). This word does not follow the pattern represented by e.g. *fixable* – able to be fixed or *mendable* – able to be mended. Furthermore, in the court jargon an offence is *jailable* in difference to a *fine-only offence* (Atwater v. Lago Vista U.S. Supreme Court 195 F. 3d 242 (2001)) in the sense that it may lead to detention. Hałas (1995: 53) referred for the Polish legal language to a parallel process concerning the formant (PL) *–lny,* e.g. in (PL) *karalny* able to be punished/that should be punished or (PL) *zaskarżalny* able to be charged/that should be charged. The example concerning the word *payable* demonstrates that the meaning of some complex words is not composed of the meanings of their parts (Akmajian 2001: 49). We are able to grasp the meaning of such words only in the context of their use. Here, once again, our pragmatic approach facilitates also the understanding of morphological implications in the legal terminology and prevents cumbersome analyses of isolated lexical units. Morphonological problems can also emerge in situations where two terms such as *insistence* and *insistency* are perceived as synonymous in a language, but could have been used to mark conceptual differences in the legal language. Traditional legal terminology of Germanic or Romance languages is rather strict in this respect, whereas the Finnish terminology is much more flexible (Galdia 2003: 13). Furthermore, in the morphology of the legal language one can mention the general absence of verb forms in the second person plural or singular (Hałas 1995: 42). Additionally, Tiersma (1999: 87) points out the antiquated morphological formations, e.g. *This policy witnesseth that…*

2.3.2.3 Syntax: in sentences composed by lawyers is specific (Gustafsson 1975; Hiltunen 2001). Simple sentences are rare in law. A typical sentence is a composed one; often build up in accordance with complicated syntactic patterns (Hiltunen 1990: 70-74). It seems that the syntax of the legal English became more transparent with time; e.g. a phrase in the English Act of Settlement from 1700 clarifying the succession to the throne consists of 182 words, taking 13 lines in modern print (Barnett 1999: 25): *And it was thereby further enacted that all and every person and persons that then were or afterwards should be reconciled to or shall hold communion with the see or church of Rome or should professe the popish religion or marry a papist should be excluded and are by that Act made for ever incapable to inherit possess or enjoy the crown and government of this realm and Ireland and the dominions thereunto belonging or any part of the same or to have use or exercise any regall power authority or jurisdiction within the same and in all and every such case and cases the people of this realm shall be and are thereby absolved of their allegiance and that the said crown and government shall from time to time descend to and be enjoyed the same in case the said person so reconciled holding communion professing or marrying as aforesaid were naturally dead.* However, some text types such as (IT) *massime di giurisprudenza* remain amazingly resistant as to their syntactic pattern (cf. Notes and Materials nr. 14). Overall, long sentences do not necessarily impede upon the understandability of texts. In the legal texts layers of embedding make legal sentences appear longer and more difficult to parce (Okawara 2006). This can be demonstrated on the mentioned (IT) *massime di giurisprudenza* that can be easily reformulated in simple sentences. Syntactically striking is further the omission of the definite article before the terms *plaintiff* or *defendant* in judicial decisions, e.g. *...it is clear, defendant believed it could comply with the contract by delivering stewing chickens. Plaintiff asserts that it is equally plain that plaintiff's own subjective intent was to obtain broilers and fryers.* (Frigaliment Importing Co. v. B.N.S. International Sales Corp. 190 F. Supp. 116 (S.D.N.Y. 1960)). Syntactic particularities include structures common for opening in pleadings, e.g. *Comes now plaintiff* for *Here comes the plaintiff* (Tiersma 1999: 88). Word order in legal English follows occasionally the French pattern of the adjective set behind the noun, e.g.: *attorney general, court martial* or *fee simple absolute*. Reversed word order occurs also in Italian court decisions: *Ritiene questa Corte che non ...* (cf. Notes and Materials nr. 25).

2.3.2.4 Semantics: in law has been dominated by definitional questions. We can refer to the definition of *house* in an English bill (cf. Notes and Materials nr. 11). The ambition of jurists dealing with semantic questions has been to define the legal-linguistic use. Semantical processes in law usually broaden or streamline the ordinary language notions. They may include additional semantic components, e.g. (D) *Wilderei* (poaching) according to the Sec. 296 of the German Penal Code includes trafficking of parts of animal bodies such as horns which are not covered by the German ordinary language use of poaching. Moreover, *crabs* are covered by the Polish statute on fishery although they clearly are not fishes (Hałas 1995: 25). However, purely semantic analyses based on isolated terms may lead to unjustified distinctions in the terminology. When for instance Pigolkin (1990: 118) points out that the lexical unit (RU) *брак/brak* may mean in the Russian language *marriage* or *defect* so is this perfectly right. The lexical unit (RU) *brak* is used in appropriate contexts in the Russian legislation, e.g. in the legislation on marriage and in the provisions on the sale of goods with the respective meaning. Pigolkin does not show that this synonymy may lead to confusion or other problems in the understanding or in the application of laws which comprise the term (RU) *brak*.

2.3.3 Lexicology

The legal lexicology comprises isues of general nature such as choice of lexical units, lexical borrowings, synonyms and phraseology as well as etymology. The choice of vocabulary that is used in law from the vast number of words has been rarely researched (Bülow 1986: 33). Mattila (2006: 4-6) dealt with the legal jargon and the counter-language of the criminal fraternity. Overall, the lexicological research shows that lexical units undergo a process of selection and change in which they acquire a more precise meaning within the special register. We can illustrate this process on the example of the verb *pre-empt* and the noun preemption. The modified use of preempt (pre-empt) in the American legal terminology can be illustrated through its specific usage in the constitutional law. For instance, the Secretary of Administration and Finance of Massachusetts was sued by a trade association in a case concerning the constitutionality of the Myanmar-statute, enacted 1996. In the litigation the council argued that the Massachusetts "anti-Myanmar" statute was pre-empted by the Supremacy Clause of the Constitution… The Supreme Court held that *it is just this plenitude of executive authority that we think controls the issue of preemption here.* (Crosby v. National Foreign Trade Council 530 U.S. 363, 120 S.Ct. 2288, 2000 U.S. Lexis 4153). Under preemption as a U.S. judicial doctrine we understand the supremacy of federal legislation over state legislation. The U.S. Congress may when it legislates in an area of federal concern specifically pre-empt all state legislation. State legislatures may also pre-empt local governments in the same manner: *Neither Avena nor the President's Memorandum constitutes directly enforceable federal law that pre-empts state limitations on the filing of successive habeas petitions* (Medellín v. Texas, U.S. 06-984 (2007)). Originally, preemption in the common law expressed the right of the king to buy provisions in preference of others. In the American usage it concerned the right to purchase the publicly owned land on which someone is settling before others have the chance to do so. In international law, it expressed the right to detain goods of a foreigner in transit so as to afford its subjects a preference of purchase. Moreover, pre-emptive rights specified in a charter of a corporation grant to shareholders the first opportunity to buy a new issue of stock: *Most states allow the existence of pre-emptive rights to be determined by the articles of incorporation.* In fact, the original meaning of *preempt* is connected to purchasing by *preemption*, i.e. before others have a chance or rather the right to buy. The meaning of preempt as causing something to have no influence or force any more is based on the original meaning. Also the use in the ordinary language, e.g. *We were looking forward to watching our favorite television show, but it had been preempted by a political talk* or *The political movement had been preempted by a group of evil men* or in the military parlance *Several preemptive attacks on the enemy's airforce bases* ground in the legal-linguistic usage. The origin of the lexical unit is linguistically not reflected by the speakers any more; the Latin *emptio*, i.e. purchase, is not present in the meaning of the last three examples. The legal usage still refers to it, at least partly. In our entry example ordinary linguistic use apparently imposed itself upon the legal usage and established itself as a new concurring meaning of this concept in law. This new additional semantisation of the legal concept is based on its ordinary linguistic meaning.

2.3.3.1 Synonyms: The systemic synonymy of *proxy* is an example. The person authorized to vote for someone is known as *proxy,* apparently due to an abbreviation of *proxy holder.* The same term refers to the grant of voting authority and finally, also to the document which grants the shareholder the right to vote. *Equity* as a term used in accounting is not intelligible in the context of *equitable reme-*

dies or *equity powers* of courts or securities in form of *equities.* In accounting, the term *equity* refers to the ownership interest in the company (ordinary share) and derives from the equity court's recognition of the *equity of redemption.* Questions of synonymy are sometimes difficult to solve. Language use concerning for instance *obligated* or *obliged* differs considerably and native English speakers have different views about the meaning of both lexical units. They differ for some speakers as far as the intensity of the obligation is concerned or simply in respect of the solemnity of expression while others perceive them as purely synonymous. The same concerns the terms *bankruptcy* and *insolvency* of which the later one for some speakers and also for legal professionals seems to reflect the popular usage. For some others exactly the contrary is the case in English.

2.3.3.2 Definitions: Functionally closely related to concepts, the definitions interested jurists, also those dealing with Legal Linguistics, much less than terminological issues *sensu stricto*, i.e. analyses and comparison of concepts. This lack of particular interest occurs not without reasons. Since the Roman times jurists cherished mistrust towards definitions, but strangely enough relied heavily on concepts. The adage *Omnis definitio in jure civili periculosa est* - known in many versions which aim at conveying the same message namely that the definition finally does not matter much in law - was traditionally quoted in the legal doctrine, especially in works on theory of the private law. Jurists create definitions with the same idea in mind as when they create concepts; they try to minimize the risk of polysemy (cf. Mattila 2006: 66). Definition in a strict sense of the term has been characterized as a description which allows for replacement of the concept through the definiens in any context (Savigny 1981: 326). For instance, the U.S. Court of Appeals for the District of Columbia defined the hedge fund as *any pooled investment vehicle that is privately organized, administered by professional investment managers, and not widely available to the public* (Goldstein v. SEC , No. 04-1434 (2006)). This type of explicit definition does not work in law because it is too general. Equally, knowing the definition of *negligence* as tort where the violation of a statute or ordinance constitutes the breach of the duty of care, we are still unable to solve the legal question exposed for instance in Palsgraf v. The Long Island Railroad Company (cf. Notes and Materials nr. 34), whether the company acted negligently towards Ms. Palsgraf (248 N.Y. 339, 161 N.E. 99, 1928 N.Y. Lexis 1269 N.Y.). The definition provides a first orientation about the concept used in law and can be used as a framework for the development of the legal argumentation relevant in the case. Yet, it cannot replace it, where from its limited importance for jurists. Judge Randolph resumed therefore in the above case Goldstein v. SEC (p. 8 of the decision): *The lack of a statutory definition of a word does not necessarily render the meaning of a word ambigous, just as the presence of a* *definition does not necessarily make the meaning clearer. A definition only pushes the problem back to the defining terms.*

2.3.3.3 Phraseology in law: Phraseology is connected to terminological research as are analyses of adages, maxims etc. (Pigolkin 1990: 162). Again, American phraseology may differ from the British usage, cf. (UK) *called to the bar*, (US) *admitted to practice* (Mellinkoff 1963: 7). Furthermore, Mellinkoff (1963: 122) provides a list of binomials in legal English including: *save and except, final and conclusive, fit and proper, free and clear, goods and chattels, keep and maintain, peace and quiet.* Binomials may be perceived as typical for the English legal language. Historically, they were also used in the legal French, e.g. (FR) *né et natif, sûr et certain, les us et les coutumes,* or *certificat de bonne vie et moeurs.*

2.3.3.4 Etymology: Etymological issues play traditionally a role, especially in the research into legal terminology. They were even the origin of the research related to the legal terminology. The reason for this might have been the vain hope that the original meaning of a legal term might guarantee its appropriate use and function as a guideline for its application. Nowadays, we are aware of that the etymological information is interesting in terms of language change in law. It is also clear that it is perfectly neutral in the area of the application of legal provisions. For the language of law it is however crucial because it enables to discover its fundamental linguistic features. It explains why we use words which we use in law. Nevertheless, we must understand that we could use also totally different words for legal concepts and that this would in no way change the material basis of our law. Grossfeld (1990: 94) stressed that etymology attracts lawyers in comparative legal studies. In this context Mattila (2002: 178) observed however that in comparative legal studies it is more substantial to fix terms in their conceptual interrelation rather than in their time perspective.

2.3.4 Textual aspects

Textual aspects dominate the jurist's work with legal provisions. Legal analysis concerns mostly linguistic units that surpass the sentence or even a sequence of sentences. It mostly concerns texts constituted around the coherent information in sequences of sentences (cf. van Dijk 1980: 41). For instance, Art. 68 of the French Constitution that provides for the responsibility of the President of the Republic in case of *high treason* says:

Le Président de la République n'est responsable des actes accomplis dans l'exercice de ses fonctions qu'en cas de haute trahison. Il ne peut être mis en accusation que par les deux assemblées statuant par un vote identique au scrutin public et à la majorité absolue des membres les composant; il est jugé par la Haute Cour de Justice.

Both sentences in the provision are linked by their sense. This link is however not visible in the lexical structure of the provision. Therefore, its textuality is open and allows for different - at least two - readings of the provision (Carcassonne 2005: 314). Were the sentences linked by e.g. (FR) *Dans ce cas* the textual structure would be limited and it would disambiguate the meaning of the whole provision. Similarly, sec. 11 of the (US) Securities Act gives a right of action to *any person acquiring such security*. However, in the text of the Act there is no direct antecedent for *such;* therefore courts had to construe it as meaning *any security registered by the registration statement*. Generally, the readability, i.e. the understandability of texts depends on their textual structure. The more explicitly the coherence among phrases is marked, the less is the reader's margin of appreciation and the risk of misunderstandings. Textual ambiguity in constitutional provisions is rather common, although one could expect more care in avoiding it. Art. 1 of the French Constitution says: *La France est une République indivisible, laïque, démocratique et sociale. Elle assure l'égalité devant la loi de tous les citoyens, sans distinction d'origine, de race ou de religion. Elle respecte toutes les croyances. Son organisation est décentralisée.* Here, as both *France* and *République* are of feminine gender in French, it is unclear to which of them the personal pronoun *elle* actually refers. This formulation has been disambiguated by the amendment of March 28, 2003 that introduced an additional phrase into the text of the Art. 1: *Son organization est décentralisée* (Carcassonne 2005: 44). The provision is now unequivocal as *elle* refers to *République* and not to *France* in the supplied sentence. Also Art. 1 of the German Constitution saying: *Die Würde des Menschen ist unantastbar. Sie zu achten und zu schützen ist Verpflichtung aller staatlichen Gewalt...Die nachfolgenden Grundrechte binden Gesetzgebung, vollziehende Gewalt und Rechtsprechung als unmittelbar geltendes Recht,* is ambigous. The provision declares the human dignity inalienable and states in the final phrase that the *following provisions* (D *nachfolgende Grundrechte*) are binding on all public authorities. The question arose then as to whether the Art. 1 is also binding in the light of this formulation. For us, the structure of the constitutional text and the character of the Constitution as a legal text suggest the normativity of all formulations, also of Art. 1 (Galdia 1989: 330). Hence, problems of textual structure reflect themselves in the legal argumentation as a natural cause of its being. They call arguments into their legal existence.

The mentioned textual ambiguity is not regulated in law; it follows from the general structure of texts in relation to the problem of their understandability. Some textual forms in law such as the juridic decisions follow a specific pattern. For the German judicial decision the (D) *Urteilsstil,* a method of legal argumentation opposite to (D) *Gutachtenstil* which is used by law students, is perceived as the basic structure of this legal text type. In the Notes and Materials nr. 26 we provide an example of this style. According to the French tradition of drafting court decisions, the syllogism should dominate the outfit of the decision. In the Notes and Materials nr. 22 and 23 we provide an (FR) *arrêt en forme de syllogisme* constituted of three parts: (FR) 1. *règle générale applicable (majeure)*, 2. *cas particulier de l'espèce (mineure)*, and 3. *application du général au particulier (décision prise, conclusion)*.

2.3.5 Particular descriptive features

Next to the above descriptive pattern based on linguistic levels and research areas, specific descriptive features of the legal language have been determined. Research has concentrated upon establishing a catalogue of characteristic features of the language use in law (Mattila 2006: 65-103). These features are best distinguished within the framework of postulated and established features. Given that the discussion about language use in law has a long tradition often different authors mixed opinions about what language they would wish to be used in law with the language really used. On the other side, non-postulatory, i.e. descriptive research on legal language is still quite limited and it is difficult to characterize the legal language on the basis of the research already done. Most criteria are still verified intuitively. Research into legal Latin shows that results of quantitative analyses may differ considerably from intuitive opinions lawyers held about the use of legal Latin in different countries (Mattila 2002c). It may be assumed that the situation is very much the same when whatever other language than Latin is at stake. The characteristic features which dominate the discussion are: precision (tautology, definitions and enumerations), information (over)load, universality and aloofness, systemic character (references and consistent use of terms), structure and formalism (form of judgments, contracts, legislative acts), sentence complexity, archaism and solemnity, obscurity (Mattila 2006: 65-92). Some textual examples may illustrate them:

Precision: *Plaintiff asserts that it is equally plain that plaintiff's own subjective intent was to obtain broilers and fryers* (Frigaliment Importing Co. v. B.N.S. International Sales Corp. 190 F. Supp (S.D.N.Y. 1960)).

Information load: *Texas law makes it a misdemeanour, punishable only by a fine, either for a front-seat passenger in a car equipped with safety belts not to wear one or for the driver to fail to secure any small child riding in front.* (Atwater v. Lago Alto, U.S. Supreme Court 195 F. 3d 242)

Exceptions to this exemption for after-acquired property include previously non-assignable real property rights that become assignable within 6 months after bankruptcy, and property rights vesting in the bankrupt within 6 months of the bankruptcy.

Obscurity: *The distribution of the distributable residue of the movables of the deceased is (in general) governed by the law of the deceased's domicile (lex domicilii) at the time of his death* (Dicey's Conflict of Laws, 6th ed. p. 814).

The indictment is endorsed by the foreman as a true bill.

Obscurity characterizes also the professonal jargon: *Can you plead collateral estoppel?*

Schematized language: *The ECPA* **makes it a crime** *to intercept an electronic formulation at the point of transmission, while in transit, when stored by a router or server, or after receipt by the intended recipient.* (emphasis added)

Texas law **makes it a misdemeanour...** (emphasis added)

In reviewing legal insufficiency points or no evidence points, we must consider only the evidence tending to support the finding, viewing it **in the light most favorable** *to the finding, giving effect to all reasonable inferences that may properly be drawn from the evidence...Texaco, Inc. v. Pennzoil, Co. 729 S.W. 2d 768 (1987).*

Formal vocabulary is preferred in law, e.g. *timepiece* is used for *watch* (Bulova Watch Company, Inc. v. K. Hattori & Co., Ltd., (508 F. Supp. 1322 (1981). Verbs are transformed into complex structures, e.g. (D) *vorwerfen* into *zum Vorwurf machen, anklagen* into *Anklage erheben, aufrechnen* into *Aufrechnung erklären* (Dölle 1949: 71), (FIN) *maksaa* in (FIN) *suorittaa maksu* (Mattila 2008: 1150), *to accomplish an apportionment of losses* (Cooter-Ulen 2004: 6) is used instead of *to divide losses.*

Enumeration encreases the complexity of syntactically simple sentences: *Any right, power, capacity, disability or legal relationship which has been created by the law of any civilized country applicable according to the English rules of the conflict of laws is recognized and, in general, enforced by the English courts, and no right, power, capacity, disability or legal relationship which has not been so created is enforced or, in general, recognized by the English courts.* (J.H.C. Morris (ed.), Dicey's Conflict of Laws, 7th ed. 1958, Stevens & Sons, London).

Archaism and solemnity: British legal acts enacted by the Parliament begin with the formula: *Be it enacted by the Queen's most Excellent Majesty, by and with the advice and consent of the Lords Spiritual and Temporal, and Commons, in this present Parliament assembled, and by the authority of the same, as follows* – (An Act to Amend the Theft Act 1968 and the Theft Act 1978, dated 18 December 1996)

Senior officials formulate their declarations in a way that engenders solemnity through archaic language use: *Now, therefore, I, Sir William Joseph Slim, the Governor*

General in and over the Commonwealth of Australia acting with the advice of the Federal Executive Council and in the exercise of all powers me thereunto enabling do by the presents accede in the name and on behalf of Her Majesty in respect of the Commonwealth of Australia and the Territories of Papua and Norfolk Island and the Trust Territories of New Guinea and Nauru to the convention aforsaid subject to the following reservations,... (from Australia's Reservations and Declarations relative to the International Convention for the Unification of Certain Rules of Law Relating to Bills of Lading (1924)).

Oath is sworn frequently with the use of preformulated utterances that include solemn expressions: *I swear to tell the truth, so help me God.*

Abbreviations: Formulations such as *Br. Of Pet'r at 17* for *Brief of Petitioner at 17* do not seem unavoidable and rather increase the understanding problems than contribute to a more economical language use. Still more, in a newspaper report about a police intervention: (FR) *Les policiers, grâce à une collaboration exemplaire inter-service signée BRAB-CAC-BAC, sont allés de surprise en aveux* (Nice Matin, June 25, 2008) the administrative jargon is quoted. The phrase is understandable when the initialisms of the multiple police services are deciphered : BRAB – *Brigade de la répression des atteintes aux biens*, CAC – *cellule anticambriolage de la sûreté départementale*, BAC – *Brigade anticriminalité*. The administration has the tendency to produce abbreviations, possibly also due to its professional tradition, e.g.: (FR) *D.G.R.C.S.T. - Direction générale des relations culturelles, scientifiques et techniques*, a unit of the French Ministry of Foreign Affairs in charge of promotion of the French language abroad (Baylon 1991 : 193). Abbreviations, mostly in form of acronyms, may shape also the ordinary language: (D) *Bafög* for *Bundesausbildungsförderungsgesetz* is used not only among German students as a synomym of a grant, (FR) *PACS* for *Pacte civil de solidarité* led to the coinage (FR) *se pacser* largely used in informal spoken French. Abbreviations like all other linguistic means may support or hinder communication (Mattila 2006: 89).

Arcane language: i.e. specific formulations which are understandable for lawyers due to socialization processes to which they have been exposed can be perceived as an accidental element of the legal language. They are rather shortcomings than linguistic phenomena justified by the necessity of professional linguistic practices. Elderly usage such as *plaintiff in error* or *defendant in error* in cases concerning the *writ of error* are a good example of such use. Neither the plaintiff nor the defendant need to err, they take part in a litigation concerning the writ of error (cf. for instance *Plessy v. Ferguson, 163 U.S. 537 (1896)*, in Notes and Materials nr. 28). Furthermore, a specific group of arcane language represent in the English legal language French appendices which are in fact either redundant or manieristic: *A child born anywhere in a lawful wedlock is* ***(semble)*** *legitimate* (emphasis supplied), in: A.W. Scott, Private International Law, 2nd ed. MacDonalds and

Evans, Plymouth, p. 183. Such expressions have of course their hidden sense in that they signalize that the assumption is conditioned and can be challenged with legal means. Nevertheless, they provide in this arcane language a piece of information which is known to the expert anyhow and which for the non-expert will not be understandable and remain hidden. They are therefore not helpful in the legal language, although they clearly have a function in it. They namely stress the erudition of their authors. Still furthermore, decisions of the U.S. Supreme Court can be rendered a.o. as *majority* or *plurality decisions* depending upon the number of justices voting. The terminological difference is distinctive because the *plurality decision* which settles the case does not become precedent for future cases like the *majority decision.* This distinction is not marked in the terms, it is arcane. When courts refer to facts and persons unrelated to the case, the references may not be intelligible to the laypersons. For instance: *When Cardozo enunciated the standard for doing business in New York, there would have been little need to consider how, or whether, a foreign-based multinational enterprise would be found to be doing business in New York* (cf. Bulova v. Hattori (508 F. Supp. 1322 (1981)). Only a professional reader will realize that the person mentioned in the decision is Justice Benjamin Cardozo, one of the most influential judges in the history of U.S. law. However, many laypersons may not be aware of his achievements.

Redundant terms: Terminological redundancies in law have their roots in the historical development of the legal language which unlike many other scientific thesauruses has a tradition of at least two thousand years. Therefore, the legal terminology incorporates traditional terms and expressions which had their role to play in the past legal practice but sometimes lost it in the course of times. Additionally, specific features in the development of national legal languages such as binomials in the legal English (e.g. *null and void* or *last will and testament*) may lead to problems when applied in contemporary legal texts, for instance in court decisions or contracts. All these linguistic creations ground profoundly in the history of the English legal language (Beveridge 2002: 62). Today, nevertheless, they might and sometimes are perceived as redundant in the English legal language (Adams 2005: 3). To illustrate, in numerous agreements under the common law, assertions of facts are referred to as *representations and warranties.* The use of two different terms in one expression signalizes a possible conceptual difference. This difference is usually difficult to identify in contracts. In the U.S. law, only in the *Model Stock Purchase Agreement* (1995) and in the *Model Asset Purchase Agreement* (2001), both documents prepared by the American Bar Association, a distinction between both terms is established. The agreements read as far as *representations and warranties* are concerned: ***representations*** *are statements of past or existing facts and* **warranties** *are promises that the existing or future facts are or will be true* (emphasis added). Only one case had been identified in which this distinction plays a role, namely Krys v. Hendersen (69 S.E. 2d 635, 637) and it has been argued that the distinction is much more subtle than assumed (Adams 2005: 1). This leads to the conclusion that courts frequently use both terms as synonyms (Adams 2005: 2) and that therefore the terms *representation* and *represent* would be fully sufficient to convey the proper legal meaning of the concept (Adams 2005: 3). Moreover, the common law distinguishes between *conditions precedent* and *conditions subsequent.* The first ones mean that a specified event must occur before a party is obliged to perform contractual duties while the second ones relate to a situation where an event excuses the performance of an existing contractual duty to perform. This terminological difference is applied in numerous common law and international contracts (Beveridge 2002: 74). For the U.S., the Restatement (Second) of Contracts eliminates in its Sec. 224 the distinction between *conditions precedent* and *conditions subsequent.* The UCC mentions in § 2-615 *presupposed* conditions. For international contracts, especially when common law is not applicable, the use of these terms or the strict distinction between them does not make much sense (Beveridge 2002: 74). Under the U.S. law, to distinguish between both terms in sale contracts would be redundant. Next to these conceptual redundancies, especially in the legal treatises, internal reference is used to fill the empty space in texts, e.g. (ESP) *como ya emos visto, comprobaremos más adelante, ha sido ya considerado* (Lasarte 2006: 24). Also in this book expressions such as *Needless to say* or *As already mentioned* are frequently used in order to form a more coherent exposition of thoughts and to facilitate the orientation in the text. Strictly speaking, all of them are of course logically redundant.

2.3.6 Monolingual and multilingual linguistic corpus

Legal language has been analyzed either in the monolingual perspective as a special register of a given natural language or as special register contrasted with other special registers belonging to other natural languages. Legal English has been analyzed as a part of common English (Hiltunen 1990), legal English used in the UK was compared with legal English used in the USA or India (Mattila 2006: 246-249). Furthermore, legal English has been compared with legal French (Mattila 2006: 231). This research perspective has been adapted to numerous languages and valuable results have been obtained thus far. Both, the monolingual and the multilingual perspectives have their raisons d'être. The monolingual perspective explores one natural language and makes clear its complexity. The multilingual perspective shows languages in contrast and in contact and is complementary to the monolingual point of view.

2.3.6.1 Multilinguality of the legal language: Multilinguality in the legal language is rare. In the court opinions, especially those rendered within the common law, Latin and occasionally French expressions may occur. In some jurisdictions, e.g. in Germany, however, foreign or Latin vocabulary is strictly avoided mostly with reference to procedural rules providing for the use of the State language in the legal acts. A German court would never use the term (LAT) *culpa in contrahendo.* Instead, the German equivalent (D) *Verschulden bei Vertragsschluss* will be invoked, although the deciding judges may have used exclusively the popular Latin term when discussing the case before rendering the decision. Use of foreign vocabulary in the legislation is even more seldom. Nowadays, the number of direct quotes from legal English is increasing. For instance, in the Italian Civil Code, art. 2427bis the English term *fair value* is rendered in Italian in the headline of the provision as (IT) *valore equo*; later on it is used in the Italian text of the statutory provision without any translation into Italian. The term *joint venture* is rendered in English only and not marked particularly in the text, unlike *fair value*:

2427bis. Informazioni relative al valore equo **"fair value"** *degli strumenti finanziari.*

(1) – 1. Nella nota integrativa sono indicati: 1) per ciascuna categoria di strumenti finanziari derivati: a) il loro **fair value**; *b) informazioni sulla loro entità e sulla loro natura; 2) per le immobilizzazioni finanziarie iscritte a un valore superiore al loro* **fair value**, *con esclusione delle partecipazioni in società controllate e collegate ai sensi dell'articolo 2359 e delle partecipazioni in joint venture...*

Furthermore, a German statutory provision (Art. 112 Investmentgesetz) provides for a regulation of *hedge funds* which it calls (D) *Sondervermögen mit zusätzlichen Risiken.* However, it supplies the English term in brackets in the headline of the provision (D) *Vermögen mit zusätzlichen Risiken (Hedgefunds).* Furthermore, it uses the term *leverage* for (D) *unbeschränkte Aufnahme von Krediten für gemeinschaftliche Rechnung der Anleger oder über Einsatz von Derivaten.* However, it does not use the term *short sales*, and speaks instead of (D) *Leerverkauf* (cf. Art. 112 I 2 Investmentgesetz).

2.3.7 Legal language changes

A considerable part of the reflection upon law has been devoted to the issue of changes in law (cf. Mattila 2008: 1151). The fact that law changes is a practical problem with which every lawyer must cope and he also has to find out the appropriate method for the up-date of own legal knowledge. Therefore, it cannot surprise that changes in law are often also changes in the use of language in law. The interesting issue is the sort of changes which take place within the legal language. The additional tendency in the development of the legal language is its relative dependence upon the ordinary language and changes which occur there. For the English legal language Hiltunen showed the most significant transformation from Old (legal) English to legal English rooted in legal Latin and Nor-man-French heritage (Hiltunen 1990: 21-48). We include an excerpt in our Notes to illustrate this radical transformation (cf. Notes and Materials nr. 8). Both, Hiltunen (1990: 55-62) and Mattila (2006: 226-228), also showed the relative independence in the development of ordinary English and of Law French in England as well as the process of approximation of ordinary and legal English in contemporary times towards the background of the relative interdependence of both linguistic varieties. The development of the most significant legal languages for the Western tradition has been aptly characterized in the research. Mattila (2006) describes the linguistic changes in legal Latin, French, English and German as well as the development within the EU. Heller (1992) focused on the reform of the legal German in 18th century. For the emergence of legal Russian the absence of Old Church Slavonic terminology in *Russkaya pravda* has been stressed (Unbegaun 1969: 53); in turn, the Serbian legal language previously grounded in the Old Church Slavonic terminology (Bartoszewicz 1979: 50). The main discernible tendency in this development is the one of increasing specialization of language use. This tendency may be in a sense counteracted by the plain language use in the English-language legislation in the U.S. However, it may be premature to assert that this tendency - whose efficiency has not been proven yet - would dominate language use in the legislative bodies and in the judicature of the future.

2.4. Legal Terminology

2.4.1 First contact with legal terminology

The first contact with law often concerns its terminology. As already mentioned, the terminology is in our view not the most salient aspect of the legal language, nor does it dominate our conception of the Legal Linguistics. Nevertheless, it is the beginning of the reflection about law for many persons, especially for those who approach the law from the non-professional perspective. Therefore, some introductory remarks about the legal terminology are well founded at this place of our work. For many researchers the distinction between legal concepts and legal terms is fundamental for the analysis of the legal terminology in unilingual as in bi- or multilingual contexts. Paradoxically, the comparative approach to legal concepts and terms seems to be more prolific than its unilingual complement. We will therefore base our introductory remarks upon a compromise, and begin with a bilingual example. In private law, while analyzing contracts from the comparative perspective, we encounter a contract type in the common law that is called there *unilateral contract*. The French *Code civil* provides in its Art. 1103 a legal definition of a contract type called there *contrat unilatéral*. However, it would be premature and even negligent to assume that both terms cover the same contract type. The common law *unilateral contract* is a one-sided agreement whereby one party makes a promise to do, or refrain from doing something in return for a performance, not a promise. Traditionally, the common law *bilateral contract* was reduced to the formula that it concerned a promise for a promise, whereas the *unilateral contract* concerned a promise for an act. The civil law developed the concept of a unilateral contract as opposed to the synallagmatic contract in order to distinguish contracts obliging both parties to perform and those which bind only one party (cf. *contrat synallagmatique* or *bilatéral* in Art. 1102 French *Code civil*). This aim is visible from the wording and the systematics of the Articles 1102 and 1103 in the French *Code civil*:

Art. 1102 Le contrat est **synallagmatique** *ou* **bilatéral** *lorsque les contractants s'obligent réciproquement les uns envers les autres.*

Art. 1103 Il est **unilatéral** *lorsqu'une ou plusieurs personnes sont obligées envers une ou plusieurs autres, sans que de la part de ces dernières il y ait d'engagement.* (emphasis added)

The *contrat unilatéral* of the French Code civil is in terms of the common law contract doctrine not a contract at all as it lacks *consideration*. In the common law, something of value must correspond to a promise given and this corresponding element is called there *consideration*. In the civil law, there is no need for the *consideration* as a contract can bind only one party. This results not only from the Articles 1102 and 1103 of the French Code civil but also from other codes and contract doctrines on the European continent and not only there. Therefore, *unilateral contract* and *contrat unilatéral* are two different concepts as they are two different terms in English and French respectively. Needless to say that the *consideration* cannot be translated into French as (FR) *considération* because it would not refer to any concept of the French or Continental private law. (FR) *considération* as a purported equivalent of the common law *consideration* would be an empty, misleading and therefore also redundant term in the translation. Assumed the existence of a bilingual French and English uniform legal system which is grounded in the common law concepts of the *unilateral contract* and *consideration* and which uses these terms, both French terms *contrat unilatéral* and *considération* could be used in the French linguistic version of this legal system within their common law conceptual field. They would be misleading for a French user who is not familiar with this constructed legal system and who perceives the French legal terms through the French legal concepts. The risk of misconception that was described above corresponds with the nature of the legal terminology. Unilingual or multilingual legal terminology cannot be learned or understood when separated from the law in which it functions. The price to be paid for the insistence on the contrary view is the misconception of the meaning of legal rules or legal texts in general or, at least, the increased risk of such misconceptions.

Traditionally, the Legal Linguistics devoted much time and space to the analysis of legal notions. There are good reasons for this and we will also engage in conceptual analyses especially towards a comparative background. But before we make this step we should ask why actually this sort of analyses attracts the attention of researchers in law. In fact, law has been perceived by many as an ongoing debate about the content of concepts. This type of debates emerges, according to P. F Strawson (1992: 4), when the pragmatic perspective is neglected. Strawson writes: *"...disorders never arise when our concepts ideas are actually at work, but only when they are idle."* Strawson's observation concerning metaphysical concepts as used in philosophy seems to fit perfectly the embarrassing situation we are confronted with in law. As long as the legal notions are idle, i.e. are named in statutes or precedents, they seem to be at least relatively clear. Problems emerge when these notions are to be applied in new cases. There, suddenly, the notions as used in statutes or defined in the doctrine give rise to debates about their contents. When used in precedents they lead to questions about their possible applicability in new cases. In law, we operate with posited concepts whose content was apparently only partially defined by the legislator or the judge. As soon as these concepts should become operative in a new context we are confronted with the problems of application which cannot be as easily solved as misunderstandings in the daily use of language. Misunderstandings about the content of concepts that are used in ordinary language come up rarely and when they come up, they can be easily clarified in discourses (cf. 2.2.4).

2.4.2 Legal concepts and legal terms

Fundamental for the analysis of legal terminology has been the distinction between legal concepts and legal terms (Mattila 2006: 108). This distinction is of logical origin. It enables access to legal language, especially its legal terms in respect of their content and in respect of their form. More fundamentally, the general linguistics has been interested in terms in opposition to non-terms (Hałas 1995: 4). It furthermore maintained that a term is ontologically grounded in a contrast to another term without which it would not emerge. In the general linguistics, the definition of term is not finally clarified (Kesola 2007: 14). In law, however, the fascination for terms has been nourished by the vain hope that they would convey unequivocal meaning which would be independent from the context (Kesola 2007: 21). Moreover, some researchers stress that the legal terminology is numerically rather limited when compared with other sciences (Pigolkin 1990: 15). Therefore, it may surprise that it gained a central role in the legal-linguistic research. The traditional distinction between concept and term can be shown on the following examples. We can distinguish between two legal terms from business law, (US) *sole proprietor* and (UK) *sole trader*. Both terms are functional equivalents and stand for a person running business alone with unlimited liability. Thus, the common law concept represented in these two terms is the same. In addition, UK business law terms *articles of association* and *memorandum* correspond conceptually with US terms *articles of incorporation* and *by-laws* respectively. Still more, terms describing branches of law differ linguistically, e.g. (US) *corporate* law, (UK) *company* law; both however correspond conceptually. Within the UK, private wrongdoings are termed *torts* for the use in the English law and *delicts* for the Scottish law in the same legal act (cf. (UK) Private International Law (Miscellaneous Provisions) Act 1995 (c.42) Part III, 9). Moreover, in the international law the term *convention* is used in connection with multilateral agreements, as opposed to bilateral *agreements.* For instance, the Vienna Convention on the Law of Treaties defines a *treaty* as an international agreement between states that is governed by international law. Terms in law, seen in relation to concepts, appear as fairly colorless. Conceptually, it does not matter whether a person who initiates a lawsuit is called *plaintiff* or *claimant.* Neither do other terms such as *appellant* or *petitioner* influence the conceptual setting within the legal procedure. In terms of concepts, seen from the pragmatic perspective, we used to deal in an adversary judicial process with a proponent and an opponent. Even a linguistic error in a legal translation such as (D) **Verklagter* instead of (D) *Beklagter* for defendant cannot distort the conceptual framework of the legal procedure (cf. Notes and Materials nr. 12). Moreover, the conceptual framework and the user's knowledge about it restitute the right legal-linguistic usage. In our example, the professional hearer dealing with the error in the translation will without problems reconstruct the right linguistic form of the legal term used in the text. Therefore, it may seem that terms finally do not matter in law. Later on, we will demonstrate that they have a role to play in the argumentative legal discourse and in its environment, i.e. in the legal (doctrinal) systematics.

Equally, concepts created in economics prefigure the argumentative structures of the economic discourse (cf. Cooter, Ulen 2004: ix). This fundamental economic discourse oscillates in a perspective limited by linguistic constructs such as: *incentive effects, opportunity costs, risk aversion, transaction costs, free-riding, prisoner's dilemma, Nash equilibrium, dominant strategy, asymmetric information, collective choice, open-access resource, median rule, regulatory capture, rent-seeking, credible commitments, moral hazard, adverse selection, market failure, monopoly power, price discrimination, Pareto efficiency* or *cost-benefit analysis.* The universality of this fundamental economic discourse can be proved through reference to textbooks on economics all over the world that are centered around these concepts used there in their respective linguistic versions. Also legal terms such as *judgment-proof injurers* enter into the language of economics so that some expect a further convergence of both areas due to the infusion of legal language into the conceptual realm of economics (cf. Cuter, Ullen 2004: 11).

2.4.3 How do terms and concepts work in law?

The interrelation between term and concept is complex in law, especially when also the diachronic perspective is incorporated into it. Therefore, it is appropriate to ask how legal concepts expressed in terms function in the law. Let us have a look at one of them, for instance the common law notion of *adverse possession.* It refers to a situation in which someone without being owner acquires under specific circumstances full title to land against all others including the record owner. To benefit from this unusually generous proposal made by the legislator certain acts over an uninterrupted period of time which is prescribed by statute are necessary. As a rule, it is prescribed additionally that such possession must be *actual, visible, open, notorious, hostile, under claim of right, definite, continuous,* and *exclusive.* This is quite a lot for one concept. Therefore, some call the adverse possession a 'method' to obtain the title to land, and not that much a concept (cf. Barron's Law Dictionary). In addition, some constellations like possession by a mortgageor are generally not considered as leading to adverse possession because mortgage is neither notorious nor hostile. The above description includes several situations. The first set relates to different factual constellations in which persons occupy land that does not belong to them. The other one comprises a set of related situations which all together make up the circumstances of the acquisition of property by a non-owner in an exceptional situation. To determine this exceptional situation certain requirements are set up. All of them are expressed in terms of legal concepts. The last set of situations comprises those legal constellations, which like mortgage, are perceived as typically not leading to adverse possession. The concept so composed enables a regular argumentation in a case related to acquisition of property under exceptional circumstances. This argumentation must take place within the indicated sets of situations to be complete. It must furthermore test these situations towards the background of the concepts provided by the doctrine in order to exclude abuse because *adverse possession* is an exception to the general rule that protects the rightful owner. Further, the concepts used in the test must be interpreted because they, in their generality, say everything and nothing. Interpreting of those concepts follows the guidelines of the doctrine, occasionally expressed in form of definitions. For instance, the possession is *notorious* when it is open, undisguised, and conspicuous to the point where such a possession is known or recognized. Furthermore, the possession is *hostile* when it takes place without the permission of anyone claiming paramount title and is coupled with the claim of ownership, express or implied, against all others including the record owner. For instance, a holding like a lease is not a case of hostile possession. One could counter that all this is not a big help and that it rather jeopardizes the test than promotes the efforts towards a rational solution of a case related to *adverse possession.* But, we are dealing here with requirements for professional argumentation which may not be accessible to non-jurists. It nevertheless must pass the test of rationality within the legal community. And this challenge seems to matter to jurists most. The argumentative structure based on legal notions is universal. In Spanish property law following conceptual requirements are set up for the (ESP) *usucapión* according to Art. 1941 of the Código civil: *en concepto de dueño, pública, pacífica, ininterrumpida.* The argumentation concerning a possible *usucapión* based on possession, (ESP) *posesión hábil,* is developed around these concepts (Lasarte 2006: 239). Both situational and conceptual requirements of completeness are necessary to make the conceptual structure work in the argumentation. It seems that the conceptual requirements of test completeness are more difficult to fulfill than the situational ones. Their final test is the test of rationality passed within the legal community.

2.4.4 Legal notions are a shorthand script

Legal notions have an ontology that is determined by the way they come about. When we analyze the use of (FR) *prescription* we will easily find out that it precludes claims to be effectively enforced in French courts due to a certain time limit which must pass. These claims are in the terminology of the common law *statute barred* because there is a French statute which sets a time limit for the enforcement of claims of whatever sort. This is also the rationale of the term *prescription* in the French law. The fact that it is used in the legal practice does not mean that it has the same ontological status as *gravitation* or *bicycle.* Its existence is a result of a deliberate and institutionalized setting which facilitates legal operations by making them more efficient. Definitely, (FR) *prescription* does not exist in the same way as *gravitation* or *bicycle* do. What exists in a case is a claim which is statute barred, not the statutory limitation as such. This specific statutory limitation, (FR) *prescription* is the shorthand for the situation in which there exists a statute limiting the time in which claims can be enforced by courts and the claim which is allegedly barred by the statute of limitations. The legal term can be traced back to an utterance that does not include any abstract terms (Kotarbiński 1986: 20). The rest is the application of the statute on the claim. In the application process the shorthand *statute barred claim* or (FR) *prescription* can be used to facilitate the legal operation in question, i.e. the test providing the answer to the question whether a claim is actually statute barred or not. Kotarbiński's approach helps overcome metaphysical fallacies in dealing with legal concepts that have been characterized by others as *ghosts,* i.e. purely psychical phenomena (Petrażycki 1955: 123 sqq) or *hollow words* (Ross 1957: 818). The existence of a legal notion depends upon the wish of the legislator. Thus, the question whether (FR) *contract d'adhesion* exists in the French law or not depends on the legislator's intention to introduce into the legal system a notion known by legal scholars from the history of law and the comparative law. Should the French legislator not wish to introduce the notion into the French legal system, the term will exist only as a social fact or a notion used in the scientific discourse. Its legal existence depends upon the decision of the legislator to make a legal notion of it. In law, there is no such thing as a *contract d'adhesion* as such without that the legislator introduced it. It may, of course, be postulated *de lege ferenda* and would have a place in the discussion about the future of law – but only there. Nevertheless, it will exist in the legal language. This problem setting is not new for the comparative lawyer. When the comparative lawyer is dealing with the common law procedure of *discovery* in a case involving a court in a civil law country he certainly will not simply introduce the notion of *discovery* into his systemic knowledge of this particular civil law but perceive it as a part of the other, foreign law system. He is doing this because the legislator of the civil law country in case did not introduce the notion *discovery* into this civil law system. For the comparatist, the relative existence of legal notions is his daily bread. In the hypothetical case sketched above he simply will not apply the procedures of discovery, because they do not exist for him as long as they are not anchored in the legal system by the legislator. For the comparatist, it goes without saying that this anchorage in his legal system may look differently. It may be constituted by the decision to introduce the procedure of discovery into this particular civil law system, it may also be a result of a provision related to the conflict of laws or a simple result of legislation concerning recognition of foreign judgments or other court decisions. In all three cases the existence of the common law *discovery* procedure in the particular civil law system is of different nature. Yet, without the legislative decision it simply does not exist there at all. This shorthand and relative existence of legal notions has consequences for the daily work of lawyers and for the public debate about law. It makes clear what it means that law is posited, that it is set. It allows for the most vigorous sort of freedom in the discussion about law and in its creation as the limits of legal notions are the limits of our societal goals and no other boundaries exist. Simultaneously, it excludes from the debate about the creation of new laws and interpreting precedents arguments pertaining to the existence of legal notions which allegedly could not be modified. Existing legal notions can always be modified, replaced by others or simply abolished. In the legal science, and especially in the Legal Linguistics, the prerequisites of such evolution are problematic but not the issue as such. Finally, we may note that in terms of pragmatics, the interdependence between legal concepts and legal terms is unclear. It may at the end of the day be a misunderstanding, a wrongly put hypothesis with a strong metaphysical background. The linguistic principle of arbitrariness of linguistic signs may serve as a response to the problem (cf. 3.6.2 regarding the use of (RU) *brak*). The connections between term and concept are arbitrary; they cannot be further elaborated nor justified. Terms have their etymology and their inner-systemic motivation, but they do not emerge in linguistic dependence upon concepts.

2.4.4.1 Implied terms and concepts: Terminology used in the transfer of legal concepts and terms leads to theoretical problems which are a challenge within the known approaches to the Legal Linguistics. One could ask what actually happens when a common law term such as *punitive damages* is translated as (FR) *condamnation à dommages et intérêts punitifs* (Carval 1995) or (D) *Strafschadensersatz*. One could boldly counter that nothing happens because no *punitive damages* are known in the German or the French legal systems and therefore (D) *Strafschadensersatz* does not belong to the German legal language and does not mean anything there. The same could be valid for the French equivalent. This courageous and possibly even acceptable answer – at least in the perspective of some approaches to the Legal Linguistics – does not fully satisfy. Similar to this case is a situation where a term from another language, e.g. (D) *Verhältnissmässigkeitsgrundsatz* is introduced as (FR) *principe de proportionnalité* into French-language legal acts within the EU although it does not exist as a term in the French terminology. The case is even more complicated when it is considered that the French *Conseil d'État* in the decision Benjamin from 19 May 1933 clearly applied the principle of proportionality, but did not mention it in a form of a term. Berteloot (2002: 94) posits therefore: *So we can say that the concept surely existed, but without being uttered in a short and expressive way*. Yet, can we say this? We could risk an analogous remark in regards to two terms of the EU law which are rendered in (FR) with *légitimation active* and *légitimation passive* and which do not exist in the French legal system (Berteloot 2002: 94). They were coined in approximation to the (D) *Aktivlegitimation* and (D) *Passivlegitimation*. As said, they may not exist as such in the French legal system. Nevertheless, they are thinkable and would make sense in it. Yet, what sort of existence would it be? In terms of terminological research it would probably be the existence as a term because a concept - even implied - must exist in the relevant legal system should a borrowed term make sense in it. The initial example quoted by Berteloot proves this assumption; (FR) *principe de proportionnalité* even if not explicitly used in the French law is nevertheless understandable in it because it could explicitly be used there. Even (D) *Strafschadensersatz* as a postulated equivalence for *punitive damages* means something in the German legal system as it can be explained through the reference to the German system of monetary damages. In this perspective, neither the concept nor the term (D) *Strafschadensersatz* would exist as concept and term of the German system of monetary damages; nevertheless both are comprehensible towards the background of the German legal system. The difference is that (FR) *principe de proportionnalité* is understandable also in the French legal system whereas (D)

Strafschadensersatz is understandable only towards the background of the German legal system.

Professional speakers who witness the emergence of new legal-linguistic units have the rare privilege to distinguish them automatically from the classical legal vocabulary. For instance, a new tort termed *intentional infliction of emotional distress* has been added to the established list of common law torts such as *trespass, assault* or *battery*. The doctrinal aspect which means that a new tort type has been added to the classical list and that it has been accepted by the common law courts is less interesting in our context. The decisive issue is the emergence of a concept termed in this way and the choice that is exercised in its lexicalization. As an example we may mention that the Japanese law distinguishes between *injury to honor* and *injury to reputation* (Anderson/Okuda 2007: 150). Authors of legal-linguistic neologisms can be sometimes identified by their names. For instance, the term *common heritage of mankind* has been launched by the Maltese Ambassador Arvid Pardo in 1967 (Cassese 2005: 92). Does this circumstance have an impact upon our understanding of legal terminology? It certainly does. The understanding of the legal terminology, be it monolingual or multilingual, is based upon institutionalized creation and interpretation of legal concepts and terms, preponderantly by the legislator and by courts. Spontaneous and anonymous creation is limited under these circumstances.

2.4.5 Classification of terms

Terms can be classified in several ways. They can be purely technical, i.e. be used only in law, e.g. *promissory estoppel, renvoi, certiorari* or *replevin.* Furthermore, (FR) *emphytéose, préciput, prôtet,* or *sursurestarie* are counted among ca. 250-400 lexical units that are perceived as belonging to the French legal language exclusively (Cornu 2005: 62-65). Some terms in law may have a meaning that differs from the ordinary language, e.g. *consideration, characterization, equity*. Legal terms may differ within one natural language, e.g. *domicile* in the US or the UK usage where one lexical unit covers different, only partly overlapping concepts. They may display preferences in use within one natural language, e.g. *warranty* preferred in the US, against *guarantee* rather used in the UK. The same concerns (US) *antitrust legislation* and (UK) *competition legislation* or (US) *corporation* and (UK) *company.* Terms appear as polysemic within one legal language, e.g. *civil law* meaning 1. private law or 2. Continental legal tradition in the legal English. Finally, terms may be seen in a diachronic dimension, e.g. *university* or (LAT) *universitas* or (FR) *Parlement de Paris, Parlement de Bretagne* which had been *courts of law* and not *Parliaments.* In the diachronic dimension they may display some stylistic features of the legal language as is the case with the English binomials, e.g. *terms and conditions* or *null and void.* Terms as those mentioned can be compared in a multilingual perspective, e.g. (US) *promissory estoppel* and (FR) *principe de cohérance contractuelle*, (LAT) *culpa in contrahendo* and *infringment of the rules of good faith*, (US) *piercing the corporate veil* – (D) *Durchgriffshaftung* or *unjust enrichment* and (FR) *enrichissement sans cause*. The problem connected to this comparison is the systemic incompatibility of legal concepts. Nevertheless, this problem does not always appear, e.g. *voidable transfer* and (D) *Konkursanfechtung*. Functional differences can be easily overcome even if a lexical unit may belong to the *faux amis*-expressions due to its polysemy in language contact, e.g. (S) *proposition* versus (UK) *government bill* or (FR) *proposition de loi* and (FR) *projet de loi* (Carcassonne 2005: 376).

G. Cornu concentrated in his work on legal language largely on terminological issues. He showed that terms in the legal texts can belong to the legal parlance exclusively and that they can stand in a relation of internal and external polysemia (Cornu 2005: 89-111). Furthermore, he dealt with the issue of synonymy in law. According to Pigolkin (1990: 15, 73) legal terms are not particularly numerous in the legal language. Cornu however estimates that circa ten thousand legal terms are used in legal French (Cornu 2005: 53). The divergence in estimation is here not a question of differences among legal cultures, as legal Russian is definitely not less developed than legal French. It is a result of different approaches towards the definition of a legal term.

2.4.6 Diachrony and synchrony in legal terminology

We will illustrate the interplay of diachrony and synchrony in the legal terminology on few examples. Terms like *university*, *international*, *antitrust*, and *cartel* show this complexity even if approached from a purely positivist perspective. For instance, *university* in the legal context concerns also the diachronical use of the term. In the Roman law *university* was close to corporations; even in the Middle Ages it rather resembled a unity of assets than an educational institution (cf. Savigny 1840: 378, 384 about *universitas iuris* and *adquisitio per universitatem*). In the public law, *university* was a long time an organizational form of towns as opposed to municipalities. So had been the Principality of Monaco in which this book was mainly written organized in the Middle Ages as a *university*, in Latin *universitas*. Furthermore, the use of the term *international* is very specific in the legal context. It may be understood as concerning relations between states, so in International Law or to concern international cases, so in the private international law. In fact, all states have their own private international laws and their provisions regularly differ in a way that only cases which this laws concern are international because they include an international element. The law as such remains national in essence, although it refers in its structure to the rules developed in the *ius commune* for dealing with cases that contain a foreign element. In the International Business Law *international* refers rather to the type of cases than to the applicable law. In these *international* cases, frequently also international instruments such as the CISG must be applied. They are enforced by national courts and this process of enforcement is also part of the International Business Law while constituting a national element in it. Its treatment in the legislation is also different. Moreover, according to the German company law an enterprise cannot include the adjective *international* into its name when it does not develop any substantial international activities; no such restriction exists in the U.S. legislation concerning the names of American enterprises. *International* sounds like a Latin word. However, it does not belong to the lexicon of the ancient Romans; there terms such as (LAT) *mundanus* or paraphrases, e.g. (LAT) *qui/quod ad nonnullas/omnes gentes pertinet* were in use (Mattila 2002d: 273). Some specialists are therefore reluctant to use the word (LAT) *internationalis* that is a late coinage in contemporaneous Latin texts. Nowadays, also the term *cosmopoliticum* is in use in the translation of the emerging term *global law* as *ius cosmopoliticum,* apparently in order to contrast it with *international law* (Cassese 2005: 21). *Cartel* that in the legal language means an association of business persons with the purpose of maintaining prices at a high level and restricting competition comes as a term from political language. It seems that it had been first used in relation to the coalition of the Conservative and the National Liberal parties in Germany in 1887 and meant later any such political agreement. Subsequently, it has been used to denote trade agreements. *Anti-trust* which in the U.S. legal terminology designs legislation aiming at the prevention of measures impeding upon free competition has its origins in trade agreements which were called *trusts.* The legislation has been designed to counteract the trusts which were deemed as detrimental for the development of the economy. The terminological diachrony did not lead to problems in the understanding of legal texts. The reason for this seems to be that terminology adapts to synchronized legal texts in that it follows the legal knowledge of our times. Therefore, no speaker or hearer will be confused by hearing the term *university* or *cartel* even if they have been semantically profoundly modified in time.

2.4.7 Scientific terms introduced into law

Increasingly, terms from other sciences are introduced into legal texts, especially into statutes. Can these terms retain their own meaning or will they have a new meaning due to their new lexical status as parts of the legal language? One could spontaneously imagine that terms representing concepts belonging to other sciences than law must necessarily retain their initial meaning, and that every thought to the contrary would be absurd. The situation is however more complicated. A scientific term which is incorporated into a bill passes a procedure in the Parliament where not only the vote takes place but where it is also discussed starting from the very first draft. In the materials which accompany the preparatory work in the Parliament, interpretive guidelines, definitions and other information is contained which allows for the interpretation of the concept when it becomes part of a statute. The materials may introduce a specific meaning, broader or narrower than the scientific one. Furthermore, terms developed in other sciences may not be univocal there as usually several theoretical approaches compete in the particular branch of sciences for the right understanding of their methods and their conceptual basis. For instance, when the Canadian legislator passed the Multilingualism Act *multilingualism* became a legal term in the Canadian legislation. Do we understand this term properly while applying the concept of multilingualism developed in linguistics or used in anthropology or both? Which understanding of *multilingualism* used in these particular social sciences is the right one? It would be difficult to use more than one meaning when working on the implementation of the act. The same concerns medical terms like *alcoholic* or *drug addict* which may be understood in law differently. The scientific term becoming a legal term lives its own life and may acquire a different meaning from the one used in the particular science where it emerged. In this context, Pigolkin (1990: 70) differentiates between technical terms and legal terms. Technical terms are for him those introduced into law from other scientific disciplines and which remain unchanged there. In the light of the above argument it is difficult to maintain this distinction. Technical terms become legal terms and also legal notions once they entered into law. The possibility that in many singular cases they may also keep their initial meaning is not excluded. It is however not possible to generally maintain the conceptual contents of a scientific notion in law as required by Pigolkin (1990: 74). The distinction introduced by Pigolkin shows a particularity in the development of the legal terminology. Yet, finally, it proves rather the coherence of the category than the supposed distinctiveness of terms.

2.4.8 Verbs in law

Legal-linguistic analyses of legal terms and concepts usually focused upon nouns and adjectives. Even adverbs were more attractive to jurists than verbs. However, attempts to determine the relation between *obliged* and *obligated* were not particularly successful. Dworkin (1977: 19) refers to H.L.A. Hart who in his *Concept of Law* tried to define the distinction in the usage of both participles. Hart's analysis (1961: 89) is a reference to J. Austin's theoretical arguments and seems rather a scholarly founded convention than a research into the use of the two adverbs. Surprisingly, verbs, the very residue of action, were not that appealing to jurists as were concepts expressed by terms in the form of nouns. Instead, mainly pragmatists such as J.L. Austin or J. Searle turned with passionate subtlety to them in the hope of getting into the heart of our language. Fortunately, the *West's Encyclopedia of American Law* (Lehman/Phelps 2005) treats verbs on equal footing with other parts of speech; under A it lists e.g.: *adduce, adequate, accrue, accredit, abut, abet* and many others.

2.4.8.1 Verbs in Article 2 UCC and in CISG: As said, terminological research has been traditionally noun-oriented and dominated by the questions concerning the interpretation of legal concepts. Meanwhile, verbs in law offer a perspective which stresses the dynamic aspect of language in law, i.e. the aspect directed towards and based upon action. Moreover, verbs may be even more suitable than nouns to display pragmatic aspects in the legal language. We will illustrate it on examples from the UCC and the CISG. The UCC's Article 2 *Sales* as well as the CISG are dominated by verbs describing action related to sale contracts (relevant provisions of the UCC are quoted in Notes and Materials nr. 17). § 2-201 UCC introduces the Article 2 which *shall be known and may be cited* accordingly. This ceremonial formulation refers to a specific quality of verbs to convey fictitious and prospective action without that this aspect would have to be marked additionally with linguistic means. Furthermore, verbs may convey interpretive guidelines of different degree of intensity, e.g. § 2-207(2) UCC where additional terms in acceptance or confirmation of sale contracts *are to be construed* as proposals. In § 2-208 UCC the express terms of the agreement…*shall be construed* whenever reasonable as consistent with each other, in § 2-210 (4) UCC a prohibition of assignment *is to be construed as* barring a specific declaration, in § 2-720 UCC specific expressions *shall not be construed as* a renunciation or discharge and in § 2-317 warranties *shall be construed as* consistent with each other if reasonable. The expressions *are/is to be construed* and *shall (not) be construed* function as synonyms. Other fictitious expressions are used in § 2-207 (1) UCC where a definite and seasonable expression *operates as* an acceptance, in § 2-305 (2) UCC a price *means* a price to be fixed in good faith. In § 2-206 (2) UCC an offeror *may treat the offer as having lapsed* under the stated circumstances, in § 2-205 (3) UCC the party *may* at his option *treat the contract as cancelled.* In § 2-204 (2) UCC an agreement *sufficient to constitute* a contract for sale *may be found.* This fictitious use is contrasted with declaratory verbs such as *is* in § 2-308 (a) UCC where the place for delivery *is* the seller's place of business, in § 2-323 (3) where a shipment by water *is overseas* insofar as it is subject to practices characteristic for international deep water commerce and in § 2-328 (2) where the sale by auction *is complete* when the auctioneer so announces. However, from the pragmatic perspective the difference made by the drafters of the UCC between the fictitious use and the declaratory one is not convincing. In § 2-308 (a) UCC no change in the meaning would occur through the replacement of *is* by *shall be construed as* which would give that the place of delivery *shall be construed* as the seller's place of business. In the legal norms the fictitious element is an inherent characteristic of all speech acts, declarations are therefore performative even if possibly not so intended by the drafters of the UCC. Shortcut expressions as in § 2-301 UCC where the obligation of the seller *is to transfer and deliver* and that of the buyer *is to accept and pay* omit the otherwise obligatory object while subscribing to the professional parlance where the goods and the price are implied. By so doing, it modifies the rection of verbs used. This is not the case with the CISG where according to Article 30 the seller *must deliver the goods...and transfer the property in the goods* and further according to Article 53 the buyer *must pay the price for the goods.* The UCC follows the figurative professional language while allowing the buyer in § 2-711 (1a) UCC to "*cover*" and have damages, i.e. to be able to *recover damages* as stated in (1b) of the same provision. The linguistic balance between "*cover*" and *recover* is intended in the UCC and used frequently. Nevertheless, the drafters were apparently aware of this non-juridic, merchant-like use of "cover" in the legal language and decided to put it between quotation marks. Although "cover" is defined according to § 2-103 (2) UCC in § 2-712 (1) UCC and may therefore be also perceived as a legal notion, only the expression *to effect cover* is used without quotation marks. Other merchant-like expressions are incorporated into the UCC, yet they are put between quotation marks, e.g. implied warranties expressed by *as is* or *with all faults* in § 2-316 UCC.

It goes without saying that the CISG cannot make any use of such professional expressions because it is based on a universal legal language which is only vaguely based on the language spoken in a specific legal or commercial practice and does not reflect any particular professional usage or any particular national legal language. Instead, it enables the emergence of an international neutral language use which may prove in future more effective than the reference to particular local linguistic usage and practices in the UCC. However, the different goals and territorial spheres of application of both the UCC and the CISG make this difference understandable. For instance, explicitly fictitious formulations are rare in the CISG (relevant provisions of the CISG are quoted in Notes and Materials nr. 16). Article 81 CISG is exemplary for the factual statements used in the convention. The convention creates the fictitious legal reality of international sale contracts by using the factual language. It would be redundant to stress constantly in the text that all provisions of the convention should be construed as a fiction created by law and therefore binding for certain parties under specified circumstances. According to its Article 1 the convention *applies* under specified conditions, according to its Articles 2 or 3 (2) CISG it *does not apply* to certain contracts. In Article 4 CISG the regulation *governs* certain aspects of the contract and in Article 18 CISG a statement indicating an offer *is* an acceptance. In the parlance of the UCC the Article 18 CISG would probably read: a statement *should be construed as acceptance.* In some provisions the CISG falls back into the UCC wording and becomes then less transparent. In Article 1 (2) CISG a specific fact *has to be disregarded,* in Article 1 (3) CISG it *is to be taken into consideration.* In Article 7 CISG regard *is to be had* to the international character of the contract and in Article 8 (1) and (2) CISG statements *are to be interpreted.* In Article 8 (2) CISG statements are to be interpreted according to the understanding that a reasonable person *would have had,* the formulation being reiterated in Article 8 (3) CISG. Furthermore, in Article 38 (3) CISG the seller *knew or ought to have known* of a possibility of redirection or of a redispatch of the goods. The fictionality of formulations becomes however doubtful when it does not correspond any more with the context of use of certain words. It is the case in Article 43 (2) where the seller *is not entitled to rely* upon the provisions of the Article 43 (1) if he knew of certain circumstances. In fact, we rely rightfully or not on certain circumstances or features and this reliance is not further conditioned in our language. The formulation of Article 43 (2) introduces an understandable legal limitation to reliance used as a defense but it is doing it in a way contrary to the language use. This impedes upon its understanding. In Article 80 this legal position is expressed more convincingly by saying that a party *may not rely* on the failure of the other party to perform under the stated circumstances although here too the limitation of reliance that is understandable for the jurist may surprise the layperson. Legal positions can be expressed, and are in fact expressed, convincingly in the CISG in most other cases. In Article 85 CISG the seller *is entitled to retain* goods until he has been reimbursed, an expression reiterated in Article 86 (1) CISG. Being *entitled to retain* pertains to a right while being *not entitled to rely* pertains to the facts of one's inner forum which unlike the legal consequences of this reliance cannot be limited by a legal regulation.

When the CISG enters into the dialogue with the UCC and the common law its English wording marks this systematic challenge. In Article 24 CISG the acceptance becomes effective when it "*reaches*" the addressee. The provision aims at the clarification that the common law *mailbox rule* is not applicable under the convention. In the English text, the verb has been put between the quotation marks in order to mark this linguistic difference. All above verbs help determine speech acts expressed in the statutory provisions. However, a simple classification of verbs to determine speech acts is not sufficient (Baylon 1991: 276). The verb can determine the speech act solely when taken in its context. For instance, the first sentence of Art. 41 CISG reads in its English and French linguistic versions (emphasis added):

The seller must deliver goods which are free from any right or claim of a third party, unless the buyer **agreed** *to take the goods subject to that right or claim.*

Le vendeur doit livrer les marchandises libres de tout droit ou prétention d'un tiers, à moins que l'acheteur **n'accepte** *de prendre les marchandises dans ces conditions.*

The verbs *agreed* and (FR) *n'accepter* (*de prendre*) are definitely not equivalent when isolated. In the text of Art. 41 they should be construed as having a meaning that covers also tacit declarations made by the parties (Loewe 1989: 62). Hence, interpretation is unavoidable in such cases. The legal speech act in which law is expressed linguistically has some specifics. To begin with, it must be identifiable as such. Here, usually either the context or the text type signalize to the speaker that he is operating within the sphere of law. Furthermore, the legal speech act must be expressed in a form which enables its operationalization in law. It must mark linguistically its characteristic feature as a legal speech act, for instance, with a verb signalizing that the speech act is a legal one, i.e. that it introduces a binding and enforceable legal rule. The speech act operates in the legal sphere and will therefore fail when certain legal requirements are not fulfilled when it is uttered. As mentioned, the legal speech act fails especially when it cannot be institutionally enforced. Generalizing, we can say that verbs in law represent the essence of the legal language. For the aims of our deliberations we construe law as linguistically formulated social rules of binding nature. The binding nature of legal rules grounds in their institutional enforceability which constitutes their main difference in comparison with other social rules. Also the institutional enforceability is here specific because it unlike other social rules includes the legitimate use of forceful measures.

2.4.8.2 The legal 'shall' and the legal 'may': In law the binding force of a rule must be specifically expressed. Parties of a contract may, for instance, formulate a binding rule in the following way: *Any person bidding at the auction* **shall** *stand surety as for his own debt until full payment is made for purchased merchandise.* Constitutive for the speech act is the verb *shall* which institutes the binding character of the contractual clause. Its enforceability depends on many factors provided by the contract law which is applicable upon the contract in question. Among them can be: legality of the contractual aim, admissibility of the modifications the parties made in the applicable contract law, etc. Without taking into consideration of these requirements the distinctively constituted legal speech act will fail, i.e. it will not be enforceable. Constitutive force of an utterance must be properly identified. In the above example the meaning of *shall* cannot be properly understood when qualified as introducing future tense. In legal texts it institutes the legal speech act and introduces the binding force of the utterance, i.e. it establishes its enforceability. Therefore, the speakers must identify properly the context of the utterance to be able to grasp the message in the legal speech act. First of all, they must distance themselves from the school grammarian's perspective on the language and the possibly memorized rule that *shall* introduces future tense in the English language. Thus, the translation from English into French of such utterances will have to transform this legal-linguistic property of *shall* accordingly. In examples such a transformation may look as follows: *This Act shall apply*...(FR) *La présente loi s'applique* or *There shall be a legal committee*... (FR) *Un comité juridique est institué*...(Gémar 2004: 740). When the context of the utterance is incorrectly identified, misunderstandings will occur. The Canadian Supreme Court has perceived in a legal document the English formulation *shall operate notwithstanding* as ambiguously expressed in French with *a effect indépendemment* insisting on the meaning of *shall* as including also the element of future (Gémar 2004: 740). The court, apparently blinded by school grammarians' teaching, did not recognize the constitutive force that *shall* has introduced into the interpreted utterance. In legal-linguistic contexts also *may* is used specifically, especially in utterances concerning authority or permission. In those utterances it has the meaning of *having right to,* e.g. *In certain circumstances a police officer* **may** *ask the driver to take a breath test* (the breath test is definitely not optional for the driver) or *If convicted, an accused person* **may** *appeal* (meaning that the accused has the right to appeal).

Surprisingly, therefore, it seems to be possible to overlook the momentum of constitution of an utterance as part of the legal text. Such situations come about when speakers are misled by other interpretive rules than those at work in the legal language. It is not particularly probable to assume that judges who acted in the above case would have problems with interpreting the meaning of *shall* in ordinary utterances in their daily life. Should they - against our assumption - have such practical problems so would the explanation for their confusion have to be sought in the misleading interpretive rules they were provided from outside of the immediate factual and linguistic contexts. Such rules could, for instance, have their origin in wrongly transmitted or construed formalized information about the meaning of words in utterances. We therefore insist here upon the process of the constitution of legal speech acts and perceive the constitution of legal rules with language as one of the main linguistic operations in law because it seems not always to be evident to all the participants in the legal discourse. The role of the pragmatic Legal Linguistics is at this point to make this process of the constitution of legal rules with words transparent for the participants.

2.4.9 Towards modernized legal terminology

Another recurrent topic concerns the modernization of the legal terminology through replacing outmoded lexical units by more contemporary ones, creation of neologisms and semantic change, the modernization of the legal language through plain language rules based on principles of readability or understandability. The Legal Linguistics has to follow these tendencies and comment upon them as it is also competent to provide advice on language use. The tendency towards the development of a modernized legal terminology reflects a broader problem of modernized language use in law. Earlier we have reflected upon the use of ordinary language in shaping the legal terminology (Galdia 2003: 12). This approach is not particularly popular among jurists. For instance, Cornu (2005: 87) opposed this idea pointing to the necessity of technical legal terminology and Mattila stressed the omnipresent argumentation among jurist to preserve their special register (Mattila 2006: 52). Moreover, jurists automatically ask themselves about the legal status of provisions concerning language use in law. This status can be at least twofold, imperative or recommendatory (Pigolkin 1990: 134). These provisions are different from bills regulating interpretation of statutes like the New York Law on Statute Interpretation which are by their nature peremptory (cf. 3.6.6.1). Specifically, the Private Securities Litigation Reform Act of 1995 (15 U.S.C. § 77a et seq) regulated the presentation of information in investment prospectuses. Along the lines of the act, vague information does not engender any liability; assertions lacking a reasonable basis may result in damage claims when taken on faith by investors. In legal decisions concerning stock offerings American courts insisted upon the use of plain English, i.e. a non-technical language which would enable an untrained investor to make an investment decision on the basis of mostly written information provided to him (Lemmer v. Nu-Kote Holding, Inc., 2001 U.S. Dist. LEXIS 13987; Zeid v. Kimberley, 2001 U.S. App. LEXIS 7266). However, the courts imposed on the plaintiffs the burden of proof related to misleading language or false information. Semantic change or historical semantization like *consideration* (i.e. something of value that is given in exchange for a promise) are actually phenomena of the traditional legal language. While developing the modern terminology one nevertheless should bear in mind that they regularly give rise to misunderstandings among non-lawyers who do not expect such broadly used concepts to have totally different meaning in law and in ordinary language. In their reception by the speakers they can be contrasted with explicitly legal concepts such as *promissory estoppel* which cannot be confused by laypersons because they are used in the legal language only. This warranty has nevertheless a price, namely this of unintelligibility of specialized concepts like the *promissory estoppel* for laypersons. This example also reflects the traditional dilemma of legal language perceived by some as specialized language and by others as plain language that should be understandable for everyone. The solution to the problem would be apparently to abandon specialized language and especially expressions introduced through semantic change as well as historical coinages and use an explicit and descriptive language based on or identical with the ordinary language. Likewise, the replacement of the term *writ of certiorari* by *certification* in some U.S. jurisdictions does not increase the understanding of the legal text although it modernizes the language use. The phrase: *His conviction and sentence were affirmed on direct appeal and certification was denied* in a decision of the Superior Court of New Jersey in the matter State of New Jersey v. Marshall Roundtree (A-2043-02T1) from September 21, 2006 is not per se better understandable that the phrase: *His conviction and sentence were affirmed and certiorari was denied* because *certiorari* and *certification* are used in both phrases as technical terms, the second being a linguistically modernised version of the first. They are understandable to laypersons only when an explication of procedural details, be it of the writ of certiorari or the certification, is provided as additional information. The tendency towards establishing of neologisms in the legal language is becoming stronger: in business promotion opportunities it is represented by *mentor/ mentee* or by *tipper/ tippee* in the insider trading cases. This tendency is well established and productive in the legal English: *acquitee, arrestee, lessee* or *patentee,* furthermore *asylee, condemnee, abortee* were identified in English legal texts (Tiersma 1999: 98). In the following, we will depict problems regarding the modernization of the legal terminology and the legal language in general.

2.4.9.1 Updating legal terminology: Criticism upon the legal language in the broader public concerns mostly the legal vocabulary which is often perceived as antiquated and arcane. Regularly, governments and legal scholars provide instructions and expert advice and parliaments order changes in the legal vocabulary with help of different legislative measures. Attempts towards this goal like the Plain Language Movement in the USA and results accomplished in the application of such approaches are encouraging (Hiltunen 1990: 106-108). In the UK, terminological changes have been introduced 1999 as a result of the Woolf report in course of the reform of the civil procedure. Some typical old terms have been replaced by words taken from the ordinary language or neologisms. These changes concern foremost following old and new term pairs: *writ – claim form, pleading – statement of case, plaintiff – claimant, minor/ infant – child, in camera – in private, ex parte – without notice, guardian ad litem – litigation friend, Mareva injunction – freezing injunction, Anton Piller order – search order.* The terminology of elder Acts of Parliament, for instance the Minors' Contract Act 1987, was not changed in the course of the reform which has been limited to the civil procedure rules and *minors* survive in the earlier acts of the substantive law but they become *children* in the civil procedure. In France, the *Commission de modernisation de la langue judiciaire* introduced 1977 substantial changes into the legal vocabulary. Among numerous changes following exemplary pairs of old and new terms were concerned: *intérêts de droit – intérêts au taux légal, es qualité de tuteur – en qualité de tuteur, exploit – acte, il échet – il échoit, emender – réformer* (Gazette du Palais 1977, 2e sem.). Other French governmental directives simplified the language use in the legal acts. Some new coinage (Cornu 2005: 110), e.g. (FR) *juge aux affaires familiales,* (FR) *divorce sur demande conjointe* or (FR) *autorité parentale* follow the tendency towards the convergence of legal and ordinary language. However others, like (FR) *action à fins de subsides, régime de participation aux acquêts, administration légale pure et simple* contradict the principle. Apparently, the changes introduced in the UK and in France modernize the legal vocabulary in the sense that the new terms sound for the laypersons as if they were parts of the contemporary colloquial or literary language. However, the question whether they are also better understood by the laypersons remains open, as no research into this problem is known. The problem of understanding concerns rather the legal concept than the legal term. The legal term may appeal to the laypersons in its contemporary form as more up to date but it is not per se easier to grasp in its application as a legal concept. The fact that a judicial decision is not issued any more *ex parte* but *without notice* does not necessarily guarantee a better understanding of the notion as long as there is no additional explanation about whom or what this omitted notice actually might concern. Similarly, the (FR) *intérêts de droit* and the modernized (FR) *intérêts au taux légal* are equally mysterious for someone who does not know the notion of interest due in a litigation and the rules governing it.

2.4.9.2 Dissolution of terms or concepts? Legal terminology is steadily developing and until recently it usually followed the conceptual framework of the Roman law which it modified. This was, for instance, the case with the introduction of (LAT) *culpa in contrahendo* into the modern theory of private law in civil law countries. This tendency is stable in both continental and common law. For instance, the approach by the authors of *The Anatomy of Corporate Law* generally follows this type of conceptualization (Kraakman 2004). Some concepts are used there in a modified conceptual setting; others are added to the traditional terminology. Yet, all of them function and reflect the Roman heritage in the terminology. This tendency in the development of legal terminology is very strong. Mattila provides an example for a generally known legal maxim, that of (LAT) *lex retro non agit* which although apparently constructed upon recourse to the Roman law has been of recent origin (Mattila 2006: 154). However, a tendency towards the conceptualization of a new type is nevertheless there. In it, the term does not rigidly correspond to a concept any more. Instead, different terms in different linguistic forms reflect the content of a legal concept. In the legal-linguistic perspective, rules correspond to terms as norms correspond to concepts. The consequences for law are far reaching. For instance, metaphorical concept creation like *piercing the corporate veil* is of different lexicological type than its terminological counterpart in the German legal language (D) *Durchgriffshaftung.* In the English terminology of the (UK) Companies Act also the term *lifting the corporate veil* is used. It corresponds in terms of terminology with (ESP) *levantamiento de velo,* whereas the German term (D) *Durchgriffshaftung* is composed in a closer relation with *piercing* that is typical for the American usage. The concept *piercing the corporate veil* is not used in a petrified sense. It may vary in its linguistic form due to the syntactic surrounding of use, e.g.: *A rule permitting* **veil-piercing** *in undercapitalized firms, for example, can be seen as a penalty default that creates an incentive for firms with low net capital to disclose that fact when contracting with potential creditors, so that the creditors will be estopped from* **piercing** (Kraakman 2004: 30). Still further, the notion of *reasonable man* has been used in the common law as a standard to determine the appropriate interpretation of party intent in the contract law or the appropriate, especially non-negligent, action in the tort law. This concept creation was not unexpectedly supported by the most eminent representative of Law and Economics, Richard Posner, who characterized the *reasonable man* as average person (Posner 1973: 183). The concept gave rise to terminological modifications in the tort law of professional negligence, especially in medical malpractice. There, the notion of the *reasonable doctor* functions as an equivalent to the *reasonable man* of the general contract and tort doctrines. A related notion of the *reasonable bystander* emerged in the common law contract law as an element of the objective theory of contract formation. The notion of *reasonable bystander* is frequently used there as synonymous with the *reasonable third party.* Recently, the term *reasonable person* deemed as neutral in terms of gender relations gained some importance. It replaces occasionally the *reasonable man* in the legal writings. *Reasonable* is further developed and differentiated. For instance, in the *Principles of Corporate Governance: Analysis and Recommendation*, a set of legal guidelines on managerial duties assembled 1992 by the American Law Institute, ordinary language differences are functionalized:

§ 4.01 Duty of Care of Directors and Officers; the Business Judgment Rule

(...)

(c) A director or officer who makes a business judgement in good faith fulfills the duty under this section if the director or officer:

(...)

(2) is informed with respect to the subject of the business judgment to the extent the director or officer **reasonably** *believes to be appropriate under these circumstances; and*

(3) **rationally** *believes that the business judgment is in the best interest of the corporation*

This standard intended to provide directors and officers with a wide ambit of discretion. *Rational* has a close semantic tie to *reasonable* and, at times, the two words are used almost interchangeably. In the above standard a distinction has been made between *rationally believes* which permits a significantly wider range of discretion than *reasonable*; it might fall outside the term *reasonable* but is not so remote from the realm of reason that liability should be incurred. In this context, the (U.S.) Restatement (Second) of Contracts provides in its § 19 comment b for a distinction between *reason to know* and *should know*. The *reason to know* refers to a situation where a person has a piece of information from which someone of similar intelligence would infer that the fact in question does or does not exist. In turn, *should know* imports the duty to ascertain facts, and is relatively unconcerned with actual knowledge. The new terms *piercing the corporate veil* and *reasonable man* are dynamic; their linguistic status varies and depends upon the structural (mostly textual) circumstances of use. They rather adapt to requirements of ordinary syntax than force the syntax to follow the rules of the legal language (cf. example from Kraakman 2004 cited above).

From the theoretical perspective it would be particularly interesting to know whether the tendency to develop a more dynamic terminology is related to changes in the structure of law itself. A theoretically interesting question would be whether the linguistic turn that we propose would lead to a paradigm change in the legal sciences. Ambitious attempts to characterize a language-related paradigmatic change in law, such as Broekman's (1984: 156), insist upon *the dissolution of a syllogism-based understanding of text and reality*. Surprisingly, a new creation such as the *soft law* does not necessarily introduce a different type of language into law. *Soft law*'s main distinctive feature seems to be that it gains momentum as a legal text type although certain formal requirements for its entry into force as a legal act are not fulfilled. Its legality may therefore be based on customary use in certain situations. However, the *soft law* represents an innovation in the catalogue of the sources of law. As an innovative instrument it may also tend towards innovative language use in future. We may therefore courageously assume that the future language used in law will be more descriptive than conceptual and also closer to the ordinary language, its vocabulary and syntax. One can also expect that due to the increase in awareness about language use in law, authorities would issue more guidelines and other legal acts with reference to the linguistic aspects of creation and application of law.

2.4.9.3 Modernized legal terminology is not unproblematic: Understanding of legal texts has been addressed from the point of view of their readability and the methodological problems concerning the assessment of official texts' readability (Piehl 2002: 101). The corresponding pragmatic notion to the readability is the writeability which includes principles of drafting legal provisions in a way which increases their comprehension. Problems of (US) *unconscionability* of contracts terms or (UK) *unfair terms* have been also mentioned in this context. However, the issue of unconscionable or unfair terms in a contract is not always linked to language use. Mostly, terms are deemed unconscionable or unfair because of their content which is not in line with principles or public policy in a legal system. Modernized legal terminology has the tendency to refer to the ordinary language. However, this tendency is not unproblematic in terms of understandability of such new legal-linguistic creations. It concerns foremost the introduction of terms based on colloquial or inoffensive ordinary language. We call inoffensive terms technically advanced legal vocabulary that appears in casual dress of colloquial language. Terms such as *administrator, opinion* or *information* are representative of this type of terms. In the translation theory they are commonly referred to as *faux amis.* Conceptual differences can be introduced into the inoffensive – ordinary language – usage in groups of corresponding, mutually related terms. Thus, the U.S. corporate law distinguishes between *domestic, foreign* and *alien corporations.* A corporation is *domestic* in the U.S. state in which it is incorporated. It is a *foreign* corporation in U.S. states other than the one in which it is incorporated. Finally, it is an *alien* corporation in the U.S. if it is incorporated outside the U.S. All three terms which form one conceptual field are mutually related and provide a specific legal meaning which is restrictive of their broad semantic and pragmatic usage in the ordinary language. Next to this terminology, less formal terms are used as well, e.g. *a foreign-based multinational enterprise* (Bulova Watch Company, Inc. v. K. Hattori & Co. Ltd, 508 F. Supp. 1322 (1981)). We may mention that a new term *globally integrated enterprise* is emerging and may join this semantic field in future.

Concept creation with metaphors has also its limits as far as understanding by laypersons is concerned. In the U.S. constitutional law, plaintiffs frequently *challenge facially* a legal provision. For instance, *Anheuser-Busch, Inc., filed suit in federal court,* **facially challenging** *the constitutionality of the ordinance under the First Amendment (Anheuser-Busch Inc., v. Schmoke 63 F.3d 1305 (1995)).* For a non-lawyer it is difficult to recognize that the *facial challenge* of the constitutionality of the provision is a specific procedure in the U.S. constitutional law that is different from procedures concerning the ambit of the challenged provision. Furthermore, expressions like *issue of first impression* are usually not perceived as legal concepts from the point of view of a non-lawyer. For instance, *The precise issue before us in the case sub judice is one of* **first impression**, meaning that there is no precedent to which the court could refer (Schalk v. Texas, 823 S.W. 2d 633 1991). Another group of concepts is represented by forms composed of terms of ordinary language like *summary judgment, statute of limitations or default judgment.* Nevertheless, they are not understandable for non-lawyers due to their fragmentary form. The default in the *default judgment* is the default in participation of a party in the litigation (cf. (FR) *jugement par default*), the limitation in the *statute of limitations* concerns the time period for filing suits and summary in *summary judgment* concerns the judgment without the participation of the jury when the litigation concerns only the controversy about the law and not about facts. Thus, legal concepts expressed in terms used also in the ordinary language may still be unintelligible for laypersons due to missing knowledge about the motivation that underlies the process of their coinage. This prerequisite of understandability can be illustrated with the following example. In the U.S., state securities laws are referred to as *blue sky* laws. The term sounds appealing but is as all such terms only understandable under the circumstances of its professional use. It derives from a formulation in a court decision which described the purpose of securities legislation as aiming to prevent *speculative schemes which have no more basis than so many feet of blue sky* (Hall v. Geiger-Jones Co., 242 U.S. 539,550 (1917)). Next to the *blue sky laws*, also *lemon laws* exist. In the U.S., most states enacted statutes providing for procedures for consumers who are confronted with mechanical problems concerning their vehicles. *Lemon laws* establish a simplified administrative procedure which can be applied in cases where the car dealer does not correct a recurring defect in a vehicle within a specified period of time and a specified number of attempted repaires. In such cases the purchaser can rescind the sale contract and recover a full refund of the vehicle's purchase price. Furthermore, *long-arm statutes* extend under certain circumstances a U.S. federal state's jurisdiction to nonresidents. In the agency law, an independent contractor who is a professional, such as a lawyer, is called a *professional agent*. The more traditional usage of terms with colloquial connotation such as *winding up* in the sense of closing down the business had been generally accepted although they are perceived by some speakers as odd.

Other socially relevant domains such as informatics and computer programming boldly introduced even colloquial expressions such as *cookies* into their technical vocabulary. Despite its banal reference the technical term *cookie* is understandable only to someone who masters the programming technique or has been explained its technical implications. After having received the explanation, this person will also be able to understand the motivation behind the new term. Nevertheless, the banalization of the vocabulary formation does not lead to increased understanding or operationability of the new technical concept. It may, at best, increase its acceptability in some groups of computer programs users. Therefore, it seems rather to be an issue of fashion or taste than of modern technical language which might advance progress in sciences. The programer language, e.g. *Abort: cannot find alternate!* as a message which may appear on the computer screen is comprehensible only to some users. It, therefore, does not matter that a technical phenomenon is called *cookie* and not e.g. **claumisius ephemeridae,* as both are equally unintelligible to the uninitiated user. Likewise, terms understandable due to the reference to the ordinary language such as *trade secret* obtain legal meaning in their judicial application. They are misleading, rather than helpful, and finally join the group of polysemic expressions. An inoffensive legal term such as *trade secret* is understandable in ordinary language without further explication. Its application in law is much more complicated. In Schalk v. Texas (823 S.W. 2d 633 (1991)) the Court of Criminal Appeals had to determine whether an act constituted a violation of a trade secret under Texas law. Both appellants in this case, specialists in speech processing programs, before leaving their employer TI copied the entire contents of the directories assigned to them and transferred them to computers at their new working place. They were charged with breaking the trade secret of their prior employer and condemned. Texas Penal Code defines in § 31.05: *Theft of trade secrets: (a) For purposes of this section (4) "Trade secret" means the whole or any part of any scientific or technical information, design, process, procedure, formula or improvement that has value and that the owner has taken measures to prevent from becoming available to persons other than those selected by the owner to have access for limited purposes.* The court had to deal with the question of what detailed measures constitute the protection required by the statute, as the Penal Code does not define them further. In addition, the court had to determine whether the information disclosed by the appellants has fallen within the ambit of the provision. In the opinion of the court *it is axiomatic that the core element of a trade secret must be that it remains a secret. However,* **absolute secrecy** *is not required. A trade secret can exist in a combination of characteristics and components, each of which, in unique combination, affords a competitive advantage and is a protectable secret. We find based on the record in this case that the limited disclosure made by TI in regard to speech research lab activities merely described the application and configuration of the certain elements of the software but did not reveal the actual composition of the programs. The measures used by TI to secure its premises to prevent unauthorized personnel from admission to or exposure to its proprietary research data were reasonable under the circumstances. We need not decide today their trade secret status. We do find that the combination of employment agreements, strict plant security, restricted computer access, the nonauthorization of disclosure of the subject programs and the general nondisclosure of those programs by TI and its employees served to support the trade secret status of the computer programs that are the subject of the instant indictments. Appellants* **neither requested nor received permission** *to copy the files containing the programs.* (emphasis supplied)

The legal-linguistic innovations such as *shrink-wrap contract*, *click-wrap licence* or *browse-wrap licence* are not more comprehensible than *promissory estoppel* or *replevin* only because they refer to a banalized form of the colloquial English language. The IT-programer language is injected into the legal terminology without any attempts to provide for an alternative notion which would be closer to literary language. Judges seem to perceive the *shrink-wrap licence* as a legal term sui generis because they use it sometimes between quotation marks, like in M.A. Mortenson, Inc. v. Timberline Software Corp. (140 Wn. 2d 568; 998 P.2d 305; 2000 Wash. LEXIS 287). In the decision of the Supreme Court of Washington the new term spelled as one word is constantly used without any further description; however the distance is marked in the beginning of the decision through the constant use of quotation marks or the provisional 'so-called': e.g. *Timberline further argues that so-called 'shrinkwrap' software licenses have been found enforceable by other courts, and that both trade usage and course of dealing support enforcement in the present case* (id.). Later on, in the text of the decision the quotation marks are dropped off. Surprisingly, the dissenting opinion following the one of the majority includes a descriptive definition of a *'shrinkwrap' licence agreement* included in a note. This note says: *Vendors of computer software use plastic shrink-wrapping as a mechanism of attaching terms under which they purport to make their product available. In the mass market/ consumer context, the shrink-wrap license provides an efficient way for the software vendor to dictate the terms of each sale. When a business purchases a specialized software program, it typically negotiates, with the vendor, its rights of use in the software. In the mass market setting, however, the negotiation of terms for each sale is clearly impractical.* The note in the dissenting opinion refers to Robert J. Morrill, Contract Formation and the Shrink Wrap Licence: A Case Comment on ProCD, Inc. v. Zeidenberg, in: 32 New Eng. L. Rev. 513, 516 (1998). To clarify the legal problem discussed in the court opinion we may add that the UCITA embraces the theory of *layered contracting*, which acknowledges that while some contracts are formed and their terms are fully defined at a single point in time, many transactions involve a rolling or layered process. Under the theory of layered contracting, an agreement exists, but its terms are clarified or created over time (cf. UCITA sec. 208 cmt. 3 of the Approved Official Draft).

Overall, it seems that some efforts directed towards the modernization of legal terms may not lead to an increase in their understandability or operationability. This concerns especially the tendency towards the banalization of the language used in law that in the end rather conceals the problems than facilitates the understanding. It simply produces facile language. On the other hand, the legal vocabulary is rarely used and understood in an isolated form. Rather it is used in legal texts. Therefore, attempts undertaken to increase the understability of legal texts should primarily focus on the structure of legal texts and avoid their pseudo-democratization. Use of everyday words does not guarantee readable and unequivocal legal texts because in law precision matters particularly (Okawara 1998: 204). With all this in mind, the modernization of legal vocabulary remains a task for the legislator and should be regularly undertaken. However, its impact on the understanding of legal texts should not be overestimated.

2.4.10 Legal Thesaurus

Our analysis of the legal language and the legal terminology leads not only to theoretical results. It enables also to establish an exhaustive data basis of the legal language and to set up modalities of its use in various legal-linguistic operations. The preliminary question is, of course, what vocabulary to include; this is a choice based on the conception of legal language which is one of the foremost issues of the Legal Linguistics. The question is somehow circular as only legal terminology should be represented in a lexicon of legal language. We have realized that what is legal terminology and what it is not is in terms of pragmatics an issue of context, i.e. of the circumstances of language use. For instance, Husa (2007: 311-370) identified in his list of Greek legal vocabulary lexical units equivalent to: *sister, brother, opinion, direct, relative, equal, general, to wait* or *to end* as belonging to the legal vocabulary due to specifics of their use in the legal Greek. Gémar (2004: 738) relies upon the pragmatic criterion of language use for distinguishing of legal and non-legal terminology. He quotes (FR) *accord, acte, demande, terme* as examples of terms primarily used in ordinary language. However, when these lexical units become characterized, as in (FR) *accord synallagmatique, acte exécutoire, demande incidante, terme extinctif,* they become part of the legal terminology. The use provides first information about the semantic value of a lexical unit; the real meaning of a lexical unit is provided for in the discourse in which it is used. Gémar continues: *Si l'usage confère sa valeur sémantique première à un mot, c'est le contexte de son emploi, le mot mis en discours, qui en détermine toutefois sa signification réelle.* In our approach to language we did not stress the primary and the secondary use of lexical units as the borderline between them is sometimes relatively difficult to determine. The procedure as it was proposed by Gémar is nevertheless convincing and can be implemented in lexicographical work. The pragmatics of use as criterion demonstrates again that in Legal Linguistics we have to deal with legally relevant language use rather than with legal language (Galdia 2008: 15). The criterion of use is also the most efficient one in identifying the legal terminology which should be included into a legal lexicon. Nowadays, electronic data processing allows for broad, if not practically unlimited lexical corpus to be included into a lexicon (Galdia 2003b: 130). Formerly forwarded arguments of impracticability of broad vocabulary and the necessity to save space are not relevant any more in technologically advanced lexicographic projects. New technical possibilities make therefore the idea of a Legal Thesaurus, a lexicographic work that is broader than a lexicon, feasible. Such a work would include not only the legally relevant lexical material but also samples of context, examples of use in form of phraseological units, texts and doctrinal commentaries. It could even include language used by laypersons in legal contexts with all its intricacies. Thus, the phenomenon which we for practical use call here legal language would become perceptive in all its communicative implications. In some contemporary works such as *Encyclopaedia Iuridica Fennica* (EIF) legal concepts form the structure of the whole work. The EIF - although not primarily construed to be a lexicon of legal terminology - can occasionally function as such. Some contemporary lexicographers tend towards the adoption of concept-based lexicographic works. Therefore, Mattila (2002a: 183, 188) distinguishes between traditional lexicographic approaches based on terms (appearances of concepts) and approaches based on concepts (mental abstractions). Lexicographic works based on legal concepts may have the advantage of mapping the whole conceptual field which includes the typical terms used in it. However, they neglect the structural (inner) aspects of the legal language for which the use of various terms outweigh their conceptual background. Needless to add that practical needs of legal translators speak for the conception of a legal lexicon based on terms. This, in turn, leads back to problems reflected in this chapter.

2.4.10.1 Practical consequences for legal dictionaries: The results that follow from lexicological and lexicographical analyses in the area of the legal language are rather discourraging. First, it seems that the Thesaurus of the Legal language would be a particularly time consuming enterprise. Second, a bi- or multilingual legal dictionary appears towards the background of the contemporary research as a task which cannot be accomplished in a way which would satisfy scientific requirements. Nevertheless, legal translators need in their daily work dictionaries which would facilitate their efforts. In fact, the professional translator does not necessarely need the ambitious Thesaurus of the legal language as she usually will master the specific language and at least the basic legal terminology. She will therefore not need the corresponding terms of the words *claim* or *brother-in-law* which both may appear in a legally relevant context. She will rather need help in situations where also legal comparatists have their problems, e.g. with finding equivalents to (US/UK) *promissory estoppel*, (FR) *acte sous seing privé*, (D) *negative Drittzwischenfeststellungswiderklage*, (D) *Drittschadensliquidation*, (D) *gefahrgeneigte Arbeit*, (D) *positive Forderungsverletzung*, (S) *skuldebrev* or (FIN) *liitännäisvanhentuminen*. She needs suggestions for practically oriented solutions in dealing with the terminology. The translator may well understand that differences between legal systems and conceptual networks which are transported there make a static solution of lexicological problems impossible. She will nevertheless have to advance with her work. In such situations it would be helpful to provide in special problem-words oriented dictionaries some context-determined suggestions, e.g. (FR) *préciput* for *overhead*, (FR) *affacturage* for *factoring*, (PL) *fundusz hedgingowy* for *hedge fund* or (D) *gemeinschaftlicher Besitzstand* for (EU/F) *acquis communautaire* or (D) *gute Unternehmensführung* for *corporate governance*. The same holds true for the vocabulary close to legal contexts, e.g. (D) *nachhaltige Entwicklung* for *sustainable development* or (PL) *firma headhunterska* for *headhunter firm* which may be unknown even to translators who master their working languages very well. Some terms, e.g. (FR) *réserve légale*, (S) *laglott* are notoriously difficult to deal with due to differences between the legal systems but constantly needed in English texts where they can be rendered by *legal portion* or *statutory share*. Thus, comparative lawyers can provide effective help to these practical requirements of professonals whose tasks are connected to the law in a multilingual setting without exposing themselves to the criticism of engaging in obscure lexicographic undertakings.

2.4.11 What does terminology mean in terms of pragmatics?

Our conclusion on legal terminology and linguistic pragmatics may seem paradoxical. As a matter of fact, the study of legal terminology does not alter our view on special registers in the language. Problems in the legal terminology are centered around the notion of polysemy. Polysemy is largely known in linguistics and the legal terminology provides only some details to this knowledge. They concern especially the polysemy within one national language with different legal systems such as English within the UK and the US or German in Germany and Austria. Nevertheless, some detailed observations may also be of some importance for linguists. For instance, anaphora can function in order to avoid misunderstandings, e.g. *Plaintiff asserts that it is equally plain that plaintiff's own subjective intent was to obtain broilers and fryers.* (Frigaliment Importing Co. v. B.N.S. International Sales Corp. 190 F. Supp. 116 (S.D.N.Y. 1960)). This exaggerated intention to avoid misunderstandings may be counterproductive, as the use of *its* or *his* in the quoted example would not lead to confusion. Instead, the sentence is formulated in a way which draws attention of the reader and impedes upon the smooth reading of the text. It reaches therefore the opposite of the expected legal clarity. The pragmatic Legal Linguistics makes also clear that there is a difference between the claim to produce a precise and clear legal language and the achieved result. Thus, it makes necessary a shift in the perception of the legal language. Finally and more generally, our overview makes clear that we can use the term *legal language* as shorthand for legally relevant aspects of language use. The pragmatic Legal Linguistics shows that any attempt to freeze the relation between the word and its object in law must fail. It counteracts the tendency in law to label social facts with linguistic data for good and prevents the reification of language (Jackson 1985: 11) as well as its ossification (Mattila 2006: 58) which customarily jeopardizes legal reasoning. It furthermore depicts how the legal concepts are used as a structural background for the legal argumentation. It also opposes the banalization in modernizing the legal terminology. Finally, it makes clear that the legal language is much more than terminology. The legal language becomes operative in larger linguistic units such as speech acts. Their study is more beneficial but also more complicated. The terminology in a legal text may signalize a concrete speech act. J.L. Austin himself worked on lists of verbs which were typically used in specific speech acts. We can assume that in the legal usage the speech acts have the same property. Therefore, in the following chapter we will modify our perspective upon the legal language.

Part 3: Linguistic Operations in Law

While characterizing the language use in the preceding chapter we found out that legal terminology, although as such interesting and of practical importance, is nevertheless not the essential topic in a pragmatically oriented Legal Linguistics. Therefore, in the following chapter we will introduce another, more relevant concept of the linguistic operation in law. Subsequently, we will analyze some legal-linguistic operations such as argumentation, interpretation, and translation, mostly from the perspective of the speech act theory and the discourse theory. Finally, we will clarify why legal-linguistic operations are essential for legal discourses.

3.1 Overcoming Terminological Boundaries

In the foregoing chapter we have invested substantial amounts of time and intellectual efforts in the analysis of the legal terminology. On the other side, we regularly maintained that analyzing isolated lexical units cannot be the central task of a pragmatically oriented Legal Linguistics. Yet, there is no contradiction between our interest in the legal terminology (and in the legal 'conceptology') and our attention for the more dynamic aspects of language use in law. However, it would be insufficient to argue that we are interested in the legal terms and concepts because others – professional and non-professional users of the legal language – are predominantly interested in them. These groups of users - even if they represent an impressive number of participants in legal discourses - might have determined wrongly the significant and the non-significant problems in law. We, however, think that these groups of legal language users did not err. Rather to the contrary, we would posit that they stopped half way. For us, the legal language does not consist of legal terms or legal concepts alone. It is grounded in complex rules of use of legal arguments in speech acts where terms or concepts have an auxiliary role to play. They provide anchors for the legal arguments within the legal discourse and help determine the legal speech acts. Without the legal terms the legal discourse would be much less structured and finally also less predictable in its social consequences and also less rational. Therefore, we are here also interested in the legal terms and in the legal concepts. Nevertheless, our enthusiasm for them is limited as is limited the role they have to play in the legal discourses. We will therefore turn now to issues which seem for us essential in the Legal Linguistics. First of all, we used to approach different material manifestations of law – the signs of law – from the perspective of language use. We discovered that all these manifestations of law – judicial decisions, legislative acts, witness testimonies in courts and many others – have one feature in common. They cannot exist without the use of language and at the same time they are not intelligible when language is not used in them in a very specific way. This specific way of language use in law we called *aspects of legal language* because in all these communicative situations language use varies from case to case being more or less legal or more or less ordinary. In the legal language our interest was directed towards cases in which aspects of legal language manifested themselves rather strongly. The reason for this interest is that these cases lead to problems in law; they represent the most complicated issues in the creation and the application of law with linguistic means. Here again, we were not able to deal with all phenomena which one may observe in such situations. We therefore admit to cover only some aspects of the legal language use. Furthermore, we identified some linguistic operations in law which seem to us more urgent than others to be treated in the Legal Linguistics at this stage of its development. In this chapter we will have a closer look at the question what linguistic operations in law are actually about.

3.3.1 Linguistic operations in law

We will perceive the law as a set of prescriptive texts (mostly statutes and judicial decisions) created and implemented in a given social context, i.e. under specific social circumstances. We will furthermore posit that we are able with the help of this approach to clarify the most striking features of law, such as:

- creation of law with the help of language
- legal argumentation
- legal interpretation
- legal translation

We will hopefully arrive at the conclusion that while using pragmatic instruments we can reach the necessary and sufficient certainty in terms of legal application about the contents of legal provisions under specific social circumstances and apply them in a way which satisfies social needs and professional requirements. Many other linguistic operations, such as justification of legal decisions, providing legal advice or negotiations of private contracts, stating and commenting the law, interrogatories, and witness testimony could be included into this list. All these operations are actions performed with linguistic means. Also ethically less edifying practices such as deliberative linguistic manipulation, lies, and utterances expressed under duress make part of these operations. The task of the Legal Linguistics is to make these operations discerible. Certainly, while dealing with the selected legal-linguistic operations we will also cover some additional aspects of systematization and understanding of law which have been the object of the jurisprudence from its start as a particular scientific discipline. We will do it again in a pragmatic perspective in which they slightly change their shape. The professional reader will be confronted with things he already knows but we will color them differently. Moreover, in a more restricted pragmatic theory of legal creation, legal argumentation, legal interpretation and legal translation we will ask whether:

Legal creation consists of establishing specific speech acts;

Legal interpretation deals with identifying of speech acts;

Legal argumentation is the implementation of the interpretive speech acts;

Legal translation is a systemic transformation or qualification of speech acts between conceptual networks perceived as different.

This approach will clarify some characteristic features of speech acts used in law. It is a necessary step towards developing a more generalized conception of a legal speech act. This conception will emerge gradually towards the background of efforts undertaken in legal-linguistic and other theoretical research into law. At this point we will also have to reiterate and to reformulate one of our basic questions, i.e. could we master legal-linguistic operations without knowing the law? This question may take the reader by surprise, especially in the light of all what was said here about the legal language. We construe the legal language as spoken by specialists, by persons who were provided legal education. It would then seem that speaking this language would not be possible without the knowledge of the subject matter. This holds true especially in the case where legal language is perceived as a part of the ordinary language which features particular aspects. The situation is however different when linguistic operations begin to dominate. It seems that there this specific knowledge is decisive and more valuable than subject matter related data knowledge. This assumption may seem paradoxical but it may also show the strength of the Legal Linguistics.

3.1.2 Is systematization a legal-linguistic operation?

We use a fairly broad concept of *linguistic operation* here. It enables the incorporation of simple speech acts such as *promise* or of a complex speech act such as *text*. It can be easily adapted to include all relevant aspect of the *form of life* necessary for the determination of the speech act as well as the further development of its contents in an argumentative interpretation. Previously, we have determined several legal-linguistic operations. Is the legal systematization one of them?

For instance, in the commentary to the French Code Civil (ed. Dalloz) comments to the articles are centered around the text of the provision, e.g.:

Art. 1131 *L'obligation sans cause, ou sur une fausse cause, ou sur une cause illicite, ne peut avoir aucun effet.*

References to court opinions and comments are centered around following key notions: (FR) *détermination de la cause, absence de cause, cause illicite ou immorale.*

Art. 1133 *La cause est illicite, quand elle est prohibée par la loi, quand elle est contraire aux bonnes moeurs ou à l'ordre publique.*

Topics around which the commentary is organized are: (FR) *déontologie, fiançailles, clauses de célibat, courtage matrimonial, courtage d'adoption, liberalités entre concubins, clause de non-concurrence.*

Interestingly, also in the legal commentaries such as (D) Palandt's Commentary to the Bürgerliches Gesetzbuch (BGB) arguments from judicial decisions and scholarly writings are included as notes referring to salient concepts or terms of legal provisions commented there. Thus, a commentary of this sort reflects the structure of a possible and even of the successful legal argumentation. It provides for arguments which can or should be used in it, should the whole argumentation in regard of a legal problem be successful. It also lists arguments which were used in litigations but which proved unsuccessful there. Here, once again, we realize that Legal Linguistics is in a way a new creation, but it is simultaneously rooted in legal-linguistic operations such as argumentation. These operations were (and still are) its characteristic features in the course of its emergence along the development of legal sciences that the contemporary Legal Linguistics critically accompanies and shapes. The legal systematization is based on concepts (cf. Mattila 2006: 14). It prepares argumentation and presupposes interpretation. In our view, this result should be used for preparing the linguistic turn in law, in that the focus of systematization would shift from concepts to arguments. Similarly, A. Peczenik (2005: 1) perceived the legal science as a general legal doctrine that describes and systematizes legal sources and legal arguments. For him, the legal doctrine combines descriptive and normative elements in legal language and argumentation; systematization aims at reformulation of legal norms in an abstract manner, in relation to certain basic concepts (Peczenik 2005: 3). Such systematization would be definitely a linguistic operation and could be perceived even as one of the central tasks of the legal science.

3.2 Legal Speech Acts and Legal Discourse

3.2.1 How speech acts matter to law – from the pragmatic point of view

One of the central elements of the pragmatic analysis was the approach to language developed by J. L. Austin who focused on the speech act as the basic unit of language and of linguistic analysis. J. L. Austin concentrated in his *How to Do Things with Words* upon the distinction between performative and other utterances, mainly statements. This distinction became classical and Austin's input will in no way be diminished by occasional reference made to Hume's *Enquires* in which the later also mentioned some specific utterances subsequently named by Austin - although in a different context - *performatives* in analogy to *imperatives.* Progressively, the distinction between performatives and statements had been abandoned by Austin to the benefit of a more general notion of an 'illocutionary force' of utterances. The illocutionary force enabled to lay foundations not only for Austin's classification of speech acts but also for the later work by John Searle on the issue of their classification. Not surprisingly for jurists, J. L. Austin had stressed that the jurists should be best aware of "*the true state of affairs*" (1962: 4) as they were regularly confronted with performatives of the sort quoted by him (e.g. marriage formulae, promise, betting). Yet, they '*succumb to their timorous fiction that a statement of the 'law' is a statement of fact*' (1962: 4). This remark which includes some central issues of contemporary legal theory makes of J. L. Austin a successor of J. Austin, the classic of English jurisprudence, with whom his writing is so often confounded. Let us reiterate the simple thought J. L. Austin had expressed. He argued that the utterances of our ordinary language are not always statements of facts, a simple but rarely in his times understood idea which R. Dworkin (1975) had to elaborate upon with full strength. Indeed, jurists are regularly confronted with performatives like those quoted by J.L. Austin and with others, that are contractual in origin like *I bet* or declaratives, e.g. *I declare war.* J. L. Austin aptly demonstrated that these numerous speech acts are fundamental for the law in that they do not simply describe the legal propositions but have a constitutive role to play in them. Without the conventional linguistic formulae expressed, for instance, during the wedding ceremony by legally authorized participants no legally binding marriage would exist. As a matter of fact, utterances like the above ones are numerous in law. Our question is whether they are typical in the sense that they would characterize the relation between law and language. Were it so, then language would be constitutive for legal acts and consequently it would be also the fundament of the law. The application of law at its different stages of the legal decision making process manifests itself in a linguistic form that imposes an answer to our question which might prove premature. Language, however, may play different roles in the process of creation and application of law at different stages of the communicational process of which the legal decision making is a variety among many others. J. L. Austin has been aware of this specific variety of communicative processes. Following an observation by H. L. A. Hart, J. L. Austin compared his performatives with operative clauses used by lawyers, e.g. in acts of property conveyance which give effect to a transaction and he contrasted them with other clauses which only '*recite the circumstances in which the transaction is to be effected*' (1962: 7). Furthermore, Austin qualified direct testimony in a court of law as performative in contrast to a statement of hear-say which is not admitted as evidence and is perceived by him as a mere statement of facts. Still further, it is worthwhile mentioning that H. L. A. Hart (1961: ch. 5) spoke about *'operative utterances'* in the sense of Austinian *'performative utterances'*. In the end, both names describe slightly different facets of one and the same phenomenon. The first focuses upon the process of emergence of a speech act and the other upon its results which enables the further qualification of the speech act, e.g. as an acceptance of a contractual offer. For a jurist, the paradoxical part of J. L. Austin's theory resides in his attempt to introduce new aspects into philosophy while using among others numerous examples from law. Austin's philosophical ambition was clearly stated by himself and that was to show that philosophically relevant language use is not necessarily limited to statements. In this he succeeded fully. Much more problematic is however the input of his approach to law – a matter Austin did not think about nor did he explicitly wish to contribute to. Nevertheless, J. L. Austin's *How to Do Things with Words* can be taken for the first, although limited in scope, modern treatise on Legal Linguistics. His reception in the legal theory is complicated because Austin's lectures had followed a different goal – namely a philosophical or a linguistic one.

3.2.1.1 Following Austin: As a result of Austin's efforts, we are able to distinguish linguistically expressed norms which are not only descriptive but seem to be non-constitutive for the legal norm like rules prescribing driving on the right-hand side of the road. We used to call such rules *regulative* following the distinction introduced by Searle (Searle 1999: 123). We underline their difference from *constitutive* rules because they do not engender any legal acts but limit themselves to their prescription. They are constitutive for the emergence of the legal speech acts. Typologically, they are different from the purely constitutive rules although they also in a certain way constitute the driving on the right-hand side of the road as legal only in contrast to all other directions of driving, especially on the left-hand side of the road. Technically possible and efficient driving on the left-hand side of the road violates the provisions of the road code (as stated in most countries) and makes this driving illegal in the light of this norm. Constitutiveness of institutional speech acts in law is best understood when based on formal examples which concern extreme situations. Imagine that the U.S. Congress acting in accordance with the Constitutional provisions and procedures would declare war to a state or to a group of states. Legally, the U.S. would be engaged in the state of war with this state or the group of states even if no military actions would go on or take place until the formal termination of the Congressional declaration. In this sense we can say that purely constitutive rules differ from regulative ones although the latter may also display a constitutive legal aspect. They are linguistically constitutive by being descriptive; they are constitutive in that they are necessary for the existence of the speech act while being essentially descriptive. Moreover, no one can pretend to be legally married without exchanging the traditional formulae in the presence of the authorized clerk while the driver in our example could successfully (although illegally) drive on the left-hand side of the road. He could even drive on the right-hand side of the road by liking and not by obedience to legal rules and declare not to respect the law in general as a matter of principle and the traffic rules in particular. These paradoxical statements are possible because the rules in question are linguistically regulative and not strictly constitutive. We are now convinced about the existence of different linguistically relevant constitutive and regulative rules in law. Legal speech acts follow this distinction but they are more differentiated and go beyond of what the dichotomy of *regulative* and *constitutive* might suggest. The number of speech acts is of course enormous and classification patterns engender even manifold characterizations for one and the same utterance and this procedure increases the number of speech acts and makes limitations impossible. Such limitations would also be unnecessary in the sense of the speech act theory. The amount of possible characterizations of speech acts is dependant upon illocutionary points which function as focal points for the classification of speech acts. Also they are numerous. Searle distinguishes five particular types of illocutionary force according to which speech acts are identified and characterized (Searle 1999: 149-150):

- *assertives* are propositions representing a state of affairs in the world which can be tested and identified as being true or false

- *directives* are propositions which influence the behavior like orders, commands, requests. They cannot be true or false but can be obeyed, complied with or violated.

- *commissives* are propositions embracing commitments to undertake something like promises, pledges, contracts, guarantees. They cannot be true or false but are instead respected or not.

- *expressives* convey sincerity conditions of the speech act, e.g. apologies, thanks; truth in them is taken for granted.

- *declarations* are mostly performatives which make changes in the world when uttered like the marriage formula declaring candidates 'man and wife'. They depend usually on extralinguistic institutions.

We will not enter here into the discussion and the retrospection upon the process in which the various types of speech acts have been classified, initially by J. L. Austin, later by J. Searle and many others. The magnitude of descriptions and types of speech acts is indicative of the creative potential residing in our utterances and is per se neither embarrassing nor is it discouraging. It is one of the characteristic features of our language, its multiple functions and facets. The reason why we will not enter into the debate is primarily that we need only some of these types because not all of them are productive in legal-linguistic usage.

3.2.2 Classification of legal speech acts

For our classification certain linguistic criteria will be more decisive than others. The most popular and the most reliable criterion that determines the classification is the verb present in an utterance. When we trace a verb like *state, warn, command, contract, guarantee* or *complain* in an utterance we will at first be able to almost automatically characterize the speech act as a statement, warning, command, contract, guarantee or complaint. However, as the context of such utterances may be more complex or untypical, a revision of the characterization may become necessary. In such a situation we will be compelled to redress the initial characterization of an utterance when it has been made much too automatically in close accordance with its explicit wording alone. This - in parenthesis - is also a problem typical for legal interpretation and the daily work of every practicing lawyer. Like lawyers in their practice we will have to rely on the purpose inherent in the utterance to be able to finally classify a speech act. The number of purposes can differ, Searle proposed the five quoted above and this is acceptable for us in a research limited to language use in the legal context.

The existence of *assertives* in law is questionable. As a rule, a legal text, predominantly a statute (e.g. an Act, a Bill, a Law on…, a Decree etc.) is of prescriptive nature, statements being rare in statutes. Statutes prescribe, injunctions order etc. Legal texts may include some parts of assertives that might undergo the test of true or false like a witness testimony reported in a court decision. However, their role may be more important in soft law texts which take the form of legally binding prescriptive texts while lacking this propriety in terms of law. *Directives*, embracing orders, commands or requests are the realm of the state administration. A part of them constitute legal texts such as ordinances or decrees. Others are linked to explicitly legal texts by some elements, like e.g. official correspondence. As said, statutes (and legal texts on different hierarchical levels such as ordinances or decrees), are typical directives. *Commissives* which include commitments of the speaker are first of all found in the private law, especially in contracts. There, guarantees, pledges and promises of all sorts abound. They too, like laws, cannot be true or false, but only kept or broken. They have their own characteristics. They are framed in a language of condition with *if, subject to, on condition, provided that* or in a language of promise with *I promise, I will* etc. *Expressions* manifesting the sincerity conditions of a speech act are rare in legal texts due to the emotional element inherent in sincerity. One may assume that some texts of constitutional preambles may include expressive elements (cf. 4.3.2). Also the lack of sincerity like signing a check with the name William Shakespeare may become relevant in law. Therefore, for instance, in assignments of rights under the common law the linguistic expression must be precise. It is important to use the present or future tense, e.g. *I assign, I will assign* or *I promise to assign*. Otherwise, the validity of an assignment could be challenged.

3.2.2.1 Two examples: Performative utterances that were central in J. L. Austin's reasoning may easily create institutional facts. A well known example (Searle 1999: 115) is the text on the 100 U.S. dollar note saying: *This note is a public tender for all debts, public and private* that on the note is accompanied by a facsimile of the signature of the U.S. Federal Treasurer and of the seal of the U.S. Federal Reserve. The phrase in its institutional surrounding does not or not only describe the creation of valid money, it creates this means of payment by saying in a way authorized by the Constitution that the note in question is a means of payment, a legal tender. Adequately, it creates the fact it describes. That said, one could now ask whether it is necessary to produce this effect. The answer may be yes and no. It will generally be necessary because a declaration of acceptability of money as money by the authorized institution is a prerequisite of its existence. Of course, when the means of payment in form of banknotes became general, the public also became aware of the fact that they are issued by a competent authority and can therefore be legally used as means of payment. Nowadays no one – exception made for very scrupulous debtors and intrigued researchers – studies the text on the hundred dollar note any more. The initial performative act produced its effects; it created a medium which became a part of our legal culture in such effective way that no further interpretation in a particular case concerning payment is necessary any more. This is also the reason why on the rather sterile 100 euro note we will not find any such constructive utterance any more. It has simply been replaced by the symbolic use of banknotes in our society and is therefore redundant for its constitution. The legal institution, i.e. payment of debts with banknotes had been successfully established in society and their use had been internalized by the public. Likewise, their symbolic form is generally recognized and functionalized. Using the quoted phrase of the 100 dollars note on the recently designed 100 euro note would constitute not only a formal but a formalistic act because no additional performative effect could be reached today with the antiquated formula.

3.2.2.2 Legal speech acts in comparison: The performative character of legal speech acts is quite intricate. They exist with many variations. Mattila (2006: 32) quoting D. Kurzon provides an example of promise in three forms: 1. *I hereby promise…*; 2. *I do promise*; 3. *I promise by these presents…* The qualification of promise as legal speech act must also reflect upon these varieties. Understanding the aspects of speech act use is important. The archaic use of *do* in the above *I do promise* or in *I do appoint* may falsely suggest emphasis to speakers unaware of the intricacies of the legal English (Tiersma 1999: 207). Performativity, instead, is clearly stressed in the first example by the use of *hereby.* Comparative studies available to date show that legal speech acts largely correspond. In French, they are focused around some verbs with legal connotations, for instance (FR) *je promets, j'offre, j'autorise, je reconnais, je jure, ordonnons, condamnons* (Cornu 2005: 38). However, as long as no profound comparative effort in analyzing of legal speech acts has been undertaken, it might be premature to say that this resemblance is due to the specifics of the legal culture which in all its diversity leads back to its Roman-Greek roots and thus provides patterns for the formation of legal speech acts.

3.2.2.3 Mode of existence of legal speech acts: The evolution in the use of speech acts is evident in the above case contrasting the dollar and the euro banknotes. It also shows another characteristic feature of speech acts which might be more productive for the Legal Linguistics than the problem of their formal classification. It shows the conditions of fit for the speech acts, which are their conditions for being true or false, valid or void. Already J. L. Austin realized that the conditions of functioning are essential for speech acts. Performatives such as *promise* cannot be true or false, but only implemented, they can be broken or void, etc. The mode of their existence is different from factual statements which can be true or false. Legal speech acts function under specific conditions of which three are essential. They are: appropriate procedure, authorized actors and no abuse of procedure of use (e.g. not believing what one is saying or not meaning seriously what one is saying). Therefore, identifying speech acts in law might be perceived as a sterile exercise. And indeed, what matters is the speech act in its context. In law, speech acts are often encountered in a narrativized context (Jackson 1988: 227). For Jackson, the fact of giving evidence is less interesting than the story of the giving of evidence (Jackson 1988: 227). Again, in law, a speech act cannot become operational as long as it cannot be used in the interpretation of a precedent or a legal act. Legal interpretation has in this sense two prongs, it makes the identification of a speech act possible as a speech act and it ensures its further operativeness in the legal argumentation. Because of this implication the whole potential of a speech act must be exploited in order to make it operational in law. Procedural aspects of *telling, asserting, claiming* as well as *questioning,* e.g. in cross-examination or acts of *naming* or *adoption* are complex and should not be reduced to their structural skeleton. The same concerns the central speech act of law – the *judge's decision* which constitutes an entirely new legal speech act. The reaction of law to the complexity of the subject matter has been the increase in the complexity of legal speech act. Legal speech acts such as *promise* or *warranty* have a different degree of complexity than *argumentation* or *interpretation*. Frequently, our highly complex law is therefore simplified by using gestures and other forms of non-lexical communication. Transactions of daily life, purchasing of newspapers at a newsstand or tickets in an automat as well as withdrawing cash from a teller are reduced to gestures which replace complex transactional communication. The silent law, (IT: *diritto muto*) (Benedetti 1999: 138-139; Mattila 2006: 33), dominates standard legal transactions. Therefore, laypersons involved in such procedures are often not even aware of their entering the domain of law.

3.2.3 Implementing speech acts in law

As already mentioned, the biggest influence on the pragmatically oriented legal theory and Legal Linguistics have had the speech acts, initially identified as substantial for any natural language by J. L. Austin and further elaborated by J. Searle. Meanwhile, the speech act theory established itself in the legal theory as its uncontested element. Its domain of application, i.e. its scope and its bearing for the legal theory, however, remains somehow unclear. Some researchers concentrate on tracing speech acts in the legal language in order to prove the universal character of the speech acts which are not limited to ordinary language. Others use this theoretical approach as a vantage point of legal theories. Especially, the interrelation of social institutions and speech acts has been underlined and made prolific in the legal theory. Attempts to implement the speech act theory in law show that the number of legal speech acts which is finally dependant upon linguistic acts performed in law allows for may different, yet complementary descriptive theories of law. J. Searle distinguished *constitutive* and *regulative* rules. H. L. A. Hart developed an influential theory which grounds basically in the distinction between *primary* and *secondary* rules. Also A. M. Honoré attempted a description of legal rules which comes close to the Austinian model (MacCormick & Bańkowski 1986: 133). He also characterized the academic atmosphere of his time in a passage which we quote in our notes because it explains in an original way the beginnings of the thinking which dominates also our work (cf. Notes and Materials nr. 15). N. MacCormick added a typology of legal rules based on three different types namely *institutive, consequential* and *terminative* rules (cf. 3.2.3.2). M. Atienza and J. Ruiz Manero (1996) identified enonciations as constitutive parts of the law. They differentiated between (ESP) *enunciados permisivos, enunciados normativos* and *enunciados valorativos.* For the two authors values proclamed in the law serve as interpretive guidelines; the fact that values are present in the legislative acts explains why legal norms actually can guide human actions. Other typologies of speech acts and their underlying rules are thinkable as well (Helin 1990: 153). This multitude is the strength and not at all the weakness of a legal theory which resorts to the speech acts.

3.2.3.1 Institutionalized language use: In fact, speaking a language is engaging in a rule-governed form of behavior, i.e. performing speech acts, e.g. making statements, giving commands, asking questions or making promises (Searle 1969: 16). In the light of this theoretical approach the speech act is the most fundamental unit of linguistic communication. Fundamental in this sense is not a symbol, a word or a sentence but rather the production/issuance of symbols, words or sentences in the performance of a speech act (Searle 1969: 19). Wherever two illocutionary acts contain the same reference and predication – providing that the meaning of the sentence is the same – one could pretend that the same proposition has been expressed. A proposition must be distinguished from the assertion or statement in which it is expressed. Especially, the institutional character of legal language and legal action became clear through the examples in which they were presented by the two classics of the speech act theory. Hence, the utterance *I condemn you to ten years of prison* is appropriate in a legal setting only when the situation is a trial and the speaker is a judge (Levinson 1983: 229). Would this not be the case, the utterance like the cited would be 'infelicitous' and might occur in a joke or in a film or be another metaphor not interesting in a legal context. Furthermore, it was noted in the consequence of this observation that the entire legal language is constituted in a specific legal procedure and cannot exist independently of it (cf. Levinson 1983: 230). At this moment the concept of institutionalized language use in law became anchored in the speech act theory. This conceptual development of the legal-linguistic theory itself had a profound impact upon the view of law adopted also in the modern legal theory. This impact must, in turn, be reflected in the Legal Linguistics.

3.2.3.2 Legal speech acts and institutions: The speech act theory led to the application of its fundamental notions in jurisprudence, primarily in Neil MacCormick's and Ota Weinbergers's (1986) institutional theory of law. Following Searle, both authors maintain that legal facts are institutional facts. Our knowledge about them is grounded in interpretation along the constitutive rules which construct these facts. They could be in the view of the authors reduced to utterances which could be tested on their truth or falsity, but the test seems to be complicated as it involves our total knowledge about the world. Moreover, the legal doctrine appears to the authors as possible because of the alleged testability of rules as true or false. The authors stress that legal speech acts such as marriage formulas tend to come organized in sets or institutions like marriage (cf. Jackson 1988: 243). Therefore, rules exist to determine which speech acts are necessary to create a legally valid marriage (*institutive rules*). Other rules tell us which speech acts are permitted or required once the marriage has been created (*consequential rules*). Finally, some rules refer to the termination of a marriage (*terminative rules*). The authors also distinguish between formal and informal speech acts in law. An informal speech act is an assertion that *x might be guilty of a murder* whereas the speech act: *guilty* done by the foreman of the jury in a court of law is a formal act. The theory of legal speech acts deals with formal speech acts. They are structured like the following one: A jury foreman having the right qualification to perform the act and having the intention to perform it within the right procedure along the lines of felicity conditions for speech acts developed by J. L. Austin performs the act. Normative consequences follow from a valid legal speech act, e.g. a person declared guilty of a murder is condemned to lifelong imprisonment. Operations which we have in mind are kindred with 'acts in the law', a notion defined as *acts which often (indeed usually) are carried out by means of the utterance of words* (MacCormick & Bańkowski 1986: 122). However, the operations which interest us are explicitly linguistic and in this they differ from all other acts in the law. They are not undertaken in the vacuum and therefore all other acts in law stand very close to them. In this circumstance we can see their resemblance with all possible acts in law, the linguistic and the non-linguistic or not predominantly linguistic acts. The last group would, for instance, include legally relevant linguistic operations such as making an offer or accepting it in contract negotiations which are accompanied by threat or open use of violence. An expression of intention under duress remains for us a speech act. It fails, however, under Austinian criteria for the felicity of speech acts and therefore we would argue that finally the linguistic element is not decisive in such an act although it is undeniably present there. We have also to assume that some acts in law are not linguistic acts as not all rules can be created by rule-creating linguistic acts (MacCormick & Bańkowski 1986: 123). With MacCormick and Bańkowski (ib.) we have therefore to state that normative utterances cannot all be explicable in terms of performative utterances or in terms of acts in the law. We move here in a territory which H. Kelsen (1967) tried to apprehend with his *basic norm*, or F. Lachmayer (1979) with his (D) *präkonstitutionelles Gewohnheitsrecht*. This is the realm of power where law is constituted in other terms than the linguistic ones. This statement makes plain why a theory of norms is crucial for the theory of legal speech acts. The opposite view to this would be to assume that there can exist speech acts which are not rule-defined or derivative from norms and which are therefore called informal acts (MacCormick & Bańkowski 1986: 125). Generally, however a linguistic argument can be used against the 'imperative fallacy'; one cannot derive an *ought* from an imperative *shall* nor can one derive it from the indicative *is* (MacCormick and Bańkowski 1986: 128). Yet again, we can imagine such acts in law only where pure political will is at stake, where no established rules matter. We promised in the beginning of our work to demonstrate the realm of law without language and here it is.

As indicated, N. MacCormic developed an original analysis of legal norms while distinguishing institutive, consequential and terminative rules. Critics argued however that his distinctions were less convincing than Searle's constitutive and regulative rules. Furthermore, some critics maintained that in the terminative rules expressing prerequisites for termination of legal facts a constitutive rule has been used finally in its specific role. Thus, they questioned the necessity of this concept. The institutional theory of law found some interested researchers and successors. But, generally, it did not develop to a leading trend in the legal science. There may exist several reasons for this. Critics mentioned that the two authors – who represent slightly different philosophical positions – did not bring about any coherent theory but rather published in the work quoted above a series of articles with a programatic introduction (Helin 1990: 150). Some critics suggested that the reliance on the legal doctrine and the verification methods might have been perceived as uncritical by readers and potential successors. And indeed, the approach results in a structural theory of law which its authors rightly also call legal positivism. Dworkin (1977 and 1991) showed the limits of such theories. Efforts undertaken by N. MacCormick and O. Weinberger resulted however in raising of awareness about the specific felicity conditions for legal speech acts. MacCormick and Weinberger made explicit the institutional boundaries of any action undertaken in law (cf. Salas 2001: 226). This part of their theory is essential for pragmalinguistically oriented models of legal interpretation (cf. Kwarciński 2005) and basically also for all attempts to understand and describe the legal discourse. Finally, this is also the reason why today we can maintain that in terms of the speech act theory to work effectively with legal norms means to set up requirements for felicitous legal speech acts which would justify the entry of their normative consequences. However, as the legal speech acts do not exist in a vacuum, but are part of larger linguistic units, also their felicity conditions must be searched for there. Therefore, the conditions of an effective legal discourse and linguistic operations undertaken there, especially in the legal interpretation and the legal argumentation, determine the whole set of felicity requirements for the effective use of language in law.

3.2.3.3 Linguistic operations in law and legal speech acts: We distinguish here between linguistic operations in law as general concepts and legal speech acts as particular acts which represent law in a linguistic form. We were forced to introduce this distinction because both phenomena refer to different levels on which legal signs are constituted and interpreted. Legal speech acts concern the material aspect of language use in law, while the linguistic operations in law include also theoretical prerequisites and professional interpretive aspects relative to these acts. For instance, a legal speech act can represent an interpretation of a legal provision or its translation into another legal language. Legal speech acts are of different quality; some are simple, others particularly complex. They do not exist in a vacuum, instead, they are elements of legal discourses. There, they function according to the rules of discourse composition. In turn, the linguistic operation in law such as legal interpretation or legal translation includes the meta-level of the speech acts involved, i.e. the theory of their use. They include namely the theory of legal interpretation or the theory of legal translation. In sum, the linguistic operation in law is a speech act evaluated from the perspective of the legal theory.

3.2.3.4 Language games: Already H. L. A. Hart repeated regularly that language and the rules based on it contain both a core of settled meaning and a penumbra of uncertainty (Schauer 1993: xiv). The subsequent discussion concerned the question of how far the settled area actually is and whether the notion of core is coherent at all. Serious criticism addressed this challenging issue and it was stressed that solely a wide range of varying contextual factors enables the speaker to grasp the meaning of any item of language. We have seen that J. L. Austin had found a solution to this dilemma with his speech acts. In a parallel approach to J. L. Austin, Ludwig Wittgenstein (1984: 250) developed his notion of *language games* which were in his view constitutive for any understanding of language and were necessarily bound to vast contexts named *forms of life.* This notion was until now not as successfully used as Austin's speech acts. Nevertheless, its bearing for the understanding of the legal language as for any other variety of language remains uncontested. Law is in terms of this approach a normative language game (Minda 1995: 239). Following Wittgenstein's conception of language games Th. Morawetz (1992) characterizes law as a deliberative practice in *Epistemology of Judging. Wittgenstein and Deliberative Practices.* He developed a theory of law as a radical deliberative practice. For Morawetz, the deliberative legal practice embraces participants with different commitments to different argumentative strategies and goals. They are not bound together by shared rules but by mutual recognition of relevant rules of proceedings. Deliberation proceeds as an activity in which each participant reaches and justifies arguments and deploys his justificatory strategy in part to persuade others to adopt it but also to claim his own way of making sense of experience. The players play different plays but aim at one result (cf. Galdia 1995: 69). A. Aarnio has recognized this situation and proposed to split the players into at least two auditoria in order to better distinguish between more and less convincing arguments in the legal deliberation (Galdia 1995: 34). For jurists it is interesting to notice that Wittgenstein abandoned in his approach definitions and took *family resemblances* between different uses of a word for the basis of meaning. We identify one use as a paradigm and examine others in terms of degree and nature of divergence from paradigm. Hilary Putnam coined therefore the term *cluster concept.* Other approaches, such as Georges Kleiber's introduced the *prototype* as a framework for the determination of meaning (Kleiber 1990: 49). All of these conceptions insist on the broad, if not broadest, context of language use. A theory of legal interpretation or of the legal argumentation would not be possible would the conceptual context be defined more narrowly. The mentioned approaches based on language games are decisive for the Legal Linguistics. The normative language games established and seen in the broad context of forms of life could justify the thesis that law is actually and exclusively about language. Within the Wittgensteinian hermeneutics the human understanding occurs in language games (Minda 1995: 239). These linguistic operations are anchored in broad social practices which also are linguistic. Therefore, from the Wittgensteinian perspective we deal exclusively with language when we analyze law.

3.3 Legal Argumentation

Our utmost interest in the Legal Linguistics is directed towards two of the main linguistic operations in law, the legal argumentation and the legal interpretation. They are particularly challenging because they represent highly complex legal speech acts in discourses. Therefore, it seems to be appropriate to have a closer look at both at this stage. Argumentation as a linguistic phenomenon aims at the explanation of facts and situations or at the justification of actions. As a linguistic act argumentation is particularly complex. This is the reason why its analysis is burdensome and until now not really satisfactory although considerable research into its foundations is available. Traditionally, the *syllogism* based on premises and leading to a conclusion has been perceived as its ideal conceptual structure. Nevertheless, already the classical rhetoric recognized problems in application of syllogisms in the ordinary language. The specific rhetorical syllogism - *enthymeme* (lat. *argumentum*) - is mentioned already by Quintilian (Curtius 1996: 320). Therefore, the pervasive force of enthymemes had been stressed even there. The enthymemes cannot lead to unquestionable results like syllogisms. Their conclusions are always exposed to criticism and debates. Their argumentative force has been seen in their potential to convince the audience about the just result reached in the argumentation. The criterion for their correct application is the coherence of the proposition made. Likewise, in the traditional research, scholars dealt with linguistic and logical instruments which controlled argumentation. They were the modalities of logical reasoning, consistence of utterances, coherence and lack of contradictions or topoi. Logicians dealt with issues which excluded context and socially relevant action from the analyses of argumentation. They developed an abstract form of argumentation that only under specific circumstances can be productive in law. Especially, research concerning *topoi* which manifest themselves in maxims or Latin proverbs provided remarkable results in law. It showed how specific fixed argumentative structures can dominate the argumentation and even replace the search for rationality in it. Speech acts regularly show this implication especially in statements, recommendations, motivations, and justifications. After all, argumentation is always part of a social situation; it is bound to speech acts like those named and many others. When argumentation is not convincing, the speech act which transports its purpose fails.

3.3.1 Legal rhetoric

Argumentation has been perceived as central for law by many researchers in the past (Viehweg 1954: 29). Nevertheless, we must also admit that the studies on this issue played rather a peripheral role in teaching and applying of law. Not only in Cicero's *Topics*, but also in various other learned works on legal rhetoric questions concerning use of arguments in law have been canvassed. Legal rhetoric makes sense within the system based on the Roman civil law. In the beginning of the Middle Ages it has lost importance as a basis for legal decision making due to the decrease in quality of legal procedures. Its knowledge, nevertheless, had been upheld (Curtius 1996: 117). Numerous *modi arguendi* have been developed in the Middle Ages around Boethius' *De differentiis topicis*, written ca. 522, mostly for the use of law students (Hohmann 1998: 40). Equally, serious efforts were undertaken in the past to understand and make operative the argumentative practices in law but also to explain law in terms of argumentation. Jurists frequently construed this topic as belonging to *legal logics*. Next to the mentioned *Topica* by Aristotle and Cicero's *Topica* in the Middle Ages and later profound literature was developed to provide jurists with handy arguments and a canon for the interpretation of laws. Particularly well-known are works such as: *Topicorum seu locorum legalium opus de inventione et argumentatione* (1516) by N. Everardus, later printed as *Loci argumentorum legales*, *Legalis dialectica in qua de modo argumentandi et locis argumentorum legaliter disputatur* (1507) by P.A. Grammarus, *Topica regalia* by C. Cantiuncula (1520) and later on *Dialecticae legalis libri quinque* (1531) by Ch. Hegendorf, *De dialectica ex iure libri tres* (1546) by B. Walther, *De logica iureconsultorum libri duo* (1582) by J. Freigius, *Dialectica iuris* (1610) by M. Stephani, *Logica iuridica, hoc est regulae, precepta et modus argumentandi per inductiones et interpretationes legum* (1615) by M. Schickhard. We have quoted the above works to show how far reaching in time the discussion about legal argumentation in fact is. Today, our view on legal arguments has changed with the development of the philosophy of language. We do not believe any more that argumentation in law consists of the application of a selected set of argumentative forms and formulations. Neither do we believe that the argumentative interpretation consists of the application of a limited set of interpretive canons which automatically lead to the identification of the right content of words in law. Finally, we do not believe that jurists follow or have to develop a logic of its own, a legal logic which would be characteristic of their profession. Nevertheless, we have to admit that knowledge about most issues concerning argumentation in law we have today is a result of an ongoing scientific discussion about the legal argumentation which lasts already more than two thousand years. Definitely, there is much discontinuity in this continuity but it is fascinating to see how the paradigms of legal argumentation change while their topics remain stable since the ancient Greeks. Rare are scientific disciplines which today can still use some of their past achievements or at least read five hundred years old works without bursting into life endangering laughter.

3.3.1.1 Argumentation and rhetoric: As mentioned, argumentation has been for long perceived as a rhetorical operation, i.e. the application of specific arguments in discourses. The classification of arguments caused problems as no convincing matrix for all of them could be proposed. Denominations for arguments often covered different functions. Arguments have been divided into rational, e.g. *ad rem* and irrational, e.g. *ad hominem*; universal, i.e. directed to whatever audience and contextual, i.e. related to selected audience, e.g. legal experts; correct and uncorrect; argumentation as regards the number of argumenting persons, e.g. some, many, one person (Krasilnikova 2006: 180). In her research Krasilnikova provides for a classification based on traditional methods and retains the Latin names which are traditionally provided for arguments in rhetoric. Krasilnikova (2006: 182) distinguishes: arguments (*a.*, i.e. LAT *argumentum*) with connection to logics: *a. primarium, a. ad absurdum, a. ab exemplo, a. a contrario, a. ex silentio, a. a simili, a. minimum probant, a. a fortiori* as well as some general groups of arguments called *a. ad rem* or *a. ad oratorem.* Some arguments seem to be close to methods: *a. ad auditorem, a. ad populum, a. ad ignorantiam, a. ad socordiam, retorsio argumenti.* Another type may concern the authority of the addressed person: *a. ad hominem, a. ad personam, a. tu quoque, a. ad verecundiam, a. ad reverentiam, a. ad vanitatem, a. ad fidem, a. ad iudicium, a. ad superstitionem, a. ex concessis, a. ex consensu gentium, a. ad vertiginem, a. ad invidiam, a. ad misericordiam, a. ad passiones, a. ad ridiculum, a. ad superbiam, vexatio, a. ad amicitiam, a. ad antiquitatem.* Close to this type are: *a. ad baculum, a. ad carotam, a. ad consequentiam, a. ad crumenam, a. ab utili, a. ad quietatem, a. ad metum.* Means of persuasion are not necessarily only arguments. Also pseudoarguments, i.e.illogical arguments (fallacies) and eristic tricks are used in rhetoric. Eristic writings began apparently with the Greek rhetor Maximos (cf. Kotarbiński 1955: 6, 184), who described rhetoric tricks that may be used to win litigations to the detriment of truth and equity in his (GR) Πεϱὶ τῶν ἀλυτων ἀντιθέσεων (*Peri ton alyton antitheseon*). A. Schopenhauer concentrated on this issue in his *Eristische Dialektik oder die Kunst Recht zu behalten* (ca. 1830/31). The problems with the classification of arguments and other means of persuasion show the limits of traditional rhetoric. Schopenhauer attempted to represent argumentation in action and came already close to modern argumentation theories which focus on the procedures of argumentation rather than on the classification of traditional arguments (Wohlrapp 1995: 27). The existing classification of arguments exhibits a resemblance to speech acts. Yet, unlike the speech act classification, it remains static and even rigid. Therefore, the contemporary general theory of argumentation unites pragmatic and dialectic aspects (cf. van Eemeren/Grootendorst 2004).

3.3.1.2 Argumentation in East Asian tradition: Argumentation is not a Western invention. It seems to accompany language wherever it develops to an advanced tool of social interaction. In the traditional Chinese culture argumentation followed the dialectical principle of Yin and Yang (Zhang 2004: 5) and oscillated among pairs of opposite concepts. This argumentative scheme included especially contradictory conceptual pairs based on the idea of relativity. Among those most frequently used were: inter-promotion and inter-restraint, restriction of destruction and support to construction, safety and danger, dynamic and static, left and right, up and down, complete and incomplete, noble and ignoble, superior and inferior, sense and sensibility, as well as knowledge and practice (Zhang 2004: 5). Some other opposites were immediately relevant for the legal argumentation. Let us mention some of them such as: false and true, real and unreal, life and death, sudden enlightenment and gradual enlightenment, relative and absolute, finite and infinite, whole and part, temporary and eternal (Zhang 2004: 127). Speech formed towards the background of such dialectical mechanism animated the development of the two traditions of legal thought in China, Confucianism and Legalism. Finally, it led to their merger by the time of the Western Han (206 BC to 24 AD). At any rate, also the Chinese thinkers tended towards the absorption of rational factors structuring the speech and towards remoulding them as time went by (Zhang 2004: 127). Nothing points to any practice of argumentation in which these opposites would have been applied as a strict canon. The classical Chinese argumentation is as flexible as the European one and definitively not less efficient. This dialectic argumentation did not concern legal texts in the sense exposed by the Romans. It concerned general ethical principles and cases which sometimes would be perceived as legal in the Western sense and sometimes not. However, already in the ancient time ritual forms and the rule of law were emphasized in order to maintain social stability. Thus, rules that from the traditional Western perspective may be perceived as restricted to ethics might have been perceived by the ancient Chinese as strictly legal. The tradition of legal thinking has apparently a much longer tradition in China than sometimes presumed. The mere existence of the legalistic reasoning contradicts the occasionally expressed assumption that the traditional Chinese philosophical reasoning did not distinguish between moral and legal rules and that it construed them as one ideal entity (Upham 1990: 83). In the legalistic writings they were apparently clearly apprehended as different. Another thing is the reaction which the Chinese thinkers of the past developed towards purely legal arguments and rules. These arguments and rules had been in the past not particularly cherished and may even today not be popular among parts of the population. They have nevertheless, like other rites and rules, accompanied the development of the Chinese society and shaped the structure of the social discourse there. As far as the classical Chinese language is concerned, Granet (1934: 203) argued that it was less appropriate to conceptual analysis: *Le language vise, avant tout, à agir. Il prétend moins à informer clairement qu'à diriger la conduite.* Instead, he stressed its pragmatic dimension in which conveing feelings in order to convince and to influence behavior are fundamental (id. 1934: 82): *La langue chinoise n'apparaît point organisée pour noter des concepts, analyser des idées, exposer discursivement des doctrines. Elle est tout entière façonnée pour communiquer des attitudes sentimentales, pour suggérer des conduites, pour convaincre, pour convertir.* Therefore, classical Chinese legal reasoning can be understood solely within the pragmatic dimension (May 1980: 196). This means that it makes sense to analyze it towards the background of argumentation which aims at directing behavior and regulating action. It would not be particularly fruitful, however, to engage in complex conceptual analyses of legal and semi-legal, i.e. ethical terms, where they not have been perceived as crucial. Moreover, attention should be paid to *topoi* used in such texts (May ibid.). This reasoning has also another pragmatic connotation in that it tends to avoid the idea of subjective rights which presupposes an antagonistic conception of law (May 1980: 05). The Occidentalization of China, of its legal language and of its legal culture, has also introduced changes at this point. Nowadays, Chinese legal treatises are being developed in narrow contact with the Western legal tradition (cf. Zhang 2002). Their authors follow generally the methods known there and apply doctrinal, especially conceptual analytic legal reasoning in their works. This reasoning includes the subjective rights with all their consequences. Today, the countries of East Asia all joined the family of the Western European law and even the classics of the ancient Roman law had been translated into Chinese. Not many traditional East Asian elements remain in the laws of that region. However, the legislation is only one element of the legal culture (Munday 1983: 191). The legislation must be applied and when applied it must be justified. This holds true also for the Far East. One can assume, as research into these topics is unknown (at least to us) that some specific argumentation would be discernible even today in the written legal texts of the Far East, for instance in Japanese (cf. Notes and Materials nr. 27), Chinese, Korean or Vietnamese court decisions. Sometimes, however, this type of argumentation may be less visible because it developed, in the East and in the West, along the lines of the same logic and it is based here and there on identical dialectic distinctions which are, however, termed differently in both argumentative traditions. Any pragmatic organization of texts is subject to cross-linguistic variation (Levinson 1983: xi), therefore the assumption of similarities but also of differences is theoretically well founded. Interestingly, Krasilnikova (2006: 178) argues in her research that argumentation can differ as to the type of arguments used even between close cultures and related languages such as Polish and Russian. The same may be true for argumentation in the Far East.

3.3.2 Are legal arguments sophisms?

While attempting to use arguments we have first of all to determine the field in which we can safely move, i.e. who can bring arguments and what sort of arguments can be used. The answer of dominant legal cultures to both of these questions has been different. Ancient Greece defined the quality of participants rather broadly and allowed arguments which left room for inventiveness and creation. Ancient Rome restricted with its scientific law the spectrum of possible arguments; it also limited the number of participants and clearly determined their status. The epistemological analysis of both ancient laws makes this distinction clear. The Romans were first to delimit which opinion could be duly pronounced in a court of law and which was inappropriate. This formalization of the procedure began with the setting up of formal - if not formalistic - procedural formulae and ended with the full-fledged institutionalized framework of reference, the *Corpus Iuris Civilis,* in which the players and their text were clearly defined. Between these two stages there is a wide field of argumentative and epistemological work performed by the Romans. Its reconstruction is the legal theory of both ancient laws. Occasionally, it had been claimed that the status of jurisprudence is limited to sophisms developed in the tradition of ancient Greek protagonists of this art. We know them as Socrates' adversaries in the Platonic dialogues. Here again, the conceptual field has to be clarified. We have to ask ourselves whether the alleged difference in epistemology and argumentation in these dialogues between the Sophists and the Socratic tradition prolonged by Plato and Aristotle until Kant really exists. One could equally argue that it is the product of a compilation between both schools scrupulously designed by Plato and further developed by Aristotle and successively repeated in the scholarly institutions. The other question is whether the procedure developed by the Greek sophists – when cleared from Plato's tarnishing attempts – was really that irrational and non-scientific as argued by many. As far as the development of argumentative techniques is concerned the Sophists' contribution had been increasingly acknowledged in the research (Plantin 1996: 5).

Those two fundamental questions may help reconstruct the epistemological background of modern law and clarify the importance of argumentation in it from the historically proven beginning of this institution. To reach this aim we favor the methode of epistemological interpretation based on the works by M. Foucault. The epistemological interpretation focuses on the process of emergence and structure of interpreted notions. It shows the conceptual background and the way they had been constructed and further developed in use. It therefore concerns the most fundamental process in which signification emerges in law. We will apply it later in the chapter dealing with the global law and its conceptual background (Part 5 of this book).

3.3.3 Argumentation in legal discourse

Legal arguments do not exist in a vacuum. They are interrelated as parts of a general discourse about law. The general legal discourse may be divided into discourses and counter-discourses along the linguistic and extra-linguistic interactions in which its participants engage. Interest towards the structure of the spoken type of discourse in law has long historical roots and reaches until the legendary Greek orators Corax and Tisias (Sloane 2001: 418) and their argumentative strategy of the litigation (Plantin 1996: 4). Later on, the interest shifted towards the analysis of written court decisions and their interpretation and the spoken legal arguments were less analyzed. Only recently spoken word in the legal context, especially in witness testimony, gained momentum in the research. The discourse type which interests the legal linguist most is one comprised in institutional boundaries (Plantin 1996: 8) because law is above all an institutional phenomenon. It consists of a series of organized and planned in advance argumentative utterances which aim at obtaining a specified goal within the audience towards which they are directed. Needless to stress that the free discourse about law which is not limited by professional and institutional argumentative boundaries has basically the same structure with the difference that the acceptability of the arguments used in it is not determined by a legal institution such as a court or a professional corporation of jurists. The discourse about law outside its institutional boundaries is definitely also interesting but it relates less to the main topic of our research and it can be easily analyzed in relative independence from the professional institutionalized discourse about law. The structure of the institutionalized legal discourse interests us more because this type of complex linguistic activity constitutes a challenge for the legal theory and the legal practice. From a theoretical perspective, the extra-institutional discourse about law as a free discourse relates mainly to issues concerning the acceptability of legal norms and reactions to court decisions among the broader public. Its analysis helps develop argumentative means for the legislative work and court decisions which would increase the level of their emotional and/or rational acceptability among the broader public. On the other hand, the institutional legal discourse aims at achieving acceptance within the professional audience with professional legal arguments which multiply its complexity. Also M. Atienza made clear in his early research into the legal argumentation that it is vain to expect one single form of it in the legal discourse. The understanding of what actually is legal argumentation depends upon the theoretical position taken towards the law (Atienza 1999: 37). Relevant arguments and valid argumentation are determined by the perspective upon the argumentation that can be based on legal normativism, legal realism or natural law. He furthermore stresses that the multiplicity of arguments that is engendered by this variety of approaches to law does not mean that the results of such argumentative discourses would be incompatible; he perceives them rather as complementary (Atienza 1999: 44). In our view this assumption is strengthend also by the structure of the legal discourse in which legal arguments of different paradigmatic origin usually intertwine. Sterile legal discourses, i.e. those based on one conception of law are rare both in litigations and in legislative debates. The Legal Linguistics of today concentrates upon the elements of the general legal discourse and rather presupposes than convincingly proves the existence of such a general linguistic structure which would roof over the singular and often also contradictory legal arguments. However, the principles of textual coherence which can be identified in whatever rational legal argument as well as their provable interrelation, without which the singular arguments would not make much sense, allow introducing a general concept of a linguistic entity such as the legal discourse into the Legal Linguistics. The characteristic feature of the argumentative language is its deliberative aspect, the way in which lawyers legitimize their decisions by reference to reasons for them. They aim at convincing the recipients and other readers about the fact that their decisions were correct - just or justified - and consequently also legal. The traditional theoretical question to ask at this point would be: could they not try to achieve their means with purely logical instruments? Could not these lawyers simply demonstrate that through induction and deduction results had been achieved in their decisions which guarantee that a rational legal decision had been taken? Such a procedure would ensure the logical character of the decision and convince through its logical character alone. Apparently this is not possible and in the parts of this study devoted to interpretive aspects of law we have appraised these problems. There, we have underlined the necessity to activate other than purely logical mechanisms in order to understand the process of application of laws or understanding contracts. Moreover, criticism towards the use of normative syllogism as a basis for the legal argumentation led to the rejection of this model (Jackson 1988: 239). According to the basic structure of the normative syllogism in all cases *p* consequences *q* ought to follow. The minor premise there is a categorization of the facts of the particular case being adjudicated: this is a case of *p*. The conclusion which should follow would be: *q* ought to be applied. Even if one would assume that it is a workable tool in some cases, the so-called hard cases definitely cannot be solved with the application of normative syllogisms alone. Jackson posits that the inter-discursiveness between the general rule and the particular case is the result of an intentional model of discourse. For him, a looser logical model of subsumption, a sort of "narrative comparison" would be more appropriate for legal argumentation (Jackson 1988: 242). Unsurprisingly, therefore, specific argumentation such as the legal one emerges when pure logical induction cannot help. This is especially the case when transformations in the language take place which enable propositions of different quality. When a relation $p \rightarrow q$ is not operational than pTq is worthwhile considering (Aarnio, Peczenik 1983: 14) When *p* is indicated as a reason for *q* and *p* does not logically follow from *q*, i.e. when deductively the relation $p \rightarrow q$ cannot be justified through an additional proposition then we have to deal with such a specific construction. The transformation which took place must therefore be justified (Aarnio, Peczenik 1983: 36) and this is for some authors the basis of the rational legal argumentation.

3.3.4 Procedural aspects of legal argumentation

Some authors prefer procedural aspects in argumentation while leaving material elements of argumentation to the participants of the argumentative discourse. For them, practical rationality is grounded in the discursive practice. Robert Alexy (1983) underlined the limitation of the legal argumentation through precedents and doctrine. He concentrated on the development of rules for the rational linguistic argumentation in law. He distinguished between procedural and universal rationality. These were grounded in two different sets of rules: those pertaining to the structure of arguments (e.g. lack of inconsistency) called also monological applications and others pertaining to the procedure of the discourse, e.g. every speaker can participate in the discourse. In his view, first of all the rules of rational linguistic argumentation known from the general discourse have to be accepted by the participants. They are: lack of contradictions, coherence, sincerity of arguments, readiness to apply concepts in changing contexts and speaking the same language (Aarnio, Peczenik 1988: 43). Other rules concerning participants are: everyone is able to speak and use all possible approaches, wishes and needs and present his own views, no one should be impeded to participate. However, the rules have to assure the reasonability of the discussion (Alexy 1983: 36). Arguments used are termed in the form of the burden of proof and expressed in the procedure by general maxims, e.g. *we have always done it this way* and particular arguments, e.g. *argumentum ad hominem*. The argumentation takes place towards the background of limitations to which legal discourse is exposed. Alexy reflected in his approach J. Habermas' general discourse theory (Habermas 1988) which he transposed upon legal discourses. While doing so, he also discovered the limitations of the legal discourse as compared with the general discourse that has been described by Habermas (1988) or Aarnio (1989). O. Weinberger opposed this model of rational argumentation arguing that the discourse cannot replace or guarantee truth in or correctness of a judicial decision. Other formal approaches like A. Aarnio's stress consensus, acceptability of results and interpretation through a specialized auditorium as formal requirements of convincing legal argumentation. Their aim is equally the rationality of decisions. The higher is the justified level of rationality the higher is the readiness to accept the result. The Wittgensteinian *life form* provides the basis for the acceptability of decisions. The life form is at the same time also the natural limitation for any rationality in the general and in the particular discourse (Aarnio, Peczenik 1983: 81). All these theories claim to be able to determine appropriate conditions for making of convincing and justified utterances about law.

3.3.4.1 Façade-argumentation: When a decision does not correspond with own heuristic or justification requirements, it is perceived as a *façade*-argumentation (Aarnio 1989: 25). Alf Ross (1966: 57; 183) aptly characterized this specific type of argumentation. An illustrative example of this type of argumentation is the court opinion Kinney Shoe Corp. v. Polan (939 F. 2d 209 (4th Cir. 1991)). The defendant Polan formed two corporations, let us call them A and B. He concluded a lease agreement for office premises on behalf of A that remained passive as he apparently run his business activities exclusively with B. When sued for unpaid rent he admitted the contractual duties of A, the assetless company. The landlord Kinney sued Polan personally claiming that the corporate veil that Polan created around himself as an owner of A corporation must be pierced. The court applied in this case the doctrine of piercing the corporate veil and found that Polan was personally liable for the debts of A. The test applied included: 1) the unity of interest requirement between the company and the owner and 2) the undercapitalization of the company. Both requirements are here clearly fulfilled. However, a problem remains. The landlord is a renowned and experienced company that did not pay any attention at the financial situation of A that existed only 'on paper' when the lease contract was signed. Did he merit protection under such circumstances? One might tend to the verdict that the landlord would have to assume the risk of unsolvability of a contract partner whom he carelessly accepted. The court decided differently. It admitted that the test used is in fact three-prong and not two-prong as initially indicated and that it additionally requires that the creditor must be unaware of the potential risk. Yet, it held restrictively that this requirement is only permissive and not mandatory and that it primarily concerns financial institutions and the like, e.g. insurance companies. The landlord, a nationwide shoe dealer did not belong to this group of creditors that must be particularly vigilant while entering into contracts. However, the impression remains that the court established Polan's liability mainly to sanction his apparent business plan and prevent him from keeping the profits engendered by B. This intention is however not mentioned in the decision, because it represents an extra-legal motivation. Occasionally, dissenting opinions reveal the strategy of the majority opinion as *façade*. Thus, in Atwater v. Lago Vista (532 U.S. 318 (2001); 195 F. 3d 242) the U.S. Supreme Court had to decide whether the Fourth Amendment of the U.S. Constitution forbids a warrantless arrest for a minor criminal offence. In the case the plaintiff, a lady who drove with her two small children has been stopped by a policeman and subsequently taken into custody for not having put her seatbelt on while driving. The U.S. Supreme Court rejected her complaint. Not unexpectedly, a dissenting opinion followed. In it, the four dissenting justices held that the Fourth Amendment guarantees the right to be free from *unreasonable searches and seizures*. They saw a contradiction between the holding of the majority that the arrest of Ms. Atwater under the circumstances of the case had been a *pointless indignity* but nevertheless constitutionally permissible. The dissenting judges referred to the language of the Fourth Amendment while establishing their argumentation: "*A full custodial arrest, such as the one to which Ms. Atwater was subjected, is the quintessential seizure…When a full custodial arrest is effected without a warrant, the plain language of the Fourth Amendment requires that the arrest be reasonable.*" Certainly, the issue of reasonability had not been taken by the majority for full value. Rather, formal and historical elements dominated its finding which ended in the contradiction challenged in the dissenting opinion. One can assume that the court intended to avoid problems for policemen who sometimes under unclear circumstances and in haste have to take decisions that lead to the arrestation of suspected persons. Again, these apparent motives are not spelled out in the majority decision. Furthermore, one could perceive as complementary to a *façade*-decision all judicial reasoning aiming at distinguishing undistinguishable cases and introducing counter-intuitive interpretations about the propositions of law into judgments. Reasons for this particular phenomenon can be manifold. One of them could be the pretence to discover new legal arguments and to gain respect in the professional community. The other could be characterological inclinations to prove to others that things are different than others assume them to be. Both are equally terrifying in law.

3.3.5 More and less sophisticated argumentation models in law

Legal argumentation is by its very nature a complex linguistic operation. Were it simple, no reasons for complicated and often even controversial court decisions would exist. The first theoretical problem of the argumentation in law is therefore how to structure it and how to structure the reflection about it on a professional level. Models for structuring the argumentation in law can themselves be more or less complex and a preference for one model among many is always difficult because it necessarily leads to the loss in our understanding of the phenomenon. In short, is the model of argumentation too simple, it does not provide any valuable insights into this complex and decisive linguistic operation in law. Is it too complex, it threatens to choke the arguments to death and it will not be reflected by lawyers in their work. To be useful in law, a model of legal argumentation must be sufficiently descriptive but it must also be based on material research which shows its application in law, both in the interpretation of statutes and in its use in the precedents. We will therefore concentrate here less on purely theoretical models of legal argumentation and their discussion in the legal theory when they are not based on material (i.e. also linguistic) application of their theoretical basis. Also M. Atienza (2006: 247-279) stresses the pragmatic aspects in the legal argumentation that are for him anchored in linguistic interaction (cf. also Atienza 1999: 44). In the context relevant here he insists upon the use of arguments as a linguistic activity (Atienza 1999: 40). The linguistic activity involves a bunch of utterances that lead to a conclusion as its final point; utterances have premises as points of departure and are linked with the conclusion by specific relations (Atienza ibid.). We have adopted here a very broad definition of argumentation which is for us the process of identifying of utterances and the requirements for their acceptability in speech acts. The arguments represented in speech acts may be of different nature and here too we are very tolerant and do not exclude any. Some would say that it is necessary to distinguish argumentation which must be based on reasonable grounds from simple quarrelling of the parties or statements based on emotions. We will not do it, mainly because in practice the distinction between reasonable and emotional arguments is blurred.

3.3.5.1 Argumentation in law can be very simple: The simplest model of an argumentative action would consist of a beginning, a main part, and an end. At the first glance, this model may seem simplistic. However, it explains a lot about argumentative communication. To begin with, a situation has to emerge in which argumentation is necessary. Our daily communication does not consist predominantly of argumentative acts because we simply do not need them in many routine situations. There, rather simple reference to facts and objects is sufficient because daily practice is grounded in internalized socio-linguistic procedures, like language games or discourses. In law, the argumentation comes up mainly when a disaccord emerges between at least two parties about a proposition of law. In such a situation, the parties may enter into a discourse about valid and void in the propositions of law. They may also not do so and prefer to use other methods of persuasion such as violence, threat with use of force etc. These means are extra-legal and are therefore not interesting here. When the parties enter into a discourse about the validity of a proposition of law they have to use arguments which count in law; i.e. legal arguments (Alexy 1983: 41). As a rule, they will also use many other types of arguments but the persuasive force of such arguments is rather low. Should they not be able to reach a conclusive result they will turn to a court of law for decision. There, the process which we boldly called main part of argumentation continues until it is terminated by a judicial decision which ends formally the disaccord between the parties about the validity of certain propositions in law. That the disaccord is formally terminated means that it ends in terms of law, even if one of the parties or both of them are still convinced about their own views that were not accepted by the court. When the court procedure allows an appeal the parties can choose this way and the main part of argumentation will recommence until it will find an end in a formally final judicial decision. Does this model still seem simplistic? One could answer yes and no. It is not simplistic at all because it shows the structurally fundamental stages in the use of argumentative speech which is for us decisive from the point of view of the pragmatic theory. It also shows the communicative prerequisites of argumentative speech acts; i.e. the situation of a disaccord or controversy without which no significant argumentation in law comes about. We will not treat here situations such as legal training or doctrinary comments where controversies may be assumed or constructed to enable a professional discourse about the validity of propositions about law for educational purposes. The simple model shows us not only the disaccord between the parties as an entry stage into the legal argumentation. It also makes plain that one party alone cannot simply abandon the discourse at whatever stage once it entered into it. Participation in the legal discourse can be imposed by the means of law; it is therefore a very specific institutionalized participation in the discourse. Finally, it rather proves the necessity of a disaccord in law for the emergence of the legal argumentation than the contrary. This notwithstanding, the descriptive model presented above is simplistic because it does not show how arguments are used in order to reach the final and binding decision. This part must be explored when the legal argumentation is perceived as a linguistic operation, i.e. as rooted in rules about language use. Furthermore, procedural aspects are only mentioned there and not characterized. It is said that the court will apply procedural rules when examining the propositions presented by the parties. However, it is not said how this procedure looks like and especially what is its status as a legal-linguistic procedure. This procedure, be it civil, penal or administrative, has been described by generations of jurists in innumerable volumes, but it has been described from the legal – and not from the legal-linguistic – point of view. A legal-linguistic theory must show what is linguistic in the procedures used when courts decide controversies about law. Controversies may also concern facts and they are also solved with linguistic means. Basically, the same legal procedures are applicable there, their legal-linguistic status may however differ (cf. MacCormick 1984: 53).

Another simple model, called by Plantin (1996: 22) *schéma argumentative minimal*, has been proposed to describe the essentials of the argumentative act. It refers to the model developed by S. Toulmin (1958) and consists of data input (FR *donnée)* and of the conclusion in the most simple case. This scheme is widened by an operation where the conclusion is characterized as drawn from the data input with the help of a warrant (FR *loi de passage)* in the more advanced form of the model (Plantin ib.). Here it becomes plain that in the argumentation not the lineal sequence of linguistic acts is decisive, but the linguistic operation which allows for the conclusion to be drawn from them. Therefore, the minimal models can provide some insight into the structure of argumentation. Simultaneously, they also show that it is necessary to shift attention from the sequence of argumentative utterances to linguistic processes or operations which make argumentation of them, i.e. provide conclusions apt at terminating a disaccord.

3.3.5.2 A more complicated model of legal argumentation: This model would include the analyses of procedures in which legal arguments are used. It would concentrate upon formal aspects such as procedural beginning, procedural main part and procedural termination of situations in which the validity of legal arguments is tested. It would include participative rules which determine, for instance, the burden of proof in evidence that is provided by the parties. In addition, it would examine the tests for the material validity of propositions in law. As a pragmatic model, it would also reflect upon the persuasive aspect of the final legal decision, i.e. whether it has convinced the parties and materially – not only formally – terminated the disaccord between them. The legal argumentation is also institutionalized in the sense that the participants have no choice of argumentative models. They do not need to agree on an argumentative model either. Most ordinary discourses are also based on specific rules, yet the parties may modify or abandon them. The named three particularities of arguments used in law may as indicated not be distinctive, i.e. limited in their application to law. They are, nevertheless, frequent in legal contexts and should therefore be taken into consideration while characterizing the legal argumentation.

3.3.5.3 Advanced models of legal argumentation: The advanced models of legal argumentation free themselves from situational boundaries upon which we initially relied, while developing the simple and the less simple descriptive models. They try to describe legal arguments and the argumentative discourse in terms of logical analysis. For general argumentation, Toulmin (1958: 100,106) showed the necessity of the already mentioned warrants, grounds and qualifiers in a model of argumentation. In the reading of this model by Plantin (1996: 23) such an argumentative discourse provides the justification of the proposition in question, and considers also its modality. Through the introduction of reserves and guaranties as basic concepts into the model Toulmin developed a scheme which can be used also for the analysis of legal argumentation. Different from this type of reasoning is the justification *sensu stricto*. It is perceived by many as an argumentative operation in which the decision taken within an institution is rationalized *post hoc*. This means that a decision may be taken irrationally or within the limits of daily rationality, and is afterwards reformulated in order to match up to the requirements of professional rationality and other constitutional and procedural standards. It will be mentioned later more specifically. Toulmin's model has been used in law for the analysis of statute interpretation by Dominicy (1993: 246-249). Dominicy also stressed that the speech act theory and especially the Austinian notion of illocutionary force play an important role in Toulmin's model (Dominicy 1993: 243). This has the advantage that an argumentative speech act in order to be identified and understood has to be perceived as an integral part of the context of the utterance. This procedure makes argumentation and the understanding of arguments much easier as it prevents the dissociations of notions (Perelman & Olbrechts-Tyteca 1983: 550-609) which has been perceived as one of the most significant challenges in the model of argumentation since it is used as a tool for manipulating arguments in the argumentative practice. Dominicy also applied strategies preventing the dissociations of notions in the interpretation of a statutory provision. In our reading, he came very close to the Dworkinian model of creative interpretation applied in so-called hard cases.

Furthermore, the legal argumentation has some particular features which make it interesting for pragmatics. Yet, these characteristic features do not make it necessarily distinctive. For instance, the specific reasoning with the omission of a precise *premissa major* is typical for the judicial decisions. In Jones v. Free Flight Sport Aviation, Inc. (623 P.2d 370, 1981 Colo. Lexis 571) the Supreme Court of Colorado had to deal with the time period within which a minor who became major had to disaffirm a voidable contract made during his minority. In the case, the minor who signed a contract for the use of recreational sky-diving facilities that included a covenant not to sue and an exculpatory clause, has been injured during a flight, ten months after his 18th birthday. The court decided that the plaintiff had ratified the contract made during his minority through accepting its benefits during his majority and could not disaffirm it after the time period of ten months. The court did not determine what is the reasonable time for the disaffirmation of voidable contracts for minors becoming majors. Instead, it posited that the disaffirmation must take place *within a reasonable time*. This implies that the time period of ten months was not *reasonable* in the opinion of the court. However, no rigorous logical reasoning is possible in this case because a clearly stated *premissa major* is missing. Nevertheless, the minimal consistency requirements for a rational decision are fulfilled and the decision as such is understandable for jurists as well as for laypersons. It follows reasoning patterns in the ordinary language, and, although it is doubtful from the point of view of the formal logic, it is neither inconsistent nor is it irrational.

3.4 Argumentation in the Legal Practice

Argumentation in the legal practice raised unusual interest in the 20th century, and began even to dominate the debate about the nature of law. The argumentative approach to law began successively to replace the century old legal paradigm of law as a system based on concepts. It is therefore useful to ask whether the shift of attention from the legal system based on concepts to the legal argumentation in law is a real change in the paradigm of legal research and a result of a possible contradiction of approaches, or only a new layer added to the traditional systematic (doctrinal) legal reasoning. Answers to this question, both practical as well as theoretical are complex. It is not debatable that in critical modern societies the necessity to understand, i.e. being able to follow the reasoning in a legal decision or a statute became more important than in previous forms of society based on the affirmation of the ruling social groups and their decisions (Mattila 2008: 1151). This goal also dominates the debate about law which concerns more and more broader spheres of the public and is no more limited to a group of legal experts discussing some abstract questions of systematic coherence in law. It is therefore understandable that the attention turned towards points identified as central for the understanding of law which regard mostly the way how lawyers used to speak and write. Therefore, nowadays, a judicial decision is rarely accepted on the reason alone that it had been rendered by the competent authority.

3.4.1 Argumentation in U.S. court decisions

In order to understand the prerequisites of the legal argumentation theory, material analysis is necessary. In the following paragraphs we will therefore deal with some selected U.S. court opinions. They will be scrutinized in thematic blocks because the factual interdependence among them may illustrate or even reveal some argumentative interdependence. Such a scrutiny has to start with the question of how courts react to interpretive differences and how they reflect upon problems of argumentation in their opinions. It also includes the vision of non-judges, e.g. attorneys-at-law and laypersons on the way in which institutions act in argumentative situations. It makes plain the results of these institutional reflections, i.e. mostly the established procedures for dealing with argumentative problems, the lexicalization based on such procedures in the material argumentative structures, nature of arguments used and remedies that improve the quality of argumentation, and the rationality of the decisions taken. The essence of all such effort is the developing of tests in which arguments are used in order to prove the validity of a proposition of law. They are not easy to formalize which will be shown on the following examples.

3.4.1.1 Constitutional issues: Legal argumentation in constitutional matters may be perceived as very advanced because in the rare cases in which the U. S. Supreme Court accepts to hear a case considerable efforts on all sides are undertaken to make the best of the arguments used. Still, these efforts also have limits. For instance, in 1996, the U.S. Congress enacted the Child Pornography Prevention Act (CPPA). Section 2256 (8) (B) of the act prohibits "*any visual depiction, including any photograph, film, video, picture, or computer-generated image or picture*" that "*is, or appears to be, of a minor engaging in sexually explicit conduct.*" The section has been generally understood to include also computer-generated images known as virtual child pornography. The U.S. Supreme Court had to deal with the question whether Section 2256 (8) (B) violates the Free Speech Clause of the First Amendment of the U.S. Constitution in that it criminalizes the virtual child pornography. In its decision Ashcroft, Attorney General v. The Free Speech Coalition (2002 U.S. Lexis 2789 2002) the court scrutinized the rationale provided by the Attorney General who supported the regulation. Its first argument had been that virtual child pornography encourages the paedophiles to engage in illegal conduct. This rationale did not convince the court as it would lead to the control of thought. The court stated that "*the government may not prohibit speech because it increases the chance an unlawful act will be committed at some indefinite future time.*" The second argument provided by the Attorney General to support the regulation had been that even experts have problems to distinguish the virtual child pornography from the imaging which uses real children due to high technological standards of computer imaging, and that it therefore must be forbidden like real child pornography. This argument did not convince the court either. The court stated: "*The argument, in essence, is that protected speech may be banned as a means to ban unprotected speech. This analysis turns the First Amendment upside down. The Government may not suppress lawful speech as the means to suppress unlawful speech.*" The court limited its scrutiny to the arguments provided by the government. The arguments were rather weak and not difficult to turn down. It remains the impression that something like a third argument was missing which would make the regulation more plausible. In general, controversies about the linguistic meaning of statutes and precedents manifest themselves in constitutional law as matters relating to the constitutionality of legal provisions. In order to overcome these controversies about the propositions of constitutional law *tests* of constitutionality had been established (Tribe 2000: 6 sqq). These tests apply *doctrines*, e.g. the doctrine of substantial overbreath or the doctrine of vagueness when dealing with the semantic intricacies in the propositions expressing the content of law. U.S. Supreme Court opinions deal with these doctrines especially in cases concerning the First Amendment of the U.S. constitution that guarantees the freedom of speech. In Broadrick v. Oklahoma (1973), Board of Airport Commissoners v. Jews for Jesus (1987) and Virginia v. Hicks (2003) the court developed and specified the doctrine of substantial overbreath. The U.S. Supreme Court distinguished within its constitutionality test *protected* and *unprotected speech* under the First Amendment. The unprotected speech that may be totally forbidden by the Government comprises: dangerous speech, provocative speech (Chaplinski v. New Hampshire 315 U.S. 568, 62 S.Ct. 766, 1942 U.S. Lexis 851), speech inciting to violent overthrow of the government (Brandenburg v. Ohio 395 U.S. 444, 89 S. Ct. 1827, 1969 U.S. Lexis 1367), defamatory language (Beauharnais v. Illinois 343 U.S. 250, 72 S.Ct. 725, 1952 U.S. Lexis 2799), child pornography (New York v. Ferber 458 U.S. 747, 102 S. Ct. 3348, 1982 U.S. Lexis 12), obscene speech (Miller v. California, Jacobellis v. Ohio 378 U.S. 184, 84 S.Ct. 1676, 1964 U.S. Lexis 822). Hence, the developed test distinguishes between different types of speech, and provides a first help for dealing with such cases. The overall argumentation in such cases remains however still complex and less transparent. Therefore, more sophisticated tests were developed in other cases. For instance, in equal protection cases two major standards are used for the review of their constitutionality. The 'strict scrutiny' which allows differential treatment only if 1) drawn as narrowly as possible, and 2) necessary to achieve a compelling governmental interest. This standard is used in cases involving adverse impact on racial, religious, and national minorities. The 'rationality basis' deems differential treatment constitutional when it is reasonable and related to a permissible governmental goal. It is used in cases involving business regulation or 'nonsuspect' classes. Finally, we can retain at this stage that social values underlie all such controversial decisions. This holds true also for cases that may appear as rather technical. For instance, Art. 1 § 8 of the U.S. Constitution defines the legislative competence of the Congress. As a rule, matters that are not delegated to the Congress remain within the competence of the federal state as reiterated in Amendment X. In particular, two general clauses in sec. 8 of Art. 1 gained predominant importance in determining the scope of the Congressional competence, the *interstate commerce clause* and the *necessary and proper clause*. However, as nowadays almost all daily events are linked to interstate relations, and are at least slightly related to economic activities the semantic boundaries of both clauses have become increasingly flawed. Here one should, of course, keep in mind that both clauses had been drafted in a general manner which from the very beginning deliberately left a considerable margin for interpretive appreciation. This is understandable, because we already mentioned that values play in such decisions a preponderant role. That said, the U.S. Supreme Court in 2000 rejected the view that the U.S. Congress be authorized to regulate gender-motivated violence under the commercial clause qualifying the relation to interstate commerce as too tenuous (U.S. v. Morrison, 529 U.S. 598, 120 S.Ct. 170, 146 L. Ed. 2d 658 (2000)). The power of the Congress to regulate interstate commerce has been traditionally perceived as an issue involving advanced argumentation. Congress has passed statutes that bar discrimination and regulate business activities which are very limited in scope and which are clearly of local character. In almost all cases the courts have upheld this legislation under the affectation doctrine which states that as long as an activity which is regulated by the Congress affects interstate commerce, it is within Congressional regulatory authority. The term *affects* is quite broadly interpreted by the courts. Even if in a situation where the business is explicitly local like a small restaurant in which out-of-state purchases are minimal a federal ban of racial discrimination has been successfully imposed by the Congress due to the affectation doctrine. The provision of the Civil Rights Act (42 U.S.C. § 2000 a et sq.) which was quoted in U.S. v. Morrison had dealt with the abolition of racial discrimination, and was not based on the equal protection clause of Amendment XIV. Presumably, the legislator reflected upon the interpretation of this clause in Plessy v. Fergusson and later in Brown (1965) concerning the doctrine of 'separate but equal' (cf. Notes and Materials nr. 28 and nr. 29). The Supreme Court provided in Brown a 15 years period for the implementation of the guaranteed rights. Previously, the clause has been used to justify federal legislation aiming at the abolition of racial discrimination and established the right of black citizens to occupy the same type of seats in busses in interstate traffic as white citizens. Both decisions may not be particularly pervasive in terms of argumentation, esp. the Brown-decision is perceived sometimes as wanting (Tribe 2000: 3). This becomes evident when the majority decision in Brown is compared with the dissenting opinion. They reveal however the argumentative procedure in which the Constitution and its values are tied together.

3.4.1.2 Criminal matters: Convictions about the being of the world underlie decisions as do ethical values. In the People v. Ralph J. Tortorici (92 N.Y. 2d 757, 709 N.E. 2d 87, 686 N.Y.S. 2d 346 (1999)) the New York Court of Appeals rejected the appeal by a defendant who waived his right to participate in the trial of his case. According to Art. 730 of the Criminal Procedure Law the criminal trial of a defendant *"who as a result of mental disease or defect lacks capacity to understand the proceedings against him or to assist in his own defense"* must be prevented. In the trial the defendant clearly expressed his wish not to participate, and added a remark about alleged implants of chips in his brain undertaken by the Government in order to spy out his most intimate thoughts. Psychiatrists held the defendant therefore for mentally ill. The court, however, after having ordered to x-ray the defendant held him for sane as far as his allegations concerned the right to participation in his trial and affirmed the initial order in this case. It differentiated between the defendant's both allegations as if they were disconnected. Overall, problems associated with the insanity defense in the American penal law led to the formulation of necessary standards of proof which seem to invoke the evident fact of insanity. Thus, the federal criminal legislation provides for *clear and convincing evidence* which must be proven by the defendant (cf. 18 U.S.C.A. § 17 (16)). Some U.S. states require a proof *by a preponderance of evidence*, while others shift the burden of proof *beyond the reasonable doubt*. These formulations cover an ongoing debate about the necessary degree of proof in the American criminal law and signalize rather the contrary of what the existing standards seem to invoke; i.e. the certainty about the mental state of a person. Cases such as Tortorici make plain the necessity to improve the evaluation of argumentative standards in criminal cases. Moreover, criminal cases such as the above one or many *hate speech* cases show better than others the interrelation of professional and laypersons discours in law. Professional interpretive standards seem to be better adapted to professional discourse within which they function. Communicative frictions emerge at the contact point of both. An argumentation that does not reflect professional standards usually fails. Laypersons speech is paradoxically not understood properly because it does not fit into a discursive structure established for processing it. In such cases, the risk of language reification is eminent.

3.4.1.3 Business Law: Business law cases may be perceived as less spectacular and the argumentation in them may seem rather formalistic because of their routine nature and limited efforts that are invested into their solution by courts and other participating lawyers. Nonetheless, they reveal important characteristic features of the legal argumentation.

In Rollerblade Inc. v. U.S. (282 F. 3d 1349 (Fed. Cir. 2002)) the classification of roller skating protective gear under Harmonized Tariffs Schedules (HTSUS) became an issue for litigation because the different classification of goods under the HTSUS led to the application of different duty rates on the imports (cf. Notes and Materials nr. 33). Rollerblade Inc. had brought to U.S. roller skating protective gear which it classified under the HTSUS as *accessory* to roller skaters. This classification would lead to freedom of custom duties on these imports. In turn, the U.S. Custom Services classified the goods as *other sport equipment* which carries a duty rate of 4% ad valorem. Rollerblade Inc. perceived its roller skating protective gear as *accessory* because they were manufactured and marketed solely for the use with in-line roller skates. Moreover, Rollerblade Inc. argued that the gear is part of the roller skates because it contributes to the safe and effective operation of the skates and is designed solely with them. Under the HTSUS when a good is subject to more than one section or heading number the General Rule of Interpretation should be applied to determine the appropriate classification number. The primary rule is the rule of specificity, the rule providing the more specific characterization of the product should be applied. Is there no specific rule or is more than one rule specific then the essential character of the goods is used as criterion for the characterization whereby their function, materials or components should be reflected upon. Terms used in HTSUS should be given a common and popular meaning unless the commercial meaning was clearly intended. HTSUS do not define *accessory*. Undefined terms in the HTSUS should in such cases be given their "*common, popular meaning as set forth in dictionaries, scientific authorities and other reliable information sources.*" The court held in this case that accessories and parts must have a direct relationship to the primary article, rather than to the general activity (in casu skating) in which the primary article is used. It perceived the gear as related to the activity of skating and not to the primary article as such. Rollerblade Inc. lost its case.

What procedure has been adopted by the court to reach its result? The court did not set up any specific definitions of *accessory* and of *part*. Instead, it adopted a particular approach to the goods in question by introducing a notion of a *primary article*. Subsequently, it stated that the relation of *accessory* to the *primary article* must be direct which means for the court that it concerns the primary article and not its use. The court did not follow dictionary definitions of *accessory*. At Longman's dictionary it would read under *accessory*: something which is not a necessary part of something larger but which makes it more beautiful, useful, effective etc a black dress with matching accessories (e.g. hat, shoes). At Oxford's it could read: a thing which can be added to something else in order to make it more useful, versatile, or attractive. As can be seen from the above definitions, the lexical analysis alone cannot lead to the interpretation adopted by the court. The application of the lexicological definitions on this case leads to the result that protective gear could be perceived as *accessory* in the English language usage or could not be perceived as such with equally good reasons. The only interpretive method which can be of use in such a situation is the creative interpretation. The creative interpretation cannot function in a vacuum. A specific interpretive strategy was necessary to make the decision in this case. It was based on public interest in the interpretation of the HTSUS. In controversial cases, taxation should prevail over a possible no-tax result because this solution is more beneficial to the public interest, at least from the governmental point of view. The interpretive strategy adopted by the court is to defer to the Custom's definition. It does not take one by surprise, as the public policy rule applied in such controversial cases is as follows: rather tax than let enter tax free. Rollerblade's interpretive strategy is of course contrary to it, on reasons well understandable. Overall, our pragmatic approach to language pays here once again because it shows that we rather should speak about linguistic aspects of law than about legal language. In this case it would be difficult to draw the line between the legal and the non-legal definition of *accessory*. In contrast with the general lexicological definition the interpretation undertaken by the court is rather a pragmatic approach in this situation than a binding legal definition of *accessory*. To put it short, words may under specific circumstances have a specific meaning in law; in others they may not have it.

Analogous interpretive strategies became apparent in U.S. v. Haggar Apparel Company (526 US 380 (1999)), rendered here in Notes and Materials nr. 32. There, the appeal court defers to the interpretive guidelines to HTSUS set up by the Customs Service and perceives these regulations as binding for the otherwise independent court. The court says: *"Deference to any agency's expertise in construing a statutory command is not inconsistent with reaching the correct decision. If the agency's statutory interpretation fills a gap or defines a term in a way that is reasonable in the light of the legislator's revealed design, we give that judgement controlling weight."* In this case the parties conflicted over customs classification of reimported garments which were permapressed in Mexico. Permapressing is a procedure which involves oven-baking that causes chemical changes in the fabric and is designed to maintain a garment's crease and avoid wrinkles. Re-importing of goods assembled abroad is custom free according to HTSUS. Sec. 9802 HTSUS allows importers to deduct the value of assembly from duty assessment. The exemption is given for "*articles assembled abroad in whole or in part of fabricated components that are products of the US.*" It also extends to any advancement or improvement of goods which are result of "*operations incidental to the assembly process.*" Haggar claimed that permapressing which goes beyond pure assembling is *an operation incidental to the assembly process* and as such duty free. Customs Service contended in turn that permapressing is an additional operation which reaches beyond *assembly* and, which because of this, involves custom duties. It referred to own regulation which a.o. says: *"The following are examples of operations not incidental to assembly: Chemical treatment of components or assembled articles to impart new characteristics such as...permapressing"*. Haggar claimed that the court is not bound by this regulation as it is charged "to reach the correct decision" in determining the proper classification of goods. Haggar Co. lost its case because the court deferred to the view of the specialized agency.

Likewise, in Samsonite Corp. v. U.S. (889 F.2d 1074 Fed. Cir. (1989)) the parties conflicted over sec. 9802 HTSUS relating to re-imported metal strips which were exported in straight form and re-imported as bent and incorporated into travel bag frames. To obtain the mentioned tax deduction the good assembled abroad must according to the HTSUS: 1) be exported from the U.S. in a condition ready for assembly without further fabrication, 2) not have lost their physical identity by change of form, shape etc, 3) not have been changed except by *being assembled*, and 4) *except by operations being incidental to the assembly process such as cleaning, lubricating and painting*. The court held that the strips were not exported in condition ready for *assembly* and that the bending process to which the strips were subjected did more than adjust the article. The essence of the process has been the configuration, without the resultant shape it would not be possible to insert the frames into the bottom of the luggage. Thus, in the view of the court the process which the strips underwent constituted fabrication and not mere *assembly*. Here again, language use in the legal context is controlled by the text of the provision which provides examples for *operations incidental to assembly* in the interpretive guidelines. The distinction between *fabrication* and *assembly* is nevertheless made by the court due to its institutional privilege. The court did not provide any examples for assembly which would approach fabrication. Yet, exactly this would be a persuasive test for determining the appropriate language use. Such a reaction signalizes that the court was rather making use of its interpretive privilege than interpreting the provision in its linguistic and legal context. Procedural strategies are set up to control the ordinary language use and no reference is made in them to the subject matter. Language use is institutionalized in them and a state agency is given authority to determine whether e.g. permapressing is in fact an operation *incidental to the assembly process*. The court stated that if "*the agency provides a reasonable interpretation and implementation of unambiguous statutory provision, it must be given judicial deference.*"

By contrast, in Lamb-Weston, Inc. v. McCain Foods, Ltd. (78 F.3rd 540 (1996)) the United States Court of Appeals for the Federal Circuit had to decide a patent case and particularly determine whether a patent delivered by the Patent Board to the plaintiff had been properly provided for an invention which must be novel, useful, and non-obvious to be patented. The question whether the patent provided for plaintiff's process of making frozen, partially fried, lattice-shaped french fries concerned a non-obvious invention was controversial between the parties - competitors on the market. The court decided for the obviousness of the invention previously patented by the Patent Board and affirmed the decision of the court of appeals which had been challenged by the plaintiff. The court ruled that the process of making waffle fries was too obvious to be patentable. It held: "*The ultimate determination of obviousness is a legal conclusion, resting on factual determinations. ...The evidence of prior use and sale of waffle fries and parfried potato products provides sufficient motivation to combine the known waffle-cut shape and the parfry cooking method. This combination renders the '084 patent obvious.*" Unlike in the previous decisions concerning the customs regulations, the court did not defer to the view of the specialized state agency, in casu the Patent Board. Instead, it decided the question of the obviousness of the patented invention in own responsibility and according to its own knowledge. The argument used in the previous cases of a better professional knowledge about the subject matter in specialized state agencies was not used here. Still further, in J.E.M. Ag Supply, Inc., v. Pioneer Hi-Bred International, Inc. (534 U.S. 124, 122 S.Ct. 593, 2001 U.S Lexis 10949 2001) the U.S. Supreme Court dealt with the question whether sexually reproducing hybrid plants are a patentable subject matter. The court answered this question affirmatively. In its decision it expressly referred to the practice of the specialized state agency in this matter, the Patent and Trade Office (PTO). It held that "*It has been the unbroken practice of the PTO since that time to confer utility patents for plants. To obtain utility patent protection, a plant breeder must show that the plant he has developed is new, useful and non-obvious.* " Here, the court not only used but also deferred to the view and practice of the specialized state agency. Generally, in the U.S. law an administrative agency is afforded judicial deference when it interprets the statutes that enable it to act (cf. CNG Transmission Corp. v. New York State Public Service Comm'n A.D. 2d 671, 585 N.Y.S. 2d 916). This is especially the case in situations where specialized knowledge is involved (Dworman v. New York State Division of Housing, 94 N.Y. 2d 359, 70 N.Y.S. 2d 192 (1999)). Courts are usually deferential to administrative agencies in cases where the interpretation is based on *knowledge and understanding of underlying operational practices or entails an evaluation of...data and inferences to be drawn there from* (New York Telephone Company v. PSC 95 N.Y. 2d. 40, 710 N.Y.S. 2d 305 (2000)). However, this deference is by no means absolute (National Merchandising Corp. v. New York Public Service Comm'n, 5 N.Y. 2d 485, 186 N.Y. s. 2d 47 (1959) and Consolidated Edison Co. of New York, Inc. v. New York Public Service Comm'n, 417 N.Y.S. 2d 30 (1979)). Thus, balancing between deference to the knowledge of the administrative agency and the relative nature of this interpretive rule is needed. However, a rule stating general deference which nevertheless should not be perceived in absolute terms does not help. Striking the right balance is again a question of creative interpretation. Apparently, legal arguments are of a volatile nature; they do not change their structure, but are largely undetermined as to their contexts of application. In a specific context the same argument appears almost by tradition while in some cases positioned in the same or at least analogous context the expected argument is missing. This is the lesson learned from above cases.

Legal argumentation reaches beyond technicalities of the concept-oriented legal sciences. Legal and purely imaginary language may also cross in the court argumentation. Descriptive language which refers to facts is contrasted with interpretive language which refers to statutes or rules developed from precedents. In Two Pesos, Inc. v. Taco Cabana, Inc. (505 U.S. 763, 112 S.Ct. 2753, 1992 U.S. Lexis 4533) the court had to decide whether a trade dress had been distinctive and thus protected under the Lanham Act. This would be definitely the case had the trade dress in question acquired *secondary meaning*. The court had to ask whether the trade dress in casu had been so distinctive that it could have acquired protection even without the proof of secondary meaning. Finally, the court affirmed this view stating that: "*We see no basis for requiring secondary meaning for inherently distinctive trade dress protection. Adding a secondary meaning requirement could have anticompetitive effects, creating particular burdens on the start-up of small companies.*" Rule interpretation is here dominated by the non-linguistic imaginary which the court has acquired from witness and photographic testimony during the litigation. The description of the necessary grade of distinctiveness yields the way to the imaginary impression which is decisive and which underlies the language used in the justification of the result. The two areas of linguistic argumentation based on imaginary, non-linguistic impressions may, however, be transformed into a purely linguistic argumentation. In Ty, Inc. v. GMA Accessories, Inc. (132 F. 3d 1167 (1997)) the judge had to compare two toys, small stuffed pigs, to determine whether one was a copy of another. The court held its observations in the decision which affirmed the copyright infringement claim: "*The two pigs are so nearly identical that if the second is a copy of the first, the second clearly infringes Ty's copyright. But identity is not infringement. The Copyright Act forbids only copying; if independent creation results in an identical work, the creator of that work is free to sell it...But identity can be a powerful evidence of copying. The more a work is both like an already copyrighted work and - for this is equally important - unlike anything that is in the public domain, the less likely it is to be an independent creation...GMA's pig is strikingly similar to Ty's pig but not to anything in the public domain- a real pig for example...Preston resembles only Squealer, and resembles him so closely as to warrant an inference that GMA copied Squealer.*" The language used in the decision lexicalizes the impression which the court acquired by viewing the two stuffed pigs. There is no reference to the objectively invisible realm of imaginary but a clear description of intertwingled visual impression within the interpretive language. The lexicalization of the visualized material clearly increases the persuasiveness of the decision. Unlike in Two Pesos v. Taco Cabana, this sort of language warrants the justification test in that in makes the decision plausible in its entirety. It does not force the reader to imagine what sort of visual evidence must have been presented to the court to achieve the imaginary impression that underlies the decision. The higher is the degree of lexicalization in a decision, the higher is also the effectiveness of the rationality test in it. As a result, the increased level of acceptability is reached by the improved quality of argumentation. The pig case was decided in the U.S. Court of Appeals for the Seven Circuit by Chief Justice R. Posner.

Legal argumentation which stresses emotions increases the interest towards the case. In Barnett v. Merck & Co., Inc. (MDL no. 1657) the judge of the U.S. District Court of Louisiana criticized in one of the so-called Vioxx cases the jury verdict awarding the plaintiff USD 50 million compensatory damages as *"excessive under any conceivable substantive standard of excessiveness...No reasonable jury could have found that the plaintiff was entitled to USD 50 million in compensatory damages."* The judge ordered upon the motion for judgment notwithstanding the verdict that a new trial should take place. In casu, the plaintiff suffered a heart attack after being treated with a drug manufactured by the defendant. Evidence was presented in the case showing both the causal relation between the product and the heart attack and defendant's liability for the product. The formulation criticizing the amount awarded by the jury became famous through the media which quoted it regularly while reporting this case in 2006. However, the public interest which increased due to the emotional formulation chosen by the judge does not necessarily increase the effectiveness of the rationality test. The judgment would have been more persuasive if the judge would have explained the reasons why he deemed the amount in question as outrageous towards the background of other jury verdicts in U.S. in cases concerning product liability. The judge reflected in the case only upon the relation between the illness suffered by the plaintiff and the amount of compensatory damages. The judge did not criticize the jury verdict concerning the punitive damages, although this part might be perceived as problematic. Therefore, an argumentative gap is perceptible between the judge's opinion that the jury has issued the right verdict concerning all matters of law and especially the three theories of product liability which were central for the legal debate in this case. At the same time, the judge referred to precedents in South Carolina according to which a damage award is grossly excessive if it appears *"to be the result of passion, caprice, prejudice, or some other influence outside the evidence."* The role of the judge would be to show that the jury acted upon influence of at least one of the named motives. Unsurprisingly, in this case he limited himself to quote the amount awarded which should apparently speak for itself. However, the impressive amounts of money which attract magnetically the attention of readers are per se not a proof of unreasonable jury verdicts. The lexicalization of the essential problem in this case did not take place. Therefore, the decision taken by the judge is not particularly convincing. All in all, the emotional argument seems rather to draw attention to the case than to pave the way to the appropriate solution of that case.

3.4.2 Argumentation in concurring and dissenting opinions

In some jurisdictions, and especially in the common law, concurring and dissenting opinions make part of the legal tradition. Their very existence proves the argumentative nature of law; i.e. its dependence upon argumentation. Their role in the legal science and in the Legal Linguistics is different because they are not perceived as sources of law. For the legal linguist, however, they are perfect sources of the legal language. We will illustrate their usefulness on few examples:

In State of Spain v. Treasury Solicitor (All LR 1953 vol.2 p. 1579) the House of Lords dealt with the question of characterization in a case concerning the conflict of laws. The State of Spain applied for the letter of administration to intestate succession of a Spanish citizen deceased in England while the English Crown claimed the estate for itself perceiving it as bona vacantia. The legal question grounded in a problem from what legal point of view, i.e the one of the Spanish or the English substantive law the characterization of the claim to intestate succession should be undertaken in cases where there is no other heir but the State. The House of Lords opted for the law of citizenship of the decedent. The Master of the Rolls, Sir Raymond Evershed, held that "*If by the law of Spain it is possible to limit or to define the individuals who can claim to be successors, that is, individuals having some connection by blood or marriage with the deceased, I can see no reason why the law of Spain should not nominate or constitute as heir, in default of such individual, any person or corporation, including the State itself... There is before us no evidence of what the law of Spain would be in the converse case of an English national dying domiciled in England intestate without next of kin under the English law and leaving movables in Spain. I am, however, not able to reject the argument of counsel for the State of Spain on the ground that this question has not been subject of any direct decision but the distinction might not be reciprocal in Spain. I think the appeal fails and must be dismissed.*" In the concurring opinion the second judge stated: *Accordingly, for the reasons stated by Sir Raymond Evershed, M.R., and for such additional reasons that I have been able to offer, I agree that this appeal fails and should be dismissed.*" The third judge continued in his concurring opinion: "*It is, I think, well settled that where a person dies domiciled in a foreign country our courts will follow and apply the law of that country when dealing with the succession...The substance of the matter, as it seems to me, is that by the law to which reference is made, the property in England is not left ownerless, but is to pass to an heir, that heir being the State of Spain. I think that this appeal fails.*" The preceding case belongs to the group of leading English cases in the area of conflict of laws. The House of Lords has taken in it a sound position which can be easily justified. However, the mere fact that the three judges who decided the case delivered three different justifications impedes upon the readability of the decision and limits its persuasiveness. It would look differently when the arguments would be collected in a synthesized opinion. Such a decision would be easier to test under the requirements of rationality. Otherwise, one could have the impression that the judges who agree in principle follow different conceptions of legal rationality. At this point, this decision is particularly interesting because it shows that different arguments, sometimes even arguments grounded in different conceptions of legal rationality, can be successfully integrated in one legal decision as long as no disagreement about the result comes up.

In Grupo Mexicano de Desarrollo S.A. v. Alliance Bond Fund, Inc. (No. 98-231: 1999) the U.S. Supreme Court had to decide whether a preliminary injunction preventing the transfer of assets situated abroad can be obtained under federal law. The court denied this question. Its main argument has been that preliminary injunctions in federal law are possible under the limits set by the Judiciary Act of 1789 and that they must be based on equity measures acknowledged at that time. The court argued that no preliminary injunctions in equity were in use in the common law of England by 1789 and therefore cannot be issued today by U.S. federal courts. It referred furthermore to the English Mareva-injunction established around 1975 as an additional proof for the absence of such an equitable remedy before that date in the common law. In the dissenting opinion this view which may be qualified for mechanical jurisprudence has been challenged. It may be, so the dissenting judges, that the English common law before 1789 did not know and did not consider any equitable remedies like the preliminary injunction to freeze assets abroad. Yet, it included principles enabling the issuance of such an injunction which is proven by the subsequent development leading to the issuance of the Mareva-injunction. Here, the rule in the interpretation is not the mechanical one. It is constructive and is based on the aim to find the best interpretation which would fit the situation we have to deal with today.

Textually, the dissenting opinions include usually the final formula of the dissenting judge *I respectfully dissent,* sometimes *respectfully* is ambiguously omitted, e.g. *I dissent* in the dissenting opinion by Sanders, J. in M.A. Mortenson Company, Inc. v. Timberline Software (2000 Wash. LEXIS 287). Sometimes the dissent remains ambigously respectful while simultaneously providing reasons for professional disrespect, as in J. Breyer's dissenting opinion in Medellín v. Texas (552 U.S. 06-984 (2008)): *In sum, a strong line of precedent, likely reflecting the views of the Founders, indicates that the treaty provisions before us and the judgment of the International Court of Justice address themselves to the Judicial Branch and consequently are self-executing. In reaching a contrary conclusion, the Court has failed to take proper account of that precedent and, as a result, the Nation may well break its word even though the President seeks to live up to that word and Congress has done nothing to suggest the contrary. For the reasons set forth, I respectfully dissent.* Justice Harlan in Plessy v. Ferguson (in Notes and Materials nr. 28) terminated his dissenting opinion with: *For the reason stated, I am constrained to withhold my assent from the opinion and judgment of the majority.* Sometimes, however, a neutral modification such as *For the foregoing reasons, I must respectfully dissent* is supplied. Hence, the final formula is at times employed as an argumentative tool, at times it remains a pure formality. This is one more example for the volatility of legal arguments.

3.4.3 Argumentation in International Law

Rules of the International Law are created and applied slightly differently than the legal rules of the domestic law. Also the legal argumentation in the international law displays some characteristic features. The first of them seems to be that the existence of a routine case in the international law is denied. The argumentation around an international case is usually developed as a unique event towards which all political influence and legal skills have to contribute. Second, an international case is like a constitutional case prominent in the sense that particular care is involved in dealing with it. In this sense it is furthermore perceived as rhetorical and as analogical (Reus-Smit 2005: 356). It is like all legal argumentation rhetorical in the sense that it grounds in an interpretation developed by an interested party and does not provide any purely logically deducted arguments which subsequently might be automatically applied on the case. Reus-Smit quotes F. Kratochwil who emphasized that in the international legal argumentation turns on the issues whether the interpretation is acceptable rather than true (Reus-Smit 2005 : 356). The framework for this argumentation has been characterized as pending between apology of the established order and the utopian view that international law could civilize nations (Koskenniemi 1989). Moreover, the argumentation in international law is also analogical in the sense that it seeks to establish similarities and dissimilarities between rules, actions and cases (Kratochwill as quoted by Reus-Smit 2005: 356). All in all, the argumentation in international law restricts the argumentative framework as well as it limits its own methodological spectrum. Therefore, it constitutes a special type of legal argumentation.

3.4.4 Argumentation in negotiations

Legal language or at least some of its characteristic features are also used in commercial and diplomatic negotiations. Both domains of its application are a mixture of different registers, but elements of the legal language play definitely a role in it. Both are related towards the making of a final decision which would be perceived by involved parties as binding, i.e. as law set by them. In commercial negotiations the parties will frequently use commercial language as an addition to legal formulations or as dominating register. A. Koskensalo (2002) dealt with business correspondence in respect of functionality in the globalizing world. She argued that modern communication techniques such as e-mail strengthen dialogue-like communication (Koskensalo 2002: 57). She contrasted them with the monologue-like traditional business letters and posited a more contemplative element in them. She also stressed that the legislator reacted to these changes in communicative habits in the business life and introduced provisions such as § 126a BGB. Also in the U.S., new legal provisions addressed issues related to the electronic signature in the Electronic Signatures in Global and National Commerce Act (E-Signature-Act) from October 2000. Furthermore, in diplomatic negotiations the final decision is found in an amalgam of linguistic registers reaching from political to legal (cf. Kovačević 2004: 26). The use of arguments there is close to the procedure in international law, with the modification that political arguments may play a stronger role than the legal ones. Interests, attitudes and strategies structure the process of negotiating like any other linguistic operation. Positional bargaining, trade-offs and linkage of disconnected issues are typical strategies in diplomatic negotiations (Kovačević 2004: 113). Other general strategies aim at ensuring the maintenance of the negotiating process. The preformulated diplomatic notes and other samples of diplomatic correspondence (Feltham 1998: 31) reduce the risk of tensions because they limit the risk for interpretive discrepances. Aboundant courtesy is their most salient element. The obligatory use of titles, e.g. *Your Excellency* (Feltham 1998: 15) and the use of final formulas in diplomatic notes: *The Embassy avails itself of this opportunity of assuring the Ministry of its highest consideration* may reduce the negative impact of disadvantagous messages. However, some countries like the U.S. omit the final courtesy formula in their notes (Feltham 1998: 31). The formal politeness of the diplomatic note (official note or note verbale) is emphasized by the lack of any identifiable signature as the notes are solely initialized and sealed. Formulations perceived as particularly polite, especially *understatements* such as *I'm afraid that the continuation of such practices might reflect negatively on relations between our two countries* or deliberative emotional graduation, e.g. *I view with concern...* towards *I view with grave concern...* enable to express negative attitudes without that the other party loses its face and terminates the negotiation. Diplomatic discourse focuses on conceptual creations such as: *new world order, foreign affairs, equilibrium, Realpolitik, containment, geopolitics, international system, national state, balance of power, collective security, détente* or *peaceful coexistence, quiet diplomacy* (cf. Kissinger 1994). Fixing the results or interim results in *protocols* or *memoranda,* esp. in a *memorandum of understanding* reduces the uncertainties as to the binding force of negotiated results. Including a *road map* helps maintain the dialogue despite of political changes. Hence, content wins over form.

3.5 Successful Legal Argumentation

In this chapter we will return to theoretical issues whose exposition has been interrupted by our case studies. We will introduce the results obtained in the case analysis into the theoretical remarks upon legal argumentation. We will deal with elements of argumentation and with the quality of arguments as preconditions for successful argumentation. Finally, we will sketch further possible developments in this field.

3.5.1 Theoretical problems

The first structural element in the legal argumentation is the development of tests within interpretive standards as a reaction of courts to interpretive differences. In these tests the validity of arguments is tested. As the initial tests mostly prove to be too general, additional test criteria are included into them. Finally, however, social values as interpreted by the court and the view it takes upon the facts in its institutonally privileged way determine the decision taken. Not only the legal linguists but also citizens at large may have problems with this sort of argumentation. Furthermore, it remains open whether the courts are satisfied with the results they reach because judges usually do not mark in their decisions any doubts about the argumentative strategies they have used. What is more, the right to argumentative interpretation is by its very nature not particularly well adapted to be exercised in an authoritative way. Still, a valid legal norm is one identified as such by the authorized institution on the basis of the sources of law enforced by a legal system or legal culture. The validity of the norm is tested according to constitutive rules applied in a given society. The law in force is not pure rationality but is linked to the society, its culture and last but not least to the constitutive rule which states which rule in a society is perceived as a valid rule of law and which is not. Here, one could have the impression that the process is circular. Yet, society is a living which means a dynamic organism. Values in legal cultures change. Hence, also constitutive rules provide changing answers to like questions. Therefore, an authoritarian argumentation, i.e. one which is based on the institutional privilege alone cannot be perceived as particularly appealing in modern societies. Apparently, a better argumentation is needed and should be nowadays also prescribed by laws in order to ensure that argumentation exercised in courts reaches the convincing standards of rational argumentation. Overall, our case material demonstrates that this improved argumentation will also include emotions. There is no linguistic communication without rhetoric and this is equally valid for law. Rhetorical means vary with times and correspond to the culture in which they are used. Practising lawyers have always been aware of this challenge. Also the legislator became slowly but steadily aware of the fact that legislation must be linguistically appealing to citizens should it be more readily accepted. Captions from the U.S. American legislation like the Oregon *Death with Dignity Act,* the *Government in the Sunshine Act* or the *Americans with Disabilities Act,* not to speak about the *Patriot Act,* abound nowadays in emotions and are in blatant contrast with the style of most European legislators who still prefer bureaucratically bleak formulations. Overall, the improved argumentation must convince through its quality and not through the deference to authoritative bodies. Its core is the rationality in the application of legal rules. This rationality is not technical. Instead, it is grounded in ethical values and convictions shared in the society at a given moment. Law is therefore more than social engineering; it develops still more complex mechanisms for legal argumentation. These mechanisms are linguistic in essence. Therefore, the legal argumentation is one of the most important if not the central legal-linguistic operation.

3.5.2 Elements of legal argumentation

In the analyzed cases some central structural features such as: arguments, selection rules for application (validity) of arguments, participants and forum, rationality test, argumentative gaps and argumentative volatility, chains of arguments as a part of legal reasoning became apparent. Their legal-linguistic status is different as is different their weight in the legal theory. However, they allow for the first tentative description of the legal argumentation towards the background of the analyzed materials. Generally, the arguments are the fundamental elements of argumentation. This holds true even if the procedural rules concerning the selection of arguments and participants in an argumentative practice, e.g. the court proceedings, may occasionally impose themselves upon the subject matter of the argumentative act. Arguments are embodied in legal speech acts which transfer them into legal arguments and ensure their operationability within the institutionalized process of the application of law. They are employed to increase the rationality of the legal argumentation. In the modern legal argumentation the pure victory does not matter. Decisive is the victory of best arguments, i.e. those which advance socially relevant goals. However, even modern argumentation is provided in traditional forms; for instance in majority or dissenting opinions. This process is visible in decisions such as Martin v. PDA (case VI of our Introduction, cf. 1.3.2) where the majority opinion was anchored in the public policy that empowers disabled citizens. There, the remnants of the argumentative positions which reflect overcome views are traceable in the dissenting opinion. Arguments are provided in a procedure, and are tested and retested in appeals where different judges participate in the review of arguments. Rules concerning the participation are central; the right to participate is debated as an issue independent of the main subject matter, as in the already mentioned case the People v. Tortorici (cf. 3.4.1). Arguments are furthermore advanced in chains; a court opinion is rarely based on one sole argument. To solve the argumentative challenge the court applies a rationality test and uses, as in Martin v. PDA, expert opinions to clarify facts viewed in the perspective of the legislative intent. Thus, the circle of participants is broadened by the participation of nonlegal experts in the decision making. Arguments are not always used in a perfect way, sometimes an argumentative gap is perceptible in a court decision or in the views expressed by the parties, e.g. in the mentioned decision Ashcroft v. Free Speech Coalition (cf. 3.4.1). Qualitative differences and the volatility of arguments are specific for the legal argumentation that is part of discursive practices, i.e. that it is not a monologue.

3.5.3 Towards a more convincing argumentation

3.5.3.1 Quality of arguments: The cases analyzed above enable us to argue that the quality of professional argumentation in them differs. We were able to identify texts in which the argumentation was more adapted to the solution of the case and therefore more convincing than in other cases. In other words, argumentation in some cases has been more successful than in others in the sense that it better suited the goals of professional justification than in some other cases. We have also reflected the recipient level and found out that some arguments of the justification may promote the decision within the non-professional audience, whereas others may be perceived as less persuasive. Indeed, the formal legal obligation imposed upon judges to justify their decisions in writing can be fulfilled in different ways. Some types of justification are of a formal type, while others are material in the sense that the judge tries not only to document the way in which he has reached his decision, but also to convince his professional surrounding that his decision has been right. The judge may furthermore try to convince the broader public that the legal solution embedded in his decision is the most appropriate one in the case. In turn, the quality of arguments used cannot depend on the result achieved with them for instance in a litigation. This has been the case in the area of the traditional rhetoric that provided argumentative schemes that would lead to a success in litigations. The question who has won or how to win in a litigation is not central for the modern Legal Linguistics. There, it is more interesting which arguments are rational and which are not because the legal argumentation should primarily advance the level of rationality in law. Nevertheless, victories achieved with better, i.e. rational arguments, are welcome in the Legal Linguistics.

3.5.3.2 Inferential model of linguistic communication: The above case analyses demonstrate also that legal argumentation cannot be integrated into a communicational model based on sending encoded messages by a speaker that are received by a hearer who simply decodes them. The message model of communication must be broadened and encompass strategies which at least enable it to cope with the disambiguation of complex messages. The inferential model of linguistic communication widens the conceptual framework of the message model (Akmajian 2001: 370). It is directed towards the identification of speaker's intentions and is therefore suitable for the analysis of communication in legal contexts. Strategies of successful communication which are based on this model stress that the communication is to be perceived as successful when the hearer recognizes the speaker's intention. They are grounded in the conviction that the successful communication is possible only when the speaker and the hearer share a system of inferential strategies leading from the utterance of an expression to the recognition of the communicative intent (Akmajian, ibid.). These strategies enable us to distinguish between expressions communicated directly and indirectly and include strategies for differentiation between literal and nonliteral meaning. However, such strategies would not work were they not grounded in common presumptions about linguistic communication (Brandom 2000). Thus, in the legal argumentation their foundation must be searched for in the institutional nature of the argument use. The analyzed cases showed that without taking this particular feature into consideration the specific rationality of the judicial decisions cannot be successfully construed. Neither is it possible to successfully apply arguments in law without taking into account this major structural feature of the legal argumentation.

3.6 Legal Interpretation

3.6.1 Why we interpret?

After having extensively treated the legal argumentation let us now turn to the legal interpretation. In the above chapter we were not inclined to artificially distinguish argumentative and interpretative language use where both coincide or come very close to each other. In fact, interpretive and argumentative language is often used in related speech acts. Since antiquity, the interpretation has been treated in the context of logic, argument and dialectic, e.g. in Aristotle's Περὶ Ἑρμηνείας, known better under its Latin title *De Interpretatione*. However, in the legal disciplines traditionally a distinction has been made between argumentation and interpretation. Here, we maintain the traditional distinction between argumentative and interpretive speech acts, although doubts might come up about such necessity. These doubts are caused by the complexity and the lack of transparency in argumentation and interpretation. In the Legal Linguistics it would be important to ask whether this distinction can be proved in the language use. Infact, interpreting linguistic utterances is part of our daily experience. This daily experience may also be the reason why we do not know much about interpreting (Baylon 1991: 208). Furthermore, some knowledge we have is frequently rather confused and inconsistent. Apparently, we are inclined to underestimate the daily experience and turn, rather, to lofty ideas to understand interpretive action. We seem to conceive such ideas, doctrines or theories as more promising because they are not directly anchored in our daily experience which for many equals banality or trivia. Also the modern analytical philosophy showed how deeply we had erred and still occasionally err while neglecting the most fundamental daily experience in our individual and our social practice (Engel 2000: 63). A part of it is, as mentioned above, the interpreting of speech with which we are confronted. It could also be that we have reached perfection in interpreting and this is why we scarcely realize this activity in everyday life. Nevertheless, no one would argue that we are not constantly involved in the interpreting of linguistic utterances, both spoken and written, i.e asking for their meaning. Occasionally, however, when confronted with issues or notions which are explicitly equivocal for us we consciously engage in interpreting. In these situations we are also usually less perfect than in the daily life. Why does this happen? In controversial situations, in which one proposed meaning of an utterance is contested we are shaken up in our life form which regularly provides us the right guiding for the everyday interpreting of utterances. This last situation interests us particularly. Its fundamentals are the lack of knowledge – which sometimes manifests itself in the form of contradictory propositions – about the meaning of a concept in a given context. Semantics and pragmatics deliver a host of examples for such situations. The question whether the Buckingham Palace is also a *house* is a typical example of such a situation in daily life. This presupposes, of course, a conversational context in which such a proposition could be expressed meaningfully or be contested. The solution to such questions through definitions is difficult. Legal definitions may sometimes provide a remedy, but they also cause new interpretive problems because they either make plain the meaning in a language or determine it (Savigny 1973: 30). The controversial cases are very special but still they do not mean that interpretation concerns exclusively controversial or *hard cases* in the legal parlance and that it excludes daily routine. Sometimes we wish to discover the initial meaning of things in texts or in other artifacts with a long history and ask ourselves what that original meaning had been. This happens regularly when we interpret a literary work, especially one which was written in times remote from ours or which belongs to a different cultural tradition (Juhl 1986: 3). In such cases we used to interpret because we do not know the meaning or we have an impression that the meaning we intuitively grasp cannot be the historically or culturally right one. This necessity to interpret which is embedded in our cultural context led however in law to the conviction that a search for objective meaning – the only right one - would be possible in the legal science. This assumption had some formal prerequisites, the first being that things are as they are (which is definitely true as a tautology) and that this being so is a fact which can be known in an uncontroversial way (and this is, of course, a problem). Another extreme situation is the deference to the purely subjective meaning which dominated the notion of meaning adopted by some theorists. Lawyers had been aware of these problems and they were also piecemeal and increasingly becoming aware of their own ignorance in this matter (Atria/MacCormick 2003). We could describe this shift in attitudes from the conviction that lawyers simply knew the law as their profession to the conviction that lawyers were ignorant about law – but this in a very professional way (Galdia 1995: 62). What the lawyers knew was the method of how to acquire knowledge about law needed in the case, how to use argumentatively statutes and precedents, as well as the legal doctrine including general principles upon which the law was based, in the deliberation about the appropriate solution of a legal case. Their arguments were specific and sometimes they were not understandable for the bigger community of laypersons, simply because they were part of a professional argumentation. We realize already at this stage that the community of interpreters was split in at least two organisms (cf. 3.2.3.4).

3.6.1.1 Interpreting statutes and precedents: Attempts to interpret statutes and foremost their terminology concentrated methodologically on a canon composed of: *grammatical* interpretation, *logical* interpretation, *systematic* interpretation and *teleological* interpretation. These interpretive methods do not lead to convincing results in controversial cases (Alexy 1983: 19; Wróblewski 1988: 128-148). They may at best characterize features of interpretation in a daily language game, in a given context of a life form. Therefore, from the 'use' as it is, it is not possible to infer the 'use' as it ought to be; a paradox of traditional doctrine of interpretation valid in this form both in the civil law and in the common law. Apparently, more was necessary to deal with interpretation, a further step had to be taken and the prerequisites of a language game of legal interpretation had to be revisited if not discovered. Legal interpretation emerged as a challenging language game played by skillful players, professionals who master complex interpretive rules. Lawyers fully realized that they had to adopt their interpretive rules to the *text type* they interpreted. Legal professionals approach statutes differently than contracts and witness testimonies or other factual declarations. Research projects such as *Interpreting statutes. A comparative study* by Neil McCormick and Robert Summers (eds.) from 1991 as well as *Interpreting precedents. A comparative study* prepared in 1997 by the mentioned editors, make plain this difference. Interpreting statutes and interpreting precedents or contracts are close but finally distinct activities. They are methodologically connected by the factor of intention which is decisive in all of them. In interpreting statutes the legislative intention plays traditionally a major role. In interpreting contracts, the intention of the parties should prevail when legally possible. Otherwise, the concluding of private contracts would not make much sense. In precedents, the intention of the deciding court is the focal point of every professional interpretation. There, however, most problems emerge because courts often do not provide detailed explications for their motives.

As already noted, while interpreting we identify the institutionally determined speech act (cf. 3.1.1). Determination of meaning concerning ordinary language can be undertaken by courts or by the legislator. In Frigaliment v. B.N.S. (Notes and Materials nr. 30) a court decided the meaning of *chicken* in a contract between the parties. It used the procedure of the burden of proof for this. The plaintiff argued that with *chicken*, the parties meant only young birds, whereas the defendant contested it and argued that all types of birds such as fowls, broilers and the like were meant in the contract among the parties. The plaintiff had to meet the requirements of the burden of proof but the witness testimony provided by him did not convince the court. He therefore lost his case. This means that *chicken* retained its meaning in the contract between the parties as suggested by the defendant. The determination of the meaning of a term belonging to the ordinary language has been procedural. Also the legislator may determine the meaning of concepts of ordinary language which he introduces into the legal language. This has been done by the British legislator concerning the notion of *house* (cf. Notes and Materials nr. 11). This determination differs from the previous one as it takes the form of a definition. The *house* is defined in terms of the legal act in which it is used. The determination here is institutional. Like the courts in our previous cases analyzed under 3.4.1, the legislator determines his own position due to his institutional powers. Clearly, the legal interpretation is more than a decoding of a meaning in a particular concept. It is also more than the disambiguation of concepts (Juhl 1986: 93). Therefore, the creative interpretation in Dworkinian sense is rather a rule in interpretation than an exceptional or metaphorical use of the concept (Dworkin 1991: 51). In law, the limit of this interpretation is problematic. Its limit seems to be an arbitrary decision about the meaning. Legal paradigms cannot be easily challenged without the blame of unprofessionality or adventurism: *Every community has paradigms of law, propositions that in practice cannot be challenged without suggesting either corruption or ignorance* (Dworkin 1991: 88). Already H. Kelsen (1960: 353) pointed to the structural limits of interpretation in his *Reine Rechtslehre* by saying: *„Rechtswissenschaftliche Interpretation kann nichts anderes als mögliche Bedeutungen einer Rechtsnorm herausstellen.“* The difference between the interpretation in the legal sciences mentioned by Kelsen, and the interpretation undertaken by the judge, resides in the character of their work (Carcassonne 2005: 294). The legal scholar may limit her work to mentioning of various possible semantic varieties whether the judge must decide the question which party wins in the litigation. The judge is therefore obliged to draw conclusions from interpretive analyses. In Frigaliment v. B.N.S. (Notes and Materials nr. 30) we have seen that the judge interprets within the boundaries of procedural rules. He may therefore use the rule of the burden of proof in the litigation as a specific semantic limit.

Interpretation requires the necessity to understand. Argumentation, in turn, requires the need to convince that the knowledge advanced in case is the right one. Interpretation as a linguistic mechanism is uniform in character. It does not differ due to changes in its object, e.g. natural phenomena, arts or social issues. It does not change as the character of the sale contract does not change when we purchase cars, bread, airplanes or computer programs. It adapts to the situational circumstances like the sale contract adapts to its different objects without changing its nature. It differs doubtlessly as its validity criteria change. Different criteria reign among literary critics or general public; similarly the legal criteria applied among laypersons differ as well. In law, the interpretation is problematic exclusively in terms of its acceptability by a community (validity in this community), not by the character of the operation itself. These criteria exclude eccentric or radical interpretations. Institutional justifications of propositional statements differ as well. The increasing number of forums competent to interpret the law, especially in the international setting, may lead to an increase in quality of argumentation in the legal decisions rendered because it stimulates courts and tribunals to hand down better-reasoned judgments and to provide explicit and convincing arguments (Cassese 2004: 286). Furthermore, the court hierarchy warrants a more effective use of arguments in the interpretation that makes it more rational (cf. Medellín v. U.S. commented here under 3.8.2).

3.6.1.2 Exegesis: The method of textual exegesis is rarely used as a sole instrument for identifying the meaning of a legal text. In literary criticism however it is used frequently. The exegesis aims at clarifying the initial, i.e. original meaning of the text, mostly based upon the author's intention (subjective approach) or the general understanding in times of the composition of the text (objective approach). The use of the terms is restricted to historical texts (Đorđević 2002: 16). Nevertheless, the exegesis of religious texts – especially in its modernized dress – often transgresses these boundaries and approaches general interpretation.

3.6.2 Do utterances which need not be interpreted exist in law?

In law, traditionally, utterances are divided into those which are unequivocal per se and others which must be interpreted. In this context the classical devise (LAT) *interpretatio cessat in claris* is regularly invoked by the legal theorists. While speaking about the distinction of hard and routine cases we already expressed doubts about the possibility of such a structural devide. The pragmatics and the legal theory provide for further arguments against this classical but still less and less convincing view of the interpretation which is needed only when a text is unclear. This presupposes logically that texts can be divided into clear and unclear ones. J. Searle is quoted by Levinson (1983: 8) with following words: *There is no such thing as the zero or null context for the interpretation of sentences...We understand the meaning of such sentences only against a set of background assumptions about the context in which the sentence could be appropriately uttered.* This concerns also utterances in law. In many cases the interpretation of legal rules or precedents may not be particularly challenging. Nevertheless, it must take place. Wróblewski (1988: 117) posits that doubts concerning the content of legal provisions can principally always come up; also clear texts are interpreted. The question whether a text is clear or unclear depends upon its evaluation by the user (Wróblewski 1988: 117). According to Wróblewski the interpretation is not a part of the process of application of a legal norm. This could mean that is should be perceived as purely linguistic. He however accepts views expressed by N. Bobbio and many others who described the interpretation as an inherent part of the application process. The conceptual separation upon which Wróblewski seems to insist is neutral in our context where the unavoidable interpretation is perceived as a linguistic operation in law. It may have, however, consequences for the mainstream legal theory.

3.6.3 Limits of legal interpretation

Interpretation is a linguistic operation. Thus, its limits are the limits of our language. They are first of all formal, i.e. syntactic (Davidson 2001: 270). What cannot be formulated in line with syntactic rules cannot be said. This at least holds true for the language of law which is shaped along syntactic rules. In daily life, these rules are of course frequently violated, for instance by children or by foreigners who master only the rudiments of the language in which they try to communicate. They are regularly modified by poets as well (Juhl 1986: 108). These groups of speakers are not particularly relevant in our context. Beyond syntactic boundaries no other limit of interpretation is imposed upon us as our brain can provide us with an unlimited number of syntactically correct utterances with arbitrary contents (Searle 2004: 19). They may include paradoxes, lies, or other consciously manipulative language use. Legal interpretation, however, has its particular intrinsic limits. It is determined through the use of specific arguments. These arguments are: first, those generally perceived by professional lawyers as legal arguments (received opinion of lawyers), second, some arguments with uncertain or controversial status like the arguments of professional minorities (e.g. dissenting opinions), and third, arguments which are generally not perceived as professional but which at the end of the day lead to changes in the adjudication, especially in supreme courts. All other arguments regarding law are usually perceived as lay arguments. They are not considered in the legal decision making process. Legal interpretation also has other limits. These are the limits of our inventiveness as jurists. Jurists learn in their professional training a number of specified arguments, and some of them learn also arguments used in the remote past, for instance in the classical Roman law. Later on, in their professional life jurists tend to rely on this knowledge and are not particularly inventive. On the other side, most cases they deal with are routine cases where particular inventiveness is limited by the structure of the subject matter and the minimal chance that the practice concerning a routine case could engender innovative legal decisions. Legal arguments ground in our social values. Legal theorists such as R. Dworkin have demonstrated it with sufficient persuasiveness. R. Dworkin also showed the way how the best argumentation should be formed in order to achieve the best available legal decision. Finally, the seemingly unlimited freedom of jurists to interpret appears as determined by so many minor burdens and more substantial constraints that one could have the impression that a free interpretive legal decision can only be an arbitrary one. After all, this is not necessarily an unwelcome result. Work done on the establishing of requirements for legal arguments has been accomplished with the aim in mind to exclude arbitrary and irrational legal decisions (Alexy 1983: 36). The constraints imposed upon legal interpretation shall guarantee that arbitrariness becomes evident in the decision and that such a decision will be corrected in appeal. As far as these constraints are linguistic, they are of pragmatic nature.

3.6.3.1 The implicit in law: A further limit to legal interpretation is a warning against dealing with legal provisions in their literary sense that are legion in all legal traditions. This holds true for the past as well as for the contemporary legal methodology. For jurists the legal text, be it a statute or a contract between private parties, had always a meaning situated somewhere else, i.e. not in itself. Therefore, nowhere law had been studied as an amalgam of provisions which when read through could function as a basis for solving legal cases. In the civil law tradition, French, Italian and German civil codes underline both for legal provisions and for contractual stipulations that their literary meaning is often immaterial, that judges have to look into the intentions of parties and the intention of the legislator rather than to the written lines of a legal document (cf. Notes and Materials nr. 19). It is surprising, but also illuminating, that totalitarian regimes like, for instance, the Soviet one also stressed this aspect of law. In the Soviet legal methodology not the text of the law but the understanding of its sense, issue, idea or problem had been central (Pigolkin 1990: 187). For us, the written legal text is constituted by material text elements and also the immaterial ones which are parts of its context. Therefore, we have fewer problems with the theoretical part of the question. It is perfectly understandable for us that a written legal text, like all other types of texts, cannot be interpreted exclusively on the basis of its material elements. But, this does not solve the practical question that jurists, especially judges are exposed to texts which can be understood only in their appropriate context and this is practically a challenge for them. This experience could justify the thesis of the implicit law in the legal provisions (Pigolkin 1990: 180). The implicit or hidden, non-public element of law is for Pigolkin inherent in whatever text. It is for him a means of economy in a linguistic utterance. The text includes information which is not explicitly formulated in it but understandable for the professionals or for the parties concerned. An example would be a formulation in a contractual clause such as *This contract is governed by the laws of France* where it is not mentioned that the contract in question is a lease contract. That the contract in question is in fact a lease contract may become apparent either from its headline, from another clause in the same contract, or from its sense. Pigolkin distinguishes the implicit from *latent* elements which he would like to have banned from laws. The latent information is according to this view not inherent to the text, it is connected to it. An example for it is a reference in a legal act to other legal provisions not included into it. Basically, all provisions or circumstances not expressed in the legal text and not inherent in it could be perceived as latent (Pigolkin 1990: 183). However, blanket norms are deemed by Pigolkin as bearing an implicit element and not a latent one, because they refer to the general context of legislation and cannot be interpreted by using univocal terms from other sources of information (Pigolkin 1990: 184). This argumentation is less convincing and it seems to qualify the blanket norms rather as a borderline case between implicit and latent than clearly belonging to one of the named categories. The latent information can be a source of problems for the application of law because for its identification the broad systemic legal and factual contexts have to be analyzed. This is the reason why Pigolkin supports in his theoretical approach the implicit information but opposes the latent one (Pigolkin 1990: 183). In terms of semantics, the distinguishing between implicit and latent may be of some interest for the development of the legal language. However, an approach based on pragmatic parameters focuses on the material law as it is. Law, in statutes and in contracts includes elements which Pigolkin names as latent. They will not disappear from the legal texts because they are parts of the pragmatics of language use in law. Theoretically, it would be possible to forbid the legislator or parties of a private contract to refer to latent elements or to omit them in contracts. This procedure has been used by several legislators, for instance in the Chinese Unified Contract Law's Art. 12, where detailed information is required for the contract to be valid. However, this sort of legislation would never be able to identify all possible sources of latent information in a statute or a contract. Its result may be the increase of the informational load of a legal text but not a solution of the problem of latent elements in law. The speech act theory integrates successfully both the implicit and the latent aspects of law in that it identifies legal speech acts in their contextual surrounding. Its advantage over the approach proposed by Pigolkin et al. is that it does not exclude any data from law. It is therefore realistic and applicable unlike the interesting approach presented by Pigolkin et al. which remains prescriptive and therefore idealistic. Such models simply never work in law. Whatever position we would take towards the assumption that law consists also of implicit and latent elements, one issue remains uncontested. Law, when expressed in legal provisions cannot be studied or applied under the impression reached from reading experience of legal texts. The methodology of the legal science is grounded in this principle. Because law is definitely not only what is written on a piece of paper but much more than that, interpretation and argumentation will be always crucial for its studies and its application.

3.6.3.2 Aporetic character of law: Another potentially discouraging aspect of the legal interpretation is the aporetic character of law which manifests itself in the circularity of right and wrong law among judicial instances in the legal process. Inferior courts are bound by the precedents of higher courts and especially the Supreme Court until they are overruled or at least substantially expanded. They provide wrong law when their decisions are overruled by the Supreme Court when it changes its constant practice, e.g. in Brown v. Board of Education (347 U.S. 483, 74 S.Ct. 686, 1954). In fact, while saying the law in conformity to the legal practice of the moment they are wrong, although they were right in following precedents acknowledged by higher courts of their times (Dworkin 1991: 6). When right is wrong and wrong is right, ancient Greeks used to speak about απορία (aporia). We will do the same but we will not fear this notion as it is symptomatic for laws made with words. The situation may be described differently, for instance with a paradox introduced by Dworkin (1991: 453) about the law which seems to be different for the higher courts and for the lower ones. Dworkin asks himself how to solve this linguistic and legal complexity. As an interpretive practice it can be generally right or wrong, its propositions valid or void, sound or unsound. In its institutional setting which imposes constraints on its argumentation it is aporetic. Aporia is one of the characteristic features of law, not its paradox. Therefore no evasive theory is needed to drive it away. Meanwhile, does this circumstance not mean otherwise that law was what it was in the first instance but than the judges in the higher instance simply changed it? The decision of the lower court becomes invalid due to the ruling of the higher court. Nevertheless, the fact that two different laws - 'propositions of law' - existed simultaneously in a legal system remains a challenge for the theoretical reasoning about law. Having this challenge in mind, Th. Viehweg referred in his *Topik und Jurisprudenz* (1954) to the classical rhetoric sources of legal argumentation that go back to Aristotle and Cicero. He stressed the development of legal rhetoric in the Middle Ages and later on in Gian Battista Vico's *De nostri temporis studiorum ratione* (1708). In making this part of argumentative legal thinking discernible Viehweg has successfully shaken up the traditional system-oriented approaches. A. Siitonen (1989: 130) remarks that according to Vieweg's conception legal argumentation cannot be based on an axiomatic-deductive system but rather on a problem oriented discussion method. He puts nevertheless Viehweg's approach and the results of his analysis in the right light. In his view, Viehweg's thesis should be perceived as complementary to systemic approaches (Siitonen 1989: 131). The cognitive technique of problem thinking and problem solving in law cannot be perceived as totally system-free. Problem thinking can be a basis for systematization which proceeds along logical rules and principles (Siitonen 1989: 132). There exists however distinctions between both approaches in that in the logical systems arguments are demonstrated and the topical structures are used to invent arguments. Their focal point could be seen in the division of labor as the logical reasoning proceeds from premises to conclusions, whereas the topical reasoning is a method of searching for premises. Therefore, for Siitonen, in jurisprudence not a system but a vague plurality of systems is at work. To avoid conflicts between these systems interpretation is needed (Siitonen 1989: 131).

3.6.3.3 Inferentialist explication of meaning: The necessity of interpretation and the concept of meaning can be further explained in an inferentialist model. This model has been used here already to characterize aspects of advanced legal argumentation (cf. 3.5.3.2). The inferentialist model is based on certain preconditions which hearers and speakers must share in order to understand each other. It is based on context sensibility, process sensitivity (interaction of speakers, lawyers, judges) as well as the account of contextual constraints and correctness conditions (Canale and Tuzet 2007: 40). The model is therefore in its essence pragmatic. Any assertion in it can be seen as a speech act that commits the speaker to a determinate set of inferences which are in turn considered by hearers who keep track of them and use them when they become involved in communicative situations (Brandom 2000). In order to characterize meaning within this model Canale and Tuzet (2007: 36) referred to Wilfrid Sellars for whom the meaning of a concept is determined by a set of material inferences; conceptual contents are understood in inferential roles. For instance, to grasp the concept of *contract* we must analyze the inferences speakers and hearers take to be correct when they enter into communication regarding a contract. Kwarciński (2005) argued that procedures and principles of the multi-level model of legal interpretation that were developed in the Polish jurisprudence were in many respects homologous to central concepts of the inferential version of the speech act theory. The multi-level model comprises descriptive, prescriptive, and presuppositional levels on which three different worlds are reconstructed by the interpreter respectively; they are independent and hierarchically structured (Kwarciński ib.). The legal text both describes and creates a possible legal world. At the descriptive level, legal provisions can be interpreted by anyone with sufficient linguistic competence, at the directive level legal training is necessary in order to engage in the interpretation (Kwarciński ib.). The multi-level model – when limited to the elements described here – makes plain that legal interpretation is an institutionalized type of utterance understanding.

3.6.3.4 Parties' intent: Courts customarily use pragmatic strategies to determine the intent of parties. The parties' intent is interestingly apt to set limits to the professional legal interpretation. Three classical English cases are illustrative of this procedure. All three cases date from the 19th century, i.e. from times where scholars could only dream of linguistic pragmatics or inferential model of meaning. First, in Dashwood v. Magniac (1891) one party devised to the other party an estate with *a power to cut timber for the repair of the estate.* Subsequently, the parties conflicted about the meaning of the term *timber* used in their locality. Evidence was therefore admitted in this case to find out the local meaning of *timber.* As a result, the court held that *timber* in the locality in question included beech in addition to the usual meaning which comprises oak, ash, and elm. Second, in Grant v. Maddox (1846) the parties interpreted differently the provision in an employment contract for an actor which stated that it was concluded *for a year.* The theater representative pretended that *year* in theatrical usage means those parts of the year during which the theater is open. This interpretation has been endorsed in court by evidence. Third, in Smith v. Wilson (1832) evidence was admitted to prove that in a lease of a rabbit warren the words *thousand rabbits* meant in that particular locality twelve hundred. The approach which takes into consideration rather the parties' intent than objective semantics is general in the legal methodology and is in no way limited to the common law. In the opinion of the German *Reichsgericht* (RGZ 99, 148) the Norwegian word (NO) *haakjöringsköd* which means objectively in English *shark meat* was interpreted as *whale meat* due to the common (objectively wrong) understanding of the parties which had in mind *whale meat* while agreeing on the delivery in a sale contract drafted in German where only the product as such had been named in the Norwegian language. The subjective meaning that the parties attached to the Norwegian word has been decisive for the (D) *Reichsgericht.* Thus, the parties' intent determined in an objectively inacceptable way the meaning of a Norwegian word. However, the linguistic reflex of the contract law is to establish the intent of the parties and not to reconstruct the semantics of the English or the Norwegian language at a particular moment. The decisive point is the meaning which the parties provided to terms they had used (cf. Guimezanes 1995: 204). The courts follow this intent even if the choice of the parties is not particularly convincing or might even be perceived as incorrect from the point of view of standard English or Norwegian language speakers. Only the use established among the parties matters for the judge. Overall, the language used in private contracts which are not always or not entirely drafted by legal professionals represents a hybrid form and is a challenge to every conception of the Legal Linguistics, but especially to the one based on linguistic pragmatics. It is necessary to maintain that its analysis in law has been regularly pragmatic; i.e. context-sensitive.

3.6.4 Interpretation and linguistic manipulation

Too frequently persons confronted with the deliberative character of law construe this characteristic feature of creation and application of law as linguistic manipulation. They, and many of them are students, argue that this characteristic feature in academic or other public usage is called interpretation in order to make it sound more objectively. This is definitely not our intention. We distinguish between legal interpretation and linguistic manipulation. Legal interpretation is a linguistic operation which necessarily has to be applied in linguistically ambiguous contexts when a univocal meaning is required. Manipulation is an abuse of this procedure. While manipulating arguments linguistic strategies are used in order to confuse the recipient of the message and impose on him a solution which may be detrimental to him. Let's have an example. When the X Corn flakes corporation established a subsidy in a country formerly belonging to the Soviet Union its manager criticized in an interview the consumers for not buying the products in sufficiently high rates. He pretended that the local consumers would "not understand that they had to eat the X Corn flakes for breakfast". Additionally, he argued that it took his company 20 years to make it clear to Brazilians that they had to buy the flakes and renounce their traditional breakfast habits. The corporate official pretended in the formulations he used that buying his products was a necessity, a mere automatism due to the fact that it was produced for being used as breakfast food. Not explicitly addressed but subliminal is there also the message that the product developed by a Western food company is of better quality and more appropriate for being taken at breakfast than the traditional food. This linguistic manipulation is grounded in the strategy to disorient the recipients of the message and conceal from them the possibility of choice and of manifesting personal preferences. In his argumentation the corporate officer suggested that the consumers had no choice. Manipulating of meaning is also accounted for in courts. For instance, in Goldstein v. SEC (discussed under 3.9.5) the court states explicitly: *That the Commission wanted a hook on which to hang more comprehensive regulation of hedge funds may be understandable. But the Commission may not accomplish its objective by a manipulation of meaning.* This means that manipulative linguistic practices are identified in legal procedures through tests in which the correspondence of arguments with underlying values of legislative acts is verified.

3.6.4.1 Interpretation and misinterpretation: How to distinguish an interpretation from a misinterpretation? In times dominated by approaches like the famous *everything goes* formula the very participation in interpretive practices may seem vain. Conventions for interpretation are mostly of social nature. Methods and regulative standards (Glass 1988: 454) are set up through numerous educational and sanctioning processes in which the legal community produces "agreements about certain interpretive conventions". Legal interpretations, therefore, are an institutional legal practice (Glass 1988: 454). Standards, criteria of evidence, procedures and awareness of what is reasonable are provided by the interpretive community (Glass 1988: 451). Dworkin argues that the notion of interpretive community cannot operate as a check upon the indeterminacy of interpretation, for it just makes a good interpretation one which is accepted by this community and he cannot imagine a weaker constraint (Glass ibid.). Interpretation requires, like all language use, fairness and openness towards its message. When the interpreter is ill intentioned and manipulative or blinded or incapable to understand the complexity of a text, then the interpretation procedure is simply misused, it is a misinterpretation. With this in mind, Perelman and others established the connection between interpretation and argumentation by referring to rationality (Plantin 1996: 10). Exactly because there is no interpretive method which would provide incontestable interpretive results argumentation is necessary. This is also why we usually do not treat judicial disagreement as irrational (Glass 1988: 453). Infact, the legal rationality is multiple, it is also complex.

3.6.4.2 Over-interpretation: Close to linguistic manipulation is the over-interpretation. One could perceive as *over-interpretation* an attempt to interpret into the text what is semantically not included there. It is a bold standing as criticism may come up as to the right to control what is and what is not semantically included in an utterance. Contexts of language use are broad and difficult to limit, therefore it is impossible to exclude in pragmatics an utterance as incorrect or meaningless without inquiring into the context of its use. However, it is necessary to insist on the meaning as a conventional feature of language (Searle 1999: 140). Whatever other transformations an utterance may experience in its use, it is primarily understood through the reference to linguistic conventions. The speaker meaning must be and usually also is explicated because conventionality is inherent in language. When a speaker claims *It is raining now* and means with it *A car accident took place* she will have to explain her specific use of language (that may be justified) and she will do it with reference to the conventional meaning. Otherwise her explication would not be understood. When both, speaker meaning and utterance meaning are made plain, no communicational problems exist any more. Understanding of legal-linguistic utterances follows the same track. For instance, Art. 1, 1st sentence of the French Declaration of Human Rights says: (FR) *Les hommes naissent et demeurent libres et égaux en droits* (Men are born and remain free having equal rights.) Some interpreters wished to see in the phrase that men are *born* (FR *naissent*) the foundation of the principle of equality between men and women (Carcassonne 2005: 398). They claimed that when men are born they are necessarly born of men and women who jointly form the basis for humanity. One would nevertheless claim that the conventional meaning of the sentence does not include such semantic alternatives. We would be ready to acknowledge the interpretive variety were we provided further contexts of use that would indicate such possibility. This is however not the case here. The interpretation remains a contention in law, and such unproven contentions are over-intrepretations. Over-interpretation concerns the textuality of law; it comes close to linguistic manipulation because it pretends that the text includes a meaning that for most speakers is not recognizable there. Creative interpretation, in turn, admits the shortcomings of the text and develops it further. It is therefore one thing to pretend that Art. 1 of the French Declaration of Human Rights provided for parity between men and women, and another to say that nowadays such a text that did not provide for this right should be interpreted in terms of law as including the principle that men and women are equal. Such an interpretive strategy is perfectly acceptable because it reveals the linguistic mechanism in which it emerged. Additionally, interpretation may also concern the conceptual rather than the textual basis. The above fundamental provision has been perceived as logically deficient in that it seems to set freedom over equality. For many, equality is the basis and source of freedom and other rights (Carcassonne 2005: 397). Some would therefore wish to reformulate the text that should say *equal and free* instead of *free and equal.* They refer to Art 1., 2nd sentence of the current French Constitution that mentions equality, yet not freedom: *Elle* (la République - suppl. author's) *assure l´égalité devant la loi des tous les citoyens, sans distinction d'origine, de race ou de religion.* Such a conceptual interpretation is free from textual constraints and comes close to creative interpretation. It is not an over-interpretation but an interpretation of a different sort.

3.6.4.3 Lies: Lies are the stronger form of linguistic inadequacies; they are stronger than over-interpretations because they ground in intentional manipulation of truth that is usually not the case with over-interpretations. Lies are frequently represented in legal-linguistic contexts and it is therefore surprising that they did not attract any attention. Especially, lies may constitute the factual basis for cases and dominate witness testimony. Sometimes also lawyers provide in their briefs objectively non-existent information about the law, e.g. reference to precedents which allegedly prove their contentions while knowing that this is not the case. Lies are particularly dangerous in the witness testimony because the proof of the contrary is frequently impossible since the witness may have been the only person who has acquired factual experience about a past event. Sometimes, lies can be detected through the linguistic analysis of the coherence in the testimony. However, illogical formulations, especially the contradictory ones do not necessarily prove that the witness is lying because he/she may not be a good speaker but they signalize that the witness should be asked further questions in order to clarify unclear formulations (cf. Bronston v. U.S. in Notes and Materials nr. 37). Needless to mention that a skillful witness usually has no linguistic problems to lie successfully in a court of law and to remain unmasked. In terms of the linguistic pragmatics lies are speech acts characterized by the abuse of the communicational procedure. They are possible because no linguistic mechanism hinders the formulation of utterances about facts performed with the speaker's intention not to state the facts but their contrary while pretending to state the facts. Pragmatists were not particularly interested in such cases because the speech act theory is based upon felicity conditions for speech acts which are fulfilled only when the speaker says what he intends to say and when he is convinced that what he is saying is true (Baylon 1991: 238; Davidson 2001: 273). Speech acts may also be formulated under less prosperous circumstances but then these circumstances make explicitly part of an utterance. Thus, in such situations the speaker would say *I doubt, I could imagine that...* etc. These formulations guarantee that the speech act is felicitous even in less determinate situations. The same concerns other deliberately unclear formulations applied with the goal to deceive especially where they are not easily identifiable as unclear or are not identified as unclear by certain recipients. A typical communicative situation of this sort is illustrated by the mentioned case Bronston v. U.S. In law, misrepresentation is the most prominent example of such a speech act (cf. Jareborg 1972: 445). The contrary constellation is the *self-deception* (Searle 1999: 71) where the speaker deceives himself, e.g. claiming not to be jealous although the contrary is evident for every observer. Related errors such as *misinterpretations* and *temporary infatuations* (Searle ibid.) follow suit. Meanwhile, truth in law is procedural. Bańkowski (1981) speaks of a *truth certifying procedure* that is formalized in the verdict. What is said in the procedure is taken as an established truth for all ulterior purposes of the law, unless and until it is quashed on appeal (Bańkowski 1981: 129). Therefore, objectively false declarations of the parties that may both wish to avoid the confrontation with the truth in a court of law become true through the procedure in which they function as a basis for the application of law. As indicated, it seems that lies do not have any future in the pragmatic research. They do not interest particularly because they are preconditioned by the sincerity requirement; without the hearer's trust in what is said there is no possibility for lying (Baylon 1991: 238). The case Bronston v. U.S., in Notes and Materials nr. 37, shows this interpretive mechanism in action. In law, however, lies matter in a specific way. The legal process based on lies makes of law a hopeless enterprise. When lies remain undiscovered, law loses any sense and perverts the society which it is expected to guide and to protect. Research on lies is therefore extremely important for the Legal Linguistics.

3.6.4.4 Half-truths: In the legal practice, the so-called *half-truths* are particularly common in witness testimony and in utterances made by corporate officers, especially in forward looking statements. Cases such as First Virginia Bankshares v. Benson (559 F.2d 1307, 1314; 5th Cir. 1977), Backman v. Polaroid Corp. (910 F.2d, 10; 1 Cir. 1990), Cooperman v. Individual Inc. (171 F.3d 43; 1st Cir., 1999) illustrate the discrepancy between the legal obligation to speak completely when making a statement and the strategy to avoid the plain disclosure of material facts. Therefore, in law, the half-truths emerge in situations where the duty to speak completely is violated (Langevoort 1999: 87). Close to the duty to speak completely is the duty to update relevant information which has been made public (Cox 2006: 690). The test of factual materiality in such a case is that the disclosed information is still relied upon by the third party, that it is 'alive' (Weiner v. Quaker Oats Co., 129 F.3d 310; 3d Cir., 1997). A further constellation concerns a duty to correct when information disclosed was objectively false but relied upon by the maker of the statement who only later discovers its falsehood. The legal consequences, at least in securities litigations, should be the same as in cases concerning the duty to update (Cox 2006: 691). False information can be furthermore disseminated by or through third parties. Again, especially in securities litigations, when the party endorses statements done by third parties that subsequently turn out to be wrong, it may have the duty to correct them (Elkind v. Ligget & Myers Inc., 635 F.2d 156 (2d Cir. 1980)). This can occur today through the creation of a hyperlink connection to the information (e.g. a report) issued by a third party. The situation becomes even more complicated when the party which establishes the link to an electronically available report which is favorable to its economic interests (and which is objectively false, e.g. too favorable) simultaneousely places a warning or a disclaimer that it is not responsible for the information provided by the third party. This again comes close to a constellation that a party is disseminating false information through the third party. Overall, the requirements for a complete testimony developed by the legal science correspond with the principle of exhaustivity in discourse that requires the information maximally compatible with the truth (Baylon 1991: 239). In a declaration *I have three children*, the existence of the fourth child or even more children is logically not excluded; nevertheless the declaration will be understood in this narrower sense under the circumstances of testimony; i.e. as limited to three children. The classical rhetoric knows a corresponding figure called *litotes* which consists in saying less than one would like to be understood. Through the *litotes* the thought is often expressed by its opposite, especially by adding *not* to the speech act. Such utterances modify the application of the principle of discursive exhaustivity. Summing this up, the pragmatic conditions of a speech act aiming at avoiding the half-truth are: speaking completely within the boundaries of confidentiality and making clear that some information may be hold back due to its confidentiality, updating and correcting issued information when the information is material and is still relied upon, possibly also correcting and updating information provided by third parties and avoiding any reference to it which is limited by disclaimers. Disseminating misleading and false information through third parties is the most blatant example of the violation of the procedure to speak completely when making a statement which is relevant for the public.

3.6.4.5 Controlling lies: Lies are rarely named as such by courts. Nevertheless, the way in which judges evaluate witness testimony frequently suggests that they perceive the party or witness depositions not as inadequacies or misunderstandings, but as lies. Courts apply rationality tests based on linguistic and extralinguistic knowledge to detect lies. In MCC-Marble Ceramic Center v. Ceramica Nuova d'Agostino, S.P.A. (144 F 3d. 1384, 11th Cir. (1998)) the court had to decide whether the parties agreed upon the application of the defendant's terms and conditions of sale. The terms of the sale contract between the parties were set upon a preprinted order form provided by the defendant with terms and conditions on the reverse side. The plaintiff provided affidavits by three of his employees. There, the court was ensured that the employees involved in the signing of the contract on behalf of the plaintiff did not take notice of defendant's terms and conditions because they were entirely in Italian. The court remarked: *We find it nothing short of astounding that an individual, purportedly experienced in commercial matters, would sign a contract in a foreign language and expect not to be bound simply because he could not comprehend its terms. The general proposition is that they will bind parties who sign contracts regardless of whether they have read them or understand them. ... Affidavits of MCC acknowledged that D'Agostino's representatives were aware of MCC's subjective intent not to be bound by the fine print terms...What a judge or a jury does with the parol evidence once it is entered into evidence is within their discretion as the weighers of the evidence. A reasonable finder of fact is free to disregard the parol evidence that conflicts with the written contract. Thus, it may disregard testimony that sophisticated international merchants signed a contract without intending to be bound as simply too incredible to believe and hold MCC to the conditions printed on the reverse side of the contract. However this is for the trier of fact to determine.* Further, in Finnish Fur Sales Co., Ltd. v. Juliette Shulof Furs, Inc. et al (770 F. Supp. 139, S.D.N.Y. (1991)) one of the defendants denied liability under the contract and claimed that conditions of the public sale did not become part of the contract due to their unconscionability. The defendant took part in a fur auction and was given there a booklet with sale conditions which a.o. provided for personal liability of bidders in the auction until the full payment of the price by the represented party. The court remarked: *Nevertheless, the perusal of the Conditions reveals that their entire text is only a single page long, and that all of the Conditions, including section 4, are printed in the same size print, which, although small, is legible. Under these circumstances, it seems unlikely that a New York court would refuse to enforce Section 4 in an arm's-length commercial transaction involving a sophisticated defendant accustomed to bidding at fur auctions.* Here, the defendant did not argue that he did not know about the contractual condition providing for his personal liability. Instead, he challenged the legality of the clause. The situation is nevertheless similar to the preceding case. The resemblance is situated in the denial to properly qualify the facts of an event. The court's opinion therefore resembles the preceding one, especially in that it underscores the commercial experience of the party denying the facts which underlie the legal defense. Overall, the contentions analyzed here are in terms of private law and procedure defenses against claims. In the pragmatic perspective they become interesting in that they show how parties manipulate facts they present to the court. By doing so, they abuse the legal procedure. This abuse is discovered by courts and sanctioned such that the parties lose their cases. It happens because they do not play according to the rules of the procedure. The underlying rule of the procedure is that facts presented by the parties must correspond with the reality. Their quality of being an efficient defense is not decisive in a legal process. Lies discovered in private litigations rarely lead to criminal prosecution as *perjuries*. Regretfully, oath is rarely sworn in courts on such occasions.

3.6.4.6 Professional errors: One of the most problematic issues within the discussion of the legal interpretation is the possibility of a professional mistake in the application of law by courts. Generally, we have adopted the point of view that the only one right interpretation in law does not exist. We have therefore to accept divergent judicial decisions of one and the same case rendered in the hierarchy of courts as well as divergent decisions made by different judges concerning similar cases. All these decisions are rooted in the mechanisms of the professional application of law. They differ as far as choices done by judges in the application of interpretive rules and goals may differ. Does this view, however, exclude the possibility of a professional error in law? With other words, are divergent judicial opinions results of the differences in the legal interpretation or the professional use of this interpretation? For instance, in Filanto S.P.A. v. Chilewich International Corp. (789 F. Supp. 1229) the issue of the validity of an arbitral clause incorporated into the sale contract between the parties has been decided according to the CISG and especially its Article 8 (2). However, the

CISG provides for its own application according to the Article 4 (1) upon issues concerning the formation of the international sale contract. The validity of the arbitration clause which is an autonomous part incorporated into the sale contract document would have to be decided according to the substantive law identified with help of the conflict of law rules. Several courts, among them OLG Frankfurt, stressed this view after the Filanto-decision has been rendered in 1992 by a Court in New York (cf. OLG Frankfurt NJW 1992: 633). The Filanto-decision is therefore perceived by many as wrong due to a professional error and not as an interesting or innovative court opinion. Furthermore, in international contracts which are frequently drafted in the English language the unreflected use of common law terminology leads to serious interpretation problems (Beveridge 2002: 55-79). There, use of foreign, e.g. Italian legal terminology, by an attorney-at-law in a contract drafted in English where constantly common law terms are used may be perceived as a professional error. Overall, the result of a legal interpretation is deemed as being professional when it is accepted as such by at least one part of the professional legal auditorium. This legal auditorium can be construed as composed of judges, attorneys-at-law or legal scholars. Is a judicial decision wrong in the sense of the law in force when the result of the legal interpretation is not approved by any of the corporative legal bodies? Or is this a very original, innovative interpretive proposition about the law in force?

3.6.5 Creative interpretation in Legal Linguistics

Unlike in many other areas of life, people - lawyers and laypersons alike – used to argue what the right law is about. This fact demonstrates again that law is at its core an interpretive (creative and argumentative) social practice. People argue about the propositions of law in different ways. Laypersons argue unprofessionally, they often mix arguments *de lege lata* and *de lege ferenda*, natural law postulates and positive law. The social dimension of these arguments cannot be underestimated. Political majorities in democracies are constituted of legal laypersons who, in turn, influence legislative mechanisms and contents. They shape the law. We retain from this that in law also the unprofessional argumentation matters. Legal argumentation used by professionals in their work shows how it matters and we will concentrate on this specific question. According to R. Dworkin professional legal argumentation consists in the best justification of our legal practice (Dworkin 1991: preface). It engenders competing narrative stories with different levels of persuasiveness. This mechanism shows best in complicated borderline cases (hard cases) but is equally operational although less perceptible in routine cases as well. Legal argumentation is limited by the constraints of the legal profession. However, it is the indeterminacy of law that enables judges to be more creative (Minda 1995: 33). The evaluation of different legal narratives, competing stories and the search for valid legal propositions in them are the real challenge for the judge because they are rooted in the social and political reality which is sometimes vague and elusive. In turn, this difficulty proves that argumentation about law is necessary and unavoidable and that it is not a result of a simple lack of knowledge about law. All lawyers must be perceived as unknowledgeable in this sense. Their lack of knowledge is part of their profession; it is the unknowlegeability *lege artis*, (according to the state of their art). In the Legal Linguistics, we do not artificially limit the scope of linguistic mechanisms in law but rather intervene where they manifest themselves most profoundly. This is also why we will treat the interpretation itself as an explicitly linguistic process while keeping in mind its social and ethical implications. Conceptions about law, about what it is and what it is not are all linguistic. However, we cannot follow a conception which is purely semantic, i.e. which seems to decode the language of law in the application process. This form of positivism is dangerous because it encourages obedience to immoral law (Minda 1995: 51) that is not the intention behind the Legal Linguistics. Dworkin also clearly demonstrated that the positivist approach does not work, at least in hard cases. Dworkin's theory of interpretation in law and its concept of integrity are central for any general conception of linguistic aspects of law, aiming at describing the legal argumentation as a merely linguistic mechanism. Therefore, we will have to dwell longer upon it and trace its linguistic foundations which make part of the approach adapted here. Some evolutionary steps in these theoretical conceptions – even if not Dworkinian in their core – will be taken as well.

3.6.5.1 Law as integrity: Based on some legal material, mostly court decisions under common law in borderline cases and criticism of dominating conceptions of the 20th century named as conventionalism and pragmatism as well as the earlier conception of the legal positivism treated in *Taking Rights Seriously* (1977), R. Dworkin arrives at a conception of law called law as integrity. In his conception of law he unites aspects related to the past and the necessary prospects of modern application of law that is adapted to the requirements of the contemporary society. He views the integrity as a coherent set of legal rules which enable the law to function in its historical setting as well as in its tendency to shape future developments and provide acceptable solutions for contemporary legal problems. The mechanism which ensures this application of law is the constructive interpretation. At least in hard cases the interpretive approach is based on an inevitable interpretive attitude which the interpreter (in Dworkin's cases the judge) takes when trying to find a solution to legal intricacies. Its goal is to adapt an attitude which would guarantee the best proposition of law in a case. The integrity of the legal system functions as a background correlative element in the interplay of views about the best proposition of law. We may again expose ourselves to the suspicion of nihilism while advocating the preponderant role of linguistic mechanisms in law to the apparent detriment of material socio-political implications. Here, it might again look like that law is not only about words but, even more so, that it is exclusively words. The hypothesis which we used to mention here regularly that there is nothing more in law than words must be scrutinized. It is much less destructive than supposed. In fact, our ordinary language reflects perfectly our form of life – the conditions under which we live in a society – it incorporates its social practices and does not exist beyond these practices. When we follow linguistic practices in a society we almost certainly also subscribe to the most substantial values which shape these linguistic practices. Even when creating legal terminology we do not create extralinguistic reality. Terms like *causality*, *constitutionality*, or *mailbox rule* do not change the order of the real world. They help us – due to their reistic background as metaphors or hypostases (Kotarbiński 1955: 16) – to cope with the linguistic complexity in law. They create law with words and not with objects. These words, in turn, fit perfectly into the legal language as they function in linguistic mechanisms (e.g. language games, speech acts) of the general linguistic practice. A linguistic conception of law is therefore not unrealistic. Dworkin insists in his jurisprudential theory of law as a creative social practice on integrity as a basic concept of this theory. With 'integrity' he means that a system of rights must be interpreted as a coherent vision of justice in a country (Dworkin 1991: 368). He stresses rather the integrity than the systemic character of law and this with good reasons. For the interpretation of law, which is for him the test for the best available proposition of law, its formal and material elements are more pertinent than a purely logical systemic approach based on formal logical mechanisms. With the same idea in mind, we insist here on a linguistic rather than systemic approach to law, its interpretation i.e. creation of propositions of law by means of legal argumentation. We are doing this because we do not believe that formal systemic argumentation would produce convincing, i.e. best eligible propositions about the law in a given social context at a particular moment. Formal and material arguments about the valid - right - sound propositions of law must merge in a legal narrative if it is aimed at persuading the legal community or the public at large. We do not exclude the aspects of material justice in a society or legal culture as accidental but rather integrate them into the larger spectrum of legal decision making, both in the legislation and in the adjudication. Otherwise, our debate about the propositions of law would remain sterile and purely academic. We try to avoid this result and strive to elaborate a general conception of law towards a pragmatic philosophical background which means for us an unconditioned anchorage in the legal practice. We can imagine law thought as a pure and coherent system of principles and rules beyond the social practice. At the same time, we are opposed to this reasoning as we deem it counterproductive in the society exposed to concrete problems hindering its progress.

3.6.5.2 Hard and routine cases: Dworkin is specifically interested in situations where law books are silent, where law is ambiguous or unclear. This makes plausible his interest for hard cases. We have nevertheless tried to show that law even when applied in line with presumed clear statutes or precedents is not less fascinating than the hard cases where alleged gaps in law must be filled by courts with legal substance. Issues like gaps in law and judicial discretion (a positivist term according to Dworkin in the preface to his Law's Empire) merge in the interpretive approach and seem to be rather metaphors in legal argumentation than legal problems or necessary legal doctrines. In our view, the linguistic potential of a case makes the distinction between hard cases and routine cases blurred and even more, it shows that this distinction is only temporary. It is based on a problem finding procedure – an analysis undertaken by a lawyer – which might in any case lead to the discovery of a legal problem in it (cf. Saarenpää 1980: 25). The legal problem will be one of interpretation. Dworkin describes a situation in which a single argument might be decisive to solve a case and addresses the situation where it might not have struck the judge in the right moment. This situation is regularly the source of the emergence of hard cases out of daily routine in the courts. The process is largely accidental as it is based on invention, professional creativity of judges and attorneys. To understand better the temporary character of the distinction between routine and hard cases let us have a look at the rules of the German Traffic Act. Art. 2 of the statute provides, like in most countries, for driving on the right-hand side of the road. At a first glance there is nothing clearer than that. However, precedents concerning road accidents show that the rule of the traffic code may be violated when the driver comes closer to the edge of the road than 60 cm. Sometimes, the driver on a narrow road at the countryside may be more on the left-hand than on the right-hand side or in the middle of the road and not violate the rule. Traffic rules were popular as examples among legal theorist because they were held by many as being unequivocal. Historically, a debate engaged H. L. A. Hart (1958) and L. Fuller (1958) about the indeterminate meaning of an inoffensive phrase *No vehicles are permitted in the park*. As a result, the semantic and the pragmatic intricacy of this banal formulation became plain. What makes our traffic cases and all analogous cases to hard cases is not that much the inherent semantic indeterminacy as such but the discovery of it, i.e. their pragmatic aspect, the result of an inevitable interpretive attitude we adapt when applying law in a professional way. Thus, the interpretation remains dependent upon the lawyer's aptitude to discover legal problems in cases while he is applying law. In this sense, every case is potentially a hard case and its qualification as a routine, simple case is temporary. While insisting upon the temporary distinction between routine and hard cases we support a more general strategic goal. Would we advocate the contrary view, i.e. argue that the routine cases are ontologically different from hard cases, we would also have to answer the question how then the legal-linguistic theory which should comprise all creation and application of law should match up to these requirements when it concentrated upon hard cases which undeniably represent the absolute minority of cases decided by courts all over the world. Routine interpretation is not possible in law because it would presuppose the determination of all contexts of application of the legal rules in advance which is clearly impossible (cf. Glass 1986: 458). Yet, our choice spares us this sort of a puzzle solution. Add to this that it would be then difficult to defend the thesis accepted by most legal theorists that law is an argumentative social practice. What role would the legal argumentation have to play were law comprised in terms of routine which does not accord much place to reasoning? In a world governed by such a law there is no place for legal theory, neither for Legal Linguistics. In fact, the obstinacy about the distinction between hard and routine cases is typical for defendants of law as a system based on concepts. For those opponents of an argumentative approach to law the system guarantees the right judicial decisions; for them problems with the application of law are due to the lack of legal knowledge. Dworkin and many others showed that the positivist and the systemic approach to law which is close to it are untenable both of them. Definitely, law and also the legal science need order to remain operative, yet this order is not necessarily a formalized system. We occasionally use here the term network and speak nevertheless about systematization efforts in law which we support with some reservation. This reservation concerns not that much the activity as such as the role it plays in law. For us, systematization concerns first of all the realm of arguments, not of concepts. We have therefore no problems with backing it in this form.

3.6.5.3 Why follow Dworkin? In countries dominated by the common law the questions of interpretation are dealt with towards the background of the court, esp. appellate decisions. Statutes play in this reasoning a less decisive role (Munday 1983: 192). In civil law countries interpretation is associated mostly with statutes and meaning attributed to them by jurists. Judiciary decisions are in their entirety rarely analyzed in this context (Glass 1988: 460). Glass observes that for Dworkin the necessity to interpret a text is strictly differentiated from the changing of the text into a different one. The criteria which Dworkin set up for the interpretation follow from this fundamental distinction (Glass 1988: 444). An acceptable legal interpretation in line with Dworkin's assumptions is one which satisfies the two dimensions of fit. They are formal features of coherence and correspondence with the existing legal rules and the dimension of value involving substantive considerations of policies and morality that make one ruling preferable to another. According to Glass, both Fish and Dworkin tried to describe interpretation in ways which avoid presenting it as being either determined or undetermined, objective or subjective, rule bound or free. In doing this, both consider the useful analogies which can be drawn between literary criticism and legal interpretation. Moreover, Glass criticized Dworkin for not looking closely to the legal practice and the rules according to which judges interpret statutes and precedents (Glass 1988: 455). Instead, he pretended, Dworkin would set up a normative-prescriptive theory of legal interpretation. Glass also pointed to the fact that Dworkin does not analyze the traditional method of interpretation in common law or the doctrine of stare decisis. Why is this so? We can scarcely assume that Dworkin had not been aware of those aspects of the legal practice. Why then is he not interested in them? For Dworkin, the legal interpretation is about controlling the context of the interpretation. The controlling institution is the court authorized to render decisions on the subject matter in question. As we have seen from above examples, courts do not hesitate to exercise their power to interpret precedents and statutes. The result of their work is the institutional interpretation which becomes law. This is its characteristic feature and the distinction from all other types of interpretations including other traditional forms of legal interpretation. Lawyers not vested with the authority to decide a subjudicial case like attorneys-at-law, legal scholars or judges not involved in the case may also be able to interpret statutes and precedents and they may do it in a convincing way. However, their professional interpretation will not obtain any legal force even if it were more persuasive than decisions rendered by the authorized court. Dissenting opinions in common law countries are the best example of the institutionalized character of legal interpretation. They are often appealing, yet they are not law. Also laypersons may interpret the law in their unprofessional way. Their interpretation either, although it is sometimes highly convincing, cannot become part of the law, due to the institutionalized nature of the phenomenon itself. A legal decision rendered by a competent court grounds in the normative character of this type of texts. Also in this way it strictly differs from all other types of interpretation.

We tried to incorporate R. Dworkin's views into our preliminary thoughts about the theory of the legal interpretation. The concepts of *constructive interpretation* and *law as integrity* correspond with the main ideas of interpretation perceived here as a legal-linguistic operation. We do not forget that R. Dworkin did not wish to establish a Legal Linguistics. His approach to law in terms of theory is different than ours. It developed in contrast to H. L. A. Hart's theory of legitimacy in law. R. Dworkin contributed to it a theory of justification. We, in turn, deal with all the issues mentioned by those and other legal theorists from the linguistic point of view. Our linguistic approach is based on language use and therefore cannot be applied to projections of law because future language use is undetermined yet. Here, again, formal and material arguments merge in our conception. Likewise, in a typical case analysis such as the following one legal and legal-linguistic issues merge (cf. 3.6.5.4). The Legal Linguistics is particularly interested in linguistic operations in such an analysis. Lawyers and legal theoreticians may prefer other aspects of systematization in law that are equally helpful because they may display other unexpected aspects of language use in law.

3.6.5.4 Controversies about law or language? We will illustrate the interrelation of legal and linguistic aspects on short case studies. The American securities market regulations have been previously interpreted as providing for the private right of action in cases of aiding and abetting in securities transactions. Since the Supreme Court decision Central Bank of Denver v. First Interstate Bank of Denver from 1994 this is not the case any more. Moreover, the Supreme Court reiterated its view 2008 in Stoneridge v. Scientific Atlanta. The case involved a cable company which inflated its revenues by using bogus transactions with two suppliers. Investors sued the suppliers claiming that they participated in a scheme to defraud them. The U.S. Supreme Court had to decide the question whether the securities laws allow shareholders to sue third parties who, knowingly or unwittingly, participate in a scheme to defraud – even if they did not directly mislead investors. The court stated that under the Securities Exchange Act Sec. 10 (b) and Rule 10b-5 there is no private right to sue the *secondary participants* as the provision establishes the right against *primary participants* only. Shareholders can therefore be succesful in this type of securities litigation only if they prove that the involved party (e.g. an accountant or an attorney-at-law) should be perceived as *primary participant* and not as a *secondary* one due to his particular involvement in the securities transaction. Also the SEC can sue in such cases. It can according to Sec. 20 (f) Private Securities Litigation Reform Act (PSLRA) sue "*any person that knowingly provides to another person substantial assistance*" in committing a securities violation. The Sec. 20 (f) PSLRA covers therefore the constellation of aiding and abetting and clearly encompasses *secondary participants.* As a result, it could happen that shareholders would be able to convince the court that their defendant is a *primary participant,*and the SEC would enforce a claim running parallel to it that would be based on aiding and abetting in a securities transaction against a participant which it qualifies as *secondary participant* (Cox 2006: 764). The same defendant could theoretically and simultaneously appear in terms of securities regulations as *primary* respectively as *secondary participant.* Shareholders as plaintiffs would have a problem in their litigations to refer to the SEC enforcement actions in which their prospective defendants have been perceived as *secondary participants.* Here, legal and linguistic problems intertwine.

An involved person cannot be perceived linguistically as *primary* and *secondary participant* in the same event, as it cannot be perceived in law as both at the same time. Concededly, the perception of participation as *primary* or *secondary*, both linguistically and legally, is a question of perspective. And, the legal argumentation can support only one view taken from a perspective that offers several options. Otherwise, it would become meaningless. Hence, the above basic contradiction is a limit to the legal argumentation. However, it remains open what is a contradiction in law. Logics and pragmatics may have different views upon this question because they relate to it from different perspectives. This constellation is therefore a challenge for the legal argumentation and the legal interpretation. Meanwhile, in Reves v. Ernst and Young (494 U.S. 56 1990) the U.S. Supreme Court while interpreting the notion of *security* under the U.S. financial market regulation provisions recognized that interpretive issues in law are well settled within the concept of *family resemblance*. J. Marshall who wrote the court opinion quoted the concept of family resemblance probably without any specific thoughts for L. Wittgenstein's innovative talents. However, he made plain that legal interpretation does not consist of the analyzing of isolated legal concepts. In recognizing this he comes close to B. Cardozo who in *Hynes* (in Notes and Materials nr. 35) referred to argumentative forms such as *concentric spheres* in facts and doctrine which led to the emergence of more complex interpretive methods than it had been frequently assumed in approaches dominated by legal positivism. The judge uses the notion of *family resemblance* as a test in order to determine whether promissory notes payable on demand by the holder can be perceived as *securities*. He says: "the "family resemblance" and "investment versus commercial" tests are really two ways of formulating the same general approach. Because we think the "family resemblance" test provides a more promising framework for analysis, however, we adopt it. The test begins with the language of the statute; because the Securities Act defines "security" to include "any note," we begin with the presumption that every note is a security. We nonetheless recognize that this presumption cannot be irrebuttable...Congress was concerned with regulating the investment market, not with creating a general federal cause of action for fraud. In an attempt to give more content to this dividing line, the Second Circuit has identified a list of instruments commonly denominated "notes" that nonetheless fall without the "security" category. See *Exchange National Bank*, supra, at 1138 (types of notes that are not "securities" include "the note delivered in consumer financing, the note secured by a mortgage on a home, the short-term note secured by a lien on a small business or some of its assets, the note evidencing a 'character' loan to a bank customer, short-term notes secured by an assignment of accounts receivable, or a note which simply formalizes an open-account debt of the customer of the broker, it is collateralized)"; *Chemical Bank*, supra, at 939 (adding to the list "notes evidencing loans by commercial banks for current operations"). The judge then applies the test in several steps: "First, we examine the transaction to assess the motivations that would prompt a reasonable seller and buyer to enter into it...Second, we examine the plan for the distribution of the instrument...Finally, we examine whether some factor such as the existence of another regulatory scheme significantly reduces the risk of the instrument, thereby rendering application of the Securities Acts unnecessary." Based on the four above factors, the judge draws his conclusions: "We conclude, then, that in determining whether an instrument denominated a "note" is a "security", courts are to apply the version of "family resemblance" test that we have articulated here: a note is presumed to be a "security," and the presumption may be rebutted only by a showing that the note bears a strong resemblance (in terms of the factors we have identified) to one of the enumerated categories of instrument. If the instrument is not sufficiently similar to an item on the list, the decision whether another category should be added is to be made by examining the same factors. Applying the family resemblance approach to this case, we have little difficulty in concluding that the notes at issue here are "securities." Ernst & Young admits that "a demand note does not closely resemble any of the Second Circuit's family resemblance examples." Nor does an examination of the four factors we have identified as being relevant to our inquiry suggest that the demand notes here are not "securities" despite their lack of similarity to any of the enumerated categories." The above U.S. Supreme Court decision from 1990 shows an advanced degree in legal argumentation and legal interpretation. First of all, it interprets legal concepts within their context of use and not in a splendid isolation of doctrinal debates. Moreover, it makes its approach also plain to those who – like the four partly dissenting justices in this case - may for whatever reasons prefer other interpretive strategies. One may observe on the margin that the notion of family resemblance as used here comes close to *prototype* analyzed by Kleiber (1990) and others (cf. 3.2.3.4).

3.6.6 Particular problems in interpreting statutes and contracts

Problems regarding the interpretation of statutes and other related legal documents such as governmental decrees appear in an at least three-fold constellation of language use. First, courts competent to decide complaints in which such issues arise are institutionally competent to provide a binding interpretation of an open statutory issue. The courts determine the meaning in an interpretive speech act (Savigny 1973: 30). Second, all persons dealing in a professonal way with legal statutes have to interpret them in order to grasp their meaning. Such persons elaborate the meaning or meaning alternatives for an open legal issue (Savigny 1973: 30). This is, for instance, the case when a legal scholar engages in the systematization of legal provisions and discovers interpretive problems in a statute that have not been decided in courts. Systematization and interpretation were therefore perceived as interrelated operations (Aarnio 1989: 301). Third, legal statutes can be read in an unprofessional way, e.g. by writers or other interested persons for the use in essays, novels or parodies. In the following, the two first varieties will be dealt with and the third one will be mentioned in the chapter on Literature and Law.

3.6.6.1 Statutes on interpretation: The legislative answer to the problem of statute interpretation could be the legislation on the interpretation of statutes. Why should the legislator not regulate the issue of statutory interpretation when all other essential aspects of the social reality are regulated by norms? The first problem connected with this issue is of logical sort. The statute would necessarily include legal concepts in a form which requires interpretation. Should these concepts be interpreted according to the interpretive guidelines provided by the statute in question or would a new statute on interpretation of the Statute on Interpretation become indispensable? Even if the concepts of the Statute on Interpretation would be interpretable according to the statutory provisions of the named statute, would this increase legal certainty or guarantee the appropriate interpretation of statutes by the authorized institutions? It seems that such legislation would not substantially contribute to the question of statute interpretation because the theoretical issue of interpretation remains unchanged notwithstanding whatever statutory regulation. The sporadically existing legislation on interpretation is illustrative upon the theoretical implications of interpretive operations that are explicitly regulated by the legislator. The New York Statute's § 94 provides an explanation on how to construe conceptual meaning in statutes in that it states that *legislative intent is to be ascertained from the words and language used, and the statutory language is generally construed according to its natural and obvious sense, without resorting to an artificial and forced construction.* The general approach of the legislator is understandable in this formulation. The legislator intends to increase the awareness of interpreting institutions to the text of a statute they deal with. But, the instrument which it provides to achieve this goal is disappointing. It does not explain how to distinguish between the natural and obvious sense and to protect the interpretive attempts against artificial and forced constructions. It is not surprising that § 94 had been subjected to numerous decisions of New York courts which had to determine what is the appropriate interpretation of the legislative intent. In Debevoise & Plimpton v. New York State Department of Finance (N.Y. 2d 657, 593 N.Y.S. 2d 974 (1993)) the Court of Appeals stressed that *words of ordinary import in a statute are to be given their natural and commonly understood meaning, unless it is clear from the statutory language that a different meaning was intended.* In course of the application of the interpretive rule the court then rejected the Tax Departments' interpretation of New York Tax Law § 1105. The Tax Department had to interpret the term *refrigeration and steam service* which according to the court did not include rent by the plaintiff to its landlord for overtime heating and air conditioning. The methodological gap which has to be bridged between the interpretive rule and the application in casu is evident. The result could be achieved also without resorting to the interpretive rule. Furthermore, in Manhattan Pizza Hut, Inc. v. New York State Human Rights Appeal Bd., (51 N.Y. 2d 506, 434 N.Y. S. 2d 96 (1980)) the Court of Appeals dealt with the interpretation of the term *marital status* in New York Executive Law § 269. It held that the term *marital status* did not include questions concerning the identity of occupation of a spouse but only the characterization as single, married or divorced. Here again, the court quoted the interpretive rule stating that *words of common usage are to be given their ordinary meaning.* Subsequently, it interpreted the legal notion *marital status* in terms of the legal language and did not reflect upon the ordinary usage which might, as a matter of fact, not include identity or occupation of a spouse but might include the category of widow/widower or even bigamist. In addition, the New York Statute's § 93 regulates the temporary aspect of interpretation by stating that *a statute speaks, not from the time...when the courts are called on to interpret it, but as of the time it took effect.* It prevents the adaptation of statutes to changing circumstances and by doing so it also reflects the approach to legislative acts in the Anglo-American legal tradition where statutes should be interpreted narrowly (Mattila 2006: 36). Moreover, in a situation of changed circumstances a change of the statute by the legislator is preferred to the adjustment of the statutory provision by the authorized institution to the changes occurred as it is frequently practiced in the civil law countries. Although the New York Statute on the interpretation of legislative intent has been perceived as an interesting approach to the challenge of statutory interpretation and had been even admiratively mentioned in the then Soviet legal literature (Pigolkin 1990: 130), it clearly shows the limits of a legislative measure directed towards structuring of the statutory interpretation. Other countries have also introduced provisions to the same aim. The (UK) Interpretation Act from 1978 is a statute which includes provisions regarding the construction of statutes and provides definitions and rules for their understanding. It states among other things that words importing the masculine gender include females, words in the singular include the plural and words in plural include the singular, the expression *person* includes a body corporate etc. Some U.K. statutes include sections expressly incorporating the Interpretation Act. Some statutes include interpretation sections, such as the (UK) Theft Act of 1968 where in sec. 34 the definition of *goods* is provided. Courts also use preambles of statutes as an aid to interpretation. As already stated, these interpretive instruments do not replace interpretation; they may however render it less opaque. Additionally, in Notes and Materials nr.19 some French, Italian and German provisions concerning interpretation are quoted. Particularly relevant for the French law is Art. 1156

French Civil Code as contrasted with Art. 111-4 French Penal Code that provides for strict interpretation in criminal law, (FR): *La loi pénale est d'interprétation stricte.*

With all this being said, it seems to be preferable to develop guidelines for interpretation of legislative acts wherever needed. Their positive impact can be seen in raising awareness of jurists towards the problem of statutory interpretation. Nevertheless, problems concerning creative interpretation as characterized by Dworkin will remain in the center of the interpretive activities. Those activities cannot be reduced to applicational schemes which in a situation where statutory interpretation is needed would automatically lead to an acceptable solution. They are complex legal-linguistic operations. Some effort and professional skills must always be invested in the legal interpretive activities.

3.6.6.2 Interpreting statutes: Interpretive strategies used by courts are centered around the notion of *creative interpretation* introduced into the legal theory by R. Dworkin. They are less visible than the traditional interpretive canons (Alexy 1983: 19) because courts usually do not mark explicitly in their decisions the creative moments in the interpretation. These strategies are centered around the notion of *creative interpretation* rather loosely because the dose of creativity in them differs. Structurally, they ground in the idea of the probability of meaning. For instance, in Goldstein v. SEC (p. 13) the court observed that: "*it may be that the strict dichotomy between clarity and ambiguity is artificial, that what we have is a continuum, a probability of meaning.*" The legal theory structures the statute interpretation more systematically. In MacCormic and Summers (1991: 512 sqq) following arguments types were held characteristic for statutory interpretation: argument from *ordinary meaning*, argument from *technical meaning*, argument from *contextual harmonization*, argument from *precedent*, argument from *analogy*, argument from relevant *principles of law*, argument from *history*, argument from *purpose*, argument from *substantive reasons* and argument from *intention*. The interpretive strategy to determine the meaning of a statutory provision may be based on existing precedents and interpretive standards. In such a case, it is rather based on professional argumentative skills than on particularly creative linguistic innovations. The pertaining interpretive strategy used to be based on the legislative intent. It is equally centered around the *creative interpretation* because the legislative intent itself is a creative argument. For instance, in Water, Waste & Land Inc. dba Westec v. Lanham (955 P.2d 997, 1998) the Supreme Court of Colorado had to interpret the section 7-80-208 of the Colorado Limited Liability Company Act (1997). The section states: *The fact that the articles of organization are on file in the office of the secretary of state is notice that the limited liability company is a limited liability company and is notice of all other facts set forth therein which are required to be set forth in the articles of organization.* In the case, managers of an LLC acted without revealing that they represent the LLC and were therefore sued personally. At trial, they admitted the liability of the LLC. The court had therefore to decide whether the fact that the managers failed to disclose the existence as well as the identity of the LLC led to their personal liability under the rules of agency. The court had to consider the above section which places third parties on constructive notice of the character of the company and especially its limited liability. The court decided that the personal liability of the managers was established by their acting without a clear reference to the LLC. Otherwise, so the court, third parties which relied on the personal liability of their interlocutors could easily become victims of deceit and outright fraud. Thus, the court asked first of all for the rationale of the provision which - when literarily interpreted - could also justify the opposite result. Finally, the court grounded its interpretation in the authority of the General Assembly which as the court presumed "*did not intend to create a safe harbor for deceit*". Apparently, the court expected that its interpretation may not be sufficiently persuasive and needed a stronger argument which it also found in the form of reference to an authority vested with broad powers. In sum, it is typical for statutory interpretation that different arguments are used in it. Their choice depends on the selected interpretive strategy.

Frequently, statutes are interpreted by jurists without reference to an authoritative interpretation in situations where no precedents exist for an issue. To illustrate, the Act to Ensure Truth in Music Advertising enacted by the U.S. State of Maine and effective September 2007 (rendered in Notes and Materials as nr. 18) has not been subject to judicial scrutiny. The act strategically anticipates interpretive issues in its § 1157 and provides definitions for notions which may lead to interpretive problems, e.g. performing group, person, recording group or sound recording. However, definitional guidelines regarding nouns used in a text usually do not solve interpretive problems; they allow for a shorter formulation of the statutory text (Savigny 1983: 26) and are the basis for the notional shorthand script mentioned by T. Kotarbiński (cf. 2.4.4). When the application of the statute concerns its main case constellation, i.e. the forbidden live musical performance or production through the use of a false, deceptive or misleading affiliation according to § 1158, the definitions of the previous section cannot help. Professional interpretation of the notions *false*, *deceptive* or *misleading affiliation* becomes necessary. Thorough research is needed to determine the difference between false, deceptive, and misleading. Procedurally, statute interpretation by courts is limited by the doctrine of stare decisis. This fundamental common law doctrine which is more fully formulated as (LAT) *stare decisis et non quieta movere* is the background of judicial decisions in the common law. Dworkin describes it as "giving gravitational force to past decisions" (Dworkin 1991: Preface). In the case law, cases are perceived as data subjected to interpretations which, again, depend on the strategies selected by their interpreters. The exception to it is the technique of overruling and distinguishing which enables to avoid following a precedent perceived as not helpful for the solution of a case. K. Llewellyn in *The Common Law Tradition* (1960: 77-91) described 64 techniques for the justification of following or not following of precedents. Among them are arguments such as the following: the ambit of the norm is too broad, the *ratio legis* is not clearly stated, the rule elaborated in the precedent is grounded in erroneously analyzed precedents, the precedent concerns only exceptional and not regular situations, only some material facts should be taken into consideration and finally that the precedent has been overruled already. Llewellyn claimed also decades before Dworkin that every rule must be set in its context of use to be interpreted properly (DiMatteo 2005). For the Legal Linguistics, the doctrine of *stare decisis* is a principle that stresses the intertextuality in law and ensures the coherence of texts produced in it. In terms of legal argumentation it is based on the principle of analogy.

3.6.6.3 Contract interpretation under the common law: Courts interpret contracts by pointing to their written texts, other evidence of prior dealings, course of performance and trade usage. In the doctrine the notion of *contract* has been perceived as not defined in a satisfactory way (Perillo 2003: 1). Traditional legal methods on which contract interpretation is based are: *four-corner analysis*, the *totality of circumstances analysis* and the *reasonable person standard.* The first stage in interpretation comprises studying the language of the contract to determine its meaning according to the four-corner analysis or plain meaning rule. This totality of circumstances analysis includes several steps; in case when the language is unclear the court will analyze the relationship and the actions of the contracting parties. The judge will look at the evidence of the 'course of performance' and analyze the post-formation conduct of the parties in order to clarify what the parties believed their contract meant. If the contract is still unclear, the judge may study any prior contracts or dealings between the parties to infer a previously established meaning. At the final stage, the meaning will be inferred from outside the contract by referring to the trade usage or custom. If no clear meaning in the sense of the plain meaning rule can be established the plaintiff will lose his case because of his failure to meet his burden of proof regarding the meaning of a clause or a concept in the contract. The totality of circumstances analysis was defined in commercial contracts by the English House of Lords as the need *"for the court to know the commercial purpose of the contract. This presupposes knowledge of the genesis of the transaction, background, context and the market in which the parties are operating"* (Lord Wilberforce in: Reardon Smith Line Ltd v. Ingvar Hansen-Tangen (W.L.R 989, 996 (1976)). Furthermore, the *reasonable person* standard reflects the totality of circumstances analysis because it is usually constructed around usages, customs or practices among business people in a particular trade or ordinary customers outside commercial contracts. Its role is increasing as many contracts nowadays are based on standard forms and are not a product of complicated negotiations and elaborated agreements. It takes into consideration: 1) terms expressly negotiated by the parties; 2) what non-negotiated terms must be reconstructed or expelled because of unreasonableness; 3) what terms are to be implied to fill gaps. We provide an example for the mechanics of the four-courner analysis in the Frigaliment-case in our Notes and Materials nr. 30. Certain expressions in contracts, e.g. *as is* are commonly understood to exclude all implied warranties, but do not bar an action for deceit or restitution (Perillo 2003: 354). In such a case the judge will regularly not enter into their new interpretation but rather use the result of interpretations provided in existing court decisions. In case of differences about the linguistic interpretation the judge determines the meaning of a word used by the parties. Breyer, J. underlined in his dissenting opinion in Medellín v. Texas, 552 U.S. 06-984 (2008): *Imagine that two parties to a contract agree to binding arbitration about whether a contract's provision's word "grain" includes rye. They would expect that, if the arbitrator decides that the word "grain" does include rye, the arbitrator will then simply read the relevant provision as if it said "grain including rye."* Parties's intent therefore dominates contract interpretation (cf. 3.6.3.4).

3.6.6.4 Interpretation in International Law: For a long time, the international law relied solely on 'rules of logics' and national interpretive methods when dealing with international treaties (Cassese 2005: 178). Jurists mostly referred to the intention of the draftsmen of international instruments and some vaguely formulated interpretive maxims such as (LAT) *in dubio mitius* that aimed at protecting the sovereign decision of states in cases when a broader or a narrower interpretation of a provision regarding their international obligations was at stake. The Vienna Convention on the Law of Treaties from 1969 has systematized and modernized the interpreation methods in regard of treaties. Its Art. 31 provides that *a treaty shall be interpreted in good faith in accordance with the ordinary meaning to be given to the terms of the treaty in their context and in the light of its object and purpose.* The convention embraces the traditional interpretive canon termed in three components: literal, systematic and teleological (Cassese 2005: 179). Art. 32 mentions the preparatory materials that can be used to lighten obscure formulations in treaties when the literal, systematic and teleological methods did not lead to satisfying results. Art. 33 presumes the same meaning in treaties drafted in different linguistic versions; in doubtful cases the meaning that best supports the text of the treaty as regards its object and purpose is preferred. The convention recommends a guiding interpretive principle of effectiveness of the treaty - (LAT) *ut res magis valeat quam pereat* - to the detriment of the mentioned maxim *in dubio* *mitius* that emphasized the sovereign right and the least unfavorable content of a controversial provision for the state as an addressee of legal duties under a treaty (Cassese ibid.). Next to the Articles 31-33 of the Vienna Convention also some interpretive standards developed under national law were incorporated into the interpretive strategies in the international law. The *implied powers doctrine* that had been developed by the U.S. Supreme Court in the case McCulloch v. the State of Maryland in 1819 has been applied upon problems of determining the tasks and prerogatives of international organizations. Hence, a doctrine of domestic law that aimed at elaborating the ambit of state law in the confrontation with federal provisions has been applied in analogy upon relations between the international organization and its member states. This interpretive strategy called *federal analogy* has been sometimes criticized as providing excessive powers to international organizations (Cassese 2005: 180).

3.6.7 Is law based on interpretive or argumentative practices?

The relation between interpretation and argumentation is still unclear (Atienza 1999: 45). In research works and in specialized encyclopedias both topics are usually treated separately. This occurs because apparently no logically necessary link is perceived between both operations. One can therefore try to discuss issues related to interpretation without explicitly enter into the debate about argumentation. In such a debate, argumentation would provide the tacit background to the discussion about preference given to one or another interpretive variety of a text. Argumentation might be in this context perceived as the formal part of interpretation, an issue concerning the structure of arguments used in the interpretation and specifically in a situation where preference must be given to one of different available varieties. Conversely, interpretation may be described as practical argumentation (Eriksson 1997: 14). This interrelation is particularly interesting in law. Others tried to link interpretation and argumentation while using the structural model of emission and reception of messages. For A. Greimas, interpretation is the linguistic activity *(faire interpretatif)* of the receiver of the message, argumentation (*faire persuasif*), in turn, concerns the emitter of the message (Jackson 1985: 57). For Greimas, this distinction did not play any particular role because he was primarily interested in the signification act itself, where it does not matter whether it is interpretation or argumentation. Both distinctive notions belong to the pragmatics of discourse (Jackson 1985: 57) and might play a significant role there. Is the interpretation understood in a narrow, philological sense as a search for the initial meaning of the text, then law can be meaningfully construed as an argumentative and not as an interpretive praxis (Grasnich 2001: 33). Some argumentative features may require interpretive preparation; analogical arguments in law rely on interpretive acts as their essential preliminary (Nerhof 1992: 23). When the different approaches to signification, argumentation and interpretation are taken into consideration, the indistinctive model relating to signification as such might be useful. It would integrate both the interpretive results and its argumentative form and elucidate conditions for signification processes in them. This is particularly persuasive in the model developed by Greimas. Apparently, it would not be necessary to distinguish between creation and translation in law either and it would be possible to view these processes through the unifying concept of signification. Nevertheless, we are here more interested in the pragmatic aspects of language use and will therefore use and distinguish both notions for practical reasons. Furthermore, we will also use the notions creation and translation of law. While doing so, we are aware that the underlying processes in which signification comes about are constitutive for whatever form of language use, i.e. for every speech act. We believe that through the procedure of distinguishing between different speech acts we remain closer to our material which is the language as it is used in legal contexts. The other procedure, advocated by A. Greimas, has the advantage that it allows to construct a coherent semiotic model of signification processes while including legal contexts. By so proceeding, it proves that it is universally applicable as a semiotic theory. Yet, it benefits more the semiotic theory than it benefits law. Our ambition is different. While being admirative of several semiotic and pragmatic models we try to make them operational for the law. As a result of our efforts, linguistic operations in law should become more transparent and also controllable in a more rational way. Unsurprisingly, the case analyses, even those not particularly numerous which we undertook here, show the interdependence of argumentative and interpretive issues. Law is a discursive practice and cannot be created nor applied without recourse to arguments. Interpretive contexts which are also argumentative in its character will remain the central problem of the application of law.

3.6.8 Interpretation in natural sciences

In terms of methodology, interpretation in natural sciences follows experimentation and concerns primarily data which emerge as a result of an experiment. Interpretation is perceived as explication, i.e. attributing sense to data gathered in experiments and in particular theories set up subsequently. One and the same fact (data) can be interpreted differently in the light of the theory shared by the interpreting scientists (Searle1999: 6). A new theory causes new interpretation of data. Social and cultural factors definitely play a role in the evolution of theories in natural sciences as well as in their internal paradigmatic developments. Theoretical and empirical levels are interrelated there. However, data may also give raise to different theories. The problem does not concern the access to data, but the inherited categories used for their interpretation (Searle 1999: 69). In natural sciences the dependence of interpretation and facts has never been questioned as had been that of interpretation and theorems on which it is based. By contrast, legal sciences had been dominated by the view that a written legal rule could be interpreted univocally and that it could lead to the only right legal decision in a case. The classical idea of justice makes it understandably difficult to accept that a legal provision can be interpreted differently in the light of different approaches or interpretive strategies. Nevertheless, the legal science cannot guarantee more than the best possible decision which is reached in the recourse to legal-argumentative mechanisms and the specific creative potentiality in interpretive techniques which only increase their legitimacy. The main difference between the legal science and the natural sciences is therefore not of qualitative art. It is grounded in different attitudes towards interpretation of data within the respective professional communities.

3.7 Legal Translation

3.7.1 Linguistic transformations of law

Legal translation is for us one of the central linguistic operations in law, especially in all its international contexts. While identifying the most fundamental linguistic operations in law we departed from the creation of legally binding rules through the legal speech acts. Subsequently, we have identified one more central process in law, i.e. the application of the legal rules expressed through language. However, this process is too complex to be incorporated into the Legal Linguistics with all its implications. We focused therefore upon the two main and inevitable legal-linguistic operations in the application of law; i.e. argumentation and interpretation. In the international context another central legal-linguistic operation must be added to those already discussed dominant varieties of legal-linguistic operations. Frequently, law in the international context cannot be applied directly in a case, but must, instead be linguistically transformed in order to become operative. This additional indirect variety of a linguistic operation in law is the legal translation. In pragmatic terms, this linguistic transformation regards the legal speech acts responsible for the creation of legal rules. Our main concern will therefore be the procedure in which legal speech acts of the source language are transformed into meaningful and equivalent legal speech acts in the target language. This operation, seen also beyond the legal context, has been perceived as one of typical language games (Wittgenstein 1984: 250). Therefore, researchers pondered intensively how to preserve the speech act's original meaning in the specific context as defined by the law to which it refers and which it also shapes with linguistic means. The starting point for an analysis of this type is the identification of the legal speech act which must be transformed. In the case when this seems to be evident, its classification within the two respective legal-linguistic contexts has to take place. This activity has a long background that is worth mentioning in the following paragraph.

3.7.2 A retrospective upon legal translation

The translation of legal texts is a practice boasting a long history. The best known artifacts in this field include the peace treaty between Egypt and the Hittite Empire concluded 1271 BC as well as the translation of the *Corpus Iuris Civilis* into numerous languages after its initial translation into Greek. We are also told that the Assyrian king Kargon let the laws of his kingdom be translated into the languages of his subjects around 3000 BC; 2100 BC a group of translators worked on the preparation of the linguistic varieties of the Babylonian Hammurabi code (Arsova-Nikolić 1999: 13). Some artifacts that played a preponderant role for other disciplines such as the Rosetta Stone that enabled the deciphering of the Egyptian hieroglyphes included text types that would be classified today as legal texts (cf. Spiegelberg 1922: 11). The Rosetta Stone bears a decree issued by the pharao Ptolemeus V in 196 BC in two variants of the Egyptian script and in Greek. The translators of these and other legal texts from past centuries – most of whom remain unknown to us – must certainly have reflected on the methodological problems associated with their complex and demanding task. Unfortunately, these reflections have not been handed down in history. Systematic study has only recently begun in the field of legal translation, but most significant problems have already been identified and the research has certainly shown its practical applications with the help of comparative law, Legal Linguistics and legal data processing (Stolze 2005: 9). It would be tempting to assume that translation of texts actually began with the legal translation as even today some specialists mention the legal translation as the beginning of studies about the general translation of texts (Arsova-Nikolić 1999: 13). This assumption is very probable because the need for legal translation emerges with trangressing the borders of one's own culture that in the past were also frequently borders of one's own state. Nowadays, a parallel process that is based on transgressing national borders emerges within the European Union (Mattila 2006: 25). Although the development of the European Union law has undeniably stimulated the discussion of legal translation, officially bilingual or multilingual countries (for instance Canada, Switzerland or Finland) have been familiar with the problem for some time. In these countries, the subject makes up one of the standard topics for legal research and education.

3.7.3 Terminological equivalence

To date, legal translation has primarily been researched through the perspective of terminology. In this regard, the emphasis has fallen largely on the question of how terms indigenous to one legal system can be conveyed in the equivalent terms of another legal system. Research aimed at demarcating areas of semantic correspondence among legal terms, e.g. (IT) *beni*, (FR) *biens* or (UK/US) *goods*. Moreover, Legal Linguistics has shown that the transfer of information not only takes place within the context of legal systems, but also concerns two predominantly technical language systems. This poses two significant problems. First, there is the question of the conditions under which the target legal text corresponds to the source legal text, whereby the requirements of equivalence must be ascertained in the context of a technical language. Second, specific problems must be resolved, depending on which source language is being translated into which target language. After all, a legal system with numerous institutions that have developed over time represents only one of the challenges for the translator. The language system itself with its syntactic and semantic implications places certain demands on the translator and even creates limits for the translation. The theory of translation has to solve this intricacy. It is based on an understanding of two texts: a source text which is to be translated and a target text which is the result of the actual translation process. The task of the translator is to establish a relationship of equivalence between the source and the target texts, i.e. a substantive homogeneity.

The term *equivalence* has been discussed in numerous linguistic works. In this regard, the spectrum of opinions ranges from an 'everything goes' approach to the assertion of the fundamental impossibility inherent in the act of translation – in other words, the factually contingent and unavoidable failure through intermediary approaches presenting requirements for approximate equivalence, or suggesting the redefinition of the concept of equivalence (Torop 1998: 137). Occasionally, equivalence has been described as an illusion (Snell-Hornby 1986: 13). For all intents and purposes, this diversity of opinion is neither surprising nor accidental. It is the natural result of different linguistic approaches which have proposed various solutions for the problem of equivalence on the basis of conflicting theorems (Mounin 1963: 9). However, once the term *equivalence* has been clearly defined, as for instance in Reiss-Vermeer (1984: 140), it performs an important function in the science of translation. There, *equivalence* is formulated in terms of the *skopos*-theory. This theory focuses upon the aim under which the translation is effectuated (cf. also Madsen 2007). For instance, a Japanese poem may be translated primarily as regards its form or rather its content, dependent upon the aim of the translation. The problems relating to legal translation – especially in the field of terminology – can be more easily presented with the help of the definition proposed by Reiss and Vermeer that can be perceived as introducing functional translation into terminological work. It is largely operative in law when e.g. (FR) *acte sous seing privé* is translated as (D) *mit Unterschrift versehene*

Privaturkunde or (FR) *dépeçage* is translated as (D) *gespaltene Anknüpfung*. As there are no German legal terms corresponding to the French ones an innovative translation that renders the meaning of the French concepts can be used in accordance with the *skopos*-theory. *Skopos*-theoretical choices must be exercised for instance in translating names of institutions, courts etc. The name of a Swedish court (S) *hovrätt* can be transformed 1) literally, 2) while taking into consideration its historical background, 3) in a descriptive way and 4) functionally (cf. Mattila 2002d: 277). Mostly, the functional translation will be needed; therefore (S) *hovrätt* will be translated as (FR) *cour d'appel* or (FIN) *hovioikeus*. While translating (S) *Svea hovrätt* a descriptive or a mixed functional/descriptive translation (with a description in brackets or in footnotes) may be better suited. The needs of the translation determine the choice. Nevertheless, functional equivalence depends not only on the terminology but also on the legal text, with all its syntactic, semantic and pragmatic implications; e.g. (S) *talan om äktenskapsskillnad väcktes* corresponds with (D) *die Scheidungsklage wurde eingereicht*. Thus, the claim that has been filed is rendered with (D) *eingereicht* or (S) *väcktes*. In this case, there is no need for *skopos*-theoretical choices because both legal languages, German and Swedish, dispose of exact context-bound syntagmas used in respective speech acts.

Many such background notions have been largely discussed in the research. Weisgerber (1961) launched the debate on translation problems as an analysis of errors, working from the premise of the fundamental impossibility of textual translation. Weisgerber's perception is paradoxical insofar as the editorial suggestions he makes in his critique of an international treaty text actually manifest the possibility of translation, rather than the impossibility that he maintains. Kielar (1977) makes an insightful link between the problem areas from the analytical point of view. She perceives the technical legal language as interconnected with the systematic structure of the law and the language. This specialized and technical legal language can be separated from the general language by the means of contrastive analysis. This formal approach may initially satisfy the requirements of a descriptive model. However, our remarks about legal terminology show that formal boundaries are difficult to draw. *Promissory estoppel* is definitely a legal concept; *mother-in-law* may turn to a legal concept depending on the context of use. When a court decision is taken in a French court (FR) *en chambre du conseil* is this formulation legal-linguistic or simply linguistic in its essence? The translation *behind closed doors* or (FIN) *suljetuin ovin* (Mattila 2002b: 505) may indicate the possibility of a non-professional translation. Yet, this sample of translation of the French sophisticated phrase requires legal knowledge. Also Vogel (1988) made an attempt at describing the legal translation. His analysis of the translation process differentiates between general language terms and legal terminology. The choice of non-technical words such as (D) *Verbindung* or (D) *Bindung* – made with reference to a text concerning the relationship between West Germany and the then West Berlin – can contain as much legal relevance as legal concepts, e.g. a trading company or partnership (*Handelsgesellschaft* in German) or public limited company (*Aktiengesellschaft* in German) (Vogel 1988: 43). For instance, (D) *Verbindung* or (D) *Bindung* both mean 'ties', but they were understood by negotiators of the Berlin Agreement as conveying varying degrees of intensity. (D) *Verbindung* suggests 'ties' such as 'connections', e.g. train connections while (D) *Bindung* – literary a 'knot' – denotes a stronger bond. Some other conceptions of legal translation also focus on the area of legal terminology. In these views, legal terms refer to the relevant areas of a legal system; a technical translation therefore requires a descriptive language that can render the incompatible legal terms without any material losses in terms of content. De Groot (1987) follows a similar track. He discusses the problems of legal translation in terms of comparative law, which in his view comprises the key element in legal translation. In his view, the level of difficulty of a legal translation does not primarily depend on linguistically determined differences, but rather on structural differences between legal systems (de Groot in Balkema/de Groot 1987: 18). In this respect, the relationship between the languages is only of secondary importance in comparison with the relationship between the legal systems. As an example, de Groot cites the largely unproblematic case of translations from Danish into Norwegian, and in the case of multilingual states with a single legal system – such as Finland – where the problem falls anyway entirely, despite the linguistic differences between Finnish and Swedish, the two national languages. Making legal language uniform at the international level is of utmost importance for de Groot. He therefore advocates the development of a legal metalanguage to convey legal terms that are defined by national laws (de Groot in de Groot/Schulte 1999). A complete equivalence between the terms of two legal systems can only be attained if both legal languages refer to the same legal system, positing an acceptable equivalence between two legal systems and not two languages. If no equivalence can be established, de Groot suggests several alternatives: citation of the non-translated term, paraphrasing, and the creation of neologisms or a combination of these.

Finally, the structural similarity between translation of legal terms and the process of qualification - (US) characterization - in the private international law is obvious for jurists. It can be exemplified on the Maldonado case rendered in Notes and Materials nr. 38. The qualification of a legal concept transforms it into an equivalent concept of the other law in order to make it understandable for foreign lawyers. Initial discussions of this problem in the conflict of laws doctrine pointed to the fundamental impossibility of qualification (Bartin 1897) due to incompatibility of legal systems. The mere fact that the qualification of legal concepts regularly takes place outside of static classification processes already runs counter to the fundamental impossibility of qualification (Rabel 1956: 13). Thus, the problem of qualification can basically be resolved. This presupposes, however, the application of methodologically sound techniques. Rabel (1956: 23) defined it as a comparison of conflict of law's concepts with those belonging to other jurisdictions. For the translator, this means having to rely on a methodical resource in answering questions of qualification which may arise in individual cases. Nevertheless, the significance of the act of qualification in private international law in the descriptive model of legal translation has not been conclusively defined. It must be therefore determined whether qualification is the method of legal translation or whether it is only an aid in the translation process. Finally, it is not sure that the legal transformation of concepts also necessitates their linguistic transformation as the conditio sine qua non of translation. Should this not be the case, both the qualification and the legal translation would be interrelated but essentially independent operations.

3.7.4 Descriptive model of legal translation

While describing the legal translation it is helpful to distinguish the subject matter oriented research and research about the discipline proper on a meta-level of reflection; this is rather a demanding task as the translation theory is not a consolidated field (Borja Albi 2004: 1-2). New linguistic approaches – of which the analysis by S. Šarčević may be paradigmatic – concentrate rather on pragmatic aspects of legal texts and underscore the need for the development of general translation strategies. In contrast, examinations undertaken from the legal perspective by authors such as H. Mattila place the emphasis on comparative law elements, although textual aspects are increasingly included in these comparative legal analyses (Mattila 2002b). Increasingly also interpretive strategies are mentioned in prefaces to the translations and terminological problems are discussed in footnotes to translations (cf. Anderson/Okuda 2007). However, both of these trends are characterized by increased tendency towards approximation and efforts to discuss legal translation problems within a broader context, more in keeping with the complexity of legal and linguistic problems (Galdia 2003a: 21).

The discussion of the terminological problems of legal translation revolves around the term 'denotation'. A legal concept under legal system A, understood as a systemic concept, is transformed into another concept under legal system B, by finding a term that corresponds with the function of the legal concept under legal system A. This allows, for example, the English legal term *trust* to be translated into German as *Treuhand* in certain instances. In the translation of legal terms, one often resorts to pairs of terms which appear somehow connected by a relationship of equivalence. The legal denoters which have to date been applied in the descriptive model - e.g. (D) *Versäumnisurteil* for *default judgment* and (FIN) *yksipuolinen tuomio* have the same legal meaning, but the question is what do they denote? The difficulty of answering this question may provide more fertile ground for further analysis than the eventual answer itself. At the very last, the difficulty may illustrate that the two designated terms might lack a common denoter. They function differently than synonyms; the terms 'mean' the same things to jurists, even though they are not identical. They are also not really similar because they exist in the context of different legal and language systems, but still they remain comparable. It can be safely said that the functional method of comparative law has proven the comparability of such legal terms. The aforementioned concepts can also be compared by reference to their connotations. In respect of the first term, it would be sufficient to provide a linguistic basis for the functional comparative law term in order to determine the connotations of the legal terms.

How could one characterize the elements of the descriptive model for legal translation? It follows from the various above mentioned studies that legal translation is primarily characterized by the denotative components of the technical language, whereas the legal system itself guarantees the basis of the translation. Denotation forms only a part of the entire process of translation, although its importance cannot be denied. In fact, an entire text – and not just terms – is the subject of translation, even though many translators concentrate only on the terms as such. Every text also has a connotative level, which is semantically as important as the denotative level. Furthermore, the text is defined by tense, mood and other linguistic categories (van Dijk 1980: 24). It is constituted but also limited by the specific linguistic system. The descriptive model which up to now has been based on denoters is weighed down by one problem. It is unclear how the denotation referred to by the denoters is to be understood. The denoters depicted as the pillars of the descriptive model – i.e. the relevant legal terms – must refer to a common subject matter in order for the descriptive model to function. Since this fact has generally been acknowledged, a call emerged for a metalanguage as the descriptive 'instrument' for the individual legal languages. References were made in this regard to civil law theory, comparative law and the exemplary description of all legal systems in order to produce a usable object for denotation. Naturally, connotative aspects of a legal language are incorporated into the translation. Thus, the denotation and connotation of legal terms enable the determination of the feasibility of functional equivalence. The relevant legal term in the source text denotes and connotes a position or an area within its own legal and language system. Furthermore, this term forms a part of a complex technical language structure, which in turn also defines it. In practice, existing conceptions point to a translation which is of a technical nature. The relevant technical legal language is marked by lexical, semantic and often intercultural facets which must be taken into consideration in the translation process. The syntactic implications for translation – a much neglected area in the study of translation theory – will most certainly gain importance as research in this field continues. Towards this complex structural background the legal speech act can be properly identified and linguistically transformed.

3.7.5 Legal metalanguage

Another model for technical translation is the translation into a metalanguage as the universal descriptive language for the propositional content of legal texts. The framework for developing this language is found in comparative law, which examines basic terms and legal structures in an international context (cf. Rabel 1956: 66). By taking into account the legal-linguistic components of the legal languages – in particular, the syntactic structure and the pragmatic meaning of legal texts, a metalanguage will emerge that not only contains a few succinct legal words, but also represents a thesaurus of the legal language. A metalanguage already exists with regard to legal terminology for fundamental problems of contemporary continental civil law: the Latin of the Roman law. At most, however, the Latin legal language allows only for an understanding of certain basic problems relating to traditional legal doctrine which are seldom the topic of legal translations. For instance, a quasi-contractual obligation such as (FR) *gestion d'affaire,* (D) *Geschäftsführung ohne Auftrag,* (JAP) *jimu kanri* can be referred to as (LAT) *negotiorum gestio* where a description, e.g. *management of affairs without mandate* or a comparative explication, e.g. *it is roughly similar to liability for agency by necessity* seem less helpful or cumbersome (cf. Anderson/Okuda 2007: 148). This problem has lent increasing support to arguments for a metalanguage based on comparative law as the best medium for legal translation. An antithetical concept of technical legal translation could be based on the fundamental structure of the ordinary language. We mentioned this possibility also in the context of the emergence of the legal language as a thinkable alternative to the special register favored by most jurists (cf. 2.2.4). Here we may therefore ask again one of the central legal-linguistic questions: if the ordinary language offers an adequate guarantee for the meaning of the words, then why should it not qualify as the universal descriptive language of the law? This especially holds true for areas such as international legal relations that are still wrestling with their own language. However, this concept has not been given much consideration in research to date (Galdia 2003a: 11-12). As mentioned already in the chapters on the legal argumentation and the legal interpretation, the ordinary language is an alternative tool for building all legal speech acts, i.e. argumentative, interpretive, translative and so on. The future will show what role it will play in the legal communication, especially in the global law.

3.7.6 Interdisciplinary aspects

The question arises as to the extent that the discussion to date has helped to solve problems relating to the translation of legal texts. In essence, it concerns the question of whether the problem of legal translation can be solved by means of the application of linguistic theorems or only through an interdisciplinary approach. Although a clear answer to this question might seem obvious, it should be nevertheless explicitly formulated. The current discussion of legal translation could create the impression that the discussion concerning the substance of foreign law and its comparability, which was originally the foreground, has become less important, given the slew of description models with a purely linguistic orientation and debates on argumentation. However, this initial impression is deceptive, since legal translation is and remains at its core linked to the contents of the respective legal institutions. Therefore, the legal-linguistic studies which highlight the comparative law method seem to point in the right direction. These include for instance research on *unjust enrichment* (Mattila 2002b: 515), a private law institution in numerous legal systems, which was aimed at establishing the relevant contents of the term for translation purposes before translation into the applicable legal terms (NL) *onrechtvaardige verrijking* or (FR) *enrichissement sans cause* is possible. These decisions, which form an integral part of the translation process, are made by taking into account the structural differences, between the relevant legal systems and the functional embodiment of the respective terms in the national law framework, which contextually either allow or preclude the relevant systemic concepts. However, such an analysis can only be applied broadly, since structural and functional differences do not become obvious otherwise, thereby prompting the translator to use terms that are lexically related, but inappropriate from a comparative law perspective. This problem is also illustrated by reference to criminal law terminology. For example, based on the former system of differentiation prevailing in French law, the general term (FR) *infraction* (German: *Straftat*, Italian: *reato*; English: *crime*) has three subcategories, represented by the terms *crime, délit* and *contravention* (English: *felony, misdemeanour, petty offence*), which in turn correspond with historical legal terms in Italian (*crimine, delitto, contravvenzione*) and German (*Verbrechen, Vergehen, Übertretung*). However, in both Italian and German criminal law, the terminological structure has changed to the extent that (D) *Straftat* in German law is now classified as either (D) *Verbrechen* or *Vergehen* and the general category of (IT) *reato* in Italian law is subdivided into *delitto* or *contravvenzione*, although the subcategories in Italian and German no more overlap in terms of their content. Comparative research on terminology in German and Finnish criminal law yields similar results

(Galdia 2003a: 17), which goes back to the fact that the Finnish system has only one standard term that can be rendered in legal German as *Straftat*, as Finnish criminal law no longer distinguishes between concepts comparable with (D) *Verbrechen* and *(D) Vergehen.* Overall, the approximation of law that was illustrated in the above example often takes place via indirect avenues, and comparative legal research has shown that the historical *ius commune* sometimes better reflected the current perceptions of harmonized law than its modern counterpart. Of course, the complexity of legal relations was of different nature then, which in turn makes some of the more ambitious developments in national legal systems understandable. Nowadays, the structural feature common to legal translation that focuses on terminological analyses – the absence of universally operative terms of reference in the sense of Beaudoin (2002: 119) – can be overcome only through the comparison of legal institutions on a case-by-case basis, as illustrated above.

3.7.7 Translating legal speech acts

The focus upon the legal terminology in the Legal Linguistics and in the theory of legal translation may lead to the false conclusion that while translating we replace some words by some others. In fact, translating is not based on words or lexicology as language does not consist solely of words. The bricks of the translation are the speech acts which must be rendered in the target language. This is equally evident in literature as it is in law. Examples borrowed from the CISG may illustrate this procedure. The Art. 25 of the convention deals with the breach of contract. Its wording in English, French and German reads in the official translation as follows:

Art. 25 A breach of contract committed by one of the parties is **fundamental** *if it results in such detriment to the other party as* **substantially** *to deprive him of what he is entitled to expect under the contract, unless the party in breach did not foresee and a reasonable person of the same kind in the same circumstances would not have foreseen such a result.*

Art. 25 Une contravention au contrat commise par l'une des parties est **essentielle** *lorsqu'elle cause à l'autre partie un préjudice tel qu'elle la prive* **substantiellement** *de ce que celle-ci était en droit d'attendre du contrat, à moins que la partie en défault n'ait pas prévu un tel résultat et qu'une personne raisonnable de même qualité placée dans la même situation ne l'aurait pas prévu non plus.*

Art. 25 Eine von einer Partei begangene Vertragsverletzung ist **wesentlich**, *wenn sie für die andere Partei solchen Nachteil zur Folge hat, dass ihr im* **wesentlichen** *entgeht, was sie nach dem Vertrag hätte erwarten dürfen, es sei denn, dass die vertragsbrüchige Partei diese Folge nicht vorausgesehen hat und eine vernünftige Person der gleichen Art diese Folge unter den gleichen Umständen auch nicht vorausgesehen hätte.*

In the above text, lexical units corresponding to the terms *fundamental* and *substantial* have been emphasized. It would be however vain to discuss here the possible differences between *fundamental, substantial* and eventually also *essential,* and favor one to the detriment of others. Loewe (1989: 11) argues that the choice of the terminological equivalents in Art. 25 does not influence its meaning, especially when compared with the German variety that uses one and the same word to render *fundamental* and *substantial,* namely (D) *wesentlich* and the Spanish translation that follows the French dichotomy of *essentielle* and *substantielle* by writing accordingly (ESP) *esencial* and *substancialmente.* The sense of the translator's work is to render the meaning of the speech act concerning some circumstances of the breach of the contract. An intersection between sentence and utterance must be reflected, but the utterance remains the dominating force in the determination of the speech act (Stolze 2005: 125). Moreover, an isolated lexicological analysis would not help the translator, because the application of general terms upon a contract is a matter of interpretation. There, the difference may or may not matter, as the breach of the contract depends upon the circumstances of the case and not upon the preformulated meaning of a word in a specific language. The translator's task is to focus on the difference that may matter. As an example, it can be assumed that the difference between the English and the German versions where the party is perceived as being of male gender *he* in the English text or of female gender (D) *sie* in the German text would not matter for the meaning of the legal speech act that constitutes the Art. 25 of the CISG. Legal speech acts manifest themselves in the application of linguistically determined legal norms. Only in the dynamics of the application process that - dependent on the legal-theoretical view may or may not include interpretation (cf. 3.6.2) - words acquire their proper meaning. Therefore, the possible difference between *fundamental, substantial* and *essential* becomes interesting when they are used. In the translation, when the words are not confronted with facts that may constitute a breach of contract, i.e. while being idle, their use may be well founded. An idle speech act adopts its meaning according to the circumstances of the use that confine the limits of the legal translation and of the work the translator is able to achieve.

3.7.8 Intentionality in translation

In terms of pragmatics, the legal translation can be therefore best characterized as a translation of a legal norm, a legal decision or a legal act with subsequent volitive consequences (Herbots 1987: 814). These legal constructs with volitive features are linguistically reflected in legal speech acts. And exactly these volitive features must be transferred from the legal source language into the legal target language. The volitive element is connected to intention, and intentionality in language is the essence of every speech act. The appropriate transformation of the source speech act into the target speech act is the pragmatic goal of the legal translation. Therefore, the principle of expressionability as developed in the speech act theory by J. Searle (Searle 1969: 68; 87 sq) is fundamental for the pragmatic view upon the translation of legal texts. Searle also posits that whatever can be mentally construed can be expressed with linguistic means. Extreme views mentioned above about the principal impossibility of translation prove therefore inconsistent at least with pragmatic mechanisms. The same concerns philosophical experiments where a language intranslatable into English is imagined as well as 'translations' from Saturnian into Plutonian that cause problems to some eminent scholars in contexts different from ours (Davidson 2001: 186). In less sophisticated circumstances, when (FR) *je promets* can be translated into English with *I promise* it is possible only due to the existing common performance rules in both languages (cf. Searle 2004: 66-74). Therefore, different languages can be perceived as realizations of linguistic conventions which in their diversity refer to one rule system, it is one of conventions (Searle 1969: 39-40). Forms of life in which rules of ordinary speech acts are rooted are not more diverse than are different legal systems expressed in legal speech acts. At the first sight, the above view could be perceived as contrary to the views expressed by W. Quine (1983) and R. Davidson (2001) about the indeterminacy of translation. However, it seems that the indeterminacy as developed by Quine in his '*gavagai*' example concerns rather the semantic and not the pragmatic perspective in language. Quine discussed in his almost proverbial example the situation where a linguist tries to understand an indigenous pronouncing the word (*) '*gavagai*' and pointing in the direction of a running rabbit. Indeed, it is at first undetermined what this '*gavagai*' may mean. It could mean, *rabbit* or *rabbit is passing* or *let us hunt this rabbit* or whatever. As such, in this situation, it is undetermined and cannot be translated. However, the context which will be explored by the linguist and his observations of use of the word '*gavagai*' will sooner or later clear up the meaning of the expression which at first may seem hazy. Here again our broader concept of pragmatics helps overcome some theoretical problems which have been perceived by many as principal objections to translatability of texts, and especially legal texts. Legal texts may seem untranslatable in the sense of the '*gavagai*'-example provided by Quine but they become meaningful and translatable in the process of the identification of legal speech acts in them. These identified legal speech acts are subsequently translatable, and this is guaranteed by the principle of expressionability and it is rooted in the functionability of speech acts in the cultural context that includes law. Equally, when Saturnian is translatable into English and Plutonian while Plutonian is not translatable into English (as supposed by Davidson 2001: 186) the Plutonian-English translation will become gradually possible in the process of the indentification of speech acts in these languages. Were it not so, neither English nor Saturnian nor Plutonian could qualify for being counted among languages in equal degree.

3.7.9 Avoiding translation

The legal translation is a specific text type within translating and it can be compared with the literary translation; yet it remains independent of other text types in its essence (cf. Arsova-Nikolić 1999: 291). Therefore, it can also use techniques that are unusual for other types of translating. An innovative approach to the translation of legislative acts is the bilingual drafting, (FR) *corédaction bilingue* (Gémar 2004: 744) where the text is rather drafted in a parallel way in the respective language versions than translated from one version into another. The process of parallel drafting includes at least a reflection upon the linguistic versions in question which is close to that of a translator. Here, the transformation of the speech acts takes place earlier than in the ordinary speech acts of translation. The illocutionary act in the drafted texts must be identified properly in order to enable the bilingual legislative text to emerge in this process. The classical translator is doing exactly the same thing; she identifies the legal speech act of the source language and transforms it into a legal speech act in the target language. We can assume, as no precise research into this question is known, that the bilingual translator in reality identifies and qualifies speech acts more or less simultaneously with the process of their transformation. Otherwise, simultaneous interpretation would not work. The action undertaken by the interpreter is therefore identical; the time factor makes the difference. In the classical translation the professional steps are better discernible, but they are not qualitatively different. Therefore, the pragmatic approach to legal language is well adapted to cover these specific linguistic operations which may induce some translation studies specialists to ask the question whether the type of operation such as parallel drafting can be perceived as translation at all. Yet, it seems to be an efficient answer to the problem of legal translating. Therefore, an approach which integrates drafting and translating appears in the light of recent experience in legislative or administrative bodies concerned by this activity to be the best practice to follow. Additionally, ZhaoYuhong (2008 :3, 24) stressed the necessity of bilingual drafting of the Chinese language versions of laws enacted in Hong Kong, mostly in order to avoid Anglicized Chinese and a Europeanized syntax in modern written Chinese. Moreover, some formalized international terms such as the *Incoterms,* e.g. *FOB* or *CIF,* are usually not translated in the legal acts and documents (Mattila 2002b: 492). Likewise, names of institutions are frequently left in their original linguistic form and their origin is marked by an abbreviation, e.g. *The Korkein hallinto-oikeus (FIN) referred the following question to the Court of Justice for a preliminary ruling* or *The Överklagandenämnden för högskolan (S) referred…,* or *The Tribunale di Larino (IT) decided to stay proceedings* …or *The Tribunal de grande instance de Nancy (FR) granted all of Céline SA applications....* These samples are also examples of a translating strategy that avoids the translating process or the translation of cumbersome terms. Doubtlessly, the informativity of the target text suffers under this innovative technique. Therefore, it might be preferable to engage into legal comparative studies instead of avoiding translation in such cases (cf. Mattila 2006: 264). Close to the above technique is the *constructive translation* (Stolze 2005: 238) in which the translator renders the meaning with her own words. This method is best suited for professional recipients because the knowledge of the constructive principles is necessary to understand correctly the product of the constructive translation. Otherwise, the risk for misunderstandings persists as to the shape of the original. We did not identify any constructive translation of statutes or court decisions. In turn, scholarly writings that pertain to the law are frequently translated with help of this technique.

3.7.10 Prospects for legal translation

The existing findings of mostly terminology-oriented studies on the translation of legal texts have defined the essential problems in the legal translation as the linguistic equivalence and the legal qualification of legal notions. The linguistic equivalence can be achieved under the *skopos*-theory. The problem of the legal qualification (characterization) understood as the reinterpretation of mostly incompatible legal notions can be solved only by comparative law methods. More generally, however, the legal translation grounds in the legal interpretation and the legal argumentation. Legal speech acts that form the legal discourse in one legal language are transformed there into equivalent legal speech acts of the target legal language. Difficulties in rendering legal speech acts in other legal languages lead to strategies of avoidance of translation or modified methods such as the constructive translating. Likewise, the scope of debates surrounding the legal translation is characterized by an increasing amount of questions which relate to the technical language and its pragmatic aspects, especially the translation strategies. These are, in turn, elements of the Legal Linguistics – which is indeed an evolving field of study for which the conditions and methods we try to clarify in this book. The conceptual convergence of two parent disciplines of the Legal Linguistics may result in procedures that will facilitate the methodically sound translation of legal texts. Still, the classical legal translation remains a reliable legal-linguistic operation provided that its pragmatic prerequisites and its limits are taken into consideration. From today's perspective, it seems justifiable to say that the legal translation is in practice as well as in theory a secure profession demanding special technical knowledge because of its complexity.

3.8 Other Legal-Linguistic Operations

Other legal-linguistic operations such as *justification*, *fact description* and *legal research* will be noted here in passing. The main reason for this spatial restriction is that there exist numerous other legal-linguistic operations in pure form or as mixtures of some others so that an exhaustive description of them is equally difficult as the description of all possible speech acts in a natural language. The focus on two selected samples should primarily enhance further research into this topic.

3.8.1 Justifying argumentation

The *justification* as a specific type of legal argumentation is used mostly in situations where professional views compete directly. There, status questions become relevant, especially in decisions where the professonal quality of the opinion can be explicitly challenged. This is for instance the case in concurring and dissenting opinions in relation to the majority opinion. In the U.S. Supreme Court opinion *Medellín v. Texas* (552 U.S. 06-984 (2008)) a concurring and a dissenting opinion were delivered. The concurring opinion begins with the words complimenting the dissent: *There is a great deal of wisdom in Justice Breyer's dissent* which places the whole following text in a close relationship to the dissent. This argumentative strategy stresses the intertextuality of the concurring opinion and builds up the distance to the majority opinion that it, nevertheless, finally endorses. Initially, the concurring judge signalizes the support for the dissent with additional assertions constructed around *I agree, I also endorse, I think this case presents a closer question than the Court's opinion allows*. The following phrase *In the end, however, I am persuaded that...* reverses the argumentation to the detriment of the initially admiratively treated dissent. The dissent itself is even more pronounced in its respect or disrespect of the majority opinion and uses language that directly questions the professionality in the criticized decision: *At best the Court is hunting the snark. At worst it erects legalistic hurdles that can threaten the application of provisions in many existing commercial and other treaties and make it more difficult to negotiate new ones.* The majority opinion is more independent from the concurring opinion and the dissent in its argumentation that is primarily structured as a dialogue with arguments provided by the petitioner, a Mexican citizen sentenced to death for murder, e.g. *Medellín argues that..., Medellín first contends..., He argues that..., Medellín and his amici nonetheless contend that.., Further, Medellín frames his argument as though.., Rather, Medellín argues that..., What is more, on Medellín view....* While developing a fictitious dialogue with the petitioner whom it also linguistically treats as the author of highly complex legal arguments due to a textual convention of drafting court opinions, the majority decision remains in a relation of expressed intertextuality to the concurring and the dissenting opinions through direct and frequent reference to them. It devotes a whole chapter (B) to the dissent and starts the justification of the own decision by quoting a convincing critical phrase from the dissent: *The dissent faults our analysis because it "looks for the wrong thing (explicit textual expression about self-execution) using the wrong standard (clarity) in the wrong place (the treaty language)."* This strategy is surprising as it does not reflect the experience made in the classical rhetoric that discouraged the mentioning of critical quotes which may be perceived as particularly convincing by the reader. The *justification* is built around the most salient arguments provided in all three opinions which form one text that is understandable only when all three opinions are taken into consideration due to internal references in them. This textual feature makes of the *justification* a specific legal-linguistic operation. We should also mention that there exists also a *justification sensu stricto* that has a slightly different background from the main type depicted here (cf. 3.3.5.3).

3.8.2 Describing facts

The *fact description* which will be treated later on in the part of this book devoted to Literature and Law is equally specific as it provides more than facts for the reader. In the above majority opinion the judges feel obliged to report the circumstances that led to petitioner's conviction to death. The description reads as follows: *Petitioner José Ernesto Medellín, a Mexican national, has lived in the United States since preschool. A member of the "Black and Whites" gang, Medellín was convicted of capital murder and sentenced to death in Texas for the gang rape and brutal murders on two Houston teenagers. On June 24, 1993, 14-year-old Jennifer Ertman and 16-year-old Elizabeth Pena were walking home when they encountered Medellín and several fellow gang members. Medellín attempted to engage Elizabeth in conversation. When she tried to run, petitioner threw her to the ground. Jennifer was grabbed by other gang members when she, in response to her friend's cries, ran back to help. The gang members raped both girls for over an hour. Then, to prevent their victims from identifying them, Medellín and his fellow gang members murdered the girls and discarded their bodies in a wooded area. Medellín was personally responsible for strangling at least one of the girls with her own shoelace. Medellín was arrested at approximately 4 a.m. on June 29, 1993. A few hours later, between 5:54 and 7:23 a.m., Medellín was given Miranda warnings; he then signed a written waver and gave a detailed written confession.* The subjudicial case concerned the question whether a decision issued by the International Court of Justice in the Hague can be applied in the U.S. directly, i.e. whether it is self-executing in the U.S. as the supreme law of the country. This is rather a formal issue and, it is definitely not related to the crime committed by the petitioner that lies outside the purview of the court. The court is free in such a case to relate the background of the matter that concerns the petitioner without being obliged to quote all details. The majority chose a detailed referral to Medellín's crime in the opinion. By reference to particularities such as the time frame of Medellín's first interrogation that is irrelevant for the decision as such the Supreme Court marks its apparent distance and exactness in an effort to prove an unbiased, professional approach to the petitioner's case. The descriptive strategy adapted in the majority opinion tends towards creating an emotional atmosphere of repugnance towards Medellín whatever the legal question of his case may be. It is introduced into the majority opinion with the intention to show that the petitioner is a particularly abominable murderer and that his guilt was proved beyond doubt. Sympathy with the victims is expressed a.o. by reference to their age. In turn, Medellín's age is not indicated in the court decision on any of its 37 pages. (It is known from newspaper reports that he was born in 1975; hence, while perpetrating the murder he was 18; he was executed on August 5, 2008 in Texas). After the decription of the crime committed by the petitioner the court has most readers on its side. The readers wish the petitioner's request to be turned down whatever its content may be. Finally, the petitioner's request is indeed turned down by the court, unsurprisingly based on rather technical reasons. In the light of the above short analysis, the specific facts quoted by the court appear therefore as representing more than facts. Their nature will be elucidated later on.

3.8.3 Legal research

It goes without saying that the activity like the one exercised here is also a linguistic operation in law. All academic research, e.g. analyses of court opinions or legal provisions belong to it. Paradigmes of this research change as changes the language used in them. These epistemic legal-linguistic transformations are best researched within the legal theory and the theory of legal sciences that focus on the paradigmatic changes in the legal sciences. Legal Linguistics reflects the linguistic attitudes in the paradigmatic change. It signalizes the change in language use that may be perceived as a beginning of a tendency towards paradigmatic change.

3.9 Legal-Linguistic Operations in the Legal Discourse

3.9.1 Centrality of the legal discourse

It has been mentioned already that the legal-linguistic operations such as the legal argumentation or the legal translation do not exist in a vacuum. They form bigger textual units and can be adequately understood within the boundaries of these superimposed units, such as the *legal discourse*. The legal discourse is fundamental for the Legal Linguistics because all legal-linguistic operations can be construed as contributions to it like bricks that are used for the construction of a house. Undeniably, most time and space has been spent here on analyzing of the singular legal-linguistic operations. Their contribution to a higher organizational level has been until now only assumed. Finally, the legal discourse consists of different legal-linguistic operations as a house consists of bricks. Arguably, though, the higher unit of textual organization has its own ontology and also own rules which govern it. The legal discourse is not a simple amalgam of legal-linguistic operations as a house is not a heap of bricks. We used to live in houses and not in heaps of bricks piled upon another as we create and apply the law in legal discourses, and not in one or more particular legal-linguistic operations. Therefore, when talking about the legal-linguistic operations in law we implicitly also kept in mind the legal discourse. All analyzed samples of the legal-linguistic operations in this book are parts of such a discourse.

3.9.2 Notion of the legal discourse

The definition of the legal discourse which can be found in the legal-linguistic scholarship is rather general (cf. Notes and Materials nr. 2). Cornu (2005: 207) develops the notion of the legal discourse in contrast with the legal vocabulary. For him, the legal discourse is the legal language in action – *Le discours juridique est, par opposition au vocabulaire juridique, l'autre versant du language du droit: c'est le language du droit en action* (Cornu, ibid.). He insists also on two different aspects of the legal discourse, the linguistic and the juridical one and undertakes a first attempt to categorize it by identifying the legislative (FR *discours législatif*), the juridical (FR *discours juridictionnel*), the customary (FR *discours coutumier*) discourses as well as the corporal expression in the discourse (Cornu 2005: 211). It is understandable that his research is based on a rather general concept of the juridical discourse, because all judicial activity makes in one way or another part of it. This seems also to be the reason for the absence of this overall notion in a standard legal-linguistic work like Mattila's *Comparative Legal Linguistics* where it is mentioned solely in the cover text. This generality allows for different forms of classification of legal discourses as undertaken by Cornu (2005: 213-419). One may also adapt a more abstract notion of the legal discourse that would comprise the totality of the linguistic activity in law which seems to be compatible with Cornu's preliminary general definition. The flexibility of the notion of the general, not necessarily only legal discourse that has been construed in this way by Michel Foucault (1966: 102) and others has a further advantage. It allows for a more specific conceptualization of the context to which frequent reference has been made here. Foucault employed it to characterize the transformation of primary texts into discourses which necessitate interpretation (Foucault 1966: 93). It is worth mentioning that also historically the discourse has been defined rather broadly, e.g. by Dionysius of Halicarnassus as an arrangement of words such disposed that they forme a complete sense. The general notion of the discourse says at least that utterances must follow in an arrangement and cannot stand freely in the speech and that the discourse constitutes a larger unit of sense called already by Dionysius, not unproblematically, complete sense. Moreover, the discourse provides information of different provenance and quality. Therefore, it can be understood as a structured context (Baylon 1991: 222) that constitutes a part of the reality such that it creates the context or represents what the participants know already (Baylon 1991: 278; 280). It has also a practical component because it links closer what is said with what is done (Baylon 1991: 253). This specific feature is important within the modern conception of the legal argumentation which should promote the rationality of the discourse and avoid empty or intentionally false arguments that are employed solely in order to win and without any attention paid to the socially relevant subject matter within a legal question. Furthermore, the discourse provides rather for a contextual than for syntactic information (Baylon 1991: 276). This, in turn, favors the general concept rather than the classification of varieties because the discourse provides an unlimited number of vantage points that could be used for its classification. Cornu's analysis of the numerous possibilities to classify the legal discourses on two hundred pages illustrates best this problem.

3.9.3 Structure of the legal discourse

Analyzing discourse has been described as a banal activity (Baylon 1991: 235). And, as a matter of fact, this unusual characterization holds true because we analyze discourses every day when reading our morning newspaper, listening to the radio or reading documents in the office. We need this ongoing analysis because the meaning of messages - especially those addressed to an undetermined circle of recipients - is not always immediately clear. Due to our linguistic competence we are able to identify communicative situations where we must hold on and think about the content of messages that we received. We do it in order to avoid misunderstandings. The whole process may be called the interpretation of the discourse (cf. Baylon 1991: 235). This discourse can be understood and ambiguities in it can be clarified because it is structured. We distinguish *cohesion*, *coherence* and *relevance* as the most caracteristic features of its internal organization (Baylon 1991: 236). These elements have a specific meaning in the legal discourse that is based on an institutional and professionally restricted argumentation. Hence, the legal discourse displays at least the following internal elements: legal cohesion, legal coherence and legal relevance. The legal cohesion concerns its textual form that is usually prescribed either by statutes or by the legal culture generally. For instance, legal discourses must take place in a specific form as trials or court decisions must be drafted in a professional manner and in accordance with pre-established textual patterns. Legal coherence concerns the way arguments are presented in the discourse. The legal argumentation is efficient only because arguments are presented in a coherent way, i.e. that they are interrelated. The legal relevance refers to suppositions and implications that the interpreter of a legal discourse needs in order to be able to understand it. It means that arguments will be effective when they affect the subject matter as closely as possible and when they also take into consideration the knowledge of their recipients (Baylon 1991: 238).

3.9.4 Legal discourse and creativity

The legal discourse does not only represent or form the context in which legally relevant utterances are made (cf. Notes and Materials nr. 3). It is also the framework in which linguistic creativity takes place (Baylon 1991: 237). Next to its mentioned constitutive elements it has further conditions of being. It is limited by the linguistic constraints; i.e. only issues that can be lexicalized in a grammatically correct way can be uttered in it and by the conditions of its resurgence in broader social and political contexts. Thay are analyzed from different perspectives by M. Bakhtin, J. Habermas, R. Dworkin and other researchers mostly representing political sciences or sociology. These fundamental constraints have linguistically relevant consequences. First, the exigence of linguistic exactness and extreme correctness in drafting statutes or court opinions may lead to the reification of language. The reification is the most dangerous consequence for the users of language (Jackson 1985: 11) because language ceases to function as a means of effective and creative communication and becomes a rigid cast where pre-formulated utterances are repeated over and over without precise reference to their context. Second, the legal discourse is not simply formed on the street but in complex political and other professional structures that provide interpretive ingrediences into its context. If this constraint is ignored, then law is not understood or applied properly because creativity in it is limited by the conditions of its constitution. The broader context of the resurgence of discursive practices is however not our main topic. While dealing with the legal discourse it is nevertheless necessary to remember that it is equally preconditioned and does not exist in a vacuum like the legal-linguistic operations that are our recurrent issue.

3.9.5 How the legal discourse works?

It is easier to show the legal discourse as a linguistic action than to propose an exhausitive definition of it. Such an enterprise may help disambiguate and also possibly demystify the notion. To this aim one may use a court decision as a starting point, e.g. Goldstein v. SEC rendered 2006 by the U.S. Court of Appeals for the District of Columbia Circuit (451 F.3d 873). In it, the D.C. Circuit invalidated the so-called Hedge Fund Rule and described it as an example of arbitrary rulemaking by the SEC. The main legal question in this litigation has been the notion of *client* of a hedge fund under the Investment Adviser Act of

1940. The petitioner Goldstein and the SEC have interpreted the notion differently. The background of the interpretive disagreement has been that the section 3 of the mentioned act has been construed by many as allowing most hedge fund advisers to avoid registration with the SEC because in practice they had fewer than fifteen clients when *client* means limited partnership that invests money in a fund. The SEC's hedge fund rule of 2004 reinterpreted the notion of *client* in that it equated it with *investor.* This would have the consequence that most hedge fund advisers would have to register with the SEC before starting their activities. However, the court held that *client* for purposes of the fifteen-client rule of § 203(b) (3) means the investing limited partnership and not the individual partners. The decision has been commented in Harvard Law Review, vol. 120, pp. 1394-1401. The sense of such a comment is the systematization of the decision within the structure of the American public law under its principles and precedents. The decision has been criticized in the comment as contrary to the American doctrine of administrative law that tends towards obliging courts to pay deference to administrative agencies' reasonable views (cf. 3.9.1). This follows, as mentioned here in the chapter on legal argumentation, from case law represented mainly by Chevron U.S.A., Inc. v. Natural Res. Def. Council, Inc (467 U.S. 837, 844 (1984)) of which the argumentatively crucial topic is characterized with the words: *"We accord deference...because of a presumption that Congress, when it left ambiguity in a statute meant for the implementation by an agency,...desired the agency (rather than the courts) to possess whatever degree of discretion the ambiguity allows."* The comment criticized the decision as being *improper under Chevron* (p. 1398), i.e. it systematized it under a particular classification of relevant precedents. These specific aspects of the internal structure of the American law are not reflected upon in the broader discourse about the decision, be it among professional fund advisers or the broader public. Next to the internal perspective, the comment includes also a reflection of ethical consequences the decision may have: *More importantly, the court missed an opportunity to adapt its jurisprudence to a rulemaking context that may be unique to the financial sector, in which systemic risk is high and regulated parties face strong incentives – and have substantial power - to avoid regulation* (p.1397) and, additionally: *The Amaranth debacle, occurring less than three months after the court handed down its opinion, illustrates the dangers that motivated the rule in the first place, and the need for a doctrine of administrative law that recognizes the importance of agency flexibility in meeting the goals that Congress has set* (p. 1401). In the comment, ethical arguments are never articulated in isolation from the systemic recurrences of the American law. Instead, they are tied to arguments related to the internal structure of the law, e.g. *deference, longstanding administrative law doctrine, Congress intent, eliminate abuse, permissible construction of a statute, fundamental purpose, policy standpoint,* etc, in order to stress that not only an emotional opinion about the court decision has been expressed. This strategy makes clear the attempt towards gaining acceptance within the community of legal experts (judges, scholars, attorneys-at-law etc.) where a purely ethical evaluation of the decision might be perceived as non-professional. The decision has been also commented by the interested financial institutions and an emotive discussion on this issue can be easily traced in the internet. The professional discourse led to the proposal of a new rule 206(4)-8 that would lead to the initially envisaged aim. In turn, the emotive discourse within the professional community of investment advisers seems to have ended rather inconclusively. For instance, the rhetortic question *Goldstein: a hero or a fool?* has been raised there towards the background of a possible 'revenge' the SEC would take on the whole branch of hedge funds managers for the lost litigation.

The short case study illustrates the complexity of the legal discourse. It takes place within the legal procedure in a court of law and the rendered court decision is binding. It includes smaller discourses concerning the interpretation of *client* where the parties bring arguments that may back their views. It includes furthermore the systematizing discourse within the academic community which must find a place for the court decision within the complex structure of the law and cope with a decision that is legally binding although it does not find support by the professional commentator of the Harvard Law Review. The discourse outside the community of the legal experts is rather egotistic than focused on the legal issue. It mainly concerns the possible steps which could be and were actually taken by the SEC after the unfavorable court opinion has been rendered. This discourse did not address the general legal problems in the opinion because it is exclusively concerned about the outcome. As is so often the case, the discourse about law is divided between the professional legal community interested in the inner perspective of the law and the non-professional one interested in the results of litigation. It is unclear in how far the particular discourses are interrelated. A special research would be necessary to find out this circumstance. Overall, a socially productive legal discourse would be one that integrates both perspectives into a discourse that comprises the internal view on the law where only professional legal arguments matter and the external one that focuses on the repercussions that the legal decision may have on the society. The legal discourse in the Western societies seems to be still characterized by the mentioned dichotomy and argumentative selectivity.

Part 4: Literature and Law

In the preceding analysis of the linguistic operations in law we found out that textuality is one of the most specific features of law. It is also the conditio sine qua non of literature. In both, stories and narratives about concrete and abstract issues are composed and developed. In the following chapter we will therefore ask whether the Legal Linguistics can learn from literary criticism and the literature which is grounded in fictitious worlds. The most challenging question in this respect could be therefore reduced to the formulation: are novel writers pursuing a creative activity unlike judges who apply law and nothing more than that? When namely both the writer and the judge are equally creative then the Legal Linguistics is of primordial importance for the legal sciences. Are only writers creative? If so, then the legal linguist would have to satisfy his ambitions with being occasionally mentioned in footnotes.

4.1 Writing and Reading in Law and Elsewhere

4.1.1 Resemblances and differences

In this chapter of our study we will be dealing with aspects common to law and to literature as well as with issues which clearly distinguish the one from the other. This initial statement is made here without further proof for the fundamental resemblances and differences between both phenomena because indices are there which provide, at least, for the impression that law is not only literature as literature cannot be perceived like law. On the other side, amazing analogies were discovered between fictitious literary texts and legal non-fictitious texts. With literature we mean here mainly *fiction* but we are ready to accept other *narrative forms* like reports or news which refer to social reality. They use a specific form for the purposes of narration which is not a simple reference to the discourse of ordinary language. Partly, we could even perceive scholarly legal research as narrative as well. We have also reversed the traditional order of topics in our heading. And there are good reasons for this. We will namely be looking for forms in legal texts which resemble fiction and we will have to do it from the point of view of literary theory. At this stage we would not be able to proceed differently because no classification of legal texts due to their literary aspects exists to-date. Our approach differs slightly from the widespread tendency in Law and Literature to look into how certain novelists, e.g. Franz Kafka or Fyodor Dostoyevski, dealt with legal issues in their work. We do not oppose this tendency as such. Substantial knowledge about law can be reached through such comparative analyses. However, for the specific reasons of our approach we have to adopt a different perspective. We will look mostly at legal texts and ask whether they could be read as literary texts. The answer seems to be obvious. One could pretend that we can read whatever text as literary and abstain from reflecting upon its foundations in its subject matter. Yet, our experience shows also that we do not read legal texts in the way we used to read literary texts. The reader adopts a specific perspective towards legal texts and distinguishes literary/fictitious texts from non-fiction in legal texts. The reader seems to know or even to have internalized the appropriate approach to every type of texts. He is able to identify a text as literary; i.e. fictitious and construe it accordingly. Similarly, he reads a court decision in a way which does not resemble his reception of fictitious texts. And indeed, *facts* claim to be true and not merely credible, *events* in novels do not (Jackson 1988: 246) and the reader seems to identify this distinction almost automatically. Sincerity is not assumed in literature (Baylon 1991: 238), while in law it is. In this extra-textual criterion may lie the reason for the different perspectives readers adopt towards literary and legal texts. The distinction between facts and events makes sense for us and in the following paragraphs we will not try to establish that facts are as fictitious as events might be and pretend that no borderline between both could be proven convincingly. With Searle (1999: 32) we believe that facts exist in reality and we will therefore reflect upon the specific nature of social facts which jurists mostly used to deal with. However, language use in dealing with facts will dominate our deliberations because we try to find out in what relation facts or events stand to the final narrative product and how language contributes to it. We mentioned already the fundamental role language plays in shaping our view upon reality; i.e. mainly upon our view of natural and social facts. Both sorts of facts could not be expressed without language, be it only the formal language of mathematics. Our perception of facts clearly depends upon the language used in their *description.* This description is in a very specific way also their *creation*, at least in many cases. And exactly these cases are the most interesting for jurists. Yet, in the paragraphs which will follow we cannot reflect upon all the approaches and ideas which emerged in the past debate on Law and Literature. We may remind that we have committed ourselves to a specific perspective upon language and law, i.e. to the pragmatic approach. We will try to show that language and law seen in the pragmatic perspective not only reflect the past debates, but also serve to pave the way towards an understanding of the subject which reflects the textuality of both. In spite of or rather due to our linguistic perspective we will show that law even when viewed from the linguistic perspective remains a social phenomenon and that it therefore cannot be separated from the society in which it is growing.

4.1.2 Rules in texts

Indeed, the unique feature of law is its *textuality*. Laws nowadays rarely exist in non-written form. In the Western legal tradition the written judicial decisions usually must be provided with a written justification. And, this textual requirement determines our perspective upon law. Legal texts must be created along specified rules, otherwise they would not be perceived as legal. For us it is crucial to observe that both law and language are rule-oriented. A speaker can understand a sentence he has never heard before only due to the linguistic rules he masters. Likewise, we understand the law only because we master rules which enable us to identify and to apply it. We insist here on textuality as characteristic for the modern law, although social sciences may add to it many other features pertaining mostly to power structures in state and society. Nevertheless, wherever law is applied, it is also invoked and determined in its textual form. If the textual form is missing, then we usually have to do with the enforcement of the legal decision that belongs to the context of law or an action with relation to law that itself is not part of it, such as the non-verbal perpetration of a crime. What is more, law may create with texts linguistic and political entities as well as legal notions. For instance, the (English) Treaty of Union from 1706 states in its Art. I: *That the two kingdoms of England and Scotland shall be united in the kingdom by the name Great Britain.* Occasionally, additional criteria are needed to figure out whether a textual sample is creative in terms of law. For instance, in the absence of a written constitution in England it may at times be difficult to determine whether a particular text belongs to the constitutional law, i.e. forms the corpus of legal constitutional acts of England (Barnett 1999: 19). Doubtlessly, also the legal argumentation grounds in textuality. Prefigurations such as procedural concepts, e.g. *summary judgment, default judgment, demurrer* or *judgment notwithstanding the verdict* determine the argumentation which is applied in them. The legal argumentation develops around the inherent structural elements of those concepts. These conceptual prefigurations are texts that are operative in law.

4.1.3 Reading texts and applying rules

As said, textuality is the largest common denominator which can be found for literature and law. There exist of course numerous logical or semiotical common features of both areas such as signification processes (Jackson 1985: 13), but they also manifest themselves primarily or secondarily in written or oral texts. Textuality is an extremely reliable criterion for both law and literature. Meanwhile, although law frequently functions through the spoken word and literature is sometimes read aloud, their only uncontested form is the written one. All other forms of their existence including meaning varieties can be questioned. This does not mean that the written textual form would be dominant for the signification processes or for the application of law. Rather the contrary seems to be the case. Nevertheless, the written textual form is useful as a departure for all comparative approaches to literature and to law due to its unconsealed materiality. The written text is immediately traceable, although meaning is distilled from it after time-consuming analyzing and testing. The textuality as a fundamental feature is also an intermediate phenomenon. In law, our main problem with textuality is that it seems to be pragmatically uninteresting. Lawyers do not apply *texts* on cases; they apply legal *rules* which are developed on the basis of legal texts. These rules have doubtlessly also a written textual form, but they are applied as rules and according to the structure of rules and not of texts. Textuality lacks the dynamic force which drives pragmatics and all other operations undertaken under its auspices. It is pragmatically mostly perceptible in intertextual contexts which will be demonstrated later on examples. However, the textuality of rules has a pragmatic component that is the text of the rule stated as a part of a speech act which constitutes it. This may appear not to be much, because it comprises only the material formulation of the legal speech act, the locutionary act. Yet, the material formulation is not without importance due to the limitations to which legal texts are exposed and to the institutional limits of their application.

4.1.4 Complexity of literary texts

Complexity which for us comprises the information load of a text is definitely not a characteristic feature of legal texts. Generally, also all scientific texts are perceived as complex. The problem is to find the right example for simple texts. This is difficult to achieve as daily spoken or written texts beginning with conversations and newspaper reporting manifest intricacies which were rather late discovered by the researchers. It seems that no simple-structured text type exists, but that texts under specific circumstances can be simpler or more complex. Thus, the legal text is not by definition complex and the daily conversational text by definition simple. Generally, there exist simple and complex legal texts as there exist simple and complex conversational texts. The same can be posited in relation to literary texts. In fact, the material formulation of the legal texts, the thoughts expressed in them can be formally determined (Laurén 2002: 18). For instance, two texts of which one belonged to the area of electrical engineering and the other to legal writings were transformed into lines of x-signes and compared in Laurén's mentioned research. The design of the legal text, its long paragraphs, complicated syntax and advanced layering were easily discernible in this form. The contrastive approach showed that thoughts expressed in them are formulated differently in the process of lexicalization. In the legal texts the form reflects the specific legal argumentation (Laurén 2002: 19). This argumentation and its form are not accidental. Therefore, Laurén reflects upon the Roman law and Latin's specific influence upon the syntax of the contemporary legal language. The specific form of the legal text allows Laurén to talk about its *iconism*; i.e. that signs used resemble the represented object, the law (Laurén 2002: 16). However, also this specific form may be dynamic and vary according to the circumstances of language use or be expressed with other terms according to linguistic strategies adopted for the creation of legal texts. In the literary fiction the situation is analogous. There too, the form can be represented as a model and is due to the specifics of the epoch or the writer's personal style that is also discernible from his other texts. The particular iconic form demonstrates the interrelation between the object and the signs representing it. And we can assume that texts generally display this feature. However, the mere belonging to one of customarily established technical or legal categories does not establish their pragmatic difference, i.e. the different circumstances of their use. Technical texts like the legal ones can and certainly also do establish rules for application of specific procedures. And, both texts are used as a source of information. Novels as well are used in this sense, the information there is applicable in the socially relevant practice. The influence literary fiction has had on the social life proves this circumstance.

4.1.5 Written legal texts

We have adopted a rather broad working definition of a legal text which for us, at least at this stage, includes all utterances oral or written which are relevant in the legal context. As far as narrative forms are concerned, especially the written form is interesting in a contrastive approach because it is characteristic for advanced literary texts. The question how oral narrative forms may be contrasted or made instrumental for law would also be interesting. We assume that its complexity structure would substantially differ from the written structure of contemporary legal texts. Additional research would be needed to clarify this question. We will illustrate the problem with an example. A written legal text, for instance a court decision, may read:

Petitioner Edmondson sued respondent Leesville Concrete Co. in the District Court, alleging that Leesville's negligence had caused him personal injury. During **voir dire,** *Leesville used two of its three* **peremptory** *challenges authorized by statute to remove black persons from the prospective jury. Citing Batson v. Kentucky, 476 U.S. 79, Edmondson, who is black, requested that the court require Leesville to* **articulate a race-neutral explanation for the peremptory strikes.** *The court refused on the ground that Batson does not apply in civil proceedings, and the empanelled jury which consisted of 11 white persons and 1 black, rendered a verdict unfavourable to Edmondson. The Court of Appeals affirmed, holding that a private litigant in a civil case can exercise* **peremptory** *challenges without accountability for alleged racial classification.* (Edmondson v. Leesville Concret Co. 500 U.S. 614 (1991))

Emphasis has been supplied to the text to mark parts of it which a layperson may not understand. A layperson should be able to infer from the above fragment of the case syllabus that the respondent attempted at eliminating black persons from the jury and that the petitioner ultimately lost his case. Probably, the layperson will not understand the procedural questions related to the peremptory challenges which make it clear for the lawyer why exactly the court refused petitioner's request during the voir dire. The layperson should be furthermore capable to understand that Batson is a precedent decided by the U.S. Supreme Court and that in the view of the deciding court it does not apply to civil proceedings like the one in question. Furthermore, we may assume that not only legal notions such as *voir dire* or *peremptory challenges* may not be understandable for a non-lawyer but also formulations like *to articulate a race-neutral explanation for the peremptory strikes* or the holding of the Court of Appeals. The layperson will furthermore not know what has exactly happened to the petitioner as the syllabus informs only that he suffered personal injury. What does this understanding mean in terms of literature? First of all, it shows a parallel because literary texts are 'incomplete' in the sense that they do not include the information some readers would like to become. They are, however, complete in the sense of the authorial intention. They are as they are, hermetically delimited and fenced off against intruding questions. For such texts no extra-contextual information can exist. The same concerns in our example the inquiry into the injuries suffered by the petitioner. They are not part of the information provided in the case neither are they a part of the legally relevant context of the case. It does not matter what really happened to petitioner because this is not the issue in question. The issue of the case are the peremptory challenges. Of course, the interested reader could inquire into the factual background of the case and find out the sort of injuries allegedly caused by the respondent and by so doing fill the alleged gaps in the text (cf. regarding the so-called gaps in literary texts Juhl 1986: 198; Rimmon-Kenan 1989: 128). Beginning law students sometimes act in this way and attempt to fill the alleged informational gaps, and by overarching their inquisitorial skills unwillingly manifest that they do not understand the legal issue of the case, here notably the peremptory challenges. In terms of a literary narrative one could say that those inquisitive readers do not understand what the text is about. No difference exists between the syllabus formulation regarding the injuries and a literary text in which the information about the profession of a protagonist is missing. In both cases, the text does not deal with this sort of information and it does not matter that in the legal text the information could be discovered and in the literary text not. One could however imagine a situation in which the author of a literary text would be asked about the profession of his protagonist which was not indicated in the text and which he nevertheless imagined while writing his text and which he wilfully would provide to the enquiring reader. But, this information would be extra-contextual as well. Would the author not be alive any more or be unwilling to provide the answer, the situation would be comparable to the practical impossibility to find out factual information, for instance in the internet. It remains the situation in which the writer did not imagine any profession for his protagonist and willingly informs the reader about it, but this case is quintessentially extra-contextual. Insofar, we did not discover any difference between the legal and the literary text including their structures, although we might have caused the impression to have traced at least one.

4.1.6 How are good legal texts written?

As said, the legal texts are - like good literary texts - written according to established criteria for exemplary legal texts. They have to follow their constitutive linguistic rules. In law, these rules are less transparent than in literature because criticism of legal texts is less developed than is the literary criticism. Yet, professionals dealing daily with legal texts could easily establish a set of criteria based on textuality and intertextuality as well as compositional standards developed for legal texts, such as statutes or judgments. For instance, in the U.S. jurisprudence the texts written by Benjamin Cardozo are perceived as qualitatively better than average production delivered by judges (Weisberg 1992: 12). There must exist reasons for this interpretation. Legislators and their staff, judges, attorneys-at-law, legal translators constantly compose texts. They also use spoken word, and, as long as research into the proportions of spoken and written word in law is missing, we can assume that the written word is equally important that the spoken one in all legal activities. While writing all jurists follow professional rules, and while so doing, they behave like their colleagues, the writers of belles-lettres. In law as in literature we distinguish among well and poorly written texts. However, the criteria for their distinction are clearer in literature than in law due to shortcomings in the research.

4.1.7 Intertextuality in law

Texts follow specific formal and substantial patterns that can give rise to other texts. Novels look as they look like because their authors read certain novels before and during the time they wrote them. Literary criticism has devoted impressive energy towards the discovery of texual links between different literary texts. So are parts of F. Scott Fitzgerald's *Great Gatsby* influenced by Petronius' *Satyricon.* Wherever there is literature, intertextual links emerge. Intertextuality is also common in law, but sometimes less obvious. It concerns first of all the textual form of legal texts. Like the *sonnet* or the *short story* the *code* and the *statute* spread around the world from the culture of their origin. The content of legal texts is equally subject to intertextual relations. For instance, the Bill of Rights from 1689 that is perceived as a document of constitutional importance in England (Barnett 1999: 24) states in its Art. X: *...excessive bail ought not to be required, nor excessive fines imposed, nor cruel or unusual punishment inflicted.* The formulation *cruel and* *unusual punishment* is currently used in the U.S. Constitution's VIII Amendment that states: *Excessive bail shall not be required, nor excessive fines imposed, nor cruel and unusual punishment inflicted.* The above quotation can be perceived as the most obvious example of legal intertextuality, as the quotation of the English bill is almost literally reiterated in the VIII Amendment of the U.S. Constitution. Moreover, the intertextuality does not concern exclusively one legal system or one language in which different systems may be expressed linguistically. It appears regularly in legal acts which are created with open or concealed reference to legal provisions contrived in other legal systems and in other languages. The existing international cooperation in the area of legislative development favors this type of text creation. The copyright does not protect legal provisions from being copied or translated by others, and rightly so. For instance, some provisions of the Italian and of the French civil codes concerning interpretation are almost identical (cf. Notes and Materials nr. 19). Art. 1156 French Code civil saying: *On doit dans les conventions rechercher quelle a été la commune intention des parties contractantes, plutôt que de s'arrêter au sens litteral des termes* and Art. 1362 Italian Codice civile: *Nell'interpretare il contratto si deve indagare quale sia stata la comuna intenzione delle parti e non limitarsi al senso letterale delle parole* are that close as to their content and linguistic form that one may assume that the one is the translation of the other. Furthermore, the formulation of the Art. 1161 French Code civil: *Toutes les clauses des conventions* **s'interprètent les unes par les autres**, *en donnant à chacune le sens qui résulte de l'act entier* corresponds with Art. 1363 Italian Codice civile : *Le clausole del contratto* **si interpretano le une per mezzo delle altre**, *attribuendo a ciascuna il senso che risulta dal complesso dell'atto* (emphasis added). As this resemblance cannot be coincidental because it even comprises set phrases, it can be posited that they stand to each other in a relation of intertextuality; i.e. that the one has been developed because the other existed already. As the French Civil code dates from 1804 and the Italian Codice civile entered into force only 1942 one can claim that the Italian provision is the translation of the French one. Examples of intertextuality such as the preceding ones are very frequent in the legislation of countries belonging to the civil or to the common law traditions respectively due to their common legal heritage and regular borrowings from legislative acts which are perceived by legal comparatists as particularly well formulated. They prove again a close structural link between legal and literary texts.

4.2 Textuality and Interpretation

4.2.1 Is there only language in literature?

We asked already an analogous question regarding the law. As an intermediary result, we may invoke that literature is grounded in textual rules for its creation. There, also the plot is identifiable as a creation in language with specific means.

These means are called literary techniques. Plots and literary techniques (rules of composition) produce literary genres. It seems therefore that there is quite a lot in literature, but all this may be a very specific use of complex language. In law, we may recall, language is also used as being anchored in language games as a part of life forms. We found out that in this sense law is about language and nothing more than that. In literature the situation is analogous. The decisive hinge is the view upon language and not upon the subject matter that we discuss here. Yet, literature as well as law may have other limits.

4.2.2 Limits of legal and literary texts

Legal texts are not constructed freely under the impression of a given moment of time and in a contextual vacuum. Legislative techniques provide forms for their creation. They keep ready textual patterns for laws, decrees, ordinances etc. They also determine their textual composition and partition in chapters, sections, subsections until the determination of the use of Arabic or Roman numbers in them (cf. the French administrative instruction on these issues in Notes and Materials nr. 20). Moreover, their formulation depends upon the legal language of the specific legal culture. They are formulated in a way which is usually predictable for any professional involved in text creating activities specific for the given legal culture. When applied, the rules embodied in written texts are incorporated in forms of judicial decisions, injunctions and judgments, which are petrified in the most productive legal cultures. Not much room for textual inventiveness or creativity for drafters or judges is left there. Similarly, literature develops under the constraints of literary techniques. Good literature is good only if it matches up to the requirements established for good literature which are grounded in the existing patterns for writing novels or poetry in a specific period of time. Inventiveness and creativity operate within these boundaries. These boundaries are not only textual, they are also institutional because they are set by the literary experienced professional public, like literary critics, scholars or editors. A writer may not accept these boundaries and write as he desires but then the result of his efforts will not be perceived as good literature within the institutionally constituted audience. Exactly the same happens to a judge who does not accept textual forms of legal texts or other institutional boundaries in his activity. His judgment will still remain a judgment in the opinion of his peers, only a bad one. In fact, such a court decision displays also the juridical intertextuality in action. This aspect did not interest jurists until now and was not discussed in the legal theory either.

4.2.3 Legal and literary interpretation

A judge interprets a case or a statute in order to apply the results of the interpretation on another case while a literary critic interprets the literary work for itself, although not out of context. He is like the judge bound by the rules of interpretation specific to his profession. No reader or writer is free or independent of the interpretive context. The magic triangle of literary reception *writer – text – reader* provides the necessary framework for the discussion of all issues concerning the meaning of a literary work. It includes, but is not limited to, and this confession will not surprise here, the creation, the interpretation, the argumentation and the translation of and in literary texts. We have realized that in a text that is a linguistic product no inherent mechanism is apt to prevent whatever interpretation. The text usually bears whatever interpretation provided that persuasive argumentation has been prepared. The acceptability of an interpretation depends upon criteria in the professional community which under specific circumstances may favor some interpretations to the detriment of others. This process is especially striking in law where the professional community (foremost in the supreme courts) sets up institutional mechanisms that determine which interpretive rules can be applied and which results be accepted. The community of laypersons uses different mechanisms in interpreting legal texts which lead to divergences in the social discourse about right and wrong in judicial decisions (cf. 3.9.5). These mechanisms are less visible in literature because the literary criticism is less formally structured. The mechanisms that allow for certain interpretations while excluding others are analogous in literature. Interpretive constraints are therefore not in the text, but in the context. In the literary criticism, the ambit of inquires into the context is disputed (Juhl 1986: 90). In law, the creative interpretation that we favor is also disputed. Moreover, it is limited by the institutional mechanisms that set requirements for what is acceptable interpretation and what is not. This is especially the case in the so-called *hard cases* where the interpretation method applied is the one of pure creativity in law perceived according to R. Dworkin as integrity. Therefore, for R. Dworkin interpretation is not reconstruction of meaning. Instead, the need of understanding to determine the meaning in its social context undermines interpretation there. Similarly, for G. Gadamer, a forestructure of understanding, (D) *Vorverständnis*, determines this process (Gadamer 1965). In literature, it merely makes sense to find out the writer's initial idea whereas in law, especially in cases of explicit creative interpretation, it would be redundant to search for the initial meaning. Nevertheless, such interpretive practice would be legitime in any case. Only that it would be finally irrelevant for the decision taken. Therefore, the necessity to interpret creatively in law should not be understood as an impediment but as a precondition of understanding. Here again, law and literature meet.

4.2.4 Aren't we able to cope with narrative or textual ambiguity?

Traditionally, avoiding of polysemia, homonymy and lexical, textual or narrative ambiguity makes part of the claims for the development of a model legal language or at least its terminology (Mattila 2006: 111). The claim has been rarely challenged, but when questioned it leads to results contrary to the received opinion. Indeed, it may surprise that lawyers – usually skillful users of language – should not be able to overcome the ambiguity of language used in legal contexts and make a step towards a more univocal and precise language use. Is this a coincidence? Or is it a strategy of language use and legal argumentation? As far as lexical vagueness or ambiguity is concerned some researchers claimed that this is an intentional strategy of language use that aims at reaching the optimal application range of the propositions about law (cf. Den Boer, in an unpublished paper). Nevertheless, until now, the lack of linguistic univocality is perceived as a negative feature, and rather a shortcoming of language use in legal contexts than a characteristic feature of their textuality (Mattila 2008: 1150). Also the transparency in legal texts is perceived by many as problematic. Transparency, however, is a feature of the textuality in which the text is created. Its degree therefore differs and also this has reasons. In literary texts, some question the need of transparency, e.g. in poems (Baylon 1991: 251). Yet, even the most individualistic poet usually wishes to be understood by her readers; at least it seems improbable that she ignores the problem of transparency in texts. Therefore, transparency and ambiguity in different degrees of their manifestation seem to be structurally tied to the legal textuality. Hence, every criticism on their degree must be formulated with care. Similarly, yet in another context, Schauer (1993: xi) remarks that researchers are rather preoccupied with linguistic breakdown than with linguistic success in law. Doubtlessly, much would be won through the change in perspective upon ambiguity or transparency in legal text. Law, in fact, has never been simple and it apparently never will be perceived as such whatever efforts would be undertaken to simplify it (Mattila 2006: 99). Law addresses complex issues in complex societies. It cannot be simpler than the society it reflects. However, the Legal Linguistics can contribute to the process of reducing the complexity to a level which makes law operational and effective while clearly structured.

4.3 Creating Laws and Creating Fiction

One distinctive feature of law and literature could be seen in the supposed free creation of a novel writer limited only by his phantasy and the work of a judge who applies the law without interfering into it. The first activity would be creative, the other purely mechanical. Our analysis of the linguistic operations in law brought about results which clearly contradict such an assumption. A comparison with literature, i.e. with the creation of belles-lettres makes plain why the assuption that until today is shared by many cannot hold place. In fact, we persistently claim that legal texts are created through linguistic rules. Yet, what are the results of such creation? As to their form they are mostly statutes and related legislative acts as well as court opinions (precedents). These forms are very rare in literary fiction. Occasionally, writers invent legal provisions or create court decisions but such text types have a marginal role to play in the complexity of a literary work. The legal texts may however come closer to literature as far as their contents are considered. In such cases, law and literature would again come closer to each other than often assumed.

4.3.1 Narrativity of legal texts

Narrativity is not a concept which traditionally would be associated with technical or scientific texts. Recipients are used to categorizing texts along the difference of telling stories from life or about life and those relating facts. However, all texts have a specific narration; all have a story to tell. These stories are alike. To jurists legal texts tell many legal stories. Recipients of literary fiction are sometimes not used to reading other scientific or technical texts and they identify them therefore as different because the subject treated in them is different, or because for them they lack a story, a plot. All texts have a narration and this narration can be read and analyzed (Jackson 1985: 13, 57). We can assume that the narration of the text allows us to keep it in mind (Laurén 2002: 12). The more concrete a text is, the more material becomes the law. Therefore we usually understand and easier keep in mind cases than abstract legal provisions. The less abstract a legal provision is, the easier it is read and understood. Abstract provisions are not less narrative than others; their story is generalized and is readable only with the use of complex analytical instruments that comprise the legal methodology. Like complex literary fiction generalized legal texts cannot be read by whomever. A substantial part of the population is not able to read Joyce or Proust. For those readers, these texts when technically decoded through pronouncing the printed letters of the written texts do not say much even if they master the respective languages of both works. Yet, it is possible to learn the appropriate methodology and then these texts become accessible like all other texts. It is like through learning a foreign language we obtain gradually access to texts in this language, beginning with simple door inscriptions, when our efforts start, until the arcane historical layers of classical texts in this language, when we reach excellence in mastering it.

4.3.2 Literality of legal texts

What legal texts are also about? Legal texts, e.g. judicial decisions or statutes, include enonciations which in every culture are perceived as essential, ethically fundamental and therefore representing specific truths, values basic for the society. Let us have a look at some examples:

Generally know are Roman legal maxims that teach us that:
Salus rei publicae suprema lex.
Ubi societas, ibi ius.

Ulpian's maxims in the first volum of the *Corpus Iuris Civilis* are even more specific:

Iustitia est constans et perpetua voluntas ius suum cuique tribuendi.
Iuris praecepta sunt haec: honeste vivere, alterum non laedere, suum cuique tribuere.
Iuris prudentia est divinarum atque humanarum rerum notitia, iusti atque injusti scientia.

Constitutional preambles create texts that are perceived as visionary and are frequently invoked by citizens, cf. The U.S. Constitution:

We the People of the United States, in Order to form a more perfect Union, establish Justice, insure domestic Tranquility, provide for the common defence, promote the general Welfare, and secure the Blessings of Liberty to ourselves and our Posterity, do ordain and establish this Constitution for the United States of America.

The preamble of the French Declaration of Human and Citizen's Rights is not less visionary:

Les représentants du Peuple Français, constitués en Assemblée Nationale, considérant que l'ignorance, l'oubli ou le mépris des droits de l'homme sont les seules causes des malheurs publics et de la corruption des Gouvernements, ont résolu d'exposer, dans une Déclaration solennelle, les droits naturels, inaliénables et sacrés de l'Homme, afin que cette Déclaration, constamment présente à tous les Membres du corps social, leur rappelle sans cesse leurs droits et leurs devoirs ; afin que les actes du pouvoir législatif et ceux du pouvoir exécutif, pouvant être à chaque instant comparés avec le but de toute institution politique, en soient plus respectés ; afin que les réclamations des Citoyens, fondées désormais sur des principes simples et incontestable, tournent toujours au maintien de la Constitution, et au bonheur de tous. En conséquence, l'Assemblée Nationale reconnaît et déclare, en présence et sous les auspices de l'Être suprême, les droits suivants de l'Homme et du Citoyen.

And finally, statutes are equally fundamental in their formulations:

§ 1621 Perjury generally (U.S. Code Title 18 Part I Chapter 79 § 1621):

Whoever –

(1) having taken an oath before a competent tribunal, officer, or person, in any case in which a law of the United States authorizes an oath to be administered, that he will testify, declare,

depose, or certify truly, or that any written testimony, declaration, deposition, or certificate by him subscribed, is true, willfully and contrary to such oath states or subscribes any material matter which he does not believe to be true; or

(2) *in any declaration, certificate, verification or statement under penalty of perjury as permitted under section 1746 of title 28, United States Code, willfully subscribes as true any material matter which he does not believe to be true; is guilty of perjury and shall, except as otherwise expressly provided by law, be fined under this title or imprisoned not more than five years, or both. This section is applicable whether the statement or subscription is made within or without the United States.*

The quoted texts are not less fundamental, ethical, or true for society than other texts traditionally perceived as literary or philosophical. Benjamin Cardozo's decisions such as Hynes (in Notes and Materials nr. 35) or Palsgraf (in Notes and Materials nr. 34) - both already mentioned here - are examples of this sort of fundamental texts. And, they do not lack certain dramatics either. To illustrate this dramatics or literality we will now turn to precedents.

4.3.3 Literality of precedents

Court opinions may include or even mainly consist of texts with substantial dramatic input. The following is an excerpt from Hynes v. New York Central Railroad Co. (231 N.Y. 229, 131 N.E. 898, 17 A.L.R 803) decided by Benjamin Cardozo in 1921:

On this day Hynes and his companions climbed on the top of the bulkhead, intending to leap into the water. One of them made the plunge in safety. Hynes followed to the front of the springboard, and stood poised for his dive. At that moment a cross-arm with electric wires fell from the **defendant's** *pole. The wires struck the diver, flung him from the shattered board, and plunged him to his death below.*

No linguistic element of this fragment of the court decision, except for *defendant,* indicates that it does not make part of a novel. Yet, can occasional use of legal terminology qualify a text as a legal one? Literary parodies which use legalese in order to caricature language used by jurists would rarely be qualified as making part of legal texts, mainly because the intention of their authors has not been seriously directed towards the creation of a legal text. Is therefore Cardozo's opinion or the quoted paragraph of it a legal text because it has been created by a judge intending to establish a legal text? What do we know about Judge Cardozo's intention? We know quite a lot about his ambitions and his specific style. Can we assume that he had no intention to create a text which would be acceptable as being (also) a literary text? Can we assume that he excluded the idea that his opinion might be perceived as a literary text? Can we exclude that Cardozo has seen no particular boarderline or contradiction between legal and literary texts? In fact, also some samples from Cardozo's academic writings taken from *The Nature of the Judicial Process* (1928) show that the author was not primarily concerned with fitting into stylistic criteria of the genre but with pragmatic aspects of his writing, namely that it should convince the reader about the rightness of the proposition of law made there:

Back of precedents are the basic juridical conceptions which are the postulates of judicial reasoning, and further back are the habits of life, the institutions of society, in which those conceptions had their origin, and which, by a process of interaction, they have modified in turn.

All this may be true, but we must not press the truth too far. Logical consistency does not cease to be a good because it is not the supreme good. Holmes has told us in a sentence which is now classic that "the life of the law has not been logic; it has been experience." But Holmes did not tell us that logic has to be ignored when experience is silent.

Property, like liberty, though immune under the Constitution from destruction, is not immune from regulation essential for the common good. What that regulation shall be, every generation must work out for itself.

The case of Benjamin Cardozo, as judge and as legal writer, shows that not all jurists feel the necessity to distinguish strictly between legal and extra-legal literary genres. Even if this approach was unreflected it would still be most illustrative of inherent structural potentialities of texts, legal and non-legal ones.

Let us return now to Hynes. The Hynes-case can be easily reformulated and re-edited in the sense of a literary text through omitting of the specific legal terminology. It looks then like this:

Harvey Hynes, a lad of 16, swam with two companions from Manhattan to the Bronx side of the Harlem River. Along the Bronx side of the river the New York Central Railroad operated its trains by high-tension wires, strung on poles and cross-arms. Projecting from a bulkhead above the waters of the river was a plank or springboard, from which boys of the neighborhood used to dive. For more than five years swimmers had used it as a diving board without protest or obstruction. On this day Hynes and his companions climbed on the top of the bulkhead, intending to leap into the water. One of them made the plung in safety. Hynes followed to the front of the springboard, and stood poised for his dive. At that moment a cross-arm with electric wires fell from the pole. The wires struck the diver, flung him from the shattered board, and plunged him to his death.

We may contrast the above text sample with a citation from F. Scott Fitzgerald's *Great Gatsby,* written 1926, a few years after Cardozo's *Hynes*:

The wind had blown off, leaving a loud, bright night, with wings beating in the trees and a persistent organ sound as the full bellows of the earth blew the frogs full of life. The silhouette of a moving cat wavered across the moonlight, and, turning my head to watch it, I saw that I was not alone – fifty feet away a figure had emerged from the shadow of my neighbour's mansion and was standing with his hands in his pockets regarding the silver pepper of the stars. Something in his leisurely movements and the secure position of his feet upon the lawn suggested that it was Mr Gatsby himself, come out to determine what share was his of our local heavens.

The reformulated part of the original Cardozo text concerns facts. Legal issues were not paraphrased there. This is however possible. Let us look at the continuation of the court opinion:

His mother, suing as administratrix, brings this action for her damages. Thus far the courts have held that Hynes at the end of the springboard above public waters was a trespasser on the defendant's land. They have thought it immaterial that the board itself was a trespass, an encroachment to the public waters. They have thought it of no significance that Hynes would have met the same fate if he had been below the board and not above it.

Here, too, the transformation into ordinary language is not particularly complicated:

His mother sued the Railway company in a court, but lost. Judges there thought that Hynes entered the land without permission and therefore was himself responsible for his fate. They did not care about that the board itself was not fixed by the Railroad and was actually illegal because it reached over the river where everybody has the right to swim. They did not realize either that Hynes would have died were he swimming in the river below the plank.

And, also here we may continue with Scott Fitzgerald's *Gatsby*:

The little dog was sitting on the table looking with blind eyes through the smoke, and from time to time groaning faintly. People disappeared, reappeared, made plans to go somewhere, and then lost each other, searched for each other, found each other a few feet away. Some time towards midnight Tom Buchanan and Mrs Wilson stood face to face discussing, in impassioned voices, whether Mrs Wilson had any right to mention Daisy's name.

We could be exposed to criticism because we have chosen as an example a text largely known among American jurists as a masterpiece of a judicial opinion. Moreover, our transformation may not live up to the expectations of some readers used to read English classics, either. Yet, its sense is only to show the possibility of a transformation of a judicial opinion into literary or ordinary language. And this task is surprisingly easy. What is more, we quoted *Gatsby* here as a sample of a literary text that is doubtlessly fictitious. The narration in it does not differ from *Hynes*. Both tell us a story. And, we discovered that reader's perspectives in both are interchangable. Legal texts can be read as fiction as well as novels can be read as factual reports. The difference is again, as in interpretation, not in the text but in the context. The interpretive context includes choices of attitudes which their readers exercise in order to be able to cope with texts. As they are part of social practices, readers's choices are well settled within daily conventions. This means that the readers more or less automatically adopt the socially adequate interpretive attitude to texts. They read legal texts as reports about social facts and novels as social fiction. Nevertheless, the problem is one of choice, not of structure.

4.3.4 Reading cases as if they were stories

Samples from routine cases prove the regularity we insist upon. We engage in them to show that the choice of interpretive attitudes is not limited to cases written by prominent and particularly talented judges. In Walker v. Quillen (622 A. 2d 1097 1993) the imagery is steering the decision making process in the case. The Supreme Court of Delaware had to decide whether the plaintiffs could claim an implied easement or an easement by necessity to pass defendant's land which was their only means of access to the public road. The plaintiffs owned a tract of land, the Bluff Point, which previously belonged also to the defendant's dominant estate. The tract of land owned by the plaintiffs was surrounded on three sides by a bay and on the fourth side by the defendant's estate. It could not be reached from the bay due to the shallowness of the water there. Thus, it was completely landlocked. The defendant did not allow any access through the dirt road leading through his estate to the tract of land owned by the plaintiffs. It is not surprising in the light of the description of facts in this case that the court finally granted the implied easement. The facts seemed to speak for themselves and the court relied on them as if they would be programing the decision. Descriptive imagery dominates some decisions to a point that the decision making seems more or less automatic. In Nollan v. California Coastal Commission (483 U.S. 825) the U.S. Supreme Court dealt with the question whether the easement upon the estate of the plaintiffs ordered by the authorities amounted to taking which is illegal when imposed without compensation. The plaintiffs owned a beachfront lot in the neighborhood of an Oceanside public park. They tried to obtain a costal development permit in order to demolish a bungalow on their lot and replace it by a new one. The defendant granted them the permit subject to the condition that they allow the public an easement to pass across their lot to get to the public park and the neighboring beaches. The plaintiffs objected this decision. The U.S. Supreme Court reacted in an emotionally loaded language to the facts: "*The building restriction is not a valid regulation of land use, but an out-and-out plan of extortion. We therefore find that the Commission's imposition of the permit condition cannot be treated as an exercise of its land-use power. To obtain easements of access to private property the state must proceed through its eminent power domain."* Clearly, the court did not oppose the idea that an easement could be imposed upon the plaintiffs when there is sufficient public interest to be served. But it excluded a procedure that links an administrative decision to acts amounting to taking.

However, the imagery is not always the best predictability test for the court decision. In Michigan Mutual Insurance Co. v. Marriott Corporation (1992 WL 82498 N.D.III.) the court dealt with an insurance case. The owner of the insured Probe Prevost customized coach attempted unsuccessfully to park the coach in the hotel's valet parking area. At the request of the hotel's personnel he moved the coach to the hotel's general parking lot across the street, in front of the hotel. There, the coach had been stolen at night. The owner's insurance company claimed compensation from the hotel under the doctrine of bailment. However, the claim failed because the plaintiff could not prove that the defendant had accepted delivery and possession of the coach which are the prerequisites of bailment claims under Illinois law. As the coach owner kept the keys to the coach, he and not the hotel had the control over it so that no bailment existed. The imagery without the 'key' element is thus deceptive.

4.3.5 Facts in law

Questions of fact and issues of law are regularly distinguished in the legal argumentation and rightly so. They are different in nature and pertain to different aspects of adjudication. Another issue is whether they are as strictly isolated as the judicial practice would like us to believe. For us, they are rather interrelated. Furthermore, we would have to ask what sort of interrelation determines their symbolic appearance which is at least textually contingent because issues of law emerge where also facts are in question. In the adjudication abstract legal issues are rarely discussed, and should this happen, so they are related to the legal questions of the case. Moreover, under the common law, precedents map the way in which facts are stated in the decision and they constitute the focus of the decision when the judge distinguishes between precedents in the case at bar. The skill of a legal writer, such as a judge or an attorney-at law, in describing facts depends upon the identification of relevant events and chains of events in terms of the legal discourse. The legal discourse determines what is a relevant fact in terms of law and what is irrelevant (Broekman 1984: 159). The skillful legal writer distills from the social reality those facts of the story. This is the reason why sometimes a layperson may have the impression that something is missing in a legal narrative. What is 'missing' is simply irrelevant and therefore not a fact in terms of law. It remains a piece of information, but a redundant one. We already dealt with the situation that a novel reader has an impression that some information is missing there. This feeling is equally misleading, and we have explained the reasons for it. Like the novel writer who sees only the fictitious world of his narration, the legal writer sees only the legally relevant facts. This comes to be so, because both master the institutionalized rules of their profession.

4.3.5.1 A case study: In Torres v. Reardon (3 Cal. App. 4th 831, 5 Cal. Rptr. 2nd 52, 1992 Cal.App. Lexis 198, in Notes and Materials nr. 36) the parties disagreed about the liability for consequences of an accident that occurred to the plaintiff when he worked on the defendant's plot. The plaintiff was a self-employed gardener and was contracted by the defendant to take care of his garden in weekly turns. Some day, he had to trim a tree in their garden. While at work, the plaintiff fell from the tree due to a misfortune caused by a person who assisted him. This accident rendered him a paraplegic. He sued the defendant for damages pretending to have acted as his employee and being without the necessary workers' compensation insurance which the plaintiff allegedly was obliged to provide but did not. The defendant however contended that Torres had acted as an independent contractor to whom he had not been liable. In fact, the case as such is not particularly complicated in terms of law and it will not surprise any jurist that the plaintiff lost in all instances. It is nevertheless typical for language use in judicial decisions, and for this reason we will dwell a while upon it. The narrative provided by the court in its decision refers to aptly visualized scenery. Torres arrives as every week at the estate of the Reardons to take care of their garden. The Reardons are not at home but their neighbor instructs Torres what is to be done. A branch that overhung the neighbor's house should be cut. Torres climbs on the tree and the neighbor holds a rope tied to the branch in order to pull it out of his house when it would fall. The neighbor pulls on the rope when Torres does not expect it; Torres falls down and is made invalided for life. As a legal question, the court had to establish whether Torres worked as employee or as independent contractor. It examined evidence and held that Torres was self-employed and was doing business under the name of Jose Torres Gardening Services and was working for the plaintiff as well as for numerous other clients. He provided tools and equipment for the work and owned a truck which he used for the business. He himself had employees who assisted him in his business. Thus, the court denied Reardons' liability for the injuries Torres suffered because he was not an employee, but rather an independent contractor in the light of facts established. However, we have here two sorts of facts. First; the scenery of the accident and second; the facts establishing the background of Torres' business and his relation to the Reardons. The first group of facts is not controversial. These facts are easy to find out and to relate in the judicial decision. The second group of facts establishing the legal relation between Torres and the Reardons are of different nature. They are based on the distinguishing of employees and independent contractors under the doctrine of agency. Therefore, it is the doctrine of agency which dictates the way in which the court examines the background facts and it provides criteria for inclusion or exclusion of facts from the description. Moreover, fact finding is law finding. The court of appeals put it unsurprisingly short: "The evidence establishes *as a matter of law* that Torres was not an employee of the Reardons, but was an independent contractor at the time he was injured" (emphasis added). With help of this formulation the court establishes the difference between legal and other facts. The other facts could, in turn, become legal facts would the court ask whether a tort had been committed here. However, it did not as it did not establish any sufficient ground for defendant's liability towards the plaintiff. Some facts remained a pure narrative while others were decisive for the judgment rendered by the court. The metamorphosis of facts makes plain the narrative potentiality of the judicial decision. It does not matter in terms of law that the accident occurred on June 20, 1988. Yet it could, had data relevant in the light of the statute of limitations for torts been the issue. It does not matter that the accident happened at 11.00 AM, it furthermore does not matter whether June 20, 1988 had been a Wednesday or not. The interplay between legal rules and facts with all their potentiality for transformations is constitutive for the structure of judicial decisions as narratives. This interests us here. Words create law not only for Cardozo (Weisberg 1992: 6). They are not a mere translation of a holding into words (Weisberg ib.). While writing a court opinion the judge makes choices and determines facts interesting for the decision. The facts like the law are not simply there, they are created. Judges create them as they create the law on the basis of their professional knowledge. In this they resemble writers who create novels based on their professional knowledge of literature, its techniques, its history and the literary criticism. It appears that the legal linguist can learn from literature one essential thing about law; i.e that legal writing is a creative process. This discovery also explicates why the decription of the work that judges undertake with linguistic means is so complicated. Were it a simple, mechanical application of law and nothing more than that, no reason would exist for legal-linguistic activities. In this hypothetical case, the jurist interested in the legal language would have to limit her inquisitive mood to etymological issues. Therefore, legal conclusions in court decisions are always a mixture between law and facts. And court decisions also prove this mechanism: "*The failure of the defendant to respond to the intestate's outcries is immaterial*" stated the judge in Osterlind v. Hill (231 N.Y. 229, 131, N.E. 898, 17) after having distinguished between precedents pertaining to assistance under private law (contracts and torts) to persons not incapacitated and thus responsible for their own fate. Here, a non incapacitated had fallen into the lake from a canoe and was in vain crying for help from the renting agent Hill. According to the judge, no duty to rescue the drowning person could have been established on the basis of the facts that were provided by others, as the interested *'intestate'* could not contribute to the litigation by reasons well understandable. Undoubtedly, facts and law can easily be separated in Osterlind v. Hill but in the judicial decision they nevertheless constitute an interwoven entity.

4.3.6 Judges apply law and more than that

Every court opinion documents the way in which judges create the law. Creative narration emerges when the act of adjudication generically rhetoric does not assist the argument but is the argument (Weisberg 1992: 16). In the world of growing multimedia communication the importance of law in the media should not be overestimated, because possibilities of visualisation of law are limited. Nevertheless, legal cases and lawyers as protagonists and characters fascinated many writers and led to the emergence of the lawyer as a literary type (Weisberg 1992: 54). What might be the reason for this rather one-sided fascination? Is it that lawyers use language more carefully than do novelists? Or are rather the social implications law makes clear in society the reason for novelists to deal with the law and the lawyers? Novelists approach the law from the outside perspective; they are less interested in doctrinal intricacies of the legal practice. There, they provide reflections on the interpretive background of law, especially its ethical underpinnings. But still, is this a convincing explanation of the relation between law and literature? Weisberg insists on the textual parallelism grounded in a structure-oriented interpretation of both literary and legal texts. Indeed, as he posits, some formulations in ambiguous contracts or statutes may force the interpreter to refer to the structure of the text in order to identify its meaning (Weisberg 1992: 11). This structure is a broad term. When analyzing Melville's *Billy Budd, Sailor* Weisberg refers to the naval law and uses the Articles of War in order to provide an interpretation about sound or unsound, humane or legalistic legality of the plot. Finally, he joins Dworkin who also provides a broad concept of interpretation within his conception of law as integrity where a simple look into a statute would not enable to solve the Billy Budd case. In fact, deconstructive terminology is helpful in determining certain traits of interpretation in law. First of all, the specific limitations judges adopt when reading and composing legal texts can be characterized as a professional strategy of dealing with texts (Weisberg 1992: xiii). It follows from it that the plain textual meaning and the indeterminacy of meaning always enjoyed a hidden life in law and had finally to be addressed in order to end the myth of a professional judge strictly applying the law and nothing more than that. Postmodernist theory had at least an impact on jurisprudence in that it substantiated the occasionally expressed suspicion against the positivist ideal of an honest judge applying the law and nothing more than that. They established the conceptual instruments which make it possible to prove the anti-positivist claim. One of the foregoers of this attitude had been the Danish legal theorist Alf Ross who described the legal decision as a *façade*. He came close to the perspective of the American legal realists while pointing at the social and personal background of the judicial decision (cf. 3.3.4.1).

4.3.7 Literality and the institutional character of judicial opinions

Judicial opinions differ from other literary texts in that they are bound to judicial institutions. The texts produced by judges materially link the judicial decisions to the judicial institutions. Procedural rules assure the legality of this relation. Therefore, would a judge write a fictitious judicial opinion and publish it, e.g. in a literary magazine, the opinion would never become a precedent for the solution of other cases, whatever its professional quality would be. Would, furthermore, a judge who has no jurisdiction over a case issue an opinion, this opinion would not become precedent and would not be able to reference the law in force. However, would the parties not oppose this opinion and would it enter into force, then it would matter as a source of law. Apparently, procedural rules determine the quality of a text as a binding and valid judicial opinion. Statutes share the fate of judicial opinions in this respect. The best draft of a law prepared outside the legislative body remains a private initiative and cannot become law, even if it provides for highly persuasive and innovative solutions to social problems. Constitutional rules clearly determine its character as private and not binding in the public sphere. In terms of Legal Linguistics we could speak here about a text related to law rather than about a legal text. Juridical and other texts traditionally perceived as literary differ in the sense that they are engendered under boundaries imposed by different social institutions, be them the literary world or the justice system. Therefore, institutionality is their common characteristic feature. The texts produced within those institutions provide the missing material link between both areas. The materiality of a text is in essence linguistic (Todorov 2007: 9) and it is its most fundamental characteristic. Therefore, other cultures such as the Chinese did not distinguish formally between belles-letters, philosophy and legal scholarly writings. Instead, they relied on the most characteristic features of all these texts which is their linguistic basis. The European tradition of dealing with texts introduced distinctions which formally are well justified. However, one may ask oneself to what aim all these differentiations were actually undertaken? We therefore questioned here - not without a dose of personal courage - the traditional differentiation of texts and achieved results which challenge the received opinions about the nature of legal texts. Indeed, legal texts have been classified as a specific literary genre (Todorov 2007: 32) which has its own rules and conventions. This is a particularly convincing approach. A judicial opinion differs from a novel like a poem differs from a detective story. None of them are or could become true in the sense of the correspondence theory of truth (cf. Todorov 2007: 74). They are based on the proper rules of their particular ontology. In fact, the structural difference between a judicial decision and a literary text is the reference to sources. In judicial decisions this reference is mostly explicit, especially in common law countries where court decisions abound in references to precedents. In literary texts which - as we already pointed out - are composed within textual traditions explicit reference is rare. Sometimes, an understatement refers to the literary source, in other cases the textual parentage in recognizable only to an expert. Both, however, have one more feature in common, namely, that they cannot develop outside their textual reference.

4.3.8 What is then specific in legal texts?

Are legal texts specific in the sense that they are results of a specific reasoning? Basically, all texts are grounded in a specific reasoning, e.g. poetic texts are anchored in the specific reasoning of poetry and other fictitious literary texts are created analogically. Science fiction novels follow the pattern of a science fiction reasoning, medical treatises follow patterns of the medical science etc. Texts of whatever sort are preconditioned by the specific material rules for their construction. The legal reasoning is specific in that it grounds in rules of the legal argumentation which set limits for the valid legal speech acts engendered in such operations. We have already mentioned such limitations; among them are precedents issued by supreme courts and exceeding scholarly writings. Yet, all other texts, as we have seen, are equally limited in their constitution. Some constructivists therefore question even the distinctiveness of legal rules (Finnemore 2000: 701). Our result seems therefore to be trivial, because it suggests that legal texts are legal because they refer to law and medical texts are medical because they deal with medicine. Within the constructivist perspective upon law, Franck's 'compliance pull' for legal norms consisting of the elements: pedigree, determinacy, coherence and adherence may function as a test for the 'oughtness' in distinguishing norms (Finnemore 2000: 703). At the end, this test too concentrates on institutional criteria for distinguishing between norms and identifying legal norms among them. It seems to be explicitly pragmatic and therefore useful also for the Legal Linguistics. It would mean that legal texts are determined as legal due to extra-linguistic factors. What is more, we have also identified the specific extra-linguistic factor that is responsible for the change in attitudes writers and readers take when dealing with texts that are anchored in the institutionality of law. Writers write these texts and readers read them differently because both – at least ideally – are committed to *sincerity* as a condition of applying law and making the process of the application transparent in legal decisions. On the same reasons statutory provisions are received differently by their recipients than sonnets or science fiction. The sincerity as an ethical moment in law makes the distinction between fictitious texts and the legal ones. To put it short, legal texts create social facts whereas fiction does not. It may only influence the creation of such facts.

4.3.9 Literature and Law as part of Legal Linguistics

We have scrutinized here Law and Literature, the sister discipline of Law and Language, in the hope to be able to learn from it and use some of its results. We have to admit that we looked at Law and Literature from a very specific point of view and that we focused mostly upon some methodological aspects concerning the law as expressed in the written textual form. To avoid misunderstandings we also modified the heading and called this part of the book Literature and Law. The sense of this modification has been foremost to signalize that we will not enter into some specific issues of Law and Literature such as the question of how law, i.e. its institutions or its professonals are rendered in novels. While focusing on the textuality as a common feature of law and of literature we were nevertheless able to identify some pertinent structural resemblance between both. We found out that writing literature and writing law are kindered activities. Texts are produced in both according to specific professional rules. The rules and mechanisms in which they are applied differ; the procedure is the same. Moreover, argumentation in law is not limited to doctrinal issues. Facts described and evaluated in law are presented in judicial decisions towards the background of factual-linguistic imagery which is, in its core, argumentative. Additionally, legislative acts display narrative ambitions which can be meaningfully accessed by means of literary analysis. Therefore, in order to understand the language of the law and its use by the legal professionals it is necessary to understand also this specific imagery. Since this imagery is embodied in texts which show a striking resemblance with literary fiction, methodological approaches developed in the literary criticism are equally operative in this field of the Legal Linguistics. All these specific features make plain that textuality and its pragmatic consequences are part of the prolegomena to a pragmalinguistic theory of linguistic aspects of law. This result permits us to count Literature and Law - seen from the pragmatic perspective - as a part of the Legal Linguistics.

Part 5: Global Law and its Language

Law and the Legal Linguistics are aim-oriented. Among the aims of the Legal Linguistics are those of theoretical nature, e.g. the clarification of the tantalizing relation between the language and the law in general as well as in all detail. The main part of this book was dedicated to these problems. Finally, the Legal Linguistics has also a practical dimension which is not less important. It can be namely expected to contribute to the emergence of the global law. This practical activity may be duly perceived as one of the noblest tasks for the legal-linguistic research in the decades to come. The Legal Linguistics describes the linguistic requirements of the globalization process in law from the diachronic and the synchronic perspective. Hence, it scrutinizes the attempts to conceptualize the law in competing national languages as well as the conceptual language of the law, i.e. the language behind languages. It also looks back to times when the legal language had been formed in order to facilitate all attempts to advance the globalization process in law and to avoid unnecessary frictions. Moreover, as law regulates also its own language, the Legal Linguistics has the task to assist the legislator at this point and to contribute to the linguistic legislation. In the debate about the global law numerous specialists representing many different branches of law will have their word to say. Ultimately, and predominantly, legal linguists should be among them.

5.1 Converging Laws and Converging Languages

5.1.1 Globalization of law

The expansion of transnational and international law ranging from trade to human rights alongside the creation of new worldwide legal institutions such as the International Court of Justice or the International Criminal Court is indicative of an emerging global legal order (Cassese 2005: 5). This process is a part or a tendency in the general process of globalization (Reus-Smit 2005: 358). In that the different legal cultures converge or merge in it, it also illustrates the main theoretical problems related to the general process of globalization, its advantages and disadvantages. The task of the Legal Linguistics is to reflect upon the linguistic presuppositions of the globalization process in law. For these reasons and more, one could assume that merging of national laws, laws of supranational and international institutions into the global law should not be particularly difficult. Laws are – as we have seen – made of words and include a volitive element. Their merger would mostly require a political commitment to conclude the process because practically only two main legal traditions, i.e. *civil law* and *common law* are productive in this sense (Mattila 2006: 106). However, work on the merger of these two systems has been sluggish and cumbersome. Presumably, the volitive element in law; i.e. that it is a mechanism through which power is exercised in society (cf. Mattila 2006: 31; Husa 2007: 1) rather impedes than supports the process. The globalization process in law was launched on different levels of the international exchange including informal *consultations*, more formal *co-operation*, formal *harmonization* and *uniformization*. All these steps in the international exchange relations aiming at an approximation of the two dominating systems of civil law and common law are political in essence, but there are also explicitly linguistic in nature. It is therefore necessary to find the appropriate language for this law. The comparative law deals with issues which are very close to this task. In its core, seen from the perspective of the Legal Linguistics, comparative law is about comparing legal languages. This in turn is, as we have seen in above chapters, mostly the comparison of the legal argumentation applied in different legal traditions. We do not have until now any exhaustive repertory of argumentative forms in the Western law, in its dominant traditions common law and civil law. We miss this sort of knowledge also regarding other cultures which either totally or partially adopted Western approaches to law, such as the Japanese (cf. Notes and Materials nr. 27) or the Chinese one. Last but not least we do not know much about legal argumentation in traditions which developed differently than the Western legal culture. The practical work on the globalization in law concerns the rules of the substantive law, the procedural rules and the rules of the conflict of laws. Within the substantive law the most crucial legal-linguistic question is connected to the textuality of law and the text types. It mostly concerns the issues whether it is useful to codify legal provisions which means, from the legal-linguistic perspective, to establish the *code* as a global text type. In some approaches to the *uniform law* or (D) *Weltprivatrecht* the issue of the textuality of law is left open and harmonization of the content of provisions is stressed instead (Linhart 2005: 3, 13). It is nevertheless maintained that equal texts do not guarantee equal application due to differences in interpretation (Linhart 2005: 2). Legal Linguistics can provide some input at this stage. The procedural rules, in turn, pose another sort of problems as they involve also non-lawyers. The way how people speak, describe facts, etc., is culturally different. It may be therefore risky to postulate without further research that one set of procedural rules could become operative globally. Yet, results of the international co-operation, such as the *Principles of Transnational Civil Procedure* prepared by UNIDROIT and the American Law Institute in 2006 are interesting initiatives which pave the way towards an effective international co-operation. Finally, the rules of the conflict of law are relatively easy to harmonize.

Under regular circumstances, language does not seem to be an obstacle to unification processes in law. Languages generally can be adapted to the received legal tradition. The Swiss Civil Code had been transformed into Turkish law (cf. 4.9.2). The Japanese and the Chinese contemporary legal terminology are based on the European tradition. The Chinese terminology has been successfully adapted to the international demand and to the systemic necessities of the Occidentalization of law against all fears to the contrary (cf. David 1978: 538). The languages of India adapted to the English common law terminology. South Korea adopted the German conception of administrative law including the administrative process. Unsurprisingly, some problems remain on the level of understanding of these new texts by their readers and especially by those who shall apply them in cultures different from those in which these rules emerged. Laws refer to values and cannot be applied without them. However, values expressed in general terms can be successfully applied in different, sometimes even diametrically opposed societies. This had been the case with the German Civil Code applied in West and East Germany until 1975, the year of the entry into force of the East German Civil Code that became obsolet after the German unification. The abstract general language of the law adapted by other countries in cultures different from the European one show that the unification should proceed on the basis of the generally broadest common conceptual denominator. This strategy would not challenge the existing cultural diversity. It would, by necessity, rather focus on the common heritage than on differences. The results of unification of law will occasionally lead to differences in interpretation (Linhart 2005: 2). However, these differences can be easier overcome than conceptual dichotomy. Within our perspective on language - which is comparative - one more fundamental problem exists. It concerns the homogeneity of legal language in the comparative perspective. Apparently, the major legal languages have a lot in common, especially common technical terminology. However, they differ also in many respects. Legal German applies a more abstract language than legal Finnish (Galdia 2003: 18), legal Russian follows sometimes other paths than other languages (Mattila 2006: 93-96), some judges in Islamic law countries tend to a more solemn expression than for instance judges in Scandinavian countries. The style of judgments rendered by judges in the Anglo-American law tradition differs significantly from the French or the Scandinavian decisions. Sarcastic and even humorous remarks are not unusual in the common law decisions while on the European continent they could jeopardize the judicial decision that could be perceived as rendered by a biased judge (cf. OHG v. Kolodny in Notes and Materials nr. 31). These are pragmatic aspects of legal language use which may oppose its uniformization.

5.1.2 Legal Linguistics and Comparative Law

We are aware of that the process in which global law is constructed will take quite a long time. And, as it is the case already today the international legal order will coexist with national laws all over the world (Cassese 2005: 21). Some researchers underline in this context the high level of internationality that has been already achieved in the contemporary national legal systems (Pigolkin 1990: 11).

This systemic duality makes the work of lawyers difficult because they are dealing with a changing object both on a national and international level. Law, of course, always changed. But, it was mostly an evolution of the national legal system which lawyers had to face. Today, the national legal systems still evolve and simultaneously they also disappear. Consequently, they are replaced by rules of supranational organisms such as the European Union or by the international legislation, for instance the CISG whose 'internationality' is limited to the states that have ratified it. What is more, comparative lawyers like specialists in private international law (conflict of laws) are conscious of that their special disciplines have one finality, the one to disappear. It is, in fact, an exciting task to participate in the destruction of one's own profession because is serves a good cause. This destruction will pass several stages until the final result will be attained. The named formalized processes of the bilateral and multilateral consultations, co-operation between national states, harmonization and unification with formulas of opting-in or opting-out will gradually dissipate any need for the comparative law in its contemporaneous shape or the conflict of laws in the international arena. Therefore, a gradual transformation of comparative studies into comparative legal-linguistic and later on to legal-linguistic studies is recommendable because the legal language will resist to all changes in the globalizing subject matter. Paradoxically, civil law and common law may differ in their methodology; as far as their language is concerned they seem far less remote. Comparative law showed that systemic difference does not play any particular role in the light of results achieved in both legal traditions. Methodological differences seem in practice to be much less decisive than in some theoretical explorations based – often artificially - on an opposition between civil law and the common law. This opposition in description and analysis of both Continental civil law and the Anglo-American common law is an issue for the Legal Linguistics. It is best addressed under the caption Literature and Law as it concerns problems of the textual conceptualization in comparative legal research. Here, we shall maintain some of its possible consequences. As said, the long-term goal of the legal globalization will not be achieved over night. Therefore, the conception of Legal Linguistics as Comparative Legal Linguistics in the sense proposed by Mattila (2006) remains a realistic option for the research in the times to come. The Comparative Legal Linguistics will have to develop a legal language which can be used in the forming of the global law. This language is first of all based on the morphology of law. It will have to cover all its morphological elements such as contracts, torts or delicts, property, etc., with their inherent structural elements. One could call this auxiliary language a meta-language of the law. But it concerns also the adaptation of the main natural language of international relations, the English language, to function in this role. Criticism on the English language as a tool able to express the conceptual totality of international law is not new. Due to its links with the common law tradition it tends towards retransformation of whatever conceptual apparatus into common law. Within the European Union considerable progress has been achieved to develop a more neutral legal English (cf. 5.1.5). The same concerns legal relations within private law, especially within the UNIDROIT, e.g. the *Principles of International Commercial Contracts* (Beveridge 2002: 77) and the draft of the *Principles of the European Contract Law* prepared 1999 by the Commission on European Contract Law. As an alternative to a natural language as bearer of the global legal language one can imagine an auxiliary language such as Esperanto to take over this role after all necessary adaptation. In comparative diachronic research the differences in development between different national and legal languages may lead to complications, especially in terms of terminology. This is, for instance, the case when in the diachronic research notions with long history, such as the German ones must be transferred into Finnish which is a language with relatively short tradition of specialized legal terminology (Letto-Vennamo 2002: 29). In such a case there is a risk that whatever new term would be used in the linguistic transfer it will always be perceived as anachronistic.

5.1.3 Legal terminology and cultural diversity

Nowadays, the legal terminology – seen from the global perspective – develops under a strong influence from the civil law and the common law traditions. This concerns also countries which are not perceived as European or having strong cultural links to the European culture. We already mentioned that the legal terminology had been perceived by many as the heart of the Legal Linguistics. It could be analyzed in many different ways. First, it could be approached in a monolingual scheme and be based on the contrast between the special register and the ordinary language or second, it could instrumentalize the same perspective while including two or more natural languages. Third, it could focus on an exclusive comparative analysis of the special registers. Fourth, it could include the diachronic perspective and focus on the changes in the special register in time or fifth, it also could concentrate on language contacts concerning the emergence of the special register be it synchronically or diachronically or both. Very often, and rightly so, the named perspectives are combined in the research and they lead to substantial results. Generally, legal terminology developed within one cultural tradition in the process of linguistic contacts. In the Turkish legal language Persian loan words such as *şartname* (TR document containing terms and conditions) are frequent. This holds also true for the Chinese signs used in Japanese (Okawara 1998: 199). The same process concerns legal English or legal French which were influenced by the Latin terminology and to some extent by the Greek language (cf. Husa 2007: 97). Terminological influence from outside the cultural reference in Europe is rare. In the legal French words rooted in Arabic or Persian like *douane* or *avarie* (Cornu 2004: 142), in the legal Russian Tatar words like *tamozhnja, kazna, jarlyk* or *karaul* (Pigolkin 1990: 45) have been identified in the research. One could add to them also (FR) *tarif* from Arabic *tarif (notification).* The legal terminology in former Yugoslavia had been influenced by Turkish, e.g. (MAC*) ortach (partner).* Furthermore, for legal English the process of introducing of Islamic legal terminology into legal texts written in English in Pakistan is characteristic (Mattila 2006: 249). In Chinese, one of the legal terms meaning *sale,* (CN) *mǎimai* corresponds literally with (LAT) *emptio-venditio.* However, this linguistic contact is a one-sided process.

The multilingual perspective has the advantage that it paves the way towards developing of a legal language for the emerging global law. English language terms rooted in the constitutional system of the common law countries such as *state of law*, *good governance*, or *checks and balances* find entry into legal languages which belong to civil law. Specifically, *corporate governance* may be rendered as (D) *verantwortungsvolle Unternehmensführung.* One can also follow this lexical creation in a broader comparative perspective. To illustrate, *parent company* corresponds in (S) to *moderföretaget* as a pendant to (S) *dotterföretaget* and to (D) *Muttergesellschaft* and (D) *Tochtergesellschaft* respectively. The distinction in the German terminology is due to the feminine gender of (D) *Gesellschaft* (company) whereas the Swedish language terminology is based on (S) *företaget* and sometimes (S) *bolaget* which are both of neutral gender. Therefore, the Swedish form – unlike the German terms - seems to be rather a calque, a foreign borrowing than a linguistic creation motivated in the linguistic system. In the Japanese terminology (JAP) *oyagaisha* (i.e. parent company) and (JAP) *kogaisha* (i.e. child company) are used respectively. Comparative law studies began in some cases with the process of the emerging of the legal terminology. David (1978: 554) reports that during the Meiji era in Japan (beginning 1868) Japanese terminology has been invented in the process of translation of the European codes into Japanese. Terms such as (JAP) *kenri* for *subjective right* and (JAP) *gimu* for *legal obligation* date from this period. Less interest had been brought towards the existing legal Japanese terminology before the time of Europeanization of Japan's legislation. Igarashi (1990) accounts for a specific Japanese legal vocabulary or vocabulary with legal connection including terms such as: *assen, horei, iriai, iriai-ken, jori, kaisha, kanji, kankai, karitoki-tampo, kojoryo-zoku, kokutai, kumiai, mansion, meinin-hoko, menso, nainen, ne, onsensarakin, shiho-shoshi, shinpan, shinto, tenno.* They are difficult to translate; sometimes a description is necessary as in the case of *jori* which may be translated as customs or the nature of things (Igarashi 1990: 2). Analogous remarks can be found concerning the legal Chinese terminology (Escarra 1936: 55) as independent terminology, e.g. (CN) *yong dian quan* (eternal lease) is rare there. The development of the modern Chinese terminology in the international law (*ius gentium sinense*) was sketched by Zhang (2002). He concentrated on concepts such as *international law, state, nation, international, inter-state* (all p. 4), *war* (233), *immunity* (54), *human rights* (47), *treaty* (185), *larger freedom* (211), *obligation* (177), *ius cogens* (212), *security* (209), *individual* (53), *person* and *thing* (53), *extradition* (74), *hot pursuit* (128) or *self-executive* (24) and demonstrated that these concepts can be clearly termed in the Chinese language. For this type of analysis Mattila's (2006: 108) methodological distinction between term and concept has proven to be an indispensable matrix. The acceptablility of the international legal terminology which is written mostly in English and subsequently translated into some official languages could be increased through loan words borrowed from beyond the borders of the European culture. Rules for such a linguistic policy should be preferably developed by international organizations. They could, for instance, include also percentage limits for vocabulary representing different legal traditions and cultures, as it is the case with rules for the development of Esperanto.

5.1.4 Argumentation in Comparative Law

Furthermore, as we have indicated, the development of a more neutral legal terminology with English as its basis or with whatever other language is not necessarily the final solution to the problem of the global legal language. Crucial for the creation of law is the appraisal of the linguistic processes which anticipate the interpretation and the use of arguments in the legal language. Central for the application of law is argumentation, and this operation is until now not universal in its application. Argumentation as such is an extremely complex linguistic speech act. The results and the profile chosen here for the analyses of the legal language lead to the conclusion that the argumentation research is substantial for the development and the transformation of comparative law in times of globalization. Differences and parallels in the argumentation in different legal traditions and between legal cultures have been discovered in the research and every contact of a comparatist with a legal decision rendered in a foreign country shows both the differences and the similarities in the use of arguments (cf. Galdia 2008: 24 regarding German and Greek court decisions). Also, the degree of formality involved in interpretive practices may differ (cf. Atiyah/Summers 1987: 15). However, intuitive conclusions are not satisfying any more and comparative law as well as all other legal branches will have to turn to the argumentation research for fundamental advice how to develop their disciplines in times dominated by qualitative changes. Comparative research into the legal language must therefore aim at canvassing the argumentative mechanisms at work in the different national legal systems and in the international law. Otherwise, the law in the future risks becoming a law of a part of the globe imposed upon other legal traditions.

5.1.5 Linguistic aspects of the E.U. law and the law in the U.S.

The convergence processes in law can be well observed on the example of the European Union and the U.S. Within the European Union, linguistic issues and matters of policy intertwine. Political decisions are necessary for any legislative break-through. Attempts had been undertaken in the research to determine the nature of the law ruling the European Union. Apparently, the law of the European Union does not develop towards a conceptual background which would guarantee its fundamental cohesion. Text types were perceived to be mostly of French origin. Most leading concepts like (FR/EU) *acquis communautaire* are of French origin or new coinages made initially in French. However, some interpretive approaches are perceived as typical for the common law. The European Union tried therefore to develop a more coherent legal terminology (Mattila 2006: 102). These efforts culminated in the Inter-institutional agreement on common guidelines for the quality of drafting of Community legislation from December, 22 1998. The Inter-institutional Agreement on common guidelines for the quality of drafting of Community legislation (Official Journal C 073, 17/03/99) recommends in its Section 5: *Throughout the process leading to their adoption, draft acts shall be framed in terms and sentence structures which respect the multilingual nature of the Community legislation; concepts or terminology specific to any one national legal system are to be used with care.* Likewise, the Principles of European Contract Law (PECL) reflect the spirit of the drafting instruction. J. M. Smits (2005: 568) characterizes the PECL as an attempt to draft a common European private law code. He also stresses that the PECL create a common language through which the European scholars can communicate and European students be educated (Smits 2005: 573). However, provisions in plain English that is largely independent of the common law are difficult to draft even if their neutrality is expressly postulated (Smits 2005: 568). For instance, a linguistic plan scheduled in steps for a regulated action is developed in PECL Art. 6: 111 (*Change of Circumstances*):

(1) A party is bound to fulfil its obligations even if performance has become more onerous, whether because the cost of performance has increased or because the value of the performance it receives has diminished.

(2) If, however, performance of the contract becomes excessively onerous because of a change of circumstances, the parties are bound to enter into negotiations with a view to adapting the contract or terminating it, provided that:

(a) the change of circumstances occurred after the time of conclusion of the contract,
(b) the possibility of a change of circumstances was not one which would reasonably have been taken into account at the time of the conclusion of the contract, and
(c) the risk of the change of circumstances is not one which, according to the contract, the party affected should be required to bear.

(3) If the parties fail to reach agreement within a reasonable period, the court may:

(a) end the contract at a date and on terms to be determined by the court; or

(b) adapt the contract in order to distribute between the parties in a just and equitable manner the losses and gains resulting from the change of circumstances.

In either case, the court may award damages for the loss suffered through a party refusing to negotiate or breaking off negotiations contrary to good faith and fair dealing.

In the above provision notions such as *performance* or *agreement* may, even if read independently from their meaning in the common law, nevertheless cause in the common law reader connotations that are different from the civil law perspective. Moreover, this risk of misunderstanding increases when notions typical for the common law such as *good faith and fair dealing* are included into a language that purports to be neutral. In addition, the formulation in Art. 9: 201 PECL *Withholding Performance* or Art. 9: 303 PECL *Anticipatory Non-Performance* are probably understandable only to lawyers who know the respective common law and civil law equivalences of this concept. Furthermore, the *prescription* of PECL 14th chapter that corresponds to the common law *statute of limitations* is clearly grounded in the civil law terminology. It is therefore not really neutral, although it pretends to be it. In fact, a drafted language may be free from specific denotations due to explicit drafting guidelines that are known also to the users; language-specific connotations remain however unavoidable. Expressions in Art. 6: 111 PECL such as *to fulfil the obligation*, *excessively onerous* or *within a reasonable period of time* will usually be construed within language-specific limits of use by the English speakers. Alleged neutrality of language use in drafting different and often contradictory legal provisions in one language, e.g. CISG, UCC, PECL or EU legislation in English will always lead to interpretive divergences because language cannot be used out of its context. If the context is overburdened by too many interpretive guidelines then the language will not fulfill its goal to function as a means of effective communication. Instead, misunderstandings that cause harm to the legal certainty will emerge. More specifically, most problems concern the legislative drafting of the EU secondary law (Cordeiro 2004). Meanwhile, the legislative drafting concerns all sorts of official documents, beginning with the constitutional provisions, laws, decrees and ending with the particular decisions taken in singular cases. Another aspect concerns the correctness of language use – which doubtlessly exists in language – that is also part of language use in law and therefore part of the Legal Linguistics. Text editing has also its part to play there. The full stop or the colon should be put in a legal text at the right place and no adventurous spelling can be allowed in official texts. Official texts, and the legal texts are official *par excellence*, are characterized by increased level of intersubjectivity. They are aimed to be read, understood and enforced by other persons than their authors. They must therefore follow as close as possible the rules of linguistic correctness in order to avoid subjective or privative, hermetically close language use. Banalities such as correct spelling or right use of diacritic signs are part of this sort of correctness, and therefore also of the legal language, although they definitely are not its most fascinating part. Editing of legal texts comprises these tasks – as trivial as they may seem – and constitutes a link between both involved disciplines, i.e. national language philology and Legal Linguistics.

Translation of the EU law into the official languages of the member states is not unproblematic either although the legal languages refer basically to the same object. However, it seems to be difficult to find the appropriate national legal language for this task. For instance, the Swedish language version of laws drafted in Finland is as a rule a translation from Finnish. However, according to the Finnish Constitution's Section 79 all legal acts are to be enacted and published in the Finnish and Swedish languages. According to the Government Bill concerning the new Constitution (no. 1/1991, p. 131) the enactment of the legislation in two languages means that both linguistic versions have an equal legal status. Thus, due to the enactment procedure the translated text acquires a legal status which in terms of law transforms its very nature from a translated text to an original text (Palmgren 2002: 157). Nevertheless, in terms of text type the Swedish text will remain a translation. The EU develops a Swedish language terminology which is common for Finland and Sweden (Palmgren 2002: 159) despite persisting differences between the legal Swedish language terminology in Sweden and in Finland.

Where the EU insists upon *transparency*, the U.S. Government stresses the necessity of the *plain language* use. In the U.S., the *plain language* of the legislation dominated the linguistic discussion of legislative problems. Already 1978 the U.S. President J. Carter issued an executive order to all government departments regarding the use of plain language. Likewise, U.S. President W. Clinton issued 1998 an administrative order requiring that laws be drafted in plain language as of January 1999. The (US) Securities and Exchange Commission adopted 1998 amendments to the Securities Act Rule 421 and required that the prospectus disclosure comply with the principles of plain English, including the use of active voice, short sentences, definite, concrete everyday words, tabular presentation or bullet lists, without legal or highly technical business terminology or multiple negatives (cf. Sec. Act Rel. 33-7380/1997).

The *plain language* requirements in Europe concern mostly the UK and the Scandinavian countries. Elsewhere, the postulates for the understandability of the legal language are expressed in less assertive terms. Comparatively, the guidelines developed in Finland in regards of the use of plain Swedish language include following recommendations (cf. Palmgren 2002: 158):

a) The official texts (including legislation) are written for the citizen's sake;
b) They must therefore have a linguistic style that is understandable at least for people who are willing to enter deeper into the substance;
c) The linguistic style is 'present-day, ordinary Swedish prose'.

Within the *plain language* tendency legal linguists could have a role to play. They could develop linguistically founded mecanisms for legislative drafting in a way which takes account of understandability and avoids banalizing of the legal language.

The harmonization of the U.S. American law resembles in many respects the European development. However, in the U.S., convergence processes, e.g. within the adoption of the UCC, were easier because they took place in the same language and the same political system, even if the legal tradition of Louisiana is different from most other U.S. federal states. In the confrontation between federal states and the federation a compromise has been achieved in the Erie-doctrine. According to this doctrine, federal courts apply the law in the limits of the federal state law in which they function. Predominant in the development have therefore been the strategies developed by the federal government and some prominent lawyers within the American Law Institute to proceed peacemeal, yet to insist on progress.

5.1.6 Lessons learned

Searching for the language of the emerging global law may happen on different levels. First, the conceptual language, i.e. the language behind national languages must be defined. The task includes the identification of textual forms for this language, e.g. *codes*. Its basis is the *meta-language of law* that is scrutinized and developed in the linguistically oriented comparative law. Second, a national language or a set of national languages must be defined to carry the concepts of the global law. Alternatively, an artificial language like Esperanto or Legal Latin may function in this role. This language must be neutral enough in order to cope with the autonomous terminology of the global law. Third, as the linguistic operations in law are dominated by the argumentation, the argumentative specifics in different legal cultures must be reflected upon while drafting common provisions of substantive and procedural law. Fourth, linguistic strategies of drafting shall be developed in order to put in line the language of law with the realities of communication, especially as far as understandability and acceptability are concerned. Increasing the overall level of internationalization in drafting will also improve the acceptability in politics and among the citizenry. Research on legal argumentation in different legal cultures would also show which parts of the language use in law are particularly resistent to unification efforts and which parts fit smoothly into innovative conceptualizations of law. For all these tasks the conception of Comparative Legal Linguistics developed by Heikki E.S. Mattila seems to be the appropriate intellectual vehicle.

5.2 *Épistémologie* of Law as Search for the Original Legal Language

The above scrutiny of some pertinent linguistic problems in the process of globalization in law ended with the postulate to adopt a coherent set of legal-linguistic strategies adapted to the requirements of the modern societal conditions. Additionally, we could also ask whether the legal linguist may be able to learn something essential from past law. The answers will often be elusive as we have also experienced the limits of cultural phenomena like Greek philosophy, Roman law or the Biblical texts which are perceived by many as essential foundations of the Western culture. It seems that the retrospective upon the Biblical tradition is the least promising for law because ethical and legal issues are treated there authoritatively as received law (Gaudemet 2001: 10). They are not subject to deliberation which is the essence of law as it functions nowadays. But we can assume that the Greek philosophy as the fundamental discourse about man and the world could provide some insight into the discursive operations of law. The Roman law as a discourse of jurists about the content of law - especially in the textual form of the *Corpus Iuris Civilis* – is a deliberation which did not lose its impact until today. However, theoretically more giving are epistemological inquiries into the linguistic side of law. They show its initial grammar, i.e. processes of emerging of legal speech acts, their terminology and textual forms which made them to a success story in the Western world. Knowledge of epistemic regularities may help avoiding disorientation, frustration and reluctance towards the new legal language of the globalized world. This task can be approached from different perspectives; we will remain close to a method developed mostly for the scrutiny of humanities by Michel Foucault that in the French scientific tradition is called *épistémologie*. We call it also in the following by an English name *epistemology* although mainly another philosophical discipline claims this denomination in the English speaking academia. Moreover, we limit ourselves to law and will therefore speak only about the *legal epistemology*. Legal epistemology (FR *épistémologie juridique*) has been developed in France foremost by Christian Atias (1986) who referred to the work by Fr. Gény (Atias 1994: 24) as far as the coinage of the term is concerned. In parenthesis, we may mention that in the same work Fr. Gény also used the term *linguistique juridique* which was transformed here into Legal Linguistics (cf. 2.1.2). Atias sees the role of the legal epistemology in tracing the legal knowledge in terms of its scientific formation. However, he rather relies on the conceptual foundations set by G. Bachelard (Atias 1994: 44) and G. Canguilhem than on the discursive approach developed by M. Foucault and expounded by Fr. Ewald.

5.2.1 Épistémè in law

Legal epistemology is equally deep as is the legal language. To create notions such as *plaintiff* or *defendant* a linguistic and legal practice of a court procedure is necessary. The emergence of this practice which reflects exactly the general linguistic patterns of emergence of speech acts in forms of life proves the interdependence between the legal language and the legal institutions. In this circularity there is method and it consists in introducing or modifying the linguistic practice along the societal evolution where changes in the perception of values and norms occur. In the research, it has been regularly stressed that the process of emergence of the legal language is central for every perspective upon the legal language (Hałas 1995: 6). In fact, the reconstruction of the original language of law which in the Western tradition had been expressed in Latin is one of the most fascinating projects within the Legal Linguistics. It fascinates not because of its backward orientation or nostalgia towards a better or more reliable law of times past. It fascinates because it makes language used in contemporary legal practice transparent, it provides for its inner motivation. Law has qualitatively never been as efficient or humane as it is today. There is, therefore, no reason to glorify the past of the law. Nowadays, Western-type societies reached a level of reasoning upon law which provides for the most appropriate solutions to legally relevant social problems. These solutions may not seem perfect, but they have never been as perfect as they are today.

Epistemological research into law also includes other legal languages and cultures than Latin and the Roman law. It starts with ancient Chinese (Escarra 1936), Babylonian (Gaudemet 2001: 3-8; cf. also Notes and Materials nr. 4), Egyptian (Spiegelberg 1892, 1907, 1922; Lippert 2004), Hebrew (Gaudemet 2001: 8-10), Greek (Gaudemet 2001: 11-24, 28-29; Thür 2003), Nordic (Amira 1882/1895), and Mediterranean (Ladjili-Mouchette 1990). The note nr. 4 shows that textual forms typical for law, such as contracts have a long epistemological history of continuity and discontinuity. Although religious traditions may deny creational elements in law because they perceive it as received (e.g Bible, Koran), they use rhetorical elements in the discourse about law. Hebrew rhetorical tradition produced neither theoretical works nor handbooks on rhetoric; meanwhile the Hebrew Bible as well as commentaries thereto abound in rhetoric figures (cf. Sloan 2001: 325). Hence, the epistemological conception of law and the discourse about law concern different linguistic practices. The linguistic aspects of the law of Occidental type are, however, best reconstructed through the Roman law to which the Occidental law is directly tied.

5.2.2 Legal-linguistic aspects of the Roman Law

The legal epistemology in the sense of identifing of legal-discursive practices and their roots is historically based on the Roman law. The Roman law is for jurists what the Greek philosophy is for philosophers. It means that both jurists and philosophers may exercise their respective professions without knowing the Roman law or the Greek philosophy but they will never understand why their disciplines became what they are should they decide to ignore their epistemological foundations. Moreover, one could claim that the beginning of the research into the Roman law marks also the beginning of the Legal Linguistics. It included at least studies of the legal vocabulary, categories and concepts used in law (David 1978: 51). In the sense of the above, the legal theory of the Roman law is archeology of linguistic forms rather than other phenomena. Archaeology of thought is most effective under the criteria introduced by M. Foucault (1969). We will try to identify some forms that shaped this discursive reality and we will again strongly rely on terminology. In this context, R. Arntz (2002: 39) remarks that influences from the Roman law on the terminology are not always immediately apparent. Sometimes the terminology may have undergone fundamental changes and it may have been transformed into the national language in form of a *calque* or a neologism which is not perceptible as such any more. Therefore, it is necessary to look into the 'inner form' of the language in order to discover the conceptual and terminological legacy of other languages (Arntz 2002: 44). Yet, what does it mean to understand the inner motivation of a language? It means to be able to follow its conceptualization and lexicalization patterns. For instance, expressions like *to subpoena someone* show that the motivation in the special register is not understood by the speakers any more.

5.2.2.1 Romans conscious of legal language: The specialized language creation in law includes practices of language creation on different levels of linguistic exchange. A specific pronunciation or use of antiquated vocabulary, use of honorifics, etc., are examples regularly quoted in the Legal Linguistics. Cicero complains in his *De Oratore* (I-193) about the antiquated language in the Law of the Twelve Tables which sometimes was difficult to grasp for his contemporaries. Others do not complain but rather contribute to the specialized legal register and they increase its complexity but also its optimal use in legal-linguistically relevant situations. The list of abbreviations, known as *De Juris Notarum* by Valerius Probus or Gaius Aelius Gallus' lexicon *De verborum quae ad jus pertinent significatione* (Mattila 2006: 7) are artifacts of the later type. Gallus' work was appreciated in Rome and it was also commented upon (cf. Auli Gellii Noctes Atticae,

Liber XVI in Notes and Materials nr. 6). Valerius Probus justifies the reasons for the existence of his work and he elaborates with a theoretical ambition unusual for the Roman jurists upon the use of abbreviations in legal texts, including both legal acts and legal actions. His short text could be perceived as one of the first legal-linguistic treatises in the development of the Legal Linguistics. We render therefore its entire theoretical part which constitutes its introduction in a note (cf. Notes and Materials nr. 5). One reason for the express theoretical ambitions in *De Juris Notarum* could have been that its author had been a grammarian, not a jurist. We can assume that a Roman jurist, had he been an author of the list of abbreviations would had set up an uncommented register, and by so doing, he would expose us to one more riddle about the origins of the Roman law and its language. As for Gallus and his successors, Mattila (2006: 7) remarks that the lexicographic method once established remained productive later on in Byzantium and in the Western Europe of the Middle Ages.

5.2.2.2 Formal legal education: Professional legal language is closely related to the emergence of formal legal education in ancient Rome. Aulus Gellius mentions in his *Noctes Atticae* the beginnings of this rudimentary and adventurous education in same places in Rome, (LAT) *in plerisque Romae stationibus* (cf. Notes and Materials nr. 7). Besides, from this quote it becomes plain why even today young lawyers in Germany used to article in courts in (D) *Stationen*, such as (D) *Zivilstation* or *Strafstation.* In CIC, book I. 2. (Pomponius libro singulari Enchiridii) the subsequent phases of the legal education are presented under the broader heading of the chapter *De origine iuris et omnium magistratuum et successione prudentium.* This succession of experts is possible only when there exists a notion of formal education based on the transfer of knowledge in a systematic way (Ladjili-Mouchette 1990: 423). Furthermore, the Constitution *Omnem* from 16 December 533 includes even a more binding scheme with a complete curriculum for the legal education in the Byzantine Empire under Justinian. This education is based on the studies of texts in Latin and Greek and survives in the medieval legal education revigorated in Bologna in a form reduced to commentaries upon foremost Latin legal classics (Berman 1977: 903). However, it would be a risky undertaking to pretend that the details reported for in the ancient sources quoted above can all be taken for face value. For us, they are interesting mostly as a testimony of an epistemological tendency in the upcoming legal reasoning. This legal reasoning was construed as "*a conceptual system of law, which presupposes clarifying connections between specific legal concepts*" and, consequently, also makes defining of terms for the expression of legal concepts unavoidable (Mattila 2006: 7). In its application is has been perceived mostly as forensic rhetoric. This formal division of tasks survived in the legal sciences in a slightly modified and occasionally even modernized form until today. The division between the legal reasoning as a task for the doctrine and the legal theory on the other side, has been complemented by the legal rhetoric which in the eyes of some would be the domain of the Legal Linguistics of today. This is an unhealthy dichotomy as it splits what should not be divided, namely reasoning and language (cf. Recanati 2008: 10). Mattila (2006: 108) has persuasively shown the interrelation of term and concept in law.

5.2.2.3 Use of legal Latin in contemporary statutes and court decisions: Nowadays, classical studies which traditionally comprise Latin and Ancient Greek are no longer perceived as an obligatory part of the academic education. However, the Latin legal terminology is still present in many statutes or precedents. One can find legal Latin used in an international instrument such as the Geneva Convention on the Status of Refugees which is applicable also in countries far remote from European educational traditions. The use of Latin terms in an international instrument indicates that legal Latin is perceived as part of the general legal cultural tradition and education. In this respect, legal Latin, like Greek philosophy, succeeded to overcome traditional cultural boundaries.

The Convention Relating to the Status of Refugees states in its Article 16 (2):

A refugee shall enjoy in the Contracting State in which he has his habitual residence the same treatment as a national in matters pertaining to access to the Courts, including legal assistance and exemption from **cautio judicatem solvi**. (emphasis added)

Also in the legal acts of the European Union Latin is present. For instance, Art. 16 of the European Takeover Directive (2004/25/EC) refers to the right of the sell-out of securities and it provides in its paragraph 3: *Article 15 (3) to (5) shall apply* **mutatis mutandis** (emphasis added). The Latin expression is printed in italics in the English language text of the directive. It is risky to interpret such language use. However, it seems possible to assert that the European legislator assumes the knowledge of basic Latin among the users of the directive. It is not possible to assess how realistic the assumption is. In turn, it is well founded to assert that it reflects the legislator's conviction that Latin makes part of the general legal culture. In English and American court decisions Latin formulas and expressions are still occasionally used. In the Maldonado-cases (quoted in Notes and Materials as nr. 38) the formula *mobilia sequuntur personam* or the terms *bona vacantia* and *jus regale* are quoted without any English translation although they are central for the decision and without the knowledge of their meaning in English the court opinion cannot be understood properly. This language use again presupposes the assumption of the authors that its readers know these Latin expressions. In sum, the use of Latin in current legislation and court opinions allows the conclusion that the Latin legal language is still perceived by many jurists as part of their professional culture.

5.2.2.4 Incorporation of legal Latin into national legal languages: Latin maxims and Latin legal terminology are incorporated into texts in other languages than Latin in different ways. In the Maldonado-case (quoted in Notes and Materials nr. 38) the mentioned Latin expressions and maxims such as *mobilia sequuntur personam* or by virtue of *jus regale* over *bona vacantia* (p. 1582) are quoted without translation and are not even italicized in the main English language text. Sometimes their use is adapted to their English language syntactic surrounding, e.g. a *persona ficta* (p.1581), such *personae* (p. 1581), claiming *jure regali* (p.1585), not as *ultimus heres* but *jure regali* (p. 1582), or (B)ut *non constat* that (p.1586). In some cases the Latin expressions were put between quotation marks, in others left unmarked in the English text. The differences in the treatment of the Latin expressions and maxims show that the judges sometimes perceive those lexical units as foreign and wish to mark this impression in the text. In other cases, they may identify those expressions with the national legal language which does not necessitate any differentiation. This comes close to the terminology which grounds in the legal Latin and which provides for the multitude of variations in national languages: *avocat, advokat, advokaat, advocate, avvocato, advogado, abogado* for *attorney-in-law*. The created concepts refer to the original (LAT) *advocatus* that is transformed in line with the phonetic rules of the involved languages. This procedure for creation of the legal-linguistic vocabulary is relatively simple. More complicated are notional correspondences such as the (D) *Rechtsanwalt* or the English *attorney-at-law* which function in the textual contexts of (LAT) *advocatus*. Moreover, it is challenging to trace and to prove the genetical link between, e.g. (LAT) *persona legalis* and (CN) *fărén* or (LAT) *emptio-venditio* and (CN) *măimai* that correspond literally. The Latin terminology survives in the legal language apparently in times and places far remote from the space where it emerged.

5.2.2.5 Systematization in the Roman law: In the Legal Linguistics aspects of systematization that are related to language must be analyzed because the systematization is one of the fundamental legal-linguistic operations. In the diachronic perspective the systematization is primarily related to the formation of concepts. It is linked on the synchronic level to the legal argumentation (cf. 3.1.2). In the diachronic perspective on law, the Roman law is central for this undertaking. Indeed, the idea that something different from 'systematization' had been in the center of the Roman legal thinking was often claimed in the research. In this context especially the 'casuistic nature' of the early Roman law had been stressed. As J. Gaudemet (1986: 11) put it: *Que les Romains aient envisagé le droit sous son aspect casuistique, nul ne saurait le contester.* Nevertheless, the Roman law offers more than a casuistic inventory and this is the reason why it has fascinated generations of jurists from the very Middle Ages until our own days. One of the particular reasons for this fascination was the presence of many concepts used nowadays in the writings of classical Roman legal writers like Gaius, Ulpianus or Paulus or in the *Corpus Iuris Civilis*. The Roman law seems to be edified as a legal system when seen in the retrospective taken from the CIC (Ladjili-Mouchette 1990: 421). The Roman jurists did not explain in their writings – at least in those disponible to posterity – their conceptual method (Glendon 1999: 39). Thus, it has to be reconstructed.

5.2.2.5.1 Possible reconstructions: The roots of such a reconstruction are far reaching. For instance, a concept such as *res publica* has been used by the Romans without any distinction of the regime. Its lexical form is strikingly simple and is therefore apt to cover whatever form of governance. Concepts, however, function in contrast. The networks in which these contrasts can be observed are the basis for their linguistic and epistemological reconstruction. The epistemological reconstruction of the Roman law would have to start in the private law with the dichotomy of *actor/reus* as the dialectical source of litigation perceived by the Romans as contradictory and its instrument, actions of different sorts. Thus, where the *actor* (plaintiff) brings the suit, there should also be a *reus* (defendant) to be held liable. Furthermore, a specific procedure is needed which includes the *actio* as its main argumentative element. *Actor* does not simply complain to the *praetor* about someone; he enters into litigation with *reus*, who in case of a contested demand *(exceptio)* becomes himself *actor* (cf. the rule *excipiendo reus fit actor* in a case of *probatio*). The litigation continues until the claim or the exception is proven. That *reus* must correspond with *actor* may be understandable, the necessity of *actio* will forever remain a special feature of the Roman law, which interfered with and sometimes even confused the legal thinking until our times. Furthermore, are documented in the sources the background and the emerging of one of the most important concepts of private law, the *obligatio*. Gaius (3, 88) says about it: *Omnis enim obligatio vel ex contractu nascitur vel ex delicto. Obligatio est iuris vinculum, quo necessitate adstringimur alicuius solvaendae rei secundum nostrae civitatis iura.* Gaius' words were additionally commented in *Corpus Iuris Civilis* (I. 313). Kaser (1983: 149) claims that Gaius' words were rather a description than a definition. However, the more the concept was used the more it was commented upon. Paulus (D 44, 7, 3) says: *obligationum substantia non in eo consistit, ut aliquod corpus nostrum aut servitutem nostram faciat, sed ut alicui nobis obstringat ad dandum aliquid vel faciendum vel praestandum.* This approach comes already very close to the later commentary (interpretation) of concepts before they were applied in practice. The analysis of the dialectical procedure for emerging concepts is different from anthropological or ethnological analysis of *obligatio* as a mental state of being bound by a promise which may not be accessible to all minds in all cultures. Undoubtedly, somewhere in the lowest layers of our and Roman legal consciousness there must have been an identification with the idea of *obligatio*, although even today not everyone and not everywhere feels equally bound by a promise. The same concerns the tendency to create concepts out of common language, such as *possessio* (...) or *dominium/proprietas* (...). In this context, Ulpian (D 43, 17, 1, 2) stresses the necessity to distinguish between these legal concepts and the daily use which apparently differed from it:...*separata esse debet possessio a proprietate: fieri etenim potest, ut alter possessor sit, dominus non sit; possessor vero non sit: fieri potest, ut et possessor idem et dominus sit.* Legal concepts, once created, could have been replaced by others, such as *pignus* which was later replaced by *hypotheca* in its most contexts whereby its meaning was again modified in Institutiones Iustiniani (I 4, 6, 7). Nowadays uncertainty reigns as to the scope of both concepts (Kolańczyk 1986: 328). The Romans had apparently less problems with understanding them. As mentioned above, the Roman jurists did not teach us their methodology. We used to learn their concepts as we go along reading the ancient sources. There, systematization efforts increase with time. A typical procedure for the Romans was to enter *in medias res*, and, for instance, introduce a sale of goods contract *(emptio venditio)* without defining it otherwise than by the description of its components. It was stated that parties of the contract *(conventio)* had to agree about the price *(pretium)* and the object of the contract (*res*), (cf. Gaius 3, 139-141: *Emptio et venditio contrahitur, cum de pretio convenerit, quamvis nondum pretium numeratum sit, ac ne arra quidem data fuerit; nam quod arrae nomine datur, argumentum est emptionis et venditionis contractae...et I. 3, 23: Emptio et venditio contrahitur, simulatque de pretio convenerit...*).

5.2.2.5.2 Case study: res incorporales: The concepts of the Roman law usually emerge in the form of a simple introduction which coincides with their creation. We are not told how they came about nor what their theoretical origins are. Gaius' writing is the most striking example of such a procedure. In his Institutes 2,12 and 2,14 he introduces the distinction between corporeal and incorporeal things:

12. Quaedam praeterea res corporales sunt, quaedam incorporales. Corporales hae sunt quae tangi possunt, velut fundus, homo, vestis, aurum, argentum et denique aliae res innumerabiles...14. Incorporales sunt quae tangi non possunt, qualia sunt ea quae jure consistunt, sicut hereditas, ususfructus, obligationes quoquo modo contractae.

Whereas some of the named institutions in sentence 14 may be perceived as prelegal and thus not particularly interesting in the context of the emergence of the legal terminology, the statement that also *obligationes* were among incorporeal things provides insight into the creation methods in the Roman conceptual world. However, some scholars such as M. Kaser (1983: 90) claimed that the above distinction proved to be without any particular influence on the Roman law: *"Praktische Bedeutung hat diese schulmäßige Einteilung in Rom nicht gehabt."* This opinion may surprise because the distinction and the example of *obligatio* as an incorporeal thing enabled various transactions on them in analogy to corporeal things. Thus, it became possible to sell *obligationes*, to claim rights on them in an action or to assign them. Furthermore, the distinction allowed jurists such as Gaius, and later on also Justinian's compilators, to treat both in one chapter as *ius quod ad res pertinet.* Therefore, the importance of this distinction cannot be overestimated. According to Gaius the incorporeal things existed through the law in force (*...quae in iure existent,* Gaius 2.2). This is amazing as a sophisticated, if not a Greek, idea. And indeed, the traditional research into Roman law stresses the Greek character of this thought (Kolańczyk 1986: 262). The scarce sources of the classical Roman law do not allow claiming Gaius's authorship of the concept. However, in the discussion about the distinction it can be treated as one introduced by Gaius, at least for the audience of later centuries. It had been assumed that until Gaius the Romans did not make any distinction of this kind (Girard 1928: 273). Moreover, it had been claimed that this distinction may have been opposed by Cicero in his *Topica* (27). Cicero's words may rather prove his ignorance of the concept. They do not prove his criticism on it. In his philosophical analysis Cicero rather concedes the possibility of existence of incorporeal things:

26. Definitio est oratio, quae id, quod definitur, explicat, quod sit. Definiendum autem due sunt genera prima: unum earum rerum, quae sunt: alterum earum, quae intellegitur. 27. Esse ea dico quae cerni tangire possunt, ut fundum, aedes, parietem, stillicidum, manicipium, pecudum, supellectilem, penus, cetera; quo ex genere quaesdam interdum nobis definienda sunt. Non esse rursus ea dico, quae tangi demonstrarivae non possunt, cerni tamen animo, atque intellegi possunt. Ut, si usucapionem, si tutelam, si gentem, si agnationem definias: quarum rerum nullum subest quasi corpus: est tamen quaedam conformatio insignita et impressa intelligentiae: quam notionem voco.

The French classic of the Roman law research Stroux refers in this context to the work of the grammarian Charisius (Gaudemet 1986: 23). All above findings show that it is possible to trace the lexicalization of concepts undertaken in the ancient Roman law. Overall, the creation of the concept 'res incorporales' is what G. Deleuze and F. Guattari call *l'art de former des concepts* in their work where they characterized the way how philosophical concepts were formed. They posited that *la philosophie est l'art de former, d'inventer, de fabriquer des concepts* (Deleuze/ Guattari 1991: 8 ; cf. also Searle 1999 : 159). In philosophy this view may be controversial, but in classical Roman law it hits the nail on the head. Consequently, we encounter here a process deemed as philosophical by its nature, namely creating concepts. It is aiming at tracing the way how concepts of which many still remain essential to our law were invented by Roman jurists and applied in the Roman jurisprudence.

5.2.2.5.3 The rule in Roman law: It is not only that the Roman jurists did not display any particular interest towards the idea of a system; they also omitted the reflection on another central legal concept of modern jurisprudence – the rule. The CIC (50. 17.1) provides Paulus' definition of a rule: *Regula est, quae rem, quae est, breviter enarrat. Non ut ex regula ius sumatur, sed ex iure, quod est, regula fiat.* As is so often the case, they lay the ground for future elaboration of theories (Ladjili-Mouchette 1990: 456). The Roman legal rule that is rooted in interpretation emerges at a point where the disparate rules are positioned in a context (cf. Ladjili-Mouchette 1990: 423); they function as the epistemological background of systematization. This extraordinary intellectual capacity has been soon instrumentalized politically; the personal authority of the interpreter to determine the meaning of legal rules on behalf of public authorities (LAT *jurisconsultum*) has been replaced by an officially attributed privilege (LAT *ius publice respondendi*, cf. CIC 1.2.2.47). In modern legal thinking *system*, *rule* or *concept* compete with each other for the supremacy in the realm of jurisprudence. Indeed, creating legal concepts appears to be its very essence and applying those concepts remains the main task of the legal practice. Applying the law – or its concepts – includes interpretation (lege artis) of its rules; creating concepts involves knowledge of specific techniques which by their very nature are extra-legal. That *concept* attracted the Roman jurists more than rules may be connected with the partition of tasks among the legislator and the legal writers. The legislator usually does not introduce self-made concepts, e.g. *negotiorum gestio.* He rather decides that in the case of *negotiorum gestio* the costs of an operation of law shall be borne by one of the parties concerned. This means that he sets up a rule.

5.2.3 Following ancient Greeks or Romans and their law?

In a work perceived as prolegomena to an emerging branch of legal science and/or linguistics, we spent a lot of time upon issues which are perceived as belonging to history. And indeed, the reflection upon the Roman law or the development of rhetoric in ancient Greece are definitely topics which can be perceived as historical. We nevertheless mentioned that we perceive historical experience and testimony, especially the written one, in a specific perspective. We concentrated on them from the epistemological point of view and tried to understand how legal terms or concepts as well as forms of legal argumentation emerged and developed as parts of the legal language. We also mentioned that interpretive methods in law which have a long history can be perceived as a part of the legal metalanguage in that they enable to understand utterances formulated in a special register which is different from that in daily use. The epistemological interpretation made it possible to grasp some aspects of this development. Therefore, the retrospective made sense for us in a research which is not predominantly historical but rather methodological. Could this retrospective contribute also to a prospective view, to the view of law in the future? Does it allow identifying tendencies in the development of the prospective law and its language? We think it does. The retrospective taught us, roughly speaking, that the Romans concentrated their efforts on constructing their law upon concepts. The ancient Greeks stressed rather the legal argumentation. Of course, this assertion, when expressed that sweepingly, invites opposition. Were not the Greeks also masters of the concepts? Yes, they were. Were not the Romans among the best court orators? Yes, without any doubt. Nevertheless, in our epistemological perspective upon the law and the legal language in the Antiquity they appear as pertaining to two conceptions of law. The propositions of law have been clarified differently in both traditions of the Western Antiquity. The Greeks maintained that what is right or wrong in their society is defined in the agora (GR αγοϱά) as a result of the free deliberation among citizens. Their legal reasoning had been based on the ideas of justice and coherence (Ladjili-Mouchette 1990: 421) that grounded in the Greek dialectics. The Romans discovered the law through conceptual analysis based on the scrutiny of legal texts. What can we learn from this experience? We have seen that legal concepts and legal terms which represent them in legal texts have an essential role to play in the legal argumentation. Legal argumentative texts, oral or written, are centered on crucial legal terms which condition their structure. Legal argumentation and legal systematization are therefore not opposite, they are complementary operations. In both of them, the Roman and the Greek legal landscapes merge into a law that is understood as a discursive practice. We do not pretend that the ancient Greeks or Romans did not understand this ontological implication of law and its language. However, we posit that nowadays we (which means here not only the author of these lines but persons dealing with legal theory and Legal Linguistics) understand these two landscapes in a particular way in that we are able to explicitly describe them in an epistemological perspective. Our inquiry ends, therefore, with a happy end.

5.3 Some Tentative Results of the Retrospective View upon Law and its Language

5.3.1 What means creation in the legal language?

Generally, legal language emerges in legal discourses with different degrees of speciality depending on their participants. Discourses of lawyers differ in quality from discourses about law between lawyers and laypersons and from discourses about the law among laypersons. The professional skills of participants do not determine the complexity of the discourse. Laypersons may develop complicated argumentative structures as lawyers may remain tied to insipid *topoi* that are perceived in their community as particularly professional. Interpretive and argumentative legal speech acts are formed in these discourses. They focus on terminology of different kind, some terms are professional, others innovative or spontaneous. The process of emergence of these phenomena is the formation of the legal language. Legal-linguistic practices are value-laden, therefore the legal language changes. The main features of this transformation are semantic change and lexical innovation. More complex legal speech acts such as legal argumentation or legal interpretation undergo fewer changes as they are in their use less exposed to the evolutions of social values. Creating legal language is therefore not creation of words. It is a discursive practice in which among other things also words emerge.

5.3.2 Creation and interpretation in law

The creation of legal provisions and the making of legal decisions were less frequently analyzed in the research than were the interpretation of existing legal provisions and the impact legal decisions (precedents) have had on their actual interpretation. The idea that law should be written by trained legal scholars is not new and, in fact, many civil codes in Europe were construed and drafted by famous legal scholars (Gaudemet 2001: 369). To date, a scientific law which would provide statutes or rules for the legislator as competing projects that might convince him or not is not existent, although it is thinkable and even recommendable. Apart from these facts, in most countries guidelines for ministerial and parliamentary administrative bodies dealing with the drafting of legal provisions have been developed.

5.3.2.1 Legislative drafting and understandability: Creation of legislation is the most challenging task among legal activities mainly because jurists usually have only a limited role to play in the whole process which remains in its nature political. Democratic processes within the legislative follow their own rules that are far remote from our subject which is related to language and law. The auxiliary role jurists play is much more demanding than the adjudication in which they can follow and apply professional rules which they master. Within the legislative process they play the role which other professions rarely accept. They are reduced to the role of advisers and secretaries who transform the wishes of their clients in words but they are also limited by these wishes. They liken physicians observing their patients indulge in self-medication and non-indicated treatment, but are unable to stop them. This state of affairs may wonder even more, because jurists will in future apply laws that were passed with at best their partial participation. What is more, statutes are regularly results of political compromises. Were jurists participating more actively in these processes, statutes could be formulated in a more professional way. The lack of professional standards about statute drafting, especially in the form of a generally studied and developed legal discipline, are visible in the problems of legislation. Statutes drafted according to administrative guidelines for ministries along the line of political instructions cannot harmoniously fit into the legal world occupied by jurists. Instead, they constantly will lead to problems in interpretation and application. Already in ancient Rome the opinion that jurists as professionals of law have a particular role to play in the development of law has been recognized. Attempts to relativize this view are not particularly convincing (Gaudemet 2001: 11). Nothing prevents jurists to present to the interested or to the broad public drafts of legislation which may compete with others. Views on what is the best law *de lege ferenda* often prevailed in ancient Rome due to the high quality of the work done and not necessarily due to the position of the drafter in the state administration.

The linguistic aspect of the legislation is another problem. Nowadays drafts are regularly controlled with respect to their linguistic correctness. The legislator apparently understands this correctness in terms of grammatical and orthographic rules and at best in terms of readability. The form of judicial decisions has been perceived, especially within the judicial body, as particularly important. Legal decisions in many countries follow a rigid, sometimes formalistic pattern (cf. Arntz 2002: 37). Sometimes even the use of a specific tense is regulated by internal guidelines of courts or through professional usage. Pragmatic aspects of legislation concern its acceptability among the persons concerned. Therefore, a scientifically founded practice of legislation should include mechanisms enabling it to increase the acceptability of legislative acts among citizens. Thornton (1996: 47) characterizes the aims of the legislative drafting as delimiting the law and communicating the law to society and in particular to persons affected by it. The communicative aspect in the legislative process has been an issue for the legal theory. Some legal theorists pretended that law is communicated to jurists, i.e. primarily to judges who are charged with its application. For instance, H. Kelsen (1991) differentiated between *direct* and *indirect addressees* of legal acts; J. Sager (1990: 102) argued in the context of terminology understanding that the knowledge base of producers and receivers in the specialized communication is presumed to be the same. Others insisted upon the rights of citizens to be communicated the law and added also recently the right to an understandable legislation (cf. Mattila 2006: 18). Needless to stress that problems connected to the *understandability of law* depend on the *recipient issue*. Jurists, judges or attorneys-at-law alike, will obviously have less problems with the understanding of legislative acts than citizens without legal training. Jurists will doubtlessly have other problems with the understanding of law; yet these problems are anchored in the specifics of their profession and not in the understandability of the text as a linguistic entity produced in a natural language. In a modern democratic society the idea of law that is written in specialists' language and directed to specialists is not appealing any more. Jurists are among the addressees of legislative acts and may have a special role to play in their application; they are however not the exclusive target group of the legislative intent any more. The acceptability of law among the citizenry would be jeopardized would this citizenry be excluded from the circle of addressees, i.e potential readers of legislative acts. Over long, the idea of expressing the law in ordinary langage that has been occasionally mentioned in this book (c.f. 2.2.4) may be perceived as a practicable solution to problems discussed today under the topics of *understandability* or *readability* of legislative acts.

5.3.2.2 Discursive parameters: This general retrospection allows us to sketch parts of the development of the legal language. It concerns legal concepts in legal arguments, i.e. the legal terminology which is discourse-dependent. Concepts facilitate the argumentation and are more visible than complex speech acts. Therefore, they also draw most attention upon themselves. This circumstance led in the past to excessive focusing on concepts in the legal sciences and in the emerging legal-linguistic deliberations. For concepts the Roman law provides the best source of materials. Let us return to some of them and deal with their discursive parameters. For instance, the creation of the concept of *person* has been fundamental for the development of law. It enabled to create and to center subjective rights and duties around the bearer of these rights and duties. These *rights* are a creation that makes legal operations in law necessary; as *rights* have an abstract content and can be construed differently only the legal discourse can provide a solution that, however, will not satisfy everyone (cf. Koskenniemi 1999: 99). The concept of *person* had been specified through the creation of *legal* or *juridical persons* and distinguished from *natural persons*. The creation of an artificial *person,* i.e. the *legal* one, has been admired by lawyers and by non-specialists as an impressive conceptual construction which enabled to maintain legal systems operational in complex societies. Ladjili-Mouchette (1990: 454) refers to J. Gaudemet who held that the term *legal person* had been coined upon *universtitas.* It seems, however, that the creation of the general concept of *person* which had been provided subjectivity had been the most challenging step in the creation of the original legal language and its structure, i.e. the network of legal concepts. In the legal language *person* means in terms of law that it can be a bearer of rights and duties independently of the community (social group, corporation) to which it more or less voluntarily belongs. The creation of the concept of *legal person* as a separate legal entity depends – as always in law – upon its acceptance by the legislator. He is the formal creator of legal concepts in law, even if the concept as such is created by a specified author who might under more favorable circumstances claim an intellectual property right for his creation. The creation of the corresponding *object* of rights and duties which subsequently materialized in multiple forms had been its rather evident follow-up. The object can be a contract, a property right or forbearance. The *object* is therefore a corresponding, secondary creation in the conceptual network. The multitude of rights and duties related to *objects* and focused in a *person* has been formalized in *procedural rules*. Procedural rules are linguistic programs in which rights of legal subjects (persons) towards objects are exercised. They include organizational rules as well as *claims* and *defenses* with which the parties act within the procedure. Procedure in law is based upon the rule that equal situations should be processed in an equal way in courts of law. In legal discourses, procedure links concepts with argumentation. The legal doctrine established *sources of law* which it perceives as indicators of the legal validity of rules grounded in them. It means that a rule established upon reference to a source of law has a bigger chance to be approved in a court of law as a rule stating the law than one which cannot be based on an acknowledged source of law. For the U.S., the sources of law are: the U.S. Constitution, state constitutions, federal and state statutes, ordinances, administrative agency rules and regulations, executive orders, and judicial decisions by federal and state courts. In France, international treaties, the constitution, laws, and (FR) *règlements* are generally accepted by the doctrine as sources of French law. Other possible sources, such as usages or general principles of law or legal decisions are subject to controversies as to their status as sources of French law. Overall, through establishing a source of law the legal doctrine endorses it as a text with legal force. It creates a specific category of texts which are 'more legal' than others because sanctioned by the doctrine with specific functions which are, first of all, to state the law of the country better than other possible sources. In terms of the Legal Linguistics this operation of the doctrine means that certain texts are declared as belonging doubtlessly to the type of legal texts while others are subjected to discussion. The process in which this determination takes place is institutionalized. At any rate, it would be difficult to postulate that a text perceived by the doctrine as a source of law is not a legal text. However, the scientific dispute about the quality of court decisions as sources of law in various non-common law countries shows that the institutionalized procedure of determining what is a legal text has its limits and may be challenged. Wherever language use is not analyzed in its entirety and selective procedures are preferred instead, conflicts about the quality and acceptability of results will emerge. – When the legislator or the doctrine call a cat "a dog" there will emerge problems with the acceptability of the result and additional argumentation will be needed to balance the lack of credibility caused by such a procedure. - The dispute about the quality of legal decisions as the source of law in several countries is an illustrative example of a shortcoming described in terms of linguistic pragmatics. From this perspective it appears advisable to adopt as sources of law all linguistic sources used for the formulation of a legal rule. It is possible and even beneficial to introduce a hierarchy of legal sources which prevents conflicts in case when conflicting results would emerge from different legal sources. However, the selective process of artificially terming some documents legal sources and denying this quality to others is at least from the perspective of the pragmatic Legal Linguistics not justified (cf. 2.3.5).

Contractual legal language oscillates around the formation of the promise and its enforcement. The problem of contract enforcement emerges mostly when one party entirely or partly denies the relevant circumstances described by the other party. For this, the general linguistic scheme of a contract composed of *offer* and *acceptance* provides a first remedy. When one party offered something to the other party and the other party accepted it, it is already very probable that the parties have concluded a contract. Other elements of a valid contract such as the *consideration* in common law countries, the capacity of the parties and the legality of the contractual transaction follow suit. Jurists used to say that in order to have an agreement the minds of the parties must meet. With this formulation the jurists achieve a description of an agreement which could not be better expressed even by most prominent pragmatists. Also, as a matter of fact, in order to agree both parties must mean exactly the same. First of all, the parties must have the intention to create legal relations. This is a fundamental pragmatic requirement for a contract which is a legal institute. The interlocutors cannot simply chat just about whatever subject or make situational jokes; both must know that they engaged in contract negotiations which may result in reciprocal rights and obligations. They must be aware of the fact that they negotiate in a situation in which customarily binding agreements come about. The validity requirement however would not be realistic would it concern all circumstances of offer and acceptance. It is not particularly probable that two interlocutors agree about absolutely everything in a discourse even if they manifest agreement and are subjectively convinced to agree with each other. The legally relevant part of these circumstances is therefore limited in law to the *essentialia negotii*, i.e. to those topics without which a contract cannot be identified as such. The linguistic formulation of the basic concepts in the contract law serves this goal. It goes even further and provides tests and remedies for the situation when the minds of the parties did not or not entirely meet. A mistake can happen, and can under certain circumstances be invoked by one of the parties. Some terms of the contract are express, they are explicitly mentioned by the parties while others are implied and must be reconstructed when judicial enforcement is required by one of the parties.Formalities imposed upon the parties by the legislator and the precedents facilitate the enforcement of the contract, they make the contract visible for others and make testing of the parties' intentions more reliable. Furthermore, *torts* are a linguistic creation connected to compensation for losses. Only an action which is perceived as a tort can lead to monetary compensation. In the common law a set of intentional torts like *battery, assault, trespass* or *infliction of mental distress* were created to characterize the wrongful action. In the civil law a unified type of (FR) *délit* fulfills this function. This type refers to certain typical situations for which monetary compensation has been provided. Later on, *negligence* and *unintentional torts* were added to the existing types. They covered situations in which a duty of care has been violated so that a damage occurred which was caused involuntarily. A particular problem here is the causation. It is important for us because it could be that this is not a linguistic problem. This would be the case when causation would not be primarily determined by linguistic means but with other extra-linguistic methods. It seems however that negligence like causation is - at least in law - a linguistic construct (cf. Palsgraf v. Long Island Railroad in Notes and Materials nr. 34). They are based on certain formulations and texts which - when compared - allow the judge to say that a party had acted negligently or that it has caused damage. *Strict liability* goes even a step further and imposes liability through a linguistic formulation without any intent to harm because it creates liability without fault. Still further, *property* law attributes and protects property. It establishes with linguistic means the protected objects, such as the *intellectual property rights.* Property is equally defined in rights, not in goods (cf. Koskenniemi 1999: 91). It is conceptually more stable than other branches of the private law due to conservative relations of ownership that rule in the Western society.

We have canvassed above some characteristic discursive parameters used in law and the prerequisites of their use. A fully-fledged Legal Linguistics would comprise a broad catalogue of such elements as part of the general grammar of law.

5.4 Other Language-Related Areas of Globalizing Law

Language has been regularly the object of legal regulation. Therefore, within the Legal Linguistics issues concerning regulation of language use are perceived as belonging to its realm (Mattila 2006: 18). Three issues have attracted particular interest in the research. They are: *linguistic legislation*, *language risk* and the *professional liability of translators.* All the three issues have a pragmatic dimension in that they show law in action. In our context of emerging global law they also provide insights into some particular problems related to this process and especially to the distribution of languages in the globalization process. The dominating topic in this special area of the Legal Linguistics has been the linguistic legislation.

Studies in linguistic legislation have at least a two-fold goal. First, from the point of view of applied linguistics, they should prepare a model of linguistic legislation which would reflect linguistic presuppositions of such type of legislation. Second, from the point of view of human rights protection, they should advance the level of international standards and their application in national legislative projects. A successful piece of national linguistic legislation has to combine both perspectives. In addition to these issues, it is worthwhile mentioning that research related to clarity and understandability of the legal language for ordinary citizens is perceived by some as belonging to the linguistic legislation because it posits a right to clear language (Mattila 2006: 18). In the following, this issue will not be treated because it has been discussed passim in other chapters and in different contexts. Language risk and professional liability of translators may seem purely legal in essence as they pertain to legal questions. The legal-linguistic interest in them is equally two-fold as is the legal-linguistic position towards the linguistic legislation that is doubtlessly also legal in its essence. In both areas, it is necessary to show the linguistic element in the legal debate and stress the professional linguists' input into it. Moreover, the specialists' view on language should be taken into consideration while solving language-related cases in courts which only rarely happens nowadays (Salmi-Tolonen 2008: 391).

5.4.1 Linguistic legislation

The linguistic legislation has been perceived in the academic research as either belonging to the Legal Linguistics or to the international law and human rights protection. For legal linguists such as Cornu (2005: 11) the linguistic legislation is a necessary part of Legal Linguistics because it deals with the norming of language use. For him, legal language cannot be characterized efficiently without taking into consideration the operation in which linguistic elements, words, phrases as parts of the legal discourse became elements of the legal discourse by a legislative decision. In this sense, linguistic legislation would comprise not only issues of distribution of language use in the society that is linked to human rights protection but reach much further and include legislation relating to the creation and the interpretation of law. Pigolkin (1990: 5) adds to it the determination of the authentic linguistic version of a piece of legislation, both national and international. Chinese legal linguists stressed that language in law is power that must be regulated (Zhou 2003: 2). Cornu's vision is helpful in shaping a coherent conception of Legal Linguistics. It does not impede upon research into specific aspects of linguistic legislation under other topics, especially in the public international law (cf. Mattila 2006: 18). Generally, issues addressed in the Legal Linguistics are also topics of research in the specialized branches of law such as human rights protection and they are addressed there in a methodologically different way. Purely technical legal issues may also be better settled there; the legal linguist has an interest in contributing to the linguistic legislation her professional knowledge about the role and the use of language.

The part of the linguistic legislation which focuses upon the societal distribution of language use emerged towards the background of a multilingual world divided into national states. This state of affairs resulted in linguistic or religious conflicts in many parts of the world. There is no tendency perceptible on the international arena towards a more distanced approach to ethnic issues and language use in multilingual societies. Linguistic legislation seems therefore to be necessary in countries in which linguistic problems persist and occupy the citizens. In countries where problems with language choice and language use do not exist (such countries are not particularly numerous) no linguistic legislation is necessary. In the U.S., no legislation concerning the official language of the country exists on the federal level. Nevertheless, most citizens concerned do not have any problems with identifying English as the official language of their country. In Germany, the main language is of course German although no legal guarantee exists to this extent there. Elsewhere, countries such as France opted for precise legislative regulation of language use. Other multiethnic states like the Russian Federation have federal and regional legislation on language use. Multilingual states like Switzerland regulate the use of languages regionally, while others, for instance Finland or Belgium adopted a functional approach. Consequences of these different approaches are visible in the respective national linguistic policies and in daily attitudes towards multilingualism in these countries.

5.4.1.1 Idea of a linguistic legislation: The fact that some countries introduced linguistic legislation into their legal systems while others did not indicates that such decisions are not unproblematic. The importance of linguistic legislation and its connection with the rising of social tensions and violent conflicts in societies and states has been recently recognized also in the area of conflict prevention. However, the idea that minority or linguistic legislation can have a negative impact on societies and states and even on inter-state relations is definitely not new. The history of bilateral treaties dealing with the status of ethnic minorities is proof of the relevance of this issue as it can be traced back to the 16th century (De Varennes 1996: 24). Yet, in the 20th century the issue gained renewed importance because of increasing tensions and conflicts directly related to ethnicity and language use. This was the reason why within the field of the international law, in the preventive diplomacy and in the non-governmental sector great attention has been paid to this issue especially over the last two decades. As a result, the need arose to develop mechanisms which could facilitate conflict prevention work in this area. Therefore, the contemporary approach to the issue includes also the socio-political background of linguistic legislation. Below, some developments in this area shall be traced. Additionally, mechanisms for practical work in the area of international law, conflict prevention, be it preventive diplomacy or non-governmental action, will be canvassed.

5.4.1.2 Minority legislation and European culture: The emergence of minority and especially linguistic legislation is a case study in and of itself. Historically, multicultural contacts, migration and the reception of cultural achievements or linguistic proficiency must be perceived as almost natural phenomena in the European context. Cultural exchange shaped the life form of modern day European nations while daily language contacts formed the languages spoken today in Europe. Therefore, it comes as a surprise how any tensions or conflict could arise on a basis which constitutes a common denominator in the development of the European culture and one of the most fruitful processes in the development of mankind. Even conflicts of interests and social contradictions need not necessarily end up in violent conflicts. Civilized societies and well governed states establish mechanisms which enable social cohesion under circumstances which may be perceived as antagonistic. In order to guarantee the effective functioning of state and society social practices must additionally include a culture of conflicts with elements of protection against acting in the heat of the moment. These tasks seem to have been neglected in some parts of the world. In addition, it has become pertinent that some conflicts are not based on aggressive motivation but on purposely calculated uses of force and manipulation of emotions. However, research on linguistic legislation also shows that the regulation of the language use had in certain societies a selective and even a discriminatory role to play (De Varennes 1996: 32). The character of linguistic legislation in many countries is perceived as repressive in terms of linguistic diversity (Mattila 2006: 18). Again, this should take as a surprise given that European history beares witness to a multiethnic and multicultural development of the continent for ages. Negative historical experiences need not necessarily determine the action of successive generations, however. Rather a reflected reaction to dysfunctional social practices could be expected in a world which is increasingly governed by laws and international standards.

5.4.1.3 Social and scientific perspectives on multilingualism: Societal multiculturalism and multilingualism have a long and only partly examined history. Some researchers have tried to reconstruct our historical perspective on multiculturalism and multilingualism, an inquiry typical for our reasoning which asks for (GR) *αρχή*, i.e. the beginning of things. Some connect it even to the biblical myth about the Tower of Babel. Others, still interested in the very beginning of things, thought about the multiplicity of languages on the planet and speculated about an original language of mankind while others have reflected the fears of peoples confronted with multilingualism which sometimes came up even in monolingual societies. Many of them have tried to advocate monolingualism, but in vain. It has been, for example, the case in Finland where the statesman J.V. Snellman (1806 - 1881) tried to disseminate his ideas with the slogan (FIN) *yksi kieli, yksi mieli*, i.e. one language, one mind. As different as these approaches may be, they show that language use and societal interaction are closely connected. And indeed, the linguistic community has overcome a long time ago the view of primal linguistic confusion in the linguistic landscape and perceives it nowadays as transparently structured. The linguistic landscape includes some monolingual areas and vast multilingual regions with or without diglossia (Hoffmann 1991: 157). Thus, in the historical perspective multiculturalism and multilingualism involve in our context a structured language use and a cooperative social interaction, rather than social chaos introduced by cultural and linguistic plurality. Nevertheless, linguistic conflicts continue to be part of political developments all over the world. Speakers react on linguistic issues and they react often in a different way than scientists would. They sometimes share views on language use concerning, for example, the prestige or usefulness of a language which may seem controversial for linguists. In our scientific tradition particular languages were for a long time perceived as pure sign systems and also analyzed as such. This perspective seemed to have been sufficient for scientific research. Only recently linguistic research realized that languages and their use have an emotional component for their speakers as well as their listeners and began to reflect upon these aspects. Speakers have namely a tendency to identify with sign systems such as languages, however unscientific or irrational this tendency may seem. The consideration of the behavior of speakers led to a shift in the attention or at least to the broadening of the linguistic perspective which in turn has resulted in the interference of emotional aspects of language in such austere areas as international and domestic legislation.

5.4.1.4 Minority legislation and linguistic legislation: Linguistic legislation is a part of a bigger legislative branch of minority legislation. This legislation comprises, in addition to linguistic legislation, legislation governing education and legislation affecting the participation of ethnic minorities in public life. Additionally, it includes international and domestic legislation concerning statelessness and obtaining citizenship, migration, and protection of stateless children. Also the alien's legislation provides a broader legal perspective in which the problems of ethnic minorities are embedded. The traditional approach to this part of legislation which distinguishes between the subjects and the objects of rights and their legal protection shows already some characteristic features of this branch of law. The subject of the law may be a person or another legal entity, like a group and this issue constitutes a new problem in minority legislation (Giordan 1992: 12-15). The issue is further made difficult since a definition of a national or ethnic minority is not resolved in the professional discussion. Capotorti (1991: para. 568) defined it as *a group numerically inferior to the rest of the population of the state, in a non-dominant position, whose members – being nationals of the State possess ethnic, religious or linguistic characteristics differing from those of the rest of the population and show, if only implicitly, a sense of solidarity, directed towards preserving their culture, traditions, religion or language.* This definition that has been developed for the purposes of Art. 27 ICCPR had been watered down considerably in the academic research (Engel 2002: 57). The aspect of the object protected by the state is also difficult to determine as obligations of a state are often described in an ambiguous way, e.g. the states "*should as far as possible*" or "*under specific circumstances*" guarantee specific minority or linguistic rights (Yacoub 1998: 173). This aspect is reflected also in the area of monitoring and protection of minority rights where blurred provisions lead to uncertainty in their interpretation and application. Moreover, national legislative acts are often incompatible in their structure and terminology and therefore difficult to compare or to evaluate (Engel 2002: 31). Legal standards for the minority legislation are set in international instruments. The most important international legal instruments in this area are: the Universal Declaration of Human Rights (1948), the International Covenant on Civil and Political Rights (1966), the International Covenant on Economic, Social and Cultural Rights (1966), the International Covenant on the Elimination of All Forms of Racial Discrimination (1965), and the Declaration on the Rights of Persons Belonging to National or Ethnic, Religious and Linguistic Minorities (1992). For the member states of the Council of Europe its European Convention on the Protection of Human Rights and Fundamental Freedoms (adopted in 1950) is the basic document. This document has been approved for the CIS countries in Resolution 1249 (2001) of the Parliamentary Assembly of the Council of Europe on the Coexistence of the Convention on Human Rights and Fundamental Freedoms of the Commonwealth of Independent States and the European Convention on Human Rights. Within the Council of Europe the possibility to appeal to the European Court of Human Rights in Strasbourg constitutes one of the most effective mechanisms of implementation of the Convention (Wildhaber 2002: 72). Furthermore, in the European Union a relevant role is played by Article 13 of the Treaty establishing the European Community, Article 21 of the Charter of Fundamental Rights of the European Union, the anti-discrimination directives 2000/43/EC implementing the principle of equal treatment between persons irrespective of racial or ethnic origin, 2000/78/EC establishing a general framework for equal treatment in employment and occupation and 2003/9/EC laying down minimum standards for the reception of asylum seekers and the Council Decision 2000/750/EC establishing a community action program to combat discrimination. Another group of sources with legal impact consists of political documents which due to their practical importance in shaping international relations have reached a position similar to that of legal acts. Those documents belong to the area of the so-called *soft law* and are becoming more and more influential in this sphere. Among them are: The Final Act of the CSCE Conference in Helsinki (1975), the Copenhagen Document on the Human Dimension of the OSCE (1990) and several OSCE HCNM recommendations. Recently, these documents which were meant as interpretive guidelines that belong to the soft law have attained a status of much more practical importance (Kemp 2001: 28). Among the most frequently used documents are: The Hague Recommendations Regarding the Education Rights of National Minorities issued in October 1996, The Oslo Recommendations Regarding the Linguistic Rights of National Minorities dating from February 1998, and the Lund Recommendations on the Effective Participation of National Minorities in Public Life, adopted in 1999, regarding participation in governance of the state as well as self-governance. Additionally, Guidelines on use of minority languages in broadcast media were launched in October 2003. These documents were issued by the OSCE HCNM and are based on well founded and balanced expert opinions on the issues they discuss. Presumably, this is the reason why - in a relatively short time - they have reached the position of standing as reliable reference works when standard and exceptional legal problems concerning ethnic minorities are at stake. Excerpts of these documents are quoted in Notes and Materials nr. 21.

Overall, minority legislation is already a vast area of legal provisions, which can be in their majority applied by courts to protect rights established by the provisions. Although some criticism has been expressed as to the extent of those rights, one has to admit that considerable progress has been achieved in this domain since the establishing of the UN and some regional organizations such as the Council of Europe or the OSCE. Another issue is, to what extent additional measures can be claimed in courts. In legal terms, the question how far a state can be forced to take positive action on behalf of linguistic minorities is here at stake. This is to a large extent a question of domestic legislation. Moreover, one should not forget that the linguistic legislation provided in domestic and international instruments is a part of an ongoing legislative evolutionary process with a determined direction towards ever more generous improvement of these standards. The last word on its contents and implementation has by no means been spoken yet. While working with international instruments one should therefore bear in mind that they are a product of a political compromise of states on issues perceived as problematic and reflect rather a legal minimum of rights than a full-fledged system of minority protection. A domestic legislator should therefore never feel limited in an attempt to provide a more generous legal status to minorities and further develop this area of legislation. By doing so, the domestic legislator contributes also to the development of international standards and paves the way for new tendencies adapted to the needs of new generations.

5.4.1.5 Nature of linguistic rights and their background: Linguistic rights are by their very nature human rights. The concept of linguistic human rights is widely used and rightly so (Skutnabb-Kangas 1995: 1). Nowadays, the commitment to non-discrimination on the basis of language is general and as such a major standard of the linguistic legislation. In most developed societies the idea that exceptions from the rule must be made to protect the minorities has been understood and accepted (Kymlicka 1995). No substantial discussion about "equal rights for all" can be expected under these circumstances. The new dimension in the discussion is represented in the research concerning the language death (Crystal 1997; Nettle and Romaine 2000; Skutnabb-Kangas 2000). As many languages are disappearing the discussion about language protection becomes a new and unexpected component within the area of linguistic legislation. The current discourse on linguistic human rights has also other characteristic features which are worth to be mentioned. First, if we don't consider the marking events associated with the adoption of bilateral treaties, the area lacks a history and a tradition. Second, it concerns mostly linguists as lawyers often refuse to participate in it due to the alleged linguistic character of the problem which is approached with purely political means. Furthermore, it starts on the highest possible level – which in terms of our political organization as species is the UN – and works downwards reaching sometimes the grass root level, but this is rare. Add to it that initiative for legislative measures comes often from the states, and not from the speakers concerned. This circumstance will not change until legal aspects of minority problematique reach a higher level of knowledge in the societies concerned, mainly through strengthening of the linguistic component in the discussion. Due to its novelty, there is a far-reaching confusion between arguments *de lege lata* and *de lege ferenda* which unfortunately contributes to uncertainty in the resulting debate. This uncertainty may also arise from the fact that the discourse is inter-disciplinary and methods implemented in it may vary. Textually, linguistic rights are mostly formulated in a negative way as non-discrimination prescriptions. Sometimes, however, the states take upon themselves the obligation to ensure specific rights. This formulation may, when taken concretely and not only as a programatic phrase, enable both sorts of implementation of rights, negative as well as positive one.

Linguistic rights are scattered among various international agreements, but this fact does not impede upon their application. The lack of one binding codification is caused by the fact that several international – universal and regional – organizations are in charge of different aspects of minority legislation. As a result, some globally valid legal instruments were constructed within the UN and supported by provisions issued, for example, by European organizations. Among them are the OSCE and the Council of Europe which has a slightly more legalistic approach to the issue than the OSCE which works with political instruments and soft law measures. When applying these norms it is necessary to verify whether the state in question has ratified the specific document. Most important among the international legal provisions are: Articles 25 and 27 of the International Covenant on Civil and Political Rights according to which persons belonging to ethnic, religious or linguistic minorities shall not be denied the right to use their language. The same right is guaranteed to children belonging to minorities in Article 30 of the Convention on the Right of the Child (1989). The UNESCO Convention against Discrimination in Education (1960) provides in Article 5 para.1 lit. c) for the right to use the own language in education. Article 5 para. 1 of the Framework Convention for the Protection of National Minorities (1995) obligates the states to protect language as part of the identity of persons belonging to minorities; further relevant provisions are Articles 12, 13 and 14 regarding education. Furthermore, the European Charter for Regional and Minority Languages (1992) regulates the right to use a minority language in its Articles 2, 7, 9 and 10. In addition, the European Convention on Human Rights concerns also the protection of language use, e.g. in Article 8 para. 1 in conjunction with Article 14 and another Article 10 concerning the freedom of expression and Article 11 concerning names, language signs and other inscriptions. Still further, the Copenhagen Document of the OSCE as a part of the soft law includes in its par. 32 passages regarding linguistic guarantees to minorities.

Following the systematics developed by Francesco Capotorti (1991), it is essential to distinguish in a legal analysis at least four spheres: language use in the private sphere, language use in the public sphere, language use in media and language use in the educational system. It goes without saying that no state can interfere in the use of any language in the private sphere (Engel 2002: 81). Language use in the public sphere may be subject to limitations when there is a clearly proven need for such measures. In such a case the burden of proof must be carried by the state. Language use in education and media can be limited in certain cases and it is decisive to determine the cases in which this limitation is admissible. Researchers are of the opinion that only the official status of a language can secure to its speakers the enjoyment of all linguistic human rights. This argument is used when linguistic legislation is planned. On the other side, countries without linguistic legislation exist and no significant legal problems with the protection of their languages are reported there. Occasionally, especially when it is politically impossible to provide a strong legal status for a language, the determination of its linguistic status can be replaced by a *guarantee of development* for the language in question (Wydra 2008: 86). However, this formulation seems to function only as a temporary solution. What is more, the specific structure of minority problems and their relation to majorities may demand additional efforts, such as *affirmative actions* or development of *integration strategies* which are worthwhile considering within the scope of linguistic rights. They may include: a broad discussion in the society on minority-majority issues in the situation where there is a lack of, or confusion in the information the society has from the state agencies on possibilities of multicultural/multilingual biographies.

Towards the background of the concept of linguistic human rights, linguistic legislation with its topics concerning prescribed language use in different spheres emerged at the same time on different levels of hierarchy in international and domestic law. The more effective and substantial the legislative measures in the area of linguistic legislation have been, the more specific terminology they engendered. Most concepts introduced into linguistic legislation have their origin either in linguistics or in ethnology/anthropology. This is why the current discussion about linguistic legislation is dominated by the infiltration of the conceptual instruments of different scientific disciplines (esp. linguistics, socio- and psycholinguistics, ethnology and others) into the legal language. But again, the discussion about prescribed or guaranteed language use – and this is the essence of linguistic legislation – has to follow its own methodological rules as it is a legal discourse, i.e. a discussion about the content of law which has to follow the interpretive guidelines of this art. Unfortunately, often the methodological aspects of disciplines which willingly offer their concepts to lawyers are disregarded. The most striking feature in it is that the linguistic and the ethnological terminology is mostly descriptive, legal terminology in turn is a part of prescriptive texts. While entering into legal texts ethnological or linguistic concepts become legal concepts with all consequences (e.g. application by authorities, interpretation by judges, etc.) Thus, when the Canadian legislator passed the Official Languages Act or the Canadian Multiculturalism Act (1988) he simultaneously introduced new legal concepts like *official language* and *multiculturalism* into the domestic legal system. Furthermore, what remains unclear is the question as to what extent the legislator is bound by the achievements of scientific research in the field of different scientific disciplines like linguistics or ethnology. The answer may be surprising; it seems, to some extent. This is because of the fact that the state has an overall and a long-term policy to follow in which the inter-ethnic relations are only a fragment. The state understandably has multiple tasks and has to balance different, often contradictory interests. It cannot always reflect upon and react immediately to the state of the art in one particular discipline, especially when consensus among scientists has not been reached in that area. Yet, in accordance with the principle of good governance, the state should have an interest in following closely the development of scientific research and keeping in mind the results of new studies.

5.4.1.6 Structure of linguistic legislation: In states where it is deemed useful or politically helpful, language use in the linguistic legislation is determined along the lines of the linguistic policy of such states. This policy, implicitly or explicitly, is reflected in the legal norms and constitutes their contextual background. This policy is also determinative for the legislative process in which the prospective legal norms are construed and voted. Through linguistic legislation the state influences the communication processes in the given society by attributing certain functions to specific languages. By so doing, it often relies on domestic legislative techniques and foreign and international experience. Thus, certain concepts and topics can be perceived as characteristic instruments of the domestic linguistic legislation which underlie its structure. The conceptual instruments traditionally associated with this legislation include the following: *national language* – an elderly formulation still in use, sometimes used in association with the situation in the U.S., where no specific federal legislation on the status of the English language exists, *official language* (*state language*) – language of intra-state communication, language of official acts and administration, so to say the language in which the state speaks to its citizens and vice versa, *official state language* – a European Union term regarding a language used in an E.U. country which is at the same time an official language of the E.U., *administrative language* - language used by public authorities and regularly also courts, *working language* - a subset of the term official language which encourages the use of other languages, e.g. conference language, regional language, *minority language* – a concept closely connected to different definitions of minority, *lesser used languages, language of international communication* – language used in formal contacts among states. Other forms also exist, but are rarely used in European settings, such as: *language of court decisions or pronouncements, literary language defined in laws, religious language, language of alphabetization.* The use of the above terminology is closely linked to the policy of states and international organizations like the UN and the EU. Consequently, it is linked to priorities clearly defined by the drafters of the legal acts. Some concepts, such as *working language* provide an elastic tool for the shaping of the legislation and help avoid dogmatism. This issue is particularly important when the linguistic norms are shaped in a conflict-like atmosphere. Through the use of elastic concepts the legislator may avoid many problematic decisions and refer to particular situations in which interlocutors involved can freely decide on the language to be used in their public communication. These concepts bear in themselves a great potential for future legislation. International organizations use the concept of *working languages* already in their political practice in order to avoid frictions and to increase their daily practical operational efficiency. Linguistic legislation all over the world follows a pattern where the above terminology is used and sometimes specifically defined. Furthermore, special topics like language use in the public sphere, jurisdiction, education, broadcasting and advertisement as well as sanctions for the violation of the law are included in it. A model language law could be easily developed on the basis of analysis of the existing legislation. However, it would be premature to cherish high expectations regarding such piece of legislation and to believe that linguistic problems in a state or a society can be solved solely through using certain sterile legislative techniques. Therefore, no legislator will be able to hide behind these concepts without presenting a clear linguistic policy. One could pretend that linguistic legislation is blind when there is no linguistic policy to refer to. It is conceivable that a multilingual state might not have any linguistic legislation at all, but should it decide to introduce it, it will have to develop an explicit linguistic policy upon which it may rely when shaping the law and implementing it. Thus, linguistic legislation provides for a framework of formal rules and concepts concerning the status and the use of languages in a society which are necessary prerequisites for the implementation of a state's linguistic policy.

5.4.1.7 Linguistic policy: The international instruments such as Art. 1 of the UN Charter and other provisions named above prohibit any discrimination based on language use. In addition, international practice in shaping and implementing the linguistic legislation provides reliable guidelines to tackle the most upcoming issues. The blindness mentioned above is therefore curable because there exist many examples of successful linguistic policies and integration strategies for ethnic minorities developed along the lines of some descriptive and prescriptive properties.

The linguistic policy should:

1. reflect common views on language use in the linguistic community (descriptive element),
2. encourage social debate on issues concerning inter-ethnic relations and provide the appropriate conceptual framework for it (integration of minorities, multiculturalism, multilingualism),
3. include an overall strategy regarding use of language and inter-ethnic relations involving both minorities and the majority,
4. propose measures of active promotion of language (prescriptive element) where inadequacies formed in historical processes can be compensated for,
5. increase public awareness about issues concerning multiculturalism and multilingualism in the educational system,

6. develop professional skills among legal professionals and state officials dealing with multiculturalism and multilingualism

It is advisable that a linguistic policy of a country closely follows the state's linguistic realities. In a stable multilingual landscape official multilingualism is usually the most adapted basis for the development of a long-term linguistic policy. States like Finland or Switzerland have proved that official bi- or multilingualism is neither a burden to the state nor to the society. Tensions with a linguistic background in the post-Soviet area, however, show that the non-application of this concept leads unavoidably to serious social frictions. In areas where bi- or multilingualism appears in regional boundaries, appropriate measures like establishing locally limited bilingual areas should be implemented. Once again, the experience, be it Canadian or Finnish, shows that introducing and implementing official regional bi- or multilingualism does not confound the state structure nor the society but makes it more stable and efficient. Undeniably, situations can occur where the linguistic landscape of a country may become inadequate due to former linguistic policy which may even have been introduced forcibly. In such situations measures to compensate for linguistic losses, like the active promotion of a formerly suppressed language by state agencies and increased teaching of the language in the educational institutions should be taken. An additional problem is the legal status to be given to a linguistic policy which may appear as a purely political document binding solely the government in power during its adoption. Rather, it is advisable that the policy is endorsed by the Parliament as a document binding the state or that it is passed as a framework law on language use in the state. This issue is decisive because without a legal status the linguistic policy risks to become a short-lived phenomenon.

5.4.1.8 Role of legislation in conflict prevention: The recent experience from the conflict prevention work, especially in the OSCE region, shows that legislative initiatives in the area of minority legislation and foremost in the linguistic legislation have to be based on a solid linguistic policy developed by state agencies in a dialogue with minorities concerned and the broader interested public. Most tensions concerning linguistic legislative initiatives emerge due to one-sided and uncompromising approaches by legislative bodies which have preferred quick action instead of a long-term policy and broad social dialogue. An assessment of this type of action makes the development of preventive mechanisms necessary. Many preventive measures have been developed to this aim. First of all, *early warning* based on systematic monitoring and awareness rising on issues concerning minorities enables an efficient early response to the upcoming tension and blocks a possible escalation into a conflict. Concrete and determined political action must be taken as well. Here, steps taken within the *quiet diplomacy* seem to be particularly efficient. In order to prevent tensions and even conflicts around legislative initiatives it is essential to interfere at the earliest possible stage of the development so that legislative initiatives can be stopped early, preferably before their first reading in the Parliament takes place. A series of consultations with national and international experts can be proposed to legislative bodies with the aim to work out a coherent approach to the planned piece of legislation. Such an approach must be based on strict observance of human rights and especially on international instruments concerning the rights of national minorities and international standards which proved to be effective during longer time in the practical work of the application of linguistic legislation. Furthermore, harmonization of domestic legislation with international standards can help avoid tensions as it shows to the minorities that work is done on their issue and that their legal situation shall reflect the general standards of legislation which, even if sometimes perceived as insufficient, guarantees their equal treatment in international comparison. Awareness rising among minorities and in the majority on existing international standards in minority and language protection is one of the fundamental tasks within conflict prevention activities. It goes even beyond pure information on legal issues, because due to the quality of some standards the feeling of discrimination may persist in a case where specialists are of the opinion that international and domestic legislation have been observed but the minority does not share the view of the experts. Here, political measures like reconciliation activities and strengthening social dialogue can help. Minorities concerned must take into account the well founded advice to learn the state language in order to better integrate into the life of their surrounding that is structured by the linguistic needs of the majority. On the other side, majorities should be informed in the educational system about the situation of neighboring minorities. Occasionally, it is worthwhile to consider teaching the minority language to majorities as it constitutes a language of the closest cultural neighbor and enables the speakers belonging to a linguistic majority to cope much better in their social surroundings. Problems concerning migrants, especially those undocumented or those perceived as being illegal residents, must be addressed by the legislator and should not be shifted to the police or the broader society. Migrants must be provided a clear legal status (even gradually) and should be involved in integration measures, as well as integration courses on civic education and the language of their new country of residence. It is naive to believe that migrants will out of themselves develop the most appropriate behavioral strategies for their integration. Additionally, it is not reasonable to expect the majority of traditional residents to be prepared for life among changing ethnic circumstances. Work in the educational sector and with media can help to stabilize the situation. In turn, the experience shows that when linguistic legislation is a part of a coherent linguistic policy of the state and that it reflects international standards the risk of social tensions or violent conflicts diminishes radically or can be assessed as highly improbable.

5.4.1.9 Soft law, recommendations and promotional measures: Laws are the strictest instrument of governing in a society, if arbitrariness is set aside. In a democratic state, exclusively legalistically defined decisions are perceived as largely admissible. Such decisions are deemed as a sufficient protection against arbitrary, i.e. undemocratic decisions. Indeed, arbitrariness has an opposite side which is rationality. Both legality and rationality must coincide in order to produce legislation worth bearing this name. However, in the course of the development of social techniques of governing other instruments close to the legal ones came up and were used with some success. For instance, *soft laws* are sometimes mentioned as one example of such modern and effective means of governing. Other tools, such as *promotion programs* and *promotion projects* are still not sufficiently used to be perceived as an appropriate counterweight to laws. Meanwhile, laws in their very essence are coercive by structure, tone and even more, they are coercive in their application. This may make them less popular among citizens who are rather surprised by changes in the society and its leading scientific institutions. This seems to be the case in many issues concerning law and ethnicity, and especially with the legislation pertaining to language use. Changes in our views upon ethnicity which had happened in the last century, changes in our comprehension of the cultural diversity and multiculturalism/multilingualism as a mass phenomenon became sometimes more visible in the political and legislative processes than in the social practice. Here, rather informal, educational and promotional measures can reach more than coercive mechanisms which involve state structures and which in the end force them to persecute with sanctions those who act in disaccord with the coercive legal mechanisms. Alternative measures make this approach unnecessary and fill the gap between the coercive measures and the arbitrary action in the society. They are not neutral as they show the direction recommended by the state and make ethically determined choices towards multilingualism and cultural diversity and against ethno-nationalism or allegedly existing monoculturalism. *Promotion of multiculturalism*, especially in a situation where local languages get into a disadvantageous situation was undertaken in the Republic of Ireland and in Welsh speaking areas of the U.K. The results of these measures expressed in figures may be perceived as limited but coercive measures of language use would scarcely bring about better scores, especially when their destructive impact upon the society is taken into account. In addition, setting up laws without sanctions makes no sense, as they rest programatic and decorative in use. Actions increasing the public awareness such as the granting of the Cultural Harmony Award by the Canadian town of Vancouver or EU programs promoting tolerance can under specific circumstances influence the society more than legislative or purely political measures.

A specific help for interpretation are guidelines and recommendations developed to support the work of lawyers applying the linguistic legislation. Often such documents are classified as *soft law* (Lukashuk 1996: 104), a term which may prove useful in determining the legal character of a document without changing the concept of law. Sometimes, they may play a role of temporary guidelines until a formal solution is found and incorporated into law. In this spectrum other documents of purely consultative character such as the OSCE HCNM *recommendations* have gained substantial practical importance. They are as a rule drawn up for issues deserving particular elucidation and care. For the area of the linguistic legislation the OCSE accumulated serious experience in dealing with tension-loaded issues due to its involvement in preventing ethnic conflicts (Kemp 2001: 28). The task of drafting guidelines has been addressed by a group of experts on the request of the OSCE HCNM. This group set up in 1998 the Oslo Recommendations regarding the Linguistic Rights of National Minorities. These recommendations are further elucidated in an explanatory note. The international legal standards on language use in minority contexts concern first of all issues linked to names, religion, community life and NGOs, media, economic life, administrative authorities and public services, independent national institutions, judicial authorities and deprivation of liberty. The issues highlighted in the recommendations represent the areas in which problems used to occur in the national legislation of numerous countries.

5.4.1.10 Interpreting minority and linguistic legislation: As already noted, no international legal standards obliging states to adopt linguistic legislation exist. Many countries, such as Germany and the United States do not have any such legislation. Unlike in many others branches of law, e.g. in the penal or in the family law, there is no such international standard of norm setting which would provide for the introduction of linguistic legislation into the legal system of the country. Thus far, a state can choose whether it needs linguistic legislation or not. Such a choice should be a matter of profound analysis of needs by the legislative body in a given society. Usually, it is worthwhile considering other instruments of language promotion and strengthening the position of one selected language than to determine the use of a language which in practice means also to limit the use of other languages than the promoted one. It is difficult to say in what way the existing linguistic legislation all over the world has proven useful or unavoidable. Nevertheless, the impact of this specific legislation on human behavior is unquestionable. On the other side, it goes without saying that states act within their sovereign rights when they adopt such legislation, should they deem it necessary. The approach of states towards this topic is apparently as different as are their experiences with or without this type of legislation. At the end of the day, the matter concerns a legitimate purpose of legislation and the adoption of such a law by a state is, therefore, generally speaking legitimate. Another problem concerns the interpretation of language laws. It is, of course, first of all limited by professional procedures. Interpretation of laws is a part of the everyday activity of members of the legal profession, and such work does not take place in an empty space. As stressed in the main part of this book, interpretation of laws has its own premises and consequences. This is especially important in our context where many non-lawyers have to deal with the interpretation of laws. Regarding the language laws, one must take into account their concrete background. The primary purpose of this kind of law is to protect and promote the language as a part of the protection of human rights. Human rights are closely connected to linguistic, educational, and political rights. This helps understand the background of the interpretive activity. The protection of human rights and the fulfillment of the specific obligations guaranteed in the international instruments must also be guaranteed as the primary goal of the interpretive process. While interpreting we have to bear in mind that international standards reflect a legal minimum and thus their *restrictive interpretation* would be unfortunate as it would contradict their main aims. It is also important to distinguish between legal obligations based on international instruments and other social goals. The question is to determine what is allowed by international or domestic law and what measures seem to be aim-oriented in terms of policy or the everyday practicalities of the given society. First of all, it must be made clear what is legally allowed, and then which restrictions are imposed on a person's professional activities. These requirements must be reasonable and correspond with the principle of legality. In fact, interpretation of legal norms is an unavoidable activity. It is therefore necessary to choose an appropriate approach to it. Purely structural or linguistic interpretation of the legal provisions proved to be insufficient when changing needs of a complex society are at stake. The interpreting person will have to go a step further and keenly define the goals of the legislation in an attempt to interpret it. A constructive interpretation is vital if the provisions with human rights character shall remain vivid in the society (Dworkin 1991: 87). Terminology plays a special role in it. We may speak about terminology at the political level or handle it in legal terms, we may speak of national majorities at the cultural, historical or political levels but first of all it is important to determine from which definition we proceed. Legal standards and definitions differ very much from those used in historical-political or other contexts.

5.4.1.11 Specific aspects in the interpretation of linguistic legislation: The linguistic legislation is determining the use of languages in the society. Its background is rooted in the public policy on language use in State structures and society. It is formed like all other acts of legislation in the Parliamentary legislative process, and is afterwards implemented through competent State agencies. The two sides of the phenomenon, i.e. the legislative one (norm setting) and its subsequent application are closely interrelated. In fact, deficiencies in the legislative process regularly show up within the application of the law. Thus, the overall linguistic policy must anticipate problems of law setting and its subsequent application, if the linguistic legislation is to be efficient. In the theoretical perspective, the problems of application coincide with the problem of interpretation of legal norms. They focus upon the issues which have to be considered in this specific legislation towards the background of the international legal standards. These standards form – next to the public linguistic policy – the landmarks for the domestic linguistic legislation and its interpretation. At first, the interpretation of norms perceived as belonging to linguistic legislation follows the general procedures of professional interpretation of legal norms. Due to the characteristic features of the legal-linguistic norms, some specifics must be also borne in mind. In fact, only a skillful interplay between the general rules for interpretation and the specific features of their subject matter guarantee a solid and convincing result of the interpretation of norms belonging to the linguistic legislation. Here, once again, the creative interpretation of norms proves to be a reliable instrument in dealing with a subject which frequently gives raise to tensions and conflicts.

All too often, the legislator tries to determine the language use in all spheres of the societal life. As far as the public sphere is concerned, this approach is in many cases understandable. Problems usually emerge when the legislator enters into the private sphere, be it business life, private mass media, private schools, or other cultural institutions. Here, interference is legally allowed only upon limitations. Moreover, the legislator can be recommended not to enter into this field when avoidable. In the legislation of many states, especially in transition economies, separation of public and private sectors, which may indeed be complicated in certain cases, is very important. A clear definition of private and public sector is possible and it is important to interpret the provisions accordingly. At the same time, standards of the public sphere cannot be transferred automatically into the private sector. This concerns e.g. private and public schools which are often organized differently and have specific goals. Any analogy should be applied extremely cautiously. At the same time, the social background of some provisions must be considered when legal acts are developed in a legislative tradition of a country involved in a systemic transition and they shall function under the conditions of market economy. The language used in the linguistic legislation is an additional problem. Especially, very general norms granting rights *within the possibilities of the State,* or *as far as possible* are not particularly effective and should be omitted. It goes without saying that the inclination for this sort of formulations is rather of a political than of linguistic nature. However, the flawed language of such norms results regularly in problems of interpretation. To be able to interpret this kind of legislation additional background information is needed which can be found either in recommendations or guidelines of specialized bodies or in soft laws providing general rules for understanding and application of this type of legislation.

5.4.1.12 Interpretive methods: Research on legal interpretation brought about not only specific methods but also a distinguished set of legal texts which differ in content and due to these circumstances also demand different interpretive techniques. Consequently, we used to interpret statutes differently than precedents and these again differently than contracts. Still, the classical list of interdependent methods is traditionally referred to as a canon of interpretation. The traditional techniques of interpretation, (i.e. grammatical, logical or systematic) are of limited importance for the linguistic legislation. Some role could be ascribed to the teleological (aim-oriented) technique, but even there limits clearly show up very soon. The linguistic legislation is rarely unclear in grammatical or logical terms and its systematics is rather limited. Nevertheless, some help can be provided via the analysis of the legislative intention when exploring the aim of the statute. As said, it is impossible to avoid interpretive attitudes while dealing with laws (Dworkin 1986: 46). These attitudes are inherent in our dealing with all social practices. We interpret unclear statutes always from a determined point of view; we rely on our interpretive attitudes with all implied values and experience.

Roughly, interpretive problems include:

- unclear concepts due to limited legal tradition or their roots in either ethnology or linguistics (e.g. *multilingualism/multiculturalism*, *official bilingualism*, *ethnic/national minority*)

The unclear concepts can be clarified by using recommendations and guidelines issued by specialized state agencies and expert bodies.

- clearly sounding concepts which are often of unlimited scope such as *state language*

Above general concepts pertaining usually to the constitutional law can be clarified within the domestic procedures set up for solving of such legal interpretive problems. Hereby, the main principles of the democratic legal systems, especially the rule of law and good governance as well as the goals of the state policy such as strengthening of multiculturalism provide guidelines which enable to find a workable interpretive variety of a general concept.

- a special case of the linguistic legislation form open-ended formulations like *The state shall whenever possible enhance...*

These formulations constitute a real challenge for the interpreter. They are the classical area for the creative interpretation. They shall be interpreted towards their background in human rights. This background and the aim of this type of legislation pertaining to protection and to strengthening of human rights in the society will show the interpreting lawyer the appropriate criteria for his work. Within the problematic type of formulations some changes are necessary in the course of times. Aims and principles once accepted such as affirmative actions may not be productive any more. This is one of the reasons why the reference to the legislative intentions does not always lead to acceptable results. It is also worthwhile to make the interpretive principles visible in the final result. The interpretation gains on legitimacy and acceptability when rules and principles on which it has been based are clearly stated in it. Furthermore, it should be stressed that the result of the interpretation is not only a recommendation of "a certain notion or meaning" (Juhl 1986: 3). It is also the best possible result of the interpretation that is able to pass the constitutionality test, and that finally corresponds with international standards. In sum, interpreting linguistic legislation is a challenging task. Nevertheless, it can succeed when the aims of the legislation are clearly understood and their interference with the international instruments and the broader background of human rights protection finds an appropriate place in the constructive work of the interpreter.

5.4.2 Comparative language law

Due to the amount of statutes pertaining to language use a new discipline called comparative language law has been suggested in the academic research (Turi 1995: 111). This discipline should support the further systematization of the legal material in the international settings, and elaborate general principles of the linguistic legislation. Case studies upon which such a comparison is to be based would make a model linguistic law possible and prescribe law setting standards in the international legislative practice. Within the comparative studies, Finnish and Swiss legislation have gained particular importance. Furthermore, Canadian and Russian legislation which reflect an extreme cultural variety on their political territories were also considered. French linguistic legislation gained momentum in recent years as well. A closer look at different legal conceptions of determining language use makes some general remarks possible. It signalizes also possible interpretive problems inherent in the structure of the statutes. Below the

French, Russian, and Finnish linguistic legislation is contrasted to illustrate the role the comparative linguistic legislation could play in future.

5.4.2.1 French linguistic legislation: The French linguistic legislation has been approached with some reservation by the experts (Baylon 1991: 190). It is nevertheless worthwhile studying because it displays some structural problems of classical treatment of this subject by national legislators. The first structural problem is the determination of the goal towards which such legislation should be interpreted and applied. In France, it has traditionally been the protection of the French language (Cornu 2005: 422). Never any other goals have been advanced in the legislative materials nor in the public policy statements. Therefore, all statutory provisions and court decisions relating to them are structured around the idea of the protection of the French language. This fact may be surprising as in France no serious challenge to the preponderance of the French language in the public sphere (be it political or cultural) has been perceived since the French revolution, the obligatory point of reference of any thought about the French Republic. Usually, reference has been made - mostly by French researchers - to regionalist and autonomist political claims in areas where Occitan, Breton, Alsatian, Basque or Corsican are spoken (Cornu 2005: 427). However, no political evaluation of these movements has been undertaken. Such an evaluation would probably show their rather folkloristic character and limited political impact as well as their isolation among the majority of citizens. Furthermore, it would attenuate the legislative fervor and fears based on the illusionary assumption that a risk exists for the position of the French language within the French state and the French society.

The history of the French linguistic legislation and the linguistic policy is visible in its contemporary legislation. With the ordinance of Villers Cotterêts from 1539 France embraced the linguistic legislation which for centuries remained basically oriented towards the strengthening of the French language as spoken in the capital and the surrounding provinces. The ordinace replaced Latin by French in legal matters including court proceedings. Moreover, 1694 the first normative *Dictionnaire de l'Accadémie française* drew the final line under the attempts to control language use by the state. Hence, historically, two perspectives on language have been anchored in the French legislation; i.e. the necessity of one state language and the right of the state to determine this language and survey its development. The mentioned goal of protection of the French language structures basically the whole legislation. In addition, the goal to make France a unilingual country is manifest as well (Cornu 2005: 425). Art. 2 of the French Constitution states since 1992 that French is the language of the Republic: *La langue de la République est le français.* Surprisingly, it does not perceive the French language as a national language, unlike its national anthem *Marseillaise* or its national flag, the *tricolore*. This circumstance has also been interpreted in the sense that the French language still plays a role in international communication (Cornu 2005: 424). It is interesting to compare the formulation of Art. 18 of the Swiss constitution from 1999 applied in a country where the French language is one of the dominating idioms: The freedom of language is guaranteed, *La liberté de la langue est guarantie*. As a result, it can be inferred from the comparison of the two fundamental constitutional provisions that in the Swiss legislation the use of the language is not connected to politically determined preponderance of a language. Neither is in a profoundly multilingual country, that Switzerland undeniably is, any reference been made to the necessity to protect a language against others or to a risk for a language, imagined or proven. Regional languages did not play any particular role in the French legislation. However, in 2008 regional languages have been declared part of the national heritage (FR *patrimoine de la France*) and a provision with the corresponding content has been introduced into the French constitution's Art. 75. The position of the so-called regional languages is still unclear as governmental directives mostly deal with facultative teaching of those languages in public schools. The *Conseil Consititutionnel* decided 1999 that the European Charter on Regional and Minority Languages is not compatible with the French constitution and therefore should not be ratified by France (Dec. nr. 99-412 DC, dated June 15, 1999). The *Conseil Constitutionnel* referred to the indivisibility of the Republic, the unity of the French people and the egality of all citizens while rejecting the aims underlying the European Charter as well as the spirit of the Charter altogether. A further Parliamentary Act, the Law on the use of the French language no. 94-665 (*Loi relative à l'emploi de la langue française)* from 1994 determines the use of the French language in the public sphere which is however rather broadly conceived in the act. It includes certain contracts and publications as well as public advertisements and notifications accessible to the broad public.

Additional and very specific aspects of the French linguistic legislation concern issues such as neologisms and the orthography reforms which are dressed in legislative forms, decrees or laws. Orthography reforms have been regularly initiated by the *Académie française* in 1694, 1718, 1740, 1762, 1798, 1835, 1878, 1932-35 and also recently, in 1990. The recently proposed changes have a character of recommendations; however, they are mandatory for the public educational institutions. As a result, orthography reforms remain within the State domain and the reforms are undertaken on behalf of the government. Spelling is not perceived as a private matter or a question which should be decided among cultural elites, scholars and writers, mostly interested in such issues. Lists of neologisms are prepared by state agencies, predominantly within the Ministry of Culture. Moreover, France's linguistic policy embraces the idea of *francophonie* which makes also clear why the constitution does not perceive the French language as a national medium of communication. Promotion measures are developed within the *francophonie* which has also a pronounced political dimension. The *francophonie* as an idea is of interest because it reflects the international perspective in the linguistic legislation. Unlike in France, in most other countries the linguistic legislation relates exclusively to the internal distribution of language use. The French linguistic legislation is an illustrative example for the initial presupposition advanced here, that in the linguistic legislation the politically determined goal pre-structures all further legislative effors. It shows furthermore that the argumentative practice in the application of this legislation is clearly determined by its initial goal.

5.4.2.2 Russian federal linguistic legislation: Overall, the linguistic legislation of the Russian Federation has been deemed as acceptable in the light of international standards (Galdia/Wydra, in: Galdia/Voronina 2004: 334). Basically, only the provision of Art. 3 (6) of the Language Act prohibiting the use of other alphabets than Cyrillic for languages spoken in the Russian Federation have been qualified as clearly violating international standards. However, acceptability of a set of norms in the international perspective does not automatically mean that the legislation perfectly fits local needs or does not lead to problems in application. Particular problems connected to the Language Act reflect its roots in the Soviet legal techniques which produced overlong laws in flawed terms and little essence. Clearly, the intention of the legislator has been to describe the linguistic use in the country and mark more or less precisely to what extent the free choice of the language is permissible. As the law is overburdened with situational descriptions it is difficult to interpret and to apply. Moreover, terms in provisions referring to permitted use of a language other than Russian are formulated in extremely general wording, e.g. Art. 21 (RUS) *с учетом местного населения* (while taking into account the local population), Art. 16 (3) (RUS) *в необходимых случаях* (in necessary cases), or 15 (3) (RUS) *в случае необходимости* (in case of necessity). In situations, in which this wording may lead to difficulties in determining the scope of the application of the concerned provisions a broad interpretation can be recommended. Indeed, in the domain of human rights when the legislator is using terms which are difficult to interpret, he will also have to accept the risk that more rights can be attributed to citizens than he actually intended to provide to them. In all countries, Russia included, the general rule should be that human rights cannot be interpreted restrictively.

5.4.2.3 Finnish linguistic legislation: The Finnish linguistic legislation has been perceived by many as an advanced system of norms regulating language use in a satisfying way and rightly so. Approaches to address language use issues in Finland date back to 19th century (Mattila 2002: 156). The long legislative tradition in Finland and the experience made with the linguistic legislation there led to a model-like language law which is interesting in several ways. The new language law (FIN Kielilaki 6.6.2003/423) entered into force on January 1, 2004. It develops the main contents of Art. 17 of the Constitution stating that Finnish and Swedish are national languages of the Republic. It may at the first glance appear surprising as this law does not address very many questions which use to come up in numerous other countries at least in the last decade. This is definitely not a coincidence, but rather the result of experience made in a bilingual country in the last century. Indeed, efficient linguistic legislation requires first of all limitation. Once the needs for legal regulation are explored and determined, it is possible to curtail the legislation which suits the country and responds to legitimate social needs in the society. The legislator must ask himself, what part of linguistic relations between the state and its citizens and the relations between citizens shall be determined in laws. By far, no speculative range of situations or a general approach aiming at regulating everything everywhere makes sense. This is the lesson learned by the Finnish legislator who introduced a streamlined set of rules which correspond to the situations which must be determined in the Finnish society. They are as a matter of fact fundamental, but not particularly numerous. Thus, the law determines in its Art. 1 the state languages and in its Art. 2 the scope of the regulation which is the use of the state languages in courts and administrative bodies. Additional acts such as the Act on the Knowledge of Languages Required of Personnel in Public Bodies (424/2003), the Church Act (1054/1993), the Act on Judicial Appointments (205/2000), and the Act on General Language Examinations (668/1994) address specific issues relevant for the civil service. This legislative program may look from the perspective of the linguistic legislation passed in the last years in many European countries as very reduced. However, it may also pave the way for the development of modern linguistic legislation in other countries.

5.4.3 Conclusions on linguistic legislation

At least one result emerges from our analysis of the comparative language law. It seems that the limitation of the scope of the legislation has a positive effect upon the application of the statutes and on their acceptability in the societies concerned. On the other side, it becomes also plain that the differentiated structures of the legislative acts in the three countries in question make comparative efforts difficult. Therefore, the mentioned model linguistic legislation would also provide a useful basis for comparison of existing national legal acts. Moreover, the recommendation "*the best laws are those that legislate the least, especially regarding unofficial use of language*" (Turi 1995: 114, 116) remains a reliable guideline for the legislators in this domain. Linguistic legislation is a double edged sword; it may lead to solving problems in a society or instigate tensions and ethnic conflicts.

Therefore, the state has to consider twice the necessity of legislative acts regarding language use and set up a linguistic policy which accompanies the implementation of such acts. A legislation that regulates language use must be shaped also by linguists. Their advice that multilingualism and multiculturalism are characteristic features of developed societies must be heard. Linguistic legislation must reflect the structure of the linguistic landscapes it regulates. Historical inadequacies must be balanced by soft law and promotional measures. In sum, the linguistic legislation may - after having reached the phase of an apparent triumph which culminated in abounding legislation regulating all thinkable details of language use - become in future a domain of limited and much more relaxed application. The growing acceptance of the principles of multiculturalism as guidelines for state and society among legislators might in some time from now lead to less tense relations between ethnic groups and limit the necessity of decision making regarding language use in legislative bodies. The interpreters of the linguistic legislation could reflect this tendency in their works and influence the further development of interpretive standards along the lines of cultural diversity. Thus far, it is the legislation which relies upon the cultural diversity and not the other way round.

5.4.4 Language risk

The tendency towards developing legislation which could be some day called global law is in our view not questionable. Problematic are, however, methodological insufficiences in practical and theoretical approaches to this task. Especially, frustrations caused by the globalization in some countries may hinder the legislative progress. Certainly, they will not be able to impede significantly upon the development of the global law. The emerging globalized world is multicultural and multilingual and this fact cannot be changed. The global law will be therefore a multilingual law. This is one of the reasons why in this book the problems of the legal translation were discussed as one of central issues of the Legal Linguistics. Other consequences of this fact are the legal liability related to the use or the omission to use a language, called especially in the private international law *language risk*. Until now, no clear rules exist for cases concerning the language risk. In times, when the population on a territory was relatively culturally homogeneous and migrants played only a peripheral role, linguistic problems in law, be it in the public or in the private sphere, were not perceived as crucial. Today, it would be simplistic to claim that the knowledge of the main language of the country is a practical necessity if not a legal obligation for every resident upon its territory. The diversity of biographies and the diversity of cultures make clear even for uninterested lawyers that such a rule would oversimplify the social reality in an inadmissible way. Finally, as a result of this uncertainty about right or wrong language use the language risk became an increasing issue in law. The most problematic cases in multilingual contacts concern negotiations in a language which is less understandable to one party than to another one or when one party uses a language dominant in a specific branch which is also its native language whereas this language is a foreign language to the other party. The basic constellation can be more complicated; due to cases which emerge in such situations we are able to distinguish between situations where the linguistic incompetence of one party is (manifestly) recognizable or where it is well hidden in the subject matter and manifests itself as misunderstanding, e.g. after a contract has been concluded. The first constellation concerns mostly consumer related issues (Dreißigacker 2002), the second one is rather specific for advanced business practices such as negotiations among enterprises.

The first constellation can be exemplified on the court opinion Ramirez v. Plough, Inc. (15 Cal. App. 4th 1110, 12 Cal. Rptr. 2d 423 (1992)) where the Court of Appeal of California had to decide a product liability case. A Spanish-speaking mother of a sick baby bought aspirin in a pharmacy. On the package the standard Reye's syndrome warning was printed, and this in English only. The mother administered the drug to her baby who developed the Reye's syndrome and was damaged for life. She sued the manufacturer for damages. The manufacturer argued that no duty to warn in any other language than English existed in the U.S. and insisted on this practice pointing to the fact that ca. 148 languages were spoken in the U.S. The court however adopted a differentiated point of view and asked whether the warning given in English only was adequate under the circumstances of the case. It stressed that the public policy in the U.S. is directed towards the treatment of English as official language of the Union. However, *nothing compels the conclusion that a manufacturer of a dangerous or defective product is immunized from liability when an English-only warning does not adequately inform non-English literate persons likely to use the product.* In this case, the manufacturer was aware of the fact that the product was distributed also in pharmacies situated in areas where Spanish-speaking population dominates. Moreover, he even advertised it in Spanish-language media. Therefore, the court denied Plough the summary motion without stating, however, that a warning in foreign languages is necessary on certain products: *In deciding that Plough did not establish its right to judgment as a matter of law, we do not hold that manufacturers are required to warn in languages other than English simply because it may be foreseeable that non-English literate persons are likely to use their products. Our decision merely recognizes that under some circumstances the standard of due care may require such warning.*

The second constellation can be illustrated by the already cited MCC – Marble Ceramic Center v. Ceramica Nuova d'Agostino, S.I.A. (144 F3d. 1384, 11th Cir. (1998)) where a more stringent standard is developed (cf. 3.6.4.5). The parties, an American enterprise as buyer and an Italian enterprise as seller agreed to terms and conditions of a contract that were preprinted on the reverse side of the order form prepared by the seller in the Italian language. Later, the buyer pretended that he did not understand the clauses and that the parties agreed to remove them from the contract. The court however assumed it as improbable that a professional buyer would sign a contract including terms and conditions in a foreign language that he did not understand. MCC had therefore to bear the language risk. In Ramirez, the approach to the language risk issue is based on circumstantial appreciation and this seems to be an effective criterion for a liability test. In MCC v. Marble, the test is more formal as it can be based on commercial practices among enterprises involved in international business; nevertheless, it also stresses the role of circumstances for answering the question of who bears the language risk. It may be assumed that in future decisions in this area the differentiating test will be applied which would enable to avoid a rigid legislation on the matter.

5.4.5 Professional liability of translators

Translators are, like all other professionals, liable for damages caused by their products; i.e. texts in the target language (Mattila 2002b: 487). However, the legal issue regarding the liability of translators is complicated due to the nature of the legal texts and problems of the legal translation which were discussed above (cf. also Kinnunen 2006: 25). Therefore, the question when a translation is erroneous is not always easy to decide. Legal texts may lead to misunderstandings, and cause damage due to the formulations in the source text which deliberately or negligently might have been formulated in an ambiguous way. Is the translator obliged to discover such ambiguities and signalize them to his client? Is this his legal or professional obligation? Where is the borderline between translating and detective work to be drawn? Another set of problems concerns translations into lesser used languages with underdeveloped or missing legal terminology such as some Uralic languages spoken in Russia. There, a general description of the meaning included into the source language document or direct borrowings from Russian are used to render the meaning. The third possibility is to shape neologisms in the hope that they will be understood properly by the readers. In many other languages the description with words from the ordinary language is preferred to the forming of neologisms. The translation of a promissory note from English into Hawaiian from 1917 is an example of such a procedure (Notes and Materials nr. 9). Another legal-linguistically relevant problem is the translation of international conventions into languages that lack the necessary legal terminology and where the terminology is invented by their first translators. Are these new coinages binding also on future translators of international instruments related to these documents even when the new translators have better proposals for rendering the original terminology in the texts that they develop? The standards for professional translation are unclear at this point. In all such cases the central legal question is whether the lack of equivalent terminology or legal-linguistic features in a language increases or diminishes the translator's professional liability. Liability standards in some countries may suggest increased liability linked to the contractual acceptance of an offer to translate. Indeed, who accepts an offer, accepts also the risk inherent in it. The nature of the legal translation would, however, require rather an increase in tolerance towards legal translation into languages that are problematic from the point of view of their legal-linguistic features. The proper test for such translations must therefore focus on the essentials of the message, and not on the legal terminology.

In the legal-linguistic research, work concerning the standards of a correct legal translation in the light of professional liability has only begun. The most reliable criterion to determine professional liability would be court decisions about the acceptability of variations in legal translations. However, very few legal translations have been challenged in courts of law (Gémar 2004: 743). Therefore, the limits of interpretive creation in the translation of legal texts remain the professional risk of translators. In some cases, such as Falcoal, Inc. v. Kurumu (660 F. Supp. 1536 S.D. Texas (1987)) the translation error is evident. In casu, the Turkish language clause in the contract between the Turkish and the U.S. American parties – here retranslated into English - provided that *the final jurisdiction for the settlement of any disputes, in the case of the Purchaser submitting a claim, lies within the jurisdiction of the Houston commercial courts and, in the case of the Supplier submitting a claim lies within the jurisdiction of the Ankara commercial courts.* The English version of the clause stated that any dispute *shall be settled in Houston and submitted to the jurisdiction of the courts of the U.S.A. if the claim is put forward by Supplier and in Ankara, Turkey, and submitted to the Turkish Courts if the claim is put forward by Buyer.* Hence, the forum selection clauses in the source and in the target language directly contradicted each other. This resulted in the impossibility for the plaintiff to sue in Houston which led to damages. In such a case where the translation error is evident also for a non-specialist, the determination of liability is not problematic.

Liability issues may emerge also in the case of a translation that does not comply with professional standards of the language knowledge and which includes numerous grammatical errors. Such a translation may not lead to direct damage because it is usually understandable notwithstanding its numerous grammatical errors but may indirectly tarnish its user's image. The liability claim would in such a case be based on bad quality of work provided by the translator. The translation into the German language of a Turkish court decree (Notes and Materials nr. 12) that was mentioned here in another context is illustrative of this set of problems. The translator of this text would almost certainly not be able to claim her honorarium for the work done because her work does not even approach the lowest standards set up for a professional translation. Overall, at this stage of the legal-linguistic development one would have to ask whether different standards of professionality should be accepted within the evaluation procedure of the legal translation depending on the languages from and into which the texts are translated. Today, practically, different standards govern the translation from French into English than from Russian into Mari or Italian into Hawaiian. Should a more differentiated standard for the evaluation of the professional work emerge among the professionals themselves, it would also become easier to determine who shall bear the risk for misunderstandings caused by translation into languages with limited legal terminology.

Part 6: Conclusions

Linguistic turn in law In this study we have proposed a *linguistic turn* in dealing with issues of creation and application of law (cf. 1.2.11). As a matter of fact, our initial idea is not new. Generations of researchers, lawyers, philosophers, and others were perfectly aware of the specific relation which law entertained with language – here we allow ourselves to use the metaphor one last time. Indeed, law and language cannot but artificially be separated. Until now, much too frequently this artificial separation took place. Law was perceived as a logical system where the systematization of provisions and concepts had to prevail. The civil law tradition devoted itself sometimes even excessively to the task of conceptual systematization and took the risk to lose the contact with the social practice. The alleged logical legal system represented by systematized provisions, legal concepts, and their requisites dominated the legal research and the legal education. In the common law tradition the importance of court procedures and judicial decisions for the developing of law prevented to some extent the exaggerated interest towards pure systematization of legal concepts. It takes time to understand the consequences of this state of affairs, as it took time to discover this anomaly in perception of the essential features in creating and applying of law. The temporary factor is particularly beneficial for the proposed shift of attention. The past century was dominated by the linguistic turn in philosophy, the ordinary language philosophy, and the following developments in philosophical and linguistic pragmatics. Time has shown the limits of these approaches as well. Nevertheless, the achievements of the scientific research based on the pragmatic conceptions are undeniable, although other concurring or even contrary movements also contributed to the renewal of the perspective in which we used to perceive the social reality.

Our material analysis allows the first important conclusion that legal argumentation prevails over conceptual systematization in law. It must therefore be perceived as central for the legal research as well as for the legal education. We are not inclined to deny the necessity of systemizing work in law as systematized concepts provide a reliable matrix for the legal argumentation. Our idea is limited to the necessary shift in the attention towards law. The shift in the attention towards linguistic implications of law is due to the fact that the legal argumentation is as such a linguistic phenomenon. Therefore, while undertaking the linguistic turn in law we actually re-establish the necessary balance of cognitive interests towards law. Our analysis has also demonstrated that jurists have been always dealing with language but did not take law's linguistic foundations seriously. They rather construed language as a decoration which was added to the legislative or judicial decision after the legal work was accomplished. In order to balance this inadequacy, the center of interest must shift towards argumentation. This, in essence, is the linguistic turn in law.

Methodology of Legal Linguistics At the initial stage of theory building, the Legal Linguistics has to answer two fundamental questions; first, what is law and second, how is language used in law. In the first task it is assisted by the general legal theory while being itself a particular theory of law. The second task is best performed with help of pragmalinguistic approaches because they show the closest affinity to law among all linguistic perspectives. We have therefore adapted the analytic conceptual apparatus of the speech act theory and the discourse theory, and we have shown that it serves perfectly its purpose also in law. Law and language seen in the perspective of the speech act theory are not artificially separated any more. Creation and application of law as explicitly linguistic operations can be described with theoretical means of the linguistic research. This description is justified because it touches upon the most essential feature of law; i.e. its embodiment in institutionalized discursive social practices. These social practices remain unclear until perceived as argumentative practices. This result may, at first, disappoint because it seems to concern rather the scientific paradigm in the legal theory than the social practice. However, through the shift in perspective we will be gradually able to improve rationality tests for the legal argumentation and subsequently we will be able to produce law of better quality. This result, which may seem limited to theory, satisfies the demand expressed in the society for good governance, which means in essence a demand for law created along the principles of an advanced democracy and the application of the modern law according to principles of rationality in which the best available arguments will be used.

Conception for the Legal Linguistics The conception of the Legal Linguistics proposed here is based on language use in opposition to studies of linguistic utterances, for instance particular legal provisions or legal notions, without reference to their context of use. This approach has the advantage to be broad enough to capture not only the legal language but also the law as a social phenomenon. Law's most distinctive features, (i.e. its link to power as well as to language), are best understood when the use of linguistic devices and not the use of abstract declarations is perceived as the central field of the legal-linguistic research. Theoretically, the choice exercised here means the preference for a pragmatically oriented perspective over the semantic one that is dominated by the tendency to denote meaning in legal concepts. Many semantic problems can be solved or simply disappear when the shift from the semantic to pragmatic perspective occurs because in law meaning is created in the application of legal rules within complex linguistic operations. Therefore, meaning cannot be simply decoded or distilled from legal provisions or court opinions.

We tried to expand the core legal theory by explicitly linguistic elements. We started with the question how are laws made with words and ended with a more complicated problem setting, namely how we speak about law. Legal terms which we have analyzed turned to be vantage points for arguments, the later being elements of a discourse about law which takes place in different professional and less professional settings. Complex speech acts such as legal argumentation, legal interpretation or legal translation proved to constitute such discourses. The main field of the Legal Linguistics are legal operations in law developed around legal speech acts. Legal speech acts are qualitatively different in that they reach from simple utterances like a promise to complex argumentative and interpretive structures. Legal terms that represent legal concepts function as focal points for these complex structures. The linguistic operations are organized within legal discourses on different levels of discursiveness as they involve legal professionals, professionals and laypersons or laypersons solely. These legal discourses take place in preformulated textual patterns; the stricter is the discursive pattern organized, the more professional the discourse will be. Laypersons' discourses about law are less strict in the choice of argumentative or interpretive devices, but they are also less effective in their impact upon the creation and application of law. There, formal aspects may dominate the debate to the detriment of the subject matter. In turn, they are less exposed to the risk of the reification of language than professional discourses about law. These discourses demonstrate that law seen from the linguistic perspective appears as a discursive practice that is subject to institutional limitations. We would wish to provide an exhaustive overview over legal arguments used in the discursive practice. Yet, the Legal Linguistics in the modern sense of the term is only in its beginnings. We have at least sketched its possible development.

Morals in law and morals of law We have equally shown the importance of moral values in law. This holds true for society as a whole as well as for the social group of lawyers who create and apply the law. This circumstance is actually the guarantee for the operationability of law in whatever democratic society. Again, while making it clear we did not express anything particularly new. We simply made plain that values and value-laden language are inherently integrated in law. They are so deeply merged that law cannot be perceived or applied *more geometrico,* i.e. without taking into consideration the values which underlie the legislation or the legal decisions in general and in the professional discourse about law. By identifying the values embedded in law we approached the legal argumentation which differs in many ways from other types of language use. Arguments used in it are of volatile nature; they are grounded in the plurality of views on ethical issues (ethical diversity). The modern Legal Linguistics supports argumentative and interpretive strategies that further the socially relevant issues and does not focus any more on discovering devices that engender success in litigation with formal procedures; it reflects upon the quality of arguments. The Legal Linguistics is therefore not neutral in terms of morals.

Future issues in Legal Linguistics Creation of language used in the public sphere will remain one of the central issues for the future legal-linguistic research. Notions such as *intentional infliction of emotional distress* or *common heritage of mankind* will be elucidated in respect of the way they are constituted. Traditionally, signification processes had been characterized only in general epistemological terms. The reason for this has been that only limited data was available allowing a research into the linguistic processes of their immediate constituence. Today, in the public sphere it is occasionally even possible to identify the creator or the first group of users of a specific term as well as the strategies which guaranteed the use of the new term in the language of the public sphere. Similarly, the interpretation strategies directed towards these texts as well as the argumentative strategies used by the issuers of texts composed of a language that is specific for the public sphere and especially for legal contexts will remain substantial for the research. The part of conversational analysis will probably increase as access to and recording of oral sources within legal institutions become technically and legally less prohibitive. Under these circumstances, the legal discourse will be characterized materially and enable further theoretical insights into law which may become useful for the legal theory.

The author's last word In this book we have focused on issues which we perceive as central in law, and we have determined the legal argumentation as methodologically fundamental for all reflection upon law. In this sense, law is for us a matter of language. We have also proposed a vast research program into argumentation in the area of the national and the international law. Finally, it is tempting to ask whether, provided exhaustive results of such a research program would become available, the legal problems, i.e. problems of the legal theory would be perceived as solved. Is it realistic to assume that we would be able to reach a stage where we would know everything about law and witness the end of the reflection upon it? There exist several hindrances to this result. The first one is inherent to the phenomenon law itself. We have excluded from this study material issues of law, i.e. questions why law is as it is or why it says things it says. We do not underestimate these questions, yet the Legal Linguistics deals primarily with the language in which propositions about law are expressed. Nevertheless, even in the Legal Linguistics we would be theoretically able to address the issue from a praxiological point of view. We would argue that law has to address subject matters it aims to regulate in an efficient way because efficiency is the central principle of activities in social contexts. This efficiency can be construed in different ways. R. Posner in his fundamental works on the economic analysis of law showed the complexity of the material side of law. Posner intended to reduce the efficiency to economic arguments (Posner 1987). However, the results of his innovative approach were not equally encouraging in all areas of law. One would nevertheless have to insist on the legislation that is adequate; i.e. which matches best to the standards of the modern democratic society. Our claim for efficiency would be therefore satisfied by the adequacy reached in institutionalized argumentative processes. The second inherent hindrance is of legal-linguistic nature. As constantly stressed here, material issues in law are based on argumentation. There is no limit to our inventiveness of arguments so far. Moreover, in a modern society it does not make much sense to use whatever arguments. Reliable residues for modern arguments are the human rights which provide subject matter related solutions. Yet, again, these recipes are argumentative in nature. In fact, also many limits to civil rights have been obtained through reference to the human rights. Therefore, strategies adopted in argumentative reference to the human rights or other central issues in the discourse about the appropriate law are equally relevant as is their material basis, i.e. what the legal provisions actually say. Therefore, in order to avoid traps in argumentation we have to master its most fundamental mechanics. The third hindrance is anthropological in essence. Law is an ongoing project in the development of mankind. One of the most impressive achievements in its long history is the strengthening of its discursive nature. Laws are nowadays lesser imposed than they are agreed upon. Furthermore, the discourse about the content of law will definitely continue. To reduce tensions in the battle of arguments and transform it into a discourse about good governance and effective sustainable development in economical life and protection of human rights would be a move forward. Legal linguists can prepare the society to participate in legal discourses in a more civilized and rational way than it has been the case to date.

Part 7: Notes and Materials

In Notes and Materials the reader will find some general remarks on legal-linguistic and related issues that are connected to the main topics of this book. They should be consulted by the reader upon the reference indicated in the main text. They are not construed as an ongoing text and should therefore not be read separately from the main text. All notes presented here are in a way relevant for the Legal Linguistics without necessarily making part of it. Additionally, commented quotes from research papers as well as some longer statutory texts which were not introduced into the main text due to their volume can be found here. Furthermore, legal decisions issued by French, Italian, German, Japanese, English and U.S. courts that were analyzed in the main text are quoted here at length. Some of them, especially those which show interesting legal-linguistic features irrelevant to the particular topic dealt with in the main text, are provided with additional comments. Other decisions are quoted in selected paragraphs which are of interest for the legal linguist. Meanwhile, the main text of the book refers in its analyses exclusively to original versions of the materials used. Therefore, no translation of these texts into English has been supplied here, with the exception of lesser used languages. Otherwise, new interpretive problems resulting from the linguistic diversity could emerge which, in turn, would necessitate further theoretical comments. In the end, such a procedure would not be in the reader's interest.

(1) On the relation between pragmatics and semantics

The relation between pragmatics and semantics has been addressed by many researchers in different ways. Levinson's classical textbook *Pragmatics* focuses in its introductory part upon the distinction between pragmatics and semantics; it accentuates pragmatic contributions into the area that has been perceived by many as the realm of semantics. Moreover, Levinson (1983: 372) stresses in his conclusions that pragmatics can even simplify semantic analyses or broaden the ambit of understanding of linguistic phenomena. Other prominent researchers attempted at defining this distinction or at least made plain the ambit of pragmatics. As can be seen from the quotes below it would be difficult to construct an integrative definition of pragmatics based on these views. Some of the views rendered below are of conciliatory nature, e.g. (Verschueren/Östman 1995), some perceive pragmatics rather as an appendix to systematic linguistics (Akmadjan et al. 2001), while others plead for autonomous pragmatics (Bülow 1988). This diversity of views is encouraging because it shows that the area of pragmatic research is actually quite broad. We are not interested here in counteracting this tendency.

Morris, Ch. *Foundations of the Theory of Signs. In: Writings on the Theory of Signs, The Hague: Mouton* (1938/ 1971: 35; 43): Semantics deals with the relation of signs to...objects which they may or do denote... Pragmatics concerns the relation of signs to their interpreters. May *op. cit* (1980: 195) characterized Morris' semiotic distinction of linguistic dimensions as follows: An den allgemeinen Zeichencharakter von Sprache anknüpfend, können drei Dimensionen bezeichnet werden, die pragmatische, die syntaktische und die semantische Sprachdimension. Unter der pragmatischen Dimension ist der externe Beziehungsbereich zwischen Zeichen und Zeichenbenutzer in unbeschränkter Rücksicht auf den gesamten situativen Zusammenhang der Zeichenbehandlung zu verstehen. Demgegenüber beinhaltet die syntaktische Dimension die Beziehungen zwischen Zeichen, während die semantische Dimension den internen Beziehungs- und Deutungsbereich zwischen Zeichen und Bezeichnetem ausweist. May stresses the pragmatic dimension in his characterisation of Morris' conception primarily through quoting it on the first place. This is definitely not a cosmetic shift of phrases. Instead, it comprises the fundamental idea that pragmatics has the first as well as the last word in language. Language without the pragmatic dimension is an empty hull. No natural language has been meaningfully characterized without the pragmatic dimension nor can it be properly spoken without it. The lack of knowledge about this dimension makes a full characterization (and also the full command) of ancient languages like Latin or Greek impossible. This theoretical problem is even more manifest in the case of artificial languages such as Esperanto which cannot be fully determined in terms of pragmatics simply because they are artificial. An artificial pragmatics, in turn, would not make much sense.

Stalnaker, R. *Pragmatic Presuppositions, in: Munitz, M. and Unger, P. (eds.) Semantics and Philosophy, New York University Press: New York* (1972: 383): Syntax studies sentences, semantics studies propositions. Pragmatics is the study of linguistic acts and the contexts in which they are performed. There are two major problems to be solved within pragmatics: first, to define interesting types of speech acts and speech products; second to characterize the features of the speech context which help determine which proposition is expressed by a given sentence... It is a semantic problem to specify the rules for matching up sentences of natural language with the propositions that they express. In most cases, however, the rules will not match sentences directly with propositions, but will match sentences with propositions relative to features of the context in which the sentence is used. These contextual features are part of the subject matter of pragmatics.

Katz, J. *Propositional Structure and Illocutionary Force, Crowell: New York* (1977: 14): (I) draw the theoretical line between semantic interpretation and pragmatic interpretation by taking the semantic component to properly represent only those aspects of the meaning of the sentence that an ideal speaker-hearer of the language would know in an anonymous letter situation,...(where there is) no clue whatever about the motive, circumstances of transmission, or any factor relevant to understanding the sentence on the basis of its context of utterance.

Gazdar, G. *Pragmatics: Implicature, Presupposition and Logical Form, Academic Press: London* (1979: 4-5): What we need in addition is some function that tells us about the meaning of utterances…The domain of this pragmatic function is the set of utterances, which are pairs of sentences and contexts, so that for each utterance, our function will return as a value a new context – the context as changed by the sentence uttered…And we can treat the meaning of the utterance as the difference between the original context and the context arrived at by the sentence.

Bülow, E. *in a duplicated commentary to own lectures* (1988): Die Pragmalinguistik (PL) ist das zentrale wissenschaftstheoretische Paradigma, das die "Nach-Chomskysche Linguistik" charakterisiert. Sie markiert den Paradigmawechsel von der „C-(=Chomsky)- zur P-(=Pragmatik) Matrix" und hat die wissenschaftstheoretische Selbstreflexion der Linguistik wesentlich vorangetrieben. Die PL versteht sich als eine Performanzlinguistik, die den Sprachgebrauch, das sprachliche Handeln von Sprechern in den unterschiedlichen gesellschaftlichen Gruppen und deren kommunikativen Handlungsspielen sowie deren Regelsysteme untersucht. Sprechakttheorie, sprachliche Handlungstheorien und Interaktionstheorien allgemein (Sozialpragmatik), Konversationsanalyse, Kommunikations Kommunikationstypologien bilden den Kern der PL.

Kempson, R. *Grammar and Conversational Principles, In: Newmeyer, F. (ed.): Linguistics vol. II, Cambridge University Press: Cambridge* (1988: 139): Semantics provides a complete account of sentence meaning for the language, by recursively specifying the truth conditions of the sentences of the language…Pragmatics provides an account of how sentences are used in utterances to convey information in context.

The Oxford Companion to Philosophy (Fotion 1995: 709): Pragmatics is the study of language which focuses attention on the users and the context of language use rather than on reference, truth, or grammar.

Verschueren, J., Östman, J.-O. et al. *op. cit.* (1995): Pragmatics is the cognitive, social and cultural study of language and communication.

The Cambridge Dictionary of Philosophy (Lycan 1995: 588): Pragmatics studies the use of language in context, and the context-dependence of various aspects of linguistic interpretation…(Its branches include the theory of how) one and the same sentence can express different meanings or propositions from context to context, owing to ambiguity or indexicality or both,…speech act theory, and the theory of conversational implicature.

The Blackwell Companion to Philosophy (Davies 1996: 124): The distinction between semantics and pragmatics is, roughly, the distinction between the significance conventionally or literally attached to words, and thence to whole sentences, and the further significance that can be worked out, by more general principles, using contextual information.

Akmadjan *op. cit.* (2001:361) Therefore, we will take the term pragmatics to cover the study of language use, and in particular the study of linguistic communication in relation to language structure and context of utterance.

Gémar *op. cit.* (2004 : 738, 739): Si l'usage confère sa valeur sémantique première à un mot, c'est le contexte de son emploi, le mot mis en discours, qui en détermine toutefois sa signification réelle. De là l'importance du processus d'interprétation de textes, particulièrement poussé chez les juristes...Ce que presque tous les spécialistes appellent « le language du droit » posséderait au moins trois éléments fondamentaux analysable dans tous leurs aspects, soit un lexique...une syntaxe...et une sémantique (sens des unités significatives/mots et morphèmes : signifiés) ; ou encore, selon le point de vue (linguistique, sociologique, communicatif, sémiotique, philosophique, littéraire, etc) une « pragmatique », soit l'étude du language par l'usage qui en est fait, autrement dit l'étude des phénomènes énonciatifs.

Recanati *op. cit* . (2008: 93): Dans la conception traditionnelle inspirée des idées de Carnap et de Morris, la pragmatique (l'étude de l'emploi des formes linguistiques) présuppose la sémantique (l'étude de leur sens, identifiée à l'étude de la relation entre les mots et les choses qu'ils représentent), et la sémantique présuppose la syntaxe. En revanche, la syntaxe ne présuppose pas la pragmatique. Recanati (2008: 95) refuses this conception: ... on ne peut accorder un contenu représentationnel aux phrases types, indépendament du contexte; however, he maintains the distinction between semantics and pragmatics in the notion of *sémantique pragmatique* where functions or types of use are assigned to utterances. This, in turn, results in a partition of tasks: L'explication pragmatique a donc besoin des résultats de l'analyse sémantique, et c'est en ce sens qu'on peut dire de celle-ci qu'elle est présupposée par celle-là (Recanati 2008 : 98-99). This view is in our reading compatible with the conception of the *integrative pragmatics* that embraces semantic questions in its conceptual framework, as it is the case in this book.

(2) Discourse and discursiveness

The notion of *discourse* is used in philosophy and in linguistics in different contexts with broader or narrower meaning that comes close to *text* or *utterance*. Baylon (1991: 235-236) has identified some of them:

"Le mot *discours* est:

- synonyme de la parole saussurienne dans la linguistique structurale ;
- une unité linguistique de dimension supérieure à la phrase (transphrastique), un message pris globalement, un énoncé ;
- l'ensemble des règles d'enchaînement des suites de phrases composant l'énoncé (Harris)
- ce qui s'oppose à l'énoncé : « L'énoncé, c'est la suite des phrases émises entre deux blancs sémantiques, deux arrêts de la communication ; le discours, c'est l'énoncé considéré du point de vue du mécanisme discursif qui le conditionne » (L. Guespin, Language 23, « Le discours politique », sept. 1971, p.10) ;
- « toute énonciation supposant un locuteur et un auditeur, et chez le premier l'intention d'influencer l'autre en quelque manière » (E. Benveniste, Problèmes de linguistique générale, I, Gallimard, 1966 ; p. 242)
- ce qui s'oppose à la langue. La langue s'oppose alors, comme ensemble fini, relativement stable d'éléments, au discours entendu comme lieu où s'exerce la créativité, lieu de la contextualisation imprévisible qui confère de nouvelles valeurs aux unités de la langue."

Following the Saussurian concept of (FR) *langue* as a limited domain of the linguistic science and (FR) *parole* as a residue of a speaker's liberty, the discourse analysis in pragmatic sense concerns rather the *parole*. It concentrates on elaborating of constraints or regularities of such a discourse and envisages the way in which things are said rather than what is said (Baylon 1991: 237). They can be found in the language itself, in history, ideology, habitus, mentality, and since M. Foucault's works also in the knowledge (FR *savoir*). This broader conception of discourse, especially in the sense introduced by Foucault, combines linguistic and extra-linguistic elements. Therefore, Foucault (1966: 102) stresses rather the discursiveness than the discourse: « Ce que nous laissent les civilisations et les peuples comme monuments de leur pensée, ce ne sont pas tellement les textes, que les vocabulaires et les syntaxes, les sons de leurs langues plutôt que les paroles qu'ils ont prononcées, moins leurs discours que ce qui les rendit possible : la discursivité de leur language. » When applied to law, the broader conception of discourse provides for an overarching analytic concept apt at integrating the two most significant ingrediences of law, i.e. power and language.

(3) Context in Legal Linguistics

The notion of *context* is not less ambigous than the one of *discourse.* It can mean interpersonal (FR *contexte interpersonnel)* or social context (FR *contexte social*). *Context* may also extend to the physical environment and it can encompass general knowledge (Akmajian 2001: 388). Baylon (1991: 236-237) stresses that the research in the English speaking countries favors the interpersonal context, whereas the French linguistic research, represented mainly by D. Maingueneau et O. Ducrot relies more on social contexts in the tradition initiated by the writings of Mikhael Bakhtin. It has been also claimed that the context should not be specified in advance but rather discovered in a pragmatic analysis (cf. Levinson 1983: 22). For the Legal Linguistics a broad notion of context is needed due to the involvement of institutionalized and non-institutionalized elements that compete or coexist in legal discourses.

(4) Sale contract from Mesopotamia

A contract for the sale of a slave, dating from the reign of Rim-Sin, c. 2300 B.C. says in its English translation:

Sini-Ishtar has bought a slave, Ea-tappi by name, from Ilu-elatti, and Akhia, his son, and has paid ten shekels of silver, the price agreed. Ilu-elatti, and Akhia, his son, will not set up a future claim on the slave. In the presence of Ilu-iqisha, son of Likua; in the presence of Ilu-iqisha, son of Immeru; in the presence of Liku-lubishtum, son of Appa, the scribe, who sealed it with the seal of the witnesses. The tenth of Kisilimu, the year when Rim-Sin, the king, overcame the hostile enemies.

(in: George Aaron Barton, "Contracts," in: *Assyrian and Babylonian Literature: Selected Transactions, With a Critical Introduction by Robert Francis Harper* (New York: D. Appleton & Company, 1904: 256) quoted after *Ancient History Sourcebook: A Collection of Contracts from Mesopotamia, c. 2300-428 BCE; www.fordham.edu*)

The text enables to distinguish purely linguistic and the legal-technical mechanisms of law in interaction. It identifies the legally relevant action *S-I bought x* and establishes a legal mechanism to guarantee the property of the new owner by the seller's guarantee *not to claim the slave back.* To ensure the enforcement of the guarantee the written form of the contract is chosen and the presence of witnesses assured. Unlike in modern contracts, all actions undertaken are reflected or commented upon; e.g. *ten shekels of silver* is commented as *the price agreed* and fixed in writing. The seal is not only put on the document, the action of putting the seal is also mentioned in it. This procedure of reference to action taken seems to be characteristic for early periods of sense constitution in law where everything must be explained because law is only emerging. Our short commentary is obviously influenced by the English translation, its presumably anachronistic language, spelling etc. The legal linguist shall never work with translations alone; we take here the risk of linguistic misconception in order to show that textual forms such as contracts to which we frequently refer in the main text of this book are deeply rooted in the history of linguistic conceptualization.

(5) Valerius Probus' *De Juris Notarum*

Valerius Probus' note on legal abbreviations is known in the classical literature under the heading *De Juris Notarum.* It consists of a short note of a few lines quoted below and a list of abbreviations with their explications.

Valerii Probi DE JURIS NOTARUM

1.- Est etiam circa prescribendas vel paucioribus litteris notandas voces studiorum necessarium. Quod partim pro voluntate cujusque fit, partim pro usu publico et observatione communi. Namque apud veteres cum usus notarum nullus esset, propter scribendi difficultatem, maxime in senatu qui scribendo aderant, ut celeriter dicta comprehenderent, quaedam verba atque nomina ex communi consensu primis litteris notabant, et singulae litterae quid significarent, in promptu erat. Quod in praenominibus legibus publicis pontificumque monumentis et in juris civilis libris etiam nunc manet. Ad quas notationes publicas accedit etiam studiosorum voluntas. Sed unusquisque familiares sibi notas pro voluntate quas signarit, comprehendere infinitum est: publicae sane tenendae, quae in monumentis plurimis et in historiarum libris sacrisque publicis reperiuntur, ut: ...

(in : F. Girard (1923): Textes de droit romain)

(6) Aulus Gellius on legal vocabulary

Auli Gellii Noctes Atticae Liber XVI :

V. Vestibulum quid significet; deque eius vocabuli rationibus...

III. C. Aelius Gallus in libro de significatione verborum, quae ad ius civile pertinent, secundo vestibulum esse dicit non in ipsis aedibus neque partem aedium, sed locum ante ianuam domus vacuum, per quem a via aditus accessusque ad aedis est, cum dextra sinistraque ianuam tectaque sunt viae iuncta atque ipsa ianua procul a via est area vacanti intersita.

(7) Aulus Gellius on legal education

Auli Gellii Noctes Atticae Liber XIII :

XIII. Quod in libris humanarum M. Varronis scriptum est aediles et quaestores populi Romani in ius a privato ad praetorem vocari posse. I. Cum ex angulis secretisque librorum ac magistrorum in medium iam hominum et in lucem fori prodissem, quaesitum esse memini in plerisque Romae stationibus ius publice docentium aut respondentium, an quaestor populi Romani ad praetorem in ius vocari posset.

(8) A legal text in Old English

The text in Old English which follows and in which king Alfred describes the circumstances and the motivation why he let collect the ancient laws and ordered them to be written down, makes plain that no new laws have been instituted by the king but rather a selection was preferred where the most suitable laws were collected and other ancient laws discarded. The translation of this text into modern English is provided in Hiltunen (1990: 22).

Old English: Ic đa Aelfred cyning Þas togaedere gegaderode awritan het, monege Þara Þe ure foregengan heoldon, đa đe me locodon; manege Þara Þe me ne licodon ic awearp mid minra witena geđeahte, on ođre wisan bebead to healdanne. Forđam ic ne dorste geđristlaecan Þara minra awuht fela on gewrit settan, forđam me waes uncuđ, hwaet Þaes đam lician wolde đe aefter us waeren. Ac đa đe ic gemette awđer ođđe on Ines daege, mines maeges, ođđe on Offan, Mercna cyninges ođđe on Aelelbryhtes, Þe aerest fulluhte onfeng on Angelkynne, Þa đe me ryhtoste đuhton, ic Þa heron gegaderode, Þa ođre forlet.

(in: Whitelock, D. (1979: 49, 9) (ed.): English Historical Documents, vol. I (London: Eyre Methuen).

(9) Promissory note in English and Hawaiian

Legal terminology is introduced into languages that did not develop any specific legal language in the sense of the Western legal culture through neologisms and descriptions. The following text of a promissory note displays such translation problems from English into Hawaiian in 1917. The unequal length of both texts signalizes that many terms of the English text have been described in the Hawaiian translation, e.g. the term *promissory note* is rendered by a lengthy *he palapala hooia e uku aku.*

Promissory note, Honolulu, May 20, 1917

Twelve month after date, I promise to pay Henry Philip, the sum of One Hundert Dollars, with interest at 1 per cent, per month, value received.

John Kapena

He Palapala Hooia e Uku Aku, Honolulu, Mei 20, 1917

He umikumamalua malama mahope aku o keia la, ke hooia nei au e uku aku ia Hanale Pilipo, i na Kala Hookahi Haneli, me ka ukupanee ma ka 1 pakeneka no ka malama, no ka waiwai i loaa mai.

Ioane Kapena

(10) Excerpts from Japan's Constitutions

The Occidentalization of the Japanese legal language and its law is manifest in text samples from the different Constitutions of Japan which are in terms of language and legal thought typical for the different time periods in which they emerged (cf. Upham 1990: 304):

(1889)

Art. I The Empire of Japan shall be reigned over and governed by a line of Emperors unbroken for ages eternal.

Art. III The Emperor is sacred and inviolable.

(1908)

A. The prerogatives of the monarch

1. The Ta Ch'ing Emperor will rule supreme over the Ta Ch'ing Empire for one thousand generations in succession and be honored forever.

(1947)

Art. 1 The Emperor shall be the symbol of the State and of the unity of the people, deriving his position from the will of the people with whom resides sovereign power.

Art. 3 The advice and approval of the cabinet shall be required for all acts of the Emperor in matters of State, and the Cabinet shall be responsible therefore.

Art. 4 The Emperor shall perform only such acts in matters of State as are provided for in this Constitution and he shall not have powers related to government.

(11) Examples of legal definitions

Definitions are in terms of the text analysis akin to generalization and conceptualization (cf. Rimmon-Kenan 1989: 60). They may occasionally illustrate the process of gradual emergence of a concept rather than provide the final result. The static impression which the authoritative legal definitions usually provide is alleviated by the process of defining which is shown in the definition. The definition below is illustrative of such a procedure. It is also quoted and commented by Mattila (2006: 68).

The legal definition of *house* in the (UK) Leasehold Reform Act (1967):

2. Meaning of "House" and "House and Premises", and Adjustment of Boundary.-

(1) For purposes of this Part of this Act, "house" includes any building designated or adapted for living and reasonably so called, notwithstanding that the building is not structurally detached, or was or is not solely designed or adapted for living in, or is divided horizontally into flats or maisonettes; and –
(a) where a building is divided horizontally, the flats or other units into which it is so divided are not separate "houses", though the building as a whole may be; and
(b) where a building is divided vertically the building as a whole is not a "house" though any of the units into which it is divided may be.

(2) References in this Part of this Act to a house do not apply to a house which is not structurally detached and of which a material part lays above or below a part of the structure not comprised in the house.

(3) Subject to the following provisions of this section, where in relation to a house let to and occupied by a tenant reference is made in this Part of this Act to the house and premises, the reference to premises is to be taken as referring to any garage, outhouse, garden, yard and appurtenances which at the relevant time are let to him with the house and are occupied with and used for the purposes of the house or any part of it by him or by another occupant.

(4) In relation to the exercise by a tenant of any right conferred by this Part of this Act there shall be treated as included in the house and premises any other premises let with the house and premises but not (...)

The classical definition such as the one below does not illustrate the way in which it came about. The defining as such is a semiotic process which took place before the final text was put on paper. It provides, therefore, a rational and authoritative impression of a final and supra-temporal generalization. In order to facilitate the interpretation of the general concept of *security* the definition below proceeds by presentation of examples. It comes close to indirect presentation of *security* rather than to an abstract description *per genus et differentiam*. In its attempt to create an abstract and general concept it stops half way; cf. the definition of *security* in Sec. 2 (1) of the (U.S.) Securities Act of 1933:

Any note, stock or similar security, certificate of interest or participation in any profit sharing agreement, pre-organization certificate or subscription, transferable share, voting trust certificate or certificate of deposit for an equity security, limited partnership interest, interest in a joint venture, or certificate of interest in a business trust; or any security convertible, with or without consideration into such a security, or carrying any warrant or right to subscribe to or purchase such a security; or any such warrant or right; or any put, call, straddle, or other option or privilege of buying such a security from or selling such a security to another without being bound to do so.

Examples in definitions may occasionally impede upon the readability of texts, cf. the definition of *discrimination* under ADA § 12182(b)(2)(A)(ii):

A failure to make reasonable modifications in policies, practices, or procedures, when such modifications are necessary to afford such goods, services, facilities, privileges, advantages, or accommodations to individuals with disabilities, unless the entity can demonstrate that making such modifications would fundamentally alter the nature of such goods, services, facilities, privileges, advantages, or accomodations.

The Italian legislator, in turn, deals specifically with the definition of *window* in Artt. 900 sqq of the Codice civile. The linguistic operation in question is classical defining through creation *per genus et differentiam*:

Art 900. Specie di finestre. – Le finestre o altre apperture sul fondo del vicino sono di due specie. Luci, quando danno passaggio alla luce e all'aria, ma non permettono di affacciarsi sul fondo del vicino; vedute o prospetti, quando permettono di affacciarsi e di guardare di fronte, obliquamente o lateralmente.

Art. 901. Luci. – Le luci che si aprono sul fondo del vicino devono: (1) essere munite di un'inferriata idonea a garantire la sicurezza del vicino e di una grata fissa in metallo le cui maglie non siano maggiori di tre centimetri quadrati; (2) avere un lato inferiore a un'altezza non minore di due metri e mezzo dal pavimento o dal suole del luogo al quale si vuole dare luce e aria, se esse sono al piano terreno, e non minore di due metri se sono ai piani superiori; (3) avere il lato inferiore a un'altezza non minore di due metri e mezzo dal suolo del fondo vicino, a meno che se tratti di locale che sia in tutto o in parte a livello inferiore al suolo del vicino e la condizione dei luoghi non consenta di osservare l'altezza stessa.

Moreover, also the *enterprise*, (IT) *azienda* is defined by the Italian legislator in the classical sense: Art. 2555. Nozione. – L'azienda è il complesso dei beni organizzati dall'imprenditore per l'esercizio dell'impresa.

(12) A translation from Turkish into 'German'

The following text, published August 9, 2001 in the German newspaper *Hamburger Abendblatt* could be characterized as an attempt to translate a Turkish court decree into legal German. The linguistic errors are not marked in it due to their overburdening number; the initial asterisk marks therefore the general quality of this linguistic experiment. The text as such is nevertheless understandable and is clearly identifiable as representing a legal text type. The Turkish court wishes to communicate through its decree to the defendant who is presumably residing in Germany that her marriage was dissoluted in Turkey and that she can appeal against this decision within 15 days counted from the day of publication. The text is apparently binding in terms of law because its legally relevant sense is intelligible also to a layperson with some effort. For purposes of the below quotation, family names that are rendered in full in the decree were reduced to initials, also some addresses were omitted as irrelevant.

(*) Republik Turkei

Karakoçan

Juristischerechtgericht

Grund Nr. : 1997/126

Urteil Nr. : 2000/30

Ankläger : Ziyattin D., Sohn von Şeyho und Hanife, 1967 geb. Karakoçan, Elaziğ/Karakoçan-Bazlamköyü gemeldet.

Vertreter : Rae. Aziz K., A. Cad. Nr: 137/a Karakocan

Beklagterin : Adriane M…, Tochter von Roswit, 1969 geboren

Klage Art : Von heftigen Ehestreit Scheidung.

Klagedatum: 29.07.1997

Urteildatum: 22.03.2000

Durch den Vertreter von Ankläger gegen die Beklagterin gegebene Scheidungsantrag, das Gericht hat zwischen den Parteien haben heftigen Ehestreit. Nach dem Zivilgesetz (M.K.) 134/1 das Gericht hat die Parteien scheiden gelassen. Die Adresse von Beklagterin ist unbekannt, das Gerichtsurteil konnte an sie nicht mitteilen können, darum die Mitteilung durch öffentliche Bekanntmachung Urteil gegeben. Die Frist von öffentlichen Bekanntmachung von 15 Tagen und nicht Widerspruchseinlegung, das Gerichtsurteil wurde rechtskräftig gerechnet und mitteilen. 24.05.2000

Stempel und Unterschrift

Richter-34006

(13) Abbreviated language of a German code

The Palandt Commentary to the German Civil Code, (D) *BGB Kommentar*, is written in an abbreviated language. In the connotation to Article 29 BGB abbreviations of legal terms and words belonging to the ordinary langage are used in order to save space. As a result, the text is readable only for jurists and persons with full command of the German language because many words must be reconstructed out of the context of their use. The connotation is provided below in the original quote and, subsequently, with the transformation of the abbreviations into the full text with deciphered abbreviations.

Original text of Sec. 29 BGB:

Fassg des RPflG 1957. Zust is das AG, das gem § 55 das Vereinsregister führt. § 29 ist, sow keine SonderVorschr bestehen, auf alle JP des PriR anwedb, so auf die GmbH, Genossensch, bergrechtl Gewerksch, wg Akt 85 nicht auf die AktGes.

Full text in German:

Fassung des Rechtspflegergesetzes 1957. Zuständig ist das Amtsgericht, das gemäß § 55 das Vereinsregister führt. § 29 ist, soweit keine Sondervorschriften bestehen, auf alle juristischen Personen des Privatrechts anwendbar, so auf die GmbH, die Genossenschaft, die bergrechtliche Gewerkschaft, wegen § 85 Aktiengesetz jedoch nicht auf die Aktiengesellschaft.

(14) Italian *massime di giurisprudenza*

Italian synthetic versions of court decisions (IT. *massime di giurisprudenza*) are frequently worded in over-long phrases, e.g.:

(a) Nel caso di danno cagionato dall'alunno a se stesso, la responsabilità dell'istituto scolastico e dell'insegnante non ha natura extracontrattuale, bensì contrattuale, atteso che – quanto all'istituto scolastico – l'accoglimento della domanda di iscrizione, con la conseguente ammissione dell'allievo alla scuola, determina l'instaurazione di un vincolo negoziale, dal quale sorge a carico dell'istituto l'obbligazione di vigilare sulla sicurezza e l'incolumità dell'allievo nel tempo in cui questi fruisce della prestazione scolastica in tutte le sue espressioni, anche al fine di evitare che l'allievo procuri danno a se stesso; e che – quanto al precetto- re dipendente dell'istituto scolastico – tra insegnante e allievo si instaura, per contratto sociale, un rapporto giuridico, nell'ambito del quale l'insegnante assume, nel quadro del complessivo obbligo di istruire ed educare, anche uno specifico obbligo di protezione e vigilanza, onde evitare che l'allievo si procuri da solo un danno alla persona. (*Supreme Court of Italy, June 27, 2002*)

(b) La responsabilità nei confronti del beneficiario di un assegno circolare non trasferibile in cui incorre la banca girataria per l'incasso qualora, violando l'obbligo di diligente accertamento dell'identità e della legittimazione del presentatore del titolo, paghi l'assegno a persona diversa dal predetto (artt. 43 ed 86 del r.d.n. 1736 del 1933), non ha natura né extracontrattuale, in quanto non consegue dalla violazione di una norma di condotta, né contrattuale, poiché non sussiste tra dette parti alcun rapporto negoziale, dato che detta banca è estranea sia alla convenzione di assegno sia al rapporto di emissione del medesimo, bensì constituisce violazione di un'obbligazione “ex lege”, riconducibile, in base all'art. 1173 c.c. ad ogni altro atto o fatto idoneo a costituire fonte di obbligazione in conformità dell'ordinamento giuridico, siccome derivante dalla violazione dell'obbligo posto a suo carico dall'art. 43 r.d. cit., di pagare l'assegno esclusivamente all'intestatario, titolare del diritto di agire per il risarcimento del danno eventualmente subito, con la conseguenza che siffatto diritto è soggetto alla prescrizione ordinaria decennale. (*Supreme Court of Italy, October 6, 2005*)

(c) Mentre la convenzione contenente una promessa di attribuzione di propri beni a titolo gratuito configura un contratto preliminare di donazione che è nullo, in quanto con esso si viene a costituire a carico del promittente un vincolo giuridico a donare, il quale si pone in contrasto con il principio secondo cui nella donazione l'arricchimento del beneficiario deve avvenire per spirito di libertà, in virtù cioè di un atto di autodeterminazione del donante, assolutamente libero nella sua formazione; diverso è, invece, il caso in cui un coniuge, in sede di separazione consensuale, assume l'obbligo nei confronti dell'altro coniuge di provvedere al mantenimento del figlio minore, impegnandosi a tal fine a trasferirgli un bene immobile, ponendo in essere con il detto coniuge un contratto preliminare a favore del figlio, con la conseguenza che l'atto scritto con cui il coniuge obbligato, in esecuzione di tale contratto, dichiara di trasferire al figlio quel bene, essendo privo dello spirito di liberalità, non configura una donazione, ma una proposta di contratto unilaterale gratuito e atipico, che, ai sensi dell'art.1333 c.c., in mancanza del rifiuto del destinatario in un termine adeguato (alla natura dell'affare o stabilito dagli usi), determina l'irrevocabilità della proposta e quindi la conclusione del contratto, nonostante che la volontà di accettazione non risulti da atto scritto, dovendosi ritenere assolto l'obbligo della forma attraverso le modalità con cui è stata formulata la proposta. (*Court of Appeals, Rome, June 15, 2005*)

(15) A. M. Honoré on the way how people speak and write

A.M. Honoré, Real Laws, in: P.M.S. Hacker and J. Raz (eds.) Law, Morality and Society (Oxford, 1977: 117):

In the balmy days of the 1950s Hart was a central and I a peripheral figure in the movement called 'linguistic philosophy' which has since passed from fashion but from which lawyers can still learn much. We learned to pay precise attention to the way people speak and write. We repeated to ourselves and to anyone who would listen to the salutary maxim that everything is what it is and not something else.

(16) Excerpts from the CISG

United Nations Convention on Contracts for the International Sale of Goods

Article 1

(1) This Convention applies to contracts of sale of goods between parties whose place of business are in different States:...

(2) The fact that the parties have their places of business in different States is to be disregarded whenever this fact does not appear either from the contract or from any dealings between, or from information disclosed by, the parties at any time before or at the conclusion of the contract.

(3) Neither the nationality of the parties nor the civil or commercial character of the parties or of the contract is to be taken into consideration in determining the application of this Convention.

Article 3

(2) This Convention does not apply to contracts in which the preponderant part of the obligation of the party who furnishes the goods consists in the supply of labour or other services.

Article 4

This Convention governs only the formation of the contract of sale and the rights and obligations of the seller and buyer arising from such a contract.

Article 7

(1) In the interpretation of this Convention, regard is to be had to its international character and to the need to promote uniformity in its application and the observance of good faith in international trade.

Article 8

(2) If the preceding paragraph is not applicable, statements made by and other conduct of a party are to be interpreted according to the understanding that a reasonable person of the same kind as the other party would have had in the same circumstances.

(3) In determining the intent of a party or the understanding a reasonable person would have had, due consideration is to be given to all relevant circumstances of the case including the negotiations, any practices which the parties have established between themselves, usages and any subsequent conduct of the parties.

Article 18

(1) A statement made by or other contract of the offeree indicating assent to an offer is an acceptance. Silence or inactivity does not in itself amount to acceptance.

Article 20

(2) Official holidays or non-business days occurring during the period for acceptance are included in calculating the period.

Article 24

For the purposes of this Part of the Convention, an offer, declaration of acceptance or any other indication of intention "reaches" the addressee when it is made orally to him or delivered by any other means to him personally, to his place of business or mailing address or, if he does not have a place of business or mailing address, to his habitual residence.

Article 38

(3) If the goods are redirected in transit or redispatched by the buyer without a reasonable opportunity for examination by him and at the time of the conclusion of the contract the seller knew or ought to have known of the possibility of such redirection or redispatch, examination may be deferred until after the goods have arrived at the new destination.

Article 43

(2) The seller is not entitled to rely on the provisions of the preceding paragraph if he knew of the right or claim of the third party and the nature of it.

Article 80

A party may not rely on a failure of the other party to perform, to the extent that such failure was caused by the first party's act or omission.

(17) Excerpts from the UCC

Uniform Commercial Code (2000 Official Text), Article 2:

2-101 Short Title. This Article shall be known and may be cited as Uniform Commercial Code – Sales.

2-301 General Obligations of Parties. The obligation of the seller is to transfer and deliver and that of the buyer is to accept and pay in accordance with the contract.

2-316 Exclusion or Modification of Warranties.

(1) Words or conduct relevant to the creation of an express warranty and words or conduct tending to negate or limit warranty shall be construed wherever reasonable as consistent with each other, but subject to the provisions of this Article on parol or extrinsic evidence (Section 2-202) negation or limitation is inoperative to the extent that such construction is unreasonable.

(3) Notwithstanding subsection (2)

(a) unless the circumstances indicate otherwise, all implied warranties are excluded by expression like "as is", "with all faults" or other language which in common understanding calls the buyer's attention to the exclusion of warranties and makes plain that there is no implied warranty; and...

2-711 Buyer's Remedies in General; Buyer's Security Interest in Rejected Goods.

(1) Where the seller fails to make delivery...the buyer may...

(a) "cover" and have damages under the next section as to all the goods affected whether or not they have been identified to the contract; or

2-712 "Cover"; Buyer's Procurement of Substitute Goods.

(1) After a breach within the preceding section the buyer may "cover" by making in good faith and without unreasonable delay any reasonable purchase of or contract to purchase goods in substitution for those due from the seller.

(3) Failure of the buyer to effect cover within this section does not bar him from any other remedy.

2-305 Open Price Term.

(2) A price to be fixed by the seller or by the buyer means a price for him to fix in good faith.

(3) When a price left to be fixed otherwise than by agreement of the parties fails to be fixed through fault of one party the other party may at his option treat the contract as cancelled or himself fix a reasonable price.

(18) Statutory provisions (Truth in Music Advertising Act)

The statute rendered below has been prepared for publication by the Office of the Revisor of Statutes of the U.S. State of Maine in September 2007. The text begins with the characterization of the statute by the staff of the Office as belonging to public law. Technical details which enable to incorporate the statute into the collection of Maine laws are included as well. Following the American legislative tradition the statute has a long name (*An Act to Ensure Truth in Music Advertising*) and a short one (*The Truth in Music Advertising Act*) which is usually quoted in court decisions and in research papers. The text ends with the indication of the day on which the statute enters into force. The text including the Maine statute reads as follows:

Public Law

123rd Legislature

First Regular Session

Chapter 171

H.P. 517 – L.D. 686

An Act to Ensure Truth in Music Advertising

Be it enacted by the People of the State of Maine as follows:

Sec. 1.10 MRSA c. 202-E is enacted to read :

CHAPTER 202-E

TRUTH IN MUSIC ADVERTISING

§ 1156. **Short title**

This chapter is known and may be cited as "the Truth in Music Advertising Act."

§ 1157. **Definitions**

As used in this chapter, unless the context otherwise indicates, the following terms have the following meanings.

1. **Performing group.** "Performing group" means a vocal or instrumental group seeking to use the name of another group that has previously released a commercial sound recording under that name.

2. **Person.** "Person" means any individual, partnership, corporation or association.

3. **Recording group.** "Recording group" means a vocal or instrumental group at least one of whose members has previously released a commercial sound recording under that group's name and in which the member has a legal right by virtue of use or operation under the group name without having abandoned the name or affiliation with the group.

4. **Sound recording.** "Sound recording" means a work that results from the fixation on a material object, such as a disc, tape or other phonorecord, in which the sounds are embodied.

§ 1158. **Production**

A person may not promote, advertise or conduct a live musical performance or production in this State through the use of a false, deceptive or misleading affiliation, connection or association between a performing group and a recording group unless:

1. **Authorized; federal service mark.** The performing group is the authorized registrant and owner of a federal service mark for that group registered in the United States Patent and Trademark Office;

2. **Legal right.** At least one member of the performing group was a member of the recording group and has a legal right by virtue of use or operation under the group name without having abandoned the name or affiliation with the group;

3. **Salute or tribute.** The live musical performance or production is identified in all advertising and promotion as a salute or tribute and the name of the performing group is not so closely related or similar to the name used by the recording group that it would tend to confuse or mislead the public; and

4. **Expressly authorized.** The performance or production is expressly authorized by the recording group

§ 1159. **Restraining prohibited acts**

1. **Injunction.** Whenever the Attorney General or a district attorney has reason to believe that a person is promoting, advertising or conducting or is preparing to promote, advertise or conduct a live musical performance or production in violation of section 1158 and that proceedings would be in the public interest, the Attorney General or district attorney may bring an action in the name of the State against the person to restrain that practice by temporary or permanent injunction.

2. **Payment of costs and restitution.** Whenever any court issues a permanent injunction to restrain and prevent violations of this chapter as authorized in subsection 1, the court may in its discretion direct that the defendant restore to the recording group any money or property, real or personal, that has been acquired by means of any violation of this chapter, under terms and conditions to be established by the court.

§ 1160. **Penalty**

In addition to any other relief that may be granted under section 1159, a person who violates section 1158 commits a civil violation for which a fine of not less than $500 per violation may be adjudged. Each performance or production advertised or conducted in violation of section 1158 constitutes a separate violation.

§ 1160-A. **Exemption**

This chapter does not apply to any nonprofit corporation incorporated under the laws of this State and subject to the provisions of Title 13, chapter 81 or 93 of the Maine Nonprofit Corporation Act.

Effective September 20, 2007

(19) French, Italian, German and international statutory provisions on interpretation

The French Civil Code includes in its Articles 1156 – 1164 provisions about the interpretation of contracts:

De l'interprétation des conventions.

Art. 1156 On doit dans les conventions rechercher quelle a été la commune intention des parties contractantes, plutôt que de s'arrêter au sens littéral des termes.

Art. 1157 Lorsqu'une clause est susceptible de deux sens, on doit plutôt l'entendre dans celui avec lequel elle peut avoir quelque effet, que dans le sens avec lequel elle n'en pourrait produire aucun.

Art. 1158 Les termes susceptibles de deux sens doivent être pris dans le sens qui convient le plus à la matière du contrat.

Art. 1159 Ce qui est ambigu s'interprète par ce qui est d'usage dans le pays où le contrat est passé.

Art. 1160 On doit suppléer dans le contrat les clauses qui y sont d'usage, quoiqu'elles n'y soient pas exprimées.

Art. 1161 Toutes les clauses des conventions s'interprètent les unes par les autres, en donnant à chacune le sens qui résulte de l'acte entier.

Art. 1162 Dans la doute, la convention s'interprète contre celui qui a stipulé et en faveur de celui qui a contracté l'obligation.

Art. 1163 Quelque généraux que soient les termes dans lesquels une convention est conçue, elle ne comprend que les choses sur lesquelles il paraît que les parties se sont proposé de contracter.

Art. 1164 Lorsque dans un contrat on a exprimé un cas pour l'explication de l'obligation, on n'est pas censé avoir voulu par là restreindre l'étendue que l'engagement reçoit aux cas non exprimés.

The Italian Civil Code provides numerous and explicit provisions regarding the interpretation of legal provisions and the interpretation in law:

Art. 12. Interpretazione della legge. (1) – Nell'applicare la legge non si può ad essa attribuire altro senso che quello fatto palese dal significato proprio delle parole secondo la connessione di esse, e dalla intenzione del legislatore.

Se una controversia non può essere decisa con una precisa disposizione, si ha riguardo alle disposizioni che regolano casi simili o materie analoghe; se il caso rimane ancora dubbio, si decide secondo i principi generali dell'ordinamento giuridico dello Stato.

Capo IV *Dell'interpretazione del contratto*

Art. 1362. Intenzione dei contraenti. – Nell'interpretare il contratto si deve indagare quale sia stata la comune intenzione delle parti e non limitarsi al senso letterale delle parole.

Per determinare la comune intenzione delle parti, si deve valutare il loro comportamento complessivo anche posteriore alla conclusione del contratto.

Art. 1363. Interpretazione complessiva delle clausole. – Le clausole del contratto si interpretano le une per mezzo delle altre, attribuendo a ciascuna il senso che risulta dal complesso dell'atto.

Art. 1364. Espressioni generali. Per quanto generali siano le espressioni usate nel contratto, questo non comprende che gli oggetti sui quali le parti si sono proposte di contrattare.

Art. 1365. Indicazioni esemplificative. Quando in un contratto si è espresso un caso al fine di spiegare un patto, non si presumono esclusi i casi non espressi, ai quali, secondo ragione, può estendersi lo stesso patto.

Art. 1366. Interpretazione di buona fede. – Il contratto deve essere interpretato secondo buona fede.

Art. 1367. Conservazione del contratto. – Nel dubbio, il contratto o le singole clausole devono interpretarsi nel senso in cui possono avere qualche effetto, anziché in quello secondo cui non ne avrebbero alcuno.

Art. 1368. Pratiche generali interpretative. – Le clausole ambigue s'interpretano secondo ciò che si pratica generalmente nel luogo in cui il contratto è stato concluso.

Nei contratti in cui una delle parti è un imprenditore, le clausole ambigue s'interpretano secondo ciò che si pratica generalmente nel luogo in cui è la sede dell'impresa.

Art. 1369. Espressioni con più sensi. – Le clausole inserite nelle condizioni generali di contratto o in moduli o formulari predisposti da uno dei contraenti s'interpretano, nel dubbio, a favore dell'altro.

Art. 1370. Regole finali. – Qualora, nonostante l'applicazione delle norme contenute in questo capo, il contratto rimanga oscuro, esso deve essere inteso nel senso meno gravoso per l'obbligato, se è a titolo gratuito, e nel senso che realizzi l'equo contemperamento degli interessi delle parti, se è a titolo oneroso.

The Italian Law on the Conflict of Laws (L. 31 maggio 1995, n. 218) includes following interpretive provisions:

2. Convenzioni internazionali. - 1. Le disposizioni della presenta legge non pregiudicano l'applicazione delle convenzioni internazionali in vigore per l'Italia - 2. Nell'interpretazione di tali convenzioni si terrà conto del loro carattere internazionale e dell'esigenza della loro applicazione uniforme.

15. Interpretazione e applicazione della legge straniera. - 1. La legge straniera è applicata secondo i propri criteri di interpretazione e di applicazione nel tempo.

The German civil code (BGB) also includes analogous interpretive regulations:

Art. 133 BGB Auslegung einer Willenserklärung – Bei der Auslegung der Willenserklärung ist der wirkliche Wille zu erforschen und nicht an dem buchstäblichen Sinne des Ausdrucks zu haften.

Art. 157 BGB Auslegung von Verträgen – Verträge sind so auszulegen, wie Treu und Glauben mit Rücksicht auf die Verkehrssitten es erfordern.

Some international instruments such as the UNIDROIT Principles, CISG or PECL also include provisions concerning interpretation:

UNIDROIT Principles of International Commercial Contracts (1994), Chapter 4 - Interpretation:

Art. 4.1 – Intention of the parties

1. A contract shall be interpreted according to the common intention of the parties.

2. If such an intention cannot be established, the contract shall be interpreted according to the meaning that reasonable persons of the same kind as the parties would give to it in the same circumstances.

Art. 4.2 – Interpretation of statements and other conduct

1. The statements and other conduct of a party shall be interpreted according to that party's intention if the other party knew or could not have been unaware of that intention.

2. If the preceding paragraph is not applicable, such statements and other conduct shall be interpreted according to the meaning that a reasonable person of the same kind as the other party would give to it in the same circumstances.

Art. 4.3. – Relevant circumstances

In applying Articles 4.1. and 4.2. regard shall be had to all circumstances, including:

(a) preliminary negotiations between the parties;

(b) practices which the parties have established between themselves;

(c) the conduct of the parties subsequent to the conclusion of the contract;

(d) the nature and the purpose of the contract;

(e) the meaning commonly given to terms and expressions in the trade concerned;

(f) usages

Art. 4.4. – Reference to contract or statement as a whole

Terms and expressions shall be interpreted in the light of the whole contract or statement in which they appear.

Art. 4.5 – All terms to be given effect

Contracts shall be interpreted so as to give effect to all terms rather than to deprive some of them of effect.

Art. 4.6 – Contra proferentem rule

If contract terms supplied by one party are unclear, an interpretation against that party is preferred.

Art. 4.7 – Linguistic discrepancies

Where a contract is drawn up in two or more language versions which are equally authoritative there is, in case of discrepancy of the versions, a preference for the interpretation according to a version in which the contract was originally drawn up.

Art. 4.8 – Supplying an omitted term

1. Where the parties to a contract have not agreed with respect to a term which is important for a determination of their rights and duties, a term which is appropriate in the circumstances shall be supplied.

2. In determining what is an appropriate term regard shall be had, among other factors, to:
(a) the intention of the parties;
(b) the nature and purpose of the contract;
(c) good faith and fair dealing;
(d) reasonableness.

Art. 7 CISG: In the interpretation of this Convention, regard is to be had to its international character and to the need to promote uniformity in its application and the observance of good faith in international trade.

The PECL include in chapter V *Interpretation* following provisions regarding contract interpretation:

Art. 5: 101: *General Rules of Interpretation*

(1) A contract is to be interpreted according to the common intention of the parties even if this differs from the literal meaning of the words.

(2) If it is established that one party intended the contract to have a particular meaning, and at the time of the conclusion of the contract the other party could not have been unaware of the first party's intention, the contract is to be interpreted in the way intended by the first party.

(3) If an intention cannot be established according to (1) or (2), the contract is to be interpreted according to the meaning that reasonable persons of the same kind as the parties would give to it in the same circumstances.

Art. 5: 102: *Relevant Circumstances*

In interpreting the contract, regard shall be had, in particular, to:
(a) the circumstances in which it was concluded, including the preliminary negotiations;
(b) the conduct of the parties, even subsequent to the conclusion of the contract;

(c) the nature and purpose of the contract;

(d) the interpretation which has already been given to similar clauses by the parties and the practices they have established between themselves;

(e) the meaning commonly given to terms and expressions in the branch of activity concerned and the interpretation similar clauses may already have received;

(f) usages, and

(g) good faith and fair dealing.

Art. 5: 103: *Contra Proferentem Rule*

Where there is doubt about the meaning of a contract term not individually negotiated, an interpretation of the term against the party who supplied it is to be preferred.

Art. 5:104: *Preference to Negotiated Terms*

Terms which have been individually negotiated take preference over those which are not.

Art. 5: 105: *Reference to Contract as a Whole*

Terms are to be interpreted in the light of the whole contract in which they appear.

Art. 5: 106: *Terms to Be Given Effect*

An interpretation which renders the terms of the contract lawful, or effective, is to be preferred to one which would not.

Art. 5: 107: *Linguistic Discrepancies*

Where a contract is drawn up in two or more language versions none of which is stated to be authoritative, there is, in case of discrepancy between the versions, a preference for the interpretation according to the version in which the contract was originally drawn up.

(20) French governmental instruction on counting paragraphs in legislative drafts

A French governmental instruction dating from 2000 regulates the mode in which paragraphs in legal texts should be counted. It has been issued, according to its declared *raison d'être,* in order to harmonize and to simplify the structure of legal texts. However, the Secretary General of the Government in charge of this instruction self-critically invokes the risk that through new formal measures such as the one reprinted below the texts may not become easier to draft or to grasp.

Therefore, the instruction illustrates rather the problem of formalized measures aiming at structuring the legal texts. In the main text of this research language use strategies have been favored to the detriment of such formal, if not formalistic, rules. The instruction stresses in the last phrase of its sec. 5 the strategy to express in an article only one rule and not to overburden it with paragraphs. Such strategic rules are more efficient when introduced in a coherent body of rules about legislative drafting. Despite the efforts undertaken in the instruction, the impression comes up that it replaces one formal system by another and that it does not improve the overall quality of legislative texts. It goes without saying that a certain order in the drafting of legal text or in the usage of abbreviations in them is absolutely necessary. However, from the legal-linguistic point of view it is the approach taken to these issues which is decisive. The Legal Linguistics cannot support blind approaches which ground in mechanistic development and application of formalized rules for the drafting of legal texts. Rules for language use in texts which convey orders must be embodied in general strategies of language use in the social sphere in which they emerge and are applied. When this is not the case, new rules remain ineffective or are perceived, at best, in a comical perspective.

Circulaire du 20 octobre 2000 relative au mode de décompte des alinéas lors de l'élaboration des textes

J.O. n° 253 du 31 oct. 2000, p. 17302.

Le secrétaire général du Gouvernement à Mesdames et Messieurs les ministres et secrétaires d'Etat.

Référence : circulaire du 30 janvier 1997 relative aux règles d'élaboration, de signature et de publication des textes au Journal officiel et à la mise en œuvre de procédures particulières incombant au Premier ministre.

1. Le Parlement et le Gouvernement utilisaient jusqu'ici des règles différentes pour décompter les alinéas composant un article de loi ou de décret. Les assemblées parlementaires ont pour usage de compter come un alinéa tout mot ou ensemble de mots qui commencent à la ligne, alors même qu'ils ne constituent pas, à eux seuls, une phrase, et quels que soient les signes de ponctuation dont ils sont précédés. De son côté, le Gouvernement avait fait sien le mode de computation préconisé par le Conseil d'Etat. Selon ce dernier, il n'y avait lieu de compter un nouvel alinéa que lors de chaque passage à la ligne faisant suite à un point. A contrario, étaient regardés comme la suite du même alinéa les termes venant après une phrase introductive qui étaient renvoyés à la ligne, soit qu'ils constituent les éléments d'une énumération, soit que, placés entre guillemets, ils fussent destinés à s'insérer dans un autre texte.

2. Ce double décompte était peu satisfaisant, à deux égards. D'une part, dans le cas des projets de loi comportant des renvois à des alinéas, il conduisait à une modification systématique, lors du passage devant la première assemblée saisie, du texte préparé par le Gouvernement. D'autre part, l'existence d'une dualité de règles, selon que le texte était de forme législative ou réglementaire, n'était pas de nature à faciliter la consultation des textes et l'accès à la règle de droit. Ce sont sans doute ces considérations qui ont récemment conduit le Conseil d'Etat à faire sien le mode de comptation utilisé par le Parlement.

3. Les administrations chargées de la préparation des textes doivent évidemment tirer sans tarder les conséquences de cette évolution, qui rend caduques les indications figurant au point 1.1.3.5. de la circulaire du 30 janvier 1997 susmentionnée.

Il conviendra donc, désormais, de compter pour un alinéa tout mot ou groupe de mots renvoyé à la ligne, sans qu'il y ait lieu d'établir des distinctions selon la nature du signe placé à la fin de la ligne précédente (point, deux-points ou point-virgule) ou au début de la ligne nouvelle (chiffre arabe ou romain, tiret, guillemets…).

Il va de soi que, dans un souci de simplicité, l'application de cette règle ne saurait être limitée aux seuls textes soumis au Conseil d'Etat. Vous en ferez usage pour l'ensemble des textes préparés par votre département ministériel, décrets, arrêtés ou circulaires.

4. La simplification ainsi obtenue trouve, il est vrai, ses limites dans le fait que coexisteront, dans le droit positif, des textes réglementaires appliquant l'une et l'autre décompte, selon la date à laquelle ils auront été adoptés.

Aussi est-il souhaitable qu'à l'occasion des modifications qui seraient apportées à un texte rédigé sous l'empire de l'ancienne règle, vous vous assuriez que sa lecture ne prête pas à la ambiguïté selon que l'on applique l'ancien ou le nouveau mode de décompte des alinéas. Si tel était le cas, il conviendrait de revoir cette rédaction, par example en recourant à la numérotation des dispositions auxquelles il est renvoyés.

En tout état de cause, vous veillerez à éviter la coexistence, au sein d'un même texte, de dispositions utilisant alternativement l'un et l'autre mode de décompte. Cette alternance pourrait d'autant plus dérouter le lecteur que l'ensemble des décrets devraient prochainement être mis à la disposition du public sous une forme consolidée, par le site Légifrance. S'agissant des dispositions dont l'ampleur est telle que ce travail de révision n'apparaît pas possible, notamment le code général des impôts et les codes dont la partie réglementaire a déjà été adoptée, vous vous efforcerez, à tout le moins, de rédiger les modifications à venir de telle sorte qu'il n'existe pas d'ambiguïté dans les renvois opérés.

5. Plus généralement, je vous invite, lorsque vous élaborez un texte procedant à des renvois, à n'utiliser qu'avec circonspection la notion d'alinéa. Cette technique de rédaction, s'il en est fait un usage trop libéral, rend la lecture du texte malcommode et peut, en outre, être à l'origine d'interrogations ou même d'erreurs sur l'exacte portée de ses dispositions.

Aussi vous efforcerez-vous d'agencer le contenu des articles de telle sorte que le renvoi à certaines des dispositions qui y sont contenues puisse se faire par référence à un chiffre ou une lettre. Par ailleurs, ces références à des parties d'articles peuvent être elles-mêmes plus souvent évités, grâce à une meilleure application du principe qui veut qu'un article ne contienne l'énoncé que d'une seule règle.

(21) Excerpts from OSCE Recomendations on Minority and Linguistic Rights

Excerpts from *The Hague Recommendations regarding Minority Education Rights*:

The spirit of international instruments

1) The right of persons belonging to national minorities to maintain their identity can only be fully realised if they acquire a proper knowledge of their mother tongue during the educational process. At the same time, persons belonging to national minorities have a responsibility to integrate into the wider national society through the acquisition of a proper knowledge of the State language.

2) In applying international instruments which may benefit persons belonging to national minorities, States should consistently adhere to the fundamental principles of equality and non-discrimination.

3) It should be borne in mind that the relevant international obligations and commitments constitute international minimum standards. It would be contrary to their spirit and intent to interpret these obligations and commitments in a restrictive manner.

....

Excerpts from *The Lund Recommendations on the Effective Participation of National Minorities in Public Life*:

General Principles

1) Effective participation of national minorities in public life is an essential component of a peaceful and democratic society. Experience in Europe and elsewhere has shown that, in order to promote such participation, governments often need to establish specific arrangements for national minorities. These Recommendations aim to facilitate the inclusion of minorities within the State and enable minorities to maintain their own identity and characteristics, thereby promoting the good governance and integrity of the State.

2) These Recommendations build upon fundamental principles and rules of international law, such as respect for human dignity, equal rights, and non-discrimination, as they affect the rights of national minorities to participate in public life and to enjoy other political rights. States have a duty to respect internationally recognized human rights and the rule of law, which allow for the full development of civil society in conditions of tolerance, peace and prosperity.

3) When specific institutions are established to ensure the effective participation of minorities in public life, which can include the exercise of authority or responsibility by such institutions, they must respect the human rights of all those affected.

4) Individuals identify themselves in numerous ways in addition to their identity as members of a national minority. The decision as to whether an individual is member of a minority, the majority, or neither rests with that individual and shall not be imposed upon her or him. Moreover, no person shall suffer any disadvantage as a result of such a choice or refusal to choose.

5) When creating institutions and procedures in accordance with these Recommendations, both substance and process are important. Governmental authorities and minorities should pursue an inclusive, transparent, and accountable process of consultation in order to maintain a climate of confidence. The State should encourage the public media to foster intercultural understanding and address the concerns of minorities.

…

(22) Structure of French court decisions (1)

Cour de Cassation (Ch. Civ. 1re sect. Civ.) 20 janvier 1964

(Dame Blum C. Dlle Lassus) – Arrêt

La Court ; - Sur le premier moyen, pris en sa première branche. – Vu l'art. 1382 c. civ.; - Attendu que l'exercice du droit de propriété, qui a pour limite la satisfaction d'un intérêt sérieux et légitime, ne saurait autoriser l'accomplissement d'actes malveillants, ne se justifiant par aucune utilité appréciable et portant préjudice à autrui ; - Attendu que la cour d'appel a refusé d'ordonner la suppression d'un rideau de fougères de 1,70 m de hauteur, planté par demoiselle Lassus, à environ 0,85 m du mur de la maison de dame Blum et empêchant le passage de la lumière par une ouverture à verre dormant dont l'aménagement avait été judiciairement autorisé pour l'éclairage d'une cuisine ; que pour statuer ainsi, l'arrêt informatif attaqué (Agen, 28 mars 1962) se fonde sur ce que s'il était fait droit à la prétention de dame Blum, l'héritage voisin se trouverait grevé « d'une véritable servitude d'éclairement...contractuellement inexistante » ; -Mais attendu que la même décision, après avoir rappelé et déclaré constantes les constatations de fait de premiers juges, a relevé « qu'il apparaît bien des éléments de la cause que les parties vivent dans une mésintelligence certaine » et que « l'instance...reflète et caractérise la psychologie de demoiselle Lassus, recherchant la satisfaction d'un mobile malicieux » ; - Attendu qu'en se refusant, dans de telles circonstances, à accorder à dame Blum réparation du préjudice dont elle se plaignait alors qu'ils constataient, en même temps, à la charge de demoiselle Lassus, un exercice purement malicieux, partant, abusif, de son droit de propriété, les juges du second degré ont violé le texte visé par le pourvoi ;

Par ces motifs, et sans qu'il y ait lieu de statuer, soit sur les autres branches du premier moyen, soit sur le deuxième moyen, casse..., renvoie devant la cour d'appel de Bordeaux.

(23) Structure of French court decisions (2)

Sur la recevabilité du pourvoi:

Attendu que selon les articles 1 et 2 du décret no 67-1210 du 22 décembre 1967, le pourvoi en cassation est formé au plus tard dans un délai de deux mois à compter de la signification de la décision attaquée ;

Qu'en vertu des dispositions de l'article 46 du décret susvisé du 22 décembre 1967 et des articles 6 et 7 du décret no 72-788 du 28 août 1972, alors applicable, ce délai expire le jour du dernier mois qui porte le même quantième que le jour de l'acte qui fait courir le délai, à vingt-quatre heures ;

Attendu qu'en l'espèce le pourvoi a été formé par la dame Benet le 4 septembre 1975 contre l'arrêt rendu le 27 mai 1975 par la Cour d'appel d'Aix-en-Provence ; que, cet arrêt ayant été signifié le 3 juillet 1975 à la dame Benet, le pourvoi est tardif et doit être déclaré irrecevable ;

PAR CES MOTIFS :

DÉCLARE IRRECEVABLE le pourvoi formé contre l'arrêt rendu le 27 mai 1975 par la Cour d'appel d'Aix-en-Provence.

(24) Composition of French court decisions

The French decision quoted below illustrates the *attendu que* -technique used by French and Belgian courts. There, every paragraph in which the views of the parties and the facts provided by them are discussed, begins with the quoted formula. At times, this technique may be perceived as tiresome, especially when the *attendu que*-formula is used several times in one sentence as illustrated here by an excerpt from the decision of the French Supreme Court. Also the decision Dame Blum C. Dlle Lassus (quoted in Notes and Materials as Nr. 22) uses the *attendu que*-technique. Some other courts such as the French Conseil d'Etat use the formula *considérant que* instead of *attendu que*, but the technique of text composition remains the same. The French Supreme Court, (Court de cassation, 1ère Chambre civile), in a decision rendered on July 4, 2007, no. 05-14918 puts one of the main complaints of the appeal which it had to decide in two paragraphs following strictly the *attendu que*-technique:

Attendu qu'il est fait grief à l'arrêt attaqué d'avoir rejeté la demande de sursis à statuer et d'avoir en conséquence déclaré exécutoires en France les décisions des juridictions suisses alors qu'une décision pénale, de nature à révéler que les décisions étrangères ordonnent l'exécution de conventions constituant l'instrument d'une infraction pénale, est susceptible d'influer sur l'instance civile en exequatur; qu'en refusant de surseoir à statuer au motif inopérant que la licéité des conventions fondant les condamnations ne pouvait être discutée au regard de l'ordre public français et que la validité de ces conventions ne pouvait être remise en cause au stade de l'exequatur, sans rechercher si la décision à intervenir sur l'action pénale était susceptible d'avoir une influence sur décision à intervenir sur la demande d'exequatur, la court d'appel a privé sa décision de base légale au regard des articles 4, alinéa 2, du Code de procédure pénale et 27 alinéa 1 de la Convention de Lugano du 16 septembre 1988 ;

Mais attendu qu'après avoir rappelé que le contrôle de la conformité des décisions suisses à l'ordre public international français est exclusive de leur révision au fond, l'arrêt retient à juste titre qu'un sursis à statuer sur le fondement de l'article 4, alinéa 2 du Code de procédure pénale ne pourrait être décidé qu'en cas d'incidence prouvée de la procédure pénale sur la licéité des engagements, souscrits par Y Congo à l'égard de X, fondant les condamnations prononcées par les décisions dont l'exequatur est demandé ; que l'arrêt relève que Y Congo, qui ne s'est pas constituée partie civile, n'apporte aucun élément sur l'état de la procédure pénale, dans laquelle MM. A… et B… aurait été mis en exament, portant sur des suspicions de versement de commissions au profit de personnes physiques autres que les persones morales en cause devant les juridictions suisses; que la court d'appel, qui avait constaté un engagement irrévocable de Y Congo à l'égard de X, dont la licéité ne pouvait être discutée au regard de la conception française de l'ordre publique international, dont la validité ne pouvait être mis en cause au stade de l'exequatur, et dont l'inexécution partielle par Y Congo avait été sanctionnée par les juridictions suisses à statuer dès lors que la République du Congo et Y Congo, sur lesquelles pesait la charge de la preuve, n'établissaient pas l'incidence de la procédure pénale sur l'instance civile;

....

PAR CES MOTIFS :

REJETTE les pourvois...

The structural split between *attendu que*-arguments and *mais attendu que*-arguments is marked in the text by grouping arguments in paragraphs. The technique may seem formalistic as it is exercised with rare consequence. In the decision of the French Supreme Court which follows this technique is strictly observed. It could however be that both decisions were written by the same judge. The contrasting argumentation or rather the grouping of arguments along the mentioned split prepares also here a negative decision for the requesting party:

Cour de cassation, 1ère chambre civile, March 27, 2007, no. 05-1048

Attendu que la société X fait grief à l'arrêt d'avoir appliqué le droit français à l'action en responsabilité engagée contre elle par la société d'assurance alors qu'en l'éspece la companie Z se prévalait exclusivement des manquements aux obligations découlant de la convention conclue entre la société X et l'armateur ; qu'en statuant comme ils l'ont fait, sans s'interroger au préalable sur le droit applicable à cette convention, les juges du fond ont privé leur décision de base légale au regard de l'article 3 du Code civil et de la règle de conflit de lois applicable en matière de responsabilité quasi-délictuelle ;

Mais attendu que l'arrêt relève que le manquement du X à ses obligations contractuelles vis-à-vis de l'armateur, a causé un préjudice dont la compagnie Z pouvait demander réparation; que l'action étant de nature délictuelle, la loi applicable au contrat entre la société de classification et l'armateur, d'ailleurs non invoquée devant les juges au fond, était sans incidence sur la détermination de la loi applicable à l'action ; que le moyen n'est pas fondé ;

...

PAR CES MOTIFS:

REJETTE les pourvois…

(25) Composition of Italian court decisions

Italian court decisions are structured less strictly than the French ones and come close to the German and Spanish court decisions. Arntz (2002: 35, 37) provides a formal textual structure of these decisions. However, their textual structure is still more rigid than the individualistic form and style of common law court opinions. Furthermore, as in the (IT) *massime di giurisprudenza* which are also quoted in these Notes and Materials under nr. 14, over-long sentences occur with systematic regularity. In the decision rendered below in some relevant parts the Italian *Corte di Cassazione* had to decide the dispute between a French and an Italian enterprise concerning the appropriate jurisdiction for a claim regarding unpaid invoices.

Corte di Cassazione 27.9.2006 – n. 20887

Excerpts from the decision: Provvedendo sul ricorso, rilieva questo giudice di legitimità che deve essere dichiarato il defetto di giurisdizione del giudice italiano.

Al riguardo, si osserva preliminarmente che - contrariamente a quel che assume la società francese S. s.a. ed a quanto sostiene anche il P.M. nelle sue conclusioni – nella specie deve, ratione temporis, farsi applicazione della disciplina prevista dal Regolamento 44/2001 CE, che è entrata in vigore in data 1.3.2002, successivamente alla stipulazione dei due contratti per i quali è causa, ma anteriormente alla notificazione della citazione in data 15.5.2002.

Dispone, infatti, in proposito l'art. 66, primo comma, che "le disposizioni del presente Regolamento si applicano solo alle azioni proposte ed agli atti pubblici formati posteriormente alla sua entrata in vigore", per cui, dovendo il momento della proposizione della domanda essere determinate in rapporto al diritto processuale del foro adito, deve ritenersi che la domanda al giudice italiano, che è stata introdotta con l'atto di citazione notificato il 15.5.2002, rientra tra le "azioni proposte" successivamente all'entrata in vigore del Regolamento (obbligatorio per tutti gli Stati membri della Comunità Europea, fatta eccezione per la Danimarca nei previsti casi), la cui disciplina ha sostituito, quando alla "materia civile e commerciale", quella della Convenzione di Bruxelles relativamente alla competenza giurisdizionale ed alla esecuzione di decisioni nella predetta materia.

La questione di giurisdizione, in relazione al primo dei profili dedotti, deve essere esaminata con riguardo alla sussistenza della clausola di deroga pattizia a favore del giudice francese, deroga che, secondo la prospettazione della società ricorrente, dovrebbe derivare per le seguenti ragioni:

1) la clausola n. 11 di attribuzione delle controversie al giudice francese, inserta nelle condizioni generali del contratto predisposte dalla società francese, sarebbe stata accettata dalla società italiana per il fatto che, conoscendole, la società T. srl aveva dato successiva esecuzione al contratto;

2) le medesime condizioni generali erano riportate sul retro delle fatture, rimesse dalla società francese a quella italiana e da questa pagate, per cui la mancata formulazione di obiezioni al riguardo costituirebbe la prova dell'esistenza di un accordo sulla deroga della giurisdizione a favore del giudice francese;

3) la mancata espressa sottoscrizione della clausola da parte della società T. srl non impedirebbe l'operatività della deroga, poiché l'attribuzione di competenza al giudice francese dovrebbe farsi rientrare nell'ambito degli abituati rapporti commerciali tra le parti.

Premesso che in tema di giurisdizione questa Corte giudica anche del fatto e deve procedere all'apprezzamento diretto delle risultanze e degli atti di causa, in modo indipendente dalle deduzioni delle parti, si osserva che, nel caso in esame, la norma che disciplina il patto derogatorio è quella dell'art. 23 del Regolamento 44/2001 CE, che, con disposizione sostanzialmente analoga a quella dell'art. 17, primo comma, della Convenzione di Bruxelles 27.9.1968, stabilisce che la clausola attributiva di competenza "deve essere conclusa: a) per iscritto o oralmente con conferma scritta, o b) in una forma ammessa dalle pratiche che le parti hanno stabilito tra di loro, o c) nel commercio internazionale, in una forma ammessa da un uso che le parti conoscevano o avrebbero dovuto conoscere e che, in tale campo, è ampiamente conosciuto e regolarmente rispettato dalle parti di contratti dello stesso tipo nel ramo commerciale considerato".

...

La questione di giurisdizione è, invece, fondata in relazione al secondo dei profili esposti dalla società ricorrente, la quale ha dedotto che il difetto di giurisdizione del giudice italiano, deve essere ritenuto in applicazione, comunque, della regola di cui all'art. 5 n. 1 del Regolamento 44/2001 CE, secondo cui nella materia contrattuale, analogamente alla previsione della Convenzione di Bruxelles (art. 5 n.1), consente all'attore di citare il convenuto, domiciliato nel territorio di uno Stato membro, davanti al giudice di un altro

Stato membro se questo corrisponde con il "giudice del luogo in cui l'obbligazione dedotta in giudizio è stata o deve essere eseguita".

...

Ritiene questa Corte che non si è realizzata nessuna delle tre previste ipotesi di patto derogatorio.

In accogliamento del ricorso va, pertanto, dichiarato il difetto di giurisdizione del giudice italiano.

La società resistente è condannata a pagare le spese del presente procedimento di cassazione nella misura indicata in dispositivo...

(26) Composition of German court decisions

In Germany, the so-called juridic style is perceived by the jurists to be two-fold and to consist of a style of legal opinions, (D) *Gutachtenstil*, and a style of court decisions, (D) *Urteilsstil*. The difference, however, seems to be not that much one of style but of reasoning. Whereas (D) *Gutachtenstil* which is used mostly by law students in their written exams proceeds in an interogative mood, (D) *Urteilsstil* in which court decisions are written, is of assertive nature. The (D) *Gutachtenstil*-opinion may read, e.g.: *A could have a claim for price payment according to Art. 433 BGB. It requires a valid sale contract between the parties. The parties may have concluded a sale of a good in that they exchanged e-mails.* In turn, the same text written in (D) *Urteilsstil* would read: *A has a claim for price payment according to Art. 433 BGB as there is a valid sale contract between the parties. Through the exchange of successive and mutually related e-mails the parties agreed upon the sale of a good.* The (D) *Urteilsstil* is illustrated by the following court opinion.

OLG Hamburg 3.3.2006 – 5 U 1/05

Excerpts from the motives of the judgment: Die Parteien streiten darum, ob die Klägerinnen berechtigt sind, Wein unter der Bezeichnung REVIAN's zu vertreiben. Die Klägerinnen gehören zu der Steiner-Racke-Dujardin Getränkegruppe, die Beklagte ist eine französische Aktiengesellschaft mit Sitz in dem Kurort Evian-les-Bains in den französischen Alpen. Die Beklagte ist u.a. Inhaberin einer deutschen Wortmarke EVIAN mit Priorität vom 11.11.1985 für Mineralwasser. Sie vertreibt seit ca. 40 Jahren unter dieser Bezeichnung ein stilles Mineralwasser auch in Deutschland. Dabei verwendet sie auf den Flaschen eine Schreibweise in kleinen Buchstaben und mit einer Bergkulisse als Hintergrund.

Gestützt auf ihre deutsche Marke EVIAN hat die Beklagte in einem vorangegangenem, rechtskräftig abgeschlossenen Rechtsstreit gegen die Klägerinnen u.a. ein

Verbot erwirkt, die Bezeichnungen REVIAN zur Kennzeichnung von Wein zu verwenden und außerdem in die Löschung weiterer für die Klägerin zu 1 eingetragener Marken einzuwilligen, nämlich REWIAN und REVAN.

Bereits während des noch laufenden Rechtsstreits, nämlich jedenfalls seit September 1999, haben die Klägerinnen die Kennzeichnung ihrer Weine auf REVIAN's umgestellt. Für diese Bezeichnung haben die Klägerinnen zwei deutsche Wort/Bildmarken mit Priorität vom 1.10.98 und 14.7.98 eintragen lassen. Ferner haben die Klägerinnen am 21.9.1998 eine der letzteren Marke entsprechende Gemeinschaftsbildmarke angemeldet. Der gegen diese Marke von der Beklagten erhobene Widerspruch ist von der Widerspruchsabteilung des Harmonisierungsamtes am 23. 11. 2001 zurückgewiesen worden.

Die von der Beklagten eingelegte Beschwerde hat die Beschwerdekammer des Harmonisierungsamtes am 22. 7. 2005 zurückgewiesen. Über die hiergegen von der Beklagten eingereichte Klage hat das Europäische Gericht erster Instanz bislang nicht entschieden. Mit Schreiben vom 13. 2. 2003 forderte die Beklagte die Klägerinnen auf, die Benutzung der Bezeichnung REVIAN's für Weine zu unterlassen, da dies gegen das Urteil des Landgerichts Hamburg vom 19.3.1997 verstoße. Außerdem verlangte sie Auskunft über den Umfang der Benutzungshandlungen. Daraufhin erhoben die Klägerinnen gegen die Beklagte Klage auf Feststellung, dass die Beklagte aus dem Urteil vom 19.3.1997 keine Ansprüche wegen der Verwendung der Bezeichnung REVIAN's herleiten könne. Die Beklagte erhob Hilfswiderklage mit folgenden Anträgen:

1. die Klägerinnen zu verurteilen, es bei Meidung der gesetzlichen Ordnungsmittel zu unterlassen, die Bezeichnung "REVIAN's" zur Kennzeichnung eines Weines im geschäftlichen Verkehr zu verwenden, so gekennzeichneten Wein anzubieten, in den Verkehr zu bringen oder zu den genannten Zwecken zu besitzen, unter der Marke „REVIAN's" ein- und auszufüllen, die Bezeichnung „REVIAN's" in Geschäftspapieren oder in der Werbung zu benutzen;

2. festzustellen, dass die Klägerinnen als Gesamtschuldner verpflichtet sind, der Beklagten allen Schaden zu ersetzen, der der Beklagten aus der unter Ziffer 1. bezeichneten Zuwiderhandlung entstanden ist und/oder noch entstehen wird;

3. die Klägerinnen als Gesamtschuldner zu verurteilen, der Beklagten Auskunft zu erteilen über den Umfang der unter Ziffer 1. beschriebenen Zuwiderhandlungen in Form einer zeitlich geordneten Aufstellung, insbesondere der Verkaufsmenge, der erzielten Verkaufspreise, der Gestehungskosten und des Gewinns des unter der Bezeichnung „REVIAN's" verkauften Weins und der dafür geschalteten Werbung, geordnet nach Werbeträgern und Verbreitungsdatum.

Mit seit dem 30.5.2004 rechtskräftigen Teilurteil vom 21.4.2004 hat das Landgericht der Feststellungsklage stattgegeben. Mit Schlussurteil vom 25.11.2004 hat es auch der Widerklage weitgehend stattgegeben, allerdings alle Ansprüche auf Auskunft und Schadensersatzfeststellung auf die Zeit ab dem 30.5.2001 beschränkt. Wegen der Einzelheiten des erstinstanzlichen Parteivortrags wird auf den Tatbestand des Schlussurteils Bezug genommen…

(27) Samples of Japanese court decisions

Some samples of Japanese court decisions may indicate differences in the legal argumentation there. However, as long as systematic research into this issue is missing, it is difficult to generalize this first impression. The impression of a cultural difference may also result from the English translations, here quoted after Upham (1990: 625).

(A divorce case) Inoue v. Inoue (Japan's Supreme Court Third Petty Bench Feb. 19, 1952 6 Minshuu 110)

Reasons: As found by the High Court, the Appellee's conduct in pouring water on the appelant and beating him with a broomstick is truly vulgar and improper. It is obvious however, that the reason for this behavior was the Appellant's sexual relation with "S" resulting in her pregnancy. The Appelant reaped what he sowed, as it were the Appellee's behavior as found by the High Court was all excusable and does not constitute a conduct so cruel and humiliating that cohabitation is intolerable as set forth in Art. 813 of the former Civil Code.

Another case concerns the so-called Minamata-disease (mercury poisoning caused by eating fish which was contaminated by effluents from a chemical plant) and state agencies responsibility for injuries. The court argumentation in it seems to differ to a degree from the Western patterns.

Re. Kawamoto Teruo (Tokyo High Court 1977, June 14):

Whether or not this case constitues an abuse of the right of public prosecution and should therefore be dismissed will be discussed below. What is distinctive about this case is that the claim of bias which constitutes the essential part of the appeal does not rest on the comparison of the suspects in this case with suspects in another case of the same kind. Instead, the discrimination lies in the manner of dealing with the two parties involved. In other words, there is a so-called assailant's side and a victim's side in a pollution incident. The discrimination in this case is further complicated by the fact that pollution can be called a fatal contradiction in present day society.

(28) Plessy v. Fergusson (U.S.)

Excerpts from the U.S. Supreme Court decision Plessy v. Ferguson (163 U.S. 537 1896):

...

The petitioner was a citizen of the United States and a resident of the state of Louisiana, of mixed descent, in the proportion of seven-eigths Caucasian and one-eighth African blood; that the mixture of colored blood was not discernible in him, and that he was entitled to every recognition, right, privilege, and immunity secured to the citizens of the United States of the white race by its constitution and laws; that on June 7, 1892, he engaged and paid for a first-class passage on the East Louisiana Railway, from New Orleans to Covington, in the same state, and thereupon entered a passenger train, and took possession of a vacant seat in a coach where passengers of the white race were accommodated; that such railroad company was incorporated by the laws of Louisiana as a common carrier, and was not authorized to distinguish between citizens according to their race, but, notwithstanding this, petitioner was required by the conductor, under penalty of ejection from said train and imprisonment, to vacate the said coach, and occupy another seat, in a coach assigned by said company for persons not of white race, and for no other reason than that petitioner was of a colored race; that, upon petitioner's refusal to comply with such order, he was, with the aid of a police officer, forcibly ejected from said coach, and hurried off to, and imprisoned in, the parish jail of New Orleans, and there held to answer a charge made by such officer to the effect that he was guilty of having criminally violated an act of the general assembly of the state, approved July 10, 1890, in such case made and provided.

...

By the fourteenth amendment, all persons born or naturalized in the United States, and subject to the jurisdiction thereof, are made citizens of the United States and of the state wherein they reside; and the states are forbidden from making or enforcing any law which shall abridge the privileges or immunities of citizens of the United States, or shall deprive any person of life, liberty, or property without due process of law, or deny to any person within their jurisdiction the equal protection of the laws.

...

The object of the amendment was undoubtedly to enforce the absolute equality of the two races before the law, but, in the nature of things, it could not have been intended to abolish distinctions based upon color, or to enforce social, as distinguished from political, equality, or a commingling of the two races upon terms unsatisfactory to either. Laws permitting, and even requiring, their separation, in places where they are liable to be brought into contact, do not necessarily imply the inferiority of either race to the other, and have been generally, if not universally, recognized as within the competency of the state legislatures in the exercise of their police power. The most common instance of this is connected with the establishment of separate schools for white and colored children, which have been held to be a valid exercise of the legislative power even by courts of states where the political rights of the colored race have been longest and most earnestly enforced.

...

In his dissenting opinion Justice Harlan wrote:

It was said in argument that the statute of Louisiana does not discriminate against either race, but prescribes a rule applicable alike to white and colored citizens. But this argument does not meet the difficulty. Every one knows that the statute in question has its origin in the purpose, not so much to exclude white persons from railroad cars occupied by blacks, as to exclude colored people from coaches occupied by or assigned to white persons. Railroad corporations of Louisiana did not make discrimination among whites in the matter of accomodation for travelers. The thing to accomplish was, under the guise of giving equal accomodation for whites and blacks, to compel the latter to keep to themselves while traveling in railroad passenger coaches. No one would be so wanting in candor as to assert the contrary. The fundamental objection, therefore, to the statute, is that it interferes with the personal freedom of citizens. 'Personal liberty,' it has been well said, 'consists in the power of locomotion, of changing situation, or removing one's person to whatsoever places one's own inclination may direct, without imprisonment or restraint, unless by due course of law.' If a white man and a black man choose to occupy the same public conveyance on a public highway, it is their right to do so; and no government, proceeding alone on grounds of race, can prevent it without infringing the personal liberty of each.

(29) Brown v. Board of Education (U.S.)

Excerpts from the U.S. Supreme Court decision Brown v. Board of Education (347 U.S. 483 1954):

In each of the cases, minors of the Negro race, through their legal representatives, seek the aid of the courts in obtaining admission to the public schools of their community on a nonsegregated basis. In each instance, they had been denied admission to schools attended by white children under laws requiring or permitting segregation according to race. This segregation was alleged to deprive the plaintiffs of the equal protection of the laws under the Fourteenth Amendment. In each of the cases other than the Delaware case, a three-judge federal district court denied relief to the plaintiffs on the so-called "separate but equal" doctrine announced by this Court in Plessy v. Ferguson, 163 U.S. 537. Under that doctrine, equality of treatment is accorded when the races are provided substantially equal facilities, even though these facilities be separate.

...

Segregation of white and colored children in public schools has a detrimental effect upon the colored children. The impact is greater when it has the sanction of the law, for the policy of separating the races is usually interpreted as denoting the inferiority of the negro group. A sense of inferiority affects the motivation of a child to learn. Segregation with the sanction of law, therefore, has a tendency to retard the educational and mental development of negro children and to deprive them of some of the benefits they would receive in a racially integrated school system.

...

We conclude that, in the field of public education, the doctrine of "separate but equal" has no place. Separate educational facilities are inherently unequal. Therefore, we hold that the plaintiffs and others similarly situated for whom the actions have been brought are, by reason of the segregation complained of, deprived of the equal protection of the laws guaranteed by the Fourteenth Amendment.

(30) Frigaliment v. B.N.S. (U.S.)

Frigaliment Importing Co. v. B.N.S. International Sales Corp.

190 F. Supp. 116 (S.D.N.Y. 1960):

Friendly, Circuit Judge. Plaintiff says 'chicken' means a young chicken, suitable for broiling and frying. Defendant says 'chicken' means any bird of the genus that meets contract specification on weight and quality, including what it calls 'stewing chickens' and plaintiff pejoratively terms 'fowl'. To support its claim, plaintiff sends a number of volleys over the net; defendant essays to return them and adds a few serves of its own. Assuming that both parties were acting in good faith, the case nicely illustrates Oliver Wendell Holmes's remark "that the making of a contract depends not on the agreement of two minds in one intention, but on the agreement of two sets of external signs – not on the parties' having meant the same thing but on having said the same thing." Since the word 'chicken' standing alone is ambigous, I turn first to see whether the contract itself offers any aid to its interpretation.

Plaintiff's first contention hinges on an exchange of cablegrams which preceded the formal contracts. After testing the market price, plaintiff accepted, and sent defendant a confirmation. These and subsequent cables between plaintiff and defendant, which laid the basis for the additional quantities under the first and for all of the second contract, were predominantly in German, although they used the English word 'chicken'. Defendant's agent testified that when asked plaintiff's agent what kind of chicken were wanted, received the answer "any kind of chicken". Defendant relies on conduct by the plaintiff after the first shipment had been received. Defendant argues that if plaintiff was sincere in thinking it was entitled to young chickens, plaintiff would not have allowed the shipment under the second contract to go forward.

Plaintiff's next contention is that there was a definite trade usage that 'chicken' meant 'young chicken'. Here there was no proof of actual knowledge of the alleged usage; indeed it is quite plain that defendant's belief was to the contrary. Plainfiff endeavored to establish such a usage by the testimony of witnesses. However, one witness stated that a careful businessman protected himself by using 'broiler' when that was what he wanted and 'fowl' when he wished older birds. An employee of a company that publishes a daily market report on the poultry trade gave his view that the trade meaning of chicken was "broilers and fryers." Defendant provided a witness that said that in the trade, 'chicken' would encompass all the various classifications of chicken. Defendant also provided a regulation of the Department of Agriculture that defined 'chicken' as various classes including "Broiler or Fryer, Roaster, Capon, Stag, Hen or Stewing chicken or Fowl".

When all the evidence is reviewed, it is clear defendant believed it could comply with the contracts by delivering stewing chickens. Plaintiff asserts that it is equally plain that plaintiff's own subjective intent was to obtain broilers and fryers. Because plaintiff has the burden of showing that 'chicken' was used in the narrower rather than in the broader sense, and this it has not sustained, judgment shall be entered dismissing the complaint.

(31) OHG v. Kolodny

OHG v. Kolodny (NY County, Supreme Court 1st Jud. Dept., IA Part II (1992)):

Baer, Justice Plaintiff is an auction house dealing in works of art. Defendant is an art dealer. His gallery has purchased fine art from the plaintiff over the years, presumably with happier results than in this case. In 1988, defendant received, in New York, a catalogue sent by the plaintiff that described works of art that would be put for auction by plaintiff. Among these, defendant says, was a "bronze sculpture produced by Hilaire Germain Edgar Degas before 1990," to wit, the "Dancer Gazing". Plaintiff phoned defendant in New York during the auction and solicited a bid for the "Dancer". Without ever having set eyes on the right foot or any other part of the sculpture, plaintiff offered a bid of DM 220,000 and triumphed. Defendant was never told the identity of the consignor of the Degas. Defendant wired to plaintiff the purchase price and a commission.

The "Dancer" arrived shortly thereafter in New York, where she immediately did a pirouette and departed for London. Defendant wished to let no grass grow under either of his feet; he would put the Degas up for resale at Christie's and would, he was confident, earn a great deal of not bronze, but sterling. Eagle eyes at Christie's surveyed the work. Defendant was told, to his horror, that Christie's suspected that the statue was ersatz, in a word, a fake. Defendant contacted Herr Hanstein and advised that his heart was heavy and his wallet, he was afraid, too light. Defendant sought a refund.

Defendant allegedly secured the agreement of plaintiff that the "Dancer" would be given the once or twice over by the world's foremost expert of Degas Bronzes, whose determination would be binding. The statue was brought to New York, where an expert, like many other world's foremost experts, resides. His conclusion unfortunately was that the work was not genuine.

A German court decided in favor of plaintiff, rejected defendant's contention that he was entitled to an offset for the purchase price of the pseudo-Degas. The court held that plaintiff had disclaimed any warranty as to the authenticity of the "Dancer"; that since the job of an auction house is to sell as a commission agent many items owned by others, the authenticity of which the auctioneer cannot readily confirm, disclaimers do not violate the law; and that defendant in his letter on the Riopelle has disavowed any offset.

After plaintiff launched its "Blitzkrieg" here in New York, defendant responded with a lawsuit of his own. Defendant seeks to recover the purchase price for the ill-fated Degas. Defendant, relying inter alia upon Article 15 of the New York Arts and Cultural Affairs Law (the "Art Law"), contends that plaintiff is liable for having provided inaccurate information about the Degas and that the German judgment contravenes New York public policy, as a consequence of which its enforcement in favor of plaintiff is *verboten.* This argument, while creative and well presented, must fail.

CPLR Sec. 5304(b)(4) provides that a monetary judgment of a foreign country need not be recognized by New York if the cause of action on which the judgment is based is "repugnant to the public policy of the state". Normally, the judgment of a foreign nation will be given effect. Differences between the laws of New York and those of many sovereign nations of the world are likely to arise often, but such differences alone cannot constitute a violation of public policy. As Judge Cardozo said, "We are not so provincial as to say that every solution of a problem is wrong because we deal with it otherwise at home". Were we New Yorkers to be overly provincial, we might well inspire foreign nations to reject enforcement of New York judgments, precisely the opposite of the purpose Article 53 was created to achieve and an outcome particularly undesirable as the economy of this country grows every day more intertwined with those of other nations.

The German court applied German law in this case. This is not unreasonable since the auction occurred in Germany and defendant placed his bid during a telephone call with the auction house in Germany. In addition, plaintiff's conditions of sale stated that legal relations between plaintiff and the bidder would be governed by German law. Defendant appeared in the German action, defended, and lost. There is, of course, no claim that German law and procedures are unfair and unworthy of respect here.

The Germans are less Bismarcian than defendant contends. German law, as exemplified by the decision of the Cologne court in this case, is not indifferent to the general sale of fakes by art merchants. The court relied upon the warranty exclusion that formed a conditon of sale.

Enforcement of the German judgment would not undermine the public interest, public confidence in law or security for individual rights, nor violate fundamental notions of what is decent and fair. The German judgment is enforceable.

(32) U.S. v. Haggar Apparel (U.S.)

U.S. v. Haggar Apparel Company (526 U.S. 380 1999)

Kennedy, J. The case concerns regulations relating to the customs classification of certain imported goods issued by the United States Customs Service. The question is whether these regulations are entitled to judicial deference in a refund suit brought in the Court of International Trade. Contrary to the position of that Court and the Court of Appeals for the Federal Circuit, we hold the regulation in question is subject to the analysis required by Chevron U.S.A. Inc v. Natural Resources Defense Council, Inc., and that if it is a reasonable interpretation and implementation of an ambigous statutory provision, it must be given judicial deference.

Respondent Haggar Apparel Co. designs, manufactures and markets apparel for men. This matter arises from a refund proceeding for duties imposed on men's trousers shipped by respondent to this country from an assembly plant it controlled in Mexico. The fabric had been cut in the United States and then shipped to Mexico, along with the thread, buttons and zippers necessary to complete the garments. There the trousers were sewn and reshipped to the United States. If that had been the full extent of it, there would be no dispute, for if there were mere assembly without other steps, all agree that imported garments would have been eligible for the duty exemption which respondent claims.

Respondent, however, in the Government's view, added one another step at the Mexican plant: permapressing. Permapressing is designed to maintain the garment's crease in the desired place and to avoid other creases or wrinkles that detract from its proper appearance. The Customs Service claimed the baking was an added process in addition to assembly, and denied a duty exemption; respondent claimed the baking was simply part of the assembly process, or, in the words of the controlling statute, an "operation incidental to the assembly process". After being denied the exemption it sought for the permapressed articles, respondent brought suit for refund in the Court of International Trade. The court declined to treat the regulation as controlling. The court ruled in favor of respondent. On review, the Court of Appeals for the Federal Circuit declined to analyze the regulation under Chevron, and affirmed.

The statute on which respondent relies, Section 9802, provides importers a partial exemption from duties otherwise imposed. The relevant regulation interpreting the statute with respect to permapressed articles provides as follows:

Any significant process, operation, or treatment other than assembly whose primary purpose is the fabrication, completion, physical or chemical improvement of a component, or which is not related to the assembly process, whether, or not it effects a substantial transformation of the article, shall not be regarded as incidental to the assembly and shall preclude the application of the exemption to such article. The following are examples of operations not considered incidental to the assembly:

(4) Chemical treatment of components or assembled articles to impart new characteristics, such as a showerproofing, permapressing, sanforizing, dying or bleaching of textiles.

The Customs Service (which is within the Treasury Department) is charged with the classification of imported goods under the proper provision of the tariff schedules in the first instance. In addition, the Secretary is directed by statute to "establish and promulgate such rules and regulations not inconsistent with the law...as may be necessary to secure a just, impartial and uniform appraisement of imported merchandise and the classification and assessment of duties thereon at the various ports of entry."

For the reasons we have given, the statutes authorizing customs classification regulations of an administering agency warrant judicial deference. We turn to respondent's second major contention, that the statutes governing the reviewing authority of the Court of International Trade in classification cases displace this customary framework. The Court of Appeals held in this case, and in previous cases presenting the issue, that these regulations were not entitled to deference because the Court of International Trade is charged to "reach the correct decision" in determining the proper classification of goods. The whole point of regulations such as these, however, is to ensure that the statute is applied in a consistent and proper manner. Deference to an agency's expertise in construing a statutory command is not inconsistent with reaching a correct decision. If the agency's statutory interpretation fills a gap or defines a term in a way that is reasonable in light of the legislature's revealed design, we give that judgment controlling weight.

The customs regulations may not be disregarded. Application of the Chevron framework is the beginning of the legal analysis. Like other courts, the Court of International Trade must, when appropriate, give customs regulations Chevron deference. The judgment is vacated and the case is remanded for further proceedings consistent with this opinion.

The U.S. Court of Appeals for the Federal Circuit affirmed the above decision (U.S. v. Haggar Apparel Company, 222 F.3d 1337 Fed.Cir. 2000). The U.S. Supreme Court refused to grant certiorari in this case, so that the decision is final. The difference between *incidental* and *substantive* has been discussed and solved in the U.S. Supreme Court decision McCullough v. Maryland from 1819. In it, the Chief Justice John Marshall posed the famous question whether the Congress had the power to incorporate a bank. The part of the decision interesting here reads as follows: "The power of creating a corporation, though appertaining to sovereignty, is not, like the power of making war, or levying taxes, or of regulating commerce, a great substantive and independent power, which cannot be implied *as incidental to* other powers, or used as a means of executing them. It is never the end for which other powers are exercised, but a means by which other objects are accomplished. No contributions are made to charity for the sake of an incorporation, but a corporation is created to administer the charity; no seminary of learning is instituted in order to be incorporated, but the corporate character is conferred to subserve the purposes of education. No city was ever built with the sole object of being incorporated, but is incorporated as affording the best means of being well governed. The power of creating a corporation is never used for its own sake, but for the purpose of effecting something else. No sufficient reason is, therefore, perceived, why it may not pass *as incidental to* those powers which are expressly given, if it be a direct mode of executing them." (emphasis added)

(33) Rollerblade v. U.S. (U.S.)

Rollerblade, Inc. v. U.S. (282 F.3d 1349 Fed.Cir. 2002)

Rader, Circuit Judge. Rollerbade, Inc. (Rollerblade) appeals from a summary judgment of the United States Court of International Trade affirming the United States Customs Service (Customs) classification of imported in-line roller skating protective gear under subheading 9506.99.6080 (99.6080) of the Harmonized Tariff Schedules of the United States (HTSUS). Because Customs correctly classified the imports, this court affirms. The imports in this case are in-line roller skating protective gear, such as knee pads, ellbow pads, and wrist guards. Customs classified the imported protective gear as residual "other" sports equipment under subheading 99.6080 of the HTSUS, which carries a duty rate of 4% ad valorem. Rollerblade appealed to the Court of International Trade, arguing that Customs should have classified the protective gear as "accessories" under subheading 9506.70.2090. HTSUS subheading 70.2090 carries a 0% duty rate. Rollerblade sought this "accessory" classification because the protected gear was designed, tested, manufactured and marketed solely for use with in-line roller skates.

The Court of International Trade affirmed the Customs classification based primarily on its interpretation of the dictionary meaning of the term "accessory". According to the trail court, an accessory under subheading 70.2090 must be "of" or "to" the article (roller skates) listed in the heading, not "of" or "to" the activity (roller skating) for which the article is used. The trial court found that the protective gear had a direct relationship to the activity of roller skating, but not to the HTSUS heading, namely roller skates. Hence, the trial court affirmed Custom's refusal to classify Rollerblade's protective gear under subheading 70.2090 as an "accessory" to roller skates. Moreover, on summary judgment, the Court of International Trade concluded that Customs properly classified the protective gear under the residual "other" (sports equipment) subheading 99.6080.

Classification of goods under the HTSUS entails both ascertaining the proper meaning of specific terms in the tariff provision and determining whether the merchandise subject to tariffs comes within the description of those HTSUS terms. When reviewing whether the imports fit within those terms, this court uses a clear error standard. Universal Elecs., Inc. v. United States, 112 F.3d 488, 491 (Fed. Cir. 1997). When the HTSUS does not define a tariff term, the term receives its "common and popular meaning." E.M. Chems. V. United States, 920 F.2d 910,913 (Fed.Cir.1990). To determine a term's common meaning, a court may consult "dictionaries, scientific authorities, and other reliable information sources." C.J. Tower & Sons v. United States, 69 C.C.P.A. 128, 673 F.2d 1268, 1271 (CCPA 1982). Like the trial court, this court also observes that HTSUS offers no definition for the term "accessory". Thus, the trial court correctly consulted the common (dictionary) meaning of the term. As the Court of International Trade found, dictionary definitions indicate that an "accessory" must bear a direct relationship to the primary article that it accessorizes. In this case, under subheading 70.2090, the article accessorized is roller skates, not the general activity of roller skating. Moreover, as found by the trial court, the protective gear lacks a direct relationship to the roller skates. The protective gear does not directly act on the roller skates at all. Unlike a roller skate part or accessory, the protective gear does not directly affect the skates' operation. Thus, based on the common meaning of "accessory" and the language of subheading 70.2090, this court sustains the trial court's conclusion that Rollerblade's imported protective gear is not a roller skate accessory. Rollerblade argues that the protective gear is, alternatively, "parts" of the roller skates. Rollerblade would classify the protective gear as roller skate parts because it contributes to the safe and effective operation of the skates and functions by design solely with the skates. A "part" is "an essential element or constituent; integral portion which can be separated, replaced, ets." Webster's New World Dictionary 984 (3d College Ed. 1988). Thus, based on the common meaning, the term "part," like the term "accessory," must have a direct relationship to the primary article, rather than to the general activity in which the primary article is used. Again, the protective gear in this case has a relationship to the activity of roller skating, and not directly to the roller skates. Rollerblade's imported protective gear protects the wearer from injuries related to an activity using the article. The imports are not necessary to make the skates themselves work, nor are they necessary to make the skates themselves work efficiently or safely. At best, the protective gear adds to the comfort and convenience of the wearer while roller skating. In other words, the roller skates work in the same manner whether the skater wears the protective gear or not. Concurrent use of the protective gear with the roller skates no doubt reduces injuries to the skater from the activity of roller skating, but this observation does not make the protective gear "parts" of the roller skates.

In this case, the most applicable heading is 9506, entitled "articles and equipment for general physical exercise...gymnastics, athletics, other sports." Subheading 99.6080, entitled "other," is the so-called catch-all for this provision. The definition offered for "equipment" includes those articles that are necessary and specifically designed for use in athletics and other sports. Rollerblade's imported protective gear fits within this category because it is "equipment" specifically designed for use in the sport of roller skating. In sum, the Court of International Trade did not err in its determination that Customs properly classified Rollerblade's imported protective gear under the residual subheading 99.6080. Affirmed.

(34) Palsgraf v. Long Island Railroad (U.S.)

Justice B. Cardozo created in the following decision Palsgraf v. Long Island Railroad an imagery consisting of cases in a case. The hypothetical cases are used in the narration to clarify the legal notion of the proximate cause. Cardozo's principal professional goal is to show why the main case which has been brought by the plaintiff does not fulfill the requirements developed within the proximate cause doctrine. The part of the case that interests here is its story, therefore it would be more correct to speak about stories in a story rather than about cases in a case. Cases reflect stories within the legal framework of professional argumentation; stories have a role to play in cases but they do not interfere directly with doctrinal issues. Cardozo did not experiment with legal references nor did he reformulate them in his opinion. Therefore, his cases in the case remain within the framework of the classical legal argumentation of his times. His particular innovations within the argumention are the stories that position the plaintiff's case and her story in a specific perspective which is relevant for his final decision. Writing stories based on facts is a particularly intricate task. Next to introducing stories as a strategy for deciding cases, Cardozo develops also linguistic tests which are based on the specific features of the legal language. Cardozo stresses the instability of meanings which shift in law. He has also demonstrated how the plaintiff should use the legal language in order to comply with the juridical test that evaluates the wrong which occurred to her.

Palsgraf v. Long Island Railroad, Co. (248 N.Y. 339, 172 N.E., 1928)

Cardozo, C.J. Plaintiff was standing on a platform of defendant's railroad after buying a ticket to go to Rockaway beach. A train stopped at the station, bound for another place. Two men ran forward to catch it. One of the men reached the platform of the car, without mishap, though the train was already moving. The other man, carrying a package, jumped aboard the car, but seemed unsteady as if about to fall. A guard on the car, who had held the door open, reached forward to help him in, and another guard of the platform pushed him from behind. In this act, the package was dislodged, and fell upon the rails. It was a package of small size, about fifteen inches long, and was covered by a newspaper. In fact it contained fireworks, but there was nothing in its appearance to give notice of its contents. The shock of the explosion threw down some scales at the other end of the platform, many feet away. The scales struck the plaintiff, causing injuries for which she sues.

The conduct of the defendant's guard, if a wrong in its relation to the holder of the package, was not a wrong in its relation to the plaintiff, standing far away. Relatively to her it was not negligence at all. Nothing in the situation gave notice that the falling package had in it the potency of peril to persons thus removed. Negligence is not actionable unless it involves the invasion of a legally protected interest, the violation of a right. "Proof of negligence in the air, so to speak, will not do" (Pollock, Torts, 11th ed., p.455). "Negligence is the absence of care, according to the circumstances" (Willes, J., in Vaughan v. Taff Vale, Ry. Co., 5 H.&N. 679, 688; Adams v. Bullock, 227 N.Y. 298, 211; Parott v. Wells-Fargo Co. (the Nitro-Glycerine case, 15 Wall. (U.S.) 524). The plaintiff as she stood upon the platform of the station might claim to be protected against unintentional invasion of her bodily security. Such invasion is not charged. She might claim to be protected against unintentional invasion by conduct involving in the thought of reasonable men an unreasonable hazard that such invasion would ensue. These, from the point of view of the law, were the bounds of her immunity, with perhaps some rare exceptions, survivals for the most part of ancient forms of liability, where conduct is held to be at the peril of the actor (Sullivan v. Dunham, 161 N.Y. 290). If no hazard was apparent to the eye of ordinary vigilance, an act innocent and harmless, at least to outward seeming, with reference to her, did not take to itself the quality of a tort because it happened to be a wrong, though apparently not one involving the risk of bodily insecurity, with reference to someone else. "In every instance, before negligence can be predicated of a given act, back of the act must be sought and found a duty to the individual complaining, the observance of which would have averted or avoided the injury" (McSherry, C.J., in W. Va. Central RR. Co. v. State, 96 Md. 652, 666). "The ideas of negligence and duty are strictly correlative" (Bowen, L.J., in Thomas v. Quartermaine, 18 Q.B.D. 685, 694). The plaintiff sues in her own right for a wrong personal to her, and not as the vicarious beneficiary of a breach of duty to another.

A different conclusion will involve us, and swiftly too, in a maze of contradictions. A guard stumbles over a package which has been left upon a platform. It seems to be a boundle of newspaper. It turns out to be a can of dynamite. To the eye of ordinary vigilance, the bundle is abandoned waste, which may be kicked or trod on with impunity. Is a passenger at the other end of the platform protected by the law against unsuspected hazard concealed beneath the waste? If not, is the result to be any different, so far as the distant passenger is concerned, when the guard stumbles over a valise which a truckman or a porter has left upon the walk? The passenger far away, if the victim of a wrong at all, has a cause of action, not derivative, but original and primary. His claim to be protected against invasion of his bodily security is neither greater nor less because the act resulting in the invasion is a wrong to another far removed. In this case, the rights that are said to have been violated, the interest said to have been invaded, are not even of the same order. The man was not injured in his person nor even put in danger. The purpose of the act, as well as its effect, was to make his person safe. If there was a wrong to a property interest only, the safety of his package. Out of this wrong to property, which threatened injury to nothing else, there has passed, we are told, to the plaintiff by derivation or succession a right of action for the invasion of an interest of another order, the right to bodily security. The diversity of interests emphasises the futility of the effort to build the plaintiff's right upon the basis of a wrong to some one else. The gain is one of emphasis, for a like result would follow if the interests were the same. Even then, the orbit of the danger as disclosed to the eye of reasonable vigilance would be the orbit of the duty. One who jostles one's nighbor in a crowd does not invade the right of others standing at the outer fringe when the unintended contact casts a bomb upon the ground. The wrongdoer as to them is the man who carries the bomb, not the one who explodes it without suspicion of the danger. Life will have to be made over, and human nature transformed, before provisions so extravagant can be accepted as the norm of conduct, the customary standard to which behavior must conform.

The argument for the plaintiff is built upon the shifting meanings of such words as "wrong" and "wrongful", and shares their instability. What the plaintiff must show is "a wrong" to herself, i.e. a violation of her own right, and not merely a wrong to some one else, nor conduct "wrongful" because unsocial, but not "a wrong" to any one. We are told that one who drives at reckless speed through a crowded city street is guilty of a negligent act and, therefore, of a wrongful one irrespective of the consequences. Negligent the act is, and wrongful in the sense that it is unsocial, but wrongful and unsocial to other travelers, only because the eye of vigilance perceives the risk of damage. If the same act were to be committed on a speedway or a race course, it would lose its wrongful quality. The risk reasonably to be perceived defines the duty to be obeyed, and risk imports relation; it is risk to another or to others within the range of apprehension. This does not mean, of course, that one who launches a destructive force is always relieved of liability if the force, though known to be destructive, pursues an unexpected path. "It was not necessary that the defendant should have had notice of their particular method in which an accident would occur, if the possibility of an accident was clear to the ordinarily prudent eye" (Munsey v. Webb, 231 U.S. 150,156). Some acts, such as shooting, are so imminently dangerous to any one who may come within reach of the missile, however unexpectedly, as to impose a duty of prevision not far from that of an insurer. Even today, and much oftener in earlier stages of the law, one acts sometimes at one's peril. Under this head, it may be, fall certain cases of what is known as transferred intent, an act willfully dangerous to A resulting by misadventure in injury to B (Talmage v. Smith, 101 Mich. 370, 374). These cases aside, wrong is defined in terms of the natural or probable, at least when unintentional (Talmage v. Wells-Fargo Co., 15 Wall. (U.S.) 542). The range of reasonable apprehensions is at times a question for the court, and at times, if varying inferences are possible, a question for the jury. Here by concession, there was nothing in the situation to suggest to the most cautious mind that the parcel wrapped in newspaper would spread wreckage through the station. If the guard had thrown it down knowingly and willfully, he would not have threatened the plaintiff's safety, so far as appearances could warn him. His conduct would not have involved, even then, an unreasonable probability of invasion of her bodily security. Liability can be no greater where the act is inadvertent.

Negligence, like risk, is thus a term of relation. Negligence in the abstract, apart from things related, is surely not a tort, if indeed it is understandable at all...

The law of causation, remote or proximate, is thus foreign to the case before us. The question of liability is always anterior to the question of the measure of the consequences that go with liability. If there is no tort to be redressed, there is no occasion to consider what damage might be recovered if there were a finding of a tort. We may assume, without deciding, that negligence, not at large or in the abstract, but in relation to the plaintiff, would entail liability for any and all consequences, however novel or extraordinary. There is room for argument that a distinction is to be drawn according to the diversity of interests invaded by the act, as where conduct negligent in that it threatens an insignificant invasion of an interest in property results in an unforeseeable invasion of an interest of another order, as e.g. one of bodily security. Perhaps other distinctions may be necessary. We do not go into the question now. The consequences to be followed must first be rooted in a wrong.

Case dismissed.

(35) Hynes v. New York Central Railroad (U.S.)

Hynes v. New York Cent. R. Co.

May 31, 1921

Action by Florence Hynes, as administratrix of James Harvey Hynes, deceased, against the New York Central Railroad Company. From the judgment of the Appellate Division (190 App.Div. 915, 179 N.Y. Supp. 927) affirming by a divided court a judgment of the Trial Term dismissing the complaint, plaintiff appeals.

Reversed, and new trial granted.

See, also, 188 App. Div. 178, 176 N.Y. Supp. 795.

Hiscock, C.J. and Chase and McLaughlin, JJ., dissenting.

CARDOZO, J.

On July 8, 1916, Harvey Hynes, a lad of 16, swam with two companions from the Manhattan to the Bronx side of the Harlem River, or United States Ship Canal, a navigable stream. Along the Bronx side of the river was the right of way of the defendant, the New York Central Railroad, which operated its trains at that point by high-tension wires, strung on poles and cross-arms. Projecting from defendant's bulkhead above the waters of the river was a plank or springboard, from which boys of the nighborhood used to dive. One end of the board had been placed under a rock on the defendant's land, and nails had been driven at its point of contact with the bulkhead. Measured from this point of contact the length behind was 5 feet; the length in front 11. The bulkhead itself was about 3 ½ feet back of the pier line as located by the government. From this it follows that for 7 ½ feet the springboard was beyond the line of the defendant's property and above the public waterway. Its height measured from the stream was 3 feet at the bulkhead, and 5 feet at its outermost extremity. For more than five years swimmers had used it as a diving board without protest or obstruction.

On this day Harvey Hynes and his companions climbed on the top of the bulkhead, intending to leap into the water. One of them made the plunge in safety. Hynes followed to the front of the springboard, and stood poised for his dive. At that moment a cross-arm with electric wires fell from the defendant's pole. The wires struck the diver, flung him from the shattered board, and plunged him to his death below. His mother, suing as administratrix, brings this action for her damages. Thus far the courts have held that Hynes at the end of the springboard above the public waters was a trespasser on the defendant's land.

They have thought it immaterial that the board itself was a trespass, an encroachment on the public ways. They have thought it of no significance that Hynes would have met the same fate if he had been below the board and not above it. The board, they have said, was annexed to the defendant's bulkhead. By force of such annexation, it was to be reckoned as a fixture, and thus constructively, if not actually, an extension of the land. The defendant was under a duty to use reasonable care that bathers swimming or standing in the water should not be electrocuted by wires falling from its right of way. But to bathers diving from the springboard, there was no duty, we are told, unless the injury was the product of mere willfulness or wantonness – no duty of active vigilance to safeguard the impending structure. Without wrong to them, cross-arms might be left to rot; wires highly charged with electricity might sweep them from their stand and bury them in the subjacent waters. In climbing on the board, they became trespassers and outlaws. The conclusion is defended with much subtlety of reasoning, with much insistence upon its inevitableness as a merely logical deduction. A majority of the court are unable to accept it as the conclusion of the law.

We assume, without deciding, that the springboard was a fixture, a permanent improvement of the defendant's right of way. Much might be said in favor of another view. We do not press the inquiry for we are persuaded that the rights of bathers do not depend upon these nice distinctions. Liability would be doubtful, we are told, had the boy been diving from a pole, if the pole had been vertical. The diver in such situation would have been separated from the defendant's freehold. Liability, it is said has been escaped because the pole was horizontal. The plank when projected lengthwise was an extension of the soil. We are to concentrate our gaze on the private ownership of the board. We are to ignore the public ownership of the circumambient spaces of water and of air. Jumping from a boat or a barrel, the boy would have been a bather in the river. Jumping from the end of a springboard, he was no longer, it is said, a bather, but a trespasser on the right of way.

Rights and duties in systems of living law are not built upon such quicksands.

Bathers in the Harlem River on the day of this disaster were in the enjoyment of a public highway, entitled to reasonable protection while they were diving from encroaching objects or engaging in the sports that are common among swimmers. Such acts were not equivalent to an abandonment of the highway, a departure from its proper uses, a withdrawal from the waters, and an entry upon land. A plane of private right had been interposed between the river and the air, but public ownership was unchanged in the space below it and above it. The defendant does not deny that it would have owed a duty to this boy if he had been leaning against the springboard with his feet upon the ground. He is said forfeited protection as he put his feet upon the plank. Presumably the same result would follow if the plank had been a few inches above the surface of the water instead of a few feet. Duties are supposed to arise and to be extinguished in alternate zones or strata. Two boys walking in the country or swimming in a river stop to rest for a moment along the side of the road or the margin of the stream. One of them throws himself beneath the overhanging branches of a tree. The other perches himself on a bough a foot or so above the ground. Hoffman v. Armstrong, 48 N.Y. 201, 8 Am. Rep. 537. Both are killed by falling wires. The defendant would have us say that there is a remedy for the representatives of one and none for the representatives of the other. We may be permitted to distrust the logics that leads to such conclusions.

The truth is that every act of Hynes from his first plunge into the river until the moment of his death was in the enjoyment of the public waters, and under cover of the protection which his presence in those waters gave him. The use of the springboard was not an abandonment of his rights as bather. It was a mere by-play, an incident, subordinate and ancillary to the execution of his primary purpose, the enjoyment of the highway. The by-play, the incident, was not the cause of the disaster. Hynes would have gone to his death if he had been below the springboard or beside it. Laidlaw v. Sage, 158 N.Y. 73, 97, 52 N.E. 679, 44 L.R.A. 216. The wires were not stayed by the presence of the plank. They followed the boy in his fall, and overwhelmed him in the waters.

The defendant assumes that the identification of ownership of a fixture with ownership of land is complete in every incident. But there are important elements of difference. Title to the fixture, unlike title to the land, does not carry with it rights of ownership usque ad coelum. There will hardly be denial that a cause of action would have arisen if the wires have fallen on an aeroplane proceeding above the river, though the location of the impact could be identified as the space above the springboard. The most that the defendant can fairly ask is exemption from liability where the use of the fixture is itself the efficient peril. That would be the situation, for example, if the weight of the boy upon the board had caused it to break and thereby throw him into the river. There is no such causal connection here between his position and his injuries. We think there was no moment when he was beyond the pale of the defendant's duty – the duty of care and vigilance in the storage of destructive forces.

This case is a striking instance of the dangers of 'a jurisprudence of conceptions' (Pound, Mechanical Jurisprudence (Columbia Law Review, 605, 808, 610), the extension of a maxim or a definition with relentless disregard of consequences to 'a dryly logical extreme'. The approximate and relative become the definite and absolute. Landowners are not bound to regulate their conduct in contemplation of the presence of trespassers intruding into private structures. Landowners are bound to regulate their conduct in contemplation of the presence of travelers upon the adjacent public ways. There are times when there is little trouble in marking off the field of exemption and immunity from liability and duty. Here structures and ways are so united and commingled, superimposed upon each other, that the fields are brought together. In such circumstances, there is little help in pursuing general maxims to ultimate conclusions. They have been framed alio intuitu. They must be reformulated and readapted to meet exceptional conditions. Rules appropriate to spheres which are conceived of as separate and distinct cannot both be enforced when the spheres become concentric. There must then be readjustment or collision. In one sense, and that a highly technical and artificial one, the diver at the end of the springboard is an intruder on the adjoining lands. In another sense, and one that realists will accept more readily, he is on public waters in the exercise of public rights. The law must say whether it will subject him to the rule of the one field or of the other, of this sphere or of that. We think that considerations of analogy, of convenience, of policy, and of justice, exclude him from the field of the defendant's immunity and exemption, and place him in the field of liability and duty. Beck v. Carter N.Y. 283, 23 Am. Rep. 175; Jewhurst v. City of Syracuse, 108 N.Y. 303, 15 N.E. 409; McCloskey v. Buckley, 223 N.Y. 187, 192, 119 N.E. 395.

The judgment of the Appellate Division and that of the Trial Term should be reversed, and a new trail granted, with costs to abide the event.

HOGAN, POUND; and CRANE, JJ., concur.

HISCOCK, C.J., and CHASE and McLAUGHLIN, JJ. dissent.

Judgment reversed, etc.

(36) Torres v. Reardon (U.S.)

Excerpts from Jose Torres v. Michael Reardon et al. (Court of Appeal of California, 3 Cal. App. 4th 831; 1992 Cal. App.):

Croskey, J. Plaintiff and appellant Jose Torres (Torres) appeals from the summary judgment against him and in favor of defendants Michael and Ona Reardon (the Reardons). Because there is no evidence that Torres's injuries resulted from any act of negligence by, or attributable to, the Reardons, or that any circumstances existed that would impose upon them liability for Torres's injuries under the peculiar risk doctrine, the trial court properly granted summary judgment.

Factual and procedural background

During the years of 1980 to 1988, Jose Torres was a self-employed gardener, doing business under the name of Jose Torres Gardening Service. From approximately 1984 until June of 1988, as part of his gardening business, Torres performed weekly general gardening services at several homes on Cricklewood Street in the City of Torrance, California, including the home of the Reardons.

Early in 1988, the Reardons began discussing with Torres the possibility of employing him to trim a 65- to 70-foot-tall tree located in their front yard. In mid-June of that year, it was agreed that Torres would trim the tree for a price of USD 350. Final arrangements for the trimming were made between Torres and Ona Reardon. The Reardon's next door neighbor, David Boice, was also present at the conversation in which the arrangements were made. Boice expressed concern at that time that care be taken in the cutting of a large branch that overhung Boice's house to assure that the branch did not fall onto his roof.

At 11 a.m., on the morning of June 20, 1988, four days after agreeing to trim the Reardons' tree, Torres arrived at the Reardons' home with one helper, prepared to do the job. The Reardons were not at home when Torres arrived, or at any time while he was working. David Boice, the next door neighbor, was at home in his garage-workshop, building an electrical panel. (Boice was an electrical contractor by trade and had done electrical work on the Reardons' home.) Boice reminded Torres to take care that the large branch overhanging his house did not fall onto the roof, and he occasionally left his garage to observe Torres's work. Torres used a chain saw to cut the larger branches of the tree. At one point, Boice observed that Torres was not using safety lines, and asked why. Torres answered that he did not need them.

The branch that extended over Boice's house left the tree's trunk at a point approximately 25 feet from the ground and had a diameter of approximately 20 inches. When Torres was ready to cut it, Boice came outside to hold a rope that was tied to the branch, apparently with the intention of pulling the branch away from Boice's roof as it fell. Torres positioned himself on the branch next to the trunk and began to cut at a point just beyond where he was standing. Torres was wearing a safety belt around his waist, but it was not attached to the tree, as he did not have a line long enough to reach the branch strong enough to hold him. According to Torres, Boice pulled on the rope when Torres was not expecting a pull. As a result, Torres's chain saw "kicked back", and Torres fell from the tree, landing on his back. Torres was rendered paraplegic as a result of his fall.

On April 12, 1989, Torres filed suit against the Reardons and against the manufacturer and seller of the chain saw that he was using when he fell from the tree.

On December 7, 1990, the trial court granted the Reardons' motion for summary judgment. Judgment was entered thereon, and this appeal followed.

Contentions on appeal:

Torres contends that: (1) a triable issue of fact existed as to whether he was an employee of the Reardons at the time of the accident that caused his injuries; (2) if Torres was engaged by the Reardons as an independent contractor, rather than an employee, the Reardons are liable for his injuries under the doctrine of "peculiar risk"; (3) a triable issue of fact existed as to whether the Reardons were negligent in the hiring and supervision of Torres, and whether such negligence was the cause of his injuries; (4) a triable issue of fact existed as to whether Torres reasonably assumed the risks involved in trimming a 70-foot tree.

...

(37) Bronston v. U.S. (U.S.)

Distinguishing true from false depositions which are provided as evidence in courts is a professional task that judges have to master. The decision which follows illustrates the specific problem of distinguishing whether the answer which is on its face truthful may be perceived as perjury because it negatively implies another result. In the case syllabus, the U.S. Supreme Court provided the following holding: *Federal perjury statute, 18 U.S.C. 1621, does not reach a witness' answer that is literally true, but unresponsive, even assuming the witness intends to mislead his questioner by the answer, and even assuming the answer is arguably "false by negative implication". A perjury prosecution is not, in our adversary system, the primary safeguard against errant testimony; given the incongruity of an unresponsive answer, it is questioner's burden to frame his interrogation acutely to elicit the precise information he seeks.* The text of sec. 1621 is rendered in this book in the paragraph 4.3.2 as an example of a culturally valuable achievement in law. The U.S. Supreme Court realizes that "*(T)here is, indeed, an implication in the answer to the second question that there was never a personal bank account; in casual conversation this interpretation might reasonably be drawn.*" The court recognizes that the language is used here in a specific legal framework and that speech acts which come about under such conditions cannot be evaluated with means applied for the appraisal of speech acts made in colloquial speech. Therefore, what may be perceived as a lie in ordinary language will not automatically turn into a perjury in law. The reason for this is that language use requirements in these different speech acts differ. Ordinary language provides for very vague and simplified requirements for the distinguishing between true and false statements whereas the legal language provides an institutionally established catalogue of prerequisites, in casu sec. 1621, which enables the interpretation of the speech act in terms of law.

U.S. Supreme Court

Bronston v. United States, 409 U.S. 352 (1973)

Certiorari to the United States Court of Appeals for the Second Circuit

Mr. Chief Justice Burger delivered the opinion of the Court.

We granted the writ in this case to consider a narrow but important question in the application of the federal perjury statute, 18 U.S.C. 1621: whether a witness (409 U.S. 352, 353) may be convicted of perjury for an answer, under oath, that is literally true but not responsive to the question asked and arguably misleading by negative implication.

Petitioner is the sole owner of Samuel Bronston Productions, Inc., a company that between 1958 and 1964, produced motion pictures in various European locations. For these enterprises, Bronston Productions opened bank accounts in a number of foreign countries; in 1962, for example, it had 37 accounts in five countries. As president of Bronston Productions, petitioner supervised transactions involving the foreign bank accounts.

In June 1964, Bronston Productions petitioned for an arrangement with creditors under Chapter XI of the Bankruptcy Act, 11 U.S.C. 701 et seq. On June 10, 1966, a referee in bankrupcy held a 21(a) hearing to determine, for the benefit of creditors, the extent and location of the company's assets. Petitioner's perjury (409 U.S. 352, 354) conviction was founded on the answers given by him as a witness at the bankruptcy hearing, and in particular on the following colloquy with a lawyer for a creditor of Bronston Productions:

"Q. Do you have any bank accounts in Swiss banks, Mr. Bronston?

"A. No, sir.

"Q. Have you ever?

"A. The company had an account there for about six months, in Zurich.

"Q. Have you any nominees who have bank accounts in Swiss banks?

"A. No, sir.

"Q. Have you ever?

"A. No, sir.

It is undisputed that for a period of nearly five years, between October 1959 and June 1964, petitioner had a personal bank account at the International Credit Bank in Geneva, Switzerland, into which he made deposits and upon which he drew checks totaling more than $ 180,000. It is likewise undisputed that petitioner's answers were literally truthful. (a) Petitioner did not in the time of questioning have a Swiss bank account. (b) Bronston Productions, Inc., did have the account in Zurich described by petitioner. (c) Neither at the time (409 U.S. 352, 355) of questioning nor before did petitioner have nominees who had Swiss bank accounts. The Government's prosecution for perjury went forward on the theory that in order to mislead his questioner, petitioner answered the second question with literal truthfulness but unresponsively addressed his answer to the company's assets and not to his own – thereby implying that he had no personal Swiss bank account at the relevant time.

At petitioner's trial, the District Court instructed the jury that the "basic issue" was whether petitioner "spoke his true belief." Perjury, the court stated, "necessarily involves the state of mind of the accused" and "essentially consists of willfully testifying to the truth of a fact which the defendant does not believe to be true", petitioner's testimony could not be found "willfully" false unless at the time his testimony was given petitioner "fully understood the questions put to him but nevertheless gave false answers knowing the same to be false." The court further instructed the jury that if petitioner did not understand the question put to him and for that reason gave an unresponsive answer, he could not be convicted of perjury. Petitioner could, however, be convicted if he gave an answer "not literally false but when considered in the context in which it was given, nevertheless constitute(d) a false statement." (409 U.S. 352, 356). The jury began its deliberations at 11:30 a.m. Several times it requested exhibits or additional instructions from the court, and at one point, at the request of the jury, the District Court repeated its instructions in full. At 6:10 p.m., the jury returned its verdict, finding petitioner guilty on the count of perjury before us today and not guilty on another charge not here relevant.

In the Court of Appeals, petitioner contended, as he had in post-trial motions before the District Court, that the key question was imprecise and suggestive of various interpretations. In addition, petitioner contended that he could not be convicted of perjury on the basis of testimony that was concededly truthful, however unresponsive. A divided Court of Appeals held that the question was readily susceptible of a responsive reply and that it adequately tested the defendant's belief in the veracity of his answer. The Court of Appeals further held that, "(f)or the purposes of 18 U.S.C. 1621, an answer containing half of the truth which also constitutes a lie by negative implication, when the answer is intentionally given in place of the responsive answer called for by a proper question, is perjury." 453 F.2d 555, 559. In this Court, petitioner renews his attack on the specificity of the question asked him and the legal sufficiency of his answer to support a conviction for perjury. The problem of the ambiguity of the question asked him and the legal sufficiency of his answer to support a conviction for perjury. This problem of the ambiguity of the question is not free from doubt, but we need not reach that issue. (409 U.S. 352, 357) Even assuming, as we do, that the question asked petitioner specifically focused on petitoner's personal bank accounts, we conclude that the federal perjury statute cannot be construed to sustain a conviction based on petitioner's answer.

The statute, 18 U.S.C. 1621, substantially identical in its relevant language to its predecessors for nearly a century, is "a federal statute enacted in an effort to keep the course of justice free from the pollution of perjury." United States v. Williams, 341 U.S. 58, 68 (1951). We have held that the general federal perjury provision is applicable to federal bankruptcy proceedings. Hammer v. United States, 271 U.S. 620 (1926). The need for truthful testimony in a 21 (a) bankruptcy proceeding is great, since the proceeding is "a searching inquiry into the conditions of the estate of the bankrupt, to assist in discovering and collecting the assets, and to develop facts and circumstances which bear upon the question of discharge." Travis v. United States, 123 F. 2d 268, 271 (CA10 1941). Here, as elsewhere, the perpetration of perjury "well may affect the dearest concerns of the parties before a tribunal..." United States v. Norris, 300 U.S. 564, 574 (1937).

There is, at the outset, a serious problem in applying 1621 to petitioner's answer. The words of the statute confine the offence to the witness who "willfully...states...any material matter which he does not believe to be true." Beyond question, petitioner's answer to the crucial question was not responsive if we assume, as we do, that the first question was directed at personal bank accounts. There is, indeed, an implication in the answer to the second question that there was never a personal account; in casual conversation this interpretation might reasonably be drawn. But we are not dealing with casual conversation and the statute does not make it a criminal act for a witness to willfully (409 U.S. 352, 358) state any material matter that implies any material matter that he does not believe to be true.

The Government urges that the perjury statute be construed broadly to reach petitioner's answer and thereby fulfill its historic purpose of reinforcing our adversary factfinding process. We might go beyond the precise words of the statute if we thought they did not adequately express the intention of Congress, but we perceive no reason why Congress would intend the drastic sanction of a perjury prosecution to cure a testimonial mishap that could readily have been reached with a single additional question by counsel alert – as every examiner ought to be – to the incongruity of petitioner's unresponsive answer. Under the pressures and tentions of interrogation, it is not uncommon for the most earnest witness to give answers that are not entirely responsive. Sometimes the witness does not understand the question, or may in an excess of caution or apprehension read too much or too little into it. It should come as no surprise that a participant in a bankruptcy proceeding may have something to conceal and consciously tries to do so, or that a debtor may be embarrassed at his plight and yield information reluctantly. It is the responsibility of the lawyer to probe; testimonial interrogation, and cross-examination in particular, is a probing, prying, pressing form of inquiry. If a witness evades, it is the lawyer's responsibility to recognize the evasion and to bring the witness back to (409 U.S. 352, 359) the mark, to flush out the whole truth with the tools of adversary examination.

It is no answer to say that here the jury found that petitioner intended to mislead his examiner. A jury should not be permitted to engage in conjecture whether an unresponsive answer, true and complete on its face, was intended to mislead or divert the examiner; the state of mind of the witness is relevant only to the extent that it bears on whether "he does not believe (his answer) to be true". To hold otherwise would be to inject a new and confusing element into the adversary testimonial system we know. Witnesses would be unsure of the extent of their responsibility for the misunderstandings and inadequacies of examiners, and might well fear having that responsibility tested by a jury under the vague rubric of "intent to mislead" or "perjury by implication". The seminal modern treatment of the history of the offense concludes that one consideration of policy overshadowed all others during the years when perjury first emerged as a common-law offense; "that the measures taken against the offense must not be so severe as to discourage witness from appearing or testifying." Study of Perjury, reprinted in Report of New York Law Revision Commission, Legis. Doc. No. 60, p. 249 (1935). A leading 19th century commentator, quoted by Dean Wigmore, noted that the English law "throws every fence round a person accused of perjury," for " the obligation of protecting witnesses from oppression, or annoyance, by charges, or threats of charges, of having borne false testimony, is far paramount to that of giving every perjury its deserts. To repress that crime, prevention is better than cure: and the law of England relies, for this purpose, on the means provided for detecting and exposing the crime at the moment of commission, - such as publicity, (409 U.S. 352, 360) cross-examination, the aid of jury etc.; and on the infliction of a severe, though not excessive punishment, wherever the commission of the crime has been clearly proved." W. Best, Principles of the Law of Evidence 606 (C. Chamberlayne ed. 1883). See J. Wigmore, Evidence 275-276 (3d ed. 1940). Addressing the same problem, Montesquieu took as his starting point the French tradition of capital punishment for perjury and the relatively mild English punishment for the pillory. He thought the disparity between the punishments could be explained because the French did not permit the accused to present his own witnesses, while in England "they admit of witnesses on both sides, and the affair is discussed in some measure between them; consequently false witness is there less dangerous, the accused having a remedy against the false witnesses, which he has not in France." Montesquieu, The Spirit of the Laws, quoted in Study of Perjury, supra, p. 253.

Thus, we must read 1621 in light of our own and the traditional Anglo-American judgment that a prosecution for perjury is not the sole, or even the primary, safeguard against errant testimony. While "the lower federal courts have not dealt with the question often," and while their expressions do not deal with the unresponsive testimony and are not precisely in point, "it may be said that they preponderate against the respondent's contention." United States v. Norris, 300 U.S., at 576. The cases support petitioner's position that the perjury statute is not to be loosely construed, nor the statute invoked simply because a wily witness succeeds in derailing the questioner – so long as the witness speaks the literal truth. The burden is on the questioner to pin the witness down to the specific object of the questioner's inquiry. United States v. Wall, 371 F.2d 398 (CA6 1967); United State v. Slutzky, 79 F.2d 504 (CA3 (409 U.S. 352, 361) 1935); Galanos v. United States, 49 F.2d 898 (CA6 1931); United States v. Cobert, 227 F. Supp. 915 (SD Cal. 1964).

The Government does not contend that any misleading or incomplete response must be sent to the jury to determine whether a witness committed perjury because he intended to sidetrack his questioner. As the Government recognizes, the effect of so unlimited an interpretation of 1621 would be broadly unsettling. It is said, rather, that petitioner's testimony falls within a more limited category of intentionally misleading responses with an especially strong tendency to mislead the questioner. In the federal cases cited above, the Government tells us the defendants gave simple negative answers "that were both entirely responsive and entirely truthful...In neither case did the defendant – as did the petitioner here – make affirmative statements of one fact that in context constituted denials by negative implication of a related fact." Thus the Government isolates two factors which are said to require application of the perjury statute in the circumstances of the case: the unresponsiveness of petitioner's answer and the affirmative cast of that answer, with its accompanying negative implications.

The analysis succeeds in confirming the Government's position, but it does not persuade us that Congress intended to extend the coverage of 1621 to answers unresponsive on their face but untrue only by "negative implication". Though perhaps a plausible argument can be made that unresponsive answers are especially likely to mislead, any such argument must (409 U.WS. 352, 362) we think, be predicate upon the questioner's being aware of the unresponsiveness of the relevant answer. Yet, if the questioner is aware of the unresponsiveness of the answer, with equal force it can be argued that the very unresponsiveness of the answer should alert counsel to press on for the information he desires. It does not matter that the unresponsive answer is stated in the affirmative, thereby implying the negative of the question actually posed; for again, by hypothesis, the examiner's awareness of unresponsiveness should lead him to press another question or reframe his initial question with greater precision. Precise questioning is imperative as a predicate for the offense of perjury.

It may well be that petitioner's answers were not guileless but were shrewdly calculated to evade. Nevertheless, we are constrained to agree with Judge Lumbard, who dissented from the judgment of the Court of Appeals, that any special problems arising from the literally true but unresponsive answer are to be remedied through the "questioner's acuity" and not by a federal perjury prosecution.

Reversed.

(38) In re Maldonado (UK)

The following English court decision is known among jurists as the Maldonado-case. It is particularly complex in its linguistic and juridic structure. Although some of its paragraphs have been quoted in the main text, it seems expedient to quote here also the entire text. It perfectly illustrates many issues discussed in the theoretical part of this book. In the English private international law, the Maldonado-case concerned the problem of characterization (qualification) of legal notions and especially the issue of perspective in which this characterization should be undertaken. Here, the legal-linguistic perspective dominates the analysis. Issues relevant to this case as one of the leading cases of the English private international law of characterization are therefore mentioned only on the margin. In the main text, the Maldonado-case has been dealt with because it addresses or rather touches upon some principal legal-linguistic questions such as whether a judicial decision may be viewed as "a mere matter of words", or a "distinction without difference". In the decision there is a direct reference to such proceedings where the foreign State is perceived as one which "can constitute itself successor" (cf. p. 1585 of the decision in All E R). This makes plain that the legal language and the underlying legal reality are created and not simply found and that they are created with linguistic means. The Maldonado-case may not be the best available source for the analysis of the process in which the legal language is created. It shows, however, in a unique way how this specific language is used and how it functions in a judicial decision. It functions in this case as a piece of argumentation where a unanimous legal decision reached by a collegial body should be made convincing to the readers in a controversial case. All three judges delivered their opinions in which despite the reference to views contrary to the result reached in the case, the same main line of justification is maintained. This subliminal argument on which the whole opinion is based is that the result reached is overwhelmingly better justified than the thinkable opposite result. The fact that three concurring opinions are delivered, strengthens the impression that the decision is right or at least that it is much better than the thinkable opposite decision. Intertextual references as legal arguments are aboundantly used to this effect. References to the precedents and to the legal literature are frequent; the quotation from Dicey's Conflict of Laws is even literally quoted twice in the same decision (cf. pp. 1582 and 1584) which as such seems to be already a legal-linguistic rarity. Passages from the legal literature are perceived as "incorporated in this judgment" (cf. p. 1585) and the numerous quotes which could also be used to support the opposite view to the one reached in the unanimous decision are repeated several times in the concurring opinions as well. For the contrary view, there are apparently no convincing arguments; the third judge, therefore, concludes assertively "I can see no warrant for acceding to, nor authority to support, it." (cf. p. 1587). The final formulas repeated three times: "I think the appeal fails and should be dismissed" (cf. p. 1584), "I agree that this appeal fails and should be dismissed" (cf. p. 1587), and "I think that this appeal fails." (cf. p. 1587), let no room for doubts, especially when repeated almost literally.

Re Maldonado (deceased)

State of Spain v. Treasury Solicitor

(All England Report 1953 vol. 2, pp. 1579-1587)

Court of Appeal (Sir Raymond Evershed, M.R., Jenkins and Morris, L.JJ.) November 26, 27, 30 1953.

Conflict of Laws – Succession to estate of intestate – Foreign domicil of intestate – Personal property in England – Claim by foreign State as sole and universal heir

On Oct. 11, 1924, the deceased, a Spanish citizen domiciled in Spain died there a widow and intestate, leaving movable property in England. On June 4, 1930, the State of Spain obtained in Spain a declaration of heirship on failure of heirs on intestacy, and now claimed a grant of letters of administration of the English property. On the evidence, the State of Spain was "a true heir just as any individual heir according to Spanish law", but it was contended by the Crown that the maxim "mobilia sequuntur personam" stopped short of recognition of a State as successor.

Held: assuming that there was a valid distinction between the case where a foreign State claimed property in England of a person dying intestate and domiciled in the territory of the foreign State on the footing that it was ownerless and bona vacantia and the case where the foreign State claimed to be the successor by virtue of its own laws, in the latter case there was no rule of the English law which confined such succession to individuals having a particular quality or characteristic or had the effect of excluding a State from entertaining the capacity of an heir, and therefore, the State of Spain as true heir was entitled to a grant.

Decision of Barnard, J. (ante, p. 300), affirmed.

As to Intestate Succession to Movables see Halsbury, Hailsham Edn., Vol. 6, p. 245, para. 299; and for cases see Digest, Replacement Vol. 11, pp. 397, 398, Nos. 525-550.

Cases referred to:

(1) Re Barnett's Trusts, (1902) 1 Ch. 847; 71 L.J.Ch. 408; 86 L-T. 346; 11 Digest, Replacement, 398, 548.

(2) In the Estate of Musurus, (1936) 2 All E.R. 1666; Digest Supp.

Appeal by the defendant, The Treasury Solicitor, from a decision of Barnard, J., dated May 22, 1953, and reported ante, p. 300.

Eloisa Hernandez Maldonado, a Spanish subject domiciled in Spain, died there on Oct. 11, 1924, a widow and intestate, with no ascendant, descendant or collateral relative entitled to succeed to her estate on her death under the law of Spain. She left movable property in England valued at the time of her death at the sum of £ 31,515 5s. 4d. but now said to be worth of some £ 27,000. Article 956 of the Spanish Civil Code, as translated for the purposes of this case, and in the form in which it stood at the death of the intestate, was in these terms:

"In default of persons having the right to inherit in accordance with the provisions of the foregoing sections (which is the present case) the State shall inherit, the assets being devoted to institutions of charity and free instruction in the following order: (i) municipal charitable establishments and free schools of the place of residence of the deceased, (ii) establishment of both classes of the province to which the deceased belonged, (iii) charitable establishment and educational establishments of a general character."

On June 4, 1930, the State of Spain obtained in Spain a declaration of heirship in accordance with art. 958 of the Spanish Civil Code "to enable the State to take physical possession of the estate". The State of Spain brought proceedings in this country claiming that letters of administration to the estate of the intestate in this country should issue to the duly constituted attorney of the Spanish State as the sole and universal heir to her estate by Spanish law. The defendant in the action was the Treasury Solicitor, who claimed that a grant should issue for the benefit of the Crown as bona vacantia. On May 22, 1953, Barnard, J., held that on the evidence before him the State of Spain was a true heir just as any other individual heir according to Spanish law; that there was nothing contrary to English policy or repugnant to English law in a foreign State being permitted to take possession of the movables of one of its citizens in this country, and that, therefore, the State of Spain was entitled to a grant of letters of administration of the English estate. The Treasury Solicitor appealed.

Sir Lynn Ungoed-Thomas, Q.C., and Victor Russell for the Treasury Solicitor. Russell, Q.C. and Lindner, Q.C., for the State of Spain.

Sir Raymond Evershed, M.R., stated the facts and continued: It was agreed in the court below, and it has been conceded in this court, that the question is, as between the plaintiff, the State of Spain, and the defendant, the Treasury Solicitor: Who is entitled to the property? – since it is conceded that the right to the grant depends on the right to the property. The claim of the State of Spain is that by the law of Spain the State is entitled, in the circumstances of the case, as "successor" to inherit all the property of the intestate, and, accordingly, that the English courts will apply the principle mobilia sequuntur personam and accept the State of Spain as entitled to the property in question. On the other side, the Treasury Solicitor argues that the claim of the State of Spain is in truth not by way of a succession, but by the exercise of a paramount right of a sovereign State to take property of its nationals which has become ownerless on their deaths, and that the corresponding right of the English Crown to ownerless property is the only right that the English courts will recognise, having regard to the fact that the property in question is in England.

Barnard, J., had first to determine what was the relevant Spanish law. The material article of the Spanish Civil Code which was in force on Oct. 11 1924 (the date of the death) is art. 956. On this article there was a sharp conflict of expert testmony. Two witnesses called for the State of Spain said that the effect of the article was, as is stated by its terms, that the intestate having left no issue, parents or grandparents, surviving spouse, or collaterals within the sixth degree (for the purpose of art. 955 in force in October, 1924), the State of Spain was entitled as ultimus heres. On the other side, Dr. Colas, for the Treasury Solicitor said that, notwithstanding the language of the article, the State of Spain was not a true heir or successor but had become entitled to this property as bona vacantia. Between these two views the learned judge decided clearly in favour of the witnesses for the State of Spain. He said (ante, p. 305): "I am satisfied on the evidence before me that the State of Spain is a true heir just as any individual heir according to Spanish law". This finding has not been challenged in this court.

The Crown's argument before us may fairly be stated in the form of four propositions. (i) Prima facie, movable property situate within the limits and jurisdiction of any State is subject to the laws of the State, and if such property be found to be ownerless it will pass to and become the property of the State. This, at least, is the law of England, and in the case supposed the property in England is assumed by the Crown as bona vacantia. (ii) To the above general rule there is an exception, being a rule of private international law generally accepted by and forming part of the law of civilised States, including England. The exception is expressed by the formula mobilia sequuntur personam. Thus in the case of movables belonging, for example, to a deceased national of another country who died domiciled in that other country (as in the present case), the courts of this country will treat as entitled to the movables the person or persons who are by the law of that other country entitled to succeed thereto either under a testamentary disposition valid by the law of that other country or on an intestacy, as the case may be. But, (iii) the extent and scope of the exception expressed by the formula mobilia sequuntur personam is a matter in the case of each State for its own municipal law. And, (iv) in the case of a national of another State dying domiciled in the other State, and dying, according to its laws, intestate (as in the present case) the English courts will not recognise as having a title in this country to the movables of the intestate any persons who are not "successors" in accordance with some generally recognised nexus of personal relationship with the intestate, or, at least, will not recognise as a successor the foreign State itself which has made itself such by its own laws; for; notwithstanding the language used in those laws, the truth is that the State is exercising the equivalent of our jus regale as regards ownerless property. In further support of his fourth proposition counsel for the Crown has argued that since the rules of private international law apply to the relations inter se of individuals or, at least of subjects of States and not to the relations inter se of States themselves, the scope of the exception necessarily and logically stops short of recognition of a State as successor.

Counsel for the State of Spain has not, at any rate for the purpose of this appeal, been concerned to contest the first three of the propositions submitted by the Crown. His challenge has been directed to the fourth and last. According to this argument the successors of the foreign intestate are those persons, whether natural persons or personae fictae (including the foreign State itself) who, by the laws of the foreign State, are constituted successors. There can, according to counsel, be no justification for a requirement by our courts that the successors should have a particular quality, for example, that they should be blood relations of the deceased in some degree. Thus, to take the example used during the course of the argument, if the Spanish law decreed that, in default of any relations of the degree stated in the Code, the Archbishop of Toledo should be the next successor, the English courts must recognise the title of the archbishop to the movables here of a Spanish intestate. It follows thence that no line can be drawn to exclude a persona ficta, whether a corporation, a municipality, or the State itself, so long as, by the Spanish law, such personae are in truth made successors and do not claim their title otherwise, for example, by a right of appropriation of the property as bona vacantia.

In confining his argument to this single question, counsel accepted as good law the decision by Kekewich, J., in Re Barnett's Trusts (1) the English Crown claimed as bona vacantia movables belonging to a former Austrian citizen. But there was joined as a party for the purpose of the argument a representative of the then Austrian government who also claimed the property. The relevant art. 760 of the General Civil Code of Austria, unlike the article with which we are concerned of the Spanish Code, used this language:

"If the spouse is no longer alive, the succession is confiscated as heirless property either by the fiscus or by those persons who according to the political ordinances are justified in confiscating heirless estates"; and, having regard to the terms of that article, Kekewich, J., held that the claim of the Austrian government or its representative did not depend on his being in the guise or clothing of a successor, his claim was a claim to ownerless property, and, as between similar claims on the part of the British Crown and on the part of the Austrian government, that of the former must prevail. The argument for the Crown is set out at length (1902 1 Ch. 849), and it was observed pertinently by counsel for the State of Spain that there was no argument put forward on the part of the English Crown that no claim to "ownerless" movables by a foreign State as a successor, or in any other capacity, could, in any event, be successfully put forward in these courts. The argument of the representatives of the Crown was based on the terms of the article which I have read, and was to the effect that the right asserted by the Austrian government rested on a confiscation in the terms of art. 760 of the property as heirless (that is, ownerless) property. At the end of the argument it was said (1902 1 Ch. 852): "If in one of the countries a different principle prevailed (that is, if the State took not as on confiscation of heirless property, but as being a successor), a more difficult question might arise, because international law depends on reciprocity. But as in this country, so in Austria the State takes, not as 'ultimus heres' but 'jure regali'. It being clear that goods of this kind are taken by the Crown in both countries as bona vacantia, the law of England must apply to the English goods as the law of Austria would to goods in Austria".

The representative of the Crown cited Bar's Private International Law, Gillespie's translation, 2nd ed., p. 843, para. 387, which reads: "The question to which State property is to fall where there is no heir, whether to that in which it is situated, or to that to which the last possessor belonged, is dependent upon whether the right of the State to succeed is to be considered to be a right occupatione or a right of consolidation belonging to the feudal superior, or as a true right of succession. In either the first or the second case, the property will go to the State where the property is situated; in the last case it will fall to that of the domicil of the deceased, in so far as both States hold the theory of a universal succession, or as the estate is made up of movables. The theory which is in conformity with modern ideas of law, which is more deserving of our respect, and which undoubtedly now prevails as the theory of the law in Germany, is that, if there is no nearer in blood to be called to the succession, a man's fellow-countrymen must be regarded as his heirs. This view is supported by the fact that it is the State to which a man belongs that fixes the circle of those who are entitled to succeed to him as heirs, drawing it more or less wide, as it pleases; while, on the other hand, it has more or less of the air of robbery for a State to seize on the movable estate of a deceased person, who was by mere accident resident there at the moment of his death. Thus the State whose subject and citizen the deceased was, will be entitled to succeed him. But, beyond Germany, the other rule still prevails, and each State seizes the movables which happen to be within its borders."

In the course of his judgment Barnard, J., also referred to a passage in Wolff on Private International Law, 2nd ed., p. 579, which is as follows: "In default of the next of kin, the universal rule is that the property goes to the State or the Crown or a township or some other public body – in Germany, Italy, and Switzerland as ultimate 'heir', in England, Austria and Turkey by virtue of jus regale over bona vacantia. In the latter case the conflict rule on succession is not applicable because there is no 'succession' (inheritance)… the right to 'heirless' property is governed by the lex situs."

Other examples of a recognition of the distinction in the character in which a sovereign State may take is to be found in other text-books to which we were also referred during the course of the argument. For example, in Dicey's Conflict of Laws, 6th ed., the statement of r. 178 (p. 817): "The succession to the movables of an intestate is governed by the law of his domicil at the time of his death…" is followed by this passage (ibid., p. 818): "Where a person dies, e.g., intestate and a bastard, and under the law of the country where he is domiciled there is no succession to his movables, but they are bona vacantia, and leaves movables situate in a country, e.g., England, in which he is not domiciled, the title to such movables is governed by the lex situs, i.e., under English law the movables being situate in England, the Crown is entitled thereto. In such a case the foreign Treasury claims not by way of succession but because there is no succession. It does not follow that the decision would be the same if the law of the domicil was such that the foreign Treasury claimed as ultimus heres. That would be a true case of succession and would, it is submitted, be governed by the law of the domicil."

As will be observed in that work, the distinction, or the result, in the case of a foreign State claiming by way of succession is put as a submission. It is stated more positively in Cheshire's Private International Law, 4th ed., p. 59. But assuming that there is a valid distinction between the case where a Sovereign State claims the property on the footing that it is ownerless and bona vacantia, and the case where the State claims as being successor by virtue of its own laws, there is, at any rate, no statement, in any of the cases or the text-books, that I have been able to find, or to which our attention was drawn, that there is in England a rule which confines successors to individuals having a particular quality or characteristic, or which has the effect of excluding a State from ever entertaining the capacity.

In my judgment the real question is: What is the right or title by virtue of which the Spanish State now makes its claim? And, in my judgment, this point has been decided adversely to the Crown. That decision, the validity of which has not been challenged, I regard as conclusive against the appeal. I am unable to accept that, notwithstanding the finding of the learned judge, who said (ante, p. 305): "I am satisfied on the evidence before me that the State of Spain is a true heir just as any individual heir according to Spanish law.", these courts will reject the result on an apriori view of the necessary qualifications for succession. If by the law of Spain it is possible to limit or define the individuals who can claim to be successors, that is, individuals having some connection by blood or marriage with the deceased, I can see no reason why the law of Spain should not nominate or constitute as heir, in default of such individual, any person or corporation, including the State itself. The idea of succession no doubt imports some notion of continuity of, for example, title. But, I see no reason why this conception is inapplicable to the State which is constituted successor by the laws of the State. It is, indeed, as I understand it, conceded that if under a valid will property of the deceased were given to the State of Spain, the State of Spain would be then treated as being a successor, although in that case as the result of the testamentary disposition. Nor does the Latin word "heres" from which the word "inherit" is derived necessarily involve any notion of some blood connection. To quote a sentence from Cicero, me nemo nisi amicus heredem fecit. I add that, in my judgment, there is no question of the law of Spain amounting to such a confiscation as would be regarded as repugnant to our own laws, and therefore, not enforceable in these courts. Finally, I refer again to the passage at the end of the reported argument in Re Barnett's Trusts where the matter is put (1902 1 Ch. 852): "If in one of the countries a different principle prevailed, a more difficult question might arise, because international law depends upon reciprocity." There is before us no evidence of what the law of Spain would be in the controverse case of an English national dying domiciled in England intestate without next of kin under the English law and leaving movables in Spain. I am, however, not able to reject the argument of counsel of the State of Spain on the ground that there is no evidence that the law, as I think it should held in this country, might not be reciprocal in Spain. I think the appeal fails and should be dismissed.

Jenkins, L.J., stated the facts as set out above and continued: The general rule to be applied in a case such as this is summed up in the maxim mobilia sequuntur personam, and is thus stated in Dicey's Conflict of Laws, 6th ed., p. 814: "Rule 177. The distribution of the distributable residue of the movables of the deceased is (in general) governed by the law of the deceased's domicil (lex domicilii) at the time of his death." Thus, in the present case the personality in question should, prima facie, devolve in accordance with the provisions of art. 956. There is, however, an admitted exception to the general rule to the effect that if, according to the law of the foreign State in which the deceased is domiciled, there is no one entitled to succeed to the movable property of the deceased owing, for example, to the bastardy of the deceased, or to the failure of kin near enough in degree to qualify for succession under the law of the domicile, and, by the law of the foreign State, the State itself is, in such circumstances, entitled to appropriate the property of the deseased as ownerless property, by virtue of some jus regale corresponding to our own law of bona vacantia, English law will not recognise the claim of the foreign State as part of the law of succession of the domicil, but will treat it merely as to the assertion by the foreign State of a prerogative right which has no extra-territorial validity and must yield to the corresponding prerogative right of the Crown. That appears from Dicey's Conflict of Laws, 6th ed., p. 818, to which Sir Raymond Evershed, M.R., has already referred: " Where a person dies, e.g., intestate and a bastard, and under the law of the country where he is domiciled there is no succession to his movables, but they are bona vacantia, and leaves movables situate in a country, e.g., England, in which he is not domiciled, the title to such movables is governed by the lex situs, i.e. under English law the movables being situate in England, the Crown is entitled thereto. In such a case the foreign Treasury claims not by way of succession but because there is no succession."

But the law of the relevant foreign country may be such as to constitute the State itself the successor to the deceased in the absence of any individual with a prior right of succession under that law, and the question then arises whether the claim of the foreign State should be recognised under the general rule as the claim of a person entitled to succeed according to the law of domicil, or should be treated as falling within the exception on the ground that the claim of the foreign State as self-constituted successor does not differ in substance or in principle from a claim by a foreign State by virtue of its paramount right to ownerless property within its dominions as bona vacantia or the equivalent.

Accordingly, two questions were debated in the court below: First, whether under the Spanish Civil Code the State takes as a true heir or successor in the eye of Spanish law, or takes by virtue of a jus regale; and, secondly, if it takes in the former capacity, whether English law will recognise the State of Spain as a true heir or successor for the purpose of the maxim mobilia sequuntur personam. Barnard, J., having heard evidence on both sides in regard of the Spanish law, answered the first question in the former sense, and the second question in the affirmative, holding in effect that the answer to the second followed from the answer to the first. The decision of Barnard, J., on the first question has not been challenged by the Crown in this court. The sole issue before us, therefore, is whether or not the State of Spain, being admittedly according to its own law the true heir of, or successor to, the intestate, should be recognised as such by English law in its application of the maxim mobilia sequuntur personam. This question has not been the subject of any direct decision, but the distinction between the sovereign State claiming "jure regali" and as true heir or successor was recognised in Re Barnett's Trusts (1) and In the Estate of Musurus (2). Inasmuch as the foreign law in each of those cases was held to give the foreign State concerned a jus regale as distinct from a true right of succession, there was no actual decision on the present question, but, as I have said, the distinction was recognised. Indeed, as Sir Raymond Evershed, M.R., has pointed out, both those cases would have been susceptible of a short and simple answer if the view then taken of the law had been that in no circumstances could a foreign State claim the assets situated in this country of a deceased intestate, whether the claim was founded on jus regale or on a true right of succession. The question has also been discussed in various text-books on this branch of the law. For example, in Dicey's Conflict of Laws, 6th ed., p. 818, the page which I have quoted continues: "It does not follow that the decision would be the same if the law of the domicil was such that the foreign Treasury claimed as ultimus heres. That would be a true case of succession and would, it is submitted, be governed by the law of domicil".

There are also passages referred to by Sir Raymond Evershed, M.R., in Wolff on Private International Law, 2nd ed., p. 579, in Bar's Private International Law (Gillespie's Translation), 2nd ed., p. 843, para. 387, and Cheshire's Private International Law, 4th ed., p. 59, all of which I treat as incorporated in this judgment.

The conclusion of Barnard, J., therefore, has the support of no inconsiderable weight of learned opinion, and althought, for my part, I find it difficult to embrace with enthusiasm either side of this highly technical question, his conclusion also commends itself to me on the ground of consistency. In cases such as the present, English law professes to apply the law of the domicil to the devolution of the intestate's movables situated in this country. If the law of the domicil is that of a foreign State under whose law of intestacy the State itself is the successor, why should English law not give effect to that provision as part of the law of succession which it professes to apply? The reasons why, it is claimed, English law does not do so are expressed in a variety of ways. First, the distinction between succession by a sovereign State is said to be a mere matter of words. This argument is not without persuasive force, but I do not think the question can truly be said to be one of distinction without difference. The foreign State can only succeed under its own law of succession where the succession is governed by that law. On the other hand, where the case is not one of succession but of appropriation of ownerless property, the right applies to any ownerless property which may be reached by the law of the foreign State concerned, irrespective of the law by which its devolution is governed, provided only that by the relevant law it is in fact ownerless. Then it is said that the foreign State, being omnipotent so far as its own law of succession is concerned, can constitute itself successor in circumstances in which it could equally well rely on a claim based on jus regale. But in accepting the foreign State's law of succession, English law recognises the foreign State as arbiter of what the succession is to be. The foreign State could, for instance, enact that older relatives should be preferred to younger, or that male relatives should be preferred to female, or vice versa, or even that fair-haired relatives should be preferred to dark-haired. And to such distinctions, unreasonable as they might seem, English law would, as I understand the matter, have no objection. Why, then, should English law stop short of recognising the foreign State itself as a successor where, according to its own law, it is indeed such? The answer that English law recognises it to be the function of the relevant foreign law to regulate succession as between individual subjects or citizens, but declines to recognise rights conferred by the foreign State on itself in exercise of that function does not commend itself to me. It involves distinctions at least as arbitrary and artificial as those discerned by the

Crown in the distinction between jus regale and true inheritance by the State. For example, it was, I think, conceded in argument that if the Spanish law of succession provided that in circumstances such as those of the present case the estate of the intestate was to go to some person, or body, or corporation, other than the State itself, for application to charitable purposes such as those stated in art. 956 of the Spanish Civil Code, there would be no reason why the English courts, in applying the general rule to the inheritance, should not recognise and allow effect to be given to that provision. Why, then, should not the same result ensue where, as in the present case, the estate goes by Spanish law to the Spanish State itself for application to those same charitable purposes?

Then it is said that private international law is concerned only with the rights of individuals and not with the competing rights of sovereign States. That may well be so. But it is clear that English law recognises the legitimate proprietary rights of foreign sovereign States, and I see no reason why a right of succession to an intestate's estate should not be held to answer that description. Then it is said that English law should not recognise as "heir" or "successor" any person not bound by some personal nexus with the deceased. I cannot follow this. The heir or successor is surely the person, whether related to the deceased or not, who under the relevant law is entitled to inherit or to succeed. Then it is said that there is no reciprocity, because Spanish law would not give effect to a claim by the Crown in respect of bona vacantia. But non constat that Spanish law would not recognise a right to succession belonging to the Crown if any such right existed, and it could easily be made to exist by Act of Parliament if that were thought expedient.

There might be a case where a so-called right of succession claimed by a foreign State could be shown to be in truth no more than a claim to bona vacantia. If so, then, no doubt, it would be right to apply the recognised exception to the general rule, but this has not been shown to be such a case. On the contrary, it has been found (and the Crown has accepted the finding) that the State of Spain is, in the eye of Spanish law, the true heir, and I would add that, to my mind, notwithstanding what was said (1936 2 All E.R. 1667) by Sir Boyd Meriman, P., In the Estate of Musurus (2), the conclusion that this is a case of genuine succession is reinforced by the circumstance that the State of Spain is by art. 856 of the Spansh Civil Code enjoined to apply the property of the intestate to the charitable purposes therein mentioned. Accordingly, for the reasons given by Sir Raymond Evershed, M.R., and for such additional reasons as I have been able to offer, I agree that this appeal fails and should be dismissed.

Morris, L.J.: It is, I think, well settled that where a person dies domiciled in a foreign country our courts will follow and apply the law of that country when dealing with the succession, using that word in a strict sense, to the ownership of movables in this country. The property will go to the person who becomes heir to it according to the law of the domicil. One result is that the English court will, as a rule, make a grant of administration to the person who is constituted the personal representative of the deceased in the country where he was domiciled at his death. It is unnecessary to consider the basis of the recognised principle; it has been said to imply a fiction which deems movables to exist in the place of the domicil of the deceased. Re Barnett's Trusts (1) was a case where, according to the General Civil Code of Austria, there was no one to whom distribution of the property could be made, so that it became liable under the Code to be confiscated as ownerless. The provision to this effect was held by Kekewich, J., to be precisely on the lines of the English law as to bona vacantia. As Kekewich, J., said (1902 1 Ch. 859): "Where there is no heir, some paramount authority steps in and claims it, not against any one, but because there is no one to claim it at all." As the ownerless property was in England he held that the paramount authority was the English Crown.

The State of Spain has not found it necessary to challenge the decision in Re Barnett's Trusts (1) which has stood since 1902. It has in its favour the finding of Barnard., J., not assailed in this court, that the State of Spain is a true heir just as any individual heir according to Spanish law. Counsel for the Crown, while acknowledging that he must accept that this is the position under Spanish law, submits that the substance of the matter is that the Spanish State is to take in default of there being kindred of the deceased, and he submits that our adoption of the law of the deceased's domicil need not go beyond the stage when it legitimates to distribute among those with some personal nexus with the deceased, and, in any event, can stop short of any stage at which the State is decreed to take. Though the submission is reasonable and clearly formulated, I can see no warrant for acceding to, nor authority to support, it. It invites the court to lay down new doctrine in one of two alternative forms. It requires partial non-acceptance of the law of succession of the domicil, and the existence of the alternative submissons points to the fact that the court is really being asked to fix in arbitrary manner some limit to the extent of the adoption of the law of the domicil relating to succession. No question arises for consideration whether there might be provisons in a foreign law of such a nature that, either on grounds of public policy or of repugnance to English principles, our courts would not recognise rights to succession given by the foreign law.

I can see no reason why either this or another country should not by law provide that on intestacy the Crown or the State should in certain circumstances inherit. The line in such a case between becoming owner as heir or inheritor by a law dealing with inheritance on intestacy and acquiring movables because there is no one who is made their owner as heir or inheritor may be a fine one, but it is, I think, a real one. If in regard to the foreign law dealing with succession as such, partial non-acceptance is embarked upon, the line of such non-acceptance must be arbitrarily drawn. I can see no warrant for differentiating between a provision of the foreign law which on intestacy might, for example, give to remote relatives and a provision which, for example, might give to some public body whose activities might be generally welcome. As it is established and not in this court challenged, that the State of Spain is under Spanish law the heir of the deceased, and is as truly the heir as any individual heir would be, I can see no reason why the English courts should decline to recognise this particular heir. The substance of the matter, as it seems to me, is that by the law to which reference is made, the property in England is not left ownerless, but is to pass to an heir, that heir being the State of Spain. I think that this appeal fails.

Appeal dismissed.

Bibliography

The following bibliography includes only works quoted in the main text of this book. A general bibliography of the Legal Linguistics is included in Mattila (2000 b) and Mattila (2006). Our bibliography embraces a general part including all chapter references with the exception of the linguistic legislation and a special part where the works related to the linguistic legislation are listed. Works of classics such as Cicero's Topica, Boethius' De differentiis topicis or Corpus Iuris Civilis that belong to the universal history of thought are not included into our bibliography. Works from which only textual examples have been borrowed are mentioned in the main text.

General bibliography

Aarnio, A., Alexy, R., Peczenik, A. (1983): Grundlagen der juristischen Argumentation, in: Krawietz, W., Alexy, R. (eds.): Metatheorie juristischer Argumentation (Berlin: Duncker & Humblot).

Aarnio, A. (1987): The Rational as Reasonable: a Treatise on Legal Justification (Dordrecht: Reidel).

Aarnio, A. (1989): Laintulkinnan teoria (Porvoo, Helsinki: W. Söderström).

Adams K.A. (2005): A lesson in drafting contracts, in: Business Law Today, vol. 15, nr. 2, pp. 1-3.

Aichison, J. (1978): Linguistics (London: Wodder & Stoughton).

Akmajian, A. et al. (2001): Linguistics. An Introduction to Language and Communication, 5th ed. (Cambridge: MIT Press).

Alexy, R. (1983): Theorie der juristischen Argumentation (Frankfurt/M: Suhrkamp).

Amira, von, K. (1882/1895): Nordgermanisches Obligationsrecht, vol. I Altschwedisches Obligationsrecht, vol. II Westnordisches Obligationsrecht (Berlin: W. de Gruyter).

Amira, von, K. (1905): Die Handgebärden in den Bilderhandschriften des Sachsenspiegels (München: Abhandlungen der Königlichen Akademie der Wissenschaften).

Anderson, K., Okuda,Y. (2007): Translation of Japan's Private International Law: Act on the General Rules of the Application of Laws, in: Yearbook of Private International Law 8/2007.

Arntz, R. (2002): The Roman Heritage in German Legal Language, in: Mattila (ed.) (2002a).

Aroui, J.-L. (1993): Linguistique et sciences cognitives: Aristote ou Platon? D'un adepte confronté à l'avocat du diable, in: Recherches linguistiques de Vincennes, vol. 22 Francs-tireurs de la linguistique (Saint-Denis: Université Paris VIII), pp. 125-136.

Arsova-Nikolić, L. (1999): Preveduvanje. Teorija i praktika (Skopje: Univerzitet Sv. Kiril i Metodij).

Ashley, K.D. (1990): Modeling Legal Argument: Reasoning with Cases and Hypotheticals (Cambridge: Bradford Books/MIT Press).

Atiah, P.S., Summers, R.S. (1987): Form and Substance in Anglo-American Law: A Comparative Study of Legal Reasoning, Legal Theory, and Legal Institutions (Oxford: Clarendon Press).

Atias, C. (1986): Épistémologie juridique (Paris: puf).

Atias, C. (1994): Épistémologie du droit (Paris: puf).

Atienza, M., Ruiz Manero, J. (1996): Las piezas del derecho : Theoría de los enunciados jurídicos (Barcelona: Ariel).

Atienza, M. (1999): El derecho como argumentatión, in: Isegoría 21, pp. 37-47.

Atienza, M. (2006): El derecho como argumentación (Barcelona: Ariel).

Atria, F., MacCormick, D. N. (eds.) (2003): Law and Legal Interpretation (Burlington, Vermont: Ashgate).

Austin, J.L. (1962): How to Do Things with Words (Oxford: Oxford University Press).

Ayer, A.J. (1966): Can There Be a Private Language?, in: Wittgenstein. The Philosophical Investigations. Pitcher, G. (ed.) (New York: Doubleday Anchor), pp. 251-266.

Balkema, J., de Groot, G.R. (eds.) (1987): Recht en vertalen (Deventer: Kluwer).

Bańkowski, Z. (1981): The Value of Truth: Fact Scepticism Revisited, in: Legal Studies 257/68.

Barnett, H. (1999): Constitutional and Administrative Law, 2nd ed. (London: Cavendish Publishing).

Bartin, E. (1897): De l'impossibilité d'arriver à une solution définitive de conflicts de lois, in : Journal de droit international, vol. 24.

Bartoszewski, A. (1979): Istoria russkogo literaturnogo jazyka (Warszawa: PWN).

Baylis, J., Smith, S. (eds.) (2005): The Globalization of World Politics, 3rd ed. (Oxford: Oxford University Press).

Baylon, Ch. (1991): Sociolinguistique. Société, langue et discours (Paris: Nathan Université).

Beaudoin, L. (2002): Legal Translation in Canada, in: Mattila (ed.) (2002a).

Bench-Capon, T.J.M., Coenen, F.P. (1992): Isomorphism and Legal Knowledge Based Systems, in: Artificial Intelligence and Law 1, pp. 65-86.

Benedetti, G. (1999): Diritto e linguaggio. Variazioni sul 'diritto muto', in: Europa e diritto privato, pp. 137-152.

Berman, D.H., Hafner, C.D. (1987): Indeterminacy: A Challenge to Logic-based Models of Legal Reasoning, in: Yearbook of Law Computers and Technology, vol. 3, pp. 1-35.

Berman, D.H., Hafner, C.D. (1993): Representing Teleological Structure in Case-Based Legal Reasoning: The Missing Link, in: Proceedings of the 4th International Conference on Artificial Intelligence and Law, pp. 50-60 (New York: ACM Press).

Berman, H.J. (1977): The Origins of Western Legal Science, in: Harvard Law Review, vol. 90/ 894.

Berman, H.J. (1983): Law and Revolution. The Transformation of Western Legal Tradition (Cambridge/London: Harvard University Press).

Berteloot, P. (2002): Legal French in France and in the European Communities, in: Mattila, H. (ed.) (2002): The Development of Legal Language, pp. 81-99 (Helsinki: Kauppakaari).

Beveridge, B. (2002): Legal English. How it Developed and Why it is not Appropriate for International Commercial Contracts, in: Mattila (ed.) (2002a).

Bonsdorff, von, P. (1984): Om det svenska lagspråket i Finland, in: Tidskrift utgiven av Juridiska Föreningen i Finland, 1984/403.

Borja Albi, A. (2004): La investigación en traducción jurídica, in: García Peinado y Ortega Arjonilla (eds.): Panorama actual de la investigación en traducción (Granada: Atrio).

Broekman, J.M. (1984): Text als Institution, in: Rechtstheorie, Beiheft 4: Recht als Sinn und Institution, pp. 145-167.

Brandom, R.B. (2000): Articulating Reasons (Boston: Boston University Press).

Branting, K. (1991): Reasoning with Portions of Precedents, in: Proceedings of the 3rd International Conference on Artificial Intelligence and Law, pp. 145-154 (New York: ACM Press).

Brodziak, K. (2004): O lingwistycznym statucie języka prawnego, in: Studia Prawnicze vol.1, pp. 110-124.

Bülow, E. (1981): Materialien zu einer Bibliographie der Rechtslinguistik (Ein Versuch), in: Studium Sprachwissenschaft, vol. 5. (Münster: WWU).

Bülow, E. (1985): Interdisziplinarität, Legitimität und Finalisierbarkeit der angewandten Sprachwissenschaft, in: Peuser, G., Winter, S. (eds.) Angewandte Sprachwissenschaft: Grundfragen Bereiche Methoden (Bonn: Bouvier) pp. 17-40.

Bülow, E. (1986): Strafdrohungen und ihr magisches Potential, in: Lange-Seidl, A. (ed.) Zeichen und Magie (Tübingen: Stauffenburg Verlag).

Bulygin, E. (ed.) (1983): El lenguaje del derecho: homenaje a Genaro R. Carrió (Buenos Aires: Abaledo-Perrot).

Canale, D., Tuzet, G. (2007): On Legal Inferentialism. Towards a Pragmatics of Semantic Content in Legal Interpretation?, in: ratio juris, vol. 20, nr. 1, pp. 32-44.

Cao, D. (2008): Is the Chinese Legal Language More Ambiguous and Vaguer?, in: Wagner, A., Cacciaguidi-Fahy, S. (eds.), Obscurity and Clarity in the Law. Prospects and Challenges (Aldershot: Ashgate).

Carcassonne, G. (2005): La Constitution, 7th ed. (Paris: Éditions du Seuil).

Cardozo, B.N. (1928): The Nature of the Judicial Process (New Haven: Yale University Press).

Carrión Wam, R. (1982) Panorama de la Semiótica Jurídica, in: Investigationes Semióticas 2/3 1982-83, pp. 116-190.

Carval, S. (1995): La responsabilité civile dans sa fonction de peine privée (Paris: LGDJ).

Cassese, A. (2005): International Law, 2nd ed. (Oxford: Oxford University Press).

Cordeiro, A.M. (2004): Vernáculo jurídico: directrizes ou directivas, in: Revista Ordem dos Advogados, an. 64/vol. I/II.

Cornu, G. (2005): Linguistique juridique, 3rd ed. (Paris: Montchrestien).

Cox, J., Hillman, R., Langevoort, D. (2006): Securities Regulation, 5th ed. (New York: Aspen).

Cooter, R., Ulen, T. (2004): Law and Economics, 4th ed. (Boston: Pearson).

Curtius, E.R. (1996): Evropska književnost i latinski srednji vek, (orig. Europäische Literatur und lateinisches Mittelalter) (Beograd: Srbska Književna Zadruga).

David, R. (1978): Les grands systèmes de droit contemporains, 7th ed. (Paris: Dalloz).

Davidson, D. (2001): Inquiries into Truth and Interpretation, 2nd ed. (Oxford: Clarendon Press).

Deleuze, G., Guattari, F. (1991): Qu'est-ce que la philosophie? (Paris: puf).

De Groot, R.G., Schulze, R. (eds.) (1999): Recht und Übersetzen (Baden-Baden: Nomos).

Den Boer, M.: The Legal Art of Unambiguous Storytelling (unpublished paper).

DiMatteo, L. (2005): A Theory of Interpretation in the Realm of Idealism, bepress Legal Series, working paper 872.

Đorđević, M. (2002): Pravo u hermeneutičkom krugu (Beograd: Službeni list SRJ).

Dölle, H. (1949): Vom Stil der Rechtsprache (Tübingen: Mohr).

Dominicy, M. (1993): De Toulmin à Perelman. Analyse d'un réseau argumentatif, in : Verbum 1-2-3/ 1993.

Dreißigacker, M. (2002): Sprachenfreiheit im Verbrauchervertragsrecht (Frankfurt/M.: P. Lang).

Du, J. (2004): Forensic Linguistics (Shanghai: Foreign Language Education Press).

Duarte i Montserrat, C. (1998): Lenguaje administrativo y lenguaje jurídico, in: J. Bayo Delgado (ed.), Lenguage judicial (Madrid: Consejo general del poder judicial).

Du Bois, J.W. (2002): Discourse and Grammar, in: Tomasello, M. (ed.) The New Psychology of Language. Cognitive and Functional Approaches to Language Structure, vol. 2 (Mahwah/New York: Lawrence Erlbaum Associates).

Dworkin, R. (1977): Taking Rights Seriously (London: Duckworth).

Dworkin, R. (1991): Law's Empire (London: Fontana Press).

Eckmann, H. (1969): Rechtspositivismus und Sprachanalytische Philosophie. Der Begriff des Rechts in der Rechtstheorie H.L.A. Harts (Berlin: Duncker & Humblot).

Eemeren, F.H. van, Grootendorst, R., (2004): A Systematic Theory of Argumentation. The Pragma-Dialectic Approach (Cambridge: Cambridge University Press).

Engel., P. (1994): Introduction à la philosophie de l'esprit (Paris: Editions de la découverte).

Engel, P. (ed.) (2000): Précis de philosophie analytique (Paris: puf).

Enos, T. (ed.) (1996): Encyclopedia of Rhetoric and Composition (New York/London: Garland Publishing).

Eriksson, L.D. (1997): Att förstå och att tolka, in: Kangas, U., Timonen, P. (eds.): Juhlajulkaisu A. Aarnio, pp. 13-25 (Helsinki: Suomalainen Lakimiesyhdystys).

Escarra, J. (1936) : Le droit chinois. Conception generale, aperçu historique (Beijing: Henri Vetch).

Falcone, G. (1991): Per una datazione del "De verborum quae ad ius pertinent significatione" di Elio Gallo, in: Ann. Sem. giur. Univ. di Palermo, vol. 41, pp. 223-226.

Feltham, R.G. (1998): Diplomatic Handbook, 7th ed. (London, New York: Longman).

Finnemore, M. (2000): Are Legal Norms Distinctive?, in: Harvard Law Review, vol. 32-591, pp. 699-705.

Foley, R., Salmi-Tolonen, T., Tukiainen, I., Vehmas, B. (eds.) (2008): Kielen ja oikeuden kohtaamisia. Heikki E.S. Mattilan juhlakirja (Helsinki: Talentum).

Fortshoff, E. (1940/54): Recht und Sprache. Prolegomena zu einer richterlichen Hermeneutik (Darmstadt/Königsberg).

Foucault, M. (1966): Les mots et les choses, Une archéologie des sciences humaines (Paris: Gallimard).

Foucault, M. (1969): L'archéologie du savoir (Paris: Gallimard).

Frändberg, Å. (2001): Rättsordningen och rättstillämpningen, in: Strömholm, S. (ed.) Svensk rätt – en översikt (Uppsala: Iustus Förlag).

Fuller, L. (1958): Positivism and Fidelity to Law – A Reply to Professor Hart, in: Harvard Law Review, 71/630.

Galdia, M. (1989): Länsisaksalaisen oikeustieteen umpikujat ja oikotieet, in: Oikeus 1989/4, pp. 328-331.

Galdia, M. (1996): Der Paradigmenwechsel in der finnischen Rechtswissenschaft (Frankfurt, New York: P. Lang).

Galdia, M. (1999): Lakisaksa, in: Encyclopaedia Iuridica Fennica, vol.VII., (Helsinki: Suomalainen Lakimiesyhdystys), pp. 550-555.

Galdia, M. (2003a): Juridisten tekstien kääntäminen erityisesti suomalais-saksalaisen vertailun näkökulmasta, in: Lakimies 2003, pp. 3-22.

Galdia, M. (2003b): Flerspråkiga juridiska ordböcker, in: LexicoNordica 10-2003, pp. 119-131.

Galdia, M., Voronina, N. (2004a): Pravo i etnichnost v subjektah Rossijskoj Federacji (Moskva: EU-Russia Cooperation Programme).

Galdia, M. (2006): Review of H. Mattila, Comparative Legal Linguistics, in: European Legal Forum (I), 5/6-2006, p. 271.

Galdia, M. (2008): Oikeuskielen pragmaattiset aspektit, in: Foley, R. et al. (eds.), Kielen ja oikeuden kohtaamisia, pp. 13-29.

Gaudemet, J. (1986): Tentatives de systématisation du droit à Rome, in: Archives de philosphie du droit, vol 31.

Gaudemet, J. (2001): Les naissances du droit, 3rd ed. (Paris: Montchrestien).

Gémar, J.C (2004) : Traduire le language du droit, in : Übersetzung Translation Traduction, Kittel, H. et al. (eds), vol. 1 (Berlin: Walter de Gruyter).

Girard, P. (1929): Manuel élémentaire du droit romain, 8th ed. (Paris : Rousseau).

Girard, P. (1923): Textes du droit romain, 5th ed. (Paris: Rousseau).

Gizbert-Studnicki, T. (1979): Czy istnieje język prawny?, in: Państwo i Prawo, 1979/3, pp. 49-60.

Gizbert-Studnicki, T. (1987): Der Vorverständnisbegriff in der juristischen Hermeneutik, in: Archiv für Rechts- und Staatsphilosophie 1987, pp. 476-493.

Glass, A. (1988): Fish and Legal Practice, in: Rechtstheorie 19, pp. 443-460.

Glendon, M., Gordon, M., Carozza, P. (1999): Comparative Legal Traditions, 2nd ed. (Hong Kong: Thomson).

Goodman, N. (1978): Ways of Worldmaking (Indianapolis: Hackett Publ.).

Gorelov, B.I. (1989): Teoreticheskaja grammatika kitajskogo iazyka (Moskva: Prosvjeshtchenje).

Granet, M. (1934): La pensée chinoise (Paris: Alban Michel).

Grasnich, W. (2001): Entscheidungsgründe als Textcollage, in: Müller, F., Wimmer, R. (eds.) Neue Studien zur Rechtslinguistik (Berlin: Duncker & Humblot).

Greimas, A.J. (1976): Analyse sémiotique d'un discours juridique. La loi commerciale sur les societés, in : Sémiotique et sciences sociales, pp. 79-128.

Grossfeld, B. (1989): Rechtsausbildung und Rechtskontrolle, in: Neue Juristische Woche 1989, pp. 875-881.

Grossfeld, B. (1990): The Strength and Weakness of Comparative Law (London: Clarendon Press).

Guimezanes, N. (1995): Introduction au droit français (Baden-Baden: Nomos).

Gustafsson, M. (1975): Some Syntactic Properties of English Law Language (Turku: University of Turku).

Habermas, J. (1988): Theorie des kommunikativen Handelns, vol. 1 and 2 (Frankfurt/M: Suhrkamp).

Hare, R.M. (1952): The Language of Morals (Oxford: Clarendon Press).

Hart, H.L.A. (1958): Positivism and the Separation of Law and Morals, in: Harvard Law Review 71/593.

Hart, H.L.A. (1961): The Concept of Law (Oxford: Clarendon Press).

Hałas, B. (1995): Terminologia języka prawnego (Zielona Góra: WSP).

Helin, M. (1990): Kielitekojen teoriasta institutionaaliseen oikeusteoriaan, in: Hirvonen, A.,

Tuori, K. (eds.) Oikeus, kieli ja kritiikki (Helsinki: Itakapaino) pp. 141-157.

Heller, D., Ehlich, K. (eds.) (2007): Studien zur Rechtskommunikation (Bern, Berlin: P. Lang)

Heller, M. (1992): Reform der deutschen Rechtssprache im 18. Jahrhundert (Frankfurt/M.: P. Lang).

Herbots, J.B. (1987): La traduction juridique. Un point de vue belge, in : Cahiers de Droit 28, pp. 813 – 844.

Hiltunen, R. (1990): Chapters on Legal English. Aspects Past and Present of the Language of the Law (Helsinki: Suomalainen Tiedeakademia).

Hiltunen, R. (2001): Some Syntactic Properties of English Law Language, in: Hiltunen, R. Battarbee, K. et al. (eds.): English in Zigs and Zags: A Festschrift for Marita Gustafsson (Turku: University of Turku).

Hirvonen, A., Tuori, K. (eds.) (1990): Oikeus, kieli ja kritiikki (Helsinki: Helsingin yliopiston julkisoikeuden laitoksen julkaisuja).

Hlouch, L. (2007/8): Teorie a realita právní interpretace (unpublished PhD-thesis, University of Brno).

Hohfeld, W.N. (1913): Fundamental Legal Conceptions as Applied in Judicial Reasoning, in: Yale Law Journal 23/16.

Hohmann, H. (1998): Logic and Rhetoric in Legal Argumentation: Some Medieval Perspectives, in: Argumentation 12, pp. 39-55.

Holtgraves, Th. M. (2002): Language as Social Action. Social Psychology and Language Use. (Mahwah, N.J., London: LEA Lawrence Erlbaum Associates, Publishers).

Husa, J. (1998): Johdatus oikeusvertailuun (Helsinki: Kauppakaari).

Husa, J. (2007): Kreikan oikeus ja oikeuskieli (Helsinki: Suomalainen Lakimiesyhdistys).

Igarashi, K. (1990): Einführung in das japanische Recht (Darmstadt: Wissenschaftliche Buchgesellschaft).

Jackson, B. (1985): Semiotics and Legal Theory (London: Routledge).

Jackson, B. (1988): Narrative Models in Legal Proof, in: International Journal for the Semiotics of Law 1/3, pp. 226-246.

Jareborg, N. (1972): Vilseledande genom antydningar, in: Festskrift till P.O. Ekelöf (Stockholm: Kungl. Boktr.).

Jopek-Bosiacka, A. (2006): Przekład prawny i sądowy (Warszawa: Wydawnictwo Naukowe PWN).

Juhl, P.D. (1980): Interpretation. An Essay in the Philosophy of Literary Criticism (Princeton: Princeton University Press).

Jyränki, A. (ed.) (1999): Oikeuden kielet (Turku: Turun yliopiston oikeustieteellisen tiedekunnan julkaisuja B: 71).

Kaser, M. (1983): Römisches Privatrecht (München: Beck).

Kelsen, H. (1960): Reine Rechtslehre, 2nd ed. (Wien: F. Deuticke).

Kelsen, H. (1991): General Theory of Norms (Oxford: Clarendon Press).

Kennedy, D. (1982): The Stages of the Decline of the Public/Private Distinction, in: Univ. of Pennsylvania Law Review, vol. 130, pp. 1349-1357.

Kesola, E. (2007): Valtiosopimusten termistö ja sen käyttö (unpublished thesis, Tampere University, Finland).

Kielar, B. (1977): Language of the Law in the Aspect of Translation (Warszawa: Wydawnictwo UW).

Kielar, B. (1979): W obronie koncepcji "języka prawnego" jako rejestru języka naturalnego, in: Państwo i Prawo, nr. 8-9, p. 172 sqq.

Kinnunen, T. (2006): Käännös oikeudenkäyntiaineistona. Lakitekstien tulkinta oikeuskäsittei-den kääntämisen näkökulmasta (Tampere: Tamperen yliopisto).

Kirchmann, von, J. (1938): Die Wertlosigkeit der Jurisprudenz als Wissenschaft (Stuttgart, Berlin: Kohlhammer).

Kissinger, H. (1994): Diplomacy (New York: Simon and Schuster).

Kleiber, G. (1990): La sémantique du prototype. Catégories et sens lexical (Paris: Presses Universitaires de France).

Koch, H.J. (ed.) (1976): Juristische Methodenlehre und analytische Philosophie (Kronberg Ts.: Athenäum Verlag).

Kolańczyk, K. (1986): Prawo Rzymskie (Warszawa: PIW).

Koskenniemi, M. (1999): The Effect of Rights on Political Culture, in: Alston, P. (ed.) The EU and Human Rights, pp. 99-116 (Oxford: Oxford University Press).

Koskensalo, A. (2002): The Functionality of Business Letters in the Face of Globalisation, in: Satzger, A. Poncini, G. International Perspectives on Business Communication. From Past Approaches to Future Trends, pp. 55-64 (Frankfurt/M: P. Lang).

Kotarbiński, T. (1955): Kurs logiki dla prawników (Warszawa: PIW).

Kotarbiński, T. (1965): Praxiology. An Introduction to the Science of Efficient Action (New York: Pergamon Press).

Kotarbiński, T. (1986): Drogi dociekań własnych. Fragmenty filozoficzne (Warszawa: PWN).

Kovačević, Z. (2004): Međunarodno pregovaranje (Beograd: Diplomatska akademija MSP SCG).

Kraakman, R., Davies, P. et al. (2004): The Anatomy of Corporate Law. A Comparative and Functional Approach (Oxford: Oxford University Press).

Krasilnikova, K. (2006): Problem stworzenia klasyfikacji argumentów (na podstawie rosyjskich i polskich badań), in: Rozprawy Komisji Językowej ŁTN, vol. LI.

Kredens, K., Gozdz-Roszkowski, S. (eds.) (2007): Law and the Language: International Outlooks. Lodz studies in Language series, vol. 16. (Frankfurt/M.: Lang).

Kwarciński, W. (2002): A Speech Act Approach to Legal Discourse (unpublished PhD-thesis, University of Poznań).

Kwarciński, W. (2004): Recipient Design of Statutes and Judgments, in: Studia Anglica Poznanensia, vol. 40, pp. 209-225.

Kwarciński, W. (2005): Some Parallels between Pragmalinguistic and Legal Models of Interpretation (unpublished presentation at the 7th IAFL Conference – Cardiff University).

Kwarciński, W. (2006): A Diachronic Speech Act Analysis of Sworn Testimonies in Polish Criminal Trials, in: Kryk-Kastorsky, B. (ed.) Historical Courtroom Discourse, pp. 293-314.

Lachmayer, F. (1979): Präkonstitutionelles Gewohnheitsrecht, In: Juristische Blätter 99, pp. 411- 415.

Ladjili-Mouchette, J. (1990): Histoire juridique de la Méditerranée. Droit romain, droit musulman (Tunis: Imprimerie Officielle de la République Tunisienne).

Lampe, E.J. (1970): Rechtsanthropologie I. Individualstrukturen in der Rechtsordnung (Berlin : Duncker & Humblot).

Landquist, H. (2008): Spår i SAOB: David Ehrenstråle Nehrman och Svenska Akademiens ordbok, in: Foley, R. et al., Oikeuden ja kielen kohtaamisia, pp. 157 – 171.

Langevoort, D. (1999): Half-Truths: Protecting Mistaken Inferences by Investors and Others, in: Stanford Law Review 52.

Laurén, Ch. (2002): Iconism as Special Language, in: Mattila (2002a).

Lehman, J., Phelps, S. (eds.) (2005): West's Encyclopedia of American Law, 2nd ed. (Detroit, San Diego: Thomson).

Letto-Venamo, P. (2002): Legal Systems and Legal Languages, in: H. Mattila (ed.) The Development of Legal Language, pp. 21-30 (Helsinki: Kauppakaari).

Levinson, S. (1983): Pragmatics (Cambridge: Cambrigde University Press).

Linhart, K. (2005): Internationales Einheitsrecht und einheitliche Auslegung (Mohr Siebeck: Tübingen).

Lippert, S.L. (2004): Ein demotisches juristisches Lehrbuch. Untersuchungen zu Papyrus Berlin P 23757 rto, Ägyptologische Abhandlungen 66 (Wiesbaden: Harrassowitz Verlag).

Liu, W. (2005): Illocutionary and Perlocutionary Acts in Chinese Judge's Attached Discourse (unpublished presentation at 7th IAFL Conference, Cardiff University).

Loewe, R. (1989): Internationales Kaufrecht (Wien: Manzsche Verlags- und Universitätsbuchhandlung).

Lyons, J. (1968): Introduction to Theoretical Linguistics (Cambridge: Cambridge University Press).

Mackie, J.L. (1977): Ethics. Inventing Right and Wrong (New York: Viking Press).

McCormick, J. (1997): Habermas' Discourse Theory of Law: Bridging Anglo-American and Continental Legal Traditions?, in: The Modern Law Review Limited, pp. 734-743.

MacCormick, N. (1984) : Coherence in Legal Justification, in : Theorie der Normen. Festgabe für Ota Weinberger zum 65. Geburtstag (Berlin: Duncker & Humblot).

MacCormick, N. & Bańkowski, Z. (1986): Speech Acts, Legal Institutions and Real Laws, in: The Legal Mind. Essays for Tony Honoré, in: N. MacCormick & P. Birks (eds.), pp. 120-133, (Oxford: Clarendon Press).

MacCormick, N., Weisberger, O. (1986): An Institutional Theory of Law. New Approaches to Legal Positivism (Dordrecht/Boston: D. Reidel Publishing).

MacCormick, N., Summers, R. (eds.) (1991): Interpreting Statutes. A Comparative Study (Aldershot: Dartmouth).

MacCormick, N., Summers, R. (eds.) (1997): Interpreting Precedents. A Comparative Study (Aldershot/Ashgate: Dartmouth).

Madsen, D. (1997): Towards a Description of Communication in the Legal Universe. Translation of Legal Texts and the Skopos Theory, in: Fachsprache 1/1007, pp.17-27.

Malinowski, A. (2006): Polski język prawny. Wybrane zagadnienia (Warszawa: LexisNexis).

Markhardt, H. (2006): Wörterbuch der österreichischen Rechts-, Wirtschafts- und Verwaltungsterminologie (Frankfurt/M: P.Lang).

Mattila, H.E.S. (ed.) (2002a), The Development of Legal Language (Helsinki: Kauppakaari).

Mattila, H.E.S. (2002b): Vertaileva oikeuslingvistiikka (Helsinki: Kauppakaari).

Mattila, H.E.S. (2002c): De aequalitate Latinitatis jurisperitorum, in: Revue du droit comparé pp. 717-758.

Mattila, H.E.S. (2002d): Review of R. Pitkäranta's Finnish-Latin-Finnish Dictionary, in: LexicoNordica 9/2002, pp. 271-283.

Mattila, H.E.S., Jussila, A, Kaltio, O. (2004): Oikeuselämän lyhennesanakirja. Juridisk förkortningsbok (Helsinki: Talentum).

Mattila, H.E.S. (2005): Språket och den nordiska rättsfamiljen, in: Tidskrift utgiven av Juridiska Föreningen i Finland 1/2005, pp. 43-57.

Mattila, H.E.S. (2006): Comparative Legal Linguistics (Aldershot: Ashgate).

Mattila, H.E.S. (2008): Oikeuskielen muutokset nykymaailmassa, in: Lakimies 7-8, pp. 1149-1165.

May, R. (1980): Problematik chinesischen Rechtsverständnisses, in: Archiv für Rechts- und Staatsphilosophie, vol. LXVI/2, pp. 193-205.

Mellinkoff, D. (1963): The Language of the Law (Boston, Toronto: Little).

Minda, G. (1995): Postmodern Legal Movements (New York: New York University Press).

Morawetz, Th. (1992): Epistemology of Judging. Wittgenstein and Deliberative Practices, in : D.M. Patterson (ed.): Wittgenstein and Legal Theory, pp. 3-27, (Boulder, S. Francisco: Westlaw Press).

Mounin, G. (1963): Les problèmes theoriques de la traduction (Paris: puf).

Müller, F. (ed.) (1989): Untersuchungen zur Rechtslinguistik, (Berlin: Duncker & Humblot).

Müller, F. (1997): Methodik, Theorie, Linguistik des Rechts. (Berlin: Duncker & Humblot).

Munday, R. (1983): The Common Lawyer's Philosophy of Legislation, in: Rechtstheorie 2/83, pp. 191-203.

Neumann-Duesberg, H. (1949): Sprache im Recht (Münster: Regensberg).

Nerhot, P. (1992): Law, Writing, Meaning. An Essay in Legal Hermeneutics (Edinburgh: Edinburgh University Press).

Olivekrona, K. (1969): Det rättsliga språket och verkligheten (Lund: Ekstrands Tryckeri).

Okawara, M.H. (1998): The Comprehensibility of Japanese Legal Language: the Penal Code in: Chiiki Seisaku Kenkyu, vol. 1/2, pp. 197-206.

Okawara, M.H. (2006): A Linguistic Analysis of Some Japanese Trademark Cases (unpublished PhD- thesis, University of Sidney).

Opeibi, O. (2008): Between Obscurity and Clarity in Nigerian Legal Discourse: Aspects of Language Use in Selected Written Texts, in: Wagner, A., Cacciaguidi-Fahy, S. (eds.), Obscurity and Clarity in the Law. Prospects and Challenges (Aldershot: Ashgate).

Pajula, P. (1960): Suomalaisen oikeuskielen historia pääpiirteittäin (Porvoo/Helsinki: WSOY).

Palmgren, S. (2002): Legal Swedish and Legal Finnish, in: Mattila. H. (ed.) (2002): The Development of Legal Language, pp. 153-161 (Helsinki: Kauppakaari).

Peczenik, A. (1986): Rätten och förnuftet (Lund: Nordstedts).

Peczenik, A. (1995): Vad är rätt? Om demokrati, rättssäkerhet, etik och juridisk argumentation (Stockholm: Fritzes Förlag).

Peczenik, A. (2005): Kinds of Legal Argumentation – Draft 2005 (available online).

Perelman, C., Olbrechts-Tyteca, L. (1983): Traité de l'argumentation, 4th ed. (Bruxelles: Editions de l'Université).

Perillo, J. M. (2003): Calamari and Perillo on Contracts, 5th ed. (St. Paul: Momsen West).

Petrażycki, L. (1955): Law and Morality (Cambridge: Harvard University Press).

Petzel, J. (2006): Język prawny w świetle lingwistycznej teorii rejestru językowego, in: Studia Juridica XLV/2006, pp. 153-163.

Piehl, A. (2002): The Influence of EC Legislation on Finnish Legal Langage: How to Assess it?, in: Mattila (H.) (ed.): The Development of Legal Language, pp. 101-112 (Helsinki: Kauppakaari).

Pieńkos, J. (1999): Podstawy juryslingwistyki. Język w prawie – prawo w języku (Warszawa: Muza).

Pigolkin, A.S. (ed.) (1990): Iazyk zakona (Moskva: Juridicheskaya literatura).

Pintore, A. (1995): Law and Language: The Italian Analytical Tradition, in: Jackson, B.S., Making Sense in Law. Linguistic, Psychological and Semiotic Perspectives (Liverpool: Deborah Charles Publications)

Plantin, Ch. (1996): L'argumentation (Paris: Seuil).

Podlech, A. (1976): Rechtslinguistik, in : Grimm, D. (ed.) Rechtswissenschaft und Nachbarwissenschaften, vol. 2 (München: Beck) pp. 106-116.

Pohl, I. (ed.) (2008): Semantik und Pragmatik – Schnittstellen (Frankfurt/M: P. Lang).

Posner, R. (1987): The Decline of Law as an Autonomous Discipline: 1962-1987, in: 100 Harvard Law Review 761.

Pradid, J. F. (2002): Vstup do juridichnoi lingvistiki. Navchalskij posibnik (Simferopol: Dolya).

Prieto de Pedro, J. (1991): Lenguas, lenguaje y derecho (Madrid: Civitas).

Quine, W. (1983) Wort und Gegenstand (orig. Word and Object) (Stuttgart: Ph. Reclam).

Rabel, E. (1956): Das Problem der Qualifikation (Darmstadt: Wissenschaftliche Buchgesellschaft).

Recanati, F. (2008): Philosophie du language (et de l'esprit) (Paris: Gallimard).

Reiss, K.,Vermeer, H.J. (1984) : Grundlegung einer allgemeinen Translationstheorie (Tübingen: Max Niemeyer).

Reus-Smit, C. (2005): International Law, in: Baylis, J., Smith, S. (eds.) (2005).

Rimmon-Kenan, Sh. (1989): Narrative Fiction. Contemporary Poetics (Routledge: London and New York).

Rhees, R. (1966): Can There Be a Private Language?, in: Pitcher, G. (ed.) Wittgenstein. The Philosophical Investigations, pp. 267-285, (New York: Doubleday Anchor).

Rodingen, H. (1977): Pragmatik der juristischen Argumentation (Freiburg/München: Alber).

Roehl, K. F. (2003): Das Recht nach der visuellen Zeitenwende, in: Juristenzeitung vol. 7.

Rorty, R. (1992) (ed.): The Linguistic Turn (Chicago and London: Univ. of Chicago Press).

Rorty, R. (1993): Human Rights, Rationality, and Sentimentality, in: Shute, S., Hurley, S. (eds.), On Human Rights, The Oxford Amnesty Lectures, pp. 112-134, (London: Basis-Books).

Ross, A. (1957): Tû Tû, in: Harvard Law Review 70/5, pp. 812-825.

Ross, A. (1966): Om ret og retfærdighed. En indførelse i den analytiske retsfilosofi (København: Nyt Nordisk Forlag A. Busck).

Rottleuthner, H. (1973): Richterliches Handeln. Zur Kritik der juristischen Dogmatik (Frankfurt/M: Athenäum Fischer).

Saarenpää, A. (1980): Rutiinijuttu (Helsinki: Helsingin Yliopisto).

Sager, J. (1990): A Practical Course in Terminology Processing (Amsterdam: Benjamins).

Said, E. (1979): Orientalism (New York: Vintage Books).

Salas, M. E. (2001): ¿Que pasa actualmente en la teoría del derecho alemana?, in: Doxa 24, pp. 203-234.

Salmi-Tolonen, T. (2008): Forensista lingvistiikkaa – kielentutkimuksen juridisia sovellutuksia, in: Foley, R. et al. (2008), pp. 375-393.

Šarčević, S. (1997): New Approach to Legal Translation (The Hague: Kluwer).

Savigny, von, E. (1973): Grundkurs im wissenschaftlichen Definieren, 3.rd ed. (München: dtv).

Savigny, von, E. (1981): Inwiefern ist die Umgangssprache grundlegend für die Fachsprachen?, in: Hahn v.,W. (ed.), Fachsprachen. Wege der Forschung (Darmstadt: Wissenschaftliche Buchgesellschaft).

Savigny, von, C.F. (1840): System des heutigen Römischen Recht, vol. I, (Berlin).

Schauer, F. (ed.) (1993): Law and Language (Aldershot, Hongkong: Dartmouth).

Schmidt, J. (1972): Einige Bemerkungen zur Präzision der Rechtssprache, in: Jahrbuch für Rechtssoziologie und Rechtstheorie, vol. II, pp. 390-437.

Searle, J. (1969): Speech Acts. An Essay in the Philosophy of Language (Cambridge: Cambridge University Press).

Searle, J. (1999): Mind, Language and Society. Doing Philosophy in the Real World (London: Weidenfield & Nicolson).

Searle, J. (ed.) (2004): Filosofija iazyka (orig. The Philosophy of Language) (Moskva: URSS, orig.: Oxford University Press).

Serpe, A. (2006): Analysis of language and legal rights within the Scandinavian debate. Human rights: a "hidden essence"?, in: Frónesis 13/3.

Sheriff, J. (1989): The Fate of Meaning: Charles Peirce, Structuralism and Literature (Princeton: Princeton University Press).

Shuy, R. W. (2006): Linguistics in the Courtroom: A Practical Guide (Oxford: Oxford University Press).

Siitonen, A. (1989): Problems of Aporetics (Helsinki: Suomalainen Tiedeakademia).

Sloane, T.O. (ed.) (2001): Encyclopedia of Rhetoric (Oxford: Oxford University Press).

Smits, J.M. (2005): The Principles of European Contract Law and the Harmonisation of Private Law in Europe, in: Vacquer, A. (ed.): La Tercera Parte de Los Principios de Derecho Contractual Europeo, pp. 567-590 (Valencia: Tirant).

Snell-Hornby, M. (1986): Übersetzungswissenschaft. Einer Neuorientierung. (Tübingen: UTB).

Solan, L.M. (1993): The Language of Judges (Chicago: Chicago University Press).

Spiegelberg, W. (1892): Studien und Materialien zum Rechtswesen des Pharaonenreiches (Leipzig: Vereinigung wissenschaftlicher Verleger).

Spiegelberg, W. (1907): Die Schrift und Sprache der alten Ägypter (Leipzig: Vereinigung wissenschaftlicher Verleger).

Spiegelberg, W. (1922): Das Verhältnis der griechischen und ägyptischen Texte in den zweisprachigen Dekreten von Rosette und Kanopus (Berlin/Leipzig: Vereinigung wissenschaftlicher Verleger/ W. de Gruyter).

Steinvorth, U. (1990): Klassische und moderne Ethik (Hamburg: dtv).

Strawson, P. (1992): Analysis and Metaphysics (Oxford: Oxford University Press).

Tiersma, P. (1999): Legal Language (Chicago/London: University of Chicago Press).

Thornton, G. C. (1996): Legislative Drafting, 4th ed. (London: Butterworths).

Thür, G. (2003): Recht im antiken Griechenland, in: Manthe, U. (ed.), Rechtskulturen der Antike. Vom Alten Orient bis zum Römischen Reich (München: Beck).

Todorov, T. (2007): La littérature en péril (Paris: Flammarion).

Torop, P. (1998): Granicy perevoda, in: Sign Systems Studies vol. 26.

Toulmin, E.S. (1958): The Uses of Argument (Cambridge: Cambridge University Press).

Tribe, L.H. (2000): American Constitutional Law, vol. I, (New York: Foundation Press).

Unbegaun, B.O. (1969): Iazyk russkogo prava. Selected Papers on Russian and Slavonic Philology (Oxford: Oxford University Press).

Upham, F.K. (1990): Introduction into East Asian Legal Systems (Boston: Boston College Law School).

Veronesi, D. (2000): Linguistica giuridica italiana e tedesca (Padova: Unipress).

Verschueren, J., Östman, J.-O. et al. (eds.) (1995): Handbook of Pragmatics (Amsterdam/Philadelphia: John Benjamins Publishing).

Viehweg, T. (1954): Topik und Jurisprudenz (München: C.H. Beck).

Vilar Sánches, K. (ed.) (2007): Mikrofunktionen in Arbeitsverträgen deutsch-spanisch (Bern, Berlin: P.Lang).

Vlasenko, N.A. (1997): Iazyk prava (Irkutsk: Vostochno-Sibirskoe knizhnoe izdatelstvo).

Vogel, H.-J. (1988): Juridiska översättningar (Lund: Juristförlaget).

Wagner, A., Cacciaguidi-Fahy, S. (eds.) (2008): Obscurity and Clarity in Law. Prospects and Challenges (Aldershot: Ashgate).

Warda-Radys, L. (2006): O polszczyźnie urzędowej w Gdańsku w dobie średniopolskiej, in: Rozprawy Komisji Językowej ŁTN, vol. LI.

Weinberger, O., Weinberger, C. (1979): Logik, Semantik, Hermeneutik (München: Beck).

Weisberg, R. (1992): Poethics and Other Strategies of Law and Literature (New York: Columbia University Press).

Weisgerber, O. (1961): Übersetzungsprobleme in Südtirol-Konflikt (Innsbruck: Leopold-Franzens-Universität).

White, J.B. (1990): Justice as Translation: An Essay in Cultural and Legal Criticism (Chicago: Chicago University Press).

White, J.B. (1994): Acts of Hope: Creating Authority in Literature, Law and Politics (Chicago: Chicago University Press).

Wittgenstein, L. (1984): Philosophische Untersuchungen (Frankfurt/M: suhrkamp).

Wohlrapp, H. (ed.) (1995): Wege der Argumentationsforschung (Stuttgart: problemata fromann-holzboog).

Wolf, E. (1950-1957): Griechisches Rechtsdenken, vol. I-V (Frankfur/M: V. Klostermann).

Working Group, (2001): Tuomioistuinsanasto (Helsinki: Edita).

Working Group, Cabinet Secretariat (2006): Hôrei yôgo nichi-ei hyôjun taiyaku jisho. Japanese-English Legal Terms Standard Bilingual Dictionary (www.cas.go.jp).

Wright von, G.H. (1951): Deontic Logics, in: Mind 60, pp.1-15.

Wróblewski, J. (1988): Sądowne stosowanie prawa (Warszawa: PWN).

Zhang, N. (2002): Guoji fa yuanli (The Theory of International Law) (Beijing: Zhongguo Zheng Fa Daxue).

Zhang, Q. (2004): Traditional Chinese Culture (Beijing: Foreign Languages Press).

Zhou, Q., Wang, J., Su, J. (eds.) (2003): Yuyan yu falü yanjiu de xin shiye. Language and Law in a New Perspective. (Beijing: Law Press China).

Znamenáčková, K. (2007): Fachsprachliche Wortgruppen in Textsorten des deutschen Zivilrechts (Frankfurt/M: P. Lang).

Bibliography concerning linguistic legislation

Capotorti, F. (1991): Study on the Rights of Persons Belonging to Ethnic, Religious or Linguistic Minorities (New York: United Nations).

Crystal, D. (1997): English as a Global Language (Cambridge: Cambridge University Press).

Diakofotakis, Y. (2002): Expanding Conceptual Boundaries (Athens: Sakkoulas, Brussels: Bruylant).

Engel, D. (2002): Die sprachenrechtliche Situation der Angehörigen von Minderheiten im Völkerrecht (Berlin: Berlin Verlag).

Galdia, M., Voronina, N. (2004b): Problemy pravovogo regulirovaniya mezhetnicheskih otnosheniji i antidiskriminacjonnogo zakonodatelstva v Rossijskoj Federacji (Moskva: Tacis).

Giordan, H. (ed.) (1992): Les minorités en Europe (Paris: Éditions Kimé).

Hoffmann, Ch. (1991): Introduction into Bilingualism (London, New York: Longman).

Kemp, W. (ed.) (2001): Quiet Diplomacy in Action: The OSCE High Commissioner on National Minorities (The Hague: Kluwer).

Kymlicka, W. (1995) Multicultural Citizenship (Oxford: Oxford University Press).

Lukashuk, I. (1996): Mezhdunarodnoje pravo, Obshchaja chast (Moskva: Beck).

Mattila, H. (2002c): Les materiaux non finnois dans l'interprétation juridique en Finlande, in: Sacco, R. (ed): L'interprétation de texts juridiques redigés dans plus d'une langue (Turin : Isaidat Harmattan Italia).

Nettle, D., Romaine, S. (2000): Vanishing Voices: the Extinction of the World's Languages (New York: Oxford University Press).

Skuttnab-Kangas, T., Phillipson, R. (eds.) (1995): Linguistic Human Rights, (Berlin,New York: Mouton,de Gruyter).

Skuttnab-Kangas, T. (2000): Linguistic Genocide in Education – or Worldwide Diversity and Human Rights? (Mahwah: Lawrence Erlbaum Associates).

Turi, J. (1995): Typology of Language Legislation, in: Skuttnab-Kangas, T., Phillipson, R. (eds.) Linguistic Human Rights. Overcoming Linguistic Discrimination, pp. 111-119 (Berlin, New York: Mouton/de Gruyter).

Varennes, de, F. (1996): Language Minorities and Human Rights (The Hague, New York: Martinus Nijhoff).

Wildhaber, L. (2002): Protection against Discrimination under the European Convention on Human Rights – a Second-Class Guarantee? In: I. Zemele (ed.), Baltic Yearbook of International Law, vol. 2, 2002.

Wydra, D. (2008): Autonomie auf der Halbinsel Krim. Eine völker- und verfassungsrechtliche Analyse, Ethnos vol. 68 (Wien: Braumüller).

Yacoub, J. (1998): Les minorités dans le monde (Paris: Desclée De Brower).

Index of Issues

Bold numbers *refer to pages in the main text where the relevant notions have been treated with particular attention. Regular numbers refer to the pages of the main text where the notions have been mentioned in a specific context.*

Index of Names

In this index the names of persons mentioned in the main text are listed. Names of researchers whose contributions are constantly quoted in the main text such as H.E.S. Mattila, G. Cornu or J. Searle are referred to with the page number indicating the central part of the theses that have been developed here. Names of classics, e.g. Aristotle or Boethius, are not included.